*third* | edition

# Teaching Exceptional, Diverse, and At-Risk Students in the General Education Classroom

**Sharon Vaughn**

*University of Texas, Austin*

**Candace S. Bos**

*Late of University of Texas, Austin*

**Jeanne Shay Schumm**

*University of Miami*

Boston ■ New York ■ San Francisco
Mexico City ■ Montreal ■ Toronto ■ London ■ Madrid ■ Munich ■ Paris
Hong Kong ■ Singapore ■ Tokyo ■ Cape Town ■ Sydney

*Editor in Chief:* Paul A. Smith
*Executive Editor:* Virginia Lanigan
*Development Editor:* Linda Bieze
*Editorial Assistant:* Robert Champagne
*Executive Marketing Manager:* Amy Cronin
*Editorial–Production Service:* Omegatype Typography, Inc.
*Composition and Prepress Buyer:* Linda Cox
*Manufacturing Buyer:* Megan Cochran
*Cover Administrator:* Linda Knowles
*Interior Designer:* Carol Somberg
*Cover Designer:* Susan Paradise
*Photo Researcher:* Laurie Frankenthaler
*Illustrations:* Omegatype Typography, Inc.
*Electronic Composition:* Omegatype Typography, Inc.

For related titles and support materials, visit our online catalog at www.ablongman.com.

Between the time Website information is gathered and published, some sites may have closed. Also, the transcription of URLs can result in unintentional typographical errors. The publisher would appreciate notification where these errors occur so that they may be corrected in subsequent editions.

**Library of Congress Cataloging-in-Publication Data**

Vaughn, Sharon
    Teaching exceptional, diverse, and at-risk students in the general education classroom / Sharon R. Vaughn, Candace S. Bos, Jeanne Shay Schumm.—3rd ed.
        p.   cm.
    Includes bibibliographical references and index.
    ISBN 0-205-34271-X (alk.paper)
    1. Mainstreaming in education—United States.   2. Special education—United States.
3. Children with disabilities—Education—United States.   4. Children with social disabilities—Education—United States.   5. Learning disabled children—Education—United States.
6. Inclusive education—United States.   I. Bos, Candace S., 1950–   II. Schumm, Jeanne Shay, 1947–   III. Title.

LC3981.V28   2003
371.9'046—dc21

2002020211

**Photo Credits**

Bob Daemmrich/Stock Boston: pp. 1, 292; Will Hart: pp. 16, 19, 34, 90, 102, 107, 120, 124, 130, 158 (right), 160, 166, 192, 205, 215, 221, 247, 252, 256, 273, 277, 302, 329 (top), 335, 346, 369, 377, 383, 386, 399, 404, 415, 422, 444, 451; David Young-Wolff/PhotoEdit: pp. 24, 152; Will Faller: pp. 27, 57, 111, 113, 117, 137, 172, 210, 224, 268, 282, 348, 355, 420, 439, 442; Brian Smith: pp. 41, 48, 72, 135, 143, 174, 180, 184, 287, 308, 309, 319, 409, 426 (top), 434, 437; Robin Sachs/PhotoEdit: p. 66; Robert Harbison: pp. 80, 226, 307, 329 (bottom); Nancy Pierce/Photo Researchers, Inc.: p. 85 (top); Will and Deni McIntyre/Photo Researchers, Inc.: p. 85 (bottom); Richard Hutchings/Photo Researchers, Inc.: p. 147; Kurzweil Educational Systems, Inc.: p. 196; Ed Bock/Corbis/Stock Market: p. 225; Michael Newman/PhotoEdit: pp. 240, 315, 342; Laura Dwight/PhotoEdit: p. 257; Success For All, www.successforall.net: p. 313; Peter Cade/Getty Images Inc: p. 352; Getty Images, Inc.: p. 374; Mark Adams/Getty Images, Inc.: p. 426 (bottom).

**Text Credits**

List on pp. 367–368 adapted from Raphael, T. E. (1986, February). Teaching question-answer relationships, revisited. *The Reading Teacher, 39*(6), 516–522. Copyright by the International Reading Association.

Printed in the United States of America

10  9  8  7  6  5          VHP        07  06  05  04

# contents

chapter **3**

# Teaching Students with Communication Disorders and with Pervasive Developmental Disorders  66

chapter 4

## Teaching Students with Emotional and Behavioral Disorders   102

chapter 5

## Teaching Students with Developmental Disabilities   124

chapter 6

# Teaching Students with Visual Impairments, Hearing Loss, Physical Disabilities, Health Impairments, or Traumatic Brain Injury   152

c h a p t e r  **11**

# Teaching Students Who Are at Risk and Students Who Are Gifted and Talented    302

## chapter 12

## Facilitating Reading   342

## chapter 13

## Facilitating Writing   374

c h a p t e r   **14**

# Helping All Students Succeed in Mathematics   404

chapter **15**

Teaching in the Content Areas    434

## Tips for Teachers

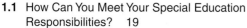

## Making a Difference

### The 60-Second Lesson

## Making a Difference

### Through Action Teaching

## Tech Talk

## Research Brief

Today's elementary and secondary teachers are assuming considerably more responsibility for meeting the educational needs of students from diverse backgrounds and with diverse learning needs. Teachers identify students with special needs as their greatest challenges and often their greatest rewards. Unfortunately, most general education teachers feel at a loss as to how to educate these students. They are eager to provide appropriate instruction, yet often feel inadequately prepared to do so. Furthermore, teachers tell us that what they most want to learn are specific instructional practices that "make a difference" for diverse learners, and that they want these practices to enhance the learning of all the students in their classrooms.

The central theme of this book is that general education teachers can make a difference in the lives of all students, particularly students with special needs, by using the tools and strategies we present. Our confidence in the effectiveness of these suggested practices comes from our ongoing and continued work in teachers' classrooms in which these practices have been successfully implemented. Many teachers whose stories appear throughout this book interpret and extend the recommended practices.

This third edition includes updated references to the latest research, allowing readers to look up the most recent studies on topics of interest. Throughout the text, we have added new information and described techniques brought to light since the second edition was published, and reexamined the ongoing issues surrounding the teaching of diverse learners in general education classrooms.

## Organizational Format

By presenting information that can be easily retrieved and applied, we hope this book will serve as an indispensable resource for teachers seeking effective strategies for meeting the needs of exceptional learners.

First, the book starts with addressing general issues regarding laws, inclusion, and suggestions for

Each chapter section includes **Tips for Teachers** features with specific advice, guidelines for teaching practice, and step-by-step procedures.

how teachers can orchestrate their classrooms for students with special needs (Chapter 1). Then, the book is organized into four major sections. The first section, Chapters 2–6, describes strategies for teaching students with disabilities, covering learning disabilities and attention deficit disorders, communication disorders and pervasive disorders, emotional and behavioral disorders, developmental disabilities, and visual, hearing, physical, or health impairments. We have presented instructional practices and specific accommodations in each of these chapters to ensure that teachers will not only better understand students with special needs but also will know what to do to meet their needs.

The second section of the book, Chapters 7–9, describes various strategies for teachers serving students with special needs. These strategies include

**Making a Difference: The 60-Second Lesson**
features throughout all chapters present a brief
minilesson that provides specific, concrete
examples of how a teacher can make a difference
for students with disabilities or diverse needs
in only a minute of time.

instructional adaptations (Chapter 7), behavioral management (Chapter 8), and collaboration (Chapter 9).

The third section of the book, Chapters 10 and 11, describes strategies for students with diverse needs and abilities. Chapter 10 focuses on teaching students who are culturally and linguistically diverse, and Chapter 11 examines students at risk and those who are gifted or talented.

The fourth section of the book, Chapters 12–15, presents curriculum adaptations for special learners. This section provides specific instructional practices for curricular areas, including reading, writing, mathematics, and content-area learning. Students in our university classes as well as practicing teachers urged us to do more than describe curriculum adaptations; they encouraged us to provide the step-by-step procedures for how to implement curriculum adaptations in the classroom. After reading this book, students and teachers will have more than increased knowledge about students with special needs; they will have the tools and confidence to adequately meet their students' academic and social needs.

The organizational structure of each chapter is the same so that readers can readily locate critical information. Each chapter opens with **Focus Questions** that provide an invitation to the key ideas presented in the chapter. Next is an **Interview** or vignette that presents a teacher's, student's, or parent's story that directly relates to the central ideas of

the chapter. Each of these stories also identifies issues and personal responses that set the tone for the material that follows.

Each chapter's figures, tables, photos, and informational sidebars are designed to stimulate interest and aid in comprehension. Each chapter closes with a **Summary** that highlights the key points contained in the chapter. **Key Terms and Concepts** are presented as a list following the summary and are highlighted in text for ease of location. A **Think and Apply** section at the end of each chapter provides questions, activities, and interesting problems that challenge the reader to integrate and apply the materials presented. **Read More about It** follows and provides a list of books and materials related to the chapter topic with brief descriptions of their content. In this edition, each list has been updated to include the most recent books and articles that discuss the chapter's topics. Finally, **Suggested Websites** for each chapter are presented with brief descriptions of their content.

In addition to the organizational features that open and close each chapter, the following features are used within chapters.

**Tips for Teachers.** Teaching tips in every chapter include lists of concrete suggestions for how to teach a particular skill or how to address a particular student need.

**Making a Difference: The 60-Second Lesson.** These brief minilessons appear in Chapters 1–11 and

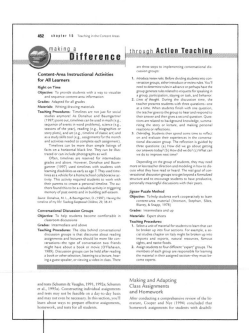

In each of the last four "content-area" chapters,
**Making a Difference through Action Teaching**
features present sample lessons that include
objectives, procedures, and application suggestions for classroom implementation.

**Tech Talk** features in every chapter describe a technological application that can be used in the classroom to enhance success for all learners, particularly students with special needs.

**Research Brief** features in every chapter highlight brief summaries of essential research studies that relate to key points in the chapter.

provide specific, concrete examples of how a teacher can make a difference for students with disabilities or diverse needs in only a minute of time.

**Making a Difference through Action Teaching.** These sample lessons are provided at the ends of the curriculum adaptation chapters, Chapters 12–15. Each lesson includes objectives, procedures, and application suggestions for classroom implementation.

**Tech Talk.** This illustrated feature, provided in every chapter, describes a technological application that can be used in the classroom to enhance success for all learners, particularly students with special needs. Since technology has undergone rapid changes since the second edition was published, many Tech Talk sections have been revised in this edition to describe the newer innovations in technological teaching and learning aids.

**Research Brief.** Every chapter highlights brief summaries of essential research studies that relate to key points in the chapter. New research briefs in this edition feature recent studies and discuss the latest findings.

To provide adequate coverage at the secondary level, we have provided examples in each chapter that illustrate how to apply accommodations and instructional practices at that level. We also designed the content-area curriculum chapter to include issues relating specifically to instruction at the secondary level. Finally, a special appendix, **Making a Differ-**

**ence through Action Learning**, contains more than 20 specific examples of how to instruct secondary students with emphasis on study skills, learning strategies, and student self-advocacy.

## Supplements

### Instructor's Manual and Test Bank with Transparency and Handout Masters

The combined Instructor's Manual and Test Bank with Transparency and Handout Masters is a comprehensive resource that comes with this textbook. Some masters are drawn from the text, but many new ones are provided to give instructors more options for augmenting chapter content. For each chapter, the Instructors' Manual also provides an instructor's overview, teaching outline, focus questions, activities, teaching strategies, and discussion questions. The Test Bank contains multiple-choice items with answer feedback and essay or case-based applications with answer guidelines.

### Computerized Test Bank

A computerized version of the Test Bank is available to adopters in CD-ROM for both PC and Macintosh computers. Please ask your Allyn & Bacon representative for details.

## Companion Website with Online Study Guide— www.ablongman.com/vaughn3e

This dynamic, interactive Companion Website includes an online study guide for students that provides learning objectives, study questions with text page references, "live" links to relevant websites, and additional enrichment material on a chapter-by-chapter basis. The Companion Website also features a "syllabus builder" that allows instructors to create and customize course syllabi online.

## NEW! PowerPoint Electronic Slide Package—www.ablongman.com/ppt

The PowerPoint package, created to accompany the third edition, is easily accessed from the Allyn & Bacon website. There are more than 100 slides, organized by chapter, for use as lecture presentations and/or handouts for students. Those instructors who already use PowerPoint as a lecture presentation tool will find this new supplement a convenient way to incorporate new slides into their existing slide package. Those instructors who have not used PowerPoint (and perhaps have no intention of doing so!) or do not have the PowerPoint program on their computers can rest assured that these slides can be easily downloaded onto their hard drive and printed out for use as traditional overhead transparencies and handouts.

## The "Snapshots" Video Series for Special Education

*Snapshots: Inclusion Video* (© 1995; 23 minutes) traces the progress of three students with disabilities—Josh, Eric, and Tonya—as they are mainstreamed into general education classes. This 23-minute video spans the elementary-school, middle-school, and high-school levels and illustrates environmental, instructional, technological, and curricular adaptations. The video also highlights professional cooperation and collaboration as parents, classroom teachers, special education teachers, and school administrators work together to help Josh, Eric, and Tonya succeed in inclusive classrooms.

*Snapshots 2: Video for Special Education* (categorical organization) (© 1995; 20–25 minutes) is a set of six videotaped segments designed specifically for use in your college classroom. The topics explored are:

- traumatic brain injury
- behavior disorders
- learning disabilities
- mental retardation
- hearing impairment
- visual impairment

Each segment profiles three individuals, their families, teachers, and experiences. These programs will be of great interest to your students. Instructors who have used the tapes in their courses have found that the tapes help in disabusing students of stereotypical viewpoints and put a human face on course material.

## Allyn & Bacon *Professionals in Action* Video Series: "Teaching Students with Special Needs"

This video is approximately two hours in length, consisting of five 15–30-minute modules. These modules present several viewpoints and approaches to teaching students of various disabilities in general education classrooms, separate education settings, and several combinations of the two. Each module explores its topic through actual classroom footage and interviews with students, general and special education teachers, and parents. The five modules are:

1. Working Together: The Individualized Education Plan (IEP)
2. Working Together: The Collaborative Process
3. Instruction and Behavior Management
4. Technology for Inclusion
5. Working with Parents and Families

## Allyn & Bacon Transparency Package for Special Education

The Transparency Package includes approximately 100 acetates, over half of which are in full color.

## iSearch: Special Education

This resource guide for the Internet covers the basics of using the Internet, conducting web searches, and critically evaluating and documenting Internet sources. It also contains Internet activities and URLs specific to the discipline of Special Education. This practical booklet is available *only* as part of a "value pack," shrink-wrapped with an Allyn & Bacon textbook. Please ask your Allyn & Bacon representative for details and ordering information.

## Acknowledgments

We have many people to thank for their generous contributions of time, knowledge, experience, and sound advice. We are deeply grateful to the many teachers who have shared their classrooms, students, and experiences with us. In particular, we would like to extend our heartfelt thanks to the teachers and principals of Flamingo Elementary School. We would also like to thank the many students in the initial teacher preparation programs at the University of Arizona and the University of Miami who have helped us better understand the important attitudes, knowledge, and skills for new teachers preparing to teach diverse learners.

Just a few of the many people whose names should be in lights for their generous contribution to this book follow. A special thanks to

- Sandra Bowen, Penny Rosenblum, and Andrea Morrison. Their expertise in educating students with hearing impairments, visual impairments, and mental retardation/severe disabilities, respectively, was a valuable resource. Sandra played an important role in writing the section on hearing impairments in Chapter 6. Penny took on a similar role in writing the section on visual impairments in the same chapter. Andrea not only worked on the physical disabilities and health impairments section of Chapter 6, but also played a significant role in writing Chapter 5 on developmental disabilities.
- Mary Hinson, for sharing her valuable knowledge as a job developer and university instructor for the mainstreaming course for secondary teachers.
- Sharon Kutok, for sharing her valuable knowledge as a speech/language pathologist.
- Judith Mesler, for her assistance with Chapter 9 on collaboration and consultation.
- Elba Reyes and Manuel Bello, for reviewing and providing insights for Chapter 10 on teaching students with cultural and linguistic diversity.
- Jeanne Bergeron and Michelle Sobol, for their help with Chapter 11 on at-risk and gifted and talented students.
- Aubrey Campbell for his assistance with Chapter 14 on mathematics instruction.
- Maria Elena Arguelles, Kristine Kalamani, Patrick Kinner, Tina Stanton Chapman, Tiffany Newell, and Amy Clark for their assistance in manuscript preparation.
- Ae-Hwa Kim and Jane Sinagub, who assisted with all aspects of manuscript preparation, including expert editorial work and good judgment. Their contribution to the book is extensive. I would particularly like to recognize the careful and thoughtful work of Ae-Hwa Kim who made a significant contribution to the third edition.

We also benefited from the suggestions and revisions of outstanding reviewers of this edition. Like all authors, we were not always anxious to rewrite but soon realized the benefits from their helpful suggestions and resources. Thank you for your generous assistance:

Patricia M. Crawford, *University of Northern Iowa*

Barbara Driver, *Virginia Commonwealth University*

MaryAnne Mackenzie, *University of New Hampshire*

Edwina Pendarvis, *Marshall University*

Melisa Reed, *Marshall University*

Jeff Sigafoos, *University of Texas, Austin*

Georgine Steinmiller, *Henderson State University*

Carolyn Stuart, *Elon College*

We would particularly like to acknowledge those reviewers who provided expert guidance and suggestions on chapters. These individuals generously shared their knowledge and expertise and the chapters benefited from their expertise: Susan Johnston, University of Utah (communication disorders); Kathleen Robins, Janice Day, and Cheryl Winston, University of Utah (vision/hearing/physical challenges); Missy Olive, University of Texas (pervasive developmental disorders); and Jeff Sigafoos, University of Texas (developmental disabilities).

The personnel at Allyn & Bacon provided ongoing support for this book. Initially, Ray Short, Senior Editor, contacted us about writing the book and provided encouragement and continuous positive feedback. He was a wonderful resource when the going got tough, assuring us we were making fine progress. We would also like to thank the following for their assistance: Donna Simons, Production Administrator at Allyn & Bacon, and Karla Walsh and the team at Omegatype Typography, Inc. The third edition of the book benefited enormously from the caring and careful work of Virginia Lanigan and her assistant Erin Liedel. Upon the sudden death of our co-author Candace Bos, Virginia was a source of social and professional support. She truly guided this third edition through completion. We are very grateful to her.

We also would like to give a very special thank you to our husbands for their steadfast support and personal sacrifices: Jim Dammann, Bob Bos, and Jerry Schumm.

Last, we would like to dedicate this book to our co-author, colleague, and friend, Candace S. Bos, who died August 13, 2001. Her loss to us personally and professionally is profound. There simply are no words to describe it.

# Special Education and Inclusive Schooling

chapter

1

# chapter | outline

# focus | questions

1. What basic laws and procedures govern special education and inclusion?

2. As a classroom teacher, what are your responsibilities toward your students with special needs?

3. What systems and resources are in place in your school to help you teach students with special needs in your classroom?

4. How are professional collaboration and family involvement critical to the success of inclusive education?

5. What concerns do teachers, parents, and schools have about inclusion, and how can these issues be addressed?

6. What are some opportunities and challenges you can expect to find in your inclusive classroom?

# inter view

## Tiffany Royal

Tiffany Royal is a fifth-grade teacher at Flamingo Elementary School in Miami, Florida. During the past two years, she has worked in an inclusive classroom in which seven of her 34 students have been identified as students with disabilities. For up to two hours a day, a special education teacher, Joyce Duryea, works in Tiffany's classroom as a co-teacher. Each week, Tiffany and Joyce also meet for an hour or more to discuss students' progress and plan instruction for the following week.

Tiffany has been successful in maintaining her students with special needs in her inclusive classroom on a full-time basis. To honor her achievement, in 1994 the Dade County Council for Exceptional Children named her "Mainstreaming Teacher of the Year."

Here is Tiffany's advice for teachers working in inclusive classrooms:

Don't worry that you have to know everything about students with disabilities to be successful with them as a teacher. At first, I was concerned that I didn't know what to do and that I hadn't been specially trained. Then I realized that they are like the other students in my class, and many of the instructional practices I use work for all students. I just have to think about the special needs of students and make accommodations. It sounds hard, but it really isn't. My advice is get to know each of your students really well, and you will learn what types of adaptations work for them. I spend a few minutes at the end of the day making a list of students I need to be sure to spend a few minutes with the next day on a one-on-one. I think about what I want to accomplish with them. That really helps a lot. Also, the special education teacher is a big help. Joyce Duryea has given me many ideas, and I learn from watching her with the students.

I think about communicating frequently with parents. Our class publishes a newsletter every other week that gets sent home to every parent. Also, the parents of students with disabilities really appreciate the weekly notes that Joyce and I take turns sending home.

Like many new teachers, I was worried about the special education laws, IEPs, and conferences. I kept saying to myself, "What if I mess something up?" Again, the special education teacher was a big help. I realized I

wasn't responsible for everything, that there are many shared responsibilities. The most important thing to remember is that the IEP is not a legal contract but a plan to define goals for each of the students with disabilities. Actually, I do something like an IEP for my entire class.

I must admit, ever since I was little I wanted to be a teacher. When I imagined myself as a teacher, I never thought about students with disabilities in my class. Now I cannot imagine teaching without them. It sounds corny, but they add so much. I'll never forget José. The teachers here tell stories about him, you know, how he acted when he first came to school and all. You should see him now. I'm not saying he does all the work other students do, but he is making great progress. When he raises his hand and gets the answer right, he just beams and looks around the room to see that everyone noticed. I don't think I could teach any other way.

# introduction

Tiffany's account reflects the philosophy of this book. Our philosophy rests on the belief that teachers make a difference, that we must teach purposefully to empower all of our students to learn, that even small steps matter, and that if we monitor students' progress we can ensure their success. The aim of this book is to offer you the basic knowledge, tools, and strategies that will empower you as a classroom teacher to skillfully, confidently, and successfully promote learning for all your students.

The basic knowledge you need includes an understanding of the laws and procedures that govern special education and inclusion, so this is where we begin.

## IDEA and the Vocational Rehabilitation Act

Legislation for individuals with disabilities has provided them with education, employment, housing, and other rights that they previously were denied because of their disabilities. You can imagine how important the following two landmark pieces of legislation have been. The Individuals with Disabilities

Education Act (IDEA), P.L. (Public Law) 94–142, and the Vocational Rehabilitation Act, P.L. 93–112, have significantly improved the opportunities for individuals with disabilities.

**P.L. 94–142,** originally referred to as the Education for All Handicapped Children Act, was enacted in 1975, later reauthorized and expanded as the **Individuals with Disabilities Education Act (IDEA)** in 1990, and once more reauthorized in 1997. This legislation was designed to ensure that all children with disabilities receive an appropriate education through special education and related services. Figure 1.1 provides a summary of the history of laws governing special education.

According to Turnbull (1990), IDEA includes the following primary characteristics:

- **Zero reject/free appropriate public education.** No child with disabilities can be excluded from education. Mandatory legislation provides that all children with disabilities are given a free appropriate public education. Before IDEA, school officials who felt that they were not equipped to address the special needs of particular students would not accept such students into their schools.
- **Child find.** States are required to identify and track the number of students with disabilities and to plan for their educational needs.

─── FIGURE 1.1 ───

## History of the Federal Laws for the Education of Learners Who Are Exceptional

1973   Vocational Rehabilitation Act (VRA) (Public Law 93–112, Section 504)
- Defines "handicapped person"
- Defines "appropriate education"
- Prohibits discrimination against students with disabilities in federally funded programs

1974   Educational Amendments Act (Public Law 93–380)
- Grants federal funds to states for programming for exceptional learners
- Provides the first federal funding of state programs for students who are gifted and talented
- Grants students and families the right of due process in special education placement

1975   Education for All Handicapped Children Act (EAHCA) (Public Law 94–142, Part B)
- Known as the Mainstreaming Law
- Requires states to provide a free and appropriate public education for children with disabilities (ages 5 to 18)
- Requires individualized education programs (IEP)
- First defined "least restrictive environment"

1986   Education of the Handicapped Act Amendments (Public Law 99–457)
- Requires states to extend free and appropriate education to children with disabilities (ages 3 to 5)
- Establishes early intervention programs for infants and toddlers with disabilities (ages birth to 2 years)

1990   Americans with Disabilities Act (ADA) (Public Law 101–336)
- Prohibits discrimination against people with disabilities in the private sector
- Protects equal opportunity to employment and public services, accommodations, transportation, and telecommunications
- Defines "disability" to include people with AIDS

1990   Individuals with Disabilities Education Act (IDEA) (Public Law 101–476)
- Renames and replaces P. L. 94–142 (EAHCA)

- Establishes "people first" language for referring to people with disabilities
- Extends special education services to include social work, assistive technology, and rehabilitation services
- Extends provisions for due process and confidentiality for students and parents
- Adds two new categories of disability: autism and traumatic brain injury
- Requires states to provide bilingual education programs for students with disabilities
- Requires states to educate students with disabilities for transition to employment, and to provide transition services
- Requires the development of individualized transition programs for students with disabilities by the time the reach the age of 16

1997   Individuals with Disabilities Education Act (IDEA) (Public Law 105–17)
- Requires that all students with disabilities must continue to receive services, even if they have been expelled from school
- Allows states to extend their use of the developmental delay category for students through age 9
- Requires schools to assume greater responsibility for ensuring that students with disabilities have access to the general education curriculum
- Allows special education staff who are working in the mainstream to assist general education students when needed
- Requires a general education teacher to be a member of the IEP team
- Requires students with disabilities to take part in state-wide and district-wide assessments
- Requires states to offer medication as a voluntary option to parents and educators to resolve differences
- Requires a proactive behavior management plan to be included in the students's IEP if a student with disabilities have behavior problems
- Limits the conditions under which attorneys can collect fees under the IDEA

● **Age.** The ages during which children with disabilities must be educated are defined by the law, and these ages exceed those provided for nondisabled students. IDEA provides for special programs and services for all students with disabilities between

the ages of 3 and 21. Infants and toddlers with developmental delays (birth to 2 years of age) are also eligible to receive early intervention services.
● **Nondiscriminatory evaluation.** An evaluation that does not discriminate on the basis of language,

culture, and students' background, must be provided for each individual identified for special education. This is particularly challenging in states such as California, Florida, and Texas, where students identified for special education services represent more than 20 languages.

- **Individualized education program (IEP).** A plan developed to meet the special learning needs of each student with disabilities must be written, implemented, and reviewed.
- **Least restrictive environment.** IDEA defines the educational settings in which students are placed. The least restrictive environment is the setting most like that of nondisabled students that also meets each child's educational needs. Inherent within the least restrictive environment is the notion of continuum of services. *Continuum of services* means that a full range of service options for students with disabilities will be provided by the school system. These service options include self-contained classrooms, resource rooms, and homebound and general education programs.
- **Due process.** Due process not only ensures that everyone with a stake in the student's educational success has a voice, but also addresses written notification to parents for referral and testing for special education, parental consent, and guidelines for appeals and record keeping. IDEA guarantees the right to an impartial hearing if appropriate procedures outlined by IDEA are not followed and parents or schools believe that programs do not meet the student's educational needs.
- **Confidentiality of records.** IDEA requires that all records and documents regarding students with disabilities remain both confidential and accessible to parents.
- **Advocacy.** Advocates are assigned for individuals with disabilities who lack known parents or guardians.
- **Noncompliance.** IDEA requires that states mandate consequences for failure to comply with the law.
- **Parent participation.** Parents' participation and shared decision making must be included in all aspects of identification and evaluation of students with disabilities.

The Individuals with Disabilities Education Act of 1990 differs from the original legislation P.L. 94–142 in that it:

- Puts the person first and the use of the term "disability" second—for example, "students with learning disabilities" rather than "LD students."

- Requires that transition services be included in the individualized education programs of all students by at least age 16.
- Provides for states, as well as school districts, to be sued if they violate IDEA.
- Includes two additional categories: traumatic brain injury and autism.
- Adds assistive technology as a support service.

Heumman and Hehir (1997) outline some of the changes brought about by the 1997 reauthorization of IDEA. The act:

- Promotes the involvement of students with disabilities in the general education curriculum.
- Requires greater accountability for results.
- Recognizes that if any student with disabilities brings a weapon or illegal drugs to school, the school has the right to remove the student to an alternative educational setting for up to 45 days. During that time, however, necessary services for the student with disabilities may not cease. That is, the student must be allowed to participate in the general curriculum, to receive services and appropriate modifications, and to receive help for addressing behavior difficulties.
- Requires that the IEP not only describe the extent to which a student will be integrated, but also detail the aids and accommodations the student will receive within the general education classroom.
- Allows states and local districts to use "developmental delay" eligibility criteria through age 9 instead of one of the specific disability categories so that students will not be classified too early.
- Provides further flexibility by allowing IDEA-funded staff who work with students with disabilities in general education classrooms to work with others who need their help as well.
- Requires states to include students with disabilities in assessments with appropriate modifications and to develop alternative assessments for the small number of students who cannot participate in regular assessments.

The **Vocational Rehabilitation Act** (P.L. 93–112) prevents any private organization that uses federal funds, or any local or state organization, from discriminating against persons with disabilities solely on the basis of the disability. This law made a significant difference in the provision of equal opportunities and services for individuals with disabilities because agencies that accept state or federal monies must comply with the law. This law prohibits discrimination not only in public education, but also in the employment of persons with disabilities and in social and health services. Because of this law, many individuals with disabilities now have greater access to colleges and universities (Cartwright et al., 1995). Take, for example, the case of Kathy Carter. "Access to facilities has opened up the world for me and Kathy," said Amy Carter, Kathy's mother.

> Since Kathy's mobility is limited to scooting around or the use of a wheelchair, there were many places we could not go. The movie theater closest to our house has a show upstairs where they often show children's movies. I either have to go with another adult who can help me get Kathy up the stairs or we can't go at all. I must say, I've noticed a big difference recently. The new shopping mall near our house is completely wheelchair accessible.

## The Concept of Least Restrictive Environment

According to IDEA (P.L. 94–142), a continuum of educational services must be available for students with disabilities. This **continuum of services** ranges from the full-time general education classroom to a special day school or residential facility. Figure 1.2 shows the continuum of services in terms of the major placement alternatives.

Consideration for **educational placement** is dynamic and ongoing. Students' placements are continually reevaluated for opportunities to move to less restrictive environments. Fundamental to the law is the notion that students cannot be educated in more segregated settings simply because it is easier to do so (Osborne & DiMattia, 1994). The principle behind the least restrictive environment is that students are best served in the settings (most like those of their nondisabled peers) in which they can learn, ideally moving to less and less restrictive settings. A checklist for determining the least restrictive environment is provided in Figure 1.3.

Most students will receive services in the general education classroom, with support services provided as necessary. There are times, however, when students' needs are best met in other

> The Steps in the Special Education Process
>
> Step 1: Initial referral
>
> Step 2: Individual evaluation
>
> Step 3: Determining eligibility
>
> Step 4: Individualized Education Program
>
> Step 5: Annual review/ reevaluation (The Office of Vocational and Educational Services for Individuals with Disabilities, 2001)

---

FIGURE 1.2

### Continuum of Educational Services for Students with Disabilities from Least to Most Restrictive

**Least restrictive**

**Level I    General education classroom with consultation from specialists:** Student functions academically and socially in general education classroom full time. Specialists provide consultation.

**Level II    General education classroom; cooperative teaching or co-teaching:** Special education teacher and classroom teacher co-plan and co-teach for part of school day. For entire school day, student is included in general classroom, where support services are provided.

**Level III    Part-time placement in special education classroom:** Student is placed in the general education classroom for part of the school day and in the special education classroom, usually the resource room, for a certain number of hours daily.

**Level IV    Full-time special education classroom in a general education school:** Student is educated in a special education classroom housed in a general education school. This arrangement—of being educated in the special education room so students have contact with general education peers only during nonacademic periods—may include part-time involvement with general education students for activities such as physical education and lunch.

**Level V    Special school:** Student is provided special education services in a special education school.

**Most restrictive**

**Level VI    Residential school, treatment center, or homebound instruction:** Student is provided special education services at home, or resides in a school or treatment center in which education is provided.

---

FIGURE 1.3

## Determination of the Least Restrictive Environment (LRE)

School district decisions are based on formative data collected throughout the LRE process.

1. Has the school taken steps to maintain the child in the general education classroom?
   - What supplementary aids and services were used?
   - What interventions were attempted?
   - How many interventions were attempted?

2. Benefits of placement in general education with supplementary aids and services versus special education
   - Academic benefits
   - Nonacademic benefits (e.g., social and communication)

3. Effects on the education of other students
   - If the student is disruptive, is the education of other students adversely affected?
   - Does the student require an inordinate amount of attention from the teacher, thereby adversely affecting the education of others?

4. If the student is being educated in a setting other than the general education classroom, is he or she interacting with nondisabled peers to the maximum extent appropriate?
   - In what academic settings is the student integrated with nondisabled peers?
   - In what nonacademic settings is the student integrated with nondisabled peers?

5. Is the entire continuum of alternative services available from which to choose an appropriate placement?

---

*Source:* Yell, M. L. (1995). Least restrictive environment, inclusion, and students with disabilities: A legal analysis. *Journal of Special Education 28*(4), 389–404. Copyright © 1995 by PRO-ED, Inc. Reprinted by permission.

settings. The decision must be made on a student-by-student basis, with any level on the continuum potentially serving as the least restrictive environment for a target student. For example, many parents of children who are deaf prefer that they be educated in settings with other children who are deaf so that their children have opportunities to learn the culture and language of deafness.

In addition to defining the continuum of services, special education laws also identify the types of services to which students with disabilities are entitled. These **related services** include speech therapy, audiology, psychological services, physical therapy, occupational therapy, recreation, early identification and assessment, counseling (including rehabilitation counseling), medical services for diagnostic or evaluation purposes, school health services, transportation, social work services, and recreation, including therapeutic recreation. Orientation (including aid in traveling to, from, and around school) and mobility services were added to the list when IDEA was reauthorized in 1997.

Related services can be an extremely important part of a student's program. The requirements for related services follow:

> The term "related services" means transportation and such developmental, corrective, and other supportive services (including speech pathology and audiology, psychological services, physical and occupational therapy, recreation, including therapeutic recreation, social work services, counseling services, including rehabilitation counseling, orientation and mobility services, and medical services, except that such medical services shall be for diagnostic and evaluation purposes) only as may be required to assist a child with a disability to benefit from special education, and includes the early identification and assessment of disabling conditions in children (U.S. Department of Education, 1997).

**Part-Time Placement in Special Education**   Some students whose educational and social needs cannot be met solely within the general education classroom receive special education and related services (that is, counseling, speech, language, occupational or physical therapy, instruction, and so on) outside the classroom. Related services may be provided individually or in small or large groups.

A common educational placement, designed to meet the educational needs of students with disabilities outside the general education classroom, is the **special education resource room.** The resource-room model provides specialized, individualized, and intensive instruction to meet students' needs. Reading, writing, and math are the three academic areas most frequently addressed by the special education teacher in the resource room. Students can work in the resource room for as little as a few hours per week in an elementary school or one period per day in a secondary setting. Depending on their needs, students may work nearly full time in a resource setting.

Some resource rooms are designed to meet the needs of students identified as having a particular kind of disability—learning disabilities, for example. Other resource rooms are designed to meet the needs of students with varying exceptionalities. The term "varying **exceptionalities**" refers to the placement of students who represent a range of disability categories (e.g., students with emotional disorders, learning disabilities, and/or physical impairments and students who are gifted).

**Full-Time Placement in Special Education**   The educational and social needs of some students cannot be met through part-time placement in the general education classroom. These students may be placed in a special education classroom located in a general education school. Students placed in full-time special education classrooms often attend electives classes (such as physical education, music, art, and vocational education) with their nondisabled peers. If there are no full-time special education classrooms in the home school, students may be transported to schools outside their neighborhood. Many educators and parents, believing that the relocation of students to another school interferes with the students' social and personal adjustment, discourage such placements. Students who are placed full-time in special education classes should be closely monitored so that they can be placed as quickly as possible in the general education classroom.

**Special School or Residential Settings**   When the problems of students with disabilities are so severe and complex that adequate education cannot be provided in general education classrooms, students may be placed in special schools. These schools may be part of the school system, or the system may contract with private schools that specialize in programs for students with special needs. One advantage of special schools is that total enrollment is usually small, with technical services and individual attention more easily provided. One disadvantage to the school system is cost: Special schools are expensive, and transportation also can be expensive. Disadvantages for students are that travel to and from the school can be time consuming and that they have limited opportunities to interact during the school day with children who do not have disabilities.

**Homebound Instruction**   Students with health or physical problems that prevent them from attending school regularly and students who have been expelled from school may receive homebound instruction. The primary role of a homebound teacher is to provide direct instruction and to coordinate instructional programs between the school and the home. Although students with disabilities sometimes receive long-term homebound instruction, it usually is a short-term remedy until the student is able to return to school. Mariel Simpson explains:

> Over the past eight years my son Jalena, who has spina bifida, has been operated on six times. Af-

ter each of these operations, he needed to stay at home for eight to twelve weeks to recover. I felt very fortunate to have the homebound teacher come to my home to work with Jalena so that he would not get too far behind in his school work.

## research brief

### Effectiveness of Inclusion

The effectiveness of inclusion has been the subject of extensive discussion in the field of special education (Fuchs & Fuchs, 1994; Kauffman & Hallahan, 1995). Although discussions about the effectiveness of inclusion are likely to continue, most of these are not based on empirical evidence (Klingner, Vaughn, Hughes, Schumm, & Elbaum, 1998). Research revealed mixed results regarding the effectiveness of inclusion for students with disabilities (Carlberg & Kavale, 1980; Klingner et al., 1998; Waldron & McLeskey, 1998; Zigmond et al., 1995). On the basis of available evidence, there are many factors that may influence the effectiveness of inclusion (e.g., what type and severity of disability, services provided in inclusive settings). Thus, it is important to decide the placement of each student individually on the continuum of services based on his or her unique needs.

## The Individualized Education Program (IEP)

IDEA (P.L. 94–142) requires that an individualized education program (IEP) be developed for each student with special educational needs. The purpose of an IEP is to provide an appropriate education. IEPs are developed and implemented by the **multidisciplinary team (MDT)**. The MDT serves two purposes. First, the team determines whether the student has a disability and is eligible for special education services. If this is the case, then the team develops the IEP, which provides the foundation for establishing the educational program for the student. The multidisciplinary team includes a representative of the local education agency, the classroom teacher, the special education teacher, parents or guardians, a person who can interpret the instructional implications of evaluation results, and, when appropriate, the student. Depending on the student's needs, the team also includes professionals from the related services (such as social workers, speech and language pathologists, psychologists, and occupational therapists) and may include other professionals, such as doctors.

Each IEP must include the following information:

- The student's present levels of educational performance, including how the disability affects the student's involvement in general curriculum
- Measurable annual goals, including benchmarks or short-term objectives that enable the child to participate in the general curriculum and help meet any other education needs resulting from the disability
- Special education and related services to be provided to the student and a statement of the program modifications or supports for school personnel that will be provided for the student not only to attain annual goals and be involved in the general education curriculum, but also to participate in extracurricular and other nonacademic activities
- An explanation of the extent, if any, to which the student will not participate with nondisabled students in the general education class and in the extracurricular and other nonacademic activities
- Individual modifications in the administration of statewide or districtwide assessments or an explanation of why those assessments are inappropriate for the student and what alternative method will be used to assess the student. Figure 1.4 provides test accommodations that teachers perceive as relatively easy to implement
- Projected date for the beginning of services and modifications and their anticipated frequency, location, and duration
- How the student's progress toward annual goals will be measured
- What method will be used to inform parents, as often as the parents of nondisabled students, of their child's progress toward annual goals and whether that progress is sufficient to enable their children to achieve the goals by the end of the school year
- Beginning at age 14, transition services are described under the applicable components of the student's IEP that focus on the appropriate course of study. At age 16, the needed transition services, including, when appropriate, a statement of the interagency responsibilities or any needed linkages must be specified.

The IEP is a method for planning and assessment that reflects the judgment and input of the school system, specialists, teachers, parents, and students themselves. The IEP is a safeguard not only for students, but also for families and school systems. An example of an IEP is presented in Figure 1.5.

---

=== FIGURE 1.4 ===

**Test Accommodations**

- Allow sufficient space for answers
- Allow additional time to take test
- Have questions from test read to student
- Give more short quizzes rather than long tests
- Create large-print test
- Reduce the number of questions on test
- Identify key words in questions before taking test
- Reword test questions if necessary
- Verbally assist the student if necessary
- Provide study guide before taking test

*Source:* Adapted from Jayanthi, M., Epstein, M. H., Polloway, E. A., & Bursuck, W. D. (1996). A national survey of general education teachers' perceptions of testing adaptations. *The Journal of Special Education, 30*(1), 106.

**Participants in IEP Meetings** IEPs are intended to serve as planning guides for the student with special needs, not as mere paperwork. IEPs provide guidelines for educators for the daily education of the individual. Unfortunately, classroom teachers at the middle and secondary levels often do not participate in the IEP process and do not know which students in their classrooms have been identified as having special needs (Schumm & Vaughn, 1992a). Carl Turner, a middle-school teacher, put it this way:

> I know that Mike has an IEP and I read it at the beginning of the year, but I haven't really used it in my planning. There may be other students who have learning disabilities in my class, but I won't know until the special education teacher tells me.

Persons who are *required by law* to attend the IEP meeting include:

- A representative of the local education agency who is knowledgeable about the special education, the general curriculum, and the availability of resources of the local educational agency
- A school representative other than the teacher, such as a person designated by the school system
- Parents or guardians to ensure that they are informed and involved in the student's placement and progress
- The student when appropriate (Involving students in the planning of their educational goals is often appropriate, particularly at upper elementary grades and secondary grades.)
- The student's general and/or special education teacher (The teacher is involved in identifying realistic and appropriate educational goals for the student.)

—— F I G U R E  1.5 ——

**Sample IEP**

## Individual Education Program (IEP)

| I. DEMOGRAPHIC INFORMATION | | |
|---|---|---|
| | DATE<br><br>(MM/DD/YY) | _____ |
| PRINT STUDENT'S NAME  (LAST)  (FIRST)  M.I.)<br><br>_____ | STUDENT<br><br>ID. NO. | _____ |

| ADDRESS | PHONE | D.O.B. |
|---|---|---|
| | | |
| HOME SCHOOL NAME | ASSIGNED SCHOOL NAME<br><br>(Complete After Section X) | |

### II. CONFERENCE INFORMATION

CONFERENCE DATE: _____ ☐ Interim Review Date: _____

(MM   DD   YY)                                          (MM   DD   YY)

CONFERENCE TYPE:   ☐ Initial   ☐ Annual Review   ☐ Temporary Assignment   ☐ Reevaluation

(Check all that apply.)

☐ Consideration to/from Alternative Education Program   ☐ Region Staffing   ☐ District Placement Committee

| PARENT NOTIFICATION: | TYPE | DATE<br>(MM DD YY) | RESPONSE |
|---|---|---|---|
| *REQUIRED | *(1) Written (Attach to IEP) | | |
| | *(2) | | |
| MODE/LANGUAGE OF COMMUNICATION OF PARENT/GUARDIAN _____ | | | |

*(continued)*

━━━━━━ FIGURE 1.5 ━━━━━━

**Sample IEP** (*continued*)

---

### III. SIGNATURES AND POSITIONS OF PERSONS ATTENDING CONFERENCE

___ PROCEDUREAL SAFEGUARDS AVAILABLE TO PARENTS OF EXCEPTIONAL STUDENTS has been received by and was explained to the parent(s) or guardian(s) of the student.

___ Parent was not in attendance.

| Position | Name | Signature |
|---|---|---|
| LEA Representative: | | |
| Parent: | | |
| General Education Teacher: | | |
| Special Education Teacher: | | |
| Evaluation Specialist: | | |
| Student: | | |
| Others: | | |

---

### IV. EXCEPTIONAL STUDENT EDUCATION (ESE) PROGRAM ELIGIBILITY

The student has been determined eligible for the following ESE programs: _____

---

### V. PRESENT PERFORMANCE LEVELS/NARRATIVE

| Area assessed | Date | Instrument | Findings (Level/Ability) |
|---|---|---|---|
| | | | |
| | | | |
| | | | |
| | | | |
| | | | |

Narrative:

FIGURE 1.5

**Sample IEP** (*continued*)

| VI. DIPLOMA OPTION (Grades 8–12 only) |
|---|
| ☐ Standard Diploma                    ☐ Special Diploma |

---

VII. PROGRAMS FOR LIMITED ENGLISH PROFICIENT (LEP) EXCEPTIONAL STUDENTS
(Complete this section only if the student is LEP.)

HOME LANGUAGE OF STUDENT _____

LANGUAGE DOMINANCE/PROFICIENCY ASSESSMENT: _____ _____ _____
                                            (MM DD YY)   (Test Used)   (ESOL Level)

ESOL ENTRY DATE _____      TEST USED _____      RAW SCORE _____
                (MM DD YY)

ESOL EXIT DATE _____       TEST USED _____      RAW SCORE _____
               (MM DD YY)

RESULTS OF MOST RECENT STANDARDIZED ACHIEVEMENT TEST (if applicable): _____

TYPE AND LOCATION OF LEP SERVICES: (Check all that apply based upon present performance levels, behavioral observations, and the language dominance/proficiency assessment.)

|  | REGULAR PROGRAM* | ESE PROGRAM** |
|---|---|---|
| ☐ English for Speakers of Other Languages (ESOL) | ☐ | ☐ |
| ☐ Curriculum Content in English Using ESOL Strategies | ☐ | ☐ |
| ☐ Curriculum Content in the Home Language (Elem. Schools) | ☐ | ☐ |
| ☐ Bilingual Curriculum Content (Secondary Schools) | ☐ | ☐ |
| ☐ Home Language Arts or ☐ Home Language Strategies | ☐ | ☐ |

*LEP Plan Required              **Attach Goals and Objectives

POST RECLASSIFICATION MONITORING (for exited students who continue to participate in an ESE program.)

Please Note: Monitoring procedures do not require parent notification or signature.

1. Date: _____  ☐ no change in status  ☐ refer to IEP committee
   (MM DD YY)
Signature: _____

2. Date: _____  ☐ no change in status  ☐ refer to IEP committee
   (MM DD YY)
Signature: _____

3. Date: _____  ☐ no change in status  ☐ refer to IEP committee
   (MM DD YY)
Signature: _____

For use by IEP committee only:

☐ reclassify
Date: _____
     (MM DD YY)

☐ reclassify
Date: _____
     (MM DD YY)

☐ reclassify
Date: _____
     (MM DD YY)

*(continued)*

FIGURE 1.5

**Sample IEP** (*continued*)

| VIII. MEASURABLE ANNUAL GOAL/BENCHMARKS OF SHORT-TERM OBJECTIVES |
|---|
| Annual Goal: |
| Benchmarks or Short-Term Objectives: |
| Evaluation Method: |
| Review Dates and Results: |
| Method of Reporting Progress to Parents: |

| IX. SPECIAL EDUCATION AND RELATED SERVICES |
|---|

| Special Education Services | Location | Hours/Week |
|---|---|---|
| | | |
| | | |
| | | |
| | | |

| Related Services/ Supplementary Aids and Services | | Hours/Week |
|---|---|---|
| | | |
| | | |
| | | |
| | | |

— FIGURE 1.5 —

**Sample IEP (*continued*)**

---

### X. GENERAL EDUCATION PARTICIPATION
(Regular/vocational education teacher(s) should be included in, or informed of, results of IEP development.)

Description of participation (e.g., specific subjects, art, assemblies, yearbook, lunch, field trips, fund-raising, recess, etc.):

_____

_____

_____

Modifications required:        ☐ Increase/decrease instructional time        ☐ Use of special communication system
(select as appropriate)
                               ☐ Vary instructional methodology             ☐ Modification of tests

                               ☐ Consultation                               ☐ Other(s): Specify below

_____

_____

_____

Mainstream Cost Factor (specify):

(1) services, aids, and/or equipment        (2) applicable subject(s)        (3) amount of time per week

_____        _____        _____

_____        _____        _____

_____        _____        _____

---

### XI. LEAST RESTRICTIVE ENVIRONMENT PLACEMENT

Extent to which the student will not participate in general education:

Program                                                    Hours/Week

_____

_____

_____

Rationale for excluding the student from participation in general education:

____ Student frustration and stress

____ Student self-esteem and worth

____ Disruption of students in general classes

____ Disruption of students in special classes

____ Distractibility

____ Need for lower pupil-to-teacher ratio

____ Time required to master educational objectives

____ Need for instructional technology

(*continued*)

─── FIGURE 1.5 ───

**Sample IEP (*continued*)**

___ Mobility problems in a large school setting

___ Safety concerns due to physical conditions

___ Health and safety concerns requiring adaptive equipment

___ Emotional control causing harm to self and others

___ Social skills causing increased isolation

___ Difficulty completing tasks

___ Other(s):

_____

_____

---

**XII. PARTICIPATION IN STATEWIDE OR DISTRICTWIDE ASSESSMENT**

___ Student will participate in statewide or districtwide assessment.

___ Student will need modification to participate in assessments.

Modifications:

___ Flexible Scheduling   ___ Flexible Setting   ___ Recording of Answers   ___ Revised Format

___ Auditory Aids   Others:_____

Rationale for modifications:

If student will not participate in assessments, methods by which the student will be assessed:

_____

_____

Rationale for excluding the student from participation in assessments:

_____

_____

FIGURE 1.5

**Sample IEP (*continued*)**

| XIII. OTHER INFORMATION |
|---|

___ Medication(s):

_____

_____

___ Other (e.g., allergies, restrictions):

_____

_____

___ Board-approved physical restraint procedures may be used if student presents a danger to self and/or others or property.

| XIV. IEP IMPLEMENTATION |
|---|

Persons responsible for the implementation of this IEP include:

☐ ESE Teacher    ☐ Occupational Therapist    ☐ Physical Therapist    ☐ Orientation and Mobility Specialist    ☐ Speech/Language Pathologist

☐ Other(s): _____

_____

| XV. INITIATION/DURATION DATES |
|---|

Services delineated on the IEP, unless otherwise indicated:

• will initiate _____,
    (MM/YY)

• and have an anticipated duration through _____.
                                              (MM/YY)

| XVI. PARENT(S)/GUARDIAN(S) COMMENTS |
|---|

Parent(s)/Guardian(s), if present, please indicate:  ☐ agreement  or  ☐ disagreement

Comments: _____

_____

_____

_____

Notes: _____

_____

_____

_____

_____

# TechTalk

## Individual Education Programs Made Easy

Numerous software programs are designed to facilitate the creation of Individualized Education Programs (IEP), and many new programs and packages are being added rapidly. Several institutes produce software targeted at teachers. Some of the software currently available is described below.

Educational Software Institute provides three kinds of IEP software: *IEP WorksPro, IEP Manager,* and *IEP Writer Supreme. IEP WorksPro* tackles the task of automatically cutting selected items from the database of goals and objectives and pasting them into the new IEP document. The new IEP is then saved for modification

and updates. It allows the user to create his or her own database of objectives and modify it for each student. Perhaps the best feature is that IEPs can be created during parent conferences so that parents and teachers can leave with the new IEP document at the end of the meeting. Purchase of this program includes a site license allowing unrestricted use within a building. A run-time version of *FileMaker Pro* is included.

*IEP Manager* handles the redundant annual work involved in creating an IEP. The *IEP Manager* provides password-protected storage of sensitive data while allowing rapid, decentralized access to the IEP by authorized support service personnel. Features include user-modifiable goals and objectives, needs, and characteristics libraries. Data screens include demographics; needs; procedural dates; psychological, physical, and social primary provider information; consent for placement; goals/objectives; characteristics of service; services to be provided; behavior and study habits; communication—oral and written; persons attending; and more. It also includes a site license. It is easy to use and requires minimal training.

*IEP Writer Supreme* makes it easy to write a computer-generated IEP. It is flexible and contains a complete collection of forms for generating the IEP. There is even an option to hire the publisher to create an exact duplicate of the forms your district uses. The program also comes with a wide variety of goals and objectives that are completely editable. Goals and objectives can be copied and pasted directly into the IEP form. The program supports online services so you can share goals and objectives with teachers from all over

---

- An individual who can interpret the instructional implications of evaluation results
- Others whom the parents or school believe can help develop the IEP (As was mentioned earlier, this may include representatives from a range of related services and professions, e.g., medicine, physical therapy, and psychology.)

The school should ensure that parents attend IEP meetings by making every reasonable attempt to contact parents and accommodate their schedules. This includes scheduling meetings at times that are convenient for parents, giving ample advance notice of the meeting, securing mutual agreement for the time and place of the meeting, meeting through phone calls or home visits if parents cannot attend,

and providing a copy of the IEP to parents on request. If parent involvement cannot be obtained, the school should document all attempts to involve parents, including correspondence and a log of phone calls and visits. Some school districts have a placement specialist who takes responsibility for managing the placement and program development for students with IEPs. In other schools, the special education teacher takes this responsibility.

The role of the general education teacher in the IEP process varies because each school district handles IEP meetings a little differently. As the classroom teacher, however, you will be an important resource.

Each person is at the meeting because he or she has knowledge and experience that can assist in designing the best educational program for the student.

the country. This program also contains a set of diagnostic checklist forms as well as a skills checklist editor that permits the design of observation checklists for various skill areas such as visual, auditory perception, and more. The Student Profile Module includes a pre-IEP conference planner, which allows teachers to keep track of all contacts with the students, maintains a daily schedule for each student, and contains a complete database for keeping track of personal information (including a student photo). It also helps teachers prepare the specialist's report, with a checklist to ensure all pertinent areas for the report are covered. The Resource Specialist Notebook provides a well-documented and organized format, using a collection of forms for planning, assessing, programming, and evaluation for each student. The Resource Specialist Aide's Notebook provides a way to train an instructional aide quickly in basic educational practices, making the aide immediately useful. Use of this program on a Macintosh requires an LCIII (or better), System 7 (or higher), and a color monitor. Windows users need a 486 (or faster), and a color monitor.

ESI also produces *A+LS—Advanced Learning System Complete Series*, which is a dynamic product family of fully managed educational software. All core curricula for elementary, middle school, high school, and adult literacy are covered in depth in the 67 *A+LS* titles for reading, writing, mathematics, language arts, science, history, and geography, and their 2,700 lessons and 32,000 exercises. All titles operate under a single, highly advanced class and student manager that will launch third party software and allow the development of IEPs with outstanding and extensive reporting capability.

Details regarding *A+LS* can be obtained from Educational Software Institute, 4213 South 94th Street, Omaha, NE 68127, by phone at 1-800-955-5570, or by fax at 1-402-592-2017.

Parrot Software also provides software to facilitate writing IEPs and reports. The IEP software is for speech pathologists with IEP reporting responsibilities. A free demonstration disk is available on the World Wide Web at www.parrotsoftware.com. The demonstration is the actual program with the print function disabled. This software requires Windows 3.x, 95, or higher, a 486 processor or faster, and 8 MB RAM, which is available on most computers. Information regarding software to write reports can also be obtained at this site. *Instant IEP* and *Report Writer Plus* are designed to help the teacher compose personalized individual plans in seconds. The teacher can add a child's name to the list, select a goal from the list within the 1,100-item database, and then highlight the objectives, procedures, and criteria to include in the report. The report is automatically generated and appears in a Windows-style word processor. Users can format the report with a variety of fonts, including bold and italic, and print it. Orders can be placed for Parrot Software at 1-800-PARROT1 (1-800-727-7681). Online discounts are available.

Another site of interest to teachers is www.edsoft.com. This site contains information regarding software focusing on IEPs, reports, and other timesaving software for teachers. See also www.ieptrack.com, http://classiep.com, http://lserver.aea14.k12.ia.us/sped/sped.html, and www.arlington.k12.va.us/departments/IMT/Eshops/material/iep.html.

Not everyone knows the same things, so each person's contribution is unique and necessary. For example, the school psychologist often provides expertise on diagnostic test results and interpretation. You, however, are the expert on the curriculum for your content areas and grade levels. Your responsibility is to ensure that the goals that are designed to be implemented in your classroom reflect appropriate content and skills for your classroom. At the same time, everyone's knowledge of the student is useful to establish high, realistic behavioral and academic goals.

**The IEP Process**　Most school districts have developed their own format and procedures for writing IEPs. All members of the team contribute to the IEP, which should include everyone's ideas about the educational goals and objectives. The person who most frequently incorporates what the team agrees upon and who writes the IEP is the special education teacher.

 ## Responsibilities of Classroom Teachers

General education teachers often express concerns about the extent to which they need to know and understand the law as it pertains to individuals with disabilities. Daniele Ferguson put it this way:

> As a classroom teacher, I'm concerned about all of the children in my classroom. I want to do as good a job as I can, but I also realize that I cannot know

everything about every difficulty, learning and behavioral, that the children in my classroom will manifest. I know that I need to know who to contact when I have questions. But I suppose what is of the most interest to me is exactly what I'm responsible for and what I need to know so that I can successfully implement education programs for the students with special needs. Probably my biggest questions center around the law and what I need to do.

When asked what questions she had, Daniele provided the following list:

*Who is responsible for the IEP?*
The multidisciplinary team is responsible for developing the IEP; the person who is principally responsible for the IEP, however, is the special education teacher. The general education teacher and the parent might be responsible for particular objectives described in the IEP.

*Can I be held responsible if a student in my class does not accomplish all of the objectives in the IEP?*
The IEP is not a contract but rather is an agreement by which the teacher undertakes the optimum educational procedures to help ensure that the student meets the IEP objectives. Teachers cannot be held responsible for students' lack of progress on IEP goals unless it can be proven that teachers have not made efforts to fulfill their responsibilities.

*What if I was unable to attend the meeting at which the child's IEP was developed?*
Obtain a copy of the student's IEP from the special education teacher or meet with the special education teacher to identify the IEP objectives for which you are responsible.

*What should I do if I feel a student is not making adequate progress on his or her IEP?*
Communicate your observations to other members of the multidisciplinary team. Regular meetings with the special education teacher and other professionals who are providing services to the student will ensure that the student's progress is monitored. Also, meetings that involve parents or guardians will help you explain a student's progress and find ways to enhance his or her performance.

Although knowledge of the law is important, you should also be aware of the resources available to you when you have questions and need further information. Many people in your

school and district can help you. Experienced teachers tell us that their best resources are the special education teachers in their building, other teachers, the school psychologist, and the principal (Schumm & Vaughn, 1992a). IDEA is a law aimed at enhancing the quality and equity of education for all students. The law requires reasonable expectations of teachers. Your role is to help students fulfill the objectives in the IEP and to provide an appropriate education for all students (see Tips for Teachers 1.1).

Octavio Gonzalez, a ninth-grade English teacher, has three students with disabilities in two of his five sections of English. These students receive support services during the school day from the special education teacher, and Octavio meets occasionally with the special education teacher to plan and get suggestions for accommodating their needs in his English class. Octavio comments:

At first I was nervous about having students with disabilities in my class. One of the students has a learning disability, one student has serious motor problems and is in a wheelchair, and the third student has vision problems. Now I have to say that the adaptations I make to meet their special learning needs actually help all of the students in my class. I think that I am a better teacher because I think about accommodations now.

An eighth-grade teacher, Lin Chang, put it this way:

At first I was worried that it would be all my responsibility. But after meeting with the special education teacher, I realized that we would work together and I would have additional resources if I needed them. Furthermore, I think more about keeping in touch with the parents so that they are always informed of progress. Doing all of this communication on the telephone is not always possible, so I send a lot of notes home.

Unfortunately, monitoring the progress of students included into general education sometimes becomes the sole responsibility of the special education teacher. This is not an effective procedure. An appropriate education for the students with disabilities is most likely to occur when the special and general education teachers work together. Our studies with middle- and high-school teachers reveal that obtaining access to students' IEPs and psychological reports (to be used to guide teacher planning for students with disabilities) is difficult (Vaughn & Schumm, 1994). Teachers believe that their best sources of information are parents, former teachers, or the students themselves (Schumm & Vaughn, 1992a). Thus, middle- and high-school teachers need to consider adaptations that provide for the special learning needs of students with disabilities and also enhance instruction for all their

*The IEP is a plan, not a contract, and teachers cannot be held responsible for students' lack of progress toward IEP goals if they do everything feasible to ensure that the plan is implemented.*

## Tips for Teachers

### 1.1  How Can You Meet Your Special Education Responsibilities?

- Ask the special education teacher what reports are relevant to successful instruction of students with disabilities in your class, then read these reports.
- Ask the special education teacher for suggestions for enhancing the learning of students with disabilities in your classroom.
- Ask the special education teacher to co-teach your class or demonstrate lessons that show how his or her suggestions can be implemented.
- Attend relevant meetings (about your students with disabilities) that involve parents and other school personnel.
- Reexamine IEPs quarterly and check that you monitor the progress of students with disabilities in your classroom.

- For each student with disabilities in your classroom, keep a folder of relevant work samples to document progress.
- Maintain parent contact through occasional phone calls and written notes.
- Meet regularly with the special education teacher. If he or she does not already work in your classroom, extend an invitation to come in and help you instruct students with special needs.
- If you are concerned about a student's progress, don't hesitate to inform the special education teacher.

students. Remember, a few minutes of one-on-one purposeful teaching is an effective way to assess progress and provide directed instruction. We have found several accommodations that general education teachers can make that not only assist students with disabilities in the general education classroom, but also enhance instruction for all students. These approaches, described in detail later in this book, are summarized in Tips for Teachers 1.2.

## Participating in the Referral and Planning Process

Approximately 13 percent of the school-age population receives special education services (U.S. Department of Education, 2000). These are students whose educational and social/emotional needs are not expected to be met through traditional instructional procedures alone.

The term "disabilities" refers to conditions that include mental retardation, hearing impairments, vision impairments, speech and language impairments, learning disabilities, serious emotional disturbance, orthopedic impairments, other health impairments, autism, traumatic brain injury, deafness and blindness, and multiple disabilities. The classification of students into categories of disability is controversial. Many people believe that labels are nec-

essary because they provide a common understanding of the student's needs and help to identify appropriate special education services. Others believe that the labels conjure up negative stereotypes, harm students' self-concepts, and cause confusion because each category subsumes many different defining characteristics. Regardless, labels and categories can be used in ways that are helpful as well as harmful. You need to consider how to think of the person first, rather than the type of disability. Figure 1.6 shows the system of federal categories and the percentage (by category) of students who are provided with special education.

How do classroom teachers participate in the IEP process? What are three ways that teachers participate in the referral and planning process for students with special needs?

# Tips for Teachers

## 1.2   Adaptations for Students with Disabilities Included in the General Education Classroom

- Respect all students as individuals with differences (e.g., be aware of their capabilities and problems, and make exceptions accordingly), and encourage all students to respect included students.
- Establish appropriate routines (e.g., establish a setting so that students know what is expected; be consistent).
- Adapt effective classroom management strategies for students with special needs (e.g., time out, point systems).
- Provide reinforcement and encouragement (e.g., encourage effort, provide support when students get discouraged).
- Establish personal relationships with students (e.g., get to know students as individuals, determine student interests and strengths).
- Help students find appropriate ways to deal with feelings (e.g., by expressing their feelings through drawings or writings; provide brief periods of time away from class).
- Communicate frequently with included students (e.g., plan frequent short, one-on-one conferences, and discuss potential modifications with students).
- Communicate with the special education teacher (e.g., exchange notes and talk informally with the special education teacher).
- Communicate with parents of included students (e.g., exchange notes and talk informally with parents, encourage parents to provide support for students' education).
- Establish expectations for all students (e.g., expect the best from every student).
- Make adaptations for students when developing long-range (yearly/unit) plans (e.g., establish realistic long-term objectives).
- Make adaptations for students when developing daily plans (e.g., be alert to problems that could pose special difficulties for students).
- Plan assignments and activities that allow included students to be successful (e.g., try to structure assignments to reduce frustration).
- Allot time for teaching learning strategies as well as content (e.g., test-taking skills, note-taking skills, and so on).
- Adjust physical arrangement of room (e.g., modify seating arrangements).
- Adapt general education classroom materials (e.g., different textbooks, supplemental workbooks).

- Use alternative materials (e.g., different textbooks, supplemental workbooks).
- Use computers to enhance learning (e.g., as a tool for writing, as a tool for practicing skills).
- Monitor the included students' understanding of directions and assigned tasks (e.g., ask students to repeat or demonstrate what you have asked them to do, check with students to be sure they are performing assignments correctly).
- Monitor the included students' understanding of concepts presented in class (e.g., attend to, comment on, and reinforce understanding of vocabulary, abstract ideas, key words, time sequences, and content organization).
- Provide individual instruction (e.g., plan for one-on-one sessions after school, allocate time for individual instruction during class).
- Pair students with a classmate (e.g., to provide assistance with assignments, to provide models for behavior and academics, and for social support).
- Involve students in small-group activities (e.g., allow students from different levels to work in small groups).
- Involve students in whole-class activities (e.g., encourage class participation of included students).
- Provide extra time (e.g., schedule extra time for skill reinforcement and extra practice).
- Adapt pacing of instruction (e.g., break down materials into smaller segments, use step-by-step approaches).
- Keep records to monitor students' progress (e.g., keep a folder of students' papers, keep a progress chart).
- Provide students with ongoing feedback about performance (e.g., meet periodically with students to discuss academic and behavioral performance).
- Adapt evaluations (e.g., use oral testing, give more time for tests, modify administration procedures).
- Adapt scoring/grading criteria (e.g., alter criteria for grades).

*Source:* Adapted from Schumm, J. S., & Vaughn, S. (1991). Making adaptations for mainstreamed students: General classroom teachers' perspectives. *Remedial and Special Education, 12*(4), 18–27. Copyright © 1991 by PRO-ED, Inc. Adapted and reprinted by permission.

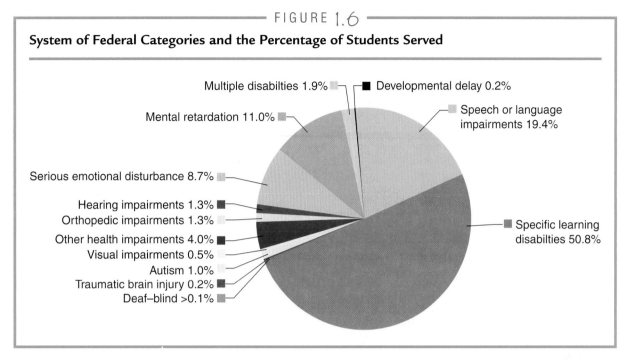

FIGURE 1.6

**System of Federal Categories and the Percentage of Students Served**

*Source:* U.S. Department of Education, Office of Special Education Programs, Data Analysis System (DANS). (2000). *Twenty-Second Annual Report to Congress on the Implementation of the Individuals with Disabilities Education Act.*

While there has been over-representation of psychiatric disabilities in Hollywood (54 percent of Academy Award–winning films), none of the Academy Award–winning films has depicted the most frequently identified disabilities category: learning disabilities (Safran, 1998).

Students are identified as having special needs through a system of referrals. Students who have obvious disabilities (such as significant hearing, visual, or physical impairments or significant mental retardation) are usually referred and identified before age 5. For these children, the disabilities are obvious to parents and pediatricians, and intervention begins early in the child's life. Students with mild to moderate disabilities are often identified by classroom teachers or parents after they begin school.

**The Prereferral Assistance Team**   Referrals for assessment and appropriate intervention services are often initiated by classroom teachers. Many schools have established school-based **prereferral assistance teams (PATs)** to screen students for assessment. The prereferral assistance team is a group of teachers from the same school who meet regularly to discuss the specific progress of students whom other teachers in the school have brought to their attention. This school-based, problem-solving team is designed to help teachers make classroom accommodations that maximize opportunities for students to succeed in the general education classroom and might make referral for special education unnecessary. The model provides

a forum where classroom teachers can meet and participate in a collaborative, problem-solving process.

Prereferral assistance teams work toward the following goals:

● Provide suggestions to the classroom teacher
● Accommodate students' academic and behavioral needs
● Reduce the need for referral to special education
● Assist the teacher with the referral process if necessary

Although prereferral strategies take different forms in different school districts, there are three general models (Strickland & Turnbull, 1990):

● The resource consultation model
● The special education teacher as part-time consultant model
● The teacher assistance team (TAT) model

**Consultation Models**   The special education teacher as a consultant is a traditional prereferral intervention model. Classroom teachers who have students with learning and behavioral difficulties and other disabilities in their classrooms frequently look to the special education teacher for advice and support (Schumm & Vaughn, 1992a). Teachers might ask the special education teacher to observe students in the classroom and in other settings to provide initial suggestions for assistance.

In a second consultation model, the special education teacher works part-time in general education classrooms to assist teachers with students who have been identified as requiring special education but whose needs generally can be met in the general education classroom. The special education teacher also assists teachers in implementing practices to enhance academic and social outcomes for students at risk for referral to special education.

**The Teacher Assistance Team**   The teacher assistance team (TAT) (Chalfant & Pysh, 1989, 1993; Chalfant et al., 1979) provides initial strategies and support for classroom teachers prior to referring a student for assessment for special education services. According to Chalfant and colleagues, schools may benefit in several ways by using teacher assistance teams:

- Classroom teachers have considerable knowledge and talent and can assist each other in meeting the needs of targeted students.
- Classroom teachers can and do help many students with disabilities. Every effort should be made to meet students' needs in the classroom before referral for special education.
- Teachers who work together can solve more problems more effectively than teachers who work alone.
- Teachers can increase their skills and knowledge through solving the academic and social problems of students.

Figure 1.7 provides an example of a form that might be used to assist with prereferral. During a TAT meeting, team members (using the guidelines in Tips for Teachers 1.3) participate in a problem-solving process that lasts approximately 30 minutes.

FIGURE 1.7

**Prereferral for Special Education Services**

**Directions:** Please complete all sections of this form. The form should be sent to the Teacher Assistance Team. Complete and provide specific information that will assist the team in providing as much assistance as possible. Use behavioral descriptions whenever possible.

**Teacher** _____

**Grade/Class** _____

**Date** _____

**Student** _____

**Age** _____

1. Describe what you would like the student to be able to do that he or she does not presently do.
2. Describe what the student does (strengths) and what he or she does not do (difficulties).
3. Describe what you have done to help the student cope with his or her problem.
4. Provide background information and/or previous assessment data relevant to the problem.

## Adapting Instruction

In addition to participating in planning, prereferral, and referral procedures, the chief responsibility of classroom teachers is to adapt curriculum and instruction to accommodate students' special needs. "What does it mean to adapt instruction for students

# Tips for Teachers

## 1.3   Problem-Solving Guidelines for TAT Meetings

- Present and review summary information about students from your prereferral form or notes.
- Identify the primary concern and describe interventions you and other teachers have tried.
- Brainstorm and evaluate ideas for potentially solving the problem.
- Select a goal to address the problem and identify objectives and procedures for solving it.

- Discuss suggestions with the classroom teacher and further refine your classroom intervention plan.
- Develop a means of measuring the success of the intervention plan.
- Establish a date and time for a 15-minute follow-up meeting to evaluate the effectiveness of the plan.

with disabilities?" asked Anna Schmidt, a tenth-grade social studies teacher. "I have certain objectives I need to meet for all of my students. Does this mean I alter these objectives?" Anna's questions are relevant to issues related to effective interventions. Classroom teachers can greatly help their students with special needs by making adaptations that positively affect learning for all students in the classroom.

> This book takes a cross-categorical approach—that is, accommodations for exceptional learners are discussed in terms of their shared needs rather than in terms of their identification as members of a disability category.

Many of the adaptations you make for students with disabilities will enhance learning for all students in your classroom. For example, Maria Arguelles, an eighth-grade teacher, develops an outline of her lectures. She projects this outline on a screen, pointing out her location in the outline as she presents key information. This procedure not only helps students with disabilities who have difficulty organizing information, taking notes, and identifying key ideas, but also enhances learning for all the students in her classroom.

Looking for students' strengths and ways to say "good job" also promotes learning for all students. Jane Gordon, a fourth-grade teacher, was a pro at this. She realized that motivation is the key to success, particularly for the students with disabilities in her classroom, and she put considerable effort into knowing the strengths and interests of each student and recognizing those strengths and interests whenever possible.

## r e s e a r c h **b r i e f**

### Models for Adapting Instruction

A study of 53 teachers who planned and developed a program to integrate students with moderate or severe disabilities into general education schools and classrooms yielded guidelines for key stakeholders at the school (Janney et al., 1995).

*District Administrators*—(1) Provide a clear and open message that you want to support what is best for all students and that you want to encourage integration of students with moderate or severe disabilities. (2) Teachers do not want a mandate that they must include every student full-time in general education no matter what. (3) Provide a "green light," when appropriate, to go ahead with integration of students with moderate to severe disabilities.

*Principals*—(1) The key to success is a positive tone from the principal regarding integration and acceptance of students with moderate or severe disabilities.

(2) Start with teachers who volunteer to participate, rather than forcing all teachers to participate. (3) Involve everyone in the planning and preparation for the inclusion of students with moderate and severe disabilities. (4) Provide information, new resources, and training so that teachers feel knowledgeable and prepared to meet the needs of exceptional learners. (5) Provide the resources so that the program can be implemented effectively, and handle the logistics from central administration, parents, and other key stakeholders. (6) Start small (a few teachers and students) and then build the program as it succeeds.

*General Education Teachers*—(1) Have an open mind about the process. Many teachers reveal that their anxieties and concern were not warranted. (2) Work collaboratively with other teachers, especially the special education teacher. (3) Help the student with disabilities to acquire full membership in the school and class community.

## Transition: Expanding the Impact of IDEA

With the amendments of IDEA, the impact of IDEA has expanded to include (1) services for infants, toddlers, and young children from birth to age 5 and (2) transition planning and services for adolescents as they move from high school to postsecondary education, adult life, and the world of work.

**Early Intervention and Transition from Early Childhood to School**  The 1986 IDEA amendments mandated services for young children with developmental delays (beginning at age 3) and also made infants and toddlers with or at risk for developmental delays (birth to 2 years of age) eligible to receive early intervention services. **Early intervention services** are comprehensive services that incorporate goals in education, health care, and social services (Hanson & Lynch, 1989). The important role that the IEP plays in program planning for school-age students with disabilities is taken on, for children from birth to 3 years of age, by the **individualized family service plan (IFSP)**. As the name suggests,

> The National Association for the Education of Young Children (NAEYC) has more than 103,000 members who provide services to young children (birth to age 8). NAEYC has developed guidelines entitled *Developmentally Appropriate Practice in Early Childhood Programs Serving Children from Birth through Age 8.*

however, the IFSP broadens the focus to include not only the child, but also the family and their needs in supporting a young child with disabilities.

If you are a kindergarten teacher, you probably will have the opportunity to teach young children who, having received early intervention services, are making the transition from preschool to your classroom. It is important for you to remember that for families and children with disabilities, these transitions are among the most significant times in their lives, filled with uncertainty and concern. Following are some comments from parents:

> "I was scared to have him go to public school. I worry about him a lot. . . . If I had it my way, I'd never send him to school" (Johnson et al., 1986, p. 15).

> "I saw making the transition to a preschool program in the school district as an extremely traumatic experience, second only to learning of Amy's diagnosis" (Hanline & Knowlton, 1988, p. 116).

As a teacher, you can help parents of children with special needs by recognizing that their fears and concerns are expected and realistic and by providing information about your classroom and the school to help alleviate their concerns (Fowler et al., 1991; Wolery, 1989). You can also help to facilitate this transition by doing the following:

- Attending the IEP or IFSP meeting before transition so that you are aware of the child's strengths, the goals planned, and techniques and strategies that have been successful. You can meet the child's parents and current teachers, ask questions, and determine how this child's goals fit with goals for your other students.
- Meeting with the child's parents before the transition to learn about their goals for their child, the child's strengths and needs, and strategies they have found that help their child succeed in preschool.
- Setting up a regular means of communication with the child's parents and former teachers, particularly for the first several months. Invariably, questions will arise that can be answered easily by the parents and those who have been working with the child. Do not hesitate to use these resources.

**Transition from School to Work and Other Postschool Activities**   The 1990 amendments to IDEA mandated transition planning and transition services for students from 16 years of age (or 14 years and even younger if appropriate) to age 21. In IDEA, transition services are defined as "a coordinated set of activities for a student with a disability, designed within an outcome-oriented process, which promotes movement from school to postschool activities including postsecondary education, vocational training, integrated employment (including supported employment), continuing and adult education, adult services,

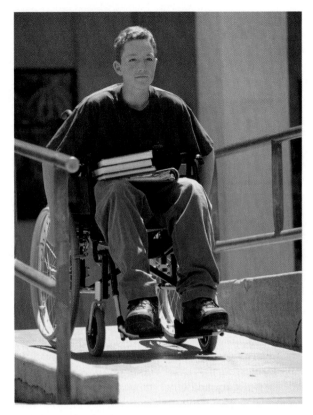

Why was IDEA expanded to include eligibility for transition planning for individuals with disabilities from birth to age 21? In what transition activities might this student be involved when he is in high school?

independent living, or communication participation" (P.L. 101–476, 602[a][19]). The law also notes that these activities should be based on the student's needs, preferences, and interests. The activities include instruction, community experiences, the development of employment and other adult-living objectives and, when appropriate, vocational evaluation, rehabilitation counseling, and the acquisition of daily living skills.

This emphasis on transition planning and services came in response to the growing concern about the number of students with disabilities who were unemployed or underemployed as adults and the limited emphasis on vocational education and adult living in many secondary programs for students with disabilities. For example, a 1994 Harris poll found that 3 of 10 adults with disabilities were working full- or part-time and that 79 percent of those not working who were of working age indicated that they would like to have jobs (Harris & Associates, 1994). A study in Vermont linked successful employment and higher wages following school to vocational education and support services during high school (Hasazi et al., 1989). As the Vermont study implies, an important part of changing this pattern is the provision of transition services, including supported employment during high school, so that students can develop the social and job skills they need to obtain and continue employment.

A key component of these transition services is the **individualized transition plan** incorporated into the IEP. This transition plan should state what transition services are necessary and, when appropriate, should include a statement of the interagency responsibilities and linkages (P.L. 101–476, 1990). Many districts interpret this by including in the IEP specific goals and objectives for transition, then adding a list of classes and activities that would provide opportunities for students to meet these goals and objectives. Sample objectives follow:

- By the end of the semester, Jason will develop the skills to complete job applications successfully. (Taught in career exploration class and by completing job applications with job developer.)
- By the end of the school year, Nancy will develop positive work habits (e.g., arriving on time, interacting with co-workers). (Taught in career exploration class and during work experiences supported by the job developer.)
- Within the next three years, Maria will develop computer skills in word processing, databases, and spreadsheets to the degree that she can effectively use them on a job. (Taught in computer classes and during work experiences supported by the job developer.)

With the increased emphasis on transition, vocational education, and work experience opportunities during high school for students with disabilities, many districts have special education personnel who work in this area. Mary Hinson, a job developer at Catalina High School, is one such person. She comments on her job and the difference it makes for helping students:

> I believe that the work I do as a job developer makes the difference for many students with disabilities and lets them leave high school already employed and adjusted to the world of work. I also believe that the opportunities provided through Catalina's transition program are the best dropout deterrent for students with disabilities, particularly with learning and emotional disabilities. What I do is work with the students, their teachers, and parents to plan a program that allows them to develop job and independent living skills, take relevant coursework both at the high school and at the community college, and have relevant work experiences. I also network with agencies and postsecondary institutions. For example, I will assist college-bound students in exploring possible community colleges and universities, in learning about support programs for students with disabilities at those institutions, and in completing the application process.
>
> A big part of my job is developing partnerships with businesses that will provide initial training and "the first job" for students with disabilities. One of these partnerships that I am particularly proud of is with AutoZone. Through this partnership, we have a classroom that is set up like an AutoZone store. Students with disabilities and their nondisabled peers take this class and learn the various facets of running an auto parts store. The class is co-taught by the marketing teacher and myself. I've learned more about sales and

> Important to making a successful transition from school to adult life is developing self-determination and self-advocacy skills, including the skills of considering options, making appropriate choices, and communicating choices to others (Schloss et al., 1993; Van Reusen et al., 1994).

## making a Difference

### Teaching on Purpose

The philosophy of this book is that classroom teachers can help their students with disabilities by teaching "on purpose," that is, by being mindful and proactive in using opportunities to make a difference in these students' classroom experiences. Contrary to common belief, purposively teaching students with special needs does not

## The 60-second Lesson

need to take a great deal of time. You can make a difference in only a minute. For example, think about having one or two 60-second lessons with each of your special-needs students every day. How is Darnell progressing on a given IEP objective? What directed feedback can you provide to Marlene to help her achieve her goals? To reflect the value of 60-second lessons in classroom practice, a feature called "Making a Difference" provides an example in every chapter of this book.

fixing a car in the last four years than you can imagine. And the students participating in this class find themselves prepared not only in general job skills but also specific skills related to sales and auto repair.

Clearly, Mary has a different role from that of a typical special education teacher. If you teach in high school, you will want to take the time to find out about transition services and the job developers or persons in charge of transition planning and services. Knowing about a student's transition goals will help you tailor your accommodations so that they are relevant for the student's long-term career goals. For example, if a student with a learning disability is planning to enter the field of drafting, then emphasizing measuring skills in basic math class and computer-assisted design in computer classes may be particularly beneficial for this student.

## Role of Collaboration in Meeting Students' Special Needs

Collaboration between general and special education teachers is occurring in schools across the nation (Dettmer, Dyck, & Thurston, 1999). Greater collaboration among education professionals has grown out of increased awareness that students with disabilities are more likely to succeed in general education classrooms if they receive targeted support services in the classroom. The goal of collaboration models is to ensure that included students remain in the classroom while continuing to receive the accommodations they need to succeed. The goal of collaboration is to achieve ongoing dialogue between all persons who can provide support for the education and social needs of the students.

At the center of the collaboration model is the classroom teacher. Research suggests that three conditions must be met for collaboration models to work (Idol, Nevin, & Paolucci-Whitcomb, 2000; West & Idol, 1990):

● Teachers need access to opportunities for training and professional development.
● School administrators need to support the model.
● Teachers' and students' schedules must be flexible.

With increased interest in including students with disabilities in general education classrooms full time, there has been increased movement toward a collaboration model. Despite this increased interest,

---

FIGURE 1.8

**Benefits and Challenges of Consultation and Collaboration Models**

**Benefits**
- Students with special needs are served in the classroom.
- Learning for all students is enhanced through spillover effects.
- Social stigma of exceptionality is reduced.
- Teachers gain new knowledge and skills.
- Teachers develop more integrated curriculum and instructional variety.
- Teachers share both burdens and rewards of working with students with disabilities.
- Importance of labels and categories of disability decreases.
- Models work at all grade levels.

**Challenges**
- Teachers need greater communication and problem-solving skills.
- Special educators' case loads need to remain realistic.
- Expectations of results need to remain realistic.
- Results need to be evaluated for effectiveness.
- Students need continued access to the continuum of services.
- Adequate funding, administrative support, and flexible scheduling need to be maintained.

---

there is limited research data documenting the effectiveness of this approach to meeting the needs of students with disabilities (Fuchs & Fuchs, 1988; Klingner et al., 1998b). Many administrators support consultation and collaboration models because they view them as opportunities to cut the costs of educating students with disabilities. This is a misunderstanding because the consultation and collaboration model, when appropriately done, does not reduce costs. Figure 1.8 outlines some perceived benefits and challenges of collaboration models that you should be aware of.

## Cooperative Teaching

**Cooperative teaching,** or **co-teaching,** occurs when general and special education teachers work together to coordinate curriculum and instruction and to teach heterogeneous groups of students in the general education classroom setting (Dettmer et al., 1999; Idol et al., 2000). The benefits of cooperative teaching are that the teachers have the opportunity to co-plan and co-teach and thus to coordinate and assess the ongoing educational programs of all students. Furthermore, the responsibilities and rewards

In what type of professional collaboration are these teachers engaged? What other forms of collaboration are important for achieving goals in meeting students' special needs?

of meeting the needs of students with disabilities are shared. Finally, all students in the classroom are likely to benefit from the teachers' expertise and coordination.

The teachers broadly plan their overall goals and desired outcomes for the class, identify students for special accommodations, and design adaptations and supports to meet the individual needs of students and enhance the learning of all students. The teachers also decide which instructional period they will co-teach and when and how they co-plan.

How might co-teaching actually work in the classroom? While one of the teachers delivers some instruction to the group as a whole, for example, the other teacher works with small groups or individual students. The special education teacher is not limited to working only with students who have disabilities but can include in the group other students who benefit from the accommodations provided.

Patty Cohen is a special education teacher who works in a cooperative teaching arrangement with Karen Feller, a fifth-grade teacher. Karen has six students with disabilities in her classroom, and Patty spends two hours each day in her room. Additionally, Karen has a teaching assistant for four hours a day. During a 90-minute language arts period, three teachers are in the classroom. Patty and Karen take turns as lead teacher and small-group teacher. Patty has time to work with students individually or in pairs to teach specific skills. Patty and Karen make cooperative teaching look simple. As you observe them in the classroom, you are aware of how easily the class grouping arrangements flow from one configuration to the next and how comfortably the teachers move from lead teacher to small-group in-

structor. "It's very easy for us," they say almost in unison. "Both of us have very high expectations for the students, and we strive never to waste a minute of instructional time. This requires planning on our part, but it's worth it."

Zigmond and Baker (1995) have investigated the many ways in which special and general education teachers work together to meet the needs of students with disabilities. As was described in the preceding paragraph, sometimes co-teachers share responsibilities for small-group and large-group instruction. This is not always the case, however. In some settings, the special education teacher works only with the students with disabilities. A series of research studies on cooperative teaching revealed that cooperative teaching may not always work (McIntosh, Vaughn, Schumm, Haager, & Lee, 1993; Schumm & Vaughn, 1991, 1992a; Schumm et al., 1995; Vaughn & Schumm, 1994). Some general education teachers at secondary level stated that they had little contact with the special education teacher and were unaware of IEPs (Bos & Vaughn, 2002). However, communication between general education teachers and special education teachers is important for successful inclusion for students with disabilities.

## Family Collaboration

Parents are the most influential persons in a child's life. This is particularly true for exceptional students, whose parents serve multiple roles, including those of advocate and information source. Fundamental to the implementation of IDEA is parent involvement and collaboration (Knoblauch, 1998). Parent rights in the educational decision-making process include the following: (a) Parents should be notified and their permission should be obtained before identification, evaluation, or educational placement; (b) parents may request an evaluation when they think their child needs potential special education and related services; (c) parents may request an independent evaluation at public expense when they disagree with the educational evaluation of the school; (d) parents may request a reevaluation when they think their child's educational placement is no longer appropriate; (e) parents may request their child to be tested in his or her primary language; (f) parents may participate in the development of IEP or IFSP, including placement; (g) parents may request a due process hearing to resolve differences with the school; and (h) parents should be informed about their child's progress at least as often as parents of children without disabilities (Knoblauch, 1998; Yell, 1998). During the middle- and high-school years, students are encouraged to participate with their parents (Van Reusen & Bos, 1994). Even though the literature clearly suggests the benefits of parent involvement, actual parent–teacher collaborative practices are not as comprehensive as they could be (Hilton & Henderson, 1993). In their study of parent involvement, Bennett, Deluca, and Bruns (1997) found that parents prefer to be physically present at the school, while teachers would rather make phone calls and send notes home.

The intention of the law is that parent involvement will benefit the student in many ways (Shea & Bauer, 1991), including the following:

- Parents will be able to provide knowledge about the student that should influence what and how he or she is taught.
- Parent knowledge of the student's educational program will ensure school-to-home continuity so that many skills can be reinforced in both settings.
- Parent knowledge and involvement will increase expectations for the student and result in academic and social gains.
- Parent involvement ensures a safeguard so that the needs of the student are discussed and met by the school system.

In many cases and many school systems, parents' roles are collaborative. They provide essential information to the multidisciplinary team that assists in the development of an appropriate IEP and a high-quality educational program. This, however, is not always the case. Parents often feel overwhelmed by the amount of information they are provided and the technical terms that are used; they can be intimidated by the number and qualifications of professionals present at meetings. This results in parents who are present but are not active, collaborative members (Rochelle, 2001; Vaughn et al., 1988b). Often, too much emphasis is placed on compliance rather than on genuine communication (Harry et al., 1995).

What can you do so that parents serve as active, collaborative resources? Some key ideas are provided by Dettmer and colleagues (1999):

- Remember that a teacher's place is on the parents' side as a team member working for a common goal: the student's success.
- Become aware of your own feelings of defensiveness. Taking a deep breath and putting feelings aside will help teachers to continue building positive relationships. If that is not possible, teachers should postpone interactions until the defensiveness can be handled.
- Remember that the focus must be on the needs and interests of parents and their children, not on their values. It is important to attack the problem, not the person.
- Accept people as they are and stop wishing they were different. This applies to parents as well as to their children.
- Remember that most parents are doing the best they can. Parents do not wake up in the morning and decide, "I think today I will be a poor parent."
- Respect parents' right to have their own values and opinions. Different values are not better or poorer values.

## Inclusion

How does inclusion relate to the continuum of services? Inclusion, the placement (from part-time to full-time) of students with disabilities in the general education classroom, is not required by law but is one way to achieve placement in the least restrictive environment. The essential element of inclusion is shared responsibility on the part of all educators in the school toward the student with disabilities. Inclusion provides accommodations designed to facilitate the participation of students with disabilities in all aspects of public education, including transportation, instruction, extracurricular activities, and access to facilities.

In practice, the terms "mainstreaming" and "inclusion" may be used interchangeably. They can have very different meanings, however. **Mainstreaming** refers to the participation of students with disabilities in general education classrooms to the extent that is appropriate to meet their needs. **Inclusion** refers to the education of students with disabilities with their nondisabled peers, with special education supports and services being provided as necessary. Advocates of **full inclusion** believe that all students with disabilities should be educated in the general education classroom all the time (Stainback & Stainback, 1992). Pull-out services (e.g., special education resource room models) are not options for full-inclusion advocates because students with disabilities are not educated entirely in the same setting (i.e., the general education classroom) as nondisabled students. A recent study examining the effects of various service delivery models indicates that inclusive settings can be effective for some, although not all, students with disabilities (Manset & Semmel, 1997). Similarly, Marston (1996) found that schools offering combined services, rather than inclusion only or pull-out only, had students with significantly greater progress in reading and higher levels of teacher satisfaction.

At issue is the extent to which a continuum of services is maintained. Earlier in this chapter, the range of educational options for students with disabilities (e.g., the self-contained special education classroom, homebound instruction, and resource room) was presented. This is the continuum of services, which advocates of inclusion want to maintain. Advocates of full inclusion are concerned, however, that maintaining a continuum of services will prevent real integration of students with disabilities. The concern is that if the option for separation or pull-out from the regular classroom is available, then educators will too easily choose it. Debate continues over the extent to which full inclusion should be required for all students with disabilities. We believe that the central issue is the extent to which the academic and social progress of students with disabilities is monitored and adjustments provided if progress is not adequate (Vaughn

& Schumm, 1995). Figure 1.9 summarizes guidelines for responsible inclusion.

The **Regular Education Initiative (REI)** is a concept that promotes the placement of students with disabilities in the general education classroom for all or most of the school day. One primary thrust of the REI is that students with disabilities benefit from placement in general education classrooms. The idea is that general and special education teachers, working cooperatively to meet the individual learning needs of all students in the general education classroom, can better educate the increasing number of students who demonstrate learning problems but do not qualify for special education. The REI has not been without criticism, however, and many educators (e.g., Fuchs & Fuchs, 1994) express concern about the wholesale return of students with disabilities to general education classrooms on a full-time basis.

Recently, the movement within the REI has been expanded to include not only individuals with disabilities, but also other support services, such as Chapter 1 reading and migrant education. Individuals who support the REI believe, fundamentally, that the separation of services between special and general education creates an unnecessary burden, restricting

---

======= FIGURE 1.9 =======

### Guidelines for Responsible Inclusion

| Responsible Inclusion | Irresponsible Inclusion |
|---|---|
| **The student comes first.**<br>The priority is the extent to which the student makes academic and/or social progress. | **The place comes first.**<br>The priority is the place in which the student's education occurs. |
| **Adequate resources are considered and provided for in inclusive classrooms.**<br>Both personnel and materials are required to develop and maintain effective inclusive classrooms. | **Resources are not considered before the establishment of inclusion.**<br>Inclusion is established with little consideration of the personnel and physical resources. |
| **A continuum of services is maintained.**<br>A range of education programs is available to meet the unique needs of students with disabilities. | **Full inclusion is the only service-delivery model.**<br>All students are placed in general education classrooms, regardless of their needs. |
| **The service-delivery model is evaluated on an ongoing basis.**<br>The success of the service-delivery model is evaluated with consideration for the extent to which it meets the student's academic and social needs. | **The service-delivery model is not evaluated on an ongoing basis.**<br>When problems occur, personnel are blamed rather than the model being evaluated. |
| **There is ongoing professional development.** | **Professional development not part of the model.** |
| **The curricula and instruction meet the needs of all students.** | **Curricula and instruction that meet the needs of all students are not considered.** |

*Source:* Adapted from Vaughn, S., & Schumm, J. S. (1995). Responsible inclusion for students with learning disabilities. *Journal of Learning Disabilities, 28*(5), 267.

the use of funds and limiting the educational opportunities available to all children. Many advocates believe that too many students are identified for special programs and that these students' needs can best be served in general education classrooms.

There are some areas in which people do agree. One is that students with disabilities need to be educated in the most normalized environment available and that extensive experience with nondisabled persons is essential to the social and academic growth of students with disabilities. The extent to which these experiences can be provided, while not abolishing required special education support services, should serve as the guiding principle.

The arguments presented in Figure 1.10 are really not for or against inclusion. All advocates believe that students with disabilities should be educated in general education settings to the extent possible. Actually, an examination of data from reports to Congress regarding placement practices for students with learning disabilities over the last six years revealed that such students are educated in increasingly less restrictive settings (McLeskey, Henry, & Axelrod, 1999). However, the data do not provide insight into how schools have provided appropriate accommodations and support services to these students placed in less restrictive settings. Of con-

> Inclusion is not required by law. The law requires that youngsters with disabilities be educated in the least restrictive appropriate educational placement, which for most students includes at least partial inclusion in the general education classroom.

cern is the extent to which specialized support services aimed at meeting the learning and behavior needs of students with disabilities should be available.

Cortina Fernandez describes the strategy she uses successfully to incorporate students with disabilities into her general education classroom:

First, I work very closely with the special education teacher. Before a student is placed into my classroom, I find out as much as I can about what the student likes, what they can do, what their academic strengths are, what they enjoy doing outside of school, and what they can teach me and other students in the classroom.

Second, I find out what they need to know, where they are in terms of their academic progress, and what skills they need to learn, both academically and socially. I get this information from the student's IEP, from the previous teacher, usually the special education teacher, and, if possible, by interviewing the student and the parent before the student is placed into my classroom.

Third, I work with all of the students in my classroom to assure that every child is a member of our community. Our learning community provides support and assistance for every other member and provides social support as well. This ongoing philosophy maintains a classroom environment in which all children are accepted, an essential ingredient to the success for mainstreaming of students with disabilities. I also make the success of every student in the class the responsibility of every other student. While I'm the teacher in the

---

**FIGURE 1.10**

**Arguments for Full Inclusion and Maintenance of the Continuum of Services**

**Arguments for Full Inclusion**

- Students with disabilities should be educated in general education classes all the time.
- Students with disabilities should not be pulled out of the general education classroom to receive specialized education.
- Benefits of placing students with disabilities in specialized classes, for either their academic or social growth, have not been demonstrated.
- Comprehensive, professional development that prepares teachers to meet the educational and social needs of all students is required.
- All students with disabilities have the right to education in the most normalized setting, the general education classroom.

**Arguments for Maintaining Continuum of Services**

- Students with disabilities should be educated in general education classes to the extent that this meets their educational and behavioral needs.
- Some students with disabilities need to have their educational needs met outside the general education classroom for part or all of the school day. A continuum of services to meet the needs of students with disabilities is required.
- Benefits and pitfalls of full-inclusion models for all students with disabilities have not been empirically documented.
- General education teachers are inadequately prepared to meet the specialized needs of all students with disabilities.
- Inclusion is a philosophy, not a place. Students have the right to receive the appropriate educational services to fill their learning needs in the most suitable site.

classroom and take that responsibility seriously, our learning community is one in which each child teaches each other. Thus, it's important to find out what everyone knows and what everyone needs to know so we can all work together. I also closely monitor the progress of every student in my classroom, particularly students with disabilities. I frequently check in with them, make sure they know what they're doing, and assure that they are making expected progress.

Fourth, communication is essential to the successful mainstreaming of students with disabilities. This communication occurs between myself and all the specialists, myself and the parent, as well as myself and other students in my class. However, I do not feel the communication is solely a one-way street. I hold the special education teacher and other specialists responsible for communicating with me, as well as encourage the parents to talk to me as frequently as they feel necessary. In addition, communication is part of the responsibility of students. They need to inform me about what they are doing well and where they need help. I encourage this communication by being open and receptive when they want to talk to me. Successful mainstreaming is more than just what I do as a classroom teacher. It's how I think and how I convey this to all the students and teachers in my school.

> Parents must receive written notification before an evaluation for special education services for their child can be conducted. The notification must be in a language parents can understand.

## summary

- The Individuals with Disabilities Education Act (which incorporates and extends P.L. 94–142) and the Vocational Rehabilitation Act (P.L. 93–112) are the two primary laws that have increased the opportunities and services available to individuals with disabilities.
- According to IDEA (P.L. 94–142), a continuum of educational services needs to be available for students with disabilities.
- The principle behind the concept of least restrictive environment is that students are best served in settings most similar to those of their nondisabled peers in which they can learn (ideally, moving to less and less restrictive settings).
- A common educational placement, designed to meet the educational needs of students with disabilities outside the general education classroom, is the special education resource room. Other placements include: (1) full-time special education, (2) special school or residential settings, (3) homebound instruction, and (4) inclusion.
- The individualized education program (IEP) is developed and implemented by the multidisciplinary team, the goal being the appropriate education of all students.
- In the last ten years, IDEA has been expanded to include services for young children (birth to five years) and to incorporate transition planning and services for students in secondary schools.
- The goal of collaboration models and practices is to ensure that included students continue to receive the accommodations they need to succeed.

## key terms and concepts

advocacy
child find
confidentiality of records
continuum of services
cooperative teaching, co-teaching
due process
early intervention services
educational placement
exceptionalities
free appropriate public education
full inclusion

inclusion
individualized education
    program (IEP)
individualized family service
    plan (IFSP)
individualized transition plans
Individuals with Disabilities
    Education Act (IDEA)
least restrictive environment
mainstreaming
multidisciplinary team (MDT)

noncompliance
nondiscriminatory evaluation
parent participation
prereferral assistance teams (PAT)
P.L. 94–142
Regular Education Initiative (REI)
related services
special education resource room
teacher assistance team (TAT)
Vocational Rehabilitation Act
zero reject

# think and apply

1. Now that you have read Chapter 1, review Tiffany's account of her experience at the beginning of this chapter. If you could talk with Tiffany directly, what questions would you ask her? List any questions or concerns you currently have about teaching students with disabilities. Then, after you read each chapter, consult your list again and check off any questions that you can answer satisfactorily. File your personal inquiries in your teaching portfolio and record your answers as you progress through the book.

2. The primary components of the Individuals with Disabilities Education Act are described in this chapter. Select three of the components (e.g., zero reject/free appropriate public education, child find, nondiscriminatory evaluation) and write a brief description of what could happen to a student with disabilities if this component were not part of the legislation.

3. Obtain a copy of the IEP form used in a local school district. Work with a partner to complete as much of it as you can on a designated student. Which aspects of the development of the IEP were challenging for you? Which aspects taught you the most?

4. Interview one or more teachers who have students with disabilities in their classrooms. Ask these teachers to identify any key practices they implement that they believe make a difference. Ask also what they wish they knew more about.

5. Interview a preschool teacher who works with students with disabilities, or a secondary teacher or job developer who coordinates transition services for students with disabilities. What do they view as their major roles and responsibilities? What do they think is important for you as a general educator to know and do so that these students are successful?

# read more about it

1. Anderson, W., Chitwood, S., & Hayden, D. (1997). *Negotiating the special education maze.* Bethesda, MD: Woodbine House.

   *This book explains all phases of the special education process in easy-to-understand language. Contains a special education glossary and lists of hotlines, parent groups, state agencies, and disability organizations. Provides charts and checklists to help negotiate the "maze." Perfect for educators who are not familiar with special education.*

2. Blatt, B., & Kaplan, F. (1966). *Christmas in purgatory: A photographic essay on mental retardation.* Boston: Allyn & Bacon.

   *Though taken more than 30 years ago, the photographs in this book tell a moving story about progress for individuals with disabilities and the importance of the laws described in this chapter. This book provides pictures of individuals living in institutional settings prior to the deinstitution movement.*

3. Council for Exceptional Children. (1994). *Creating schools for all our students: What 12 schools have to say.* Reston, VA: Council for Exceptional Children.

   *Provides a practical guide for developing inclusive schools for students with disabilities. Representing the work of 12 school districts from around the United States, common themes about what practices need to be in place to implement inclusive schools for all students are described.*

4. Council for Exceptional Children. (1997). *IDEA 1997: Let's make it work.* Reston, VA: Council for Exceptional Children.

   *A helpful set of questions and answers that deal with new aspects of the law. Topics include parent involvement, developmental delay, cultural diversity, IEPs, evaluation and reevaluation, early childhood, and many more. Most sections contain comments from the Senate Committee report and resources from journals and books that will reinforce the reader's understanding of the law.*

5. Favazza, P. C., & Odom, S. L. (1997). Promoting positive attitudes of kindergarten-age children toward people with disabilities. *Exceptional Children, 63*(3), 405–418.

   *This study examines the effects of contact, books, and discussion on the attitudes of young children toward people with disabilities. The program discussed in this article appears to be an effective strategy for promoting acceptance of people with disabilities.*

6. Montessori, M. (1912). *The Montessori method.* New York: Stokes.

   *Maria Montessori was a physician in Italy who successfully developed approaches for teaching students who were "unable to learn." Her approaches have been implemented with a wide range of students, including young children, gifted students, and students with cognitive impairments.*

7. Vaughn, S., & Rothlein, L. (1994). *Books to prepare children for inclusion: Read it again!* Glenview, IL: GoodYear Books.

   *Designed for teachers and parents, to assist them in identifying children's books that address the topic of or include key characters with disabilities. Activities are provided to help children better understand individuals with disabilities.*

8. Hammeken, P. (1995). *Inclusion: 450 strategies for success: A practical guide for all educators who teach students with disabilities.* Minnetonka, MN: Peytral.

*This book provides the crucial steps for planning and implementing a successful inclusion program. Additionally, it presents a variety of modifications and teaching strategies that can be implemented for successful inclusion.*

9. Siegel, L. M. (2000). *The complete IEP guide: How to advocate for your special ed child* (2nd ed.). Berkely, CA: Nolo.

   *This book provides parents with a step-by-step description of the IEP process. It provides all the instructions, strategies, resources and forms that parents can use. Parents can use this book as a guide from the time they first suspect that their child has special needs to attending IEP meetings and then through the entire process of special education until their child completes school.*

# suggested websites

**www.ideapractices.org**
This website provides information about IDEA (Individuals with Disabilities Education Act) partnerships.

**www.ed.gov/offices/OSERS/IDEA**
This is the website of the Office of Special Education Programs, and it provides information about IDEA of 1997. IDEA 97 amendments and regulations can be downloaded at this website.

**http://circleofinclusion.org**
This website contains various resources related to inclusion (articles, guidelines, other links related to inclusion, etc.).

**www.ldonline.org/ld_indepth/icp/icp_process.html**
This website provides an overview of the IEP process.

**www.pai-ca.org/Pubs/504101.htm**
This website contains information on basic legal rights and responsibilities.

**www.pai-ca.org/pubs/504401.htm**
This website contains information on the IEP process.

**www.ldonline.org/ld_indepth/math_skills/adapt_cld.html**
This website provides information on how math instruction was adapted for students with disabilities.

**www.pai-ca.org/pubs/505001.htm**
This website contains various links related to transition (transition services, ITP, etc.).

# Teaching Students with Learning Disabilities or Attention Deficit Hyperactivity Disorder

# chapter | outline

# focus | questions

1. According to IDEA, what are the major components of the definition and criteria for determining a specific learning disability?

2. What are the characteristics of students who have learning disabilities?

3. What percentage of students in school have learning disabilities?

4. What information should you collect about a student with a possible learning disability to share at a multidisciplinary conference?

5. What techniques could you incorporate into your teaching to benefit students with learning disabilities?

6. What is attention deficit hyperactivity disorder? How does it affect a student in school?

7. What are the characteristics of students with hyperactive–impulsive type ADHD and of students with inattentive type ADHD?

8. Why is it difficult to determine the prevalence of ADHD?

9. What are some possible reasons that more boys than girls are identified with learning disabilities and attention deficit hyperactivity disorder?

10. What are some strategies you can use to help students with ADHD be successful in school?

# inter view

**Tammy Gregory**

Tammy Gregory is one of four second-grade teachers at Canyon Verde Elementary School in Tucson, Arizona. This is Tammy's third year of teaching. In her class of 31 students, Tammy has one student with learning disabilities, Adrian, and one student with attention deficit hyperactivity disorder, Lenny.

When you talk with Tammy and watch her teach, it is clear that she believes all students can be successful learners and that her job is to modify the content and the curriculum for the various learners in her classroom. This is certainly the case with Adrian, whose learning disabilities relate most to the speed at which he processes information. It takes him longer to understand what is being said during classroom discussions and presentations. He reads slowly whether he is reading aloud or to himself. His responses to questions are often slow and labored, and the ideas are not clearly stated. He also writes slowly. He is almost always the last or next-to-last student to finish a written assignment and often does not complete work in the time allowed.

Tammy regularly makes accommodations for Adrian so that he is a successful learner in her classroom. Because his writing is slow, she sometimes reduces the length of the assignment so that he can complete it in the time allowed. Tammy says, "The key is that Adrian understands and has mastered the skill. If he can demonstrate mastery answering 5 problems instead of 10 problems in math, then he has learned and reached his goal."

Tammy has also set up an informal buddy system in her room. Students regularly help each other with assignments. Tammy has Adrian sitting next to one student who is an able helper and high achiever and another student who is an average achiever and who likes to problem solve and work with Adrian on assignments. This arrangement gives Adrian the opportunity to work with two very different students who like to work with others and provide support for him. Although speed of processing can make Adrian appear slow and not very adept at many skills, his teacher has taken the time to learn about his interests and his strengths and to share those with the other students. It is not unusual to hear Tammy say to the class, "Check with Adrian on that. He's a real expert."

Tammy has also made accommodations for Lenny, a student with attention deficit hyperactivity disorder. At the beginning of the year, Tammy thought that Lenny would be "the child that led her into early retirement." He moved constantly (even when sitting) and was out of his seat, sharpening his pencil and talking to and bothering the other students. During class discussion he would answer before Tammy had a chance even to ask the students to raise their hands. He rarely completed assignments. Tammy felt that Lenny could do much of the work but that his attention problems got in the way of his being a successful learner. To help Lenny, Tammy thought about and modified the structure of her classroom and schedule. Tammy comments,

> Lenny attends best when he knows what is "on tap" for the day. Each day I review the schedule for the day and put a copy of it on the board, on the corner of Lenny's desk, and on my desk. As each activity is completed, Lenny checks it off and rates himself for that activity on three criteria: paying attention, effort, and work completed. At first I also rated Lenny, but now I am comfortable with his self-monitoring. At lunch and during the end of the day wrap-up, I take several minutes to review with Lenny his self-monitoring. Based on his performance, Lenny receives good work day certificates to take home for his parents to sign, and on Friday afternoon he can receive a "Job Well Done" pass to watch a video or participate in other activities with the other good workers in the school. For me, taking this extra time with Lenny is well worth the progress Lenny has made and the sanity that has been restored to my classroom.

Tammy also makes other modifications for Lenny, such as reducing the number of math problems assigned by having him complete only the odd- or even-numbered problems. She also helps Lenny, Adrian, and other students in her class break multiple-step or complex tasks and projects into smaller tasks. Tammy comments, "Even reading a book and writing a book report can be divided into five or six steps the students can complete one by one. This substantially increases the likelihood of students getting these projects done in a timely manner."

Adrian and Lenny have made good progress this year in school, both in terms of their learning and their positive self-concepts as learners. Tammy is concerned, however, about their transition into third grade, where more emphasis will be placed on written work and complex assignments and less time will be spent on teaching basic skills and individualizing for different students' needs. She is wondering what to communicate to Adrian and Lenny's teachers next year so that they can continue as successful learners.

# introduction

Think about Tammy's philosophy and practice of teaching students with learning disabilities (LD) and attention problems. To what extent do the practices she implements with Adrian and Lenny reflect the type of teacher you are or want to be? The first section of this chapter provides an overview of students with LD, and the second section focuses on students with attention deficit hyperactivity disorder (ADHD). As you read, think about ways the strategies suggested for these students can also be used for other students in elementary and secondary classrooms.

## Learning Disabilities

The disabilities of students who have visual impairments, are deaf or hard of hearing, or have overall cognitive delays usually are apparent. In contrast, you probably will not recognize students with LD in your classroom until you have the opportunity to see how they learn. Only in the last 35 years have learning disabilities, sometimes referred to as the "invisible disability," been recognized in our schools. This section provides definitions and characteristics of learning disabilities, as well as suggestions for meeting the needs of students with LD in your classroom.

### Definitions and Types of Learning Disabilities

The issue of how to define learning disabilities has received considerable attention in the field since 1963, when Samuel Kirk suggested the term "specific learning disabilities" at the organizational meeting of the Learning Disabilities Association (LDA) (formerly called the Association for Children with Learning Disabilities, ACLD). At that time, children with LD were referred to by such terms as "perceptually handicapped," "brain-injured," and "neurologically impaired" and were served in classrooms for students with mental retardation or, in most cases, were not receiving any specialized services in the public schools.

The term **specific learning disabilities** represents a heterogeneous group of students who, despite adequate cognitive functioning and the ability to learn some skills and strategies relatively quickly and easily, have great difficulty learning other skills and strategies. For example, students with specific reading disabilities may participate quite well in class discussions but have difficulty reading the text and taking tests. Other students may have great difficulty with math but have little difficulty with tasks that incorporate reading and writing.

The IDEA definition of learning disabilities is presented in Figure 2.1. The operational guidelines for the definition of specific learning disabilities are specified in the rules and regulations for IDEA and indicate that a multidisciplinary team may determine that a child has a specific learning disability if:

- The student does not achieve commensurate with his or her age and ability level in one or more of several specific areas when provided with appropriate learning experiences.
- The student has a severe discrepancy between achievement and intellectual ability in one or more of these seven areas: oral expression, listening comprehension, written expression, basic reading skills, reading comprehension, mathematics calculation, and mathematics reasoning.
- The student needs special education services.

> The Learning Disabilities Association is a parent and professional organization that provides many resources related to learning disabilities. Contact information: Learning Disabilities Association, 4156 Library Road, Pittsburgh, PA 15234, telephone: (412) 341-1515.

---

FIGURE 2.1

### IDEA Definition of Learning Disabilities and Major Components of the Definition

#### DEFINITION

The term "children with specific learning disabilities" means those children who have a disorder in one or more of the basic psychological processes involved in understanding or in using language, spoken or written, which disorder may manifest itself in imperfect ability to listen, think, speak, read, write, spell, or to do mathematical calculations. Such disorders include such conditions as perceptual handicaps, brain injury, minimal brain dysfunction, dyslexia, and developmental aphasia. Such terms do not include children who have learning problems which are primarily the result of visual, hearing, or motor handicap, of mental retardation, of emotional disturbance, or of environmental, cultural, or economic disadvantage.

#### MAJOR COMPONENTS

✔ Difficulty with academic and learning tasks

✔ Discrepancy between expected and actual achievement

✔ Disorder in basic psychological processing

✔ Exclusion of other causes

A student is not regarded as having a specific learning disability if the discrepancy between ability and achievement is primarily the result of any of the following:

- Visual, hearing, or motor disability
- Mental retardation
- Emotional disturbance
- Environmental, cultural, or economic disadvantage

Some professionals were concerned about the federal definition of learning disabilities because it did not specify the heterogeneous nature of the disabilities, the lifelong impact of the disability, and the ability for this disability to exist with other disabilities. The National Joint Committee on Learning Disabilities, a group composed of representatives from the major learning disabilities professional and parent organizations, developed a definition to clarify their concerns:

> Learning disabilities is a general term that refers to a heterogeneous group of disorders manifested by significant difficulties in the acquisition and use of listening, speaking, reading, writing, reasoning, or mathematical abilities. These disorders are intrinsic to the individual and presumed to be due to central nervous system dysfunction, and may appear across the life span. Problems in self-regulatory behaviors, social perception, and social interaction may exist with learning disabilities but do not themselves constitute a learning disability. Although learning disabilities may occur concomitantly with other handicapping conditions (for example, sensory impairment, mental retardation, serious emotional disturbance) or with extrinsic influences (such as cultural differences, insufficient or inappropriate instruction), they are not the results of those conditions or influences (National Joint Committee on Learning Disabilities, 1990).

Another concern has been raised about the federal criteria for determining a specific learning disability. In using the aptitude–achievement discrepancy criterion for identifying learning disabilities, professionals and parents have to wait until children have struggled with trying to learn for several years before the discrepancy between aptitude and achievement is great enough to meet the criterion of a severe discrepancy. Consequently, most students with LD do not qualify for services until late second or third grade. At the same time, longitudinal research has demonstrated that 75 percent of students who do not learn to read by third grade will continue to have reading disabilities throughout their schooling career (Lyon, 1999). Hence, these students seem set up for failure, and

there is growing concern that the use of the aptitude–achievement discrepancy may not be the most advantageous way of identifying students with LD, particularly young students (Fletcher et al., 1998; Stanovitch, 1991). One alternative might be to provide small-group, focused instruction in the area of difficulty early in the child's education. If the child does not make substantial gains with this more intensive type of instruction, then he or she may qualify as having a specific learning disability (Fuchs & Fuchs, 1998; Lyon et al., 2001; Vellutino et al., 1996).

Although many definitions of learning disabilities have been developed, secondary science teacher Joseph Blankenship's ideas about learning disabilities are similar to those of many other general education teachers. He comments that initially, these students may not seem different from other students. They participate in classroom discussions and appear to understand the content covered. But as assignments are submitted and tests given, he quickly realizes that students with LD have difficulties with reading, writing, math, studying, and organizing their time.

## Characteristics of Students with Learning Disabilities

Because learning disabilities are heterogeneous, it is difficult to list a set of characteristics that adequately describe all students with LD. You will find that students with LD seem more different from each other than alike, in relation to how they learn, but certain overriding characteristics will help you in identifying these students:

- *Unexpected* difficulty or low performance in one or more academic areas (unexpected in that your general impressions of the student would not lead you to predict that he or she would have difficulty)
- Ineffective or inefficient information-processing or learning strategies in the area(s) of difficulty

Furthermore, the reasons for this low performance vary according to the strengths and weaknesses of the learner and the learning strategies he or she employs.

For example, Tamara and Manuel, two students in Carla Huerra's third-grade classroom, were identified as having specific learning disabilities and were reading and spelling at an early first-grade (primer) level. Both students have difficulty learning to recognize and spell words automatically when reading and writing, but the strategies they use are very different, as are the individualized educational programs that Carla and the special education teacher, David Ross, use with each student.

Carla observes the students to better understand their learning patterns, including their strategies, motivation for learning, and interests. She listens to each of them as they read aloud and retell what they have read. She notes the errors each of them makes when reading and watches for the strategies they use when they come to a word they do not recognize automatically or to something they do not seem to understand. She also observes both students during writers' workshop as they compose first (and subsequent) drafts of their work.

Carla's observations reveal that Tamara has strong oral language skills. She capitalizes on these skills when she reads and uses the meaning and the syntax (word order or grammar) of the language as her primary strategies for figuring out unknown words. When she does not know a word, she skips it or substitutes a word that more or less makes sense. She shows little evidence of using phonics beyond using the initial sound to figure out unknown words. Carla notes that even though Tamara sees a word many times, either in context or written by itself, it is not easy for her to recognize it automatically so that it becomes part of her sight vocabulary. When Carla observes Tamara's writing, she notes that Tamara has wonderful ideas but spends much of her time asking other students how to spell words or changing what she was originally going to write so that she can use words she knows how to spell. She does this despite the classroom rule that "Spelling doesn't matter on drafts; spell it the way you think."

Like Tamara, Manuel has difficulty memorizing words so that they become part of his sight vocabulary and can be retrieved automatically when he reads or writes. Manuel's strategies for reading are very different from Tamara's, however. Manuel's reading is very slow because he tries to sound out the words (uses his phonic analysis skills). He is able to get a number of the individual sounds but has trouble blending them together to make a word. Although the words that result may not make sense, he does not seem to monitor this by going back and rereading. Manuel's writing also reflects his use of his somewhat successful phonic analysis, in that even high-frequency, irregular words are spelled phonetically (e.g., "cum" for "come," "wuz" for "was").

In talking with David Ross, Tamara and Manuel's special education teacher, Carla learned that her observations were the same as David's. Both students have visual-memory and auditory-processing difficulties that make it hard for them to learn to automatically recognize words. Each student, however, uses different strategies and strengths to compensate (i.e., Tamara relies on her strong oral language skills, and Manuel relies on "somewhat successful" phonic analysis).

Together, Carla and David have planned and designed educational programs to support these students. For studying content areas such as science and social studies, Carla relies on partner reading and the use of trade books written at different reading levels. She also allows students to demonstrate their knowledge through oral reports, posters, and pictures, rather than only through traditional written reports and tests. During writers' workshop, Carla has helped each student develop a spelling dictionary. For reading, Carla and David work together to help Tamara and Manuel expand the strategies they use to decode unknown words. For Tamara, this includes learning to use phonic analysis, along with meaning to help her identify the unknown word. They are also helping Tamara to see similar spelling patterns in words (e.g., word families: -*ake, make, take, lake*). For Manuel, their help includes using repeated reading to get him to build fluency and take more risks when decoding words. Manuel is also learning to ask himself the question "Does this make sense?" to monitor his decoding and comprehension.

Table 2.1 presents some characteristics that, although they might not apply to all students with LD, have helped signal to general education teachers which students might have specific learning disabilities. Several of these characteristics refer to difficulties in attention. Students with LD often have difficulties with attention and, in some cases, hyperactivity. About 35 percent of students with LD also have an attention deficit hyperactivity disorder (Barkley, 1998); these disorders are discussed later in this chapter.

Learning disabilities represent a group of disorders that cause students to have learning and academic difficulties. Currently, although no generally accepted classification systems exist for students with LD (Keogh, 1993; Speece, 1994), types of learning disabilities have been discussed in the literature and used in medical and psychological reports for many years. Some of the most frequently used terms are the following:

- **Dyslexia**—severe difficulty in learning to read, particularly as it relates to decoding and spelling
- **Dysgraphia**—severe difficulty in learning to write, including handwriting
- **Dyscalculia**—severe disability in learning mathematical concepts and computation

Reading difficulties are the most frequent characteristic of students with LD, evident in over 85 percent of the students with LD (Lyon, 1999). For students who are learning to read, evidence suggests that this problem is related to difficulties in phonemic awareness, developing the alphabetic principle, and

═══════════════ TABLE 2.1 ═══════════════

### Signals for Possible Learning Disabilities

*Signals for learning disabilities* are characteristics of students with learning disabilities. Because these students are a heterogeneous group, only certain signals will apply to any one student.

- Has trouble understanding and following directions
- Has a short attention span; is easily distracted
- Is overactive and impulsive
- Has difficulty with handwriting and fine motor activities
- Has difficulty with visual or auditory sequential memory
- Has difficulty memorizing words or basic math facts
- Has difficulty allocating time and organizing work
- Is unmotivated toward tasks that are difficult

- Has difficulty segmenting words into sounds and blending sounds
- Confuses similar letters and words, such as *b* and *d*, and *was* and *saw*
- Listens and speaks well but decodes poorly when reading
- Has difficulty with tasks that require rapid naming of pictures, words, and numbers
- Is not efficient or effective in using learning strategies

---

> Approximately 85 percent of elementary-age students with learning disabilities have difficulties reading, particularly in decoding words.

rapid naming tasks (Foorman, Francis, Fletcher, Schatschneider, & Mehta, 1998; Lyon, 1999; Wolf, 1999). **Phonemic awareness** is the ability to blend, segment, and manipulate speech sounds (for example, "trash" has four speech sounds or phonemes: t-r-a-sh). The **alphabetic principle** is learning how speech maps to print or learning letter–sound relationships. Understanding letter–sound relationships allows students to decode unknown words by making the speech sounds associated with letters and then blending them together to make the word (e.g., c-a-t is "cat"). **Rapid naming** entails having children quickly name familiar objects, letters, or numbers. This skill seems important in building reading fluency. Students with LD may also have difficulty with reading comprehension, and many students who have difficulty learning to read continue to have difficulty with decoding which affects their reading comprehension.

### r e s e a r c h b r i e f

## Developmental, Neurological, and Genetic Nature of Reading Disabilities

Currently, the National Institute for Child Health and Human Development is sponsoring a number of research centers and projects that are investigating the nature of reading disabilities, particularly as they relate to learning to read (e.g., Olson, 1999; Pennington,

1999; Shaywitz, Pugh, Fulbright, Jenner, Fletcher, Gore, & Shaywitz, 2000). This research has been summarized by Lyon (1998), with the following findings:

- Although schools identify approximately four times as many boys as girls as having reading disabilities, prospective studies show that about as many girls are affected as boys.
- Reading disabilities persist. Of the students who have reading disabilities in the third grade, about 75 percent still have significant problems in ninth grade.
- The ability to read and comprehend depends on rapid and automatic recognition of words. Slow and inaccurate decoding are the best predictors of difficulties in reading comprehension.
- The ability to decode words depends on the ability to segment words into syllables and sounds. Difficulty with this task is central to dyslexia.
- There is strong evidence that reading disabilities are inherited, with a 35–45 percent occurrence of dyslexia in the immediate birth families of individuals with dyslexia.
- Functional magnetic resonance imaging has provided evidence that activation in the brain during reading tasks is different for individuals with dyslexia than nondyslexic individuals.

Students with LD, even those who read fairly well, may have problems with written language (Graham, 1999; Graham & Harris, 1997). These difficulties can occur in the areas of handwriting, spelling, productivity, writing mechanics, organization, and composition (Gersten and Baker, in press).

Although math disabilities are not as prevalent as reading disabilities, a substantial number of students with LD experience difficulties with mathematics (Cawley, Parmar, Foley, Salmon, & Roy, 2001). This may be in the area of basic math calculations or the more complex area of mathematical problem solving. A recent large-scale study reported that students with LD have average math scores at about the 30th percentile (Miller, Butler, & Lee, 1998).

What are the lifelong outcomes for students with LD? There is no single answer for all students, but we do have evidence that some individuals with LD are quite successful in adult life and that they learn to adjust and make accommodations for the disabilities (for example, Albert Einstein, Nelson Rockefeller, and Thomas Edison all had significant learning disabilities). However, overall, students with LD have higher rates of unemployment and underemployment, fewer live independently, and fewer succeed in postsecondary programs than students in general. What are the social and education factors that predict success for individuals with LD? Research indicates that successful adults with LD make realistic adaptations for their LD, take control of their lives, are goal oriented, and persist at these goals. Successful adults with LD have indicated that one or more significant people have supported their adjustments during school, postsecondary training, and young adult life (e.g., Raskind, Goldberg, Higgins, & Herman, 1999; Speckman et al., 1993). Increased access to vocational training programs and support programs in colleges has also served to increase success (Gerber et al., 1992; Vogel et al., 1993).

What are some learner characteristics that might help you identify a student with possible learning disabilities? How might you work with an inclusion specialist or special education teacher to plan and design an education program to support such a student?

social choices. Waldie and Spreen (1993) conducted follow-up interviews with 65 individuals with learning disabilities who were diagnosed between ages 8 and 12 and reported police contact during an interview at age 18. During an interview at age 25, 62 percent had persisting problems with the law. Data analysis, which demonstrated that poor judgment and impulsivity were the two factors involved, supports the susceptibility theory.

## research brief

### Learning Disabilities and Juvenile Delinquency

The incidence of learning disabilities is generally much higher in delinquents (18–55 percent) than in the general population. Similarly, teens who have learning disabilities report more contact with the law than their non-learning-disabled peers (e.g., Bryan et al., 1989; Keilitz & Dunivant, 1986; Spreen, 1988).

Two theories have been suggested as to why this is the case. The *school failure theory* suggests that school failure, including poor academic achievement, leads to persistent delinquency. The *susceptibility theory* suggests that learning disabilities may be linked to certain underdeveloped personality skills, such as general impulsiveness and poor judgment, which lead to increased susceptibility to delinquent behavior through unwise

## Prevalence of Learning Disabilities

Today, more students are identified as having specific learning disabilities than any other type of disability, and this type of disability is recognized as a worldwide condition (Gersons-Wolfensberger & Ruijssenaars, 1997). According to the *Twenty-Second Annual Report to Congress on the Implementation of the Individuals with Disabilities Education Act* (U.S. Department of Education, 2000), approximately 10 percent of school-age children were identified as having disabilities, and just over 50 percent of this group, or approximately 5 percent of the school-age population, were identified

Although some students with learning disabilities receive instruction in a special education classroom, more and more of these students receive all their education in a general education classroom, with support from the special education teacher or a paraprofessional.

as having specific learning disabilities. During the last three decades, the number of students identified as having LD has increased substantially. For example, during the 1979–1980 school year, 1,281,379 students with LD were identified and served in the public school system. This number increased to 2,062,076 by 1989–1990 and to 2,817,148 in 1998–1999.

Why does the percentage of students with LD continue to increase? Several factors are related to the answer, including the following (Hallahan, 1992):

- *Growing public awareness of LD.* As more parents and general education teachers learn about the characteristics of students with LD, they become more attuned to watching for signs and seeking assistance within the school system.
- *Greater social acceptance.* Learning disabilities are among the disabilities viewed as more socially accepted and with fewer negative connotations than others.
- *Limited alternatives for other students at risk.* Owing to limited alternative programs, the tendency is to identify any students who are failing as having learning disabilities so that they may receive services.
- *Social and cultural influences on central nervous system integrity.* Demographics would suggest that more children are being born to parents whose income falls below the poverty level, who may be addicted to drugs and alcohol, and who are teenagers (all factors that increase chances of these children being at risk for LD).
- *Increasing needs for literacy at work and in daily life.* As we move into an information age that requires better-educated individuals, schools are demanding more of students, and higher literacy levels are necessary for jobs and the tasks of daily life.

Also of interest is the number of boys versus girls identified as having learning disabilities, boys being identified from twice to as many as eight times more often than girls. Data from the U.S. Department of Education (1998) indicate a ratio of approximately four boys to every girl. Recent research on the genetic bases of dyslexia would suggest that the ratio of boys to girls should be more equal (Shaywitz, Shaywitz, Fletcher, & Escobar, 1990) even though males do have more of a biological vulnerability than females. Males may also be more vulnerable to referral and identification, because boys generally exhibit more disruptive behaviors that are difficult to manage in school.

## Identification and Assessment of Students with Learning Disabilities

Most students with LD are identified because of difficulties with academic achievement. Teachers—usually the first professionals to notice the students' learning strengths and weaknesses and academic skills—play an important role in identifying students with LD. Louise Parra, a first-grade teacher, comments on the importance she places on being alert for students who may have LD:

> As a first-grade teacher, it is very important that I understand LD and keep alert for children who are not learning at the same rate or with the same ease that I would expect of them. If I notice these children in the first grade and begin collaborating with the special education teacher, other specialists, and the children's families, then I can assist in preventing these children from developing the poor self-esteem that frequently develops if they continue to fail and are not supported.

Of all the members of a prereferral or multidisciplinary team, classroom teachers and parents have the most experience with a student. Referral from the classroom teacher is one of the most important predictors of whether a student will be identified as learning disabled. A study of 236 referrals made by classroom teachers in an intermediate school district in the Midwest, for example, indicated that 128 students (approximately 45 percent) were identified by the multidisciplinary teams as eligible for special education because they had specific learning disabilities (Fugate et al., 1993).

Jackie Darnell, a fifth-grade teacher, shared observations and information about a student, Cassandra, at a multidisciplinary conference during which it was decided that, because of math disabilities, Cassandra was eligible for special education services (see Figure 2.2). Jackie used a variety of assessments to collect information about Cassandra, including observations and analysis of work samples, curriculum-based assessments taken from the math curriculum and textbook, and informal math assessments designed by Jackie to pinpoint skills on which students need to work to gain mastery.

The information Jackie provided clearly identified her concerns in the area of math computation. She also provided information about strategies she had already tried with Cassandra. Documenting what has been tried and its success is key to justifying that a student needs special education services.

Because Jackie thought that the computer programs were the most helpful, she and the special education teacher decided to work together to identify

—————————— FIGURE 2.2 ——————————

**Information Shared by Jackie Darnell, the Classroom Teacher, at a Multidisciplinary Conference**

**Name:** Cassandra

**Age:** 10

**Grade:** 5th

**Literacy:**

- 4th to 5th grade level.
- Enjoys reading as a leisure-time activity and uses the library on a regular basis.
- Enjoys writing fantasy and drama and uses both character and plot development; patterns many of her stories after the popular girl-oriented series.
- Participates in literature discussion groups and can answer a variety of questions about the literature, including underlying theme and application questions.
- Can write a report with introduction and two supporting paragraphs.
- Spells at fourth-grade level, using phonic and structural analysis for unknown words.
- Can use a word processor to write and revise written work.

**Math:**

- Second-grade achievement level.
- Adds and subtracts with regrouping but makes computation errors in the process and with basic facts.
- Understands basic concept of multiplication but does not know basic facts or how to use for simple word problems.
- Has difficulty understanding simple, one- and two-step word problems.
- Has not yet memorized 50% of the basic addition and subtraction facts.
- Knows multiplication facts 0, 1, 5, and 10.
- Understands concept of multiplication as repeated addition. Does not compute multiplication problems.
- Does not demonstrate concept of division and does not know division facts.
- Demonstrates concept of simple fractions 1/2, 1/3, 1/4.
- Solves word problems. Errors are generally in computation and basic facts rather than problem representation.
- Describes math as least favorite subject.
- Struggles to learn basic math facts, despite incentive program, coordination with parents, and use of computer programs at school.

**Social/Emotional:**

- Well liked by peers, both boys and girls.
- Quiet, does not ask for help when needed.
- Works well in cooperative groups but usually does not take leadership roles.
- Good sense of humor.

# Tips for Teachers

## 2.1 What to Consider in Referring Students Suspected of Having Learning Disabilities

- In which academic areas of learning (e.g., listening comprehension, oral expression, basic reading skills, reading comprehension, basic writing skills, written expression, math computation, math reasoning and problem solving) is the student successful, and in which areas is the student having difficulties?
- What are the academic achievement levels in these areas and what are representative examples of the student's work?
- How does the student compare with other students in the classroom in areas of success and difficulty?
- What factors (other than specific learning disabilities) might be contributing to the learning prob-

- lems experienced by the student (e.g., frequent moves, absences, recent traumatic life events, vision or hearing impairments, emotional disorders)?
- Are the student's first language and language of instruction the same, or is the student learning academics while also acquiring a second language or dialect?
- What learning or compensatory strategies does the student currently use to aid in learning?
- How does the student perceive him- or herself as a learner, and what is the student's attitude toward school and learning?
- What strategies and accommodations have been tried, and how did they work?

---

additional computer programs for Cassandra. The special education teacher would work with Cassandra on how to use a calculator and build skills in computation of multiplication problems. Both teachers would use manipulatives to build Cassandra's understanding of division and fractions. Tips for Teachers 2.1 suggests what classroom teachers should consider before referring a student who seems to have LD.

## Instructional Techniques and Accommodations for Students with Learning Disabilities

Because the group of students with LD is so diverse, no one approach or technique is appropriate for all students with LD. In fact, many special education teachers describe themselves as having to be necessarily eclectic in their philosophy and approaches to teaching to match the different learning patterns these students exhibit. Effective classroom teachers report that they must use their "best teaching practices" to teach students with LD. Len Hays, a seventh-grade English teacher, elaborates on best teaching practices:

When I work with students who have been identified as having LD or who are at risk, it requires my best teaching. By this I mean that I must be very organized in the manner in which I present a literature unit or an English lesson. First, I give an overview of the lesson and explain the activi-

ties and what is expected of the students. I also make sure that when I lecture, I use an overhead projector to write important information. If I want the students to understand a process, such as how to revise an essay to add "color," then using the overhead projector lets me demonstrate the process and my thinking as I edit. I find that using the overhead allows me to model not only the questions I ask myself as a writer, but to show the changes I make. It is also important that I organize the learning activities and working groups so that students have the opportunity to practice the skills that are the focus of the lesson. Whether we are working on editing skills or doing a critical analysis of a book, I always work to relate the learning to the students' daily lives. Finally, I try to be creative and humorous. That is just part of being a middle school teacher and dealing with adolescence.

In the last five years, a number of syntheses of intervention research have been conducted that give us a good indication of what are the best practices for students with LD (Swanson, Hoskyn, & Lee, 1999; Vaughn, Gersten, & Chard, 2000). For example, H. Lee Swanson and his colleagues reviewed over 1,000 research studies that have investigated the effectiveness of different type of interventions for students with LD (Swanson & Hoskyn, 1998; Swanson et al., 1999). Syntheses have also been completed in the areas of grouping (e.g., whole class, large groups, small groups, pairs, and one on one) (Elbaum, Vaughn,

Hughes, & Moody, 1999), reading comprehension (Gersten, Williams, Fuchs, & Baker, 1998), written expression (Gersten & Baker, in press), and higher-order thinking processing and problem solving (Swanson, 2001). On the basis of this work, several common practices were very powerful in predicting the academic success of students with LD:

- Control of task difficulty (i.e., teaching at the student's instructional level and sequencing examples and problems to maintain high levels of student success)
- Teaching students with LD in small interactive groups of six or fewer students
- Using a combination of direct instruction and cognitive strategy instruction

This includes instructional features such as providing a framework for learning, modeling the process and strategies needed for completing the tasks using "thinking aloud" and instructional conversations, teaching students to use self-regulation and self-monitoring, and providing for extended practice and application of new skills and strategies.

**Providing a Framework for Learning**    Students are more successful when they have a good idea of where they are going. Research on the use of **advance organizers** (i.e., activities that orient students to the task and the materials) would suggest that this is even more important for students with LD, learning problems, or limited background knowledge for the task being taught (Corkill, 1992; Slavin, 2000).

     Keith Lenz and his colleagues (Lenz, 1983; Lenz et al., 1987) developed 10 steps for using an advance organizer. Lenz found that when content-area teachers in middle and high schools used this framework for learning, adolescents with LD could experience significant improvements in both the quality and quantity of learning. Three factors seem important to the success of advance organizers. First, students with LD are taught how to listen for and use the advance organizer. Students might complete a worksheet (see Figure 2.3) as they listen to the teacher introduce each part of the advance organizer. Second, after using the advance organizer worksheet, the teacher and students discuss the effectiveness of its use and how and when it might be used in various content classes. Third, before an advance organizer is presented, the teacher cues the students that it is going to be used.

     One critical aspect of the advance organizer is that it provides basic information or activates the students' background knowledge (refer to Step 5 in Tips for Teachers 2.2). Students with LD often have in-

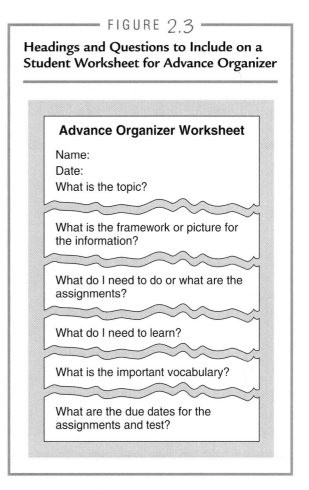

FIGURE 2.3

**Headings and Questions to Include on a Student Worksheet for Advance Organizer**

**Advance Organizer Worksheet**

Name:
Date:
What is the topic?

What is the framework or picture for the information?

What do I need to do or what are the assignments?

What do I need to learn?

What is the important vocabulary?

What are the due dates for the assignments and test?

formation about the topics, skills, or strategies being taught but do not automatically think about this information (e.g., Borkowski et al., 1989; Bos & Filip, 1984; Wong, 1991). The chapters on reading and content-area instruction discuss specific techniques for activating students' background knowledge.

**Modeling Processes and Strategies Using Thinking Aloud and Instructional Conversations**    One key to success for students with LD is to make the learning visible. Think back to your experiences as a student. How did you learn to find the main idea when you were reading? Many teachers traditionally used the technique of repeatedly asking students questions such as "What is the main idea of this story?" until a student provided the right answer (e.g., Durkin, 1978–1979). Students were expected to infer how to find the main idea. In the last 20 years, however, intervention research on teaching reading comprehension and other cognitive processes has emphasized that teachers and students should

> Modeling strategies and processes and using instructional conversations as the major means of teaching may be uncomfortable at first for teachers accustomed to more traditional lecture or question/answer formats.

# Tips for Teachers

## 2.2    Steps in Using an Advance Organizer

1. Inform students of advance organizers.
   - Announce advance organizer.
   - State benefits of advance organizer.
   - Suggest that students take notes on the advance organizer.
2. Identify topics or tasks.
   - Identify major topics or activities.
   - Identify subtopics or component activities.
3. Provide an organizational framework.
   - Present an outline, list, or narrative of the lesson's content.
4. Clarify action to be taken.
   - Explain your actions.
   - State actions expected of students.
5. Provide background information.
   - Relate topic to the course or to a previous lesson.
   - Relate topic to new information.
6. State the concepts to be learned.
   - State specific concepts and ideas from the lesson.
   - State general concepts and ideas broader than the lesson's content.

7. Clarify the concepts to be learned.
   - Clarify by examples or analogies.
   - Clarify by nonexamples.
   - Caution students about possible misunderstandings.
8. Motivate students to learn.
   - Point out relevance to students.
   - Be specific, personalized, and believable.
9. Introduce vocabulary.
   - Identify and define new terms.
   - Repeat and define difficult terms.
10. State the general outcome desired.
    - State objectives of instruction and learning.
    - Relate outcomes to test performance.

*Source:* Adapted from Lenz, B. K. (1983). Promoting active learning through effective instruction. *Pointer, 27*(2), 12. Reprinted with permission.

---

model and discuss the **cognitive strategies** (i.e., thinking processes) that they use for tasks such as finding the main idea of the story (e.g., Echevarria, 1995; Mariage, 2000; Moll, 1990; Palincsar, 1986; Tharp, Estrada, Dalton, & Yamaguchi, 1999). Teachers and students can use thinking aloud to comment on or make visible their thought processes as they are doing cognitive tasks such as finding the main idea. Teachers can use discussions (referred to as **instructional conversations**) to make visible the thinking processes needed for understanding.

In the following dialogue, the teacher is helping students to better understand story elements, using an instructional conversation to make learning more visible (Englert et al., 1994). In this example, the teacher is working with two students who have partner-read a narrative story about a bear and are now telling the rest of the students about the story.

T: Tell us about the story.
Ann: [Begins . . . by retelling random incidents from the story]
T: You already said we were going to talk about the characters, setting, and problem. Who are the characters in that story?
Dee: There is Brother Bear, Papa Bear, and . . . [Shows pictures from the book]

T: Who would you say is the main character?
Ann: They were all main characters because they were all together throughout the story.
T: When we try to figure out the main character, what is the question we ask ourselves?
Ann: What the author wants us to know.
T: Remember when we try to figure out the main character, we ask ourselves, "Who is . . . "
Ann: [Ann fills in] ". . . the story mostly about?"
T: Could you answer that question by saying it's mostly about everybody there? (p. 21)

Rather than providing the answer, the teacher is modeling what question to ask to determine who the main character is. Whether teaching reading, math, or written expression, research on students with LD has consistently demonstrated that making the learning strategies visible improves learning significantly.

### Teaching Self-Regulation and Self-Monitoring

By having students keep track of how well they are understanding or performing, they can gain incentives for learning and change their learning patterns to more effective ones. Research suggests that students with LD are not as adept as their peers at monitoring their own performance (e.g., Harris et al., 1994; Wong, 1991), and effective teachers promote self-monitoring (Pressley, Rankin, & Yokoi, 1996; Pressley et al., 2001). One way to help students with LD is to teach them to ask themselves questions about their learning and performance. General questions that students can ask themselves include the following:

- What is my purpose for learning or doing this?
- What is my plan for doing this task?
- Does what I am learning, reading, or doing make sense?
- What do I already know about this topic?
- How am I doing with my work?
- What are the main points I am learning?
- How can I use this elsewhere?

The use of **self-monitoring** and graphing has been shown to be effective for students with learning and attentional problems (e.g., Hoff & DuPaul, 1998; Martin & Manno, 1995; Trammel et al., 1994). For example, teaching students to self-monitor reading fluency can provide a means for them to set goals and see their progress. Students should read material written at their instructional to independent reading levels (e.g., word recognition 90 percent

or greater). To calculate fluency, have the students use the following formula:

$$\frac{\text{Total words read} - \text{Errors}}{\text{Number of minutes of reading}} = \text{Words correct per minute}$$

Fluency information can be plotted onto graphs like the one shown in Figure 2.4. Having students record their own progress serves as a motivation for reading, provides immediate feedback, and allows the students to set goals and see concrete evidence of their progress. Generally, for students with fluency problems, the goal should be an increase of one to two words correct per minute per week. However, use past performance to help students set goals.

**Providing Opportunities for Extended Practice and Application**   Students with LD need extended practice and additional opportunities to apply their learning to ensure continued mastery (Kameenui & Simmons, 1990; Swanson & Hoskyn, 1998). In teaching complex

Students with learning disabilities have difficulty transferring or applying skills and strategies to other learning situations (Borkowski & Turner, 1990; Wong, 1994).

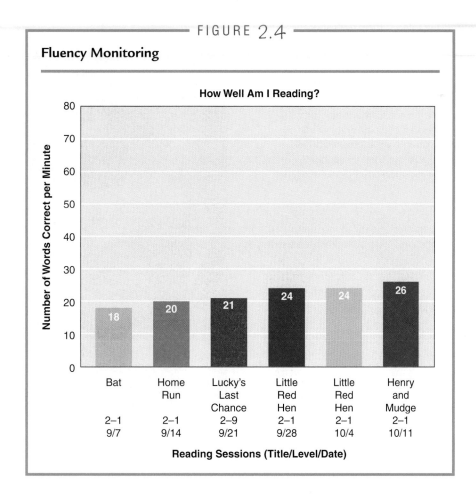

FIGURE 2.4

**Fluency Monitoring**

*How Well Am I Reading?*

materials and skills to adolescents with LD, extended practice with feedback was particularly important and helped to minimize difficulties with complex cognitive activities (Swanson & Hoskyn, 1998; Vaughn et al., 2000). To create these opportunities when other students in the class may not benefit from them, teachers must be adept at instructional management.

Margaret Duran, a fifth-grade teacher, comments on the way she organizes her classroom to promote opportunities for extended practice and maintenance of skills and strategies:

> One of the most difficult aspects of teaching is juggling the grouping of students and scheduling of activities to assure that students who need more time to learn have that opportunity available. I find that using readers' and writers' workshops has allowed me the flexibility I need. Within these workshops I embed lessons that focus on different skills and strategies. I select the skills/strategies based on students' needs, and we usually work on those skills/strategies for 1 to 3 weeks. I usually teach nine 10- to 15-minute lessons a week so that I focus on three skills/strategies at the same time. The students who are most academically at risk usually work on two of the three skills/strategies. This allows the students who need the most guidance to receive regular small-group instruction and to work consistently on a specific skill or strategy. In their writing folders, there is a list of these skills/strategies and space to record when we worked on them and for the student and me to judge mastery level. When I do individual conferences with the students, we review the skill/strategy list, update the records, monitor progress, and set goals. I find that for students with LD or who are academically at risk, I have more individual conferences to monitor progress, and we do more maintenance checks to see that the students are continuing to use the skills/strategy effectively in their writing.

As for materials, the fourth- and fifth-grade teachers have been working on these workshops for several years and regularly add text and materials, particularly materials for extended practice.

Several other instructional principles that are important for students with LD and are helpful for many students include the following:

- Using learning tools and aids
- Adjusting workload and time
- Presenting and having students demonstrate their learning in multiple ways
- Teaching students to use memory strategies

**Using Learning Tools and Aids** With the new technology and its increasing availability, more stu-

dents with reading, writing, and math disabilities are able to overcome their academic problems through the use of technologically based learning tools (Lewis, 1993; Woodward & Rieth, 1997). Also, teachers are better able to organize their classrooms and use technology to facilitate effective cooperative learning activities (Bryant & Bryant, 1998). The best-known tool is the computer, with its peripherals and programs. Students with handwriting and spelling disabilities have been helped by word processors and their built-in spell checkers. Through speech synthesizers and software, students with reading and writing difficulties have had the opportunity to hear what they write and then to read along with the computer. More and more children's literature is available on CD-ROM, an increasingly available medium that allows readers to hear as well as read the text, to have words and pictures in the text explained, and to have words provided in another language. Drill and practice programs for math facts, such as *Math Blasters Plus,* have provided students with the opportunity to review and practice their math facts in an interactive game format. See the Tech Talk for more information about **computer-assisted instruction (CAI)** and its use in building phonological awareness. Other learning

What are eight general teaching strategies that are helpful for all students but are especially effective for students with learning disabilities?

# T e c h  T a l k

## Using Computer-Assisted Instruction to Build Phonological Awareness Skills and Letter–Sound Correspondence

Students with learning/reading disabilities as a group consistently have difficulty with such phonological skills as blending, segmenting, and manipulating phonemes and learning letter–sound correspondences. Oftentimes these students need additional practice to learn these skills to the level that they become automatic and can be applied easily when reading text. A number of programs have been developed to provide practice in these areas. *DaisyQuest* and *CastleQuest* (PRO-ED) are two programs that were developed in

*Read, Write & Type*

*Source:* www.readwritetype.com. Copyright © Talking Fingers, Inc. Developed by Dr. Jeannine Herron and Dr. Leslie Grimm.

the early 1990s to promote skill development in phoneme identification and segmentation. These programs use an adventure game format to provide practice with a wide range of phonological awareness tasks including recognizing rhyming words, matching words on the basis of common first, middle, and last sounds, and counting the number of phonemes in a word. Barker and Torgesen (1995) evaluated the effectiveness of these programs with early elementary grade students who were having significant difficulty decoding. When compared to groups of students who received math practice or *Hint and Hunt,* a software program designed to improve the decoding of medial vowels and vowel combinations, students using *DaisyQuest* and *CastleQuest* made substantially more improvement in phonological awareness. Practice with these programs has also been shown to positively affect the phonological awareness skills of preschool and kindergarten students (K. Foster, Erickson, D. Foster, Brinkman, and Torgesen,1994). *Read, Write & Type* (Talking Fingers, Inc.) is another program that provides practice in phonological awareness skills and letter–sound identification, while students learn keyboarding. When used with the teacher-led instructional activities that accompany the program, this program was effective in improving the phonological awareness skills of struggling readers (Torgesen, 1999). When using these types of programs, it is important to remember that they are only a supplement and need to be part of a larger coordinated program to have their greatest impact on students with learning and behavior problems (Okolo, Cavalier, Ferretti, & MacArthur, 2000; Wise, Olson, Ring, & Johnson, 1998).

*Source:* Bos, C. S., & Vaughn, S. (2002). *Strategies for teaching students with learning and behavior problems* (5th ed., p. 124). Boston: Allyn & Bacon.

tools that are recommended for students with LD include calculators, spell checkers, tape recorders, and hand-held organizers.

**Adjusting Workload and Time** Adjustments of workload and time allocations can be useful accommodations for students with LD. Workload adjustments can include both the amount of work given and the manner in which it is given. Reducing the amount of work may be a very reasonable accommodation when the goal of an assignment or test is for the student to demonstrate mastery (and it can be

demonstrated with less work). For example, if the purpose of a math assignment is to demonstrate mastery in using addition and subtraction with regrouping to solve verbal math problems, then completing the odd-numbered problems rather than all the problems may provide adequate evidence of mastery. This type of accommodation is reasonable for students who are slow in math computation because their knowledge of math facts is not at an automatic level. Another accommodation—providing time extensions for tests or completion of large projects—has been helpful to students with LD.

Another way to adjust work is to divide it into smaller sections or tasks. Having students work on groups of 5 problems at a time rather than the complete set of 20 can make a task more manageable for the student and give the teacher additional opportunities to provide feedback and encouragement as each five-problem set is completed. Helping students to break a complex task, such as reading a book and writing a report, into smaller tasks and to develop a timeline for completing each task can also improve successful task completion.

**Presenting Information and Demonstrating Learning in Multiple Ways**   Students with LD may have difficulty processing information when it is presented in only one way. To assist these students, it is important to present the information in multiple ways. Bruce Ford incorporates a number of activities, materials, and ways of presenting information as he plans a unit on cells for his ninth-grade science class:

> When I think about planning for biology class, I think about what are the key knowledge and skills that I want the students to understand and use. I know that if I just present the information, using a lecture, and have the students read the textbook, a good number of the students will not be able to access the information. So I find myself being creative and constantly on the lookout for additional resources that I can integrate into the unit. Right now, when we do the unit on cells, I have a great video from "Nova" that I use. I have also developed a study guide that I have students complete as we go through the unit. It incorporates pictures of cells and allows them to label the parts of the cell and their functions. It also includes Internet sites that provide accurate information on cells. The study guide provides the outline for my lecture notes. The study guide is critical because many of the students in my class cannot take adequate notes, and the study guide serves as a structure for their note taking. One activity that I use is an experiment where students have to view cells during the reproduction cycle with a microscope. This activity allows the students to work in teams and develop a group report of their findings. I ask the students to be sure to include drawings. I have found that some of my students with LD excel at this activity.

Allowing students to demonstrate the learning in multiple ways is also important. The majority of students with LD have writing problems that persist over time (Graham & Harris, 1989; Mather & Roberts, 1995). A high-school teacher of students with LD explains the situation this way: "The adolescents in my program do not want to write. They do not even want to answer questions in writing. Writing a theme for a class is torture." Yet writing and tests are the major vehicles used to demonstrate learning. Modifying the manner in which students demonstrate learning enables students with LD to be more successful in the classroom. Tips for Teachers 2.3 gives ideas for presenting information and demonstrating learning in multiple ways.

**Teaching Students to Use Memory Strategies**
Research has consistently demonstrated that students with LD are less effective at employing memory strategies than their peers (Swanson, 1993; Swanson & Cooney, 1991; Torgesen & Goldman, 1977). For the classroom teacher, this means that students with LD will not automatically use **memory strategies** such as rehearsing information they are learning, categorizing the information to make it easier to learn, using visual imagery to "see" the information mentally, and using acronyms to remember lists. By teaching students with LD how to organize and associate information, how to use mnemonic devices and key words, and how to use rehearsal strategies, you can help them remember information, whether they are beginning readers developing an automatic sight vocabulary or high-school students studying for a science test. Take, for example, the use of acronyms to remember lists of information. The sentence "Kings play cards on fine green sofas," can help students remember the biological classification system:

Kingdom   Phylum   Class   Order
Family   Genus   Species

It is important not only to teach students memory strategies, but also to *cue students to use their memory strategies when they work on a task.* The 60-Second Lesson describes a fun way to have students develop acronyms.

Overall, key strategies for teaching students with LD include the following:

● Control of task difficulty
● Teaching students with LD in small interactive groups of six or fewer students
● Using a combination of direct instruction and cognitive strategy instruction
● Providing a framework for learning
● Modeling process and strategies using thinking aloud and instructional conversations
● Teaching self-regulation and self-monitoring
● Providing opportunities for extended practice and application
● Using learning tools and aids

# T i p s for T e a c h e r s

## 2.3   Ideas for Presenting Information and Demonstrating Learning in Multiple Ways

### Ideas for Presenting Information

- Demonstrate the process or strategy.
- Lecture, writing key points on an overhead projector as you talk.
- Lecture, stopping at natural breaks so that students, working in pairs, can discuss what they see as the major ideas.
- Use a graphic organizer or map to show the relationship among the ideas you are presenting.
- Use a video or movie that presents the key points.
- Have students listen to books on tape.
- Have students conduct experiments to test hypotheses or discover relationships.
- Use pantomimes and skits to explain concepts.
- Have students role-play.
- Use computer simulations.
- Use manipulatives to demonstrate and then have the students use manipulatives.
- Use analogies, metaphors, and examples to further explain concepts.
- Have students use visualization and imagery to see ideas and their relationships.

### Ideas for Demonstrating Learning for Math

- For students who have difficulties aligning numbers, use graph paper.
- Have students draw a visual representation of the story problem and then complete the math computation. Give partial credit for correct visual representation, even if math computation is incorrect.
- Allow students who do not know their math facts to use math fact matrixes or calculators.
- Allow for time extensions.

### Ideas for Demonstrating Learning for Content Areas

- Give tests orally and have students respond orally (students can tape-record their responses). (The special education teacher or paraprofessional can often assist in this activity.)
- Allow time extension on tests and projects.
- For projects, help students divide the project into steps and develop a timeline for completing each step.
- Have students use a picture or sequence of pictures to demonstrate understanding of a concept or process.
- Have students develop a skit or pantomime and present it to the class.
- Use word-processing programs and spell checkers.

---

- Adjusting workload and time requirements
- Presenting information and having student demonstrate learning in multiple ways
- Teaching memory strategies

As a teacher, you will find that many of the strategies and accommodations suggested in this section will also assist students with attention deficit hyperactivity disorder as well as other learners.

## making a Difference

### Teaching Students to Develop Acronyms

One activity that students of all ages seem to enjoy and profit from is learning to develop and memorize acro-

## The 60-second Lesson

nyms for lists of information that must be learned. When you teach a list to students, have them form cooperative groups, with each group working on developing an acronym to help them remember the list. Then each group can report on its acronym.

## Attention Deficit Hyperactivity Disorder

Many students with LD also demonstrate attention problems. Danny Moreira, a tenth-grade student, found out during the ninth grade that he has an attention deficit hyperactivity disorder (ADHD):

> It has been an enormous relief to me, because all of my life I have been called names like "spaced out," "lazy," "hyper," and "daydreamer," yet I always knew that I was doing the best I could and that it was difficult for me to behave any other way. Ever since I was very young I was very intense and had extra energy to work on areas of interest, but I also became easily bored and distracted. I've been reading and talking to my counselor about ADHD, and what they say is that people with ADHD have a hard time making friends. That has sure been true for me. I get bored with what people are saying. I interrupt. I am also somewhat impulsive so that if I am thinking something I just blurt it out and sometimes I say the wrong thing. I've gotten much better and the friends I have now understand me. I must say, though, that finding out I had an attention deficit really took the weight off of me. I feel like I've had a boulder removed from my shoulders.

> School was a disaster for me, largely because I was so bored and the work all seemed so repetitive and tedious. I've only had one teacher who I felt understood me, Mrs. Golding, my third-grade teacher. I'll never forget her. For math, she would tell me I only had to do the problems until I got five in a row right, then I could stop. At recess she would help me get involved in games with other children and insist that I be included.

IDEA does not recognize Attention Deficit Disorder as a separate category of disability. In 1991, the U.S. Department of Education clarified that students with ADD may be eligible for special education services under IDEA as "Other Health Impaired" or they may be served if they have another disability (e.g., learning disability, serious emotional disturbance).

Students with attention deficit hyperactivity disorder have been identified for well over a century (e.g., Still, 1902), but only recently have we begun to address the educational implications of their disorder in schools. The terms **attention deficit disorder (ADD)** and **attention deficit hyperactivity disorder (ADHD)** have been used to describe students with this disability. Currently, the *Diagnostic and Statistical Manual of Mental Disorders* (DSM-IV) uses ADHD, so we have chosen to use this term. Parent groups such as Children and Adults with Attention Deficit Disorders (CH.A.D.D.) have applied pressure at the local, state, and national levels so that appropriate educational services would be developed for their children (Children and Adults with Attention Deficit Disorders, 1992). Additionally, teachers and other school personnel, recognizing that students with ADHD come to school with behaviors that interfere with their successful learning, are increasingly requesting information that provides instructional guidelines that will help them meet the needs of students with ADHD. Linda Wellens, a veteran kindergarten teacher, explains her experiences with ADHD this way:

> I know that every year at least one of the students in my class will have serious attention problems. I don't mean the usual behaviors that a 5-year-old and 6-year-old display. I mean serious problems focusing on what we are doing, controlling themselves, and following directions even after everyone else in the room has caught on to the routines. I can usually tell after the first two weeks of school, but I try everything I can think of to structure the classroom for the child before I mention it to the parents or school counselor. I find that parents are relieved to discover that another adult has confirmed what they know about their child. Most of these parents are totally stressed out having to deal with the problems day and night and are looking for help.

## Definitions and Types of Attention Deficit Hyperactivity Disorder

Some teachers wonder whether there is such a disability as ADHD or whether parents and children use it as an excuse for their behavior (Reid et al., 1993). Research studies provide compelling evidence that ADHD is a true disorder (Barkley, 1998; McBurnett et al., 1993; National Institute of Mental Health, 2000). For example, magnetic resonance imaging research has demonstrated decreases in blood flow in areas of the brain associated with attention (Zametkin & Rapaport, 1987; Zametkin et al., 1993). According to the DSM-IV (American Psychiatric Association, 1994), attention deficit hyperactivity disorder has two distinct factors: (1) inattention and (2) hyperactivity–impulsivity (McBurnett et al., 1993). The current DSM-IV uses ADHD as a general term and subdivides individuals into (1) ADHD, Predominantly Inattentive Type; (2) ADHD, Predominantly Hyperactive–Impulsive Type; and (3) ADHD, Combined Type. Students who display either or both of these characteristics can be identified as having ADHD. There is increasing support for the notion that youngsters with

ADD without hyperactivity display different achievement patterns than those with both attention deficit disorder and hyperactivity (Barkley, 2000; Marshall, Hynd, Handwerk, & Hall, 1997).

**Inattention** refers to consistent (over six months) and highly inappropriate levels of at least six of the following behaviors:

- Failing to pay close attention to details and making careless mistakes that are inconsistent with the child's developmental level
- Failing to sustain attention to tasks and/or play activities
- Failing to listen, even when spoken to directly
- Failing to complete tasks
- Having difficulty with organization
- Resisting working on tasks that require sustained attention
- Losing materials and objects
- Becoming easily distracted
- Being forgetful

**Hyperactivity–impulsivity** refers to consistent (over six months) and highly inappropriate levels of at least six of the following behaviors:

### Hyperactivity
- Fidgeting or squirming
- Having a difficult time remaining seated during class, even when other students are able to do so
- Running or climbing excessively when it is not appropriate
- Having difficulty playing quietly
- Acting as though he or she is "driven by a motor"
- Talking too much

### Impulsivity
- Blurting out answers
- Difficulty waiting for his or her turn
- Interrupting others or butting into activities

These characteristics of inattention and/or hyperactivity–impulsivity should be present before the age of 7 and in two or more separate settings (e.g., at school and at home). There should also be clear evidence that these characteristics significantly impair social, academic, or occupational functioning.

The first type of ADHD is the predominantly inattentive type. Teachers recognize these students as daydreamers who are often forgetful and easily distracted. Hallowell and Ratey (1995) describe these students as daydreamers and

> the kids—often girls—who sit in the back of the class and twirl their hair through their fingers while staring out the window and thinking long, long thoughts. . . . These are the people, often highly imaginative, who are building stairways to heaven in the midst of conversations, or writing plays in their minds while not finishing the day's work, or nodding agreeably and politely while not hearing what is being said at all (p. 153).

The second type of ADHD is predominantly hyperactive–impulsive. These students have difficulty sitting still, talk out of turn, are the most challenging to parents and teachers, and are more likely to develop oppositional and defiant disorder or conduct disorder in adolescence.

The third type of ADHD is the combined type and describes students who have features of both inattention and hyperactivity–impulsivity. It is estimated that 85 percent of students with ADHD are the combined type (Barkley, 1998). Table 2.2 lists some characteristics that highlight the differences between the students with the inattentive and hyperactive–impulsive types of ADHD. Those with the combined type may exhibit features of both but are generally more like students with hyperactivity–impulsiveness.

Although many teachers and parents think that inattention is the key characteristic of ADHD, there is growing evidence and consensus that inattention, as well as hyperactivity and impulsivity, is the result of problems in behavioral inhibition and self-control (Barkley, 1998; 2000), as discussed in the next section.

## Characteristics of Students with Attention Deficit Hyperactivity Disorder

There is general agreement that ADHD manifests itself early in a youngster's life. In fact, the precursors to ADHD have been identified in infancy (Barkley, 2000). Some early indicators of ADHD include poor sleeping and eating habits, a difficult temperament, and high levels of activity. By the time youngsters are 3 years old, approximately 50 percent of those who will later be identified as having ADHD demonstrate such behaviors as high levels of activity, behavior problems, and short attention span (Barkley, 1998). Therefore, it is not uncommon for children to demonstrate many of the behaviors associated with ADHD as early as kindergarten and first grade. The core characteristics of ADHD include the following:

- Poor sustained attention and vigilance
- Impulsive or poor delay of gratification
- Hyperactivity or poorly regulated activity
- Diminished rule-governed behavior
- Increased variability of task performance

=== TABLE 2.2 ===

### Difference between Inattentive and Hyperactive–Impulsive Types of ADHD

| Trait | Hyperactive–Impulsive Type | Inattentive Type |
|---|---|---|
| Decision making | Impulsive | Sluggish |
| Boundaries | Intrusive, rebellious | Honors boundaries, polite, obedient |
| Assertion | Bossy, irritating | Underassertive, overly polite, docile |
| Attention seeking | Shows off, egotistical, best at worst | Modest, shy, socially withdrawn |
| Popularity | Attracts new friends but doesn't bond | Bonds but doesn't attract |
| Most common diagnosis | Oppositional defiant, conduct disorder | Depression, energy focused in |

*Note:* For more information, see Taylor, J. F. (1997). *Helping your hyperactive ADD child.* Rockin, CA: Prima.

Even though preschool children may be diagnosed as having ADHD at age 4, only half will have the same diagnosis by later childhood or early adolescence (Barkley, 2000). These children may no longer be diagnosed with a disability or may develop LD as the academic tasks become more challenging. However, in the majority of those children in whom this early pattern of ADHD lasts for at least a year, ADHD is likely to continue into the school-age years, including adolescence. Parents describe these young children as restless, always on the go, acting as if driven by a motor, persistent in their wants, demanding of parental attention, and insatiable in their curiosity about their environment.

The common developmental features that distinguish ADHD from mild attention or hyperactive problems are the following:

● Onset in early childhood
● Chronic over time
● Generally pervasive across situations
● Deviant from age-based standards
● Increased co-morbidity with other learning and psychiatric disorders

Typically, teachers notice that these students are restless, are inattentive, and have a difficult time with routines. These observations are often confirmed by parents. Tips for Teachers 2.4 describes what teachers and parents can do to explain ADHD to others.

In the early elementary years, teachers often view these children as having "immature" behaviors and making slow academic progress. About 20–25 percent are likely to have difficulty learning how to read. The students struggle not only with phonological processing tasks, but also with executive functioning (overall regulation of one's behavior and control over the tasks) related to both reading and behavior (Pennington, Groisser, & Welsh, 1993; Pisecco, Baker, Silva, & Brooke, 2001).

Current research suggests that the key characteristic of ADHD lies in difficulty with behavioral inhibition or self-control (Barkley, 1997, 1998; Caspi, Henry, McGee, Moffitt, & Silva, 1995). **Behavioral inhibition** refers to the ability to withhold a planned response, interrupt a response that has been started, protect an ongoing activity from interfering activities, and delay a response (Rubia, Oosterlaan, Sergeant, Brandeis, & van Leeuwen, 1998). Teachers note that these children have difficulty waiting their turn, refraining from interrupting in conversations, delaying immediate gratification, working for long-term rewards, and resisting potential distractions when working (Barkley & Murphy, 1998). The ability to delay one's response to external stimuli permits the development of the executive functions involved in self-control. **Executive functioning** is the ability to regulate one's thinking and behavior through the use of working memory, inner speech, control of emotions and arousal levels, and analysis of problems and communication of problem solutions to others. For example, students can use **inner speech** to "talk to themselves" about various solutions when in the midst of solving a problem. Consequently, students with ADHD have problems in guiding their behavior in situations that demand the ability to follow rules or instructions. These students also have more limited persistent goal-directed behavior and can find it exceedingly difficult to stay focused on tasks that require effort or concentration but that are not inherently exciting (Barkley, 1997).

As with learning disabilities, in the 1970s there was the common belief that children would outgrow

# Tips for Teachers

## 2.4 · Ten Tips for Parents and Teachers for Explaining ADHD to Children and Others

- *Tell the truth.* This is the central, guiding principle. First, educate yourself about ADHD, then put what you have learned into your own words, words the child can understand. Don't just hand the child a book or send the child off to some professional for an explanation. Explain it to yourself, after you have learned about it, then explain it to the child. Be straightforward and honest and clear.
- *Use an accurate vocabulary.* Don't make up words that have no meaning or use inaccurate words. The child will carry the explanation you give him or her wherever he or she goes.
- The *metaphor of nearsightedness* is useful in explaining ADHD to children. It is accurate and emotionally neutral.
- *Answer questions.* Ask for questions. Remember, children often have questions you cannot answer. Don't be afraid to say you don't know. Then go find the answer. See the resources in the Read More about It and Suggested Websites sections of this chapter.
- *Be sure to tell the child what ADHD is not.* ADHD is not stupidity, retardation, defectiveness, badness, and so on.

- *Give examples of positive role models.* Use role models either from history, such as Thomas Edison, or from personal experience, such as a family member (mom or dad).
- *If possible, let others know the child has ADHD.* Let others in the classroom know (after discussing this with the child and parents), and let others in the extended family know. Again, the message should be that there is nothing to hide, nothing to be ashamed of.
- *Caution the child not to use ADHD as an excuse.* Most kids, once they catch on to what ADHD is, go through a phase of trying to use it as an excuse. ADHD is an explanation, not an excuse. They still have to take responsibility for what they do.
- *Educate others.* Educate the other parents and children in the classroom, as well as members of the extended family. The single strongest weapon we have to ensure that children get proper treatment is knowledge. Spread the knowledge as far as you can; there is still a great deal of ignorance and misinformation out there about ADHD.

ADHD as they reached adolescence and adulthood. Although there is evidence that outward signs of hyperactivity may be reduced, many individuals with ADHD continue to experience attentional problems in adolescence and adulthood. From 70 to 80 percent of children diagnosed with ADHD are likely to continue to have the characteristics of ADHD during adolescence, and 25–30 percent display antisocial behavior or conduct disorder. See Figure 2.5 for a description of the characteristics of ADHD in adolescents.

Individuals with ADHD do get better as they get older, but more than half of them continue to complain of impulsivity, inattention, low self-esteem, and restlessness as adults (Barkley, 1998; Hechtman et al., 1980). As in high school, at work, adults with ADHD may have significant problems with their ability to work independently of supervision, meet deadlines and work schedules, be persistent and productive in getting assigned work done, and interact cordially with fellow workers (Barkley, 2000).

Perhaps one of the most distinctive characteristics of ADHD is the likelihood that it will co-occur

---

FIGURE 2.5

### Characteristics of Attention Deficit Hyperactivity Disorder in Adolescents

Adolescents with attention deficit hyperactivity disorder will manifest many of the following characteristics (Shaywitz & Shaywitz, 1988):

- Less activity than younger children with ADHD
- Restlessness
- Behavior problems or antisocial conduct
- Low self-concept
- Inattentiveness
- Impulsiveness
- Depression
- Academic difficulties in school
- Problems with relationships
- Difficulty maintaining jobs
- Difficulty following through on tasks
- Problems with drugs/alcohol
- Difficulty following directions
- Procrastination
- Impatience, easily frustrated or bored

with another disability, such as LD or conduct disorders. Many students with ADHD (25–68 percent of them) are also identified as learning-disabled (McKinney et al., 1993; Pisecco et al., 2001; Shaywitz & Shaywitz, 1988). Approximately 65 percent display oppositional and defiant behaviors, and as many as 45 percent may progress to the more severe diagnosis of conduct disorders (Barkley, 1998; Fowler, 1992). Thus, students with ADHD frequently have other behavioral or academic difficulties.

## Prevalence of Attention Deficit Hyperactivity Disorder

One of the most frequent reasons that students are referred for behavioral problems to guidance clinics is concern over attentional problems (Richters et al., 1995). Current best estimates of the prevalence rate of ADHD are from 3 percent to 5 percent (Barkley, 1998; NIMH, 2000). For example, a recent review of the National Library of Medicine database from 1975 to 1997 indicated that the percentage of students who are diagnosed and treated for ADHD is at or below 3 percent (Goldman, Genel, Bezman, & Slanetz, 1998). The number of individuals with ADHD is difficult to determine because many children with ADHD have not been identified. Furthermore, recording the number of students with ADHD is difficult because there is no specific category for ADHD under the Individuals with Disabilities Education Act. Students with ADHD may be identified as having a health impairment or a secondary condition when ADHD and another disability (e.g., learning or emotional disabilities) co-exist. Other students, who do not qualify under IDEA as students with ADHD, do qualify under Section 504 of the Vocational Rehabilitation Act (discussed in Chapter 1). Again, however, as in the case of IDEA, the number of students with ADHD is not recorded.

Prevalence estimates of students with ADHD consistently report higher rates for males than for females. Some reports indicate that the ratio of males to females is 3 to 1, with other studies reporting ratios as high as 6 to 1 (e.g., Barkley, 1998; Willcutt & Pennington, 2000). The ratio is highest for children referred to clinics. It is difficult to determine why the rate is so much higher for boys, but there is some reason to believe that ADHD may manifest itself differently in girls than in boys and that the identification instruments are based on the behavioral manifestations of ADHD in boys. Oftentimes, girls with ADHD are more likely to be withdrawn and diagnosed as ADHD without hyperactivity (and thus less likely to be identified) than boys with ADHD, who are likely to be hyperactive and more aggressive. For example,

Roisen and colleagues (1994) found that of girls identified with ADHD, 29.3 percent had the inattentive subtype compared to 2.3 percent of boys.

## Identification and Assessment of Students with Attention Deficit Hyperactivity Disorder

Different from learning disabilities, initial identification of ADHD often involves a medical evaluation from a pediatrician, psychologist, or psychiatrist outside the school system. This evaluation should rule out other reasons for the student's behavior problems and evaluate the student's difficulty with attention and behavioral inhibition. This is usually accomplished through the use of interviews and/or the completion of behavioral rating scales by parents, teachers, and, when appropriate, the student. The information that you provide as a teacher can be helpful in determining whether the attentional problems are severe enough to be identified as ADHD and how the attentional and behavioral problems are affecting the student in school both socially and academically. For example, keeping a record of the characteristics from the DSM-IV criteria that you observe in the child can be helpful in making initial identification and planning for accommodations.

A number of rating scales have been developed specifically for the identification of ADHD. Two frequently used scales are *Conners Teachers Rating Scale* (Conners, 1989) and the *ADHD-Rating Scale-IV* (DuPaul, Power, Anatopoulos, & Reid, 1998). Teachers and parents are asked to rate descriptive statements about the child's behavior based on presence of the behavior (not at all present, just a little present, pretty much present, very much present) or frequency of occurrence (never or rarely, sometimes, often, very often). Examples of behaviors include distractable, restless, always up, excitable, impulsive, excessive demands, unaccepted by peers, no sense of fair game, and fails to finish tasks.

Because the identification of ADHD is based on the perceptions of the raters, it is important to take into consideration cultural and ethnic factors that may result in the overdiagnosis or underdiagnosis of ADHD. Some students may have activity levels and behavioral patterns that are culturally and ethnically appropriate but differ significantly from majority-culture, same-age peers (Burcham & DeMers, 1995; Reid, 1995). For example, Hispanic students, especially those from Puerto Rico, and African American students, particularly males, may manifest more body movements, gestures, and expressions that may be interpreted as hyperactive than Anglo students

(Baumeister, 1995; Neal, McCray, & Webb-Johnson, 2001). It is important to be cautious in using and interpreting these behavioral assessments (Neal et al., 2001; Reid, 1995). Furthermore, although certain behaviors may occur more frequently owing to cultural influences, individuals vary widely within cultural groups. Instruments such as the *Child Behavior Checklist-Direct Observation Form,* a component of the *Achenbach System of Empirically Based Assessment* (Achenbach, 2000), allows for direct observation and comparison to peers from the same cultural group.

## Instructional Guidelines and Accommodations for Students with Attention Deficit Hyperactivity Disorder

Because students with ADHD are likely to spend all or most of their school time in general classroom settings (Fowler, 1992), much of their educational program is likely to be the responsibility of the classroom teacher. What are the characteristics of teachers who are effective with students with ADHD? According to Lerner and colleagues (Lerner et al., 1995), "in many respects, they are simply good teachers" (p. 96). Lerner and colleagues indicate that the following characteristics help teachers to work successfully with students who have ADHD:

- *Positive attitudes toward inclusion of students with ADHD.* These attitudes are reflected in the way teachers accept students and promote students' acceptance by the classroom community.
- *Ability to collaborate as a member of an interdisciplinary team.* Teachers who have students with ADHD in their classrooms have an opportunity to work with other professionals and family members who will be monitoring the students' academic and behavioral progress, response to medication, and self-esteem.
- *Knowledge of behavior-management procedures.* Most students with ADHD in your classroom will demonstrate difficulty following directions, remembering routines, attending to task, and organizing themselves and their work. Behavior-management skills are essential to adequately meet the needs of students with ADHD.

- *Personal characteristics.* To teach students with ADHD, you need understanding, compassion, patience, concern, respect, responsiveness, and a sense of humor.

In addition to the preceding characteristics, educational and medication-related interventions can also be helpful in your work with students with ADHD.

**Educational Interventions**    Teachers should begin any educational intervention with planning. Maria Nahmias has served as a consultant to parents and teachers on how to effectively meet the needs of students with ADHD in the classroom, and Susan Stevens is a teacher and consultant with many years of experience working with students with ADHD. On the basis of their experiences, they recommend that teachers consider the following key points when planning **educational interventions** for students with ADHD (Nahmias, 1995; Stevens, 2001):

- *Use novelty in instruction and directions.* Highlight important instructions and key points with colored pens, highlight markers, or felt-tip pens. Put key information in boldface or underline it. For example, have students highlight the operation signs on a math page before completing the page. Use oral cueing to identify key words or ideas in the directions.
- *Maintain a schedule.* As was indicated earlier, students with ADHD have a difficult time learning rules and routines; therefore, it is critical that these be changed as infrequently as possible. Change is difficult for students to adjust to and

What are some signs of hyperactivity and impulsivity in students identified as having attention deficit hyperactivity disorder? What can you do to help students with ADHD in your classroom?

often promotes behavior problems. Post rules and schedules in the room and on index cards on the students' desks.

- *Prepare students for transitions and provide support in completing transitions.* Alert students to upcoming transitions (e.g., "We'll be going to recess in three minutes. Finish what you are doing and put your materials away."). Provide guidance and encouragement as students complete transitions (e.g., "You have all your materials away. All you need to do is line up when I call your table.").

- *Emphasize time limits.* Individuals with ADHD (adults even more so than children) have a poor concept of the time needed to complete tasks. Teach students to plan ahead and use the rule that to be considered "satisfactory," assignments are to be completed according to directions, with a passing grade, and turned in on time. Any adjustments in time should be arranged well before the deadline, not at the last minute.

- *Provide organizational assistance.* Provide guidelines for how the students should maintain their desks, materials, and schedules. Provide opportunities at the beginning of each week for students to organize, and then reward them for doing so. Ask students to keep a planner and a notebook for each of their classes and to write their assignments and due dates in the notebook.

- *Provide rewards consistently and often.* All students like to receive positive feedback about their performance and behavior; however, the frequency, intensity, and consistency of rewards need to be increased for students with ADHD. Whenever possible, involve the student in selecting the rewards.

- *Be brief and clear.* Think about instructions before stating them, and provide them as briefly and in as well-organized a way as possible. Present the critical information in chunks so that it is more easily understood and remembered. Keep instructional lessons brief to maintain students' attention.

- *Arrange the environment to facilitate attention.* Consider where the student is sitting. Are there other students who might promote good behavior and organizational skills sitting nearby? Are you able to quickly and easily maintain eye contact as well as physical contact with the student? Be sure to consider how to minimize distractions.

- *Provide optimal stimulation.* There is some support for the notion that optimal stimulation facilitates learning for students with ADHD. For example, students with ADHD who were pro-

vided with background music while doing arithmetic problems performed better than non-ADHD students under the same conditions (Abikoff, Courtney, Szeibel, & Koplewicz, 1996).

- *Allow for movement and postures other than sitting.* Arrange activities so that they include movement as part of the activity, such as writing, typing, drawing, or using manipulatives. Have students demonstrate their learning by using the board or overhead projector.

Planning lessons for students with ADHD within the context of planning for the class as a whole is a challenge. The primary focus of planning should be on what accommodations are needed to make the lesson effective for all students, including a student with ADHD. Table 2.3 lists types of problems frequently manifested by students with ADHD and provides potential solutions. Figure 2.6 provides a sample lesson plan with supports identified for students with ADHD.

A problem frequently noted by parents and teachers of students with ADHD is homework (Bos, Nahmias, & Urban, 1999; Welton, 1999; Weyandt, 2001). These students have a difficult time recording assignments, knowing when they are due, and establishing an organizational sequence that enables them to complete the task on time. For this reason, homework record sheets are often developed and implemented by teachers and then monitored by parents. Figure 2.7 provides an example of a daily assignment and homework log.

The following guidelines will help reduce the trauma often associated with homework for students with ADHD.

- *Keep homework assignments separate from unfinished classwork.* Unfinished classwork should remain in class. This helps students to differentiate between classwork and homework. If unfinished classwork becomes homework (as an add-on to the already assigned homework), students can easily become overwhelmed.

- *Use homework as practice for material that has already been taught.* Don't use homework as a means for teaching new information. Homework should be on the student's independent reading level and provide for review and practice.

- *Identify the minimum amount to demonstrate learning.* Understanding and mastering the task are more important than completing an extensive amount of work. Consider shortening the task for these students. It is better that they do a small amount well than a lot of work poorly.

TABLE 2.3

**Educational Interventions**

| Problem | Solution |
| --- | --- |
| Listening | Provide visual displays (flowcharts, pictorials, wheels); prereading questions/terms at end of chapter; assigned reading; keyword note-taking system to expand memory jogs during daily review; advance note-taking organizers from subtitles in textbook. |
| Distractibility | Minimize visual distractors in the environment; don't have interesting activities going on in one corner of the room while expecting the student to do his or her seatwork. |
| Attention Span | Have student work in short units of time with controlled activity breaks (i.e., reading break or magazine break); activities need to be interspersed throughout instruction. |
| Short-Term Memory | Offer review systems in a flashcard style so frequent practice can be done independently; material may need to be reviewed frequently. |
| Task Completion | Present work in short units (i.e., five problems on paper cut into quarters rather than on one sheet); timeframes should be short, with clear deadlines and checkpoints to measure progress; have a model available so product can be examined if directions can't be retained. |
| Distractibility | Have as few distractions as possible; provide a "quiet corner" for anyone who wishes a distraction-free place to work. |
| Impulsivity | Show the student how to do the work; have a checklist for what he needs to do, and have a reward system tied to the completion of all the steps. |
| Inattention to Detail | Emphasize detail through color coding or isolation. |
| Test Taking | Have the student review critical details and main ideas in a flashcard system to support attention and practice specific retrieval. |

*Source:* Rooney, K. J. (1995). Teaching students with attention disorders. *Intervention in School and Clinic,* 30(4), 221–225. Copyright © 1995 by PRO-ED, Inc. Reprinted by permission.

● *Provide timelines for tasks associated with long-term assignments.* Rather than telling students the date a long-term assignment is due, help them problem solve a timeline for completing the key components of the assignment. Pair them with a buddy or work cooperatively with parents to ensure that each component in the timeline is completed.

Although no one educational treatment package has been demonstrated to yield successful outcomes for students with ADHD (Barkley, 1998; Guyer, 2001; Welton, 1999), the best treatment procedures to date are those that involve a range of instructional and behavioral supports and accommodations and may be in conjunction with medication.

**Medication as One Aspect of Treatment for ADHD**   The identification of ADHD in children frequently involves a pediatrician, psychologist, and/or psychiatrist. These professionals may recom-mend that the student be given medication as one aspect of treatment for ADHD. The most typical type of medication is **stimulant medication,** which includes Ritalin (methylphenidate), Dexedrine, Adderall, and Cylert. Ritalin is the most frequently prescribed drug. Concerta is a new extended-release form that requires only one dose a day. Antidepressants and alpha$_2$-noradrenergic agonists (Clonidine) are also recommended but much less frequently. About 70–80 percent of children with ADHD respond positively to stimulant medications, but it is only one aspect of a treatment plan and should be paired with behavioral and/or academic interventions (Barkley, 2000; NIMH, 2000).

The decision to use medication as one part of a treatment program can be a tumultuous one for parents who, unsure about the outcomes associated with medical treatment, fear negative side effects. As a teacher, you will want to monitor the positive and negative effects of medication and work with the parents so that the physician can be informed. It is

---

FIGURE 2.6

**Lesson Plan for Students with Attention Deficit Disorder**

---

**Objective:**
Students will understand the difference between an adverb phrase and an adjective phrase.

**Methods for Presentation:**
Demonstrations, examples, overheads, worksheets, student samples for analysis.

**Materials Needed:**
Overhead projector, worksheets, examples.

**Work Plan and Timeframes for Presentation:**

| | |
|---|---|
| 2:00 PM–2:05 PM | Review definition of adverb/adjective; have students write definition of each term from memory and then correct them to the book's definition. |
| 2:05 PM–2:15 PM | Explain and discuss the difference between an adjective phrase and an adverb phrase; demonstrate examples on the overhead. |
| 2:15 PM–2:25 PM | Have students write an operational rule and share their versions. |
| 2:25 PM–2:35 PM | Have students produce an example of an adverb phrase and an adjective phrase. |
| 2:35 PM–2:40 PM | Explain and demonstrate assignment. |

**Supports for Attention:**
Frequent shifts in activities.
Activities interspersed with instruction.
Demonstration as well as oral presentation.

**Review System:**
Record of instruction will be written in a bound notebook. Study card (homework) will be produced for the grammar review system.

**Demonstration of Knowledge (Independent Use):**
Homework. Study card from the grammar book section (pp. 54–56). The card will include the topic, the rule or instruction, and an example of each. Examples corrected in class, and errors highlighted and corrected on the card.

*Source:* Rooney, K. J. (1995). Teaching students with attention disorders. *Intervention in School and Clinic, 30*(4), 221–225. Copyright © 1995 by PRO-ED, Inc. Reprinted by permission.

not unusual that you be asked to complete behavior rating forms as the physician works to adjust the medication dosage. Linda Wellens, a kindergarten teacher, comments:

> This year I had a student, Alex, who was identified as ADHD with hyperactivity–impulsivity. His mother called me frequently to check on how he was doing in school. He had been kicked out of three preschools before he even started kindergarten, and she was worried about how he would perform. Alex just couldn't sit still. He would try to stay in his seat and then would jump up and start playing with toys or building with blocks. He just seemed to need a frequent release. He was a handful, but I managed to set up a behavior modification program that was highly effective. One of the things that helped the most is that his parents and his behavioral pediatrician agreed that he would benefit from medication. Then we worked as a team to monitor his reaction and progress.

=== FIGURE 2.7 ===

**Daily Assignment and Homework Log**

Student: _____

Week of: _____

| Day/ Subject | Class Assignment | Finished Y    N | Homework Assignment | Materials Needed | Finished Y    N |
|---|---|---|---|---|---|
|  |  |  |  |  |  |
|  |  |  |  |  |  |
|  |  |  |  |  |  |
|  |  |  |  |  |  |
|  |  |  |  |  |  |
|  |  |  |  |  |  |
|  |  |  |  |  |  |
|  |  |  |  |  |  |

| Special Projects | | | | | |
|---|---|---|---|---|---|
| Tests | | | | | |
| Materials/ Clothes Needed | | | | | |
| Teacher/ Parent Notes | | | | | |

Stimulant medication works like a pair of eyeglasses, helping the individual to focus. It can also reduce the sense of inner turmoil and anxiety that is so common with ADHD. Stimulant medication works by adjusting a chemical imbalance that affects the neurotransmitters in the parts of the brain that regulate attention, impulse control, and mood (Barkley, 1998). Figure 2.8 provides a summary of the treatment outcomes you should expect when youngsters with ADHD are given stimulant medication (Swanson et al., 1993). As a classroom teacher, your role in monitoring the medication is important. Work with the parents and doctor to observe the following:

● Changes in impulsivity, attentiveness, activity level, frustration level, organizational skills, behavioral inhibition, and interest in schoolwork

● Changes in academic performance
● Changes related to changes in dosage of the medication
● Possible side effects (loss of appetite, stomachaches, sleepiness, headaches, mood changes, irritability)
● Duration of the medication dosage

The one thing all professionals agree on about treatment of ADHD with medication is that it should always be considered one component of an overall treatment plan (Accardo et al., 1991; Barkley, 1998; Goldstein & Goldstein, 1990; NIMH, 2000). As Lerner and colleagues (1995) state, "Medication should not be considered a 'silver bullet' or the single solution to the problems the student is facing. Rather, medical treatment should

─── FIGURE 2.8 ───

**Treatment of Children with Attention Deficit Disorder with Stimulant Medication**

**What You Should Expect:**

- Improved ability to modulate motor behavior and overactivity
- Increased concentration or effort on tasks
- Improved self-regulation and reduced impulsivity
- Increased compliance and effort
- Decreased physical and verbal aggression
- Decreased negative behaviors during social interactions
- Increased amount and accuracy of academic work

- About 70 percent of children respond favorably
- Possible side effects such as facial tics, loss of appetite, difficulty sleeping, and psychological effects on cognition and attribution
- No significant improvement of academic skills
- No significant improvement of athletic or game skills
- No significant improvement of positive social skills
- No long-term improvement in academic achievement
- No long-term reduction in antisocial behavior or arrest rate

*Source:* Adapted from Swanson et al. (1993). Effect of stimulant medication on children with attention deficit disorder: A "review of reviews." *Exceptional Children, 60,* 154–162. Copyright 1993 by the Council for Exceptional Children. Reprinted with permission.

be recognized as one part of a total interdisciplinary management and intervention program" (p. 175). Schools, parents, the physician, and the counselor or psychologist all need to work as a team to develop a coordinated effort to meet the needs of students with ADHD.

## summary

- The term "learning disabilities" is used to describe a heterogeneous group of students who, despite adequate cognitive functioning, have difficulty learning, particularly academics.
- Dyslexia, dysgraphia, and dyscalculia are three types of learning disabilities that refer to extreme difficulty learning to read, write, and do mathematics, respectively.
- Students with learning disabilities represent a range of characteristics that include low performance in one or more academic areas, unexpected low performance considering their overall ability, and ineffective or inefficient information processing.
- The number of individuals identified as learning disabled is approximately 5 percent of the school-age population, which accounts for over half of all students identified as having disabilities.
- Because the characteristics of students with learning disabilities are heterogeneous, the types of learning accommodations vary. Accommodations that generally assist students with learning disabilities include teaching the students at their instructional level, using interactive groups of six or

fewer, and using a combination of direct instruction and cognitive strategy instruction. Other strategies that facilitate their learning include providing a framework for learning, modeling the processes and strategies, teaching self-regulation, providing opportunities for extended practice and application, using learning tools and aids, adjusting workloads and time requirements, presenting information and allowing students to demonstrate learning in multiple ways, and teaching students to use memory strategies.
- Attention deficit hyperactivity disorder (ADHD) refers to difficulty in attention and has two factors: inattention and hyperactivity–impulsivity. Students can display one or both of these factors.
- A conservative estimate of the number of students with ADHD is 3 percent.
- The core characteristics of ADHD are behavior inhibition and difficulty with executive functioning, or the ability to regulate one's thinking and behavior. Other characteristics include poor sustained attention and vigilance, impulsivity with poor delay of gratification, hyperactivity and

poorly regulated activity, diminished rule-governed behavior, and increased variability of task performance.

- Classroom interventions to assist students with ADHD include using novelty in instruction and directions, maintaining a schedule, providing organizational assistance, providing rewards consistently and often, communicating briefly and clearly, and arranging the environment to facilitate attention.

# key terms and concepts

advance organizer
alphabetic principle
attention deficit hyperactivity
    disorder (ADHD)
behavioral inhibition
cognitive strategies
computer-assisted instruction (CAI)
dyscalculia

dysgraphia
dyslexia
educational interventions
executive functioning
hyperactivity–impulsivity
inattention
inner speech
instructional conversations

memory strategies
phonemic awareness
rapid naming
self-monitoring
specific learning disabilities (LD)
stimulant medications

# think and apply

1. Now that you have read Chapter 2, review Tammy's experiences in working with Adrian and Lenny. If you could talk to Tammy and the parents of Adrian and Lenny, what questions would you ask them? What would you suggest Tammy tell Adrian and Lenny's third-grade teachers to help them succeed next year? List any questions or ideas you have now about teaching students with learning disabilities and attention deficit hyperactivity disorder. Discuss your questions and ideas with your fellow students, your instructors, and teachers in the field. Also check the list of questions or concerns you developed from reading Chapter 1, and see whether you can check any of them off your list. Record your answers and file your personal inquiry in your teaching portfolio.

2. Think about several students you know, have taught, or are currently teaching who are not achieving as you would expect. Using the definition of learning disabilities and the exclusionary factors, predict whether their learning difficulties are due to specific learning disabilities or other reasons.

3. Select a lesson in which you are going to teach a new skill or strategy. Think about how you can modify the lesson to provide more opportunities for you and the students to model or demonstrate the skill or strategy, and more opportunities for the students to practice the skill or strategy.

4. Modify a lesson or unit you are going to teach, increasing the number of ways students can learn the information or skills, and the number of ways in which they can demonstrate learning. Think about the needs of students with learning disabilities or attention deficit hyperactivity disorder.

5. Write, call, or visit the websites of the following organizations, request copies of their publications and resources, and keep them in a designated file for use in your classroom with parents or other teachers.

- Attention Deficit Disorder Advocacy Group
  15772 E. Crestridge Circle
  Aurora, CO 80015

- Children and Adults with Attention Deficit Disorder
  8181 Professional Place, Suite 201
  Landover, MD 20785
  (301) 306-7070
  (800) 233-4050
  www.chadd.org

- A.D.D. Warehouse
300 Northwest 70th Avenue, Suite 102
Plantation, FL 33317
(954) 792-8100
(800) 233-9273
www.addwarehouse.com

- Learning Disabilities Association of America
4156 Library Road
Pittsburgh, PA 15234
(412) 341-1515
www.ldanatl.org

- National Center for Learning Disabilities
381 Park Avenue South, Suite 1401
New York, NY 10016
(888) 575-7373
www.ncld.org

# read more about it

1. Bos, C. S., & Vaughn, S. (2002). *Strategies for teaching students with learning and behavior problems* (5th ed.). Boston: Allyn & Bacon.
*Provides specific strategies that teachers, school personnel, and parents can use to facilitate the academic and personal growth of students with special needs. Also describes the major theories and approaches to learning.*

2. Deshler, D. D., Ellis, E. S., & Lenz, B. K. (1996). *Teaching adolescents with learning disabilities: Strategies and methods.* Denver, CO: Love.
*Provides descriptions of the characteristics of adolescents with learning disabilities and specific strategies for instruction. The roles of the teacher, parent, and family members as well as appropriate programs for providing successful interventions for adolescents with learning disabilities are described.*

3. Wong, B. Y. L. (1996). *The ABC's of learning disabilities.* San Diego: Academic Press.
*This book discusses the concept of learning disabilities, as well as major research findings regarding learning-disabled children, adolescents, and adults. It also encourages the beginning student to identify the big picture and to think about implications of issues and research findings.*

4. Hampshire, S. (1982). *Susan's story: An autobiographical account of my struggle with dyslexia.* New York: St. Martin's Press.
*Provides an interesting account of a young woman's experiences in school and life. Her dyslexia was difficult for her to deal with and in many cases even more difficult for others.*

5. Moss, P. B. (1990). *P. Buckley Moss: The people's artist.* Waynesboro, VA: Shenandoah Heritage.
*Ms. Moss has become a successful artist and advocate for individuals with learning disabilities. This book conveys her feelings concerning the need to look for the creative strengths many students with learning*

*disabilities hide because of fears related to their difficulties learning in school.*

6. Smith, S. (1986). *No easy answers.* Cambridge, MA: Winthrop.
*Sally Smith is a successful woman with learning disabilities who owns a private school for students with learning disabilities. She explains the difficulties of growing up with learning disabilities and describes some of the strategies used in her school to effectively meet students' educational and social needs.*

7. Barkley, R. (2000). *Taking charge of ADHD: The complete, authoritative guide for parents.* New York: The Guilford Press.
*Provides information about ADHD, its causes, assessment, treatment, and use of medication. Discusses the teacher's role in both assessment and intervention.*

8. Cohen, M. W. (1998). *The attention zone: A parents' guide to attention deficit/hyperactivity disorder.* Washington, DC: Taylor & Francis.
*Provides information about ADHD and what parents should know about characteristics, assessment, treatment, intervention, and home–school collaboration.*

9. Flick, G. (1998). *ADD/ADHD behavior-change resource kit: Ready-to-use strategies and activities for helping children with attention deficit disorder.* New York: The Center for Applied Research in Education.
*Provides information on charting and monitoring behavior and how to set up and monitor behavior change programs for students with ADHD and other behavior problems. Forms and charts are provided.*

10. Guyer, B. (Ed.). (2000). *ADHD: Achieving success in school and in life.* Boston: Allyn & Bacon.
*Edited book that provides an overview of the definition, characteristics, assessment, and interventions for students with ADHD.*

11. Hallowell, E., & Ratey, J. (1994). *Driven to distraction: Recognizing and coping with attention deficit*

disorder from childhood through adulthood. New York: Simon & Schuster.

Designed for parents, provides information about the characteristics, identification, and interventions for students with ADHD.

12. McDonnell, K., Ryser, G., & Higgins, J. (2000). Practical ideas that really work for students with ADHD. Texas: PRO-ED.

Provides academic and behavioral interventions for students with ADHD and LD, including checklists and student monitoring forms.

13. Rief, S. (1998). The ADD/ADHD checklist: An easy reference for parents and teachers. Upper Saddle River, NJ: Prentice Hall.

Provides ideas for managing the behavior and academic needs of students with ADHD, including strategies for giving directions, arranging the environment, and student self-monitoring.

## suggested websites

**www.chadd.org**
This is the website for Children and Adults with Attention-Deficit/Hyperactivity Disorder, a parent/professional organization that provides information and instructional accommodations for students with ADHD.

**www.add.org**
This is the website for the National Attention Deficit Disorder Association, which provides information about individuals with ADHD.

**www.ld.org**
This is the website for the National Center for Learning Disabilities, which provides information on awareness, advocacy, education, and treatment of LD.

**www.ldanatl.org**
This is the website for the Learning Disabilities Association of America and provides information about state organizations, support groups, advocacy, and education of children and adults with LD.

**www.interdys.org**
This is the website for the International Dyslexia Association and provides information about and for individuals with dyslexia including branch organizations, professional development, and education.

**www.ldonline.org**
This website provides a wide variety of information about and resources for individuals with LD as well as for parents and professionals.

**www.nichd.nih.gov**
This is the website for the National Institute for Childhood Health and Human Development and provides information and research on specific learning disabilities and ADHD.

**www.nimh.nih.gov**
This is the website for the National Institute for Mental Health and provides research and general information about mental and learning disorders.

**www.rfbd.org**
This is the website for Recordings for the Blind and Dyslexic, an organization that provides books and other materials on tape for individuals who have visual impairments or learning disabilities/dyslexia.

# Teaching Students with Communication Disorders and with Pervasive Developmental Disorders

chapter

3

# chapter|outline

# focus|questions

1. Communication is a powerful tool. What are communication disorders and in what areas of communication might students have difficulty?

2. Many speech and language skills develop before students enter school. What speech and language skills develop during the school-age years? Think of language skills in terms of content, form, and use.

3. What percentage of students have communication disorders, and how does this percentage change from preschool to elementary school?

4. Language is sometimes described in terms of content, form, and use. What signs would you look for at school if students are having difficulty in each of these areas?

5. With whom would you work to determine whether a student needs further assistance in the area of communication?

6. Why is it important to take into consideration the student's culture and dialect and whether the student is learning English as a second language when making decisions about a student who might have a communication disorder?

7. How could you accommodate and support a student in your class who stutters or who has an articulation disorder?

8. What techniques could you incorporate into your teaching that would help a student with a language disorder? Are these techniques helpful only for students with language and communication problems?

9. What are pervasive developmental disorders, and what disabilities are included in this category?

10. What instructional accommodations or strategies could you consider for students with pervasive developmental disorders in your class?

11. What are the advantages of positive behavioral supports compared with reactive behavior supports?

# inter view

## Lorri Johnson

Lorri Johnson is one of five third-grade teachers at Drexel Elementary School. This is her first year of teaching. In her class of 31 students, one (Samatha) has a communication disorder. Lorri also has two students with learning disabilities, one of whom receives support from both the speech and language pathologist and the special education teacher.

Lorri believes that all children can learn and that her job is to create a learning community that supports this belief. Although she uses the districtwide curricula, she is quick to modify, supplement, and augment the curricula to fit her students' needs. For example, she uses the language arts textbook only as a resource for activities to build communication and written language skills. These activities she embeds in thematic units on such typical third-grade topics as fantasy and weather.

Samatha, the student with communication disorders, works with the speech and language pathologist, Nancy Meyers, for 30 minutes twice a week. Nancy and Lorri check with each other informally about once a week regarding Samatha's progress and what is working. This communication often occurs during lunch or when both teachers are in the teachers' work room.

As Lorri describes Samatha, it is clear that she understands Samatha's needs and makes accommodations to help her communicate successfully in the classroom. Lorri notes,

The way I would describe Samatha is as a late bloomer when it comes to language. Early in the year, Nancy and I sat down with Samatha's file, and we discussed her history and needs. Samatha did not start talking until she was almost 3 years old. Although she babbled and seemed to be talking to herself when she played as a toddler, she did not use words in her play or to communicate with others. Her mom reported that she did appear to understand what others were saying to her. At age 4, Samatha began attending Head Start and was identified as a child with speech and language disorders. She started working with a speech and language pathologist

at that time. She has continued to receive services since then. Nancy and I agree that talking is difficult for Samatha. Her sentences are short, and she continues to have difficulty producing complex sentence structures, does not use adjectives and adverbs to elaborate, and has significant difficulty with verb tenses and irregular verbs. Samatha also has a limited vocabulary when she speaks, and I am oftentimes unsure if she is getting the concepts that I am teaching.

I feel that I work to make my class successful for Samatha in several ways. First, I usually don't call on Samatha in large class discussions unless she raises her hand. We have a deal that she can't use this rule to escape listening and learning and that I expect her to contribute to large group discussions at least several times a day. But this way she gets to pick the opportunities. Second, I have a habit of frequently "checking for understanding." During lessons, I regularly ask students if they are understanding. To keep the class active, I have them use thumbs up, stand up, clap hands, and so on to indicate whether they understand. I think Samatha and the other students feel comfortable telling me they don't understand, for I encourage and praise them for the questions they ask. Third, I have Samatha take leadership roles that require her to talk when we work in small groups, and I encourage her to help other students when doing independent seat work. Finally, through reading and writing, I can focus on the areas that are difficult for her in oral language. For example, we have been working on using adjectives to make our writing more interesting. Samatha has really improved in this area of writing, and now I am asking the students to take their new descriptive written language and use it more when they talk.

I guess, overall, I feel that Samatha is a successful learner in my class, but I would like to know more about communication disorders so I can provide more encouragement and assistance.

# introduction

Many other teachers (both elementary and secondary) share Lorri's feelings. They learn a lot about teaching reading and writing but much less about the development of oral communication, the characteristics of students with communication disorders, strategies for identifying

these students, and techniques for promoting oral communication and language development in general education classrooms. This chapter focuses on those areas and should provide you with a number of techniques and strategies for working with students who have communication disorders or other disabilities that result in delayed communication development.

# Communication Disorders

Communication is the process of exchanging ideas, information, needs, and desires (Owens, 2001). Society places high value on oral communication. Both in school and in society, communication is a powerful resource. For example, we use communication to do the following:

- Develop and maintain contact and relationships with others
- Gain and give information
- Control and persuade
- Create and imagine
- Communicate feelings
- Monitor our own behavior when we talk to ourselves

Even though written communication plays a key role in school, speaking and listening are the most frequently used means of learning. Consequently, students with communication disorders may experience difficulties in many aspects of school, including both learning and social situations.

The term **communication disorders** refers to difficulties with the transfer of knowledge, ideas, opinions, and feelings (Oyer et al., 1987). Communication is thought to be disordered when it deviates from the community standards enough to interfere with the transmission of messages, stands out as being unusually different, or produces negative feelings within the communicator (Payne & Taylor, 1998). Communication disorders range in severity from mild to profound. They may be developmental or acquired through injuries or diseases that affect the brain. A communication disorder may be the primary disability, or it may be secondary to other disabilities (ASHA, 1993). For example, students with learning disabilities and mental retardation often have secondary language disabilities and receive services from a speech and language pathologist.

When students enter school, they are expected to communicate by listening and speaking. Some students may have difficulty transmitting the message or information. For example, when Sarah entered kindergarten, her speech was so difficult to understand that both the teacher and students had to listen to her for several days before they began to figure out what she was trying to communicate. Sarah has difficulty with speech, or the vocal production of language. Jeffrey, by contrast, has difficulty understanding the message of others and communicating his message to others. His speech (vocal production) is adequate, but the message is unclear. Jeffrey's diffi-culties lie in the area of language. Language, the major vehicle humans use for communicating, is a "code whereby ideas about the world are represented through a conventional system of arbitrary signals for communication" (Lahey, 1988, p. 2). The American Speech-Language-Hearing Association (1993) has divided communication disorders into the three broad categories: speech disorders, language disorders, and hearing disorders. This chapter deals with speech and language disorders; Chapter 6 discusses students with hearing disorders.

> Of students with communication disorders, 53 percent have speech disorders. By far the most typical speech disorders are articulation disorders (47 percent), with voice disorders (4 percent) and fluency disorders (2 percent) far less frequent (Leske, 1981).

## Speech Disorders

Individuals with **speech disorders** have difficulty with the verbal means of communication. The major components of speech are articulation, fluency, and voice. *Articulation* has to do with the production of speech sounds, *fluency* refers to the flow and rhythm of language, and *voice* focuses on the quality of speech, including resonance, pitch, and intensity.

**Articulation Disorders**   By far the most common speech disorders, **articulation disorders** occur when students are unable to produce the various sounds and sound combinations of language (Hulit & Howard, 1997). It is not unusual for speech and language pathologists to work with elementary-age children who have a delay in the development of articulation, because the ability to produce the speech sounds continues to develop through age 8 (Smit, 1993). Learning to produce the speech sounds, no matter what the language, usually proceeds in a fairly consistent sequence, but there may be as much as a three-year variance between the time early learners start producing a particular sound and the time late learners start producing the sound (Bernthal & Bankson, 1998; Yavas, 1998). Figure 3.1 demonstrates the developmental progression of speech sounds and clarifies why many children enter school still in the process of learning to produce such sounds as *r, l, s, ch, sh, z, j, v, zh,* and voiced and voiceless *th*.

It is also interesting to note that the production of speech sounds generally develops earlier in girls than in boys. Table 3.1 compares the development of girls and boys, noting the age at which 90 percent of girls and boys can articulate the sounds. If you teach kindergarten through second grade, you will have the opportunity to hear these sounds developing in some of your students. Even if these sounds are not fully developed, children's speech by the time they

─── FIGURE 3.1 ───

**Developmental Sequence for the Production of Speech Sounds**

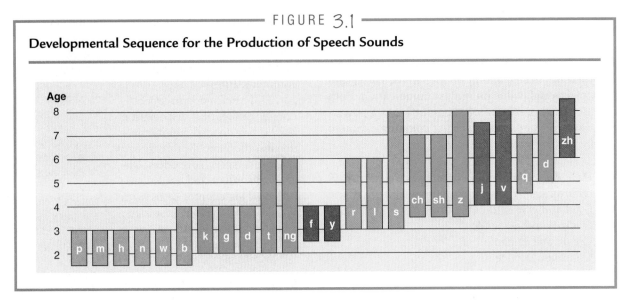

*Source:* Sander, E. K. (1972). When are speech sounds learned? *Journal of Speech and Hearing Disorders,* *37,* 62. Copyright © American Speech-Language-Hearing Association. Reprinted by permission.

enter kindergarten should be at least 90 percent intelligible.

The types of articulation errors are sound substitutions, omissions, additions, and distortions. The errors may occur at the beginning, middle, and/or end of words. Substitutions and omissions are the most common errors. In *substitutions,* one sound is substituted for another. Common substitutions at the beginning of words include /w/ for /r/ (*wabbit* for *rabbit*), /t/ for /c/ (*tat* for *cat*), /b/ for /v/ (*balentine* for *valentine*), and /f/ for /th/ (*free* for *three*). *Omissions* occur when a sound is not included in a word. Because blends are later in developing, many omission errors have the second sound in the blend omitted (e.g., *boo* for *blue, pity* for *pretty*). Final sounds also are commonly omitted, particularly the later-developing sounds such as /s/, /sh/, /z/, and voiced and voiceless /th/. As a classroom teacher, it will be important for you to listen for children whose articulation is developmentally delayed or whose articulation errors are so frequent that they significantly affect intelligibility. You will want to talk with the speech and language pathologist about these children.

Articulation is affected not only by development, but also by regional dialects and cultural uses. Variations or dialects of a language are products of historical, cultural, geographic, social, economic, ethnic, and political factors (Hedge, 1996). For example, Bostonians often use /er/ for /a/ (as in *idea/ider* and *data/dater*), and Southerners draw out vowels. **African American Vernacular English (AAVE)** is used by some African Americans and re-

flects the complex racial and economic history of the African American in the United States. The features of AAVE are characteristic of the dialect as a whole but vary in individual speakers.

Articulation of English sounds is also affected when students are learning English as a second language (ESL). Sounds made in one language might not be made in another language or might not be made in the same manner. As a classroom teacher, you must remember that differences in articulation due to regional or cultural dialects or English as a second language should not be considered disorders. (For more information about AAVE and ESL, see Chapter 10, "Teaching Culturally and Linguistically Diverse Students.")

> Variations in speech or language that are used by a group of individuals from a geographic region or from a social or cultural group are not communication disorders. Rather, these variations (e.g., Black Vernacular English and Appalachian English) are dialects.

**Fluency Disorders** Whereas articulation disorders involve difficulty with the production of the sounds, **fluency disorders** involve difficulty with the rate and flow of speech. All of us are nonfluent to some degree when we communicate. We hesitate in the middle of sentences, break the flow of language with meaningless sounds and fillers (e.g., *ah, um, you know, like*), repeat parts of words, and speak very quickly. We are more nonfluent in stressful, novel, or exciting situations. When we have difficulty thinking of a word, we may become dysfluent. However, when a child's dysfluencies become more intense and are more problematic than the dysfluencies of normal speak-

=== TABLE 3.1 ===

### Comparison of the Development for Speech Sound Production in Boys and Girls*

#### Boys

| Age | 3 | 4 | 5 | 6 | 7 |
|-----|---|---|---|---|---|
| | p | ng | y | zh | f |
| | b | | | wh | l |
| | m | | | j | r |
| | h | | | | ch |
| | w | | | | sh |
| | d | | | | s |
| | n | | | | z |
| | k | | | | th (voiceless) |
| | t | | | | v |
| | g | | | | th (voiced) |

#### Girls

| Age | 3 | 4 | 5 | 6 | 7 |
|-----|---|---|---|---|---|
| | p | l | j | sh | s |
| | b | t | y | ch | z |
| | m | | | r | th (voiceless) |
| | w | | | zh | v |
| | d | | f | f | th (voiced) |
| | n | | | wh | |
| | k | | | | |
| | g | | | | |
| | h | | | | |
| | ng | | | | |

*The age at which 90 percent of boys and girls can articulate sounds. *Note:* Vowel sounds are produced correctly by 90 percent of all children by age 3. Consonant blends—*tr, bl, pr,* and so on—develop between ages 7 and 9.

*Source:* Work, R. S. (1994). Articulation disorders. In S. Adler & D. A. King (Eds.), *Oral communication problems in children and adolescents* (p. 3). Copyright © 1994 by Allyn & Bacon. Reprinted by permission.

> Boys are four times more likely to stutter than girls.

ers, the child might have a problem of fluency referred to as **stuttering.** One of the most common types of fluency disorders, stuttering is characterized by an interruption of the forward flow of speech (Palmer & Yantis, 1990).

Most young children, at different times during the preschool years, are nonfluent in a manner that resembles stuttering. Ninety-eight percent of cases of stuttering begin before age 10 (Mahr & Leith, 1992), and more than half of all children who stutter during the preschool years recover before the age of 7 (Curlee & Yairi, 1997).

**Voice Disorders**    Voice disorders relate to the quality of the voice itself. Usually, three dimensions are considered:

- Quality (hoarse, breathy, hypernasal/hyponasal)
- Pitch (high or low, monotone)
- Intensity (loud or soft)

One common type of voice disorder found in school-age children is the presence of vocal nodules caused by yelling and other forms of vocal abuse that affect voice quality. Vocal nodules, which develop because the vocal mechanism is used incorrectly or overused, are somewhat like calluses on the vocal folds. If the nodules become too large, students can lose their voices and require surgery. Generally, it takes consistent and prolonged abuse for nodules to develop, but it is important to provide students with information about good vocal hygiene, including (1) keeping yelling to a minimum, (2) getting breath support from the stomach, (3) limiting time spent talking in noisy places, and (4) avoiding vigorous coughing (Lue, 2001).

> Students who have had corrective surgery for a cleft palate may have difficulties with resonance and often receive speech therapy to learn to control the flow of air.

Few school-age children have the other types of voice disorders, those related to pitch and intensity. Should you notice students with difficulties in quality, pitch, and/or intensity, talk with your speech and language pathologist.

## School-Age Language Disorders

**Language disorders** are the other major area of communication disorders discussed in this chapter. Language functions as an integral part of the communication process because it allows us to represent ideas, using a conventional code. A person's ability to understand what is being communicated is referred to as **comprehension** or **receptive language,** whereas a person's ability to convey the intended message is referred to as **production** or **expressive language.**

Students with language disorders may have developmental delays in comprehension or receptive language. These students frequently ask for information to be repeated or clarified. In school, these students may have difficulties with the following processes:

- Following directions
- Understanding the meaning of concepts (particularly technical or abstract concepts)

- Seeing relationships among concepts (e.g., temporal, causal, conditional relationships)
- Understanding humor and figurative language
- Understanding multiple meanings
- Understanding less common and irregular verb tenses
- Understanding compound and complex sentences
- Detecting breakdowns in comprehension

Students with production or expressive language difficulties generally communicate less frequently than their peers. These students may have difficulty doing the following:

- Using correct grammar
- Using compound and complex sentences
- Thinking of the right word to convey the concept (word retrieval or word finding)
- Discussing abstract concepts
- Changing the communication style to fit different social contexts
- Providing enough information to the listener (e.g., starting a conversation with "He took it to the fair," when *He* and *it* have not been previously identified)
- Maintaining the topic during a conversation
- Repairing communication when the listener doesn't understand

To help us think about language and language disorders, language has been divided into **content** (semantics), **form** (phonology, morphology, and syntax), and use (pragmatics) (Bloom & Lahey, 1978). It is the interaction of content, form, and use that creates language.

Grouping words by categories and using relationship words (like *if . . . then* and *because*) are often difficult for students with language impairments or English language learners. It is also the multiple meanings of words and the figurative language that holds up their learning. I consistently highlight these in our discussions of social studies. One way that I highlight them is by writing them on the overhead projector and discussing them prior to reading. Then I cue the students to look for them when they read. We discuss them after reading by finding them in the text and reviewing their use.

**Vocabulary** As students develop language, their **vocabulary,** or stock of words, and their ability to understand and talk about abstract concepts increase quickly. For example, children's speaking vocabulary at age 6 is estimated to be about 2,600 words, and their receptive vocabulary consists of about 20,000–24,000 words. By the age of 12, students' receptive vocabulary has increased to 50,000 words (Owens, 2001). In comparison, when technical words are discounted, average adult speakers use about 10,000 words in everyday conversation, and an estimated 60,000–80,000 words are known and used by the average high-school graduate (Carroll, 1964).

As Mary Armanti got to know Krista, a student with communication disorders in her third-grade class, she discovered that Krista's vocabulary was very limited. During sharing or small-group discussion, Krista used simple words and did not expand on her ideas (compared to the other students). Concerned about Krista's limited vocabulary, Mary worked with the speech and language pathologist

## Language Content

**Semantics** refers to the meaning or content of words and word combinations. When you teach a lesson (as in social studies or science), you are teaching concepts and the labels for those concepts (vocabulary). For example, students often ask for the label for an idea (e.g., "What is that?" or "What are you doing?"), and they ask about what a word means (e.g., "What is a penguin?" or "What does freedom mean?").

Teaching content focuses on teaching vocabulary, word categories and relationships, multiple meanings, and figurative language. Gloria Huerra, a high-school social studies teacher, comments,

In what ways might developmental delays in language be manifested? What aspects of communication are important in identifying students with possible language-learning disabilities?

to develop some classroom strategies to increase Krista's vocabulary. These strategies included Mary elaborating on what Krista said, that is, to model for Krista how to use a more complex, richer vocabulary. For example, when Krista volunteered, "The egg hatched," as she watched a bird nest outside the classroom window, Mary elaborated on her statement: "Yes, the bird's egg just hatched. The new bird is so tiny and fuzzy."

**Word Categories and Word Relationships**  During school-age years, students' ability to understand and organize words and concepts improves significantly (Owens, 2001). Students learn to group concepts by abstract features (such as animate and inanimate), spatial features, temporal relationships,

or function. For example, in learning about fossils, students learn to simultaneously classify different types of fossils (e.g., trilobites, crinoids, brachiopods) according to plant/animal, extinct/not extinct, and location (e.g., sea, lakes, or land). By using **semantic feature analysis**, in which the categories or critical features are placed along one axis of a matrix and the specific vocabulary along the other axis, teachers can guide student discussion about the relationships among concepts and then visually represent those relationships (see Table 3.2). Relationships can be noted as positive, negative, or no relationship or can be rated as to the degree of relationship along a scale. Instructional research shows a substantial increase in the comprehension and learning of students with learning disabilities and language disorders when

---

**TABLE 3.2**

### Semantic Feature Analysis for a Chapter on Fossils

**Relationship Chart**

Key:
+ = positive relationship
− = opposite or negative relationship
o = no relationship
? = uncertain

| Important Words | Type of Life | | Location | | | Extinct? | |
|---|---|---|---|---|---|---|---|
| | Plant | Animal | Sea | Lakes | Land | Extinct | Not Extinct |
| Trilobites | | | | | | | |
| Crinoids | | | | | | | |
| Giant cats | | | | | | | |
| Coral | | | | | | | |
| Bryozoans | | | | | | | |
| Guide fossils | | | | | | | |
| Dinosaurs | | | | | | | |
| Fresh water fish | | | | | | | |
| Brachiopods | | | | | | | |
| Small horses | | | | | | | |
| Ferns | | | | | | | |
| Enormous winged bugs | | | | | | | |
| Trees | | | | | | | |

these kinds of feature analysis are incorporated into the teaching routine (Bos & Anders, 1990a, 1992b; Reyes & Bos, 1998).

Clearly, the ability to understand the relationships among concepts is important to successful learning. Types of relationships include the following categories:

- Comparative (*taller than*)
- Spatial (*above, under*)
- Temporal-sequential (*before, first*)
- Causal (*because, therefore*)
- Conditional (*if . . . then*)
- Conjunctive (*and*)
- Disjunctive (*either . . . or*)
- Contrastive (*but, although*)
- Enabling (*so that, in order that*)

Teaching relationship vocabulary is important for students' understanding of content subjects such as science, social studies, and math.

**Multiple Meanings**    Students also learn to deal with **multiple meanings** of words during school-age years (Menyuk, 1971; Nippold, 1998). For example, the word "bank" has several meanings and can function as both a noun and a verb:

> Lou sat on the bank fishing.
> You can bank on him to be there.
> Put your money in the bank for now.

Many students with communication disorders have more limited vocabularies, and their word meanings are generally more concrete and less specific than those of other students (Bishop & Adams, 1992; Gerber, 1993; Nelson, 1998). These students also have greater difficulty understanding multiple meanings and when to apply which meaning.

**Figurative Language**    Another area of language content, **figurative language**, represents abstract concepts and usually requires an inferential rather than a literal interpretation. Figurative language allows students to use language in truly creative ways (McLaughlin, 1998; Nippold, 1998; Owens, 1995). The primary types of figurative language include the following:

- Idioms (*It's raining cats and dogs.*)
- Metaphors (*She watched him with an eagle eye.*)
- Similes (*He ran like a frightened rabbit.*)
- Proverbs (*The early bird catches the worm.*)

Table 3.3 presents some common American English idioms.

Students with language disorders, students from other cultures or regions, and students for whom English is a second language may have difficulty with figurative language. Yet figurative language, particularly idioms, prevails in the classroom. Classroom research shows that teachers use idioms in approximately 11 percent of what they say and that approximately 7 percent of the sentences in third- to eighth-grade reading programs contain idioms (Lazar et al., 1989).

## Language Form

Difficulties with the form of language are usually quite noticeable to classroom teachers. Students not only have difficulty pronouncing certain sounds and using prefixes, suffixes, and endings on words, but also use sentences that have poor word order and grammar. As was mentioned earlier, form refers to the structure of the language and includes phonology, morphology, and syntax.

**Phonology**    Phonology focuses on the sounds of language and the rules that determine how those

Shoe

## TABLE 3.3

### Common American English Idioms

**Animals**
  a bull in a china shop
  as stubborn as a mule
  going to the dogs
  playing possum
  a fly in the ointment
  clinging like a leech
  grinning like a Cheshire cat

**Body Parts**
  on the tip of my tongue
  raised eyebrows
  turn the other cheek
  put your best foot forward
  turn heads

**Clothing**
  dressed to kill
  hot under the collar
  wear the pants in the family
  fit like a glove
  strait-laced

**Colors**
  gray area
  once in a blue moon
  tickled pink
  has a yellow streak
  red-letter day
  true blue

**Games and Sports**
  ace up my sleeve
  cards are stacked against me
  got lost in the shuffle
  keep your head above water
  paddle your own canoe
  ballpark figure
  get to first base
  keep the ball rolling
  on the rebound

**Foods**
  eat crow
  humble pie
  that takes the cake
  a finger in every pie
  in a jam

**Plants**
  heard it through the grapevine
  resting on his laurels
  shrinking violet
  no bed of roses
  shaking like a leaf
  withered on the vine

**Tools and Work**
  bury the hatchet
  has an axe to grind
  hit the nail on the head
  jockey for position
  throw a monkey wrench into it
  doctor the books
  has a screw loose
  hit the roof
  nursing his wounds
  sober as a judge

**Vehicles**
  fix your wagon
  like ships passing in the night
  on the wagon
  don't rock the boat
  missed the boat
  take a back seat

**Weather**
  calm before the storm
  haven't the foggiest
  steal her thunder
  come rain or shine
  right as rain
  throw caution to the wind

*Source:* Owens, Jr., R. E. (1995). *Language disorders: A functional approach to assessment and intervention* (2nd ed., p. 347). Boston: Allyn & Bacon. Copyright © 1995 by Allyn & Bacon. Reprinted by permission. Compiled from Boatner, Gates, & Makkai (1975); Clark (1990); Gibbs (1987); Gulland & Hinds-Howell (1986); Kirkpatrick & Schwarz (1982); Palmatier & Ray (1989).

sounds fit together. **Phonemes** are the smallest linguistic units of sound that can signal a meaning difference. In English, there are approximately 45 phonemes or speech sounds, classified as either consonants or vowels. (The section on articulation disorders also includes information relevant to the development of phonemes.) The ability to listen to and produce sounds is important not only for oral language, but also for reading and writing (written language). As students learn to decode unknown words while reading and to spell words as they write, one strategy they use is to "sound out the word" or "sound spell." Students who have difficulty generating rhyming words, segmenting words into their individual sounds, or producing individual sounds and then blending them together to make words often have difficulty using the "sound out" or "sound spell" strategy. These skills develop in the preschool and early elementary years as students experiment with sounds and sound patterns while they play with words and learn to read and write. These skills, referred to as **phonological awareness,** pertain to students' ability to understand that words contain sounds and that sounds can be used as linguistic building blocks to construct words (Mann, 1984).

*Different languages have different sounds. When sounds are not made in a student's first language, the student does not listen for or discriminate those sounds. One aspect of learning a second language is retraining the ear to listen for the sounds unique to that second language.*

This difficulty with phonological awareness has been identified as a strong predictor of later reading and spelling (Catts, Fey, Zhang, & Tomblin, 2001; Passenger, Stuart, & Terrell, 2000; Van Kleek, 1995). Consequently, the ability to listen to and produce sounds plays an important role in the development not only of oral language, but also of written language.

**Morphology**   Whereas phonology focuses on sounds, **morphology** focuses on the rule system that governs the structure of words and word forms. And as phonemes are the smallest sound units, **morphemes** are the smallest units of language that convey meaning. There are two different kinds of morphemes: *free morphemes,* which can stand alone (e.g., *cat, run, pretty, small, inside*), and *bound morphemes*

(prefixes, suffixes, and inflectional endings), which cannot stand alone but, when added to words, change their meaning (e.g., *cats, rerun, smallest, transformation*).

Learning the different bound morphemes and their meanings can help elementary and secondary students to decode words, spell words, and determine the meaning of words. For example, students who do not recognize or know the meaning of the word *predetermination* can break it into the free morpheme *determine* (to decide) and the bound morphemes *pre* (before) and *tion* (denoting action in a noun). Then the students can decode the word and decide that the meaning of *predetermination* is "a decision made in advance."

Developmentally, inflectional endings are the easiest to learn, followed by suffixes and then prefixes (Owens, 1995; Rubin, 1988). Although inflectional endings can be taught through conversation, suffixes and prefixes usually require more direct instruction in both oral and written form (Moats & Smith, 1992). The most frequently used prefixes in American English are *un-, in-, dis-,* and *non-.* You can use the common prefixes, suffixes, and inflectional endings presented in Table 3.4 as a guide for teaching morphology.

**Syntax**   Syntax (sometimes referred to as grammar) focuses on the rules that govern the order of words in sentences. During the school-age years, students continue to grow in their ability to use more complex sentence structures (Owens, 2001). Even though most students understand and generate basic sentences by age 5 (McNeill, 1970; Nippold, 1998),

© 1994 Bil Keane, Inc. Dist. by Cowles Synd., Inc. Reprinted with special permission of King Features Syndicate.

—— TABLE 3.4 ——

## Common Prefixes, Suffixes, and Inflectional Endings

| Derivational | | Inflectional |
|---|---|---|
| *Prefixes* | *Suffixes* | |
| a- (in, on, into, in a manner) | -able (ability, tendency, likelihood) | -ed (past) |
| bi- (twice, two) | -al (pertaining to, like, action, process) | -ing (at present) |
| de- (negative, descent, reversal) | -ance (action, state) | -s (plural) |
| ex- (out of, from, thoroughly) | -ation (denoting action in a noun) | -s (third person marker) |
| inter- (reciprocal, between, together) | -en (used to form verbs from adjectives) | -'s (possession) |
| mis- (ill, negative, wrong) | -ence (action, state) | |
| out- (extra, beyond, not) | -er (used as an agentive ending) | |
| over- (over) | -est (superlative) | |
| post- (behind, after) | -ful (full, tending) | |
| pre- (to, before) | -ible (ability, tendency, likelihood) | |
| pro- (in favor of) | -ish (belonging to) | |
| re- (again, backward motion) | -ism (doctrine, state, practice) | |
| semi- (half) | -ist (one who does something) | |
| super- (superior) | -ity (used for abstract nouns) | |
| trans- (across, beyond) | -ive (tendency or connection) | |
| tri- (three) | -ize (action, policy) | |
| un- (not, reversal) | -less (without) | |
| under- (under) | -ly (used to form adverbs) | |
| | -ment (action, product, means, state) | |
| | -ness (quality, state) | |
| | -or (used as an agentive ending) | |
| | -ous (full of, having, like) | |
| | -y (inclined to) | |

*Source:* Owens, Jr., R. E. (1995). *Language disorders: A functional approach to assessment and intervention* (2nd ed., p. A–62). Boston: Allyn & Bacon. Copyright © 1995 by Allyn & Bacon. Reprinted by permission.

first-graders produce sentences that are neither completely grammatical (*He'll might go to jail*) nor reflect the syntactical complexities of the English language.

Some of the most difficult structures are complex sentences that express causation (*because*), conditionals (*if . . . then*), and enabling relationships (*so that*). Passive sentences (*The boy was chased by the girl*) also are developed later, often not until age 7. Students with language impairments and English language learners may experience difficulties in the area of syntax. Students who are learning English as a second language may understand complex syntax, particularly if similar syntax is found in their first language, but may be uncomfortable producing it.

Regardless of the reason for the delay, one helpful strategy for identifying children's needs relative to syntax is to listen to the students' language and determine where they are in the developmental sequence. For example, Rebecca Blair, a third-grade teacher, noticed that several of her students with language-learning disabilities were not using the past participle (*has/ have* + verb) during class discussions, on the playground, or during small-group discussions. She talked with Jean Gleason, the speech and language pathologist, who agreed that this would be a good skill to work on, since all three students were able to use the simple past tense. To teach the skill directly, Rebecca interacted with the three students as they worked together to create and write a story in which she controlled the use of verb tense by requiring them to use the past participle. The story follows:

> Once upon a time, there was a very hungry boy named Jason. Jason decided that he would eat everything he could find in the refrigerator. All day long, he has gone to the refrigerator and eaten whatever food he could find. By the end of the day,
>
> Jason has eaten 3 pickles.
> Jason has eaten 5 olives.
> Jason has eaten 8 slices of cheese.
> Jason has eaten 25 grapes.
>
> Now Jason has a stomachache.

In discussing the story, Rebecca compared the simple past tense with the past participle and had the students think of other instances in which they could

TABLE 3.5

**Average Number of Words per Communication Unit**

| | Average Number of Words per Communication Unit (mean) | | |
|---|---|---|---|
| Grade | High Group | Random Group | Low Group |
| 1 | 7.91 | 6.88 | 5.91 |
| 2 | 8.10 | 7.56 | 6.65 |
| 3 | 8.38 | 7.62 | 7.08 |
| 4 | 9.28 | 9.00 | 7.55 |
| 5 | 9.59 | 8.82 | 7.90 |
| 6 | 10.32 | 9.82 | 8.57 |
| 7 | 11.14 | 9.75 | 9.01 |
| 8 | 11.59 | 10.71 | 9.52 |
| 9 | 11.73 | 10.96 | 9.26 |
| 10 | 12.34 | 10.68 | 9.41 |
| 11 | 13.00 | 11.17 | 10.18 |
| 12 | 12.84 | 11.70 | 10.65 |

*Source:* Loban, W. (1976). *Language development: Kindergarten through grade twelve* (p. 27), Res. Report #18. Urbana, IL: National Council of Teachers of English. Copyright © 1976 by the National Council of Teachers of English. Reprinted with permission.

use the past participle. Rebecca had the students tell/write other stories with similar formats, and Jean, at the same time, worked on the same skill with the students. Rebecca also gave each student a quick "thumbs up" whenever she heard them use the past participle. Within three months, the past participle became part of their everyday language.

As sentence complexity increases, so does the average length of the sentences. Table 3.5 shows the growth in the number of words per communication unit. From early elementary school to high school, students grow from an average of 7 words per communication unit to almost 12 words. During the early elementary grades, students also continue to increase in their ability to use irregular noun plurals (e.g., *mice, sheep, men*) and irregular verbs (see Table 3.6). In students with communication disorders and other disabilities, development of these irregular forms is often delayed by several years (Koziol, 1973; Nelson, 1998).

## Language Use

The area of most important linguistic growth during the school-age years is language use, or pragmatics

(Owens, 2001). **Pragmatics** refers to the purposes or functions of communication, or how we use language in a social context (Lue, 2001). During the school years, students become quite adept in using communication for a variety of functions. Students can use language to give and receive compliments, engage in role-playing, deal with conflicts, and ask for help (Lue, 2001). Students also learn to vary their communication style, or **register**, according to the listener's characteristics and knowledge of the topic. By the age of 13, students can switch from peer register to adult register (depending on the person with whom they are talking) and from formal register to an informal register, depending on the setting and circumstances (McKinley & Larson, 1991; Owens, 1996).

Young children use language for such functions as gaining and holding attention, obtaining and giving information, directing and following others, expressing feelings, and role-playing (White, 1975). By adolescence, students demonstrate communication competence (Mobbs

TABLE 3.6

**Development of Irregular Verbs**

| Age in Years | Irregular Verbs |
|---|---|
| 3-0 to 3-5 | Hit, hurt |
| 3-6 to 3-11 | Went |
| 4-0 to 4-5 | Saw |
| 4-6 to 4-11 | Ate, gave |
| 5-0 to 5-5 | Broke, fell, found, took |
| 5-6 to 5-11 | Came, made, sat, threw |
| 6-0 to 6-5 | Bit, cut, drove, fed, flew, ran, wore, wrote |
| 6-6 to 6-11 | Blew, read, rode, shot |
| 7-0 to 7-5 | Drank |
| 7-6 to 7-11 | Drew, dug, hid, rang, slept, swam |
| 8-0 to 8-5 | Caught, hung, left, slid |
| 8-6 to 8-11 | Built, sent, shook |

*Source:* Adapted from Shipley, K., Maddox, M., & Driver, J. (1991). Children's development of irregular past tense verb forms. *Language, Speech, and Hearing Services in Schools, 22,* 115–122.

# FoxTrot · by Bill Amend

FOXTROT © 1995 Bill Amend. Reprinted with permission of Universal Press Syndicate. All rights reserved.

et al., 1993; Nippold, 1998; Owens, 1995; Wiig & Semel, 1984) in that they are able to do the following:

- Express positive and negative feelings and reactions to others
- Present, understand, and respond to information in spoken messages about people, objects, events, or processes that are not immediately visible
- Take the conversational partner's perspective
- Comprehend the speaker's mood
- Comprehend nonverbal communication
- Understand and present complex messages
- Adapt messages to the needs of others
- Use clarification and repair in conversation
- On the basis of prior experience, approach verbal interaction with expectations of what to say and how to say it
- Relate a narrative cohesively and sequentially
- Communicate a point of view logically
- Select different forms of messages according to the age, status, and reactions of listeners
- Use sarcasm, humor, and multiple meanings
- Make deliberate use of figurative language

Language is used for many different communication activities. One activity that occurs frequently in school and in other settings is conversation. To determine whether students are having difficulty with the use of language, you can assess their conversational skills. Take a few minutes to think about several students you know or with whom you are

currently working. Think about how they use language to communicate in social contexts. Do they vary their communication style depending on the listener? Do they present enough information for the listener to understand the message? If the listener is not understanding, do they take action to clarify what they said? For students who do have difficulty with these areas, working on language use may be an appropriate goal.

## Metalinguistics

Students who use **metalinguistics** can think about, analyze, and reflect on language as an object in much the same way one can describe tables or friends (Hulit & Howard, 1997; Wallach & Miller, 1988). Metalinguistics also involves understanding that language is a code for representing sounds, words, and ideas.

What competencies in the pragmatics of language do these students probably possess? How does the way children typically use language change as they mature into adolescence?

The Research Brief presents the results of developmental research on metalinguistics.

## Development of Metalinguistic Abilities

Young children learn to use language without really understanding how it operates and functions. They use the linguistic rules that govern language, but if you asked them to tell you about or explain the rules, they would have great difficulty. As children mature, however, they become more sophisticated language learn-

ers. They develop metalinguistics skills, or the ability to talk about and reflect on language as if it were an object. Berko Gleason (2001) notes that metalinguistics involves talking about words and language, seeing it as an entity separate from its function. It is the ability to judge the correctness of language and to correct it. Wallach and Miller (1988) have arranged information on the development of metalinguistic skills to correspond in rough approximation to Piaget's stages of cognitive development (see Table 3.7).

It is evident from this table that during Stage Two (ages 2 to 6), children develop the metalinguistic skills critical for decoding words (when reading) and for learning to spell (when writing) (Kamhi, 1987; Nelson, 1998;

---

TABLE 3.7

### Stages of Children's Metalinguistic Development

**Stage One (Ages 1½ to 2):**
- Distinguishes print from nonprint
- Knows how to interact with books: right side up, page turning from right to left
- Recognizes some printed symbols, e.g., TV character's name, brand names, signs

**Stage Two (Ages 2 to 5½ or 6):**
- Ascertains word boundaries in spoken sentences
- Ascertains word boundaries in printed sequences
- Engages in word substitution play
- Plays with the sounds of language
- Begins to talk about language parts and about talking (speech acts)
- Corrects own speech/language to help the listener understand the message (spontaneously or in response to listener request)
- Self-monitors own speech and makes changes to more closely approximate the adult model; phonological first; lexical and semantic speech style last
- Believes that a word is an integral part of the object to which it refers (word realism)
- Able to separate words into syllables
- Inability to consider that one word could have two different meanings

**Stage Three (Ages 6 to 10):**
- Begins to take listener perspective and use language form to match
- Understands verbal humor involving linguistic ambiguity, e.g., riddles
- Able to resolve ambiguity: lexical first, as in homophones; deep structures next, as in ambiguous phrases ("Will you join me in a bowl of soup?"); phonological or morphemic next (Q: "What do you have if you put three ducks in a box?" A: "A box of quackers.")
- Able to understand that words can have two meanings, one literal and the other nonconventional or idiomatic, e.g., adjectives used to describe personality characteristics such as *hard, sweet, bitter*
- Able to resequence language elements, as in pig Latin
- Able to segment syllables into phonemes
- Finds it difficult to appreciate figurative forms other than idioms

**Stage Four (Ages 10+):**
- Able to extend language meaning into hypothetical realms, e.g., to understand figurative language such as metaphors, similes, parodies, analogies, etc.
- Able to manipulate various speech styles to fit a variety of contexts and listeners

---

*Source:* Wallach, G. P., & Miller, L. (1988). *Language intervention and academic success* (p. 33). San Diego: College Hill. Reprinted with permission.

Smith, 1998; Tangel & Blachman, 1995; van Kleeck, 1990). These skills include ascertaining word boundaries in spoken and printed sentences, rhyming, making sound substitutions, segmenting words into syllables and sounds, and blending syllables and sounds into words. Research consistently demonstrates the reciprocal relationship between early reading and writing and the development of these metalinguistic skills (e.g., Chaney, 1998; Speece et al., 1999).

As a teacher, you will want to talk about language, how it works, and the rules that govern language. Playing word games such as the ones suggested in the 60-Second Lesson is one way to build this type of language learning into those free moments during the day.

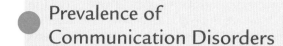

## Prevalence of Communication Disorders

Approximately 10 percent of children in elementary school have communication disorders. Furthermore, 20 percent of all children with disabilities receive services for speech or language disorders. Over 85 percent of these students are included in regular classrooms (U.S. Department of Education, 1997). Of school-age children with communication disorders, most have difficulties in the areas of language and articulation. Within this population, communication disorders occur three to four times more often in boys than in girls (National Advisory Neurological

## making a Difference          The 60-second Lesson

### Promoting Language through Word Games

Often, teachers find themselves before or just after a transition with several minutes that need to be filled. Playing word games is a great way to fill the time and to promote language and metalinguistic skills. Listed here are several word games you and your students can play. You might want to make lists based on the words you generate from these games and post them for student reference.

### For Younger Students

*Rhyming Words:* Select a word. Use a word from a word family (e.g., *-at, -ight, -an, -end*) to provide lots of opportunities for rhyming. Or have a student select a word. Then have the other students give rhyming words. You might want to write the words so that students can see the similarities between words. If you want students to select the words, put each word on a slip of paper and place them in a container such as a hat or jar, then have students draw words from the container.

*Sound Substitutions:* Select a word (e.g., *hat*). (Again, use of word-family words helps.) Say the word and write it on the board. Then ask students what word will be made if the first sound (e.g., /h/) is changed to another sound (e.g., /b/).

*Syllables:* Have a student select a word and say it. Then repeat the word slowly, and have the students clap once for each syllable in the word.

*Opposites:* Select pairs of simple word opposites (e.g., *hot/cold, easy/hard, big/little, happy/sad*). Say one word from each pair, and have students say the opposite.

### For Older Students

*Antonyms:* Select pairs of word opposites (e.g., *cool/warm, hard/soft, cruel/gentle, empty/full, tame/wild*). Write one word from the pair on a card, and put it in a container. Have a student draw a card, say the word, and have other students say or write the opposite word.

*Synonyms:* Select a word with several synonyms (e.g., *eat, pretty, pants, laugh*). Say one word, and have students name as many synonyms as they can.

*Homonyms:* Select a word with at least one homonym (e.g., *fare, sale, male*). Say and spell one word, and have students give the homonyms.

*Multiple Meanings:* Select a word that has several meanings, write it on the board, and have students give examples of sentences that use the different meanings of the word (e.g., I have a *run* in my stocking. Let's go for a *run*. In the long *run,* it isn't very important. I have to *run,* and pick up a sandwich).

*Suffixes:* Select a suffix (e.g., *-tion*). Discuss its meaning, and then have students provide examples of words that use this suffix (e.g., *determination, nomination, participation*). Have students also tell what the root word is. (You can play the same game with prefixes.)

Disorders and Stroke Council, 1990). Recall that speech sounds develop later in boys than in girls (refer to Table 3.1). This trend is evident in most aspects of communication, including the development of language, and may be responsible for the higher identification in boys than girls.

A greater percentage of preschool-age children than school-age children are identified with communication disorders as their primary disability (approximately 10–15 percent of the population or 70 percent of preschoolers with disabilities) (ASHA's Committee on Prevention of Speech, Language, and Hearing Problems, 1984; National Institute of Neurological Disorders and Stroke, 1988). Children who are identified as having communication disorders at the preschool age are often classified as having learning disabilities as they move into elementary school and experience academic difficulties (Kelly, 1998; Mallory & Kerns, 1988).

> Over 85 percent of students with communication disorders spend most of the school day in general education classes.

## Identification and Assessment of Students with Communication Disorders

Most students with communication disorders are identified in preschool or during the early elementary grades. If a communication disorder is suspected, it will be important for the student to have a hearing screening and to determine whether there is a history of chronic ear infections. One role that general education teachers play is that of observer and listener for students who have significant difficulty communicating. Particularly in the elementary grades, the classroom teacher spends more time with the students than any other individual in school.

> Evaluation of students for possible language delays or disorders often includes collecting a language sample. Sampling involves tape-recording students as they interact, then analyzing the students' utterances for characteristics such as mean length of utterance, types of utterances, vocabulary, topic maintenance, and turn taking.

When Sharon Kutok, a speech and language pathologist, spoke about what teachers should watch, she commented, "Classroom teachers are good at identifying students with language disabilities. When identifying students with receptive language problems, typical teacher comments are 'When these students are listening to a presentation they look away and don't focus. When I ask a question, they don't seem to know what is going on.

I don't know if the students don't understand me or if they can't answer my question.'"

For expressive language difficulties, Sharon noted that "Classroom teachers indicate that these students give answers that have no relationship to the question. They use short sentences or just words, and sometimes the words are out of order. Those are the kinds of symptoms that teachers notice when identifying students with language difficulties."

As a classroom teacher, you have the opportunity to observe students using language in the classroom (during both academic and social activities) as well as on the playground and during other activities such as art, music, and physical education. What should you look for in the area of language? Tips for Teachers 3.1 presents questions you can ask about your students to determine the possibility of difficulties with language. The questions are grouped according to the three areas of language: form, content, and use. If a language delay is evident, then you should consider making a referral to the speech and language pathologist.

If students are English language learners or if their first dialects are other than Standard English, consult with a speech and language pathologist and a bilingual education or ESL teacher when observing students for language differences associated with second language/dialect acquisition or possible language difficulties. (See Chapter 10 for additional information.)

## Instructional Guidelines and Accommodations for Students with Communication Disorders

Most students with communication disorders are educated in general education classrooms. Although these students may work (individually or in small groups) with a speech and language pathologist (SLP) several times a week for 30 minutes or so, they spend the rest of their school days with the classroom teacher and students. Consequently, students with communication disorders have many more opportunities to develop effective communication in the classroom than in the limited time spent with the (SLP). You, the classroom teacher, play a major role in facilitating the development of effective communication for these students.

Speech and language pathologists are one of your best resources for ideas facilitating speech and language development. As more schools adopt inclusion policies, speech and language pathologists are more frequently teaming with classroom teachers. Two ma-

# Tips for Teachers

## 3.1   Identifying a Student with Possible Language Disorders

### Language Form

- Does the student mispronounce sounds or words and omit endings more than other students in the classroom do?
- Does the student comprehend and produce types of sentences similar to those of other students in the classroom?
- Is the student's language as elaborate and descriptive as that of other students in the classroom?
- Are the student's comprehension and production of grammatical rules similar to those of other students in the classroom?

### Language Content

- Does the student comprehend and produce vocabulary as rich and varied as that of other students in the classroom?
- Does the student comprehend others' ideas and express his or her ideas as effectively as other students in the classroom?
- When talking, does the student have significant difficulty finding the word he or she wants to use (i.e., word-finding difficulties)?

- Does the student comprehend and use figurative language and multiple meanings of words similar to that of other students in the classroom?

### Language Use

- Does the student use language for different purposes, including to gain attention, ask for and tell about information, express and respond to feelings, use imagination to understand and tell stories and jokes, express opinions and persuade, and for greetings, introductions, and farewells?
- Does the student take turns appropriately in conversations?
- Does the student initiate conversations?
- Does the student maintain topic during a conversation?
- Does the student have more than one style of interacting, depending upon the listener, situation, and topic?
- Does the student recognize when the listener is not understanding, and act to clarify communication for the listener?

---

jor benefits of these teams are that you and the SLP have more opportunities to learn from each other and that students other than those identified as having communication disorders profit from the communication activities (Beck & Dennis, 1997).

## Facilitating Speech Development

Generally, specific remediation of articulation errors, voice disorders, and stuttering is provided by the SLP. The major goal of the general education teacher is to provide opportunities for the student to communicate in the classroom using the most natural, supportive situations possible (Merritt & Culatta, 1998). If students are to generalize what they are learning in therapy, you will also need to work with the SLP to get specific information on the skills students are targeting and to discuss strategies you can use to help them generalize those skills. One such strategy is to develop a personal cueing system for students who have difficulty responding in a large group. Robert Encino, a seventh-grade science teacher, explains how he developed such a system with Kim:

Kim was a student in my fifth period who stutters. I was aware that she often knew an answer and wanted to share her knowledge, but I was unsure of when she felt confident enough to do so. I met with Kim one day during planning period, and we agreed on a system where she would open her hand, palm-side up on her desk if she wanted to respond. What I found was that this reduced her anxiety, and during the semester her hand was open more and more frequently. Eventually, we discontinued the system because she felt that she didn't need it any longer.

It is also important for students with speech disorders that the classroom be a safe environment in which to practice oral communication. Tips for Teachers 3.2 provides some strategies for helping to promote a classroom community that accepts and encourages meaningful student communication.

Some students with physical disabilities and other severe disabilities cannot communicate effectively through speech and therefore rely on **augmentative and alternative communication (AAC) systems.** AAC refers to ways (other than speech) that are used to send and receive messages. We all use AAC

## Tips for Teachers

### 3.2 Creating an Accepting Classroom Community for Students with Speech Disorders

- Create an atmosphere of ease and comfortable pacing. Avoid an atmosphere that creates time pressures and tensions.
- Listen in a calm and thoughtful manner to what students have to say. Allow time for students to finish their thoughts. Don't disregard ideas just because students have difficulty expressing them.
- Do not criticize or point out speech errors. You may, however, demonstrate correct speech by correctly repeating what the students said.
- Classroom rules should not allow for ridicule of students or their speech errors.
- Take care not to place students with speech problems in situations in which their communication difficulties might interfere or are highlighted.

- Use flexible grouping so that students have opportunities to talk in small groups and with a partner.
- Allow time for students to respond. Students often need time to get their ideas organized and to plan their communication. Speech may be labored and slow.
- Develop cueing systems in which students can let you know when they are comfortable responding.
- Reading aloud in a slow, easy manner can be a good opportunity for students to practice fluency strategies or new sounds they are learning. Students become more fluent with multiple readings, so the use of repeated reading may be beneficial.
- Avoid competition among students, particularly when it highlights oral communication.

strategies such as facial expressions, gestures, and writing in our daily interactions. Individuals with severe physical and/or cognitive disabilities use these strategies as well as individualized AAC systems. Augmentative communication systems attempt to compensate for, temporarily or permanently, the impairment and disability patterns of individuals with severe expressive and receptive language disorders (ASHA, 1993). Augmentative communication is a means for students with limited or no speech to interact with peers and teachers in the classroom environment. Tech Talk describes different issues related to augmentative and alternative communication.

### Facilitating Language Development

Opportunities for teaching oral language abound during general education classroom activities—whether they occur in the classroom itself or on the playground, during field trips, or in the lunchroom. It is also in these settings that language becomes more natural and purposeful than is the case in the therapy setting.

As a classroom teacher, you are constantly teaching oral language. When you teach students new concepts and vocabulary in content area subjects, you are teaching oral language. When students learn how to give oral reports or retell a story, how to introduce themselves, or how to use irregular verbs, they are developing language skills. What are

some general guidelines you can use to facilitate language development in your classroom? Bos and Vaughn (2002) suggest the following guidelines to help shape your instruction:

- Teach language in purposeful contexts.
- Teach comprehension (receptive language) and production (expressive language).
- Use effective teaching strategies when presenting a new concept.
- Help students see the connections or relationships among concepts.
- Use conversation as the major milieu for teaching rather than questions or drill and practice.
- Give students enough time to respond.
- Adjust the pace, chunk information, and check for understanding.
- Use self-talk to explain what you are doing or thinking.
- Use parallel talk to describe what others are doing.
- Use modeling to help students get practice and feedback on a specific language skill.
- Use expansion and elaboration to demonstrate how an idea can be expressed in a more complex or mature manner, and provide more information.
- Use language as an intrinsic motivator.

Specific ideas for using these guidelines are presented in the following section.

# TechTalk

## Augmentative and Alternative Communication (AAC)

Augmentative and alternative communication (AAC) is used to replace or supplement an individual's verbal or vocal abilities. Issues to consider in designing an AAC system for a student include the following:

1. The mode of communication (e.g., a gestural mode such as American Sign Language, a graphic mode such as line drawings or the written word)
2. The availability of vocabulary that meets the needs of the AAC user
3. The method for selecting messages (e.g., direct selection, in which the AAC user directly indicates the message; scanning, in which choices are menued and the AAC user makes his or her choice)
4. The display, portability, durability, and age-appropriateness of the AAC system
5. The relative advantages and disadvantages of no/low-tech (e.g., communication boards, wallets) compared to high-tech (e.g., computerized systems with speech output) AAC systems

In situations in which a high-tech communication aid is identified as the most appropriate system for a user, Lewis (1993) suggests considering the following questions when making decisions about high-tech communication devices:

- What type of speech output does the device offer? Is the speech intelligible? Is it appropriate for the student in terms of age and gender?
- Are other types of output provided?
- What input modes are available to the student? Direct selection? Scanning? What physical abilities does the student need to operate the device?
- How are message choices presented to the user? Does the student see letters, words, graphics, or a combination of these?
- How much vocabulary can be stored in the device? Are there strategies for increasing the quantity of vocabulary? For increasing the user's speech in selecting vocabulary?
- How easy is the device for the student to use in communication situations? Can the student (or a teacher or parent) change or add messages easily?
- Is the device portable and durable enough to withstand daily use?

- Is the communication device compatible with other technologies that the student uses, such as computers and environmental control units?
- What is the cost of the device?
- Regardless of the system, the goal of AAC use is to provide the most effective communicative interaction possible.

A child uses a low-tech communication board.

A student uses an electronic communication device.

### Teaching Language in Purposive Contexts

Whether you are teaching students causal relationships such as the effect of heat on water or how to request information by telephone, it is important to teach language in the context of meaningful activities. It is difficult to imagine teaching someone how to use a screwdriver or a needle and thread without having the tools at hand, demonstrating how to use them, and then letting students practice. The same is true for language. Hence, when you cannot create a "real" situation, use such techniques as simulations and role-playing to create authentic learning experiences. Tips for Teachers 3.3 explains how to use barrier games to teach language.

### Teaching Comprehension and Production

Give students opportunities to develop both their understanding (comprehension) and their ability to express (production) the new structures (form), vocabulary (content), and ways of using language (use) that they are learning. When teaching the vocabulary associated with a new unit, for example, provide students with opportunities not only to listen to explanations, but also to discuss their knowledge of the vocabulary and to use the new terms in their discussion and writing. The pause procedure provides these opportunities (Di Vesta & Smith, 1979; Ruhl et al., 1990).

Using this procedure, the teacher pauses at logical breaks in the lecture or discussion, and the students discuss what they are learning (with a partner or in a small group) and review their notes.

### Presenting New Concepts

Critical to learning new content or concepts is the use of effective teaching strategies. As you may recall from the earlier discussion of vocabulary development, students' knowledge of concepts grows exponentially during the school-age years. By using effective teaching strategies (see Tips for Teachers 3.4), you help students with language impairments and English language learners to gain the concepts and content necessary for success in content-area classes.

### Demonstrating Connections among Concepts

One important way we learn about concepts is by understanding the relationships or connections between concepts. If you listen to a conversation in which a new idea is being explained, you'll undoubtedly hear statements such as "It's like . . . ," or "You can compare it to . . . ," or "It's like . . . except that . . . ," or "It's almost the opposite of . . . ." These phrases all help students understand and see the connections among concepts. Because students with language

## Tips for Teachers

### 3.3  Using Barrier Games to Promote Language

It is not always possible to create authentic learning environments when you teach language, but we know that the best, quickest way to learn language is when it is purposeful and taught in context. One way to promote purposeful language and to help students build their comprehension and production of descriptive language, particularly locative prepositions, is to use barrier games. These games (frequently used by speech and language pathologists to teach prepositions) can be a great activity for the entire class or used as a filler activity after students complete their work.

*The Game:* Students work in pairs, with a barrier placed between them so that they cannot see each other's work. The materials usually consist of blocks for building or paper and colors for making a picture. The lead student builds a simple structure or colors a simple design or picture. Then the lead student describes to the second student how to make what he or she has built or drawn. The second student is encouraged to ask questions when the directions are unclear.

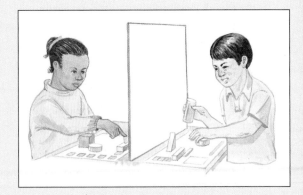

After the second student has finished his or her project, the barrier is removed, the two projects are compared, and differences are discussed. Then the roles are reversed. Students can keep track of the number of projects they make accurately.

# Tips for Teachers

## 3.4   Presenting New Language Concepts or Content

When teaching new language concepts or patterns, keep the following strategies in mind:

- Gear the activities to the students' interests and cognitive level.
- Get the students' attention before engaging in communication activities.
- Bombard the student with the concept or skill frequently throughout the day in a functional manner.
- When speaking, place stress on the target concept or language pattern.
- Pause between phrases or sentences so that the student has time to process the new concept or language pattern.
- Decrease the rate of presentation when first introducing the concept or language pattern.
- When introducing a new concept or language pattern, use familiar, concrete vocabulary and simple sentence patterns (Bloom, Miller, & Hood, 1975; Reed, 1994).

- If possible, present the new concept or language pattern by using more than one input mode (e.g., auditory, visual, kinesthetic). Gestures and facial expressions that are paired with a specific language pattern often assist students in understanding the form. For example, giving a look of puzzlement or wonder when asking a question can serve as a cue to the students.
- Pair written symbols with oral language. For instance, demonstrating morphological endings such as *-s* (plurals) and *-ed* (past tense) can be done in writing. The students can then be cued to listen for what they see.

*Source:* Reprinted with permission from Bos, C. S., & Vaughn, S. (2002). *Strategies for teaching students with learning and behavior problems* (5th ed., p. 89). Boston: Allyn & Bacon.

---

problems have difficulty making those connections, it is important that you highlight them as you and the students discuss new concepts. For example, when Peggy, a first-grade teacher, was introducing the concept of *squirm* because it was important for understanding the book her students were to discuss and read, she asked the students, "What does *squirm* mean?" "Show me with your body how you can squirm." "What other things can squirm?" "Now that we know what squirm is, what other words mean something similar to squirm?" "Is squirm similar to wiggle?" "What would be the opposite of squirm? If you weren't squirming, you would be _____."

At more advanced levels, when students make comparisons among books written by the same author, when they compare the relationships between addition and multiplication versus subtraction and division, and when they compare the similarities between the Korean and Vietnam wars, the emphasis is on making connections. These kinds of discussions help students see the relationships among concepts and better understand semantic relationships (such as contrastives, comparatives, causals, and conditionals). The use of feature analysis (refer to Table 3.2) and other graphic organizers such as semantic maps and concept diagrams (see Chapter 15) can help students see the relationships.

**Using Conversation**   As students with language impairments work, think, and play in your classroom, you need to create opportunities for them to engage in conversations with you and with other students. One way to do this is to use discussion groups rather than a question–answer format for reviews of books and current events. Nancy Meyers, the speech and language pathologist who works with Lorri Johnson, chose to work in Lorri's classroom while the literature groups meet. Once a week, she joins Samatha's literature group. As she listens and joins in the conversation about the book being discussed, Nancy has the opportunity to model language patterns on which Samatha is working.

At least several times a week, engage students in conversations. This may take some forethought and effort on your part, for observational research has shown that classroom teachers, in general, are not as responsive to students with language impairments as they are to average and high-achieving students (Pecyna-Rhyner et al., 1990). Let the students direct the topics of these conversations, which need not be long and, in secondary settings, can be accomplished as students enter the room. Tips for Teachers 3.5 provides more ideas for promoting language through conversations. Use these ideas and share them with parents.

## T i p s  for  T e a c h e r s

### 3.5    Promoting Language through Conversations

- Talk about things in which the child is interested.
- Follow the child's lead. Reply to the child's initiations and comments. Share his or her excitement.
- Don't ask too many questions. If you must, use questions such as *how did/do . . . , why did/do . . . , and what happened . . .* that result in longer explanatory answers.
- Encourage the child to ask questions. Respond openly and honestly. If you don't want to answer a question, say so and explain why. *(I don't think I want to answer that question; it's very personal.)*
- Use a pleasant tone of voice. You need not be a comedian, but you can be light and humorous. Children love it when adults are a little silly.
- Don't be judgmental or make fun of a child's language. If you are overly critical of the child's language or try to catch and correct all errors, the child will stop talking to you.

- Allow enough time for the child to respond.
- Treat the child with courtesy by not interrupting when he or she is talking.
- Include the child in family and classroom discussions. Encourage participation and listen to the child's ideas.
- Be accepting of the child and of the child's language. Hugs and acceptance can go a long way.
- Provide opportunities for the child to use language and to have that language work for the child to accomplish his or her goals.

*Source:* Reprinted with permission from Owens, Jr., R. E. (1995). *Language disorders: A functional approach to assessment and intervention* (2nd ed., p. 416). Boston: Allyn & Bacon. Copyright © 1995 by Allyn & Bacon. Reprinted by permission.

---

**Using Wait Time**   When speech and language pathologist Sharon Kutok talks about the most important principles in teaching students with language impairments, the first one she mentions is **wait time.** "For some students, waiting is important. Wait time gives students the opportunity to understand what has been said and to construct a response. These students may have particular difficulty with form (e.g., syntax) and need the extra time to think about the form they should use in constructing their response."

Students who have difficulty with content may have difficulty also with **word retrieval** or word finding (German, 1992). A word retrieval problem is like having the word on the tip of your tongue but not being able to think of it. Two examples demonstrate how difficulty with word retrieval can affect the flow of communication. The first conversation (about making an Easter basket) is a dialogue between two third-graders, one with typical language and the other with word retrieval problems (Bos & Vaughn, 2002).

> Students with word retrieval problems may use circumlocutions (talking around the word) when they are having difficulty retrieving a word, as in "It's the thing, you know, the thing you write on" (Owens, 1995).

*Susan:* Are you going to make, uh, make, uh . . . one of these things (pointing to the Easter basket on the bookshelf)?

*Cori:* Oh, you mean an Easter basket?

*Susan:* Yeah, an Easter basket.

*Cori:* Sure, I'd like to, but I'm not sure how to do it. Can you help me?

*Susan:* Yeah, first you need some, uh, some, uh . . . the things you cut with, you know . . . .

*Cori:* Scissors.

*Susan:* Yeah, and some paper and the thing you use to stick things together with.

*Cori:* Tape?

*Susan:* No, uh, uh, sticky stuff.

*Cori:* Oh, well let's get the stuff we need.

*Susan:* Let's go, to, uh, uh, the shelf, uh, where you get, you know, the stuff to cut up.

*Cori:* Yeah, the paper, and let's also get the glue (p. 79).

In the second example, an adolescent explains how to fix a tire:

> "Well . . . to fix a tire . . . or your wheel . . . you gotta take the tire off . . . you gotta lift up . . . you jack up the car and use this thing . . . it's square metal wrench . . . to loosen the bolts . . . you know the nuts . . . then you take the wheel off the axes. First you ask the guy at the garage if he will fix the tire. You lock up the car so it won't . . . you put the car in gear so it stays put" (Chappell, 1985, p. 226).

It is clear from these two examples that wait time is important for students with word retrieval problems. In addition to increasing wait time, strategies that teachers can use during classroom discussions including the following:

- Using multiple-choice formats so that students need recognize only one word in a group, rather than having to generate the word
- Providing a cue, such as the initial sound or syllable, the category name or function, a synonym or description, or a gesture demonstrating the word
- Restating a question so that it requires a yes-or-no response rather than an open-ended answer (German, 1993)

By teaching students with word-finding problems to categorize words, make visual images of words, learn synonyms, and make word associations (e.g., *bread/butter, plane/fly*), you can help them recall words, thereby increasing the accuracy and fluency of their expressive language (Gerber, 1993; German, 1993; McGregor & Leanard, 1995).

**Adjusting the Pace**    Students with language delays and other disabilities and English language learners often have difficulty comprehending what is being said during class, particularly in content-area classes. Teachers need to adjust the pace so that these students have time to process language input. The flow of instruction does not have to suffer, but when you discuss new or difficult concepts or ideas, slow the pace and highlight key ideas by writing them on the board or overhead projector and repeating them.

Reducing the amount of information in each segment is helpful also. For example, Bob Stern, a high-school science teacher, used to introduce the terms for a new science chapter by writing them on the board and discussing them as a group when he introduced the chapter. After Bob noticed that his students with language problems listened to the first five words and recorded three of them in their science notebooks, he decided to chunk the words into groups of three to five, introducing them when they were needed. Checking for understanding is also important for facilitating language development in classroom settings. Teachers generally identify a group of several students by whom to gauge the pace of instruction and the decision as to when to move on. Make sure that your group includes the students with language problems.

**Using Self-Talk and Parallel Talk**    Students, particularly young students with language delays, need to hear language that is connected to activities. In **self-talk,** teachers describe what they are doing or thinking; in **parallel talk,** teachers describe what students are doing or thinking. As you and the students work or play, describe what everyone is doing. Maria Ferraro, a first-grade teacher who works in an inner-city school, regularly uses parallel talk and self-talk when she joins students at the different centers in her classroom:

> When I join a center, I try to sit down and join in the activities rather than asking students questions. My goal is to become part of the group. As I join in the activity, I describe what I am doing and what other students in the group are doing. For example, I might say, "José is making a clay animal. It's blue and right now he is putting a ferocious snarl on the animal's face. I wonder what kind of animal it is? I think I'll ask José." In this way, the students get to hear how words can describe what someone is doing, and it focuses the attention on José and the ongoing activities.

**Using Modeling**    Modeling plays an important role in the process of learning language. Whether students are learning a new sentence structure, new vocabulary, or a new function or use for language, modeling is a powerful tool. For example, Sharon Kutok and Armando Rivera, the speech and language pathologist and the eighth-grade English teacher at Vail Middle School, decided to improve their students' conversational skills during literature groups. Both Armando and Sharon were concerned about the number of students who did not clarify what they were saying when other students obviously did not understand (but did not request clarification).

To teach clarification skills, Armando and Sharon began discussing clarifying conversations. During their discussion they role-played, first as students who could not effectively clarify what they were saying, then as students who clarified effectively. They exaggerated the examples, and the students seemed to really enjoy their modeling. Next, Armando and Sharon joined the literature groups and continued to model as they participated in discussions. At the end of the period, they asked students to summarize what they had learned and whether they thought they could become more effective at clarifying what they said and asking others to clarify if they did not understand. During the next two weeks, Armando had the students in each literature group rate the group's effectiveness in clarification. When Sharon returned in two weeks, both teachers observed a difference in the students' discussions, particularly in their ability to clarify ideas and ask for clarification. The students also thought that their skills had improved. In discussing the change, both teachers and students agreed that the modeling

Armando and Sharon had done on the first day was an important key to their learning. Peer modeling, discussed in Chapter 7, can also be a powerful tool.

**Promoting Language through Expansion and Elaboration** Language **expansion** is a technique used to facilitate the development of complex language form and content. By repeating what students say but in a slightly more complex manner, the teacher demonstrates how their thoughts can be more fully expressed. For example, Susie Lee, a first-grade teacher, is working to get Rob to use adverbs to describe his actions. As he finished several math problems, Rob reported, "I got the first one easy. The second one was hard." Susie replied, "Oh, you got the first one easily. That's good." Note that you do not want to imply that you are correcting the student; you are simply showing him or her a more complex way of expressing the thought. Note also that you should expand only one of two elements at a time. Otherwise, the expansion will be too complex for the student to profit from it.

You can use language **elaboration** to build on the content of the student's language and provide additional information on the topic. For example, Chris, a fourth-grade student with language disabilities, was explaining that snakes have rough skin. Teacher Peggy Anderson elaborated on Chris's idea by commenting, "Yes, and snakes have smooth skin on their bellies and so do lizards. Are there other animals in the desert that have smooth skin on their bellies?"

These students are working in a cooperative learning group. Which instructional accommodations described in this chapter might the teacher use for her students who have communication difficulties?

**Using Language as an Intrinsic Motivator** Language is a powerful enabling tool and carries a great deal of intrinsic motivation for students. Rather than using praise (e.g., "I like the way you said that" or "Good talking"), you can capitalize on the naturally reinforcing nature of language. During a cooking activity, for example, teacher Jon Warner asked students, "How can we figure out how much two-thirds of a cup plus three-fourths of a cup of flour is?" After Lydia explained, Jon said, "Now we know how to figure that out. Shall we give it a try?" Later, Jon asked how to sift flour. After Randa explained, Jon said, "I've got it. How about the rest of you? Do you think you can sift the flour just the way Randa explained to us?" Instead of commenting on how "good" their language was and disrupting the flow of communication, Jon complimented Lydia and Randa by letting them know how useful the information was.

When students' purposes and intents are fulfilled because of their language, their language is naturally reinforcing, and students learn that language is a powerful tool for controlling the environment (Bos & Vaughn, 2002; Owens, 1995).

## Pervasive Developmental Disorders

When Sam's teacher announces that the class should join her for group, where she will read about how dairy products are processed on a farm, Sam, a 5-year-old kindergartener, begins screaming and crying, "I want to read about dinosaurs!" This is his sixth tantrum this week, and it is only Wednesday. His teacher does not respond to the tantrum but instead tries to usher his peers to group. Sam's peers are patient about his fascination with certain objects, but they don't understand why he talks constantly about dinosaurs. This probably wouldn't bother his peers as much if he would occasionally talk about things in which they are interested. Sam has the ability to engage in conversations using words and constructs far above his age level, yet he is unable to look his peers or teachers in the eyes when he's talking. Sam knows the scientific names for a couple of dozen different dinosaurs and what they eat as well as the years when they are believed to have become extinct, but he is seldom able to finish any typical kindergarten activity. He can express his wants and needs coherently, yet when he does not get his way, he engages in severe tantrumming behavior. He has been known to hit peers from time to time. At age 3, Sam was diagnosed with Asperger's syndrome. When his teacher received Sam's school file, she was overwhelmed; her teacher preparation had never covered this disability in any of her coursework.

Ishmael is a 10-year-old child included in a second-grade classroom. On the surface, he exhibits several characteristics similar to Sam's (e.g., poor eye contact and fascination with objects), yet he has been diagnosed with autism. Ishmael never makes eye contact with peers or adults, and when he does interact, which is rarely, his voice is robotic and he often repeats exactly what he hears. Like Sam, Ishmael becomes very agitated when he does not get his way, but his tantrums are much more frequent and severe. He bites his hands and hits his head when his schedule changes without warning. Ishmael can identify all the letters of the alphabet and is beginning to recognize basic words such as *go, stop, run,* and *cat.* He can count and do simple math, but when asked what his name is, he cannot respond appropriately.

Jayshonne is an eighth-grader who is included in lunch, physical education, art, music, and math. On the surface, she exhibits many behaviors similar to those of Sam and Ishmael. She wrings her hands frequently and has very poor communication skills. Like them, she does not show interest in her peers or the environment. She is able to participate in an inclusive environment even though she has severe mental retardation, but her educational plan focuses on developing social, language, and life skills rather than traditional academics such as reading and writing. Jayshonne's parents report that she was developing typically until she was 24 months old, at which time her hand skills and language skills began to deteriorate. They also report that she has been diagnosed with Rett's syndrome, a condition found only in females.

Sam, Ishmael, and Jayshonne have disabilities that fall into a category that has become known as **pervasive developmental disorders (PDD).** Included in this category are autistic disorder, Rett's syndrome, childhood disintegrative disorder, and Asperger's syndrome. There is an additional category known as **pervasive developmental disorder–not otherwise specified (PDD-NOS).** In general, students who are diagnosed with PDD or PDD-NOS have several similar learning and behavioral characteristics. First, there are marked delays in multiple areas of development: social interaction skills, communication skills, and stereotypical behavior, interests, and activities (American Psychiatric Association, 2000). There are quantitative and qualitative differences in the learning and behavioral characteristics exhibited by individuals who have each disability. For example, all may have deficits in communication, but students with autism often lack typical language, whereas students with Asperger's syndrome have accelerated vocabularies yet are unable to use their language appropriately in conversations. Table 3.8 displays each disorder as

well as the characteristics that set the disorders apart. Delays are usually noted in early childhood and may co-occur with mental retardation. At this time, there is no identified cause for these disabilities, although some research suggests that there may be a genetic component. Given that the cause for these disabilities is currently unknown, there are no strategies for prevention at this time.

## Autism

To be diagnosed with **autism,** a child must have documented features in three areas:

1. Six or more of any combination of the following:
   a. Impairments in social interactions (e.g., poor eye contact, lack of responsiveness, inability to establish relationships)
   b. Impairments in communication (e.g., no formal language system, echolalia (repeating exactly what has been heard), robotic speech, and use of gibberish or neologisms (making up words)
2. Stereotypical behavior (e.g., body rocking, hand flapping, finger movements, or fascination with objects or object parts)
3. Delayed onset before age 3 (i.e., not as loss of skills but rather as an emergence of delay in skill development). The child must not meet criteria for Rett's syndrome or childhood disintegrative disorder, in which loss of skills is reported before age 5.

## Rett's Syndrome

To be diagnosed with **Rett's syndrome,** a child must have normal prenatal and perinatal development, normal psychomotor development for the first 5 months, and normal head circumference at birth. The child must also exhibit normal development in the following areas, in which a loss of skills occurs between 5 and 48 months: deceleration of head growth, loss of hand skills with subsequent development of stereotyped hand movements (e.g., hand washing or hand wringing), loss of social engagement, poor gait or trunk movements, and severely impaired receptive and expressive communication (APA, 2000).

## Childhood Disintegrative Disorder

To be diagnosed with **childhood disintegrative disorder,** the child must have a normal pattern of development through age 2. Between the ages of 2 and 10, the child must demonstrate a regression of

TABLE 3.8

**Comparison of Disabilities across Developmental Areas**

| | Social Interaction | Communication | Stereotypies | Cognition |
|---|---|---|---|---|
| **Autism** | Little or no eye contact<br>Autistic leading<br>Unawareness of social situations | Little to no verbal communication<br>Repetitive, echolalic, or robotic speech | Inflexible routines<br>Motor repetitions (finger flapping, body rocking) | May have mental retardation<br>May have savant characteristics |
| **Rett's Syndrome** | Loss of social skills within the first few years<br>Loss of interest in social environment | Severely impaired expressive and receptive language | Develops hand movements such as hand wringing or hand washing between 5 and 30 months | Often associated with severe or profound mental retardation |
| **Childhood Disintegrative Disorder** | Loss of interest in environment but not until 3–4 years of age<br>Lack of social or emotional reciprocity | Loss of language skills around 3–4 years of age<br>Repetitive use of language<br>Lack of make-believe play | Develops repetitive motor movements such as hand flapping and finger waving<br>Restricted interests and activities | Usually associated with mental retardation as the loss of skills in all areas is progressive |
| **Asperger's Syndrome** | Lack of ability to read social cues<br>Awkward eye contact<br>Interest in social environment | No clinically significant delay in language<br>Use of language (pragmatics) may be delayed (e.g., loudness or socially appropriate use) | Restricted areas of interest (e.g., preoccupation with a topic)<br>Inflexible adherence to certain routines<br>Repetitive motor movements | No clinically significant delay in cognition |

skills in two of the following: language, social skills, adaptive skills, bowel or bladder control, play skills, and motor skills. The child must also exhibit delays in social interaction, communication, and stereotypical behaviors. Last, the child must not meet the criteria for any other PDD or schizophrenia.

## Asperger's Syndrome

Hans Asperger is credited with first describing this population because he reported data on a group of children with different social skills (Asperger, 1944). **Asperger's syndrome** is now included as a PDD that is diagnosed by documenting behaviors in six different areas:

1. Qualitative impairment in social interaction documented by at least two of the following: impaired use of nonverbal behaviors (e.g., eye contact, body posture), failure to develop peer relationships, lack of spontaneous seeking to share (e.g., showing objects to others, saying, "Look what I did!"), and lack of social or emotional reciprocity

2. Stereotypical behavior demonstrated by at least one of the following: abnormal preoccupation with one or more areas of interest in either intensity or focus (e.g., perseverates on trucks), inflexible adherence to routines or rituals, stereotyped motor mannerisms (e.g., finger flapping), preoccupation with parts of objects

3. Presence of a clinically significant impairment in a social, occupational, or vocational area

4. No clinically significant delay in language

5. No clinically significant delays in cognition, self-help, adaptive skills, or curiosity about the environment

6. Must not meet the criteria for schizophrenia

## Pervasive Developmental Disorder–Not Otherwise Specified

A child is diagnosed with PDD-NOS when delays are exhibited in social interaction or communication or if stereotypical behaviors develop and the child does not meet the criteria for another PDD. Essentially, the diagnosis is used when no other diagnosis seems appropriate but there are obvious delays for no apparent reason such as traumatic birth or neurological development.

## Prevalence of Pervasive Developmental Disorders

Recently, these pervasive developmental disorders have received national attention as the numbers of children with disorders in this spectrum is rising. For example, between 1993 and 1998, there was an increase of 244 percent in identified cases of autism. Unfortunately, there is no clear explanation for this drastic increase. The numbers of children with autism are growing faster than the rate of population growth. Clearly, the increase should be attributed to some other reason. Fombonne (1999) hypothesized that clinicians are becoming better at recognizing early behavioral patterns or that assessment measures are improved. Others hypothesize that environmental conditions are attributing to this phenomenon, as rates of PDD are higher in some geographical locations than would be expected when compared to national averages. In general, autism is now occurring at a rate of about 1 in 1,000, and rates within the PDD spectrum are estimated to be about 1 in 200. Although Rett's syndrome is found only in females, autism, Asperger's syndrome, and childhood disintegrative disorder have higher incidences reported in males.

## Identification and Assessment of Students with Pervasive Developmental Disorders

Children in your classroom who have been diagnosed with PDD or PDD-NOS will most likely have been diagnosed in early childhood, particularly as characteristics of these disorders present before age 5. Therefore, initial identification and assessment should have already occurred. If you are involved in an initial evaluation, you may be asked to document

student performance in the areas of language, social, academic, or adaptive behaviors. You may even be asked to complete rating scales describing student behavior in your class.

If you are not involved in the identification evaluation, you will certainly be involved in ongoing assessment and reevaluation. As a classroom teacher, you may be expected to monitor progress in areas where delays are commonly reported. For example, you might have to monitor how a child with Asperger's syndrome uses language within conversations and interactions with his or her peers. You might have to document the social skills progress of a student with autism. You might have to collect data on the use of adaptive skills for a female student with Rett's syndrome.

The assessment of contextual variables is also important for this population of students. Because these students often adhere to routines, they may demonstrate skills under certain conditions in your classroom but not in others. For example, during lunch, your student with autism may be able to demonstrate appropriate use of a napkin, but he may not be able to demonstrate this in Home Economics when his class is working on table manners. You might be asked to keep a log documenting where your student performs certain skills as well as under what variables the skills are missing.

Another assessment in which you may have to participate is the ongoing data associated with functional behavioral assessment (FBA) and positive behavioral supports necessary to address challenging behaviors. For example, behavior specialists may have you complete a sequence analysis to record the events that surround challenging behavior. Figure 3.2 displays some data that Susie's teacher collected as part of an FBA. Assessment and intervention for challenging behavior are described in more detail later in this chapter.

## Instructional Guidelines and Accommodations for Students with Pervasive Developmental Disorders

Although there are no cures for these disorders, a number of educational interventions have been demonstrated to improve behaviors, allowing individuals to lead more normal lives. Generally, intervention should focus on areas of need: social interaction, language development, adaptive behavior,

— FIGURE 3.2 —

**Sequence Analysis Chart**

| Date and Time | Antecedents | Behaviors | Consequences | Comments/Notes |
|---|---|---|---|---|
| Monday, math | Students sitting in desks. Asked students to get out math workbooks. | Susie began screaming and hitting her head. | I asked her to stop and had the para-educator take her out in the hall until she calmed down. | Maybe she doesn't like Mondays. |
| Monday, reading | Students in small groups at tables for reading. | Susie began screaming and started scratching the child next to her. | I quickly ran to her group and told her that scratching was not okay. I took her to the office and called her mom. | Why are Mondays so difficult? Maybe she didn't get enough sleep over the weekend. |
| Wednesday, math | Students sitting in desks. Asked students to get out their math workbooks. | Susie started rocking back and forth and making loud noises. | I walked over and asked her to be quiet. I showed her the class picture schedule. She asked to do math with the para-educator in the hall. | She seems to respond well to her schedule. |
| Thursday, reading | Students in small groups at reading tables. | Susie began rocking again. She reached to scratch the student next to her, and the student moved her chair farther away. | I came over and reminded Susie to keep her hands to herself. I showed her the class schedule and had her sit at her own desk and read independently. | |

# Tips for Teachers

## 3.6   Working with Students with PDD

- *Use picture and word schedules for daily activities.* Use your picture schedule to help prepare students for transitions. Review your schedule several times throughout the day to prevent confusion.
- *Establish routines early in the school year.* Students with PDD rely heavily on routines. Communicate clearly about any changes in the routine, and post them in your picture schedule.
- *Learn about augmentative and alternative communication.* Students with delays in social communication often use a different mode of communication. You may have students who use picture wallets, communication boards, or even voice output communication aids to communicate. Learn to feel comfortable using these devices.

- *Establish collaborative relationships with families.* Parents know their child best, and they can assist you when you have questions or concerns. Communicate regularly with parents so that they are aware of any changes in your class. Ask them to communicate to you about changes at home.
- *Be aware of your classroom environment.* Students with PDD may be hypersensitive to environmental conditions such as noise, lighting, and temperature. Become familiar with your individual students' needs and make adjustments to your classroom environment as needed.

and cognitive development. Even though all instructional strategies and educational accommodations within classrooms should be individualized, there are a few strategies that are effective for this population, given their common learning and behavioral characteristics:

- Use augmentative and alternative communication strategies
- Provide structure and predictable routines
- Be aware of effective strategies to address challenging behaviors

## Augmentative and Alternative Communication

Given that this population of students has delays or inappropriate use of language, intervention should focus on establishing a means of effective communication. As was mentioned previously, students with Asperger's syndrome often have advanced vocabularies and language structures. However, they might not be able to use their language appropriately in social situations. You may include peer modeling or teacher reframing to ensure successful communicative interaction in classrooms. For example, ask a peer to model how to make lunch choices in the cafeteria. If you are interacting with a group of students, you may reframe what the student with Asperger's syndrome is trying to communicate so that all students in the group understand him.

Students with autism might not have any formal communication system. Therefore, they may benefit from augmentative or alternative communication strategies. For example, a communication wallet may be used so that your student can point to pictures to communicate preferences during lunch, free play, or small-group work. A voice output communication aid may be used in your class allowing the student to press a button that reads aloud to the class lunch choices for the day. Classroom intervention may focus on developing functional language skills such as asking for help, requesting preferred items, or rejecting nonpreferred items. You may be asked to prompt your student to use his wallet to communicate. You may also be asked to assist with intervention planning by listing all your classroom activities, noting which ones are conducive to peer interaction. You may also be asked to modify phrases on a switch so the device is functional in multiple activities. You could be trained to program the BIGMack, a large button that when pressed plays a prerecorded message, to say, "I'd like a hamburger, please" during lunch but to say "I need help with math" during math time.

## Structure and Predictable Routines

Another behavioral characteristic of this population of students is that they adhere strictly to routines and schedules. Therefore, addressing this rigidity within the classroom will be important to ensure successful inclusion. You may be asked to create and adhere to a consistent classroom schedule. Any change in that schedule should be communicated clearly to the student. For example, students with autism may use a

# Tips for Teachers

## 3.7    Working with Paraprofessionals

- *Keep your paraprofessional informed.* Students may have quirks such as having tantrums when they are touched. Inform paraprofessionals about these and other unique characteristics of your students.
- *Educate your paraprofessional.* Paraprofessionals may have limited formal education. They may benefit from some tips on working with students with PDD.
- *Create a schedule.* Use a schedule to help your paraprofessional understand your classroom. If you are out of the class, the schedule can still be followed.

- *Clear communication.* Just as it is important to communicate clearly with parents, you should communicate regularly with your paraprofessional so that he or she is aware of minor changes in your classroom or with your students and their families.
- *Vary responsibilities.* Paraprofessionals may become frustrated when they are expected to supervise a student in the restroom day after day. Rotate staff responsibilities so that no person gets stuck with the "dirty work" on a regular basis.

picture schedule, which is a small Velcro™ board that is used to display a picture of each activity next to a clock indicating the time activities should occur. You could communicate changes in the schedule by rearranging the picture schedule and clock along with a transition cue such as "Today we will have a special assembly after reading." Predictable routines and clear communication of schedule changes have been shown as effective for preventing challenging behaviors (Flannery & Horner, 1994; Kern & Vorndran, 2000).

Your student with Asperger's syndrome may have particularly difficult times during unstructured activities such as bus rides, class changes, lunch, physical education (PE), study hall, and before and after school (Adreon & Stella, 2001). Therefore, you may be asked to help with interventions during this time. For example, PE may be difficult because emphasis is placed on following rules within games. The poor social skills of a student with Asperger's syndrome may cause confusion around rules and thus result in disruptive behavior or social isolation. A simple intervention may include assigning the student to a particular role such as scorekeeper or equipment manager (Adreon & Stella, 2001).

## research brief

### Challenging Behaviors

Over the years, Horner and his colleagues have conducted a series of studies on the use of positive behavioral supports with students who engaged in challenging behavior. In all studies, functional behavioral assessments were conducted, a team approach to problem solving and intervention design was utilized, practical and effective interventions were implemented, new skills were taught, and ongoing data collection and monitoring were used. For example, Todd, Horner, and Sugai (2000) examined a fourth-grade student who was taught to self-monitor, self-evaluate, and self-recruit teacher attention. Teaching him these skills resulted in a decrease in frequency of challenging behavior, an increase in on-task behavior, and an increase in task completion. Vaughn and Horner (1997) compared levels of challenging behavior when students received instruction during preferred and nonpreferred tasks and when teachers rather than students selected tasks. They reported that for two students, rates of challenging behavior were lower when students were able to select tasks, regardless of task preference. Last, Day, Horner, and O'Neill (1995) described an intervention in which students were taught alternative communication in place of challenging behavior. In this study, three participants engaged in challenging behavior to escape difficult tasks or to obtain preferred items. Once a communication alternative was trained, challenging behavior decreased and new communication increased.

## Addressing Challenging Behaviors

Many students who are diagnosed with PDD engage in challenging behaviors. Challenging behavior is defined as behavior by a child that results in self-injury or injury to others, causes damage to the physical environment, interferes with the acquisition of new skills, and/or socially isolates the child (Doss & Reichle, 1991). Challenging behavior can include disruption, aggression, and self-injury. Disruptive behaviors that students most often exhibit include noncompliance, throwing materials, talking out of turn, and disturbing other students. Aggression can include any behavior that involves one student striking another (hitting, kicking, and biting). Self-injury includes behaviors in which a student strikes himself or herself (e.g., head banging or eye poking).

Challenging behaviors often serve as a form of communication for students with disabilities (Carr, 1977). Specifically, students with disabilities engage in challenging behavior because it results in desired outcomes for them. Given their delays in language, communicating their wants and needs becomes more difficult, and thus, challenging behavior becomes an effective form of communication. Students use challenging behavior to obtain desired things such as a favorite pencil, computer time, or laughter from a peer. However, students may also use challenging behavior to escape nonpreferred things such as homework, reading in front of class, or interacting with nonpreferred teachers. These consequences or outcomes of challenging behaviors are known as *functions of behavior* (O'Neil et al., 1997; Neilsen et al., 1998).

You can determine the function of a student's challenging behavior by completing a **functional behavioral assessment (FBA)**. There are three steps to an FBA.

1. Indirect assessments
2. Direct assessments
3. Functional analysis

Indirect assessments should be completed before direct assessments. Indirect assessments include interviews

# Tips for Teachers

## 3.8   Managing Challenging Behaviors

- *Understand why behaviors are occurring.* Students engage in challenging behavior for reasons, usually as a form of communication. A functional behavioral assessment will help you understand why the behaviors are occurring.
- *Be consistent.* All interventions should be implemented consistently so that the student understands what is expected on a daily basis.
- *Everyone should be aware of the student's behavior intervention plan (BIP).* Challenging behaviors usually

occur in all settings. Therefore, everyone, including bus drivers, secretaries, and parents, should implement intervention components.
- *Monitor challenging behavior closely.* It may be difficult to notice when a behavior decreases from 50 times per day to 25 times per day. Use systematic data collection and analysis to monitor your students' progress.

---

with parents and previous teachers, as well as the completion of rating scales. Direct assessments involve observing your student and documenting the sequence of behaviors around challenging behavior. Refer back to Figure 3.2 to see how Susie's teacher completed a sequence analysis in her classroom. If steps 1 and 2 do not clearly identify the function of your student's challenging behavior, you might need to seek the assistance of a behavioral specialist who can help you design and implement a functional analysis, step 3 of the FBA. A functional analysis consists of an experiment in which you manipulate one variable in your classroom to determine its effects on challenging behavior. All possible variables must be manipulated, and rates of challenging behavior must be compared across each condition. For example, if you think your student is trying to escape independent math or is trying to obtain peer attention, then you have four manipulations to implement: getting out of math, not getting out of math, getting peer attention, and not getting peer attention. Because this third step of the FBA is time consuming and often provokes more challenging behavior, it is often reserved for research purposes or for times when the function of behavior is not clear after steps 1 and 2 have been completed.

In the past, teachers and parents addressed challenging behavior by attending to the form of the behavior (e.g., hitting) rather than the function (e.g., obtaining teacher attention). The intervention was implemented after challenging behavior occurred. For example, when a student hit a peer, the teacher told the child to stop hitting. Hypothetically, this

reprimand was intended to teach the student that hitting was not tolerable and thus help the student learn not to hit anymore. Research has shown that these reactive procedures are not as effective at addressing challenging behaviors as another strategy known as positive behavioral supports (U.S. Department of Education, 2000). **Positive behavioral supports** comprise several key features. First, the approach is based on the sound behavioral science of human behavior. Second, interventions must be practical and based on FBA results. Interventions are implemented in a proactive manner rather than a traditional reactive manner. Interventions focus on teaching new skills that foster independence, improve adaptive skills, or increase effective communication. These interventions also allow individuals with disabilities to access natural communities of reinforcement. Candy and other treats are not provided following a new skill such as talking. Rather, an individual is taught to request pizza in the lunchroom where pizza occurs naturally. Additionally, these interventions are monitored with systematic data collection and analysis to determine intervention effectiveness. Another feature of positive behavioral supports is the consideration of social values during the assessment and intervention processes. Behavior change should be observed across all environments of the child's day. Behavior change should be durable, lasting through the school and postschool years. Behavior change should be relevant and result in concomitant improvements in social behavior.

## summary

- Communication is a powerful tool in school and society. For example, we communicate to develop and maintain relationships, to gain and give information, to express feelings, and to control others and the environment.
- Communication disorders include speech, language, and hearing disorders. Speech disorders involve difficulties with articulation, fluency, and voice. Language disorders involve difficulties with content (semantics), form (phonology, morphology, and syntax), and use (pragmatics). Hearing disorders are discussed in Chapter 6.
- Language can be divided into comprehension (receptive language) and production (expressive language).
- Although most basic language skills develop before children enter school, language continues to evolve through the school-age years, a process that includes a large growth in vocabulary, more complex sentence structures, use of prefixes and suffixes, multiple meanings, figurative language, complex semantic relationships (e.g., causal, conditions, enabling), and more sophisticated uses of language (e.g., adjustments to the register of communication, the use of sarcasm and humor).
- Approximately 10 percent of children in elementary school are identified as having communication disorders. Approximately 20 percent of children with disabilities receive services for speech or language disorders. Over 85 percent of these students are mainstreamed into regular classrooms.
- An important role classroom teachers play is to identify students who might have speech and language impairments.
- For students with speech disorders, the classroom teacher's role is to create a nonthreatening environment in which the students can communicate.
- Classroom teachers play an important role in facilitating the development of language. The classroom is an ideal setting to use such language techniques as self-talk and parallel talk, expansion and elaboration, modeling, and conversations. It is also important to adjust the pace and wait time.
- Including children with PDD and PDD-NOS within general education classrooms can be achieved only when there is collaboration between parents, general education teachers, and special education teachers.
- All team members have the same goal in mind: educational success of the student with PDD.
- By addressing challenging behaviors using positive behavioral supports, providing students with alternatives for communication, and structuring the environment for success by using predictable routines, students with PDD should be successful in your general education classroom.

## key terms and concepts

African American Vernacular
   English (AAVE)
articulation disorders
Asperger's syndrome
augmentative and alternative
   communication (AAC) systems
autism
childhood disintegrative disorder
communication disorders
comprehension
content
elaboration
expansion
expressive language
figurative language
fluency disorders
form

functional behavioral
   assessment (FBA)
language disorders
metalinguistics
modeling
morphemes
morphology
multiple meanings
parallel talk
pervasive developmental
   disorder–not otherwise
   specified (PDD-NOS)
pervasive developmental
   disorders (PDD)
phonemes
phonological awareness
phonology

positive behavioral supports
pragmatics
production
receptive language
register
Rett's syndrome
self-talk
semantic feature analysis
semantics
speech disorders
stuttering
syntax
vocabulary
voice disorders
wait time
word retrieval

# think and apply

1. Now that you have read Chapter 3, review Lorri's experiences in working with Samatha. If you could talk to Lorri, what other questions would you ask her? List any questions or concerns you have now about teaching students with communication disorders. Discuss your questions with your fellow students, your instructor, and a speech and language pathologist. Also, check the list of questions or concerns you developed from reading Chapter 1 to see whether you can check any of them off your list. Record your answers, and file your personal inquiry in your teaching portfolio.

2. What are the major components of oral language? Listen to a conversation between two students, and think about how the components function and interact.

3. Listen to students as they move from one school setting to another (e.g., classroom, playground, lunchroom). Determine how their use of language and its formality varies.

4. Interview a speech and language pathologist. Get information about the number and type of students served, typical ages, type of speech or language problems, and ideas for classroom teachers.

5. Teach a lesson involving new content or vocabulary. Pay particular attention to wait time, pacing, and opportunities for the students to discuss what they are learning with partners or in small groups. Notice how this affects students who usually don't respond in class.

6. When teaching, consciously use the techniques of parallel talk, expansion, and elaboration. How does this affect the expressive language of the students whose language is typically less elaborated and complex?

# read more about it

## Communication Disorders

1. Berko Gleason, J. (2001). *The development of language* (5th ed.). Boston: Allyn & Bacon.

   *Provides information about normal language development across the areas of phonology, morphology, syntax, semantics, and pragmatics. Also discusses theoretical approaches to language acquisition and atypical language development.*

2. Diamond, S. (1993). *Language lessons in the classroom.* Phoenix, AZ: ECL Publications.

   *Provides activities and lessons for general education classrooms to develop language skills for grades K–5.*

3. Langdon, H., with Cheng, L. L. (1992). *Hispanic children and adults with communication disorders: Assessment and intervention.* Gaithersburg, MD: Aspen.

   *Provides important information about speech and language assessment and intervention with Hispanic children whose first language is Spanish. Also provides information about the acquisition and development of English as a second language in Spanish speakers.*

4. Lue, M. S. (2001). *A survey of communication disorders for the classroom teacher.* Boston: Allyn & Bacon.

   *Provides information to assist the classroom teacher, direct service provider, or other professional in the understanding, identification, and remediation of communication disorders.*

5. Nippold, M. A. (1998). *Later language development: The school-age and adolescent years* (2nd ed.). Austin, TX: PRO-ED.

   *Reviews language development during the school-age years including the development of figurative language, conversation, vocabulary, and word finding.*

6. Owens, R. E., Jr. (2001). *Language development: An introduction* (5th ed.). Boston: Allyn & Bacon.

   *Summarizes child development and language development in young children, school-aged children, and adults.*

7. Owens, R. E., Jr. (1995). *Language disorders: A functional approach to assessment and intervention* (2nd ed.). Boston: Allyn & Bacon.

   *Provides a comprehensive look at language disorders and presents a model for assessment and teaching that stresses the use of functional environments, conversations as the instructional milieu, and meaningful contexts. Also provides information about second-language and second-dialect learners.*

8.  Reed, V. A. (1994). *An introduction to children with language disorders* (2nd ed.). New York: Macmillan.

    *Reviews normal language development and includes a chapter about the language of students with different types of disabilities (e.g., mental retardation, autism, learning disabilities, deaf/hard of hearing). Also includes information on language assessment and intervention.*

9.  Shames, G. H., Wiig, E. H., & Secord, W. A. (Eds.) (1998). *Human communication disorders* (5th ed.). New York: Merrill/Macmillan.

    *Provides a comprehensive introduction to the field of communication disorders, discusses language differences and disorders, and the communication disorders of special populations.*

10. Simon, C. S. (1993). *300+ developmental language strategies for clinic and classroom.* Tempe, AZ: Commi-Cog.

    *This sourcebook offers strategies for building general oral language and pragmatic skills and includes ideas for teaching English language learners.*

11. Strong, C. J., & North, K. H. (1995). *The magic of stories: Literature-based language intervention.* Eau Claire, WI: Thinking Publications.

*This program utilizes children's literature and 22 strategies to help students understand and retell stories.*

12. Wiig, E. H., & Semel, E. (1984). *Language assessment and intervention for the learning disabled.* Columbus, OH: Merrill.

    *Provides many ideas for facilitating the development of semantics, morphology, syntax, and pragmatics, as well as an overview of several language curriculums.*

**Pervasive Developmental Disorders**

1.  Mesibov, G., Adams, L., & Klinger, L. (1997). *Autism: Understanding the disorder.* New York: Plenum Press.

    *Provides a comprehensive introduction to autism and discusses various intervention approaches and treatment issues for individuals with autism.*

2.  Cohen, D. J., & Volkmar, F. R. (1998). *Handbook of autism and pervasive developmental disorders.* New York: John Wiley.

    *Provides comprehensive information about autism and other pervasive developmental disorders. Discusses characteristics, biological contributions, intervention techniques, and legal and social issues.*

# suggested  websites

**www.asha.org**
This website is for the American Speech-Language-Hearing Association. It provides membership information, feature articles, and the latest research findings in speech, language, and hearing.

**www.communicationdisorders.com**
This website has been developed and maintained by Judith Kuster, an ASHA-certified SLP and associate professor in the Department of Communication Disorders at Minnesota State University, Mankato. The website contains links and information on a broad range of topics related to communication disorders.

**www.stuttersfa.org**
This website is for the Stuttering Foundation of America. It contains information on brochures, books, videos, and the like related to stuttering and provides links to related sites.

**www.isaac-online.org**
This website is for the International Society for AAC. It provides membership information, the latest research, resources, and discussion groups.

**www.aacproducts.org**
This website is for the Communication Aid Manufacturers Association. It contains information related to work-

shops, catalogs of AAC system manufacturers, and related links.

**www.autism-society.org**
This website is for the Autism Society of America, which serves the needs of individuals with autism and their families through advocacy, education, public awareness, and research. This website also contains a variety of resources on individuals with autism (various state agencies, downloadable information packages covering various topics from diagnosis to transitional services, etc.).

**www.udel.edu/bkirby/asperger**
This website provides information and support for individuals with Asperger's syndrome. It contains a variety of information covering the definition, diagnostic scales, social implications and strategies, legal resources, software programs for this population, and more.

**www.teacch.com**
This website is for the Division TEACCH (Treatment and Education of Autistic and related Communication handicapped CHildren). It provides information on various resources on autism, educational approaches, and communication approaches for individuals with autism (medical aspects of autism, evaluation guidelines, a family's reference guide, structured teaching, inclusion, tips for

teaching high functioning people with autism, building communication around routines, etc.).

### www.autism.org
This website contains a variety of links ranging from issues (e.g., autistic savant, self-injurious behavior, social behavior, and self-stimulatory behavior) to interventions for individuals with autism (e.g., auditory integration training, music therapy, physical exercise and autism, and self-management).

### www.autism-pdd.net
This website provides the key issues associated with autism and pervasive developmental disorders. It contains information regarding diagnosis and testing, treatment, TEACCH, IDEA, computer technology, and so on.

### www.pbis.org/english/index/html
This website is for the Office of Special Education. It contains a variety of resources ranging from the definition and legal issues of positive behavioral interventions and supports (PBIS) to schoolwide PBIS and downloadable resources on PBIS.

### http://cecp.air.org/fba/default.htm
This website provides information regarding functional behavioral assessment, including an introduction to functional behavioral assessment and behavioral intervention plans, conducting a functional behavioral assessment, and creating positive behavioral intervention plans.

### www.autism-resources.com/links-methods.html
This website introduces a variety of treatments for individuals with autism, including TEACCH, the Son-Rise program, facilitated communication, the Lovaas method (applied behavior analysis), and auditory integration training.

# Teaching Students with Emotional and Behavioral Disorders

chapter

4

# chapter | outline

# focus | questions

1. What information can teachers use to decide whether a student has emotional or behavioral problems?

2. Many students may exhibit emotional and behavioral problems occasionally, but what percentage of the students in your class would you expect to have prevailing emotional and behavioral disorders? What types of problems would you expect them to have?

3. Classification of students with emotional and behavioral problems can be viewed from what two broad categories and which subtypes?

4. How should classroom teachers decide whether a student's behavior is problematic enough to warrant referral to special education or other specialized services?

5. What characteristics of the teacher–student relationship enhance positive outcomes for students with emotional and behavioral problems?

6. What types of instructional practices are likely to facilitate the learning and social development of students with emotional and behavioral problems?

# inter view

**Juline Truesdell**

Juline Truesdell has been a primary teacher for five years, during which time she has worked with many students who were identified as emotionally and behaviorally disordered. We interviewed her about one of her students who was identified as "seriously emotionally disturbed" as a preschooler.

My greatest challenge as a teacher was a student named Lenox, who was identified as seriously emotionally disturbed and placed in my classroom for part of the school day. Lenox was in my class during his first-grade year. The first day of school he ran into my classroom swinging his lunch box, bumping into other students on his approach to me. When no more than four inches from me, he looked up and shouted, "Are you my teacher?"

*Continued*

The first two months of school were difficult for both of us. Lenox was very rebellious and aggressive, and he had a very hard time controlling himself. He wanted the other children to like him, but he threw tantrums when they did not give him his way, and many of the children were afraid of him. I worked very hard with him so that Lenox could sit with one of the groups of children during the day, but I found I often had to separate him from other students. He often sat at a desk by himself, away from the other children. I always told Lenox why he was separated, but he seemed to forget seconds later. He just didn't seem to be able to control himself, and when he sat with the other students, he would call them bad names and hit them and interfere with their work. The other students would complain and say that they didn't want him to be in their group.

Because they were all so young, it was an ongoing challenge to teach the students to problem-solve and walk away rather than fight or hit when Lenox disturbed them. The special education teacher and I worked with a student team to give points to the entire group when Lenox was able to participate successfully with his group.

When he had a good day, he would get a smiley face on his report to take home, and I could tell that made a difference. But then the next day, he would come in and have a terrible day. It was very difficult to predict his behavior. Then I decided to try something new. Lenox really liked me, and so I set up a program with him where he would get a point for each of the five periods in the day. If he got all five points, I would spend five minutes with him at the end of the day. Sometimes we would talk, color together, play games, or read a book, but it would be time just for the two of us. If he got five points for four days in a row, I would bring lunch for him, and the two of us would eat together alone in the room. The program made a big difference in how Lenox behaved. He started to work better with other students, and he reduced considerably the amount of hitting and fighting. He was able to work with his group most of the day. I can truly say I hated to see him leave at the end of the year. I loved this child. I always have. He gave me so many problems and such a hard time, but there was something about him I'll never forget.

## introduction

The relationships established between classroom teachers and their students with emotional and behavioral disorders, like that of Juline and her student Lenox, are often among the more meaningful relationships experienced by both. Sharon Andreaci, a sixth-grade teacher, describes a student with emotional problems who was included in her classroom part-time and spent the rest of the day in the special education resource room:

Diana was her name, and you could just tell by looking into her eyes that something was wrong. She had been raped by a member of her family, and she never seemed to recover. She would see spirits and think evil things were coming to get her. She would say very strange things to me and to other students in the class. I felt that the support she got that year from me and the [other] students . . . really helped her feel better accepted. I have followed her in school and checked to see how she is doing. Now she is in a regular ninth-grade class and is participating in counseling.

General education teachers indicate that the students they feel are the most difficult to have in their classrooms are students who demonstrate serious emotional and behavioral disorders (Coleman, Webber, & Algozzine, 1999). As Mark Stitz, a sixth-grade teacher, says, "Teaching the content that I am interested in is the fun part. Meeting the needs of students with behavior problems is the work." Even special education teachers find students with serious emotional and behavioral problems to be a challenge. Teaching students with emotional and behavioral disorders is indeed a challenge, but for teachers who understand and implement the types of instructional adaptations necessary to meet these students' educational needs, the results can be very satisfying. And as experienced teachers have reported, the positive impact their efforts have on their students' lives can greatly reward teachers and stay with them forever.

Although some students with emotional or behavioral disorders receive at least part of their educational program in self-contained special education classrooms or in specialized settings (e.g., alternative schools for students with specific problems, hospital settings), approximately 50 percent of students who are identified as having emotional or behavioral disorders spend part or all of their school day in general education classrooms (Knitzer et al., 1990). Therefore, general education teachers must be knowledgeable in the techniques and skills necessary to work with these students.

## Definitions of Emotional and Behavioral Disorders

What does it mean to be emotionally disturbed? What types of behaviors would you expect to see? As with many other disabilities, there is no clear line between those who have disabilities and those who do not. Often the question is decided by how severe the problem is and how persistent. As a teacher, you will come in contact with students who display a range of emotional and behavioral problems.

The National Mental Health Association's National Mental Health and Special Education Coalition Workgroup on Definition (Forness & Knitzer, 1992) uses the descriptor **emotional or behavioral disorders** for students whose behavior falls consider-

ably outside the norm. Though the Council for Children with Behavior Disorders has recommended that the definition of emotional disturbance not eliminate the socially maladjusted, this change has yet to be made (Coleman & Webber, 2002). The federal government uses the term "emotional disturbance" in its criteria for placement of students in special education. The federal definition of emotional disturbance is provided in Figure 4.1.

It is not the responsibility of general education teachers to determine whether a student qualifies as emotionally disturbed, but teachers do have the responsibility of referring students for possible special education placement (by requesting evaluation of students who present significant emotional or behavioral problems in their classrooms). The federal definition of emotional disturbance can help you to determine whether a student's behaviors warrant referral for special education.

> Although the terms "behaviorally disordered" and "emotional disturbance" are often used to mean the same thing, a movement exists to emphasize the term "behaviorally disordered," which professionals believe is the less stigmatizing label. Nevertheless, the Individuals with Disabilities Education Act still uses the term "emotional disturbance."

## Prevalence of Students with Emotional or Behavioral Disorders

Higher prevalence rates are reported for mild emotional or behavioral disorders, and lower prevalence

---

FIGURE 4.1

### The Federal Definition of Emotional Disturbance

The federal government defines "emotionally disturbed" as follows:

**(i)** The term means a condition exhibiting one or more of the following characteristics over a long period of time and to a marked degree, which adversely affects educational performance including:

  **(A)** An inability to learn that cannot be explained by intellectual, sensory, or health factors;

  **(B)** An inability to build or maintain satisfactory interpersonal relationships with peers and teachers;

  **(C)** Inappropriate types of behavior or feelings under normal circumstances;

  **(D)** A general pervasive mood of unhappiness or depression; or

  **(E)** A tendency to develop physical symptoms or fears associated with personal or school problems.

**(ii)** The term includes children who are schizophrenic. The term does not include children who are socially maladjusted, unless it is determined that they are emotionally disturbed.

*Source:* Recent amendments (1997) of the Individuals with Disabilities Education Act.

In the first few years after the implementation of IDEA, McLaughlin and Owings (1992) found that rural school districts identified fewer students with learning disabilities and emotional disturbance than did more populated areas. The authors suggest that this lower identification rate is the result of social, cultural, and economic factors.

rates for more severe disorders. Prevalence varies, depending on the criteria used. Estimates for emotional and behavioral disorders range from 3 percent to 22 percent or more of the school-age population (Kauffman, 1993). Reports indicate a general prevalence rate of 3–6 percent of the student population (Achenbach & Edelbrock, 1981; Brandenburg et al., 1990). Fewer than 1 percent of students receive special education services of emotional disturbance (U.S. Department of Education, 1995). Thus, students with emotional or behavioral disorders are regarded as underserved.

The National Mental Health Association (1986) summarized the following issues as reasons for the underidentification of students with emotional and behavioral disorders:

- Social stigma is associated with the label "seriously emotionally disturbed."
- Eligibility for categorization as emotionally disordered is not clearly explained.
- There is a lack of uniformity in the identification process.
- A lack of funding may limit school districts' willingness to identify and provide services for these students.
- There is often a lack of appropriate services when students are identified.
- Adequate measures to facilitate identification are few.

Although most professionals agree that students with emotional and behavioral disorders are underidentified, there is less certainty as to why so many of the students who are identified are males. Males consistently outnumber females in all prevalence reports for serious emotional disturbance (Quay & Werry, 1986; Rosenberg et al., 1997). Particularly in specialized programs for students with emotional and behavioral disorders, males outnumber females by a ratio as high as 8 to 1.

## Types and Characteristics of Emotional or Behavioral Disorders

Think about classrooms you have observed or taught in. Which students got your attention first: those who were quiet and withdrawn or those who were acting out and disturbing others? Not surprisingly, students who demonstrate such **externalizing behaviors** as aggression, hitting, lack of attention, and impulsivity are much more likely to come to the teacher's attention and therefore to be identified as behavior-disordered than are students who exhibit more **internalizing behaviors,** such as shyness, withdrawal, depression, fears/phobias, or anxiety.

Emotional and behavioral disorders can be classified broadly as externalizing or internalizing. Students who exhibit externalizing behaviors (e.g., conduct disorders, acting out, aggression, tantrums, and bizarre behaviors) tend to interfere with others. Students who exhibit internalizing behaviors (e.g., fear, immaturity, tenseness, withdrawal, worry) tend to be less disturbing to others but still very distressing to themselves and their families.

Classifying students' behaviors as either externalizing or internalizing can be useful for classroom teachers. First, it helps you become aware that students with internalizing problems also need help, even though they do not call attention to themselves in the same way as those with externalizing problems. It is important for classroom teachers to recognize the special need of these students even though they might not interfere with instruction or the learning of others. Second, being able to identify the type of behavior problem provides a framework to establish a plan to help.

Quay and colleagues (Quay & Peterson, 1987; Quay & Werry, 1986) have identified the major subtypes of externalizing and internalizing emotional and behavioral disorders that teachers are likely to encounter. These subtypes include conduct disorder, hyperactivity and attention problems, socialized aggression, pervasive developmental disorder, immaturity, depression, and anxiety–withdrawal. During your career as a teacher, you will have students who display a range of these behaviors, some mild and some severe. Understanding these categories will help you not only to more accurately describe your students' behavior to professionals, but also to respond appropriately to your students. One classification system frequently used by counselors, psychologists, and physicians is described next.

The *Diagnostic and Statistical Manual of Mental Disorders* classification system is based on the reference book of the same name, published by the American Psychiatric Association. Currently in its fourth edition, the book is commonly referred to as the *DSM-IV.* Its purpose is to provide a uniform nomenclature that clinicians and researchers may use to discuss, research, diagnose, and treat mental disorders. The book describes specific criteria necessary for the diagnosis of each disorder as well as symptoms, indicators of severity, and any variations of the disorder. A copy of the DSM-IV should be available from the school counselor or psychologist or a local library or bookstore.

Symptoms that are affected by culture, age, sex, or other variables are discussed, along with the prevalence and progression of the disorder. Each disorder is given a code (usually four or five numbers).

Counselors, psychologists, psychiatrists, and medical doctors who have had extensive training in diagnostic procedures generally use the DSM-IV. Although teachers need not be fluent in its content, familiarity with its use can facilitate communication with school counselors, psychologists, and doctors who may use DSM-IV disorder classification titles, symptoms, and codes.

It is important to remember that the DSM-IV is an independent classification system. The disorders that are delineated and their characteristics may be different from those in other classification systems, although some overlap can be expected. Also, many students with emotional or behavioral disorders display difficulties in learning and may have learning disabilities (Rock, Fessler, & Church, 1997) and/or attention deficit disorders (Bussing et al., 1998).

What internalizing behaviors might signal the possible presence of emotional or behavioral disorders? How would you identify signals for externalizing problems?

## research brief

### Television and Violence

Violence is part of more than 50 percent of all programs on TV between 6:00 A.M. and 11:00 P.M. Children's programs, particularly cartoons, are among the most violent. Furthermore, in cartoons, the violence is most frequently portrayed in a humorous way. In summary, with respect to children and TV violence:

- Viewing violence hardens children to aggression.
- Violence is perceived as realistic.
- Violence is perceived as an acceptable means for solving problems.
- Extensive viewing of violence teaches children how to be aggressive.

*Source:* Berk, L. E. (2000). *Child development* (5th ed.). Boston: Allyn & Bacon.

## Conduct Disorders and Aggression

Behaviors associated with **conduct disorder** and aggression include hitting, fighting, throwing, temper tantrums, teasing, acting defiant or disobedient, destroying property, bullying, being physically cruel to others or animals, stealing with the victim present, lying, conning, deceiving, and serious rule violations. Some students with conduct disorders provoke peers into hitting them or others. Students with conduct disorders who are defiant often resist direction from adults. When teachers call home to describe a student's lack of compliance, they often find frustrated parents who feel that their child is not as responsive to them as they would like.

Not surprisingly, teachers have no difficulty recognizing students who display conduct disorders. Their aggressive, interfering behaviors are probably the greatest source of frustration for classroom teachers. Identifying students with extreme conduct disorders may be easy, but developing successful strategies for managing them can be difficult.

Students with mild to moderate conduct disorders can be handled through effective behavior-management strategies and cooperation with the school counselor, psychologist, and parents. Students with more extreme conduct disorders are challenging to all adults and may be removed from the classroom for all or part of the school day for special education. More than 50 percent of students with conduct disorders continue to demonstrate difficulties as adults and often have adjustment problems throughout their lifetimes (Kazdin, 1993). Although their intelligence is often well within the normal range (Sattler, 1988), students with conduct disorders often display low academic achievement (Gold & Mann, 1972; Vaughn et al., 1992b). Furthermore, the most common secondary special education service provided to students with behavior disorders is speech and language intervention (Griffith, Rogers-Adkinson, & Cusick, 1997).

**r e s e a r c h b r i e f**

## Developmental Pathways to Conduct Disorders

Loeber and colleagues (1993) conducted a long-term study of the **developmental pathways** associated with conduct disorders. Some students follow one pathway; others follow more than one. Those who follow multiple pathways are most at risk. The pathways (covert, overt, and disobedience) and related behaviors follow:

- *Covert behavior:* stealing, lying, burglary, use of drugs and alcohol
- *Overt behavior:* aggression, coercion, bullying, manipulation of others, escalated interactions with teachers, parents, and peers
- *Disobedience:* noncompliance, oppositional or defiant behavior, resistance to adult influence

## Hyperactivity

Although most parents of 2-year-olds perceive **hyperactivity** as a perfect descriptor of their child, the term refers to the restless, overactive behavior (also referred to as *motor excess*) displayed by some students. These students cannot sit still for long periods of time, even when they are doing something they enjoy. Described as acting as though they were driven by a motor, they tend to be tense, unable to relax, and overly talkative; have difficulty being quiet; and run or climb excessively. Note that hyperactivity does *not* refer to students who have difficulty remaining quiet all day or who seem restless in their seats. As a teacher, you will find that many students dislike sitting still and remaining quiet. Wise teachers build into the day brief, structured transition times during which students can move around and visit with their classmates as well as opportunities for students to work at centers or on projects. Teachers need to be concerned that many students with hyperactivity have other difficulties such as the following:

- Attention problems
- Depression
- Anxiety
- Learning disabilities

## Socialized Aggression

Few people have not engaged in some type of antisocial behavior at some point in their lives (Bullis & Walker, 1994). The term **socialized aggression** is used to refer to students who routinely engage in antisocial behavior. Adults describe them as hanging around with the wrong kinds of kids, displaying behaviors that are not typical of others in their age group, harassing others, and stealing and damaging property. School behaviors that get these students into trouble include truancy and cutting classes. Socialized aggression is also associated with **group behavior;** that is, these behaviors are displayed in the presence of other group members. Parents and teachers often worry that they have little influence over the behavior of students who are loyal to delinquent friends. Students with socialized aggression often belong to gangs. Students' attraction to gang life is apparent in many inner cities as well as in suburban and rural areas (Jankowski, 1991; Morales, 1992). Law enforcement agencies categorize **gangs** into the following four groups:

The categories of emotional and behavioral disorders described in this chapter are cultural constructs and may be regarded differently in different cultural settings. Teachers need to consider the cultural and ethnic background of students and how their behavior would be interpreted in light of that background. Students from diverse cultural backgrounds need to be assessed carefully, with consideration of their community and environment (Rogoff & Morelli, 1989), as well as their knowledge of the English language (August & Hakuta, 1997).

- *Delinquent* youth gangs, which are loosely structured and recognize each other by the way they dress and look
- *Turf-based* gangs, which are also loosely structured but committed to defending a reputation or neighborhood
- *Crime-oriented* gangs or drug gangs, which engage in robbery, burglary, or sale of controlled substances for monetary gain
- *Violent* hate gangs, whose members commit assaults or hate crimes against specific types of people

Students may be attracted to gangs through a desire for companionship, acceptance, and success. Many such students feel that they have not been accepted by traditional society (Goldstein & Huff, 1993).

A high rate of overlap exists among conduct disorders, attention problems, and socialized aggression. For example, many students who have attention problems might also display behaviors associated with conduct disorders, such as aggression and acting out.

r e s e a r c h b r i e f

## Five Types of Aggression

Lancelotta and Vaughn (1989) examined five subtypes of aggression. In *provoked physical aggression,* one student hits or taunts another, who retaliates. In *unprovoked physical aggression,* a student acts aggressively with no apparent prompting. In *verbal aggression,* one student screams, yells, or uses other verbal expression to attack another. In *outburst aggression,* a student "blows up." In *indirect aggression,* a student does something sneaky or tricky to get back at another student. Neither boys nor girls like students who use indirect aggression. Both sexes are the most tolerant about provoked aggression, but girls are less tolerant of all types of aggression than are boys. All subtypes of aggression were related to low social acceptance by classmates except provoked physical aggression. Teachers' ratings were closer to boys' ratings of peer acceptance than to similar ratings by girls.

## Pervasive Developmental Disorder

**Pervasive developmental disorder** can be classified as either externalizing or internalizing, depending on the type(s) of behavior manifested. As previously presented in Chapter 3, students who exhibit behaviors characterized as pervasive developmental disorder express farfetched, unusual, or unbelievable ideas. These students might say strange things to the teacher (e.g., "The blue dog is in the hallway, and it is going to get me when I leave.") and might also exhibit repetitive speech and unusual behaviors such as excessive rocking, nail biting, or head knocking. Students with this disorder may relate to others (including family members) as if they were inanimate objects rather than people. Students might also ignore or resist signs of affection and love and fail to interact with or adapt to others.

## Immaturity

Behaviors associated with **immaturity** include lack of perseverance, failure to finish tasks, a short attention span, poor concentration, and frequent daydreaming or preoccupation. Students might stare into space excessively; appear absentminded, inattentive, or drowsy; and seem clumsy or poorly coordinated.

Immature students often come to the attention of teachers because they show little interest in schoolwork and need prodding to participate. Teachers might feel frustrated at the amount of effort necessary to keep these students interested and involved.

Immature students often seem overly dependent on parents or caretakers and have difficulty being responsible members of a group (whether the classroom or the family). Students with severe immaturity often have difficulty interacting with other people, using social skills, and playing with children their own age. These students may frequently retreat into fantasy and develop fears that are out of proportion to the circumstances.

## Depression

Many students with emotional and behavioral disorders are also prone to **depression** (Klein & Last, 1989; Kovacs et al., 1988). Depression involves prolonged and persistent feelings of dejection that interfere with life functioning (Muse, 1990). Mental health workers and educators have realized only recently that depression is a widespread, serious problem among children and adolescents (Forness, 1988) that is similar to adult depression (American Psychiatric Association, 1994). Whereas depression is more prevalent in adult women than men, young boys are as likely as girls to exhibit depression (e.g., Lefkowitz & Tesiny, 1985; Lobovits & Handal, 1985). However, after the onset of puberty, depression in girls doubles (Rutter, 1991).

Many youngsters who talk about suicide or ending their life are at risk for suicide attempts. Phone numbers for help include:

- National Hopeline Network: (800) SUICIDE
- Survivors of Suicide/ American Foundation of Suicide Prevention: (800) 723-7985

Teachers often have difficulty identifying students who are depressed (Sarcco & Graves, 1985). The following behaviors may indicate depression:

- Acting sad, lonely, and apathetic
- Exhibiting low self-esteem
- Displaying avoidance behaviors (particularly, avoiding social experiences)
- Having chronic complaints about eating, sleeping, and elimination
- Refusing or fearing to go to school or other public places
- Talking of suicide
- Poor school performance
- Loss of interest in previously enjoyable activities

## Anxiety–Withdrawal

The term **anxiety–withdrawal** includes two highly related major behaviors. *Anxiety* refers to extreme worry, fearfulness, and concern (even when little reason for those feelings exists). Simple reassurance is rarely effective. *Withdrawal* describes the typical behavior of students who are anxious or depressed; they frequently withdraw from others and appear seclusive, preferring solitary activities. Withdrawn students are often timid or bashful around others, even people they know, thinking of themselves (and being described by others) as loners with few friends, if any. Often preferring to work alone, in class these students may avoid group work, volunteering, or answering questions. Teachers and parents often attribute such behavior to low self-confidence and poor self-concepts.

As you can see from the preceding descriptions, students with behavior disorders display a wide range of characteristics. Perhaps the most consistent characteristic of these students is their inability to maintain satisfying relationships with others (e.g., Kauffman, 1993; Walker et al., 1995).

## Causes of Emotional and Behavioral Disorders

Although the rate of sexual abuse among individuals with disabilities is unknown, 74 percent of the females and 20 percent of males with emotional disorders in one study had been sexually abused (Miller, 1993). Also, poverty is related to mental health problems in children (Tarnowski & Rohrbeck, 1993).

Despite a general understanding that the emotional and behavioral disorders of students do not reflect directly on parents, dysfunctional parenting contributes to behavior disorders in children (Kaiser & Hester, 1997). On the basis of the research we currently have, our best understanding is that emotional and behavioral disorders result from both environmental and genetic factors and that in some cases, one set of factors plays a greater role than the other. For example, a student who is exposed to family violence may be more likely to display violent behaviors (Jacobs, 1994; Sanson et al., 1993), but some students who are mentally ill may have heritable explanations for their symptoms (e.g., Lombroso et al., 1994; McGuffin et al., 1994). Regardless of the cause, early intervention is needed (Kaiser & Hester, 1997).

Whether emotional or behavioral disorders have social or organic causes, students may be treated with three groups of medications: stimulants, antidepressants, and antipsychotics.

Stimulants target the central nervous system and are believed to help the brain release certain chemicals that make it possible to focus on particular stimuli rather than be overwhelmed by all that are present at a given moment. Thus, stimulants increase attention and reduce impulsive and intrusive behav-

ior. Examples of stimulants include Cylert, Ritalin, Dexedrine, and Benzedrine. Some of the possible side effects caused by stimulants are a loss of appetite, insomnia, growth retardation, muscle tics, depression, and nervousness.

Antidepressants are often used in the treatment of depression, anxiety disorders, bed wetting, compulsive and obsessive behavior, stomachaches, anxiety attacks, and muscle tics. Antidepressants have a sedative effect; they reduce mood swings and levels of stress, making tasks seem less overwhelming. Examples of antidepressants include Elavil, Tofranil, and Prozac. Some of the possible side effects of antidepressants include nausea, dry mouth, loss of appetite, insomnia, and seizures.

Antipsychotics are tranquilizers used in the treatment of severe cases of behavioral disorders. These drugs reduce delusions and hallucinations, severe anxiety, depression, and hyperactivity. Examples of antipsychotics include Haldol, Thorazine, Mellaril, Navane, and Stelazine. Possible side effects of antipsychotics include listlessness, passiveness, impaired cognitive performance, dry mouth, increase in appetite, weight gain, enuresis, and motor difficulties.

Although not included in the preceding classifications, lithium is another medication that is commonly used in the treatment of emotional and behavioral disorders. Lithium is used in the treatment of severe mood disorders, such as bipolar disorder. Some of the possible side effects are nausea, excessive need to urinate, thirst, tremors, dizziness, diarrhea, vomiting, abdominal pain, shaking, exhaustion, and distorted or slurred speech.

## Identification and Assessment of Students with Emotional and Behavioral Disorders

How are students with emotional and behavioral disorders identified? Some students with severe disorders are recognized by parents and other adults before they start attending school. These students may receive early treatment through a combination of educational interventions, medications, play therapy, and family counseling. Other students have emotional and behavioral disorders that remain latent until students are older or that become apparent in structured settings such as the school. Older students may not have received specialized services outside the school setting.

How should classroom teachers decide whether a student's behavior is problematic enough to war-

What criteria would you use to determine whether this student's behavior warrants referral for evaluation for the presence of an emotional or behavioral disorder?

rant referral to special education or other specialized services? The following criteria provide indications of disturbance and the likelihood for referral (e.g., Clarizio & McCoy, 1983; Morgan & Reinhart, 1991):

- *Behavior–age discrepancy:* The social and behavioral problems exhibited must be unusual or deviant for the student's age. For example, clinging to adults is common in very young children but is deemed inappropriate for school-age children.
- *Frequency of occurrence of the behavior:* Under stress, all people exhibit characteristics of emotional or behavioral disorders, such as whining, withdrawal, mood swings, or depression. These behaviors and feeling states are not considered problems if they occur only occasionally.
- *Number of symptoms:* Display of one or more behavior problems at some time does not indicate that a person has an emotional or behavioral disorder, but students who frequently display several related symptoms should be considered for referral. The greater the number of

symptoms, the greater the likelihood of a serious emotional disturbance.

- *Inner suffering:* Signs of inner suffering include low self-esteem, less interaction with others, appearance of sadness or loneliness, and general malaise. Inner suffering interferes with learning, social relationships, and achievement.
- *Harm to others:* The student consistently harms others or animals intentionally and shows little remorse for hurting others.
- *Persistence of the behavior:* Persistence refers to the continuation of the emotional or behavioral problems over time, despite substantive efforts on the part of adults and the student to change the behaviors. A behavior problem is persistent when several types of interventions have not resulted in long-term change.
- *Self-satisfaction:* Students who appear to be generally happy with themselves reflect a measure of self-satisfaction. They show positive affect and the willingness to give and receive affection and pleasure. A lack of self-satisfaction contributes to problems that interfere with personal growth and development as well as academic and social success but that might not signal the presence of an emotional or behavioral disorder.
- *Severity and duration of the behavior:* All dimensions of a student's behavior can be classified in terms of two important criteria: severity and duration. *Severity* refers to how extreme the problem is and the extent to which it varies from expected behavior. *Duration* (or persistence) refers to the length of time the problem has existed. A problem that persists over a long period of time is said to be *chronic.* Most students who are identified as having emotional or behavioral disorders must deal with their problems throughout their lifetimes.

When identifying a student with possible emotional or behavioral disorders, ask the following questions:

- How often does the behavior occur? How long has the problem persisted?
- Under what conditions does the behavior occur? To what extent does this behavior occur in different settings, such as the classroom, playground, or home?
- What are the *antecedents* of the behavior; that is, what events occur before the behavior is exhibited, triggering the behavior? What are the *consequences,* that is, what occurs as an outcome

Self-stimulation—repetitive sensory stimulation, such as twirling, patting, flapping, staring at lights, and swishing saliva—is common behavior in students with severe emotional disturbance.

# Tips for Teachers

## 4.1 Making Referrals for Students with Emotional or Behavioral Disorders

- Keep a journal that includes the dates, times, and contexts of student behaviors that you regard as deviant or bizarre.
- Be specific, using behavioral terms to describe what occurs. As much as possible, avoid including value judgments. For example, a journal entry might read, "Mark got up from his seat, pushed John out of his chair, and then ran out of the room."
- Record any relevant information from parents, such as their descriptions of the student's behav-

ior at home or telephone calls concerning the student. Keep parents informed of the problem, both in writing and by telephone.
- Also record relevant information from other teachers or school personnel who know the student.
- Keep samples of the student's work in different subjects, and a record of skills the student can and cannot perform. If the student's academic performance is inconsistent, note this as well.

---

of the behavior after the student exhibits the behavior?

- Does the problem not arise in certain situations?
- To what extent does the student develop and maintain positive relationships with other people? Does the student seem happy or display satisfaction at any time?
- How severe is the problem? To what extent is the behavior deviant from that of other students of the same age?
- To what extent is this a problem in the relationship between you and the student or a problem in the student?
- What have you and/or the family done to reduce or eliminate the problem?

Tips for Teachers 4.1 offers suggestions for gathering information before referring a student with possible emotional or behavioral disorders.

## Teaching Guidelines and Accommodations for Students with Emotional or Behavioral Disorders

Many teachers realize that understanding and recognizing the behaviors of students with emotional and behavioral disorders is the first step in providing appropriate interventions. The teacher's most important role is to establish an academic community and climate that promote the learning and accep-

tance of all students, including students with emotional and behavioral problems (Walker, Colvin, & Ramsey, 1995). How can you do this? This section provides an overview of teaching accommodations to facilitate the academic and social growth of students with emotional and behavioral disorders.

Teachers usually realize that providing appropriate intervention is not sufficient but that the student's day-to-day environment must be structured to promote mental health. Students who return to abusive families or inappropriate environments that maintain or worsen their emotional or behavioral problems are unlikely to achieve much success without changes in these environments. In working with students with serious emotional or behavioral problems, some teachers feel hopeless and give up. Remember, however, that the small things you do often make a big difference in the life of a student, even if the student does not say so or demonstrate significant changes.

No single approach to intervention works for all students with severe emotional and behavioral problems. However, a systematic, well-organized plan and documentation of changes in behavior will help you determine whether an intervention is working.

### Maintaining an Organized Physical Environment

Look around your classroom or that of another teacher, and evaluate whether the physical environment supports or detracts from the student's ability to behave appropriately (Fimian et al., 1983). The physical arrangement may have a significant effect on the classroom climate as well as on student be-

What physical characteristics of the classroom environment support the learning of students with emotional or behavioral disorders? What characteristics of the classroom climate contribute to a positive emotional environment in which academic and social learning can take place?

## Establishing Positive Relationships

Think about the teachers that you remember most from your elementary and secondary school days. What made these teachers special to you? Chances are that you felt they really cared about you, what you learned, and how well you liked school, your teacher, and your classmates. The importance of your establishing good relationships with all students is important, but especially so for students with emotional and behavioral disorders. These students probably have had few positive relationships with adults and may act as if they dare you to care about them.

Trust is the foundation for success with students with emotional and behavioral disorders (Henley et al., 1993). Students learn to trust you when you act in predictable ways and do what you say you are going to do. They also learn to trust you when they believe you will do what is best for them rather than what is best for you.

Remember that disliking the student's behavior is not the same as disliking the student, who needs your respect and caring. "Respect the student, dislike the behavior" is an important motto when you work with students with emotional and behavioral disorders. Think about the language you use when you reprimand students or enforce consequences for inappropriate behavior. Be sure you convince students that it is their behavior that is unacceptable, not they. Jason Landis, a high-school English teacher, says it this way:

> When I correct students, I always talk about the behavior, and I always let the student know that anyone who behaves like this will be treated the same way. For example, the other day in class, I needed to remind a student that no one swears in the class and those who swear will get a detention and therefore, here is your detention. Later on in the period, I encouraged the same student to respond to a question and provided positive feedback for the part of the answer he got correct.

Caring for students with emotional and behavioral disorders should not come with strings attached or expectations that students will reciprocate (Webber et al., 1991). Many of these students have little experience with giving or receiving kindness and warmth. Some are hurting and cannot cope with giving to others. All children need our concern, and students who do not reciprocate need it the most.

havior, particularly that of students with emotional and behavioral problems. Consider the following:

- Is the classroom uncluttered, clean, attractive, and uncrowded?
- Are necessary materials accessible, organized, and stored appropriately?
- Is the classroom well ventilated with appropriate lighting?
- Is the noise level appropriate? What objects might be removed or changed to make the room less noisy?
- Is there evidence that housekeeping chores have been taken care of? Is the room clean and orderly?
- Does each student have his or her own physical space, desk, and materials?
- Is there a schedule posted that provides a predictable routine?
- Are classroom rules and consequences written so that students can see them?

Students with emotional and behavioral disorders work best in organized, structured environments in which materials, equipment, and personal items are well maintained, neatly arranged, and presented in a predictable way. You can establish a classroom committee composed of elected students or students you appoint on a rotating basis that allows all students to participate over the school year. This committee might meet weekly to assess the classroom environment and address issues raised by students (perhaps in a student suggestion box).

# Tips for Teachers

## 4.2    Creating an Appropriate Emotional Environment

- *Respond to students' feelings and intentions* rather than to overt behavior. When students with emotional and behavioral disorders act out or become aggressive, the teacher's first reaction might be to respond with anger or hostility, but the student is really saying, "I'm hurting. Pay attention to me."
- *Listen.* Before responding, no matter how certain you are that the student is in the wrong, give the student an opportunity to explain and give his or her version of what occurred. You may not always agree with the interpretation, but by taking the time to listen you demonstrate caring and concern to the student. Listening is a sign of acceptance, an important first step in helping students.
- *Develop a positive relationship* with the student about one topic. All students are interested in and can succeed at something that you can recognize. Discover what this area is and what the student knows about it, then make him or her the class expert.

- *Establish rules and consequences* to help provide the structure that students with emotional and behavioral disorders need.
- *Consider changes you can make.* Evaluate the classroom routines, instructional procedures, and discipline practices you use that may be contributing to the student's behavioral problems.
- *Catch the student being good.* You have many opportunities to recognize the student's inappropriate behavior. A greater challenge is to catch the student being good and recognize that appropriate behavior several times a day.
- *Use humor* to build relationships and to decrease tension. Look for the fun in the way students relate to each other and to you.
- *Create an emotionally safe classroom* environment in which students accept each other's strengths and weaknesses and treat each other with respect and consideration.

Be empathic. Empathy requires genuine concern and interest in understanding the student, no matter how deviant or difficult his or her behavior. Students know when teachers are empathic and concerned about them.

Tips for Teachers 4.2 offers further suggestions for creating an appropriate emotional environment.

## Changing Behavior

The student behaviors that teachers most want to change are those they regard as undesirable, such as those that interfere with instruction, other students, or the student's learning. Desirable behaviors—those that enhance instruction, relations with others, and the student's success—are the behaviors teachers most want to see increased. In addition to the procedures for behavior-management and behavioral supports discussed in detail in Chapter 8, the following guiding principles will help you use consequences for desirable and undesirable behaviors (Morgan & Reinhart, 1991):

- Carefully select the rules you apply, and then follow through consistently. If you try to enforce every rule strictly, you may find yourself continually at war with the student.
- Consider consequences carefully, because you must follow through on stated consequences.

Do not use threats. When you make remarks such as "You're going to do this math paper if you have to sit here all day," students soon learn that consequences are not real and that your words cannot be trusted.

- Establish consequences that are not punishing to you. If you are stressed or inconvenienced by the consequence, you might resent the student (a circumstance that would surely interfere with the quality of the relationship you need to establish). For example, staying in at lunch, giving up your planning period, or driving the student home can punish you as much as the student.
- Listen and talk to the student but avoid the trap of arguing. Listen to what the student has to say, and say what you have to say. If you are tempted to argue, recognize that you need a break and set another time to finish the discussion.
- Use logic, principles, and effective guidelines to make decisions. Avoid flaunting your authority as a teacher to make students do something without giving them a clear sense that it is the right or best thing to do.
- Focus on the problems that interfere most; that is, ignore minor misbehaviors and focus on the important things.
- Inform students that the work they complete is necessary and meaningful for their education. Avoid asking them to complete work "for you."

- As you know, each student is an individual with his or her own attributes and problems. Avoid comparing a student with emotional or behavioral problems to other students. Comparisons do not help students understand and accept themselves or be understood and accepted by others.
- Students' problems belong to them. They may interfere with your work, but they are not your problems. Resist the temptation to solve students' problems for them. Students need to learn how to resolve conflicts for themselves.
- Recognize your feelings, and do not let them control your behavior. When you are upset by a student's behavior in class, it is important not to respond by further upsetting the student. Never "strike back" by humiliating, embarrassing, or berating a student.
- Let the student know how many chances he or she has before a consequence will be applied (and do not add chances later). When you tell a student, "This is the last chance," and he or she continues to behave inappropriately, you need to follow through on whatever consequence was designated.
- Give yourself positive feedback for what you do to enhance student learning and social functioning. Do not be too hard on yourself, especially when you make mistakes. Although there are limitations to what any effective teacher can do, there are always opportunities to be successful in teaching students with emotional and behavioral disorders.

The following procedures should remind you how to target key behaviors you want students to change:

- Whenever possible, involve students and parents in identifying the target behavior. In this way, you work at changing the behavior both at school and at home.
- As when making referrals, describe the behavior in as much detail as possible, including when and with whom it typically occurs.
- Get the student's input on the behavior, as well as his or her suggestions for what might help to reduce it.
- Describe the target behavior in writing, using the terms expressed by the student, the parent, and yourself so that everyone involved understands the problem.
- Establish a procedure for eliminating the behavior and providing positive consequences when the behavior does not occur. Involve parents in distributing positive consequences as well.

Many techniques exist for helping students change their behavior. Figure 4.2 provides an example of a behavior contract between a student and a teacher. The 60-Second Lesson (page 116) shows how even simple devices can work.

Most special education teachers who instruct youngsters with behavioral and emotional problems implement a level system as a means of controlling behavior (Farrell, Smith, & Brownell, 1998). A **level system** attempts to provide a guide for managing student behavior through an organized framework based on token economies and the application of behavioral principles whereby students are provided with privileges based on their behavior. Expectations for student behavior and associated privileges are increased as the student moves up the level system. Students who reach a high enough level may be placed for part or all of the school day in the regular classroom.

## Resolving Conflicts and Promoting Self-Control

Dealing with conflict between students and between a student and a teacher is an ongoing issue for teachers at all grade levels. Conflicts are inevitable in a classroom community; they occur with students who have emotional and behavioral disorders as well as among other students.

Morgan and Reinhart (1991) suggest the use of conflict reports as a strategy for **conflict resolution.** Conflict reports not only enable students to debrief after a conflict, but also give them an opportunity to practice writing skills. A conflict report might include the following items:

- Describe the conflict you were involved in (fighting, taking an object that belongs to another, pushing).
- Briefly list who was involved in this conflict.
- Briefly list who else witnessed (but was not involved in) the conflict.
- Describe where the conflict took place (e.g., in the back of the classroom, in line going to lunch, at recess).
- Briefly describe how the conflict started. What did you do? What did they do? Describe what you said. Describe what they said.
- What else would you like to say or do to the other people involved in the conflict?
- What did you do to try to stop the conflict?
- What did they do to try to stop the conflict?
- Who do you think might be able to help stop or resolve the conflict?
- Write a brief set of procedures for resolving the conflict. Be specific. Be sure to tell who will do what and when.

FIGURE 4.2

**Sample Student–Teacher Contract**

Date: _____

Ms. Gonzalez will draw a star next to Paul's name on the bulletin board and give Paul one point when he does any of the following in her classroom:

    1) He raises his hand and waits for the teacher to call on him before talking.

    2) He stays seated in his chair while working on class assignments.

    3) When other kids in the class are bothering him, he tells the teacher about their behavior instead of yelling at and/or hitting the other kids.

After Paul has earned 12 points from his teacher, Ms. Gonzalez, he may select one of the following rewards:

    1) He may have extra time to work on the computer.

    2) He may serve as the teacher's helper for a day.

    3) He may be in charge of caring for the class pet for the day.

    4) He may serve as a peer tutor for a day (for a subject decided upon by the teacher).

After Paul has received 12 points, he begins earning the points again. Another reward will be given when 12 points have been earned.

I, Paul B. O'Brien, agree to the conditions stated above, and understand that I will not be allowed any of the rewards until I have earned 12 points by doing the activities stated above.

_____
(student's signature)

I, Ms. Gonzalez, agree to the conditions stated above. I will give Paul one of the aforementioned reinforcers only after he has received 12 points.

_____
(teacher's signature)

## making a Difference

### The 60-second Lesson

behavior in the class. Discuss with students what behaviors will be included (e.g., working, performing an assignment, asking a question, reading a text).

**Using a Timer to Change Behavior**

**Purpose:** To increase appropriate behavior, such as on-task behavior, and to reduce inappropriate behavior, such as being out of seat

**Materials:** Kitchen timer

**Procedure:**

1. Show students the kitchen timer and indicate that you will be using it to cue students to look for on-task

2. Indicate that the timer will ring at different intervals and that all groups or individuals who are on task when the timer rings will be awarded a point.
3. Set the timer initially for a range of times (from 5 to 10 minutes), then for longer periods of time.

*Source:* Adapted from Wolf, M. M., Hanley, E. L., King, L. A., Lachowicz, J., & Giles, D. K. (1970). The timer-game: A variable interval contingency for the management of out-of-seat behavior. *Exceptional Children, 37,* 113–117.

## Helping Students Establish Personal Goals

**Purpose:** To establish personal goals

**Materials:** Index card or small piece of paper, pencil or pen

**Procedure:**

1. Ask students to think about people they most admire. For younger students, discuss the meaning of "admire."

## The 60-second Lesson

2. Ask students to identify the qualities of people they admire and examples of their behavior that demonstrate these qualities.
3. Now ask each student to write on the index card one quality for which they would like to be admired.
4. Ask students to keep the card in a prominent place (taped on their assignment folder or inside their desk, for example).
5. Throughout the year, ask students to look at the card and assess the extent to which they express the quality or trait for which they most want to be admired.

One of the advantages of a conflict report is that all participants have an opportunity to write all they know about it and to give their side of the story. Furthermore, the process of reporting provides time to debrief and let anger or resentment subside. Some teachers train students in conflict resolution as part of the regular curriculum. Students serve on an informal hearing board to resolve conflicts without teacher intervention. This training lets students practice the important skill of conflict negotiation.

By teaching students to set personal goals, you also help them to develop self-control. Setting and monitoring positive personal goals contribute to students' positive self-concept and higher self-esteem. The 60-Second Lesson describes a simple activity for helping students establish personal goals.

### School-Based Wraparound

Students with behavior disorders and emotional disturbances are among the most highly segregated students with disabilities. A recent attempt to provide appropriate services to students with behavior disorders and their families has resulted in wraparound approaches that extend services to families and students (Eber, Nelson, & Miles, 1997). Wraparound planning involves considering the actual needs of the students within their home–school community rather than shopping for the program that will accept the student. Wraparound services can be used to provide supports that are coordinated through school, home, and community settings. To initiate wraparound planning, the following steps should be considered (Eber, Nelson, & Miles, 1997): issue identification, agenda setting, strengths, goal setting and needs, prioritization of needs, strategy development, securing commitments, follow-up communication, and process evaluation.

## Using the Life-Space Intervention

The **Life-Space Intervention** (**LSI**) (Wood & Long, 1994), originally discussed by Redl (1959), can be used to help students with emotional and behavioral

What steps should this teacher take to help the students resolve their conflict? What specific skills can students be taught to use in preventing future interpersonal conflicts?

problems cope with a crisis situation. According to Redl, the LSI has two primary goals:

- To provide emotional "first aid" so that the student can regain composure and return to as normal an activity level as possible
- To take advantage of the conflict situation to assist students in confronting and resolving their own personal conflicts

Although many professionals believe that the LSI is best applied by trained professionals who are familiar with counseling procedures, teachers can apply the key principles of the LSI. When the emotional problem or conflict is serious and warrants the help of a trained counselor, however, the teacher needs the good judgment to make an immediate referral.

Long, Morse, and Newman (1980) provided the following suggestions for the application of the LSI by teachers:

- Shake off or drain off the frustration and upset through the use of humor, physically shaking the problem away, or diffusing tension by allowing the student to talk about the problem. Drain off enough frustration that the student can talk about the issue.
- Be as courteous as you would be if you were dealing with a friend or another adult. Give the student time to explain his or her side of the story adequately, and listen attentively. If you ask questions, be sure to give the student time to think and respond to them.
- Conduct the LSI in as private a place as possible. No one wants to exhibit problems, throw tantrums, or be extremely upset in front of others. Find a private, quiet place to conduct the session.
- Eliminate barriers between you and the student. Position yourself at eye level, for example. With a young child, pull up small chairs and sit down so that you are at the same level.
- Ask the student to provide his or her interpretation of the event. Listen carefully, and be sure that you clarify any misunderstandings, but do not give in to the student's misperceptions of the situation. Confront the student, if necessary, to point out that there is another way to view the situation.
- Discuss what needs to be done to resolve the situation. If an apology is needed, role-play and rehearse how that can be done. If the conflict needs to be further discussed and resolved with another person, plan procedures for doing so.
- Discuss what to do the next time a similar situation develops. How can you prevent a conflict? Discuss procedures for eliminating problems in the future.

- Do not assume that you understand how the student feels. Many times, teachers assume that the student is angry, hurt, or disappointed. Ask how the student is feeling to check whether you are correct.
- Avoid invalidating students' feelings by claiming that they could not possibly feel the way they say they do. Students with emotional and behavioral disorders often say outrageous things that they mean at the time. Listen carefully without judging or denying their feelings. Allow time for students to ask you questions and to prepare a follow-up.
- Teach problem-solving skills (such as those presented in Chapter 9).

## Adapting Instruction

Students with emotional and behavioral problems often have academic difficulties (Vaughn et al., 1992b), may be underachievers in school (Kauffman, 1989), and are often missing basic academic skills (Browder & Shear, 1996). An important factor that positively affects students with emotional and behavioral disorders is the extent to which they are busy in purposeful activities. Activities need to be viewed by students as personally relevant and related to learning skills they need. Effective teachers explain to students *why* they are studying a topic, *why* they do an assignment, and *how* their learning will contribute to their success as students and in the future. Teachers can also adapt instruction in the ways described in the following sections.

**Providing Instruction That Allows All Students to Succeed** Academic failure or frustration can exacerbate a student's emotional or behavioral disorder. Without creating a parallel program or watering down the curriculum, teachers can adapt and modify assignments and expectations so that students can succeed. One simple strategy is to look for opportunities to reinforce and reward students for what they know or have done correctly. Another is to enhance motivation and performance by changing activities when students are failing. Students with emotional and behavioral disorders may have difficulty accomplishing particular types of tasks. In many cases, you can change the task so that students can demonstrate knowledge without performing tasks that upset them. Tips for Teachers 4.3 offers additional suggestions for giving students opportunities for success.

**Providing Opportunities for Students to Learn Academically and Socially** Use different groupings—individual, small groups, pairs, and large groups—to give students opportunities to acquire

# T i p s for Teachers

## 4.3    Providing Opportunities for Student Success

- When you correct papers, point out correct responses rather than mistakes.
- Before students submit papers, ask them to look carefully to see whether they can find an error. Call on students to describe mistakes they find, and praise them for finding and correcting the mistakes. Point out that everyone makes mistakes and that with practice, we can reduce the number and types of mistakes we make.
- When a student with emotional or behavioral disorders asks for help, start by asking the student to find something correct on his or her paper.

- Find opportunities for a student to "shine" in front of classmates. Even small recognitions are valuable.
- Notice improvement. If the student usually gets three right on the weekly spelling test and this week gets five right, let the student know that you notice the change. Recognition of progress toward a goal motivates students more than recognition that comes only after the goal has been attained.

academic and social skills. Students with emotional and behavioral disorders may have difficulty learning in whole-class instruction but do well in small-group or paired learning situations. Also provide opportunities for students to be tutored and to serve as tutors themselves. Learning to work with others is an important skill for students with emotional and behavioral disorders. Chapter 7 provides specific suggestions for grouping practices that enhance learning for all students.

Social learning also contributes to the success of students with emotional and behavioral disorders. **Social learning** involves observing and modeling or imitating the behavior of others (e.g., Bandura, 1971,

1973). To what extent can you expect students to imitate the appropriate behaviors of classmates, and what can you do to accelerate this process? Research suggests that students with emotional and behavioral disorders are unlikely to imitate "better" behaviors in the classroom unless teachers provide directed experiences to promote this behavior (Hallenbeck & Kauffman, 1995). Tips for Teachers 4.4 offers a strategy for guiding students to learn appropriate behaviors from classmates.

**Using a Variety of Commercial and Individually Created Materials**    Assignments designed to maximize success and capture students' interest reduce

# T i p s for Teachers

## 4.4    Guiding Students to Learn Appropriate Behaviors from Classmates

1. Identify student "models" and their behaviors that you want other students to emulate. For example, "Joaquin has his math book open to page 38 and is looking at me to indicate that he is ready. Show me that you are ready by doing the same thing."
2. Monitor whether the student with emotional or behavioral disorders follows the model. Look for approximations and provide positive reinforcement. For example, "Sheilah [student with emotional or behavioral problems] is getting her math book out. What are the next two things you need to do, Sheilah, to indicate that you are ready?"

3. Provide frequent feedback when the student performs the desired behaviors. Look for as many chances as possible to recognize desirable behaviors.
4. Students who view themselves as "like" a model are more likely than not to imitate desirable behaviors. You can facilitate this process by identifying ways in which students' behaviors are similar. For example, "Sheilah [student with emotional or behavioral disorder] and Joaquin are not talking while they are getting ready for the homework assignment. Good for them!"

# TechTalk

## Interactive Multimedia

In this era of advancing technology, interactive multimedia are playing an important role in education. Computer-assisted learning can act as a supplement to existing resources. The Vocational Rehabilitation Learning Resource Package (VRLR), a self-paced learning package, is discussed at the following website: http://ot.curtin.edu.au/research/html/vrlr.html.

Interactive Multimedia, Inc., provides educational games for all ages. Its fully interactive CD-ROM allows the user to choose the direction, action, and outcome of the overall experience. The user can explore entire areas of information through different media thoroughly at his or her convenience. The information is presented on a CD-ROM using high-impact audio, video, and animations. The CD-ROM is capable of being viewed on all Windows 3.1x, 95, 98, 2000, ME, and NT systems.

ESL/ELT Multimedia Software produces *Euro-Plus+ Flying Colours,* which is a software application for serious learners of English who favor an academic approach. The learner can do a variety of things, including listening to dialogs and taking part in them, watching video clips, and reading passages. The student can practice pronunciation by recording his or her voice and comparing it with that of a native speaker. Students can also check their understanding by doing a multitude of different exercises with immediate feedback. *EuroPlus+* is available at four levels, each providing about 150 hours of intensive study. *EuroPlus+* provides a number of supporting tools such as Audio Dictionary, Tape Recorder, Browser, and Spelling Teacher. Details regarding this software can be obtained at www.ydp.com.pl/English.

*Slim Show* is an interactive multimedia authoring software for MS Windows. It has a compact runtime engine that allows the teacher to create professional-looking multimedia projects containing graphics, text, sound, music, video clips, buttons, animation objects, and text-to-speech objects. Projects can be made for distribution on diskettes, CD-ROMs, the Internet, or other media. It can be used to create tutorials and educational programs. It requires Windows 3.1/95/98/NT and SVGA 640x480 by 256 or better. A sound card is needed to hear the audio. The program has several features, including an authoring program for making multimedia projects to run on Windows 3.1x, 95, 98, 2000, ME, and NT. It supports button objects for interactivity, includes a print option, contains an easy-to-use visual authoring environment with no programming, no scripting, and no pages—just click, drag, and drop. They have several projects, including Multimedia Playroom, that focus on educational activities for kids, such as learning to tell time, a music encyclopedia, 100 questions and answers, and more. A tutorial made with *Slim Show* can be downloaded for free, and third-party tools for creating multimedia project material can be accessed at www.pcww.com/web_mat/presentations.html. A demonstration can be downloaded at http://www.pcww.com/web_mat/slimshow.html. Software can be ordered at 1-800-242-4775

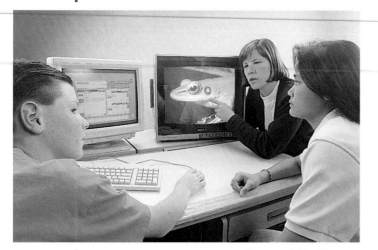
Courtesy of Video Discovery.

inappropriate behaviors. By providing high-interest materials, you can keep students involved in the task. High interest is a characteristic of educational technologies, for example. Having students compose essays, complete tests, and practice skills on a computer may provide better motivation than more traditional activities.

Also provide alternative ways for students to complete tasks and demonstrate learning. For example, students might give oral recitations, describe what they know to other students who have already mastered the material, or perform learning outcomes. Allow students to express their individual learning-style preferences. For instance, some students work better standing up, others while sitting on the floor, still others while sitting in beanbag chairs. As long as students are working, learning, and not interfering with the progress of others, providing appropriate alternatives for completing tasks makes sense.

or 1-713-524-6394. Fax: 1-713-524-6398. Mail: PSL, P.O. Box 35705, Houston, TX 77235-5705.

Educational Software Institute (ESI) provides interactive software for all ages. They produce *A+LS—Advanced Learning System* Complete Series, which is a system of fully managed educational software. The A+LS Multimedia Curriculum Authoring System provides teachers full multimedia authoring capabilities. Importantly, all of these features are integral to each and every A+LS subject title, providing schools with a true building-block approach to a fully integrated curriculum solution. Macintosh users require a 68040-based machine or better, System 7.5.3 Update 2 or higher, and 8 MB RAM. Windows users require a 486 processor or higher, Windows 3.11 or higher, Win95 Service Pack 1 or higher, 8 MB RAM for Windows 3.11, 16 MB RAM for Windows 95, Windows-compatible mouse, and Windows-compatible sound card and speakers or headphones (recommended). Contact ESI for Network/Site License policy, pricing, and availability. Floppy diskettes are available upon request at a slightly increased price. This complete series, which contains 43 titles, provides administrators, teachers, and students with a unique, fully authorable, and open instruction management and learning system. It gives teachers the flexibility to provide their students with a wide range of instructional software, along with the ability to create, for each student, an individualized lesson sequence. A+LS also provides a complete range of fully correlated instructional software in the areas of reading, writing, mathematics, social studies, and science. This entire curriculum is managed, graded, and reported through a comprehensive, easy-to-use management system with the ability to print study material, assignments, and tests. Details about this software can be obtained online at www.edsoft.com or at Educational Software Institute, 4213 South 94th Street, Omaha, NE 68127. Phone 1-800-955-5570. Fax: 1-402-592-2017.

Parrot Software provides programs that focus on speaking English. These programs can be set up to provide the directions in either spoken or written form. The number of different directions can be set between 1 and 3 to increase the difficulty of the task. The program runs on any Windows-compatible word processor. The font includes 150 characters that can be scaled between 3 and 127 points. The specific characters include those from the International Phonetic Alphabet, along with others found in scientific articles using phonetic characters. It requires Windows 95, Windows 3.x, or higher.

Parrot Software also produces an interactive version of the *Brubaker Workbook Series* on the computer. This software allows the teacher to create in seconds exactly the kind of workbook that is needed. This program provides an extensive source of language and cognitive exercises that allow the teacher to create a workbook that specifically targets a child's unique deficits. The teacher indicates the types of deficits demonstrated by a particular child by clicking on an extensive list of language and cognitive concepts. The teacher also indicates target area, cognitive and language concepts, difficulty level, response type, print size, spacing, and typeface. The program uses these options to create the most appropriate exercises from a huge database. The exercises selected can be viewed on-screen before a personalized workbook is printed. With over 1,500 new exercises on disk, the combinations are all-encompassing and comprehensive, allowing individuals to progress through the same exercise with several levels of difficulty or different exercises with one concept. The workbook can be saved and printed all or in part at any time. It requires Windows 95, 3.x, or higher; 8 MB of RAM; a printer; and a mouse. Details can be found online at www.parrotsoftware.com.

For further information, there are books that demonstrate how to create vibrant multimedia environments to enhance a child's educational and play experience, and a multimedia guide that includes a history of children's software and profiles of the latest technologies. Details regarding these and similar books can be obtained at www.amazon.com.

## summary

- Students with emotional and behavioral disorders exhibit behaviors that are significantly different from the norm and that persist over a long period of time.

- Emotional and behavioral disorders are grouped into two broad categories: externalizing and internalizing.

- Externalizing behaviors are characterized by acting out, aggression, interfering, attention-getting, and conduct problems.
- Internalizing behaviors are viewed as more self-directed, such as being anxious, worried, and depressed.
- There are six major classifications of emotional and behavioral disorders: conduct disorder and aggression, hyperactivity, socialized aggression, pervasive developmental disorder, immaturity, and anxiety–withdrawal. Some of these classifications fit the externalizing category, some fit the internalizing category, and some fit both, depending on the specific manifestation of the problem behavior.

- The criteria that are considered when interpreting emotional or behavioral problems include behavior–age discrepancy, frequency of occurrence of behavior(s), number of symptoms, inner suffering, persistence of behavior, self-satisfaction, and severity and duration of behavior(s).
- Strategies to consider when teaching students with emotional and behavioral disorders include altering the environment, targeting and changing behavior, promoting academic and social factors that enhance learning, providing successful experiences, providing ample opportunities for students to learn, monitoring and changing activities, and using alternative behavior-management strategies.

## key terms and concepts

anxiety–withdrawal
conduct disorder
conflict resolution
depression
developmental
    pathways
*Diagnostic and Statistical Manual
    of Mental Disorders*

emotional or behavioral disorders
externalizing behaviors
gangs
group behavior
hyperactivity
immaturity
internalizing behaviors
level system

Life-Space Intervention (LSI)
pervasive developmental
    disorder
social learning
socialized aggression
stimulants

## think and apply

1. Now that you have read Chapter 4, consider the behaviors of Lenox, the student in Juline's first-grade class described at the beginning of the chapter. Make a list of the types of behaviors you would expect Lenox to exhibit. Consider the suggestions provided in the chapter and list instructional and behavior-management practices you could implement to enhance this student's success. File your responses in your teaching portfolio and add ideas as you read this book.

2. Identify a practicing teacher you can interview, and ask him or her the following questions:

   a. To what extent have students in your class exhibited symptoms of emotional and behavioral disorders? What kinds of problems do you see?

   b. Do you think that more students have emotional and behavioral problems today than in the past? Why or why not?

   c. To what do you attribute students' emotional and behavioral problems?

   d. What advice would you give to teachers about working effectively with students with emotional and behavioral disorders?

   Compare the teacher's answers with your own ideas and those of your classmates.

3. Most school districts have special classrooms or programs for students with severe emotional and behavioral disorders. Make arrangements to visit one of these classrooms or programs. How do these educational settings differ from the general education classroom? What types of resources are available to meet the special learning needs of these students?

# read more about it

1. Coleman, M. C., & Webber, J. (2002). *Emotional and behavioral disorders: Theory and practice* (4th ed.). Boston: Allyn & Bacon.

   *Provides a complete overview of children and adolescents with behavioral and emotional problems, including internalizing and externalizing problems, assessment, and educational issues.*

2. Knitzer, J., Steinberg, Z., & Fleisch, B. (1990). *At the school house door: An examination of programs and policies for children with behavioral and emotional problems.* New York: Bank Street College of Education.

   *A comprehensive examination of the types of programs available for school-age children with emotional and behavioral disorders, this book also describes the educational, political, and social policies that influence intervention programs for these students.*

3. MacCracken, M. (1973). *Circle of children.* Philadelphia: J. B. Lippincott.

   *This personal account of one teacher's experiences instructing students with emotional disorders poignantly describes the frustrations and successes teachers are likely to encounter when working with this student population.*

4. Quay, H. C., & Werry, J. S. (1986). *Psychopathological disorders of childhood.* New York: Wiley.

   *A comprehensive overview of the classification, research, and intervention effects of treating students with emotional and behavioral disorders. This book*

*identifies the types of problems frequently found in students and expands on the subtypes presented in this chapter.*

5. Walker, H. M., Colvin, G., & Ramsey, E. (1995). *Antisocial behavior in school: Strategies and best practices.* Pacific Grove, CA: Brooks/Cole.

   *Provides background on identification, classification, and intervention strategies for addressing antisocial behavior of students in school settings.*

6. Penzel, F. (2000). *Obsessive-compulsive disorders: A complete guide to getting well and staying well.* New York: Oxford University Press.

   *This book provides an overview of obsessive-compulsive disorders. Topics include the definition of obsessive-compulsive disorders, causes and contributing factors to obsessive-compulsive disorders, assessment, and behavioral and medical treatments.*

7. Kauffman, J. M. (2000). *Characteristics of emotional and behavioral disorders of children and youth* (7th ed.). Upper Saddle River, NJ: Prentice Hall.

   *This is an easy-to-read book that provides an overview of emotional and behavior disorders (EBD). It provides the definition of EBD, the history of the field, and causes/contributing factors to EBD. It also introduces different types of EBD, such as attention and activity disorders and anxiety–withdrawal disorders. This book also provides instruction for teachers about how to educate students with EBD.*

# suggested websites

www.behavioradvisor.com
This website provides a number of resources related to behavior management (strategies, assessment, functional behavior assessment, discipline, etc.).

http://seriweb.com/behavior.htm
This website provides several links to information about behavior disorders (e.g., behavioral research and teaching, center for behavioral disorders).

www.mentalhealth.com/dis/p20-ch02.html
This website provides resources related to conduct disorders (e.g., definition, treatment, articles).

www.air.org/cecp/resources/20th/edenviro.htm
This website describes eligibility, characteristics, identification, and services for individuals with emotional disturbances.

http://harmony.millersv.edu/partners/millersville/students/previous/fall99/edfn333_1/vbruno/behavior_disorder.htm

This website contains several links to information about the identification and treatment of behavior disorders.

www.ed.gov/databases/ERIC_Digest/ed371506/html
This website introduces several behavior management techniques.

www.nichcy.org/pubs/bibliog/bib10txt.htm
This website provides brief summaries of a number of articles about emotional and behavior disorders.

www.pacer.org/ebd
This website introduces the project for Parents of Children with Emotional and Behavior Disorders at the PACER (Parent Advocacy Coalition for Educational Rights) center.

www.kidsource.com/kidsource/content2/behavior_disorder.html
This website provides several tips for changing problem behaviors of students with behavior disorders.

# Teaching Students with Developmental Disabilities

# chapter | outline

# focus | questions

1. What are the major concepts presented in the new AAMR definition of mental retardation? How does the new definition change and broaden previous concepts about mental retardation? Do you consider it to be an improvement? Why or why not?

2. What are some characteristics of students with autism? Of students with dual sensory impairments?

3. Describe some alternative or augmentative methods of communication for persons with developmental disabilities.

4. Describe two planning systems you could use to help plan for a student with developmental disabilities. How are the two systems different in their purposes?

5. Why are functional assessment and functional practice important for increasing the learning of students with developmental disabilities?

6. As a classroom teacher, describe how you could have peers assist students with developmental disabilities in your classroom.

# inter view

### Susie Speelman, Mary Robinson, and Steve Canty

Susie Speelman is an **inclusion support teacher** at Sunrise Elementary School, Tucson, Arizona. Susie's job involves supporting students with mental retardation, severe disabilities, physical disabilities (e.g., cerebral palsy), and visual impairments in general education classrooms. To do this, Susie works closely with the general education teachers at Sunrise to learn what the different classes will be doing and to make the necessary accommodations or adaptations so that students with disabilities can be successful and learn at their level.

Susie has been in this position for three years and therefore knows well the children whom she supports. Susie does not work alone; besides herself, there are six educational assistants (EAs) or paraprofessionals who support the 10 children with whom she works in 10 different kindergarten through fifth-grade classrooms. When talking about making accommodations, Susie comments:

> The key to making inclusion work is to have good working relationships with the classroom teachers and to assist them in feeling that they are capable of teaching students with significant disabilities. In working in the different classrooms, one generalization that I can make is that it is the attitude and knowledge of the classroom teacher that is oftentimes the key to a student's success. If the teacher has a can-do attitude and considers the student a viable member of the class, then the stage is set for the student's success. My job becomes one of providing the supports for the student's learning. This may be an EA who works in the classroom part- or full-time, using assistive technology such as a communication board, or my directly working with the student. While it may appear more challenging to support these children at the upper elementary level, where the work includes more pencil-and-paper tasks, I have found that many of my students have become fascinated with the various hands-on projects and activities that are emphasized at the upper elementary level in content subjects such as math, science, social studies, and art.

Melody's work in Mary Robinson's fifth-grade class is a good example of how a student with mild to moderate mental retardation is integrated into the classroom community. One of Melody's strengths is math. With the help of the EA and peer tutors, she is developing many functional math skills, such as reading prices and knowing how much money is necessary to make a purchase. Melody is also memorizing basic addition and subtraction facts. While the other students are working on timed tests or on the computer, Melody also works on a timed test or on computer programs for math facts. In this way, she participates like the other students, but the content of her work is different.

Many of Melody's goals focus on communication and social development and are worked on throughout the school day. Mary, Susie, and the EA know that Melody is working on asking for help instead of waiting for someone to notice her and also on looking up and speaking clearly. The team finds opportunities throughout the day to work on these goals. Mary describes how she integrates Melody's goals into the class routines:

> Now that I know Melody, it is easy to integrate her goals with the other students' goals. For example, students are expected to be independent in this classroom, and we use lots of semistructured activities such as writer's workshop and literature study groups. Each requires that the students take responsibility for getting materials, working on projects, and evaluating their own learning. Melody is responsible for getting and putting away her writing folder, her literature log, and her reading folder just like the other students. As a reminder, I have a picture of each taped on her desk. When she has difficulty remembering to get or put away her materials, I can point to the picture of what she needs to get or put away. This serves as a cue, without calling undue attention to her.

José, another student Susie supports, is in Steve Canty's third-grade class. José has severe disabilities, is nonverbal, and uses a wheelchair. One of the most difficult challenges with José is to get him actively involved in the classroom activities. Steve comments:

> José tends to let others make decisions for him, and he sits back and watches instead of participating. Therefore, making choices is one of José's major goals. Susie and I have worked hard at providing José lots of opportunities and helped his peers also give José choices throughout the day.
>
> For example, when the students were designing their own money, one of José's classmates gave him three choices of designs for their joint project.

Susie, Mary, and Steve all agree that an important key to the successful integration of Melody and José is co-planning and ongoing communication not just among themselves, but also with the EAs, with parents, and with other specialists who work with these students, including the speech and language pathologist and the occupational therapist.

# i n t r o d u c t i o n

As a teacher, you will probably have students like Melody and José in your class. This chapter provides information about these students. It also presents a process for curriculum modification and describes strategies you can use to support students with developmental disabilities in your own classroom.

## Definitions and Types of Developmental Disabilities

The populations of individuals who are considered to have developmental disabilities are quite heterogeneous, as is evident in our interview with teachers at Sunrise Elementary. **Developmental disabilities** are physical or mental disabilities that impair the person's functioning in language, learning, mobility, self-care, or other important areas of living. These disabilities may range from mild to severe. Students with developmental disabilities present a wide range of characteristics, strengths, and difficulties. This section discusses the definitions and types of developmental disabilities.

### Mental Retardation

Students with mental retardation have limited intellectual functioning, which affects their learning. These students have slower rates of learning and are particularly challenged by complex and abstract tasks. Students with mental retardation are just like other students in your class in that they are members of families, have friends and neighbors, have personalities shaped by both their innate characteristics and their life experiences, and have aspirations to become adults, get jobs, and fall in love (Orelore & Sobsey, 1996; Smith, 1998). Yet to be successful in general education classrooms, they also need additional support and accommodations. In planning for this support, it is helpful to have some knowledge about mental retardation and how it affects learning.

Historically, definitions of mental retardation focused on limitations in intellectual functioning (as measured by intelligence tests). More recent definitions are broader, focusing on four major concepts:

- *Intellectual functioning:* Individuals who have mental retardation have substantial limitations in **intellectual functioning** and have been characterized as having "significantly subaverage intellectual functioning." On measures of intellectual functioning, "significantly subaverage" has been defined as an IQ of 70–75 or less and includes about 3 percent of the population.
- *Adaptive behavior:* Students who have mental retardation also have significant limitations in adaptive skills or behavior. **Adaptive behavior** refers to "the effectiveness or degree with which individuals meet the standards of personal independence and social responsibility expected for age and cultural group" (Grossman, 1983, p. 1).
- *Developmental period:* Students who have mental retardation demonstrate limitations in intellectual functioning and adaptive behavior

during the **developmental period,** before the age of 18. Persons who acquire limited intellectual functioning after that age are referred to not as having mental retardation but as having traumatic brain injury or whatever the cause of the disability (Smith, 1998).

- *Systems of support:* **Systems of support** are the coordinated set of services and accommodations matched to a student's needs and can include teachers and specialists, specialized programs and methodologies, and assistive technology. When appropriate supports are provided over a sustained period, the life functioning of students with mental retardation will generally improve (AAMR, 1992).

Using these four themes, the American Association on Mental Retardation (AAMR) defined **mental retardation** as follows in 1992:

> Mental retardation refers to substantial limitations in present functioning. It is characterized by significantly subaverage intellectual functioning, existing concurrently with related limitations in two or more of the following applicable adaptive skill areas: communication, self-care, home living, social skills, community use, self-direction, health and safety, functional academics, leisure and work. Mental retardation manifests before age 18 (p. 1).

The following four assumptions are essential to the application of this definition:

- Valid assessment considers cultural and linguistic diversity, as well as differences in communication and behavioral factors.
- The existence of limitations in adaptive skills occurs within the context of community environments typical of the individual's age peers and is indexed to the person's individual needs for supports.
- Specific adaptive limitations often coexist with strengths in other adaptive skills or other personal capabilities.
- With appropriate supports over a sustained period, the life functioning of the person with mental retardation will generally improve (AAMR, 1992, p. 5).

In comparison to previous definitions, the current definition stresses the interaction among (1) the environment in which the person functions, (2) the person's capabilities, and (3) the need for varying levels of support (Beirne-Smith, Ittenbach, & Patton, 1998).

In addition, the new definition reflects a change in the classification system. The traditional system emphasized the individual's degree of retardation (i.e., mild retardation: IQ scores of 50–55 to 70–75, moderate retardation: IQ scores of 35–40 to 50–55, severe

─────────── FIGURE 5.1 ───────────

### 1992 Classification System for Mental Retardation

| Level of Support | Description of Support | Example |
|---|---|---|
| Intermittent | Support on an as-needed basis. Characterized by episodic nature, person not always needing the support(s), or short-term supports needed during life-span transitions (e.g., job loss or an acute medical crisis). Intermittent supports may be high or low intensity when provided. | Counseling support needed as student adjusts to school at the beginning of each year and as the student begins job training programs in high school. |
| Limited | An intensity of supports characterized by consistency over time, time-limited but not of an intermittent nature, may require fewer staff members and less cost than more intense levels of supports (e.g., time-limited employment training or transitional supports during the school to adult period). | Support provided to a high-school student with mild mental retardation as they take specially designed courses in learning strategies/study skills, functional English, and applied math. Support provided by a job developer as student works in the afternoons. |
| Extensive | Supports characterized by regular involvement in at least some environments (such as work or home) and not time limited (e.g., long-term support and long-term home living support). | Support provided to an elementary-age student with a moderate or severe disability who works in the general education classroom. An educational assistant provides the major support during reading, language arts, math, and science, with peers and the classroom teacher providing the major support at other times of the day. |
| Pervasive | Supports characterized by their constancy, high intensity; provided across environments; potentially life-sustaining nature. Pervasive supports typically involve more staff members and intrusiveness than do extensive or time-limited supports (Luckasson et al., 1992, p. 26). | Ongoing support provided to a student who is medically fragile and in need of constant support by a staff member. |

*Source:* Adapted from Luckasson, R., Coulter, D. L., Polloway, E. A., Reiss, S., Schalock, R. L., Snell, M. E., Spitalnik, D. M., & Stark, J. A. (1992). *Mental retardation: Definition, classification, and systems of supports.* Washington, DC: American Association on Mental Retardation, p. 26.

retardation: IQ scores of 20–25 to 35–40, profound retardation: IQ scores below 20–25). The new classification system emphasizes the level of supports needed to facilitate the individual's integration into the community (Meyen & Skrtic, 1995). Figure 5.1 presents the 1992 classification system, along with examples of support at each level. This classification system incorporates a multidimensional approach that includes emotional, psychological, and related health factors.

The cause of the mental retardation, although known only about 50 percent of the time (Beirne-Smith et al., 1998), is one way in which people classify different types of mental retardation. Chromosomal disorders are probably the best-known cause of mental retardation. **Down syndrome,** one of the most common chromosomal disorders, is often what people think of when mental retardation is mentioned. Yet Down syndrome occurs in only about 1 in 700 live births and accounts for fewer than 10 percent of all individuals with mental retardation (Kozma & Stock,

1993). **Fetal alcohol syndrome** (FAS), one of the top three known causes of birth defects (Griego, 1994), refers to a spectrum of birth defects caused by the mother's drinking during pregnancy and is fast becoming the leading cause of mental retardation (March of Dimes, 1993). Children with FAS may experience some degree of mental retardation, poor coordination, learning disabilities, psychosocial behavior problems, physical abnormalities, and speech and language problems (Umansky & Hooper, 1998).

## Autism

**Autism** is a developmental disability that typically appears during the first three years of life. Although people diagnosed as autistic are considered to have a severe disability, the range in ability levels within this group is varied (Powers, 1989). Some individuals with autism may function independently or almost independently. Kim Peek, the inspiration for the character

# Tips for Teachers

## 5.1　A Teacher's Advice for Working with Students with Autism

- *Don't let the behavior overwhelm you.* Develop a behavior-management plan and implement small steps. Decide what you will put up with and what behaviors must stop, and target those.
- *Talk to the student's parents and other teachers,* and find out what works and what does not work with this student.
- *Systematically expect more and more of the student.* At first, the student might be required only to sit with the class with whatever it takes (a favorite object); then the student might be required to hold the reading book.

- *Develop a picture and word schedule for daily activities.* Use this to prepare the student for transitions to new activities. Introduce changes in routine slowly, and let the student know in advance that these changes are going to occur.
- *Use peers to help redirect the student's behavior* and to interest him or her in the task.
- *Take ownership of the student* so that he or she feels like a real member of the class.

played by Dustin Hoffman in the movie *Rain Man,* is an example of an individual who has autism but generally functions independently (and even has some specific cognitive abilities in the genius range).

The physical features of people with autism might not suggest a disability. Rather, the disability is generally manifested in their language and their personal and social behavior. The Individuals with Disabilities Education Act (1997) defines *autism* as follows:

When autism was first identified in the 1940s, it was thought to be a psychosocial problem caused by parents' aloof or hostile behavior. Later, autism was classified under physical impairments. Not until the IDEA amendments of 1990 was autism treated as a separate disability category.

A developmental disability significantly affecting verbal and nonverbal communication and social interaction, generally evident before age 3, that adversely affects a child's performance. Other characteristics often associated with autism are engagement in repetitive activities and stereotyped movements, resistance to environmental change or change in daily routines, and unusual responses to sensory experiences. The term does not apply if a child's educational performance is adversely affected primarily because the child has a serious emotional disturbance (34 C.F.R., Part 300, Sec. 300.7[b][1]).

After having Jason, a student with autism, in his seventh-grade language block for several months, Robert Hernandez expressed these thoughts:

I was worried about how it would work with the other students; if it would take away from them. I was concerned that Jason would be a distraction to the students. But now that Jason has been part of our class for several months, I feel that the more he is in the classroom, the less the children even notice the noise or occasional outbursts. The stu-

dents had to learn that Jason will do things that are not okay for them to do.

Tips for Teachers 5.1 presents Robert's advice for working with students like Jason in the classroom.

## Severe Disabilities

**Severe disabilities** are often described as a condition in which typical life activities are significantly affected. The Association for Persons with Severe Handicaps (TASH) defines persons with severe disabilities as follows:

individuals of all ages who require extensive ongoing support in more than one major life activity in order to participate in integrated community settings and to enjoy a quality of life that is available to citizens with fewer or no disabilities. Support may be required for life activities such as mobility, communication, self-care, and learning as necessary for independent living, employment and self-sufficiency (Meyer et al., 1991, p. 19).

Among those who are considered to have severe disabilities are students whose mental retardation is severe or profound, whose autism is severe or profound, who have dual sensory impairments (i.e., deaf–blind), or who have multiple disabilities (e.g., significant mental retardation and physical disabilities or mental retardation and a sensory disability).

**Multiple Disabilities**　Individuals with **multiple disabilities** have mental retardation that is severe or profound, as well as one or more significant motor or sensory impairments or special health needs. For example, a person with severe mental retardation might

Fifty to sixty percent of persons with cerebral palsy also experience a mental disability.

What factors must be taken into account when planning instruction for students with severe or multiple disabilities?

also have cerebral palsy or epilepsy (Orelove & Sobsey, 1996; Westling & Fox, 2000). Types of multiple disabilities include mental retardation with physical disabilities (e.g., cerebral palsy, spina bifida, seizure disorders), mental retardation with severe behavior disorders, and mental retardation with a visual or hearing impairment. It is reasonable to expect that two of every five students with severe and multiple disabilities will have a sensory impairment (Sobsey & Wolf-Schein, 1996).

Like all students, students with multiple disabilities have learning needs that require a *holistic* approach to education (an approach in which the student is viewed as a whole person). In determining educational goals and teaching strategies, professionals consider factors such as the student's emotions, cognitive processes, and other factors that interact with the environment to produce behavior (Siegel-Causey et al., 1995).

**Dual Sensory Impairments** Students with **dual sensory impairments** (also referred to as **deaf–blind**) present unique challenges in that the two main channels (auditory and visual) of receptive communication and learning are impaired. Although difficult to determine, the cognitive abilities of students with dual sensory impairments can vary from severe retardation to giftedness. Individuals who are deaf–blind may have diverse combinations of vision and hearing impairments with normal or gifted intelligence, or they may have additional mental, physical, and behavioral disabilities (Downing & Eichinger, 1990; Orelove & Sobsey, 1996). Because these individuals do not receive clear and consistent information from either sensory modality, a tendency exists to turn inward. These individuals may appear passive, not responding to or initiating interactions with others. Tips for Teachers 5.2 provides a list of teaching strategies and guidelines for interacting with individuals with dual sensory impairments.

# Tips for Teachers

## 5.2 Environmental Accommodations for Students with Dual Sensory Impairments

- Develop a tactile schedule for your student. Each activity of the day has an object that represents it. For example: math—calculator; lunch—spoon; reading—a small book.
- Along with the schedule, objects can be used to make choices, get information from the environment or convey a message (e.g., handing the teacher a small pillow might mean the student wants his or her position changed, choosing a small ball would communicate what the student wants to do during recess).
- Tactually or visually identify your student's belongings with a consistent, meaningful symbol. This will help facilitate independence (e.g., a pencil taped on the desk, a safety pin on the tag of his or her coat).
- Have clear pathways marked with objects that serve as cues. Consistent furniture or tactile or visual runners on the wall help to promote orientation and the student's independent mobility. Important places should be distinguished by special cues.

- To encourage your student to use his or her remaining hearing or vision, add light, color, sound, vibration, interesting textures, and colors to objects.
- Firmly touch the student's shoulder to signal that an interaction is going to occur.
- Introduce yourself by using a consistent symbol for your name. This could be a ring, watch, or other piece of jewelry you always wear that the student could easily touch, or it could be a distinguishing feature, such as your hair or glasses. Name signs or the finger spelling of the first letter of your name could also be signed in the palm of the student's hand as a consistent symbol for your name.

*Source:* Adapted from Rikhye, C. H., Gotheif, C. R., & Appell, M. W. (1989). A classroom environment checklist for students with dual sensory impairments. *Teaching Exceptional Children, 22*(1), 44–46; California Deaf–Blind Services (1992). *How to interact with individuals with dual sensory impairments* (Fact Sheet). California: Author.

# Prevention of Mental Retardation

The President's Committee on Mental Retardation reported that more than 50 percent of all cases of mental retardation could have been prevented. Maternal use of alcohol and drugs during pregnancy, as well as maternal infections (such as HIV) are among the fastest-growing causes of mental retardation that can be prevented. For example, women who smoke heavily during the last six months of pregnancy are 60 percent more likely to have children with mental retardation (Bergstein, 1996). McLaren and Bryson (1987) estimated that as many as 15 percent of the cases of mild retardation are a result of child abuse or neglect and that 1 in 30 newborns will experience a serious head trauma before the age of 18. Poverty can cause mental retardation through increased chances of lead poisoning, inadequate diet, inadequate health care (including immunizations), unsafe neighborhoods, and environmental pollutants (Smith, 1998). In fact, Menolascino and Stark (1988) stated that poverty is a determinant in 75–80 percent of people with mental retardation at higher IQ levels. Following are some simple prenatal prevention strategies:

- Avoid using alcohol, taking drugs, and smoking.
- Avoid sexually transmitted diseases.
- Obtain appropriate medical care.
- Maintain good health and nutrition.
- Treat infections immediately.
- Obtain genetic testing and prenatal tests, if indicated.

Following are postnatal prevention strategies:

- Provide proper nutrition and medical care.
- Obtain proper immunizations.
- Use infant and child car seats and seat belts in automobiles.
- Prevent lead or other chemical intake.
- Eliminate child abuse and neglect.

# Prevalence of Developmental Disabilities

The prevalence of persons with mental retardation is difficult to determine because different definitions and methodologies are used to determine retardation. Generally, however, prevalence is estimated to be about 1–2 percent of the population. According to the federal government, slightly more than 1 percent of the school-age population is identified as having mental retardation and requiring special education services (U.S. Department of Education, 1997), with approximately 90 percent of those students having mild

retardation. Prevalence of multiple disabilities is difficult to determine, as different states use different classification systems (e.g., some states include students with multiple disabilities under the category of physical disabilities). The U.S. Department of Education (1994) reports that about 0.13 percent of the general population has multiple disabilities or dual sensory impairments.

It is interesting to note that the number of children born with severe disabilities is on the rise (National Center for Education Statistics, 2000). Some screening and early intervention have led to a reduction in causes (e.g., most hospitals now screen to determine whether babies have phenylketonuria, so that it can be treated before mental retardation occurs), but the number of children being born exposed to drugs and alcohol is increasing (Budden, 1996). In addition, because medical advances have also resulted in more high-risk and low-birth-weight babies surviving and living longer, more children with disabilities are reaching school age.

# Characteristics of Students with Developmental Disabilities

When you consider the characteristics of students with developmental disabilities, not every student will have all the characteristics discussed. As a group, however, students with developmental disabilities display these characteristics more often than the general population does (Mihail, 1995). The characteristics are grouped into four areas: intellectual functioning, social skills, motor skills, and communication.

## Intellectual Functioning

Although students with developmental disabilities have many diverse learning characteristics, they generally learn slowly and often fail to notice relevant features of what is being taught, do not demonstrate learned skills spontaneously, and have difficulty generalizing learned skills to new situations (Noonan & Siegel-Causey, 1990). These students also have difficulty learning complex skills and abstract concepts, and they learn less overall than other students do. Many students with developmental disabilities experience memory deficits, either remembering incorrectly or not remembering automatically. These students frequently need additional cues to help them focus their attention.

Students with mild retardation learn academic tasks such as reading, writing, and math, sometimes achieving up to a sixth-grade level in some areas by the end of high school. These students usually have more success with basic academic skills (such as decoding and math computation) than with more abstract and applied skills, such as reading comprehension and math problem solving (Thomas & Patton, 1990). Students also have significant difficulty making connections among ideas and generalizing newly learned knowledge and skills to new situations (Drew & Hardman, 2000). The following learning strategies promote skill and strategy acquisition and generalization:

- Engage students actively in learning.
- Teach the strategy or skill in small steps or segments.
- Teach students how to use the specific strategies.
- Check frequently for understanding, and provide feedback.
- Use actual materials and real-life experiences or simulations.
- Provide concrete examples in instruction.
- Have students perform the skill or strategy repeatedly.
- Provide many examples and multiple contexts to promote generalization.
- Reinforce generalization.
- Use the skill or strategy in several different learning situations to promote generalization.
- Create learning environments providing students successful experiences.
- Limit the number of concepts presented in any one period.

The Research Brief introduces a naturalistic intervention that can promote their generalizing learned skills to other contexts.

## research brief

## Naturalistic Intervention for Students with Developmental Disabilities

Naturalistic intervention is a type of environmental intervention (Hart, 1985). Naturalistic intervention has been viewed as an effective intervention that promotes generalization of learned skills to other contexts (Greenwood et al., 1991). Because many students with developmental disabilities have difficulties in generalization of learned skills to other contexts, naturalistic intervention appears to be an effective intervention to promote students' generalizing learned skills.

Recently, naturalistic intervention has increasingly appeared in the literature (Barnett, Carey, & Hall, 1993; Hepting & Goldstein, 1996; Rule, Losardo, Dinnebeil, Kaiser, & Rowland, 1998). Procedures or approaches that are described as naturalistic include incidental teaching (a naturalistic-response-prompting procedure in which a teacher arranges the environment in such a way that students need to request materials verbally; Brown, McEvoy, & Bishop, 1991; Hart & Risley, 1982), time delay (a naturalistic-response-prompting procedure used in the natural environment in which a teacher withholds materials until students use the tar-

get utterance; Wolery, Doyle, Gast, & Ault, 1993), milieu teaching (a naturalistic-response-prompting procedure in which students' interest in the natural environment is used to elicit the students' communicative responses; Warren, 1991), mand-model (a naturalistic-response-prompting procedure that involves a teacher arrangement of the environment and the use of a target utterance; Rogers-Warren & Warren, 1980), and activity-based interaction (a naturalistic-response-prompting procedure in which the teaching of language skills is embedded in the routine, planned, or child-initiated activities; Bricker & Cripe, 1992).

Over time, the procedural components investigated in earlier studies have been elaborated. Naturalistic intervention has evolved to be characterized by the following key attributes (Rule et al., 1998):

1. Naturalistic intervention typically refers to an instructional context such as routine events and everyday activities that occur in a variety of settings.
2. Interactions typically follow the student's lead or capitalize on the student's interest, and the consequences of the student's behavior are typically related to the interaction.
3. Naturalistic intervention typically focuses on functional skills, such as asking for milk, taking turns with peers, and so on.

Rule and colleagues (1998) described a set of guidelines to document specific procedural and contextual features of naturalistic intervention. These guidelines are helpful to teachers and parents by providing procedures that they can follow. These guidelines are also helpful to researchers by facilitating their replication of the research.

**Procedural Features**
Guideline 1: Describe the nature of the target behavior.
Guideline 2: Describe the number of behaviors being targeted.
Guideline 3: Describe when and how training trials are introduced.
Guideline 4: Describe who initiates teaching transactions.
Guideline 5: Describe the types of antecedents and consequences used.
Guideline 6: Describe the role of corrective feedback.

**Contextual Features**
Guideline 1: Describe the environmental arrangement.
Guideline 2: Describe the intensity of activities.

Given that students with developmental disabilities have slow learning rates and significant difficulty learning higher-level thinking skills and abstract concepts, what they learn should be necessary to their daily functioning and serve them in their adult lives. The Brigance Diagnostic Inventory of Essential Skills (Brigance, 1981) provides one means of assessing higher-level functional skills (see Table 5.1).

TABLE 5.1

### Functional Skills Assessed by the Brigance Diagnostic Inventory of Essential Skills

| Area | Subtests | Area | Subtests |
|---|---|---|---|
| Functional Word Recognition | Basic sight vocabulary<br>Direction words<br>Abbreviations<br>Warning/safety signs<br>Reads number words | Health and Safety | Medical vocabulary<br>Medical labels<br>Health evaluation form<br>Health practices and attitude rating scale<br>Self-concept rating scale<br>Warning labels |
| Schedules and Graphs | Reads class schedule<br>Reads television schedule<br>Identifies and interprets graphs | Money and Finance | Price signs<br>Computes totals for amounts of money<br>Making change<br>Comprehends and computes purchase savings<br>Computes expenses using charts and tables<br>Balancing a checking account<br>Manages a checking account<br>Computes interest on loans<br>Reads and comprehends a credit agreement<br>Application for a credit card<br>Reads and comprehends monthly credit statement |
| Forms | School information form<br>Computer base form | | |
| Measurement | Equivalent values of coins and the dollar bill<br>Total values of collections of coins and bills<br>Conversion of coins<br>Time<br>Equivalent units of time<br>Conversion of units of time<br>Equivalent calendar units<br>Conversion of calendar units<br>Calendar<br>Dates<br>Ruler<br>Equivalent units of measurement<br>Conversion of units of measurement<br>Meters and gauges<br>Concepts of Fahrenheit temperature | | |
| | | Travel and Transportation | Traffic signs<br>Traffic symbols<br>Car parts vocabulary<br>Identifies car parts<br>Application for driver's instruction permit<br>Auto safety rating scale<br>Gas mileage and cost<br>Mileage table<br>Bus schedule and map of route<br>Road map |
| Vocational | Attitude rating scale<br>Personality rating scale<br>Responsibility and self-discipline rating scale<br>Job interests and aptitudes<br>Health and physical problems/handicaps<br>Application for a social security number<br>Choosing a career<br>Employment signs<br>Employment vocabulary<br>Employment abbreviations<br>"Help wanted" advertisements<br>Simple application for employment<br>Complex application for employment<br>Job interview questions<br>Job interview preparation rating scale<br>Job interview rating scale<br>W-4 form<br>Future time on clock<br>Past time on clock<br>Time duration on clock<br>Payroll deductions<br>Federal income tax return—Form 1040A<br>Unemployment compensation form | Food and Clothing | Food vocabulary<br>Food preparation vocabulary<br>Basic recipe directions<br>Food labels<br>Conversion of recipes to different servings<br>Foods for a daily balanced diet<br>Computes cost of purchasing different quantities<br>Food quantity at best price<br>Personal sizes of clothing<br>Clothing labels |
| | | Oral Communication and Telephone Skills | Speaking skills<br>Speaking skills rating scale<br>Listening skills<br>Listening skills rating scale<br>Telephone<br>Telephone book<br>Telephone Yellow Pages |

*Source*: Brigance, A. H. (1981). *Brigance Diagnostic Inventory of Essential Skills*. North Billerica, MA: Curriculum Associates. Copyright © 1981, Curriculum Associates, Inc. Reprinted by permission.

Because students with mental retardation have many opportunities to experience failure, they can develop poor motivation for learning and set low goals (Balla & Zigler, 1979). They also learn not to trust their own solutions and look to others for cues (Zigler & Burack, 1989). Many students with mental retardation display **biased responding**—saying "yes" because they want to please the teacher or hide their confusion (Sigelman et al., 1981).

For Lilly, an eleventh-grader with Down syndrome and mild mental retardation, it is important that her teachers accommodate her slower rate, more concrete style of learning, and low level of confidence in her ability to learn. Lilly, who attends Madison High School, is included in the general education classroom for physical education, art (her favorite class), and home economics.

Grace Fong, Lilly's home economics teacher, makes several accommodations for her. Although Lilly can decode the words in many recipes, directions, and other readings in the class, Grace found that Lilly often does not understand what she is reading. To help Lilly and several other students in her class, Grace uses paired reading and has the students check often for understanding. The students read with partners, stopping at the end of each paragraph or section to discuss that paragraph (or section) and consistently using the cue "What was this mainly about?" Lilly can check for understanding as she reads instead of reading the entire assignment and then realizing that she has not understood. When reading recipes and directions for sewing, the pairs stop after each ingredient or direction and discuss what to do. Grace finds that this approach helps to increase not only Lilly's success in comprehending what she reads, but also her confidence in her reading skills. Grace also finds that in the long run, with paired reading, all her students do better (and enjoy the interactions that naturally occur).

## Social Skills

Students with developmental disabilities have friends and participate in social activities but often have difficulties developing friendships. Such difficulties may be due to behaviors that deter interactions or to lack of opportunity (Westling & Fox, 2000). With the move toward inclusive learning communities, students have more opportunities to make friends.

Circles of Friends (Forest & Lusthaus, 1989) is one example of an activity that can promote social support for students with disabilities as they are integrated into general education classrooms. In this activity, each student in the classroom completes a picture of his or her circles of friends, following the steps in Tips for Teachers 5.3.

Some students, particularly those with autism, might seem uninterested in the people around them, seldom making eye contact or initiating or responding to interactions. Students with severe disabilities often engage in isolated inappropriate behaviors such as stereotypic or self-injurious behaviors. **Stereotypic behaviors** include rocking, flapping fingers, twirling or spinning objects, and grinding teeth. **Self-injurious behavior,** which occurs in only 5–15 percent of individuals with severe retardation, may consist of head banging, scratching, or biting oneself and is difficult to understand. One of several theories about why students exhibit these behaviors is that they are a means of communicating or regulating their own level of awareness (Helmstetter & Durand, 1991; Johnson, Baumgart, Helmstetter, & Curry, 1996). Because students are unable to express their desires or dislikes verbally, they express them through their behavior.

## Motor Skills

Some students with mental retardation and most students with developmental disabilities have physical disabilities and also experience delays in sensory and motor development. The physical disabilities that are commonly found among these individuals include cerebral palsy, spina bifida, seizure disorders, hydrocephalus, and cardiovascular disorders. (Chapter 6 discusses physical disabilities in more detail.) Many students with severe disabilities cannot move independently and need assistance from wheelchairs, walkers, and braces. Other students may have limited voluntary movement of any type and may experience difficulty grasping items, holding their heads up, and rolling over.

## Communication Skills

Students with developmental disabilities often have difficulties communicating. Delayed speech and other speech problems are more common in students with severe disabilities than in other students. Additionally, language development may be inhibited or significantly delayed in students who have more limited cognitive abilities on which to build language skills, fewer experiences, and less exposure to activities than their nondisabled peers.

# Tips for Teachers

## 5.3    Providing School Support through Circles of Friends

Circles of Friends (Forest & Lusthaus, 1989) is an activity that can be used when students with disabilities are going to be integrated into general education classrooms. In this activity, each student in the classroom completes a picture of his or her circles of friends, using the following steps:

1. Students draw four circles.
2. In the first circle, students list the people closest to them, the people they love.
3. In the second circle, students list the people they really like (but not enough to put in the first circle).
4. In the third circle, students list groups of people they like or people they do things with (e.g., scouts, soccer team).
5. In the fourth circle, students list people who are paid to be in their lives (e.g., doctor, dentist).

After students have completed their own circles of friends, the teacher describes the circles for a fantasy person who is similar to the student who will be joining the class. For example, a student might have only Mom listed in the first circle, with the second and third circles empty. In the fourth circle are a number of doctors and therapists. Through discussion, the teacher and students talk about how the student must feel and how this fantasy person is similar to the student with disabilities who is going to join the class. Fi-

How might the Circles of Friends activity contribute to providing social support for students with disabilities in your classroom?

nally, the teacher and students plan how they can become part of the circles of friends for the student with disabilities through such activities as classroom ambassadors, telephone buddies, lunch buddies, and reading buddies.

*Source:* Adapted from Forest, M., & Lusthaus, E. (1989). Promoting educational equality for all students: Circles and maps. In S. Stainback, W. Stainback, and M. Forest (Eds.), *Educating all students in the mainstream of regular education.* (pp. 45–57). Baltimore: Brookes.

---

For many students with mild mental retardation, speech problems also are mild and can be corrected with help from a speech and language pathologist. Mental retardation affects not only how students communicate, however, but also the content and quality of their communication. These students use shorter, less complex sentences with fewer relative clauses and words with more concrete meanings. They also exhibit poorer recall of sentences (Bernstein & Tiegerman, 2002).

Students with severe disabilities might not acquire speech, or their speech might be difficult to understand for people who do not interact with them often (Parette & Angelo, 1996). It is important to realize that a lack of speech does not preclude communication. Communication can occur through gestures, facial expressions, eye blinks, and behavior and through alternative and augmentative communication (such as the high- and low-technology communication devices introduced in Chapter 3). Low-technology devices can involve pictures or drawings at which the student points to convey a message. High-technology devices can provide voice output (speech synthesizers) and can be programmed with many messages.

A **communication board** is one example of augmentative communication. The essential elements are the board itself and the symbols or pictures. The board can be made of sturdy paper or a board, or it can be a regular or simplified computer keyboard or a computer screen. The symbols or symbol systems that are selected depend on the learner and the environment in which he or she lives. Symbols should be selected according to what students need and want to communicate. In constructing communication boards, Lewis (1993) suggests that the following questions need to be addressed:

● What choices will the student be able to make?
● How will the choices be represented on the board?
● How will the student make his or her selections?

● How many choices will be available and how will they be arranged on the board?
● How will the communication board be constructed?

Figure 5.2 presents examples of common symbol systems, which include Core Picture Vocabulary (Johnston, 1985), Talking Pictures (Leff & Leff, 1978), Pic Syms (Carlson, 1984), Oakland Schools Picture Dictionary (Kirstein & Bernstein, 1981),

=== FIGURE 5.2 ===

**Picture Symbol Systems for Communication Boards**

| Core Picture Vocabulary | Talking Pictures | Pic Syms | Oakland | Picture Communication Symbols | Blissymbols |
|---|---|---|---|---|---|
| Man | | | | | |
| Wash | | | | | |
| Want | No symbol | | | | |
| Hello | No symbol | | No symbol | | |
| Happy | No symbol | | | | |
| House | | | | | |
| Car | | | | | |

*Source:* Glennen, S. (1992). Augmentative and alternative communication. In G. Church and S. Glennen (Eds.), *The handbook of assistive technology* (p. 100). San Diego, CA: Singular Publishing Group. Reprinted with permission.

# T e c h T a l k

## Boardmaker

Boardmaker (Mayer-Johnson, Inc., 1-800-588-4548, www.mayer-johnson.com) is a software program that allows teachers to create and print communication boards, using the Picture Communication Symbols (Johnson, 1985). This software is available for both Macintosh and PC systems. The boards are easy to design by using either a menu at the top of the screen or an index of the words for the pictures or by clicking on the find button at the bottom of the screen and typing in the desired word.

More than 3,000 picture communication symbols are available. The arrangement of the pictures can be modified. Each picture has the written word. The written word for each picture can be deleted, or it can be displayed in English, Spanish, or another language. This program provides a simple and efficient way for teachers to construct and modify communication boards.

*Source:* Adapted from Lewis, R. B. (1993). *Special education technology: Classroom applications* (pp. 388–389). Pacific Grove, CA: Brooks/Cole.

Courtesy of Mayer-Johnson, Inc.

Picture Communication Symbols (Johnson, 1985), and Blissymbols (Bliss, 1965).

This chapter's Tech Talk describes a computer program (the Boardmaker) that teachers can use to create communication boards.

Communication is an important area for students with developmental disabilities because it gives them some control over their environment and a way to fulfill their wants and needs. It is also an important key to being socially accepted.

The students in Robert Hernandez's seventh-grade class imitated the noises that Jason, a student with autism, made. Robert and the special education teacher discussed with the class how Jason is learning to communicate. "Right now he does not use words, but he makes noises and uses his communication board. The noises he makes are [the way] he

communicates, so . . . you need to respect this communication and not make fun of it. Your job is to listen closely and watch the communication board to learn what Jason is saying."

Ideas to help students with developmental disabilities develop communication skills are discussed in Tips for Teachers 5.4.

Approximately 40 percent of children with autism do not speak, and many others use **echolalia,** a repeating of what was said without necessarily understanding the meaning (Powers, 1989). For students with mild retardation, speech difficulties most often occur in articulation and include omissions, substitutions, or distortions of sounds (Beirne-Smith et al., 1998). Speech and language problems are the most frequently diagnosed secondary disability for students with mild retardation (Beirne-Smith et al., 1998).

# Tips for Teachers

## 5.4 Helping Students Develop Communication Skills

Following are areas to consider when assisting students with mental retardation and severe disabilities to develop their communication skills.

### Reason to Communicate

By anticipating the needs of students with mental retardation and severe disabilities, we often deprive them of reasons to communicate. We need to create situations that motivate students to communicate. An example might be to "accidentally" forget to give them their lunch tickets when the rest of the class receives their tickets or to have every student tell you about the drawing they just did before they can go out to recess. Working on communication skills during everyday activities is known to significantly increase the students' desire to communicate.

### Mode of Communication

We need to make sure that students have a way, as well as a reason, to communicate. If your students do

not use speech, they should have an augmentative communication device. If your students do not have a mode of communication, talk with the school's speech and language pathologist or inclusion specialist about developing or purchasing one.

### Way to Make Choices

Self-stick notes provide a quick and easy way to give students with disabilities on-the-spot choices (choosing a word to fill in the blank, choosing a color) to facilitate their participation in class. Just write the choices on the notes and stick them on the students' desks so that they can make the choices.

To help students choose a partner, take pictures of all the students in the class (or use individual class photos) and paste them in a little book or on a board, so that the student with a disability can choose the person with whom he or she wants to work on a class assignment.

## Identification and Assessment of Students with Developmental Disabilities

Before the passage of the Individuals with Disabilities Education Act (IDEA) in 1975, many students with developmental disabilities were not allowed to attend public schools. This federal legislation required that educational services be provided for all students, including students with severe and profound retardation and severe disabilities. One result was the need for better methods of identification and assessment for educational purposes. With the passage of IDEA amendments in 1986 (P.L. 99–457), these children became eligible to receive special education services as infants and toddlers and in preschool (see Chapter 1).

For students with all but mild mental retardation, initial identification is usually a medical diagnosis made at birth or shortly thereafter. For students with mild mental retardation, initial identification often occurs during preschool when the child's rate of development in cognitive, language, and motor skills is not typical. For these students, the emphasis is on developmental and educational assessment, which usually includes measures of general intelligence and measures of adaptive behavior.

Although intelligence tests are still used to determine whether students have developmental disabilities, a number of concerns have been raised. First, it can be difficult to know whether the tests accurately reflect the students' abilities, particularly given their difficulty with communication and their delayed responses. Second, there is continuing concern regarding cultural influences and biases in tests of intellectual functioning (Baca & Cervantes, 1998). In 1984, the California courts ruled that standardized IQ tests (e.g., Weschler, Stanford-Binet, and Leiter) could not be used to determine eligibility for special education for African American students (*Larry P. v. Riles*, 1984). Factors influencing student performance on intelligence tests include family history and home life, duration of study in the United States, language proficiency, socioeconomic status, prior educational experiences, and cultural background (Cuccaro, 1996). Emphasis continues to move toward a more functional definition, with intellectual functioning seen as only one aspect to consider in determining developmental disabilities.

Another area that is used to determine evidence of developmental disability is the student's adaptive behavior. One frequently used adaptive behavior scale is the second edition of the AAMR Adaptive Behavior Scale—School (Lambert et al., 1993), which includes domains for both adaptive and social behaviors (see Table 5.2).

---

## TABLE 5.2

### Domains and Subdomains of the AAMR Adaptive Behavior Scale—School

---

**Part One**

I. Independent Functioning
   A. Eating
   B. Toilet Use
   C. Cleanliness
   D. Appearance
   E. Care of Clothing
   F. Dressing and Undressing
   G. Travel
   H. Other Independent Functioning

II. Physical Development
   A. Sensory Development
   B. Motor Development

III. Economic Activity
   A. Money Handling and Budgeting
   B. Shopping Skills

IV. Language Development
   A. Expression
   B. Verbal Comprehension
   C. Social Language Development

V. Numbers and Time

VI. Prevocational/Vocational Activity

VII. Self-Direction
   A. Initiative
   B. Perseverance
   C. Leisure Time

VIII. Responsibility

IX. Socialization

**Part Two**

X. Social Behavior

XI. Conformity

XII. Trustworthiness

XIII. Stereotypical and Hyperactive Behavior

XIV. Self-Abusive Behavior

XV. Social Engagement

XVI. Disturbing Interpersonal Behavior

---

*Source:* Lambert, N., Nihira, K., & Leland, H. (1993). *AAMR Adaptive Behavior Scale—School: Examiner's manual* (2nd ed.). Austin, TX: PRO-ED. Reprinted with permission.

---

Educational assessments are also used to determine instructional goals and objectives for individual students. According to Westling and Fox (2000), the process of determining instructional needs includes the following:

- Collecting information from existing records
- Interviewing parents to determine educational goals
- Using adaptive behavior scales, activities, and skill lists to help decide students' needs
- Conducting ecological inventories of the students' learning environments

**Functional assessments** determine the skills needed to complete a particular activity or task. **Ecological inventories** assess the different skills a student needs in his or her specific environments. Related service providers also assess the student's speech and physical needs (including vision and hearing, if necessary). The needs and strengths that are determined by these assessments are then incorporated into the student's IEP goals and objectives or benchmarks.

For all students, but particularly for students with developmental disabilities, parents play an important role in assessment. This is evident in IDEA from the emphasis that is placed on the role of parents in identifying and assessing students with disabilities and in planning for the students' individual education programs. Classroom teachers can also benefit from parent input when these students are included in their classrooms.

When Anne Kiernan, a third-grade teacher, learned that she was going to have a child with autism in her class, she insisted on sitting down with the parents before school started to learn more about the student's strengths and weaknesses. She said, "I wanted to know from John's parents what John was like, . . . some of [his] habits, what works for them, what doesn't work, and what . . . he like[s]. Not to find out negative things—just to talk with them. It was very helpful."

No one knows the student better than his or her family. Remember that the family's cultural background influences their perception and attitudes about disabilities. An understanding of people's diverse views may be helpful to you before you meet with parents.

## Instructional Guidelines and Accommodations for Teaching Students with Developmental Disabilities

Teachers who have students with developmental disabilities in their classrooms are asked to participate in the development of the students' educational plans, work with the students, and communicate and work with the paraprofessionals and specialists who provide support. Douglas Akers, a fifth-grade teacher, has been working for several months with Amy, a student with Down syndrome and moderate retardation who is being included in general education classes for the first time. Reflecting about Amy entering his class, Doug comments:

> I wanted to establish a good rapport with Amy. I wanted her to take directions from me, . . . not just to rely on her aide or the special education teacher. I wanted Amy to develop a relationship with me and feel comfortable coming to me or the other students for assistance. I knew this would take time because she has always been in a self-contained special education class. But now she does come to me with her work and with questions.

The instructional guidelines and accommodations discussed here will help you to include students with developmental disabilities in your class and to develop a social support network that will facilitate these students' success.

## Role of the General Education Teacher

With the move toward inclusive schools, the roles of special education and general education teachers are less clearly defined. The role of the general education teacher is to be involved in and problem-solve adaptations and curriculum modifications for all students. In an observational study of fifteen elementary students with severe disabilities and fifteen general education students (Logan & Malone, 1998), results suggest that more individualized instructional supports were provided for the students with severe disabilities, including more one-to-one and small-group instruction that was done in coordination with the special education staff.

> Despite the movement toward inclusion, fewer than 10 percent of students with mental retardation and severe disabilities are educated primarily in general education classrooms. Thirty-five states use separate classrooms for educating more than half the students with mental retardation.

Chris Johnson is a good example of a teacher whose role changed as he worked with a student with disabilities. Chris remembers his reaction on hearing that he would have Darrell, a student with mild mental retardation, in his eighth-grade applied math class: "One of my main concerns was what am I going to do for Darrell? How am I possibly going to teach him anything? I don't have a special education degree. I feel as if I need one in order to teach him. How is Darrell going to fit in as a member of the class?"

To alleviate these feelings, Chris met with Darrell's special education teacher, Martha Anderson. They reviewed the applied math curriculum in relation to Darrell's IEP goals and objectives. What they quickly realized was that many of Darrell's goals (including skills in measurement, making change, and using fractions and percentages) could be met within the general curriculum.

Each week, Chris discussed the activities and assignments with Martha, and she gave him ideas for modifications. Once a week, Martha worked in the room with Chris so that she could keep up with the curriculum and Darrell's progress. At the end of the first month, Chris said,

> Darrell is a member of our class, just like any of the [other] students. He works on math assignments, although I usually modify them by giving him less to complete, by allowing him to use manipulatives and a calculator, and in some cases giving him different assignments from the other students. What I have come to appreciate is that Martha is there to assist me.

One of the teacher's most important roles is to take ownership of students with disabilities by demonstrating that these students are members of the class. When this happens, students with disabilities develop a sense of belonging and being accepted. The need for this sense of belonging is part of the reason that spending only part of the day in class might not work for some students with developmental disabilities. Schnorr (1990) found that part-time integration negatively affected the acceptance of a student with a severe disability as a class member. For Chris and his class, Darrell was just another member of the applied math class.

## Planning Systems

Planning, which is critical for all students, is particularly so for students with developmental disabilities, whose learning goals may differ from those of other students in the class. One planning system is the planning pyramid, introduced in Chapter 7 (Schumm et al., 1994). In the example in Chapter 7, Jeannette Robinson planned a unit on weathering and erosion (refer to Figure 7.6).

As she planned, Jeannette wrote in the base of the pyramid what she wanted *all* students to learn. This goal was appropriate for all the students in her class that year, but when Jeannette taught this unit the next year, Steven, a student with autism and limited language and cognitive skills, and Sandra, a student with mild mental retardation, were in her class. During weekly planning time, Jeannette talked about the unit with the inclusion specialist and assistant who supported Steven and Sandra. They decided that Steven's content goals would be to identify three types of weather (i.e., sunny, rainy, and snowy) and the type of clothing worn in each type, and Jeannette noted these specific goals on the unit planning sheet (see Figure 5.3).

Although Steven would participate in a number of the activities planned for the unit and continue to work on his general language and social goals (e.g., working with others and sharing, communicating wants and feelings), the assistant would work with him on these content goals. In discussion, Jeannette and the team decided that, for Sandra, a more limited

—— FIGURE 5.3 ——

### Planning Pyramid with Modifications for a Student with Significant Disabilities

| What some students will learn. | • How earth looked during Ice Age<br>• Disasters caused by sudden changes<br>• Geographic examples of slow and fast changes |
|---|---|
| What most students will learn. | • Compare and contrast weathering and erosion<br>• How humans cause physical and chemical weathering<br>• Basic types of rocks |
| What ALL* students should learn. | • Basic components of earth's surface<br>• Forces that change crust are weathering and erosion |

\* Steven— identify 3 types of weather and the appropriate clothing.

—— FIGURE 5.4 ——

### MAPS Questions and Ideas Generated for Tyrone

1. **What is the individual's history?**

   Tyrone developed meningitis shortly after birth, which resulted in brain damage. He learned to walk and talk much later than normal.

2. **What is your dream for the individual?**

   Tyrone will find a job in the community, where he can interact with many people, and a place to live with friends.

3. **What is your nightmare?**

   Tyrone will be alone after we (parents) pass away.

4. **Who is the individual?**

   Tyrone is a young man who loves music and talking to people. He is an only child. He is a sophomore in high school. He loves sports. He gets lonely and bored when alone for long periods of time.

5. **What are the individual's strengths, gifts, and abilities?**

   He loves to laugh and smiles a lot. He works hard. He has a great sense of humor. He's energetic. He is sensitive to others' moods.

6. **What are the individual's needs?**

   He needs friends his own age with whom to do things. He needs to be more assertive and ask for help, when necessary. He needs to be more independent in food preparation and in getting around the community.

7. **What would the individual's ideal day at school look like and what must be done to make it happen?**

   A Circle of Friends should be done with Tyrone so that he has friends to meet when he gets off the bus and to hang out with during lunch and breaks. Tyrone should participate in some community-based instruction. Tyrone should take a Foods class.

depth of learning and modified quizzes would be appropriate accommodations. You should find the planning pyramid helpful for planning lessons and units and making instructional decisions about how you can accommodate the various learners in your classroom.

When working with a student with severe disabilities, you might also participate in planning for the student's long-range goals, which are incorporated into the IEP. The **McGill Action Planning System (MAPS)** (Lusthaus & Forest, 1987) is one example of such a planning system. The purpose of this planning activity is to foster relationships to improve the quality of life for people with severe disabilities and to facilitate participation in inclusive settings such as a general education classroom.

In the MAPS process, the student, his or her family and friends, and special and general educators establish a team. Because peers are important to the process, students from the classroom generally participate in the team (Vandercook, York, & Forest, 1989). This team answers seven questions, using them to brainstorm methods to plan the student's future in an inclusive environment. Answers to the seven questions help to determine the goals and objectives. Figure 5.4 provides an example of the MAPS

questions and ideas for Tyrone, a high-school student with severe mental retardation.

Choosing Outcomes and Accommodations for Children: A Guide to Educational Planning for Students with Disabilities (COACH) is another planning system for developing an appropriate educational program for students with severe disabilities in the general education setting (Giangreco, Cloninger, & Iverson, 1998). COACH focuses on individualization, family participation, and the active involvement of related service providers.

For students with developmental disabilities, it is important to plan beyond the students' school experiences, particularly as these students reach middle and high school. Planning for their transition into adult life in terms of vocation and adult living are critical to their success (Hutchins & Renzaglia, 1998; Wehmeyer, 1995). Person-centered planning (Miner & Bates, 1997) builds from such techniques as MAPS and Circles of Friends to provide long-range planning and transition. As part of the process, the

student's circle of support map is developed by the student, family, educators, and other key support persons. Figure 5.5 presents the map for Robert, a 17-year-old student with moderate mental retardation. This process actively involves the student in planning, as is mandated by the IDEA.

## Functional Assessment, Discrepancy Analysis, and Task Analysis

Functional assessment, discrepancy analysis, and task analysis help to determine the skills the student needs to reach established goals. In a functional assessment, each goal or activity is broken into steps or subskills, and the student's present performance level is determined for each subskill or step in the activity. For example, the first column of Figure 5.6 shows the steps involved in the activity of getting to school, with the student's performance noted in the second column.

A **discrepancy analysis** reviews each specific step or skill and determines how the student does the step

> Adults with mental retardation and severe disabilities, most of whom lived in institutions before the 1970s, now live in group homes and supported apartments. In a supported apartment arrangement, the person chooses his or her roommates, and the apartments are located in different areas of the community.

---

FIGURE 5.5

### Robert's Circle of Support Map

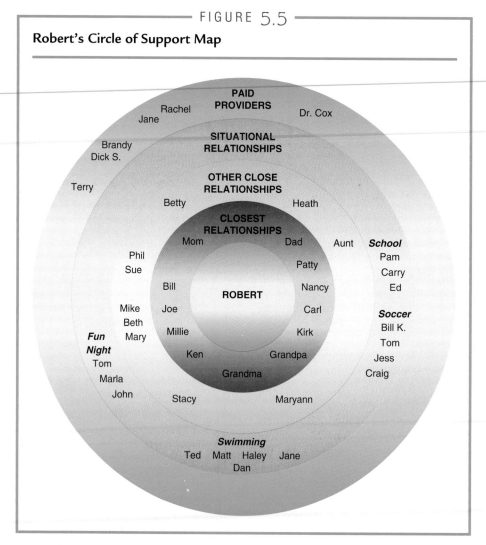

Source: Miner, C. A., & Bates, P. E. (1998). Person-centered transition planning. *Teaching Exceptional Children, 30*(1), 66–69.

or skill, compared to nondisabled peers (the third column in Figure 5.6). If the student is unable to perform a step or skill (i.e., a discrepancy exists), then the teacher determines whether the student should be taught that particular step or skill or whether an adaptation should be made to help the student perform the skill. The fourth column in Figure 5.6 shows the adaptations and instruction that will occur as a result of the functional assessment and discrepancy analysis.

Next, a **task analysis** (a further breakdown of each individual step or skill, with the necessary adaptations) is used as a guide to teach the step or skill to the student. For example, the 60-Second Lesson describes how to develop a picture task analysis.

The same goals can be assessed across the different environments in which the activities occur. Mary Hinson, Marta's high-school job developer, assessed "arriving and getting started" as part of placing Marta in her first job in an office: putting on labels and doing simple packaging. For a number of steps, the adaptations made at school could easily be made at work.

How might functional assessments have aided in placing this student in a work setting? How would you identify the skills the student needs to succeed? What opportunities does this learning situation provide for the functional practice of these skills?

## FIGURE 5.6

### Functional Assessment/Discrepancy Analysis

**Student:** Marta is an eighth-grade student with moderate mental retardation and cerebral palsy.

**Activity:** Arriving at school

| Steps of the Activity | Student Performance | Discrepancy Analysis | Teach or Adapt |
|---|---|---|---|
| 1. Arrives at school by bus | + | | |
| 2. Goes to locker | − | Cannot propel herself | Peers will wait by bus |
| 3. Opens locker | − | Doesn't remember combination | Use key lock |
| 4. Gets notebooks, etc. out | − | Can't reach items | Put items in backpack on hook |
| 5. Hangs out/does hair until class | − | Doesn't initiate conversations | Develop "Circles of Friends" |
| 6. Goes to class when bell rings | − | Can't self-propel that far | Ask classmates to help |
| 7. Listens to announcements in homeroom | + | | |
| 8. Raises hand to indicate will eat lunch | + | | |
| 9. Goes to first hour when bell rings | − | Doesn't know which class is at this time | Teach to review a picture schedule and ask for help |

Code: + = can do step　　− = cannot do step

## making a Difference

### Developing a Picture Task Analysis

Picture task analyses, by providing visual cues of the steps of a task, enable students with mental disabilities to gain meaningful skills and independence. A picture is taken of each step in a task. Then the pictures are glued (in sequential order) in a manila folder, with a number under

## The 60-second Lesson

each picture. Laminating the whole folder helps to preserve the photographs. An erasable pen enables students to cross off pictures as the steps are completed. How might you develop a picture schedule (see Figure 5.2) for Marta?

For more information, see "Using a Picture Task Analysis to Teach Students with Multiple Disabilities," by W. Roberson, J. Gravel, G. Valcante, and R. Maurer 1992, in *Teaching Exceptional Children, 24*(4), 12–16.

## Partial Participation

When you look at a skill to determine whether a student can do it, it is important to remember the concept of **partial participation,** which assumes that an individual has the right to participate in all activities to the extent possible (Downing, 1996; Falvey, 1995). An opportunity to participate should not be denied because a person cannot independently perform the needed skills; instead, individualized adaptations should be developed to allow participation and learning, even of only part of the skill. Ferguson and Baumgart (1991) stress the importance of active partial participation by having students make choices, manipulate objects, or communicate. Active participation not only helps to maintain students' physical health, but also enhances their image, as peers see them partaking in a meaningful activity. Say, for example, that a class is working on writing sentences using correct punctuation. A classmate randomly selects three small pictures and places them on Heather's desk. Heather, a student with a severe disability, has to reach out and point to one of the pictures. Her goals are to reach and point, to look at her peer, and to make decisions in a timely fashion. The peer then holds up the picture for the class to see. The class writes a sentence about it, and Heather must answer a question about it.

## Curriculum Adaptations

An important component of adapting materials or instruction is joint planning by the special education and classroom teachers. When Jeannette Robinson heard that she was going to have two students with developmental disabilities in her classroom (Steven and Sandra, discussed earlier in this chapter), she was concerned that she would be responsible for writing lesson plans and making all the adaptations. She felt overwhelmed until she realized that it was a team process and that the special education teacher and assistant would help her

plan. She said, "I'm so relieved. I feel much more positive now. I didn't know how I was going to do it." Realizing that it is a team process and that everyone has knowledge to contribute is important.

The following hierarchy of curriculum-modification questions can be used to help guide teams in making decisions about a student's participation:

1. Can the student participate in the unmodified activity?
2. Can the student participate in the activity with adapted materials, support, or modified expectations?
   - Can the student participate with peer support or with extra adult support?
   - Do materials need to be modified or substituted?
   - Do expectations of the activity (e.g., learning goals, amount of work, method of evaluation) have to be modified?
3. Can the student participate in this activity by working on embedded communication, motor, or social skills?

If the answer to these questions is "no," the team might consider a parallel activity related to the student's educational priorities (as Jeannette and her team did for Steven when planning the unit on erosion and weathering). Table 5.3 presents examples of curriculum for students with developmental disabilities.

## Peer Support and Peer Tutoring

Another important component of teaching accommodations is the development of peer support and peer tutoring. Peers may be the most underrated and underused human resource available in general education classrooms. Nondisabled peers are often creative problem solvers and staunch supporters of students with developmental disabilities (Hendrickson et al., 1996; Salisbury et al., 1995; York & Vandercook, 1991).

—— TABLE 5.3 ——

### Adapted Curriculum Outcomes for Students with Developmental Disabilities

| Grade Level | Typical Outcomes | Adapted Outcomes |
|---|---|---|
| Grade 2: Reading | Learn 10 words per week, and be able to spell them correctly. | Learn 5 grocery words (e.g., apple, shampoo), and be able to recognize them. |
| Grade 4: Writing | Read a story and write a report, using correct grammar, punctuation, and spelling. | Listen to taped story, and record a personal reaction to the story. |
| Grade 6: Social Studies | Locate all continents on a map, and name three countries per continent. | Locate own continent on a map, and name three countries on own continent. |

*Source:* Adapted from Wehman, P. (1997). *Exceptional individuals in school, community, and work* (p. 131). Austin, TX: PRO-ED.

Longewill and Kleinert (1998) provide some guidelines for setting up a peer tutoring program in a middle or high school as well as ideas on how to modify assignments for students with more significant disabilities (see Tips for Teachers 5.5). It is important, however, that students not always take the role of "helping" a student with disabilities, which can get in the way of their developing a friendship. Initially, peer support and tutoring require adult facilitation as needs and strategies are identified, but adult participation should be reduced as friendships and tutoring routines develop. Teachers using Circles of Friends for a student with disabilities often find that classmates want to add the student to their circles and try to finish their work early so that they can work with the student. Some teachers find that so many students volunteer, they must use a sign-up sheet, limiting the number of times per month peers

## Tips for Teachers

### 5.5 Using a Peer-Tutoring Program for Students with Significant Disabilities in a Middle or High School

1. Collaborate with your school administration and special education staff to create a peer-tutoring course for which the students can receive credit.
2. Inform counselors, faculty, and students of the course, and make sure it uses the typical process for enrollment.
3. Do not enroll more peer tutors than there are students to be tutored.
4. Before the students begin tutoring, teach them strategies that they can use to support their tutees.
5. Some students might want to participate in some disability awarenesss training before they begin tutoring.
6. Have tutors develop lists of ideas on how to adapt classes and assignments for their tutees:
   - In art, instead of drawing pictures, have tutees paste pictures from magazines.
   - For a written report, use picture symbols arranged in order and integrate them with written text, depending on the tutee's abilities (symbols could be from the tutee's communication system).
   - For an oral report, have the tutee and tutor develop a poster or collage that they can explain.
   - For community-based living projects, assist the tutee in learning about budgeting, nutrition, and shopping.
7. Have students report every one to two weeks on their tutee's progress and reflect on their own learning.
8. Provide opportunities for cooperative learning as well as tutor/tutee learning situations.

*Source:* Adapted from Longwill, A. W., & Kleinert, H. L. (1998). The unexpected benefits of high school peer tutoring. *Teaching Exceptional Children, 30*(4), 60–65.

# Tips for Teachers

## 5.6 Peer-Supported Strategy to Promote Classroom Survival Skills for Students with Developmental Disabilities

| Step | Description |
|---|---|
| Step 1 | Peer tutors explain why the classroom survival skills are important to learn. |
| | Example: *"In class when the bell rings, in seat when the bell rings, bring appropriate materials to class, greet the teacher, greet other students, ask questions, answer questions, sit up straight, pay attention to the teacher, acknowledge comments from other students."* |
| Step 2 | Peer tutors give one example for each survival skill. |
| | Example: *"I am going to show you how you can teach yourself to be in class when the bell rings. You need to stop what you are doing outside of the classroom during the recess and come to the class when the bell rings."* |
| Step 3 | Peer tutors give one counterexample for each survival skill. |
| | Example: *"Staying in the cafeteria when the bell rings is **not** being in class when the bell rings."* |
| Step 4 | Peer tutors explain how to count and self-record survival skills. |
| | Example: *"Were you in class when the bell rings? If you were in the class when the bell rings, mark Yes. If not, mark No."* |
| Step 5 | Peer tutors prompt for appropriate survival skills when necessary. |
| Step 6 | Peer tutors provide feedback and praise for appropriate survival skills. |

*Source:* Adapted from Gilberts, G. H., Agran, M., Huges, C., & Wehmeyer, M. (2001). The effects of peer delivered self-monitoring strategies on the participation of students with severe disabilities in general education classroom. *Journal of the Association for Persons with Severe Handicaps, 26*(1), 25–36.

can work with a student. Tips for Teachers 5.6 presents the steps of research-based, peer-supported strategy for students with developmental disabilities.

## Strategies to Support Students in the General Education Classroom

A number of general strategies can be used to support students with developmental disabilities in the general education classroom.

**Increasing a Student's Sense of Belonging**   One key to success is to create a community to which the student with disabilities has a sense of belonging. Frisbee and Libby (1992) suggest the following strategies to increase this sense of belonging:

- Give the student the same things as the other students (e.g., desk, typical seating, locker, name on classroom charts).
- Demonstrate respect for the student by using age-appropriate language and being a good role model.

- Involve the student in the typical classroom routine.
- Work with your educational team and students to find ways for the student to participate actively in classroom activities.
- Consult with specialists for ideas, and express your concerns.
- Encourage students to find ways to increase learning opportunities for classmates who are challenged.
- Promote equality and interactions with other classmates (e.g., remember to use the word "friend" instead of "peer tutor," and say "go together" rather than "take _____ with you."

**Accepting Varied Learning Goals**   The most frequently asked question about inclusion is "How are students going to benefit from my class? What will they get out of it?" Students with developmental disabilities may be working on their own goals during class activities; it is important that these goals, however different, be regarded as meeting valued educational needs. Sean Miller, a high-school biology teacher, says his biggest concern was how to grade the student with mild retardation in his class. He comments, "I didn't know what to do. The student was trying and doing her work, but it wasn't high-school level. I wondered if I gave her a passing grade, was it fair to the other students? We (the special education staff and I) ended up sitting down and reviewing her goals and determining a grade based on that. I was comfortable with that idea."

A sheet that demonstrates the relationship between the IEP goals and the activities in the general education classroom helps everyone understand that individual goals can be met through classroom activities. One example, the IEP Goal–Activity Matrix shown in Figure 5.7, is for Manny, a second-grade student with a moderate mental disability. Across the top of the matrix are the subjects and activities, and down the side are Manny's IEP goal areas. The Xs indicate the logical subject or activity in which Manny will work on his IEP goals during his school day.

**Making Environmental Accommodations** Environmental accommodations are changes made to

What kinds of accommodations should general education teachers consider when students with developmental disabilities are integrated into general education classes?

the physical learning environment so that each student can participate successfully. These changes are often as simple as having a beanbag chair so that a student with cerebral palsy can be on the floor with peers during story time or lifting the legs of a desk a few inches so that a wheelchair fits comfortably.

FIGURE 5.7

**IEP Goal–Activity Matrix**

Student  **Manny**                    Semester  **Fall 1997**

Grade  **2nd grade**                  Teachers  **Ms. Nichols, Mr. O'Brian**

**IEP Goal Areas**                              Subjects/Activities

| | Opening | Reading/ Language Arts | Recess | Math Their Way | Lunch | Science/ Social Studies |
|---|---|---|---|---|---|---|
| Writes name and functional words | | X | | X | | X |
| One-to-one correspondence | | | | X | | X |
| Decision making | X | X | X | X | X | X |
| Initiating communication | X | X | X | X | X | X |
| Functional reading | X | X | | | | X |

**Team Teaching**   Team teaching involves two or more teachers (special and general education) cooperatively teaching a class or particular curriculum or thematic unit. The teachers often have different areas of expertise that build upon each other to make a successful lesson for all students. Team teaching reduces the teacher–student ratio, thereby making small-group instruction more feasible (Vaughn, Schumm, & Arguelles, 1997). Team teaching is discussed further in Chapter 9.

**Cooperative Learning**   Cooperative learning, also discussed in Chapter 9, is an effective instructional method for including students with developmental disabilities (Putnam, 1998; Wilcox et al., 1987). In cooperative learning situations, the class is divided for learning activities into groups that have cooperative goals. Each student has a role, and it is important that each role is valued. Cooperative learning fosters interdependence and helps all involved to develop interpersonal skills (Slavin, 1995). General education teachers need to be comfortable with the idea of having heterogeneous groups for cooperative learning. Hunt, Staub, Alwell, and Goetz (1994) found that having a student with a severe disability in a cooperative group did not in any way hinder the progress of other members.

> Students with mental retardation and severe disabilities need to learn general work habits such as following directions, working with others, accepting feedback and supervision, asking for help, working steadily at a satisfactory rate, doing good work, and completing the work (Kokaska & Brolin, 1985).

**Accommodating Personal Learning Styles**   Accommodating learning styles involves letting students learn and demonstrate what they learn in ways that reflect their individual strengths. Students may share their knowledge through an oral report instead of a written one or by creating a collage about the topic being studied. High-school teacher Lynn Blankenship, who teaches independent living skills, says that because she encourages students to use various methods of demonstrating their knowledge, having Jessica, a student with moderate retardation, worked out well.

**Providing Hands-On Instruction**   Hands-on, or experientially based, instruction relates learning to what students already know and uses real-life activities as teaching tools. This type of instruction provides greater opportunity for students with developmental disabilities to be actively involved. The use of learning centers, math manipulatives, science projects, art projects, and computers are examples of hands-on activities that give students with developmental disabilities the opportunity to participate.

## Providing Opportunities for Functional Practice

In addition to hands-on activities, opportunities for **functional practice** are also important. When practice is relevant, students can easily see the connection between what they are practicing and its use in real life. For example, you can incorporate into reading instruction activities that stress reading for fun or to obtain information needed for daily life. Suggestions include the following:

- Directions (e.g., for cooking, building a model, repairing an appliance)
- Directional orientation and maps
- Menus
- Labels on foods, medicines, and clothing
- Telephone book
- Catalogs and advertisements (for selecting something to order)
- Schedules (e.g., bus, train, television)
- Signs
- Newspapers and magazines

Writing activities also can be centered on daily activities, as follows:

- Writing an email to a friend
- Writing a letter to request something or complain
- Writing a postcard or letter to a relative
- Making a shopping list
- Completing a job application or an application for a library card
- Ordering something by filling out a form
- Writing down a telephone message

Functional math activities include the following:

- Making change
- Counting money
- Making a purchase
- Using a checking account
- Using a credit card
- Budgeting money
- Telling and estimating time
- Reading a calendar
- Reading a thermometer
- Measuring
- Determining weight and height

Students' success in functional activities can often predict the degree to which they will function successfully as adults.

## Encouraging Parental Involvement

Every teacher realizes the importance of parental involvement in a student's education. This involvement is especially important for students with developmental disabilities. Their parents play a key role in determining the students' educational program and the preparation for adult life. Knowing the parents' goals for their child can help everyone work together as a team. The Research Brief presents parents' perspectives on inclusion and curriculum goals for children with severe disabilities.

## research brief

### Parents' Perceptions of Goals for Students with Developmental Disabilities

A frequently asked question is what types of goals students with mental retardation work on in the general education classroom. Parents are key members of the multidisciplinary team that determines what goals are important for the student. Knowing what parents think and feel is important information for school staff.

Hamre-Nietupski, Nietupski, and Strathe (1992) surveyed 68 parents of students (6–21 years old) with moderate or severe/profound disabilities to determine the relative value these parents placed on the following curricular areas: functional life skills (e.g., making simple meals), academic skills (e.g., addition), and development of friendships and social relationships (e.g., sharing games with peers). Parents of students with moderate disabilities ranked the areas' relative value in the following order: (1) functional life skills, (2) academic skills, and (3) friendship/social relationship development. Parents of students with severe/profound disabilities ranked the areas differently: (1) friendship/social development, (2) functional life skills, and (3) academic skills.

A survey conducted in the Los Angeles and Orange County areas of almost 500 parents of students aged 3–22 with significant cognitive disabilities reported that they were more positive about the impact of inclusion on the mutual social benefits for both their child and other children in the classroom and the acceptance and

treatment of their child (Palmer, Borthwick-Duffy, & Widaman, 1998). At the same time, the parents were more apprehensive about the quality of the educational services their child received. Parents were concerned about how meaningful the content was for their child in the general education classrooms, the difficulty in modifying lessons and materials, and the opportunity their child would have to get extra help.

What do parents of nondisabled children think about having a child with a severe disability in their child's class? Giangreco, Edelman, Cloninger, and Dennis (1993) surveyed 81 parents of nondisabled children (grades K–8) about their perceptions of their children having a classmate with a severe disability. The results showed that parents think not only that their children are comfortable interacting with a classmate with a severe disability and that this interaction has a positive effect on their children's social and emotional growth, but also that having a classmate with a severe disability has not interfered with their children's receiving a good education. Overall, the parents thought that having a classmate with a severe disability was a positive experience for their children.

As integration of students with developmental disabilities into general education classrooms increases, it is important that you learn strategies for accommodating these students in your class. You might need to adapt the curriculum or have the students work on goals that are not specified in the curriculum. A key to successful integration is collaboration with and support from the specialists who work with these students. Make time for co-planning and ongoing communication, and you can help to ensure that students are successful and that you feel positive about the learning experiences of all the students in your class.

## summary

- Students with mental retardation and severe disabilities represent a diverse group of individuals with varied learning needs and abilities.
- Although ability levels vary, difficulties often occur in four areas: intellectual functioning and social, motor, and communication skills.
- The causes of mental retardation are unknown in 50 percent of the students with mental retardation, but it is known that many of the causes are preventable.
- An important part of students' success is participation in planning systems, such as the planning pyramid and MAPS.

- Functional assessment and discrepancy analysis are means of determining how students perform a skill and whether the skill should be taught or adapted.
- A change in teaching style to incorporate more hands-on and cooperative learning activities can help you include all students in classroom activities.
- Environmental accommodations, team teaching, cooperative learning, hands-on learning, providing practice in functional activities, and getting parents involved are all strategies to promote students' involvement and learning.

## key terms and concepts

adaptive behavior
autism
biased responding
communication board
deaf–blind
developmental disabilities
developmental period
discrepancy analysis
Down syndrome
dual sensory impairments

echolalia
ecological inventories
environmental accommodations
fetal alcohol syndrome
functional assessments
functional practice
inclusion support teacher or specialist
intellectual functioning
McGill Action Planning System
   (MAPS)

mental retardation
multiple disabilities
partial participation
self-injurious behavior
severe disabilities
stereotypic behavior
systems of support
task analysis

## think and apply

1. Think about Susie's role as an inclusion special-ist in relation to your role as a classroom teacher. If one of Susie's students were to join your class, how would you plan, communicate, and work with Susie so that she could support both you and the student? List the questions you would want to ask Susie before the student joined your class.

2. Review the AAMR's definition of mental retar-dation, and think about two students with men-tal retardation. Decide which level of support they would need. Discuss with a classmate the pros and cons of this type of classification system.

3. Think about a classroom activity, then use the hierarchy of curriculum-modification questions to determine how a student with mental retar-dation and severe disabilities could participate in the activity.

4. ABLEDATA is a service with information about more than 20,000 assistive technology products and related services. Call 1-800-227-0216 or fax 301-587-1967 and ask one of the information specialists to research your area of interest. Re-port on what you learned.

5. Watch a student with a severe disability partici-pate in a general education activity. Make a list of all the embedded skills you observe the stu-dent using (e.g., communicating, reaching).

## read more about it

1. Dillon, A. D., Tashie, C., Schuh, M., Jorgensen, C., Shapiro-Barnard, S., Dixon, B., & Nisbet, J. (1993). *Treasures: A celebration of inclusion.* Durham, NH: University of New Hampshire, Institute on Disability.

   *Second in a series of these books, this thought-provoking, emotional photo essay on inclusive school-ing is a celebration for all the families, students, and school personnel who have worked hard for inclusive schooling in New Hampshire.*

2. Drew, C., Hardman, M., & Logan, D. (1996). *Men-tal retardation: A life cycle approach.* Columbus, OH: Merrill.

   *An overview of the field of mental retardation from an educational perspective.*

3. Giangreco, M. F. (1997). *Quick guides to inclusion: Ideas for educating students with disabilities.* Balti-more: Brookes.

   *This book contains five Quick-Guides, written for gen-eral educators, on topics related to inclusive education. Each Quick-Guide gives a list of 10 guidelines-at-a-glance, as well as a page of text discussing each one, and selected references on the topic. The topics covered are:*
   • *Including Students with Disabilities in the Class-room*
   • *Building Partnerships with Parents*
   • *Creating Partnerships with Paraprofessionals*
   • *Getting the Most out of Support Services*
   • *Creating Positive Behavioral Supports*

4. Graziano, A. M. (2002). *Developmental disability: Introduction to a diverse field.* Boston: Allyn & Bacon.

*This book provides an overview of developmental disabilities. It covers etiology, service delivery models, prevention, inclusion, and more.*

5. Tashie, C., Shapiro-Barnard, S., Dillon, A. D., Schuh, M., Jorgensen, C., & Nisbet, J. (1993). *Changes in attitudes, changes in latitudes.* Durham, NH: University of New Hampshire, Institute on Disability.

*First in the series of books mentioned in the first reference, this colorful publication reviews the emerging role of inclusion facilitators and provides, with wit and wisdom, many stories about their experiences.*

6. Tashie, C., Shapiro-Barnard, S., Schuh, M., Jorgensen, C., Dillon, A. D., Dixon, B., & Nisbet, J. (1993). *From special to regular, from ordinary to extraordinary.* Durham, NH: University of New Hampshire, Institute on Disability.

*This third book in the series, written to inspire and support families and professionals working toward inclusive schooling, includes strategies for beginning the inclusion process, meeting challenges along the way, and planning for success.*

7. Wehmeyer, M. L., Sands, D. J., Knowlton, E., & Kozleski, E. B. (2002). *Teaching students with mental retardation: Providing access to the general curriculum.* Baltimore: Paul H. Brookes.

*This book provides guidance, research, and practical strategies to ensure that students with mental retardation have access to the general curriculum. This book includes guidance on developing a person-centered approach to IEPs, suggestions on curriculum modifications and supports, and discussion on empowerment evaluation.*

8. *The following articles provide general education teachers' perspectives about inclusion of students with mental retardation and severe disabilities:*

Giangreco, M. F., Dennis, R., Cloninger, C., Edelman, S., & Schattman, R. (1993). I've counted Jon: Transformational experiences of teachers educating students with disabilities. *Exceptional Children, 59,* 359–372.

Janney, R. E., & Snell, M. (1997). How teachers include students with moderate and severe disabilities in elementary classes: The means and meaning of inclusion. *Journal of the Association for Persons with Severe Handicaps, 22,* 159–169.

Olson, M. R., Chalmers, L., & Hoover, J. H. (1997). Attitudes and attributes of general education teachers identified as effective inclusionists. *Remedial and Special Education, 18,* 28–35.

Smith, R. M. (1997). Varied meaning and practice: Teachers' perspectives regarding high school inclusion. *Journal of the Association for Persons with Severe Handicaps, 22,* 235–244.

Wood, M. (1998). Whose job is it anyway? Educational roles in inclusion. *Exceptional Children, 64,* 181–195.

York, J., & Tundidor, M. (1995). Issues raised in the name of inclusion: Perspectives of educators, parents, and students. *Journal for the Association for Persons with Severe Handicaps, 20,* 31–44.

# suggested websites

**www.unl.edu/spedsev/resource.html**
This website includes links to resources on students with severe disabilities. It covers topics such as autism, deaf–blind/dual sensory, and mental retardation and severe disabilities.

**www.aamr.org/index.shtml**
This website is for the American Association on Mental Retardation. It provides a variety of resources, such as the definition of mental retardation, supported employment, and transition. It also allows the readers to download its newletter and articles from *American Journal of Mental Retardation.*

**www.kidsource.com/NICHCY/severe_disable.html**
This website provides general information about severe and/or multiple disabilities, such as their incidences, characteristics, and educational implications.

**www.usu.edu/teachall/disable.htm**
This website provides useful information on students with multiple and severe disabilities. It introduces programs and interventions and provides links to other related resources on students with multiple and severe disabilities.

**http://aac.unl.edu**
This website provides a variety of resources related to augmentative and alternative communication (ACC), such as information about early intervention in ACC and tutorials for several ACC computer programs.

**www.ndss.org/main.html**
This website is for the National Down Syndrome Society. It provides general information about Down syndrome (e.g., incidences, referral information), research findings, educational implications, and so on.

# Teaching Students with Visual Impairments, Hearing Loss, Physical Disabilities, Health Impairments, or Traumatic Brain Injury

chapter

6

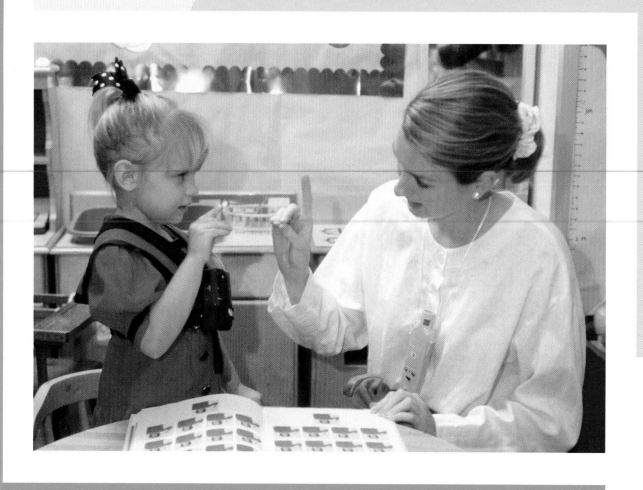

# chapter | outline

# focus | questions

1. How are visual and hearing impairments defined, both legally and functionally?

2. How are physical disabilities and health impairments defined?

3. How can you identify students with possible visual and hearing impairments?

4. What are some areas to assess when developing an education plan for students with physical disabilities, health impairments, or traumatic brain injury?

5. How can you modify instruction and the classroom environment to accommodate the needs of students with visual, hearing, physical, or health impairments or students with traumatic brain injury?

6. How can you foster the acceptance and participation of students with visual, hearing, physical, and health impairments and students with traumatic brain injury in your classroom?

7. What are the roles of the orientation and mobility specialist, the interpreter, the physical or occupational therapist, and the adaptive physical education teacher?

# interview

### Pat Childers and Diane Batson

Pat Childers, a middle-school English teacher, teaches a combination seventh- and eighth-grade class of 30 students. One of Pat's students is Brandy Walters, an eighth-grader who is legally blind and uses braille. Brandy is supported by Diane Batson, a special education teacher for students with visual impairments.

Pat first met Diane and Brandy in the early spring of Brandy's seventh-grade year. Diane scheduled a meeting with each of Brandy's eighth-grade teachers and introduced both herself and Brandy to the teachers. As part of these meetings, Diane and Brandy discussed Brandy's current classes and accommodations and requested information about the upcoming classes for her eighth-grade year. Some of the information that they obtained included the texts that were to be used in each class and the teaching style the teacher preferred. This information allowed Diane to order the necessary texts in braille and/or on tape as well as to assess the modifications that Brandy might need in each of her classes. Just as Diane and Brandy had questions for the teachers, the teachers, including Pat, had several questions and concerns for Diane and Brandy. Pat expressed her concerns about her ability to assist Brandy in learning the class content. She also wondered about the services Diane would provide and the additional equipment that Brandy might need. An open discussion followed, and as the new school year approached, many of Pat's questions and concerns were answered.

At the beginning of the new school year, it was determined that Brandy and Brandy's equipment and technology (computer, printers, braille books, tape player, etc.) would be placed in a corner of the room. As the year progressed, the accommodations in each of the classes were evaluated, and modifications were made. The arrangement of the technology center in Pat's class proved to be unsatisfactory, as Pat felt that Brandy was isolated from the other students. Pat had Brandy moved to a new desk and had her travel to her technology center when she needed her equipment to do her assignments. This change proved to be beneficial as Brandy became more involved with the other students.

By the end of the year, Pat described Brandy's role in the class as

> a part of the gang. The kids never excluded her. She followed the rules just like the rest of them. One time, when

Brandy did not follow a classroom rule, she had to pay the consequences just like the other students. In my room, students who break rules know they have to go out and run a lap around the track. When Brandy had to "do a lap," she took her long cane and used it to independently locate and travel around the track.

Pat, Diane, and Brandy recognized the importance of working as a team. This team effort allowed Brandy to be successful in her classes and built a foundation of mutual respect and trust that would also encourage some flexibility when necessary. This team learned to work together, with Brandy learning to advocate for her needs and Pat and Diane learning to work together. "Being flexible is what made it work." Diane said,

> Sometimes Pat would change a lesson at the last minute. There was no way I could get the books, notes, and other written information brailled in time, so Pat would get a peer to read it to Brandy. Somehow, it would always work because Pat was flexible in her teaching.

Flexibility and organization, Pat learned, are equally important for the class to run smoothly. When she selected reading materials for the class or wrote a test, she shared the information with Diane, giving Diane time to prepare the materials in braille so that Brandy could participate in the activity. In fact, after working together for a year, both Pat and Diane commented that they continue to need to improve their co-planning and organization. For students with visual impairments (and the other types of impairments discussed in this chapter), the teachers' preparation before teaching is what often determines the degree to which the students can be included in the learning activities of the classroom.

# introduction

This chapter provides strategies for teaching and accommodating students with sensory (hearing and vision), physical, and health impairments in your classroom. These students have individual needs (based on the extent of their disabilities) and may work with specialists. This chapter is divided into three sections: visual impairments; hearing loss or deafness/hardness of hearing; and physical disabilities, health impairments, and traumatic brain injury. When you work with these students, you will be part of a team that includes you, the parents, the student, and other teachers and specialists.

 ## Students with Visual Impairments

Both Pat and Diane learned to modify materials and the environment to meet Brandy's needs. This section's discussion of students with visual impairments focuses on instructional strategies you can use to assist these students in your classroom. So that you can better understand these students, the section begins with definitions and types of visual impairments, along with information about the characteristics, prevalence, and identification of students with visual impairments.

## Definitions and Types of Visual Impairments

The visual system is a complex system that includes (1) the surrounding structures such as the skeletal structure of the face, the eyelid, and tear system; (2) the eye globe itself, including each of the parts such as the iris, lens, and retina; and the (3) neurological system, including the optic pathways and vision centers of the brain such as the occipital lobes. In defining this system, many terms have emerged, and they are sometimes used interchangeably in the literature. Generally, the following terms and definitions are used in the field of visual impairment.

The terms visual impairment and **blindness** are generally used as umbrella terms that include all of the following:

1. **Legal blindness** is defined as a **visual acuity** of 20/200 with best correction in the best eye or a visual field loss resulting in a visual field of 20 degrees or less. An individual with good vision can stand 200 feet away to read the largest line on the standard eye chart, while an individual who has a visual impairment of 20/200 must stand only 20 feet away to read the same line. Such an individual would be classified as legally blind and may be eligible for special services. Additionally, how well an individual can see using peripheral or side vision is called **visual field**. When someone experiences a significant visual field loss that leaves the person with a field of 20 degrees or less, he or she is then classified as legally blind (Corn & Koenig, 1996). Some people who are classified as legally blind may be able to read standard print, see and identify the faces of friends and family, view objects at a distance, and discriminate details in objects or pictures. Others may have difficulty with these same tasks and may even have difficulty detecting objects, colors, and the location of light sources. Thus, each individual's visual impairment is unique.
2. **Total blindness** refers to a very small minority of individuals who have visual impairments and who are unable to see anything, including objects or light sources.
3. **Partial sight** is a phrase that was previously used to specify individuals who had a visual acuity in the range of 20/70 to 20/200. This termi-

nology is no longer used as widely as it once was (Corn & Koenig, 1996).

4. **Low vision** is the preferred terminology for individuals who have an impairment and who with standard corrective lenses (glasses) continue to have difficulty accomplishing visual tasks but who can enhance their ability to accomplish these tasks with the use of compensatory visual strategies, low-vision and other devices, and environmental modifications (Corn & Koenig, 1996).
5. **Functional vision** refers to both the way an individual uses his or her vision as well as the amount of vision the individual has. A functional vision exam evaluates how an individual uses his or her vision across multiple environments in varied tasks including academic, self-help, and mobility tasks.

The many causes of visual impairments are usually grouped in the following three areas:

- Structural impairments (i.e., damage or impairment to one or more parts of the visual system)
- Refractive errors (i.e., an inability of the eye to focus the light rays onto the retina correctly)
- Cortical visual impairments (i.e., a problem with the neurological pathways, including reception and interpretation of the visual information) (Stiles & Knox, 1996)

Students with visual impairment may have limited visual acuity, visual field, or both.

Although it is helpful to know the cause of a student's visual impairment, it is more important to know how the student uses his or her vision to accomplish desired tasks.

> In the first five years of life, vision is responsible for between 80 and 90 percent of what we learn. Only 5–10 percent of people who are visually impaired can see nothing at all.

## Characteristics of Students with Visual Impairments

Even though a student with a visual impairment is more like sighted peers than different from them, a visual impairment has an impact on all aspects of development. Its effect on each student varies considerably (Ferrell, 2000; Warren, 1994). Children with visual impairments are thought to have a more difficult time developing basic concepts, owing to their vision loss. The other senses help young children gain information about their world; however, a visual impairment will limit the range and scope of information available to the child. Additionally, a young child will have difficulty learning from the activities of others (incidental learning), as the child might not be able to determine visually what someone, such as a parent, is doing and what the results of the activity are (Ferrell, 1996). Preparing a simple snack is an example of such an activity. A child who has sight can watch a parent retrieve the food from the cupboard or refrigerator, prepare it, and then bring it to the child. A child who is visually impaired might not have access to any of the above information, as the child cannot see the location of the cupboard or refrigerator and might not even know what items are stored there. The child will not know how to prepare the food (e.g., spread peanut butter on bread) and will not know what utensils are needed. Finally, the child might not know how to open and close containers but will need repeated experiences to learn this skill.

Children with visual impairments do typically reach the developmental milestones in each of the five developmental domains of cognition (including concept development), communication, motor (fine and gross), self-help, and social and emotional development. However, students may be delayed in these areas as follows:

- *Concept development:* Areas in which the child has not had a direct experience may be underdeveloped.
- *Communication:* Young children may be delayed in using pronouns (*I, me, you*) or may use them incorrectly. Also some children with visual impairments engage in echolalia (inappropriately repeating words or phrases they have heard) (Andersen et al., 1984; Kitzinger, 1984; Warren, 1994).
- *Motor skills:* Children may be delayed in large motor (gross) skill development and may engage in fewer activities that use visual-motor skills (e.g., running, jumping, and kicking) (Bouchard & Tetreault, 2000). They may also have delays in fine motor skills (e.g., writing, cutting, and grasping small items).
- *Self-help:* If children have not been given responsibilities and guidance, they might not be able to fix a simple snack, independently select clothing, or dress themselves.
- *Social skills:* Children might not know when individuals are speaking to them. Additionally, children might be unable to see how others initiate interactions, how they give nonverbal indications of their feelings and desires, and how peers are responding to interactions and common situations (Buhrow, Hartshorne, & Bradley-Johnson, 1998). Children with visual impairments may also be more isolated than their sighted peers and less involved in after-school clubs, activities, and work opportunities (Sacks & Wolffe, 1998).

It is important to remember that children with visual impairments will need opportunities to directly interact with the environment. These children will need to touch, listen, and explore new objects.

They need to participate actively in all activities, have opportunities to talk about their experiences, and have opportunities to travel to and explore new environments. Teachers should provide additional time for these students to explore and ask questions about their environment and objects within the environment (Ferrell, 1996).

## Prevalence of Visual Impairments

Visual impairments are considered a low-incidence disability, which means that comparatively fewer students have visual impairments than have high-incidence disabilities such as learning disabilities. According to the American Printing House for the Blind (1999), approximately 55,000 students with visual impairments (less than 1 percent of the school population) were counted in the United States in January 1998. Of students with visual impairments, approximately two-thirds have some other disability (often mental retardation). Students with such multiple disabilities, including students who are deaf–blind, are discussed in Chapter 5.

It is estimated that about 25 percent of students with visual impairments are *visual* readers (use large print or some means of enlarging the print), 10 percent are *braille* readers (use braille for reading), and 7 percent are *auditory* readers (listen to tapes or others reading). The remaining students are either *prereaders* (young children) or *nonreaders* who, in addition to their visual impairment, have other disabilities (usually mental retardation) that interfere with their ability to read. According to the American Printing House for the Blind (1999), 48,399 children with visual impairments attend public schools and 4,558 children attend residential schools for children with visual impairments. It is important to realize that the American Printing House for the Blind counts only children who are legally blind, so there are children who do have significant vision impairments (acuity better than 20/200) who are not reported in the above figures.

## Identification and Assessment of Students with Visual Impairments

Certain indicators may help you identify students to refer for evaluation. Following are common characteristics that might indicate visual impairments:

- Red-rimmed, swollen, or encrusted eyes
- Excessive blinking
- Itchy eyes
- Eyes that are tearing
- One or both eyes turn inward, outward, upward, or downward
- Extreme sensitivity to light
- Tilting or turning the head to one side to see an object

- Squinting or closing one eye to see an object
- Covering one eye to view an object
- Thrusting the head forward to view an object
- Headaches, fatigue, or dizziness after doing close work
- Tripping, bumping into objects, or appearing disoriented
- Recurring sties (i.e., inflamed swelling of the gland at the margin of the eyelid)

If you suspect that a student has a visual impairment, you should refer the student to the school nurse and the school or district's teacher of students with visual impairments. To receive educational services from a special education teacher specializing in visual impairments, students must have a documented visual impairment. Written documentation in the form of an eye report is obtained from an ophthalmologist or optometrist.

After a student's visual impairment is identified, the special education teacher who specializes in visual impairments assesses the student's functional vision in multiple environments, including the academic setting. The functional vision assessment will include the student's ability to view at both near and distant points and the student's ability to sustain visual function throughout daily academic settings. Environmental conditions such as lighting, contrasts, optimal print size, seating preference, and visual features of the environment are part of a functional vision assessment. A learning media assessment to determine the student's dominant learning modality should also be included as part of the assessment battery. Compensatory skills assessments may also be appropriate to determine the services needed for the student. **Compensatory skills** include listening skills, orientation and mobility skills, social skills, and daily

living skills. These important skills must be taught in the environments in which they will be used.

## Instructional Guidelines and Accommodations for Students with Visual Impairments

Some general education teachers feel apprehensive when they see the materials and equipment that a student with visual impairments needs in the classroom. Ron Cross, an eighth-grade science teacher, was concerned when Diane and Brandy first indicated the materials and adaptations that Brandy would require. Brandy's equipment included a tape recorder, the science textbook on audiotape and in braille (twelve volumes), and a brailler and braille paper (i.e., the machine and special paper used to write braille). During the year, Diane also provided tactile diagrams of cells and insects (i.e., diagrams that are raised and textured so that the features can be felt). Diane explained that the specialized equipment and materials would enable Brandy to succeed in science class. Diane noted that many of these accommodations, presented in Tips for Teachers 6.1, are also helpful for students who have some usable vision.

**Using Braille and Braille Devices**   Some students may have some usable vision but rely on tactile and auditory information gained by using these learning channels. These students use **braille,** a system of embossed or raised dots that can be read with the tips of the fingers. The basic unit of braille is a cell that contains six dots in two vertical rows of three dots each.

> Louise Braille, who was blind, developed the braille code in France in 1829.

## Tips for Teachers

### 6.1   Modifications of the Environment for Students with Visual Impairments

**Physical Environment**

- Announce your presence and identify yourself (e.g., "Hi, girls, it's Mr. Johnson. May I join your science group to see how you are working together?"). Also announce your departure (e.g., "Thank you, girls, for letting me join you. I'm going to check in with Ryan's group now.").
- Leave doors fully opened or closed, and drawers closed so that the student does not run into them.

- Describe the location of things, especially after rearranging the classroom. Start with the door and travel around the room systematically, noting locations.
- Provide an extra desk or shelf space for the student to store materials.
- Provide access to an outlet for a tape recorder, lamp, or other electrical equipment.
- Allow early dismissal from class so that the student has time to travel to other classes.

*(continued)*

# T i p s  for  T e a c h e r s

## 6.1  Modifications of the Environment for Students with Visual Impairments *(continued)*

**Learning Environment**

- Familiarize students with classroom materials (e.g., give them time to visually or tactually explore a globe before asking them to locate the longitude and latitude of a city).
- Have concrete examples students can touch (e.g., in science, have fossils, not just pictures of fossils).
- Provide lessons with tactual and auditory components, and adapt assignments so that students can participate.
- Consider lighting conditions. Some students do best with natural lighting, others do better with lamps. Backlighting reduces visibility, so avoid standing in front of a window when you present material to the class. Low contrast in materials and between backgrounds and foregrounds reduces visibility, so make sure the contrast is as high as possible.
- Provide written copies of any materials you use on an overhead projector or board. When you use an overhead projector or board, say what you are writing as you do it.
- Allow a peer to take notes for the student, but check that the student is still paying attention and participating.
- Provide opportunities for students to work in groups, especially when the assignment has a visual component (e.g., conducting experiments in science class).
- Modify writing activities as necessary by allowing students to dictate into a tape recorder.

Combining the dots forms letters of the alphabet, numbers, punctuation marks, and contractions. Contractions are used to save space. (For example, the entire word "understand" is written as ⠥⠝⠙⠑⠗⠎⠞⠁⠝⠙, whereas the contraction for "understand" takes up only four cells: ⠥⠝⠙). When students learn braille, they learn to spell both the full and contracted forms. Figure 6.1 gives examples of braille forms.

---

### FIGURE 6.1

**The Braille Alphabet, Numbers, and Punctuation**

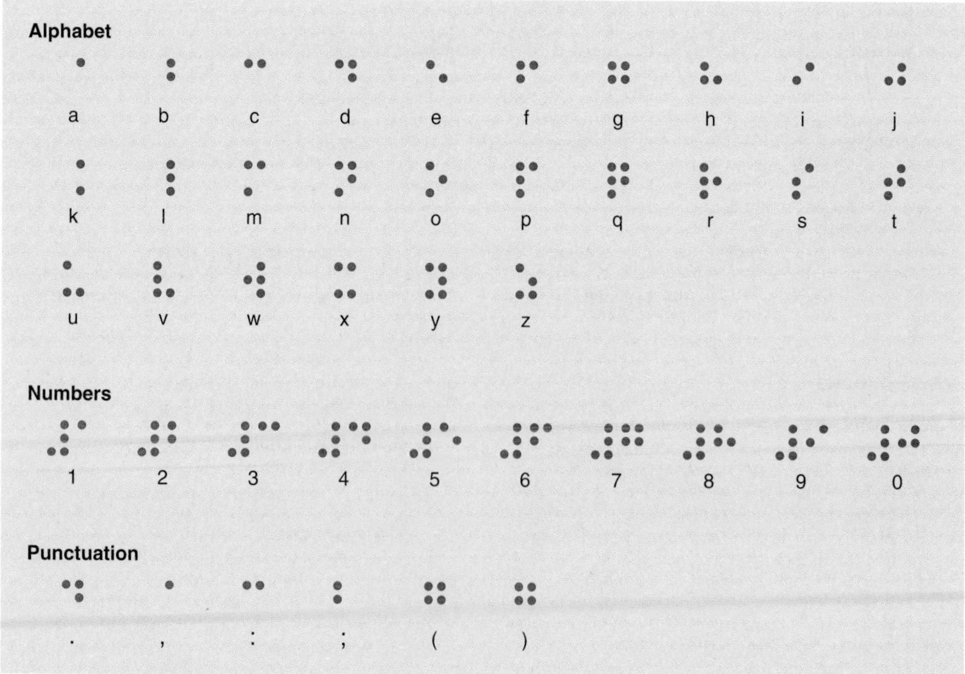

Young children who are exposed to braille before they start school are as ready to learn to read and write as their normally sighted peers (Rex et al., 1994; Swenson, 1999; Wormsley, 1997).

There are several ways to write braille: by using a *brailler* (also called a *braillewriter*), by using a noiseless portable note taker such as Braille 'n Speak or Braille Lite, and by using a slate and stylus. The Tech Talk describes these and other high-tech solutions for students with visual impairments.

**Using Orientation and Mobility Skills**   Students with visual impairments learn, from an orientation and mobility specialist, to travel independently in their environments. The goal is to enable the student to enter any environment, familiar or unfamiliar, and to function safely, efficiently, gracefully, and independently (Griffin-Shirley, Trusty, & Rickard, 2000; Hill & Ponder, 1976). Consequently, it is not unusual for the student and specialist to work not only in school, but also in the community.

# Tech Talk

## High-Tech Solutions for Students with Visual Impairments

High-tech equipment has made integrating the student with a visual impairment into the general education classroom substantially easier. The days of the teacher of students with visual impairments having to spend hours transcribing print to braille or braille to print for the student and the general education teacher to communicate quickly and effectively are disappearing, owing to the multitude of technology options now available. There are several categories of technology for individuals with visual impairment, including speech access, print enlargement, and braille output.

Speech access can be accomplished through a variety of hardware and software options. Some equipment is designed to read text aloud, such as Reading Edge (www.telesensory.com), which scans print directly from text or disk and then reads it aloud. There are computer programs available that read the characters on the computer screen aloud, including JAWS for Windows (www.freedomscientific.com).

Print enlargement can be accomplished for the individual with low vision in several ways. Software such as a program called Zoom Text (www.aisquared.com)

that is specifically designed to enlarge the print can be added to the computer system. Print can also be enlarged through the use of a closed-circuit television (www.telesensory.com), a device with an internal camera that is able to project onto a screen the image of a book, worksheet, or any other object placed on its tray (see picture bottom left).

Special portable computers also facilitate the learning of students with visual impairments who use braille. For example, the Braille 'n Speak (www.nanopac.com/brailleandspeak.htm) is a rechargeable computer, weighing less than a pound, that can serve as a word processor, stopwatch, calendar, and timer (Espinola, 1992). Other products are designed for people who read and write braille, for example, Power Braille (www.cnib.ca/tech_aids) and Braille Mate (www.telesensory.com). The keys correspond to those on a brailler. An individual with a visual impairment can braille on the Braille 'n Speak and, with the speech synthesizer, can hear the material that has been brailled—a letter, word, sentence, paragraph, or entire file at a time. Information can be transferred by connecting the device to an external braille printer, standard printer, modem, or another computer.

Courtesy of Xerox Imaging Systems.

The student needs to develop both **orientation skills** (which include understanding one's own body, one's position in space, and abstract concepts such as the layout of a city block) and **mobility skills** (which include going up and down stairs, crossing streets, and using public transportation). The orientation and mobility specialist or the special education teacher who specializes in visual impairments can help you arrange your classroom to facilitate the student's mobility.

The long cane is the mobility device that is most frequently used by individuals with visual impairments, including children. The cane has a handle (generally black or red), a shaft, which is white, and a red reflective material at the bottom of the shaft. The tip of the cane varies considerably, some being small and others quite large. The type of tip used on the cane will be determined by the orientation and mobility specialist. When students have canes at school, they are responsible for their cane. They have been shown how to store their cane when it is not in use (sometimes by hanging it on a hook, other times by folding it and placing in their bag). The cane is not a toy and is used solely for the purpose of providing the visually impaired traveler with information about the terrain as he or she walks. Instruction from the orientation and mobility specialist is essential for the child with a visual impairment to develop the skills to be a safe and efficient cane user (Griffin-Shirley et al., 2000).

> Dog guides were first introduced in the United States in 1928. Today approximately 2 percent of individuals who are visually impaired travel with dog guides.

### Using Optical, Nonoptical, and Instructional Aids

Students who have difficulty seeing street signs, building numbers, and bus signs might use a *monocular,* an optical aid that magnifies a distant object. Other optical aids include many types of magnifiers—hand-held, lighted, or with a stand—as well as prescription lenses (glasses or contacts). The special education teacher trained to work with students with visual impairments has learned techniques to employ in teaching students to use both distance optical devices such as the monocular and near optical devices such as magnifiers (D'Andrea & Farrenkopf, 2000).

Large print is another option for students with visual impairments. Large-print books are costly and difficult to store, however, and sometimes embarrass the students. Reading large print may also be tiring, in that it requires exaggerated head movements and adaptive seating positions. Optical aids, by contrast, are more compact, less costly, and let students have access to all materials (Barraga & Erin, 2001;

What low-tech and high-tech solutions available for students with vision impairments can students use in your classroom?

Corn & Koenig, 1996; Corn, Wall, & Bell, 2000). The key is to have the teacher who specializes in visual impairments assess the student's needs and abilities in multiple environments and provide appropriate training on all necessary equipment and devices. The Research Brief provides information on the use of hand-held magnifiers and other optical devices used by students with visual impairments.

## r e s e a r c h b r i e f

### Providing Access to the Visual Environment (Project PAVE)

Helen Keller's teacher was a woman named Ann Sullivan Macy who had low vision. In 1924, she was given a pair of glasses that had telescopes in them. With these, she came to realize that "I never knew there was so much in the world to see." These telescopic glasses are just one type of optical aid that children and adults with visual impairments use today. Optical aids include magnifiers (e.g., hand-held, stand), monoculars (like binoculars but only for one eye), and bioptic telescopic systems (glasses with miniature telescopes ground into the lenses). In addition, devices such as the closed-circuit television that magnifies materials placed on its tray onto a television-type screen are included in this group (see the Tech Talk).

Providing Access to the Visual Environment (Project PAVE) is a Tennessee-based project that provides children ages 4 to 21 in Tennessee with evaluations, optical aids, and instruction in how to use the optical aids. Like many other states, Tennessee is getting away from the typical classroom response of providing large-print books for children with low vision. Often, children receive large-print books because parents request these books, or teachers provide them because they can then show that they are "doing something" for the child with low vision.

The efficacy of large print is very questionable. For most children who use these books, there is no increase in reading speeds or comprehension. The large-print books are socially stigmatizing to the child, and many children hide the books or refuse to use them within the general education classroom. Optical aids, by contrast, are more readily accepted by children with visual impairments and their teachers and peers. In addition, these aids provide children with access to distance information (e.g., whiteboards, overheads, bulletin boards) and near information (e.g., worksheets, thermometers, rulers).

Corn, Wall, and Bell (2000) provided children who had low vision (acuity 20/40 to 20/600) with a comprehensive medical eye exam, a special exam called a low-vision evaluation performed by an optometrist or ophthalmologist specifically trained in how to prescribe optical aids and, most important, training in how to use the optical aids within the child's classroom. After a six-month period, the researchers found that the children perceived that they could do more things than they could before receiving the optical aids (e.g., reading maps, reading the newspaper, seeing the overheads). Teachers of visually impaired children also perceived gains. However, parents and general education teachers did not perceive gains for the children. Corn, Wall, and Bell point out that this may have resulted because parents and general education teachers were not involved in the students' learning how to use the optical aids and therefore were not aware of the many types of information the students could now access with the aids.

When it came to oral and silent reading rates and comprehension, there were gains for the children when they used the optical aids. However, these gains were not statistically significant, so the authors could not conclude that the optical aids affected reading rates and comprehension. Students were given only six months to use their optical aids before their reading rates and comprehension were retested, so not enough time may have elapsed between pretesting and posttesting. Nonetheless, the fact that there were gains for all the students is a positive indicator. The fact that they lagged behind typically sighted agemates in reading has implications for general educators. Though general educators need to have expectations for students related to reading, they must also be prepared to provide remediation and adaptations (e.g., pairing students for readings, use of audiotapes for some assignments) if a low-vision student is not reading at a speed comparable to that of classmates.

General educators, parents, and special educators must not assume that all visually impared children need large print and will benefit from it. Many children with low vision are candidates for optical aids and should be evaluated by a doctor trained in low vision. Once optical aids are prescribed, children need to receive instruction in how to use them from a certified teacher of children with visual impairments or an orientation and mobility specialist.

Some aspects to consider when selecting and preparing text is that it is clearly written, has adequate spacing between letters and words, and is on good-quality paper. Reducing the amount of background patterns on the page or providing good contrast between the color of the print and the color of the page is important (Barraga & Erin, 2001). Nonoptical aids also can help students to maximize visual potential. Nonoptical aids are devices that, although not prescribed by a doctor, promote efficient use of vision. Following are some examples of nonoptical aids:

- *Lamp* (provides additional light). Lamps with adjustable necks help to minimize glare.
- *Reading stand* (used to bring printed material closer to the eyes). Also reduces poor posture and fatigue.
- *Bold line paper* (makes writing easier for students with visual impairments). The American Printing House for the Blind manufactures writing paper, graph paper, and large-print paper with music staffs.
- *Hats and visors* (can help to reduce the amount of light). Helpful for students who are sensitive to light (photophobic).
- *Color acetate* (a plastic overlay that darkens print or increases contrast). Yellow is the color favored by many students with visual impairments.

Several nonoptical aids, available mainly from the American Printing House for the Blind, include the following:

- *Cranmer abacus:* an adapted device for the rapid computation of basic math functions, decimals, and fractions
- *Raised line paper:* writing and graph paper with raised lines that can be followed tactually
- *Writing guides:* rectangular templates designed to enable one to accurately place a signature, address an envelope, or write a check
- *Measurement tools:* such as braille clocks, rulers, and measuring kits with raised marks

**Testing Accommodations**    Classroom tests should be modified to make them accessible for students with visual impairments. Modifications may include

## Tips for Teachers

### 6.2 Accommodations for Tests in the General Education Classroom

- Provide test materials in the student's primary learning medium (e.g., braille, large print, audiotape).
- Allow extra time to complete test items.
- As a general rule, give students who read braille twice as much time as other students to complete a test.
- As a general rule, give students who read regular or large print time and a half to complete a test (e.g., if the time limit is 30 minutes, give them 45 minutes).

- Read written instructions to students with visual impairment to minimize the amount of reading they need to do (so as to reduce eye fatigue).
- Present test items orally if doing so will not compromise the integrity of the test.
- Allow students to write answers on the test material instead of a bubble sheet, or provide a large-print bubble sheet.

assigning alternative items, orally reading sections of the test to the student, using large-print or braille answer sheets, providing real objects for items shown in pictures, or coloring pictures to make them easier to see. The special education teacher who works with the student with visual impairments is an excellent resource for suggestions and help with the accommodations. Tips for Teachers 6.2 suggests several simple testing accommodations.

 ## Students with Hearing Loss

You may have the opportunity to teach a student who is deaf or hard of hearing. Nancy Shipka, a fifth-grade math and science teacher who had that opportunity, worked with a special education teacher specializing in hearing loss and a sign language interpreter. Nancy had no idea what to expect when two students who were deaf joined her math and science class. She was concerned not only that the students' academic performance would not measure up to that of the normally hearing students in her class, but also about working with a special education team. With the help of the special education team, Nancy worked with the students to determine where they could clearly see her, the interpreter, the board, and the television monitor. She also learned to face the students directly when speaking and to vary her teaching methods, emphasizing hands-on activities and demonstrations. Nancy also learned that the role of the interpreter is one of facilitating communication. Nancy told the interpreter about difficult concepts ahead of time and also provided written summaries and class notes so that the interpreter would be prepared to sign difficult or technical concepts.

During the year, Nancy asked many questions and learned about students who are deaf or hard of hearing and how to accommodate them in her class. You also may have questions about working with these students. This section explains deafness, hearing loss, and accommodating students with hearing loss.

## Definitions and Types of Hearing Loss

Hearing loss, although often associated with aging, can occur at any time, including from birth. Hearing loss can occur as the result of several factors, including heredity, illness or disease, and excessive prolonged exposure to loud noises. Many of the causes of hearing loss in infants are unknown. Young children who are identified as having hearing losses before they learn language (2 to 3 years of age) are identified as prelingually deaf. This early loss of hearing significantly affects language development.

Hearing loss can occur in one ear (unilateral) or both ears (bilateral). It can be described by type and degree. The type of hearing loss depends on where it occurs in the ear. A hearing loss is referred to as conductive when the outer and middle ears do not transfer enough acoustic energy to the inner ear fluids. Blockage of the ear canal by congenital malformation, abnormalities of the middle ear structures, and otitis media (infection of the middle ear) are some of the causes of conductive hearing loss. Medicine or surgery may sometimes help with this type of hearing loss. Students with conductive losses may benefit from and be fitted with a hearing aid. A hearing loss is sensorineural when there is damage to the cochlea (inner ear) or to the auditory nerve. This type of hearing loss is usually permanent. Typically, a student with a sensorineural loss is fitted with amplification (Boothroyd, 1988).

FIGURE 6.2

## Comparison of the Frequency and Intensity of Various Environmental and Speech Sounds

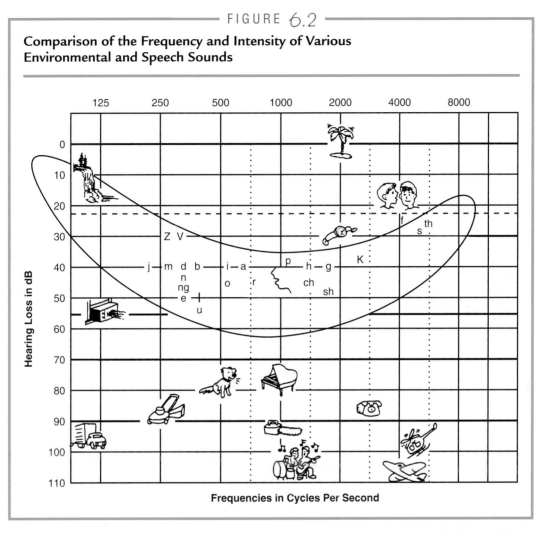

*Source:* Watkins, S. (Ed.) (1993). *Sky\*HI resource manual* (p. G9). Logan, UT: H.O.P.E. Reprinted with permission.

The degree of hearing loss is assessed by observing a person's responses to sounds. The intensity of a sound (loud versus quiet) is measured in decibels (dB); the frequency of the sound (high versus low) is measured in hertz. An audiologist tests and plots an individual's responses to sounds on a graph called an **audiogram,** a visual representation of an individual's ability to hear sound. Figure 6.2 shows a comparison of the frequency and intensity of various environmental and speech sounds, plotted on an audiogram (Stach, 1998).

## Characteristics of Students with Hearing Loss

Normal hearing falls within the range of 0–15 dB. Hearing losses are described by degree in terms such as minimal, mild, moderate, severe, and profound:

- 16–25 dB = minimal loss
- 25–40 dB = mild hearing loss
- 40–65 dB = moderate hearing loss

- 65–90 dB = severe hearing loss
- Greater than 90 dB = profound hearing loss

A person with a mild to moderate loss is usually referred to as being **hard of hearing.** Someone with a severe or profound loss is usually described as **deaf.**

Even a mild hearing loss can have significant educational effects if it is not recognized. Lauren Resnick, a first-grade teacher, commented that she was surprised at the difference hearing aids made for Rider, a student in her class who had a mild hearing loss. When Rider was not wearing his hearing aids, he was often off task or seemed uninterested in class activities. With his hearing aids, however, he functioned like the other students in the class.

Hearing loss affects normal speech and language development, which in turn affects reading development. Students who are deaf or hard of hearing may be significantly delayed in vocabulary development and reading skills. Some students who are deaf use vision as their primary mode of communication and learning. Other deaf and hard-of-hearing students develop communication and learning skills through use of **residual hearing.** Students with hearing losses to different degrees have difficulty accessing their environment and language system. Even though their vocal apparatuses function normally, they experience difficulty learning to produce the speech sounds because they might not get accurate or complete feedback from hearing the sounds they are producing. Many students who are deaf use **American Sign Language (ASL)** as their primary mode of communication. Other deaf or hard-of-hearing students use spoken English or a signed English system as their primary mode of communication. ASL is a visual, gestural language. It is not a visual representation of English, nor is it a simplified language or communication system. ASL has its own unique grammar and usage. **Finger spelling** is a system for representing the English alphabet manually. Finger spelling is used to "spell" names and proper nouns, as well as English words for which no sign exists. Figure 6.3 shows the American finger spelling alphabet.

Because many students and adults who are deaf speak a common language, ASL, and share similar backgrounds (in that they are deaf), they regard themselves as members of the Deaf culture. Members of the Deaf culture view hearing loss not as a disability but as a common characteristic among their members (Christensen & Dilgado, 1993).

FIGURE 6.3

**American Finger-Spelling Alphabet**

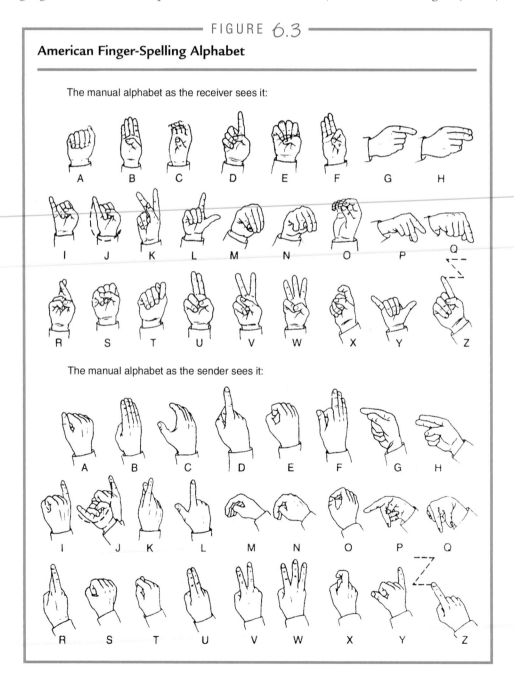

The manual alphabet as the receiver sees it:

A B C D E F G H
I J K L M N O P Q
R S T U V W X Y Z

The manual alphabet as the sender sees it:

A B C D E F G H
I J K L M N O P Q
R S T U V W X Y Z

## Prevalence of Hearing Loss

Since the implementation of the Individuals with Disabilities Education Act (IDEA), public schools have served more students with hearing loss than have state residential schools.

On the basis of an annual survey of children and youth who are deaf and hard of hearing by the Gallaudet Research Institute (January 2001), which included 43,861 students, 44.8 percent received instruction in the general education classroom and 12.6 percent received instruction in a resource setting.

## Identification and Assessment of Students with Hearing Loss

Melanie Brooks, a kindergarten teacher, recalls her first experience identifying a student with hearing loss. Chelsea had difficulty following directions, often asked that information be repeated, and had difficulty locating the speaker in group discussions. Melanie was also concerned about Chelsea's persistent colds, and she contacted the school nurse.

Together, the school nurse and Melanie began to identify ways to help Chelsea. They discovered that Chelsea had failed her kindergarten hearing screening and had incurred numerous ear infections as an infant and toddler. The district audiologist conducted further testing with Chelsea, discovering a mild-to-moderate hearing loss in both ears. Chelsea was fitted with hearing aids. Melanie and the special education teacher specializing in hearing loss, worked with Chelsea to provide resources and adaptations to help her learn better. Melanie recalls her satisfaction at being able to make a difference in Chelsea's life.

Some losses, particularly if they are mild to moderate ones, may first be detected during kindergarten screening and by classroom teachers. By the time students are ready to attend school, most moderate, severe, and profound hearing losses have already been detected and identified. Early identification and intervention are key to development of language and learning for children with hearing loss (Moeller, 2000). In 1993, the National Institutes of Health's Consensus Development Conference on Early Identification of Hearing Loss concluded that all infants should be screened for hearing loss, preferably before hospital discharge. Currently, over 30 states have passed legislation requiring newborn hearing screening for all babies born in their state (National Center for Hearing Assessment & Management, 2001). However, not all hearing loss occurs at birth, not all hearing losses are detected by a newborn hearing screening, and not all states have a systematic early detection system in place.

As a classroom teacher you may be able to assist in identifying children with hearing loss by being aware of the following warning signs:

- Daydreaming
- Inattention
- Behavior problems and frustration
- Lethargy
- Failure to follow simple verbal commands
- Using verbal expressions of misunderstanding (e.g., "Huh?" and "I don't know")
- Articulation errors
- Limited speech or vocabulary
- Inappropriate responses to questions
- Difficulties with verbal tasks
- Difficulty decoding phonetically
- Unusual voice quality (soft, nasal, high pitch, monotonal)
- Mouth breathing
- Persistent colds
- Watching other students for instructional cues

## Instructional Guidelines and Accommodations for Students with Hearing Loss

If you have a student with hearing loss in your classroom, you become an important member of a team that will make educational decisions. In addition to you, the team can include a special education teacher specializing in hearing loss, a sign language interpreter, the student, the parents, a speech language pathologist, an audiologist, and other resource personnel.

**Using Amplification**   Most students with hearing loss benefit from hearing aids. Technological advances provide many options in hearing aid selection. In classroom situations, hearing aids have limitations. They may amplify all sounds in the environment, and the student may hear other noises (background and reverberation) in addition to the desired signal such as the teacher's voice. Because of technological advances, hearing aids are available that can greatly reduce these problems. Many considerations must be taken into account in selecting and fitting amplification for children. Features unique to programmable systems and multiband compression improve the child's perception in noisy listening environments. However, background noise is not completely eliminated, and care in creating an optimum listening environment through the reduction of background noise and decreasing the listening distance of the student to the speaker is advisable. In classroom situations, students often use **assistive listening devices** such as personal FM (frequency

What are some advantages and disadvantages of amplification systems for students with hearing loss? What communication alternatives are available for students who are deaf?

modulation) units. With a personal FM unit, the teacher wears a wireless microphone, and the student wears a wireless receiver incorporated with a hearing aid. The microphone amplifies the teacher's voice 12–15 dB above the classroom noise and is not affected by distance. A sound field FM system may be another option for a student with hearing loss in the classroom. The teacher wears a small wireless microphone, and speakers are place in strategic locations within the classroom. This system creates a favorable signal-to-noise ratio and accessibility of teacher instruction (Flexer, 2000).

A new technology for individuals with hearing loss is the cochlear implant. The Food and Drug Administration has approved specific criteria for patient selection for this procedure. The cochlear implant is an electronic device designed to provide sound detection as well as improved speech understanding. Receiving a cochlear implant requires a surgical procedure. An electrode array is implanted within the cochlea. An electrical current is applied to the electrode site, which sends electrical sound directly to the hearing nerve (the auditory nerve). As with hearing aids, the success of cochlear implantation is very individual.

**Making Classroom Accommodations** Accommodation for students must be individualized. However, the following accommodations provide you, as the classroom teacher, with general guidelines:

1. Provide preferential seating.
   - Minimize listening distance by having the student sit near you. Seat students away from loud noises (e.g., high-traffic areas, doors, air conditioning and heating units).
   - Make sure the student can see you, the interpreter, and visual aids clearly.
   - Eliminate glare from windows or lights.
2. Minimize nonmeaningful environmental noise.
   - Use carpets, rugs, cork, and curtains to help absorb noise.
   - Avoid unnecessary background noise (e.g., music, hallway noise).
3. Use visual clues and demonstrations.
   - Face the student directly when you talk.
   - Use an overhead projector rather than the board so that you can face the student while you write.
   - Use natural gestures.
   - Use modeling to demonstrate how to do different procedures and tasks.
   - Use pictures, diagrams, and graphs.
   - Provide opportunities for experiential learning.
4. Maximize the use of visual media.
   - Provide closed-captioned television (see Tips for Teachers 6.3).
   - Provide access to computers.
5. Monitor the student's understanding.
   - Ask the student to repeat or rephrase important information or directions.
   - Reword statements for clarification.
   - Provide written instructions and summaries.
6. Promote cooperation and collaboration.
   - Use peer and classroom tutors and note takers.
   - Identify speakers in a group discussion.
   - Inform interpreters of topics before class, and provide study guides or teaching notes.

**Using Interpreters and Note Takers** Sign language interpreters and note takers are valuable resources in the classroom. It is important that students who use a sign language system have an interpreter in the educational setting. Although an interpreter facilitates communication between the teacher and the student, the interpreter is not a substitute for you (the classroom teacher). Students may at first rely on the interpreter for answers and guidance but will learn to shift their confidence to you, their teacher.

To understand the information being presented, students need to be visually attentive. By permitting these students to photocopy your lecture notes or a

# Tips for Teachers

## 6.3   Using Closed Captioning

*Closed captioning* is the process of encoding dialogue and sound effects from a program into readable text at the bottom of the television screen (similar to the subtitles in foreign films). *Decoders* are devices that enable you to view the words in a closed-captioning program.

In 1993, the federal Television Circuitry Decoder Act (passed in 1990) took effect. Thanks to this act all televisions marketed in the United States must be capable of decoding closed-caption signals. With this development, one does not need a special captioning machine to view closed-captioned text.

Today, not only many television programs and specials, but also many films, videos, and educational resources are captioned and available for use in the classroom. When you order a film or video, find out whether you can order it captioned. For more information, contact:

Captioned Films/Videos for the Deaf
Modern Talking Picture Service, Inc.
5000 Park Street North
St. Petersburg, FL 33709
800-237-6213

---

classmate's notes or by providing duplicating paper to a peer note taker, you allow them to focus all their attention on what is taking place in the classroom. Peer or adult note takers and tutors can also help to clarify and explain topics, preteach vocabulary, or review technical terms. Keep in mind that careful attention to teaching techniques that support language and concept development will be beneficial for all your students.

## Students with Physical Disabilities, Health Impairments, and Traumatic Brain Injury

Students with physical disabilities, health impairments, and traumatic brain injury are a small but diverse group. Disabilities can range from asthma, a comparatively mild condition, to cerebral palsy, which may involve neurological impairment that affects mobility and other functional skills, to traumatic brain injury, which may vary greatly in its effect on learning and daily functioning.

One of Lanetta Bridgewater's second-grade students, Emma, has cerebral palsy and is unable to speak but understands what others are saying and is developing academic skills at a rate similar to her classmates. In planning and working with Emma, Lanetta worked closely with Susie Speelman, the inclusion support teacher you met in Chapter 5. Among the strategies Lanetta and Susie used to facilitate Emma's successful inclusion in Lanetta's classes were time to plan together, making the class-

room more accessible for Emma and her wheelchair, use of technology (particularly of assistive devices to enable Emma to make choices and demonstrate her understanding), and reducing the amount of work (so that Emma has enough time to respond).

## Definitions and Types of Physical Disabilities, Health Impairments, and Traumatic Brain Injury

Students with significant physical disabilities, health impairments, and traumatic brain injury generally qualify for special education services under three IDEA categories: orthopedic impairment, other health impairment, and traumatic brain injury. IDEA defines **orthopedic impairment** as follows:

> a severe orthopedic impairment that adversely affects a child's educational performance. The term includes impairments caused by congenital anomaly (e.g., clubfoot, absence of some member, etc.), impairments caused by disease (e.g., poliomyelitis, bone tuberculosis, etc.), and impairments from other causes (e.g., cerebral palsy, amputations, and fractures or burns that cause contractures) (IDEA, Section 300.7[7]).

Orthopedic impairments or physical disabilities may not only interfere with the students' coordination and mobility, but also affect their ability to communicate, learn, and adjust. Section 504 of the Vocational Rehabilitation Act of 1973 defines a physical disability as an impairment that substantially limits a

Asthma is one of the most frequently cited reasons for students missing school. Another is head injury. One in 500 students is hospitalized each year for a head injury.

person's participation in one or more life activities (home, school, or work activities). By this definition, a person whose impairment is controlled by medication is not considered physically disabled if he or she can participate in home, school, and work activities.

The two general categories of physical disabilities are neurological impairments and neuromuscular disease. A **neurological impairment** is an abnormal performance caused by a dysfunction of the brain, spinal cord, and nerves, thereby creating transmission of improper instructions, uncontrolled bursts of instructions from the brain, or incorrect interpretation of feedback to the brain (Brimer, 1990). Some types of neurological impairment are seizure disorders, cerebral palsy, and spina bifida. **Neuromuscular diseases** involve both the nerves and muscles. They are neurological problems that affect the muscles. Muscular dystrophy, polio, and multiple sclerosis are examples of this type of physical disability.

IDEA also provides special education services for students with other health impairments. **Other health impairment** is defined as follows:

> having limited strength, vitality, or alertness, due to chronic or acute health problems such as heart condition, tuberculosis, rheumatic fever, nephritis, asthma, sickle cell anemia, hemophilia, epilepsy, lead poisoning, leukemia, or diabetes, that adversely affects a child's educational performance (IDEA, Section 300.5[7]).

Health impairments include conditions such as asthma, cancer, cystic fibrosis, juvenile diabetes, prenatal substance abuse, communicable diseases such as tuberculosis and HIV infection, and in some cases attention deficit disorder or attention deficit hyperactivity disorder (see Chapter 2). More recently two new subgroups have emerged within the health disabilities: **medically fragile** and/or technologically dependent. These children are at risk for medical emergencies on a regular basis and often require life support or specialized support systems such as ventilators. Medically fragile students may also have progressive diseases such as cancer or AIDS. Students with health impairments are characterized by their chronic or acute health problems that result in limited strength, vitality, or alertness.

With the 1990 amendments to IDEA, **traumatic brain injury** was identified as a category of disability and defined as follows:

> an acquired injury to the brain caused by an external physical force, resulting in total or partial functional disability or psychosocial impairment, or both, that adversely affects a child's education performance. The term applies to open or closed head injuries resulting in impairments in one or more areas, such as cognition; language; memory; attention; reasoning; abstract thinking;

judgment; problem-solving; sensory, perceptual, and motor abilities; psychosocial behavior; physical functions; information processing; and speech. The term does not apply to brain injuries that are congenital or degenerative, or brain injuries induced by birth trauma (34 C.R.F., Sec. 300.7[6][12]).

Common causes of traumatic brain injuries are motorcycle, automobile, and off-road vehicle accidents; sports injuries; and accidents from violence, such as gunshot wounds and child abuse (Russo, 1991).

## research brief

### Understanding Causes of Spinal Cord Injury and Traumatic Brain Injury

Spinal cord injuries in young children are most often caused by automobile accidents or child abuse. Automobile accidents, falls, gunshot wounds, and diving accidents cause most spinal cord injuries in adults and older children. Diseases and infections such as measles, polio, meningitis, and HIV can cause permanent damage to the central nervous system, thereby causing physical disabilities and health impairments. A lack of prenatal care and a mother's alcohol and substance abuse during pregnancy can also lead to physical disabilities and health impairments in children.

Over 50 percent of traumatic brain injuries in children and adolescents are caused by motor vehicle accidents, with falls causing another 21 percent. Sports and recreational injuries are the next major cause, followed by violence (Russo, 1991). Child abuse accounts for the majority of infant head injuries, and more than 75 percent of children under the age of 3 who are physically abused have a traumatic brain injury (Savage, 1993). Infants can also receive traumatic brain injury from being shaken (referred to as shaken-impact syndrome). In 10–25 percent of the cases, the child dies (Schroeder, 1993).

The following are typical behaviors associated with traumatic brain injuries:

- Lowered social inhibition and judgment, lowered impulse control
- Faulty reasoning
- Numerous cognitive processing difficulties
- Lowered initiative and motivation
- Overestimation of abilities
- Depression
- Flat affect with sudden outbursts
- Agitation and irritability
- Fatigue (Forness & Kavale, 1993; Tucker & Colson, 1992; Tyler & Myles, 1990; Witte, 1998).

Physical disabilities and health impairments caused by traumatic brain injury and spinal cord injury are preventable. The case for prevention of traumatic head injuries is clear:

- 63 percent of all children involved in motor vehicle accidents were not wearing restraints.
- 99 percent of those injured in bicycle accidents were not wearing helmets.
- 70 percent of those injured in motorcycle accidents were not wearing helmets.
- 54 percent of those injured while riding on all-terrain and recreational vehicles did not use restraints (Medical Research and Training Center in Rehabilitation and Childhood Trauma, 1993).

## Characteristics of Students with Physical Disabilities, Health Impairments, and Traumatic Brain Injury

During your teaching career, you undoubtedly will have students with physically disabilities, health impairments, and traumatic brain injury. This section describes some of the more prevalent of these disabilities.

**Cerebral Palsy**    Students with **cerebral palsy** are one of the largest groups of children with physical disabilities (Heward, 2000). Cerebral palsy is caused by damage to the brain before or during birth. Conditions are classified according to the areas affected and the types of symptoms. The degree of severity varies and is often evidenced by lack of coordination, speech disorders, motor problems, and extreme weakness. Cerebral palsy generally has accompanying problems in such areas as learning, vision, hearing, cognitive functioning, and social and emotional growth (Meyen & Skrtic, 1995). The condition can interfere with head control, arm use, sitting positions, balance, posture, and mobility, and these problems can be exacerbated by fatigue and stress.

As a classroom teacher, you will want to be aware of the student's level of fatigue and stress. Paul Nichols, a high-school math teacher, mentioned that his student, Allison, appeared stressed during tests, particularly if they were long or timed.

> I noticed that whenever we had a timed test with essays, Allison would have difficulty sitting up and holding up her head. At first I thought it was just a way for her to try and get out of the test so I tried to be firm with her. When I spoke to the physical therapist, he mentioned that she may be tired or stressed and then he taught her some relaxation techniques. She is doing better but it is still a difficult time for her. I did explain to her that the timed part was not as important as doing the work, so now I give her extended time by allowing her to finish the test with the special education teacher during her resource period.

**Spina Bifida**    **Spina bifida,** a birth defect that occurs when the spinal cord fails to close properly, often causes paralysis of parts of the body but seldom affects intellectual functioning. Most students with spina bifida walk with difficulty and lack complete bladder and bowel control. Some students need to use a catheter, which necessitates training in hygiene and extra time during the day to take care of the catheter. Generally, the school nurse or a special education teacher provides this training if it has not already been provided. This type of support is often provided by a para-educator.

**Epilepsy**    The most common neurological impairment in school-age children is convulsive disorders, or **epilepsy.** Epilepsy is characterized by a tendency to have recurrent seizures—sudden, excessive, spontaneous, and abnormal discharges of neurons accompanied by alteration in motor function, sensory function, or consciousness (Coulter, 1993).

There are two major types of seizures. **Absence seizures (petit mal)** are characterized by short lapses in consciousness. Students may appear inattentive and often do not realize that they are having seizures. **Tonic-clonic seizures (grand mal)** are characterized by convulsions followed by loss of consciousness. Usually, a tonic phase, in which the muscles are rigid, is followed by a clonic phase, in which the arms and legs jerk. Often the student loses consciousness and awakens disoriented and tired. Although these seizures usually last less than five minutes, they can be a frightening event for you and your students. Tips for Teachers 6.4 provides some pointers for handling this type of seizure. If a student in your class has this type of seizure disorder, be sure to help the other students in the classroom understand the condition and respond appropriately to the student (Reisner, 1988).

**Muscular Dystrophy**    **Muscular dystrophy** is a chronic disorder characterized by the weakening and wasting of the body's muscles. People with muscular dystrophy progressively lose their ability to walk and effectively use their arms and hands (Brooke, 1986; Muscular Dystrophy Association, 2000). There is no cure for muscular dystrophy at this time, and the only prevention is genetic counseling (the condition appears to run in families). Helping the student maintain independence through regular physical therapy, exercise, and necessary physical aids is important. School personnel need to be careful not to lift or pull a student with muscular dystrophy by his

## Tips for Teachers

### 6.4 How to Respond to a Student Having a Tonic–Clonic (Grand Mal) Seizure in the Classroom

- Ease the student to the floor and clear the area around him or her.
- Put something soft under the student's head to keep it from banging the floor.
- Do not interfere with the seizure. Turn the student gently on his or her side, but do not put anything in the student's mouth, and do not try to hold his or her tongue.

- Have someone stay with the student until he or she is fully awake.
- Allow the student to rest afterward.
- Seek emergency assistance if the seizure lasts longer than 5 minutes or if the student requests it.

or her arms, because doing so may cause dislocation of limbs. Most students with muscular dystrophy need wheelchairs by the age of 10 to 14, and teachers should be alert for signs of fatigue (Heward, 2000).

**HIV and AIDS** Human immunodeficiency virus (HIV) is a condition that infects and eventually destroys cells in the immune system that protect the body from disease (Colson & Carlson, 1993). A viral infection transmitted through bodily fluids, HIV is responsible for **acquired immunodeficiency syndrome (AIDS).** Students infected with HIV may eventually experience loss of stamina, developmental delays, motor problems, progressive neurological defects, repeated bacterial infections, psychological stresses, and death (Belman et al., 1988; Landau, Mangione, & Pryor, 1997). HIV progresses through stages. In the latency stage, which generally lasts from 2 to 10 years in children, there are no outward symptoms. As the disease progresses through the middle stages, individuals experience a general weakening of the immune system, which results in persistent fevers and infections. In the final stages, opportunistic infections increase in frequency and severity.

At the end of 1996, 8,000 students under the age of 13 had been diagnosed as having AIDS. About 80 percent of these children were infected by their mothers.

Most school districts have established policies regarding the inclusion of students with HIV in general education classrooms. If students in your classroom are identified as having HIV, consult with individuals knowledgeable about these policies, and work with the special education teacher and school nurse in planning for these students. One important question to ask is how the condition currently affects the stu-

dent's health. Students whose frequent absences are due to recurrent infections might need a homebound teacher. In advanced stages, students may experience a loss of knowledge and skills due to brain degeneration and a lack of vitality (Kelker et al., 1994).

By knowing and adjusting to the student's capabilities, you enable the student to participate more fully and successfully in classroom activities. For example, Shirley Meeder, an eighth-grade social studies teacher, found that she could adapt assignments for Joey, a student in the middle stages of HIV, by reducing the amount of work required, giving him the option of listening to the textbook on tape, having a note taker, and letting Joey take tests orally. These modifications helped Joey deal with his limited stamina. The special education teacher helped Shirley provide many of these accommodations. When Joey suffered from a prolonged infection, he received homebound instruction so that he could keep up with his classmates.

You might need to take some precautions with students with HIV. Casual contact among people in the classroom is not a problem, as this is not how HIV is transmitted (Wishom et al., 1989). But in situations in which you could come into contact with the blood or other bodily fluids of a student with HIV, protective gloves should be worn (Kelker et al., 1994). Most district have policies regarding precautions that need to be taken. Become familiar with those policies.

**Traumatic Brain Injury** Because traumatic brain injury may occur at different developmental stages, with a wide variety of severity and complexities and various responses to recovery, the characteristics and educational needs of these students are unique (Lash, 2000). Key points to consider about the characteristics of individuals with traumatic brain injury are the following:

- The degree of initial recovery from the injury will vary widely and require frequent review of the student's individual educational program.
- Memory, attention, and executive function difficulties are common.
- Slowed processing of information and faulty reasoning are common.
- Pre-injury skills may be preserved but are not predictive of new learning abilities.
- Lowered social inhibition and judgment, lowered impulse control, depression, and overestimation of abilities are typical.
- Less initiative and motivation are typical, as is general fatigue.
- Services and supports are often needed in at least four areas: cognition, speech and language, social and behavioral skills, and physical functioning.

For example, when Justin returned to high school three weeks after being in a car accident in which he sustained a head injury, Ms. Ruiz, his math teacher immediately recognized the changes in his cognitive functioning. His response time was slower, and concepts that had been easy for him to grasp were fuzzy and required reteaching. She worked with the special education teacher to identify key concepts for Justin to relearn and new concepts to be reinforced. Over the next three months, Ms. Ruiz recognized a significant change in Justin's learning patterns. His response time quickened, and he was able to learn new concepts at a faster rate. It was during these first three months that Ms. Ruiz stayed in especially close contact with the special education teacher and Justin's parents so that she could facilitate the recovery of his cognitive functioning.

## Prevalence of Physical Disabilities, Health Impairments, and Traumatic Brain Injury

Relatively few students have physical disabilities, health impairments, or traumatic brain injury. About 10 percent of the school-age population receive special education services for their disabilities. Of that 10 percent, approximately 67,000, or 1.2 percent, have orthopedic impairments, including students with cerebral palsy, muscular dystrophy, spinal cord injury, and spina bifida. Health impairments account for approximately 191,000, or 3.5 percent, of students with disabilities and include such conditions as HIV, asthma, cancer, cystic fibrosis, and sickle-cell

anemia. Children with asthma are the largest group of chronically ill students in the United States. At any one time, most educators have an average of two students who have asthma (Getch & Neuharth-Pritchett, 1999). It is important to remember that some students with physical disabilities and health impairments also have other disabilities and may be classified as having multiple disabilities.

While approximately 500,000 children and adolescents sustain a brain injury each year and over 150,000 are hospitalized (Hill, 1999), the number of students who receive services is substantially less, approximately 12,000 students (U.S. Department of Education, 2000). The occurrence of traumatic brain injuries increases dramatically during adolescence (15 to 24 years of age) owing to the increased participation in contact sports, greater access to and use of automobiles and motorcycles, more frequent use of racing and mountain bikes, and injuries sustained from firearms. Boys are two to three times more likely to receive head injuries than girls (Hill, 1999).

## Identification and Assessment of Students with Physical Disabilities, Health Impairments, and Traumatic Brain Injury

Medical diagnosis usually provides the initial identification of physical disabilities, health impairments, and traumatic brain injury. Assessments are carefully designed to take into account that these students may have delayed motor skills or problems staying on task for long periods of time. Depending on the student, assessments in the following areas are often appropriate:

- Activities of daily living (personal hygiene, eating, dressing, using public transportation)
- Attention, concentration, initiation, or sustained effort
- Adaptations for learning (academic and physical adaptations to help students achieve academic success and independence)
- Communication (students' ability to express and understand language)
- Mobility (students' current and potential range and mode of mobility)
- Physical abilities and limitations (positioning and necessary adaptive equipment and techniques that facilitate students' independence)
- Psychosocial development (effects of impairment on students' social and emotional functioning)
- Transition skills (skills needed for a successful transition into and from school and between grade levels)

Remember that, as a classroom teacher and a member of the education team, you are a valuable resource for information.

## Instructional Guidelines and Accommodations for Students with Physical Disabilities, Health Impairments, and Traumatic Brain Injury

Three basic principles can help you accommodate students with physical disabilities, health impairments, and traumatic brain injury in your classroom:

- *Use others as resources.* Call on the expertise of the student, parents, other school personnel, and others in health-related professions, as well as the student's classmates.
- *Be flexible in your planning.* Be willing to make last-minute changes in response to day-to-day changes in the student's condition and readiness to learn.
- *Be ingenious and creative.* One of the greatest rewards from working with students is helping them discover their strengths and ways to demonstrate them.

### Transdisciplinary Teaming and Support Providers

Because many students with physical disabilities or health impairments receive services from special education teachers, an occupational or physical therapist, an adaptive physical education teacher, and possibly a speech and language pathologist, effective

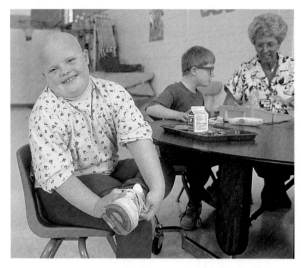

As a classroom teacher, how will you assess and address the needs of a student with a serious health impairment?

teaming and communication are crucial. In **transdisciplinary teaming,** all members of the team work together and view the student as a whole, instead of working only on their specialty area (Downing & Bailey, 1990; Orelove & Sobsey, 1996). All team members are aware of the student's goals and observe each other as they work with the student so that they can share and generalize successful techniques and strategies. Tips for Teachers 6.5 provides further suggestions for working with these and other service providers. You will find these individuals to be an important support team for you and one key to the student's success.

## T i p s for Teachers

### 6.5    Suggestions for Working with Service Providers

Giangreco (1997) provided the following guidelines for working effectively with support service providers:

- Become aware of what support service providers have to offer.
- Approach support service staff as collaborators rather than experts.
- Make sure team members agree on expectations and goals for students.
- Clarify your role as a team member and your relationship with other team members.
- Be clear about the types of supports you need and want.

- Distinguish between needing an "extra pair of hands" and more specialized help.
- Make sure support service providers understand your classroom routines.
- Participate in scheduling support services.
- Have the team evaluate the effectiveness of support services for the student.
- Make sure support services are helping you to do a better job.

*Source:* Adapted from Giangreco, M. F. (1997). *Quick-guides to inclusion: Ideas for educating students with disabilities.* Baltimore: Brookes.

**Using Assistive Technology**  Recall that the IDEA defines assistive technology as "any item, piece of equipment, or product system whether acquired commercially off the shelf, modified, or customized, that is used to increase, maintain, or improve functional capabilities of individuals with disabilities." Assistive technology devices are particularly useful for increasing mobility, communicating better, gaining access to computers, performing daily living skills, enhancing learning, and manipulating and controlling the environment (King, 1999; Lewis, 1993). By using such assistive technology as eye-gaze pointing, communication boards, and writing implements encased in plastic tubing or bicycle handle grips, for example, Lanetta's student, Emma, described earlier, is able to participate more fully in classroom life. In thinking about the use of technology and assistive technology, consider these points (Merbler, Hadadian, & Ulman, 1999):

- Determine the people who are responsible for assistive technology at your school, district, or region and use them as resources.
- Weigh the functional use of more simple technology in comparison to more complex technology.
- Opt for open-ended devices whenever possible or ones that permit customizing for different tasks and for the student's needs.
- Select devices that are gender and age appropriate. For example, the synthetic voice speaking for a high school student should be adultlike and of the same gender as the student using the voice.
- Check your school district policy on using equipment at home and on maintaining and repairing equipment.

- Ask for training on the equipment that your student will be using.
- Collaborate with others to share your knowledge and learn from others.

**Making Environmental Modifications**  In addition to the necessary accessibility modifications (wide aisles for wheelchairs, low drinking fountains, appropriate handles), other environmental modifications facilitate independence for students with physical disabilities, health impairments, and traumatic brain injury. Wright and Bigge (1991) discuss four types of environmental modifications:

- Changes in location of materials and equipment (e.g., so that students in wheelchairs can reach items independently)
- Work surface modifications (e.g., raising a desk so that a wheelchair fits under it)
- Object modifications (e.g., attaching clips to a student's desk to secure papers)
- Manipulation aids (e.g., using a page turner to reduce dependency on others)

The 60-Second Lesson provides more quick and easy ideas for helping students become more independent and successful.

**Educating Classmates**  For students with health impairments and physical disabilities, some of the most important modifications relate to informing other students in the class. Classmates, particularly younger students with rare diseases or severe disabilities, will most likely have limited knowledge and many questions. For example, Sexson and

## making a Difference

## Ways to Promote Independence in Students with Physical Disabilities or Health Impairments

- Retrace or enlarge print with a dark marker to help students see material more clearly.
- Schedule study buddies to help a student with disabilities gather learning materials.
- Assign a classmate or ask for a volunteer to take or copy notes for a student with disabilities.
- Ask students for whom writing is difficult whether they would prefer an oral assignment or test.

## The 60-second Lesson

- Ask the special education teacher to provide (or advise you on acquiring) materials for securing small objects. Velcro and a Dycem mat on a student's desk prevent books, calculators, pencil boxes, and the like from slipping off.
- Ask parents to provide a bandanna or sweatband, worn on the wrist, to help a student with limited control of facial muscles wipe off excess saliva.
- Arrange with the special education teacher for the assistance of a paraprofessional in moving a student from a wheelchair to a beanbag chair during floor activities so that the student can be both supported physically and seated on the same level as peers.

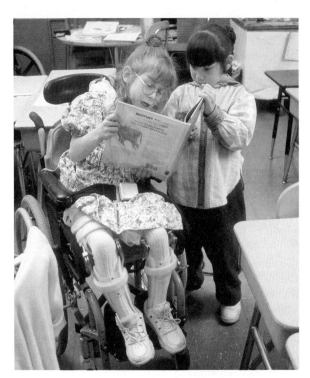

As a classroom teacher, how can you help students with physical disabilities or health impairments in their psychosocial development and peer relations?

Madan-Swain (1993) found that students most often asked the following questions about a classmate with a health problem:

- What's wrong with the student?
- Is the disease contagious?
- Will (the student) die from it?
- Will the student lose anything (such as limbs, hair)?
- Should we talk about the student's illness or ignore it?
- What will other students think if I'm still friends with this student?

It may also be helpful to talk about how a student may be different when he or she returns from a prolonged absence or a traumatic brain injury.

Using children's and juvenile literature is another way in which students can learn about different disabilities and support a student with a specific physical or health-related impairment. Prater and Sileo (2001) provide strategies for using juvenile literature about HIV/AIDS to inform students about the disease, precautions, and individuals with HIV/AIDS.

**Dealing with Death**   During your teaching career, you may have a student in your class who is dying.

In this circumstance, counseling is indicated. Open communication with the student, parents, counselor, and other members of the education team becomes very important so that you can deal with the student's feelings and fears in a consistent and open manner. You may work directly with the school counselor, but you need written permission from parents before you can contact a student's private counselor or psychologist. Children can go through stages as they move toward accepting death (Berner, 1977; Cassini & Rogers, 1990). Although not all children go through all stages and some stages may be experienced simultaneously, knowledge of these stages can help you understand the behaviors and emotions that may be exhibited by a student who is dying. The stages include the following:

- Shock and disbelief
- Crying (sometimes hysterical)
- Feelings of isolation and loneliness
- Psychosomatic symptoms, which may distract the student from the fatal condition
- Panic
- Guilty feelings that he or she is to blame
- Hostility or resentment toward others
- Resistance to usual routines and continuing to live
- Reconciliation and beginning acceptance of the inevitability of death
- Acceptance

Although the suggestions in Table 6.1 are from parents of children with cancer (Candlelighters Childhood Cancer Foundation, 1993), many apply also to children with other life-threatening illnesses, such as HIV/AIDS and cystic fibrosis.

**Providing Instruction for Motor Skills**   For students with physical disabilities, health impairments, and traumatic brain injury, working on motor skills is an important component of their education program. Many activities that support motor skills can be incorporated easily into daily classroom activities, such as increasing control by looking at a classmate during cooperative learning activities or improving fine motor skills by drawing or writing. The special education teacher, occupational therapist, physical therapist, and adaptive physical education teacher can be valuable resources in integrating instruction in motor skills into the curriculum.

**Promoting Literacy Development**   Promoting literacy development (reading, writing, listening, and speaking) is very important for individuals with physical disabilities. It provides students access to language, a means to communicate their ideas, and

━━━━━━━━━━━━━ TABLE 6.1 ━━━━━━━━━━━━━

### Parents' View: What Teachers Should and Should Not Do for a Student with Cancer

| Helpful Teachers | Less Helpful Teachers |
| --- | --- |
| ✔ Take time to learn about the treatments and their effects on school performance. | ✔ Fail to learn about the disease and its effects and treatments. |
| ✔ Demonstrate support for parents as well as student. | ✔ Show fear about having the student in class. |
| ✔ Listen to parents' concerns and fears. | ✔ Allow other students to pity the student. |
| ✔ Call or visit during absences. | ✔ Fail to keep ongoing communication with parents and student during absences. |
| ✔ Encourage classmates to call or write during extended absences. | ✔ Ignore problems classmates have in adjusting to friend's disease. |
| ✔ Before re-entry, talk with the student about any fears or concerns. | ✔ Before re-entry, fail to share information about the student and the disease with classmates. |
| ✔ Adjust lessons and assignments based on the student's endurance. | ✔ Do not give the student the benefit of the doubt on assignments and homework. |
| ✔ Follow parental and medical instructions regarding snacks, wearing a hat, bathroom visits. | ✔ Make an issue of the student's differences in front of others. |
| ✔ Treat the student as normally as possible and include the student in as many class activities as possible. | ✔ Do not give the student an opportunity to attempt what others are doing. |

*Source:* Adapted from Candlelighters Childhood Cancer Foundation (1993). Advice to educators (adapted from a survey by A Wish with Wings). In *Educating the child with cancer* (pp. 21–22). Bethesda, MD: Author.

a way to increase their experiences and knowledge. It also provides a lifelong pleasure activity (Dziwulski, 1994; Light & Kelford-Smith, 1993). Facilitating literacy development (Coleman, Koppenhaver, & Yoder, 1991) includes such suggestions as those that follow:

● *Positioning:* Adaptive wheelchairs or other seating devices may act as barriers in the students' ability to see print and pictures. Position students so that they can see the print and pictures while listening. This helps them begin to make the connection between print and speech. Ideally, the students should be situated in a way that allows them to help turn the pages so that they begin to recognize the left-to-right orientation of text. Following the text with a finger also helps a person develop this concept. Page fluffers (pieces of foam glued to the pages in a book) provide more space between pages, making them easier to turn. Gluing a popsicle stick or paper clip on the edge of the page also makes turning the page easier. A glove with a magnet

can be used with the paper clip to help the student be independent (Dziwulski, 1994).

● *Siblings and peers:* Since children with physical disabilities might not have the ability or access for questioning and retelling the story, the inclusion of peers or siblings during storytime could help make the storytime more lively. Parents have reported that children related text to real-life activities and asked and answered a greater variety of questions when peers or siblings were present. The other children also act as models for the child with disabilities.

● *Repeated readings:* Research has shown that students benefit from repeated readings, as these help them to recognize printed words and to understand the structure of written language.

● *Print in the environment:* Having print everywhere in the students' environment is important. For students with physical disabilities, remember that the print needs to be at their eye level based on their adaptive equipment.

● *Functional/recreational uses of print:* It is important for students to participate in functional and recreational literacy such as developing a grocery list, writing a note to a friend, and reading for enjoyment. Embed literacy into all activities during the day (reading the signs on the restroom door or at the grocery store).

- *Accessing literacy:* Students with disabilities need a method to independently access storybooks, writing instruments, and other literacy-related items. These could be books on tape or slide projectors with an adaptive switch that the student can independently activate. Drawing and writing can be made easier with adaptive holders for the writing utensil. Taping the paper down also helps the student draw or write. There are various writing and drawing software programs that can be accessed through Touch

Windows or switches to help students with physical impairments.

- *Assistive technology:* There is abundant assistive technology available, but it needs to be matched up with the students in their homes and schools. Books on disks, drawing and writing software, and other language programs can assist students in developing literacy.

As you work with students who have visual, hearing, physical, or health impairments, your repertoire of teaching strategies and knowledge of classroom accommodations and assistive technology will grow. With the help of a number of specialists, who can assist both you and the student, you should feel confident of success in educating your students.

## summary

- Students with visual impairment can be blind or partially sighted, depending on the degree and type of vision loss.
- It is important when planning for a student with visual impairments to consider the student's functional vision.
- The use of braille, optical aids, modified print, book on tape, and assistive technology can play a key role in integrating students with visual impairments.
- The orientation and mobility specialist, a teacher who specializes in visual impairment, provides valuable support to you in working with students with visual impairments.
- It is important to make the classroom accessible for students who have visual impairments. These students may need instruction in orientation and mobility skills.
- Hearing loss is measured by an audiologist, who plots the results of the hearing test on an audiogram.
- Although most children with significant hearing loss are identified before beginning school, it is important to watch for signs of mild hearing loss.

- American Sign Language is a visual and gestural language used by many individuals in North America who are deaf.
- Arranging the classroom to reduce background noise and to have the speaker's face visible is important for students with hearing loss.
- Interpreters and note takers provide means for students with hearing loss to better access the general education curriculum.
- When working with students who have physical disabilities, health impairments, and traumatic brain injury, you will want to collaborate with specialists such as physical and occupational therapists, speech and language pathologists, assistive technology specialists, and school nurses and other medical professionals.
- It is important to monitor the cognitive, academic, and social and emotional functioning of students with physical and health impairments and traumatic brain injury because functioning may vary dramatically.
- Assistive technology devices can enhance students' independence and learning. Devices range from low-tech items such as handles to high-tech devices such as computers.

## key terms and concepts

absence seizures (petit mal)
acquired immunodeficiency
  syndrome (AIDS)

American Sign Language (ASL)
assistive listening devices
audiogram

blindness
braille
cerebral palsy

| | | |
|---|---|---|
| compensatory skills | low vision | partial sight |
| deaf | medically fragile | residual hearing |
| epilepsy | mobility skills | spina bifida |
| finger spelling | muscular dystrophy | tonic-clonic seizures (grand mal) |
| functional vision | neurological impairment | total blindness |
| hard of hearing | neuromuscular diseases | transdisciplinary teaming |
| human immunodeficiency | orientation skills | traumatic brain injury |
|   virus (HIV) | orthopedic impairment | visual acuity |
| legal blindness | other health impairment | visual field |

## think and apply

1. In the opening interview, Pat Childers was afraid that she lacked the knowledge and experience to work with students like Brandy. Other teachers, such as Nancy Shipka and Lanetta Bridgewater, expressed the same concerns. What systems are in place to help these teachers? Make a list of your questions, the people you would ask, and the meetings or activities you would plan before a student with disabilities joins your class.

2. Interview and observe two or three of the specialists described in this chapter. Find out about the students with whom they work, their roles and responsibilities, and how they team with general classroom teachers.

3. Develop a file of assistive technology resources in your state and local district. Visit the technology center or specialist and learn more about integrating assistive technology for students with disabilities.

4. Survey a classroom and school to determine accessibility for a student using a wheelchair. List modifications that you think would improve accessibility.

5. Interview several adolescents or young adults with a visual, hearing, physical, or health impairment. Ask the following questions:
   - What impact does (the disability) have on your daily life?
   - How do your routines differ because of (the disability)?
   - How do others react to your disability?
   - What advice would you give classroom teachers about helping other students with (the disability)?

6. Check and see whether there is a classroom for students who are deaf/hard of hearing or visually impaired in your school district. Arrange to spend some time in a classroom with these students. Observe the strategies teachers use to communicate with and instruct their students. How do these classrooms function similarly to and differently than general education classrooms?

## read more about it

### Visual Impairments

1. Barraga, N. D., & Erin, J. N. (1992). *Visual handicaps and learning* (3rd ed.). Austin, TX: Pro-Ed.

   *An introductory textbook with information on designing appropriate instructional settings and programs for students who are visually impaired.*

2. Bishop, J. E. (1996). *Teaching visually impaired children* (2nd ed.). Springfield, IL: Charles C. Thomas.

   *A textbook that provides practical information for teachers who have students with visual impairments, including development, assessment, curricular needs, multiple disabilities, and technology.*

3. Corn, A. L., & Koenig, A. J. (Eds.). (1996). *Foundations of low vision: Clinical and functional perspectives.* New York: American Foundation for the Blind.

   *A practical guide with many suggestions for integrating students with visual impairments into mainstream classes.*

4. Holbrook, M. C. (Ed.). (1996). *Children with visual impairments.* Bethesda, MD: Woodbine House.

   *An introductory book for teachers and parents working with children who have visual impairments.*

5. Milian, M., & Erin, J. (Eds.). (2001). *Diversity in visual impairment.* New York: American Foundation for the Blind.

   *A guide to working with students from varied cultures who have visual impairments.*

6. Sacks, S. Z., & Silberman, R. K. (1998). Educating students who have visual impairments with other disabilities. Baltimore, MD: Paul H. Brookes.

   *A textbook that addresses the range of characteristics and needs for students who have visual impairments, including students who have other disabilities.*

## Hearing Loss

1. Lane, H., Hoffmeister, R., & Bahan, B. (1996). *A journey into the Deaf-world.* San Diego, CA: Dawn Sign Press.

   *A resource book that details Deaf culture and its role in education.*

2. Luetke-Stahlman, B., & Luckner, J. (1999). *Language across the curriculum.* Hillsboro, OR: Butte Publications.

   *A comprehensive resource providing instructional strategies for major curriculum areas.*

3. Moores, D. F. (1996). *Educating the deaf: Psychology, principles, and practices* (4th ed.). Boston, MA: Houghton Mifflin.

   *A comprehensive textbook that provides an overview of educating deaf students and discusses other aspects of deafness.*

4. Ross, M. (Ed.). (1990). *Hearing impaired children in the mainstream.* Parkton, MD: York Press.

   *Provides information to help students become mainstreamed from elementary school to college.*

5. Winslow, J., & Kozak, V. J. (1998). *Questions teachers ask: A guide for the mainstream classroom teacher with a hearing impaired student.* St. Louis, MO: Central Institute for the Deaf.

   *Offers essentials for teachers who have a student who is deaf or hard of hearing in their classroom.*

## Physical Disabilities and Health Impairments

1. Batshaw, M. L. (1997). *Children with disabilities: A medical primer* (4th ed.). Baltimore: Brookes.

   *An extensive overview of various types of physical disabilities and health impairments.*

2. Beverly, C. L., & Thomas, S. B. (1997). Developmental and psycho-social effects of HIV in school-aged population: Educational implications. *Education and Training in Mental Retardation and Developmental Disabilities, 32,* 32–41.

   *An informative article describing the developmental and psycho-social characteristics of school-aged persons with HIV and also providing educational implications and strategies to assist educators.*

3. Bigge, J. L. (1991). *Teaching individuals with physical and multiple disabilities.* New York: Macmillan.

   *A comprehensive textbook on physical and health impairments.*

4. Glang, A., Singer, G., & Todis, B. (1997). *Students with acquired brain injury: The school's response.* Baltimore: Brookes.

   *A resource for educators that provides practical information on educational issues and approaches to working with students with brain injury.*

5. Moffitt, K., Nachahsi, J., & Reiss, J. (Eds.). (1993). *Special children, special care.* Tampa: University of South Florida.

   *A practical guide for collaboration among professionals and families caring for children with complex health impairments.*

6. Witte, R. (1998). Meet Bob: A student with traumatic brain injury. *Teaching Exceptional Children, 30*(3), 56–60.

   *Provides practical information about identifying and educating students with TBI.*

7. Nevins, M. E., & Chute, P. (1996). *Children with cochlear implants in educational settings.* (School Age Children Series) Singular Publishing Group.

   *Sometimes children who are deaf receive a cochlear implant to improve their hearing. This book is a reader-friendly introduction to working with children with cochlear implants in the classroom.*

# suggested websites

**www.afb.org**

This website is developed by the American Foundation for the Blind. It provides a variety of resources on blindness and low vision (e.g., education, literacy, directory of services, and employment).

**www.aph.org**

This website is for American Printing House for the Blind. It introduces special media, tools, and materials that promote the independence of blind and visually impaired people.

**www.who.int/pbd/pbl/data.htm**
This website provides useful data on visual impairment (causes of blindness worldwide, global distribution of blindness by economic region or age, etc.).

**http://curry.edschool.virgina.edu/go/cise/os/categories/
   vi.html**
This website is for the Office of Special Education. It provides a variety of resources on visual impairments (definition, braille resources, organizations for the blind, etc.).

**www.nad.org**
This website is for the National Association of the Deaf. It provides a variety of resources on hearing impairments (e.g., American Sign Language, legal rights, Deaf culture, education, and employment).

**http://commtechlab.msu.edu/sites/aslweb**
This website contains thousands of American Sign Language (ASL) signs and provides video clips of ASL sign.

**www.inclusive.co.uk/infosite/phinfo.shtml**
This website includes information on a variety of assistive technologies for individuals with physical disabilities.

**http://apta.org**
This website is for the American Physical Therapy Association and provides information about physical therapists and their roles in schools.

**http://biausa.org**
This website is for the Brain Injury Association, Inc., and includes information about causes, treatment, and educational needs.

# Planning and
# Grouping Strategies

chapter

# for Special Learners

7

# chapter | outline

# focus | questions

1. What are the elements of the Flow of the Planning Process Model, including types of planning and factors that influence planning?

2. In thinking about long-term planning, what parameters must be considered and what resources need to be identified?

3. What are the key components of the Course Planning Routine?

4. What are the key components of the Planning Pyramid, and how can it be used for unit and lesson planning?

5. What kinds of instructional adaptations can be used in general education settings to promote learning for students with disabilities?

6. What are the differences between traditional grouping practices and current trends in instructional grouping?

7. What are the advantages and disadvantages of same- and mixed-ability groups?

8. When are whole group, small group, student pairs, and individual instruction most appropriate?

9. What is cooperative learning, and how can it be used to facilitate positive academic and social outcomes for all students?

10. How can you plan for multiple grouping structures in your classroom?

# inter view

## Lisa Geller

Lisa Geller is a third-grade teacher at South Pointe Elementary School in Miami, Florida. Of the 35 students in Lisa's class, 5 have learning disabilities. Lisa's faculty has chosen an inclusion model of service delivery for students with disabilities. Ellen Fascano is the special education teacher who works with Lisa. Her role is to provide instruction for students with learning disabilities in the general education classroom during the reading and language arts block and then to pull individual students, as necessary, to work on specific objectives identified on the IEP. Because Lisa and Ellen work daily in the same classroom, collaborative planning is a must.

Each week, Ellen and I sit down to talk about what the students with disabilities are doing. This is really important because we have parent conferences with the parents of all of our students four times a year, and Ellen and I both meet with the parents of the special education students. Although Ellen actually is responsible for the grades of the students with disabilities, we confer about their progress and decide on their grades jointly.

At the beginning of the year, Ellen and I review the IEP for all of the children and develop plans for individual students. But really our planning is ongoing. We also conduct an informal reading test at the beginning, middle, and end of the year for the students so that we can keep track of their progress in reading and make revisions and additions to our plans. We also do a great deal of informal observation and keep checklists about student progress, and we input our observations into the computer every week. The philosophy of our school is to record one observation per subject area per week. As you can imagine, this takes a great deal of work, and we need to meet every week to accomplish it all. But it is really important as we think how to meet individual student needs.

When I do my unit and lesson planning, I talk with Ellen about what areas might be difficult for the students with disabilities. She lets me know the most sensitive areas and gives me suggestions for how I can make adaptations to help students learn the material.

Part of our planning is related to how we group students for reading instruction. The philosophy at our school is for each student to feel that he or she is important and one person is not better than the other, so we use a variety of grouping patterns, including whole-class instruction to provide an overview, introduction, or review and then well-organized small groups or pairs of students. If you came into our reading class, this is what you'd see. First we do whole-class activities, such as reading a literature book together, and then some follow-up activities. Once again, Ellen is really helpful here because she lets me know where the students with disabilities might have some trouble and suggests some adaptations that I might make. I'm getting better at being sensitive to what they can and can't

do while I'm teaching and making on-the-spot changes to help them learn.

During the follow-up activities, my kids always have a "study buddy." Usually we try to choose the buddy that they work with so that a high achiever is working with a student who is having difficulty reading. It's great because the high achievers feel that they are being teachers, and they are learning something too. The low achievers are only working with one student, so they don't feel embarrassed or feel that they can't do it. It works well.

During part of the reading time we divide up into smaller groups for skill lessons. Ellen pulls all the students with disabilities into one group. The other students are placed in mixed achievement-level groups of six to ten students. I teach one group, and three other teachers come to our class to teach the other groups. This is unusual, but it really works. The other three teachers rotate from class to class to provide individual attention to students. I really like this small-group time because we can zero in on what each student in the class needs to work on.

You can see that the students with disabilities don't really feel that they are in a lower group. In our class, we just say Ms. So-and-so's group is this table, and so on. The special education group is just another group. They look forward to that time because Ellen is a wonderful teacher, she's very caring, she loves the kids.

So we have whole-class instruction, student pairing for activities, and small-group instruction for skills. We also have cooperative learning groups for special projects, and also Ellen or I pull students who might need to work on a specific skill in phonics or comprehension. As you can see, we use many different grouping formats, which involves a great deal of planning and coordination. I've been very happy with the way we grouped our students this year. Next year I probably would take even more time, pull the students who are having difficulty, and really try to focus more on the ones who can achieve more and try to challenge them. That's just my own personal goal.

# introduction

Planning for the success of all students in your class involves careful consideration of the needs of individuals as well as

of those of the class as a whole. As our interview with Lisa indicates, she recognizes that for this to happen, she needs to plan time for planning every week. Part of this planning time is hers alone, and part is for collaborative planning with other profes-

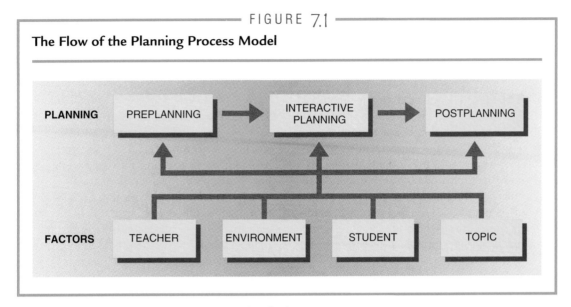

FIGURE 7.1

**The Flow of the Planning Process Model**

*Source:* Used by permission of *EEC* and the University of Calgary Press.

sionals in the school. Although Lisa is meticulous with her beginning-of-the-year planning, she also recognizes that it is important to keep setting new goals for meeting her students' individual needs.

Part of Lisa's instructional planning is the way she organizes students for instruction through grouping. She knows that sometimes whole-class instruction is appropriate and necessary, but she also realizes that at times, she must incorporate small groups and student pairing into her plans in order to meet individual student needs.

In this chapter, you'll learn strategies for planning for individual student needs within the framework of planning for the class as a whole. You'll also learn about how to incorporate a variety of grouping strategies to promote student success in your instructional planning. The focus of this chapter is not on your role in planning the IEP for students with special needs. Rather, the chapter focuses on how to make plans for your own classroom—plans that will attend to the learning needs of all students and provide you with information to group your students for effective instruction.

## Model of the Planning Process

If you ask experienced teachers how they plan, you are likely to get a collection of very different answers. Like any kind of planning (e.g., planning a budget, planning a personal schedule, planning a trip) individuals have different styles, and it is important for you to learn from other professionals

and then develop your own. In developing your own planning routines, it is helpful to think about how and when planning occurs and the factors that influence planning. The **Flow of the Planning Process Model** (Figure 7.1) can help to structure your thinking (Schumm et al., 1995a). This model indicates the sequence and relation among three types of planning and the factors that influence planning.

### Types of Planning

For most teachers, planning is not just what is written in plan books, which often includes only a general outline of what is going to happen in class. The real plan is in the head of the teacher and is developed and revised on an ongoing basis. Whether planning is for an entire school year, for a unit, or for an individual lesson, planning occurs at three stages—preplanning, interactive planning, and postplanning—as the Flow of the Planning Process Model indicates.

**Preplanning**  Preplanning involves decisions about what to teach and how to teach it. This advance preparation, which occurs at many levels, begins with progress monitoring so that the teacher has a clear understanding of what students know and need to know. Planning also includes activities such as developing unit or lesson plans, gathering materials, identifying resources, and deciding on instructional methods. Preplanning also involves

In a survey of 775 classroom teachers, 98 percent reported that their knowledge and skills for planning for general education students was excellent or good, but only 39 percent said that their knowledge and skills for planning for special education students was excellent or good (Schumm & Vaughn, 1992a).

gathering information about the students' prior knowledge of the topic being taught and their level of skill development so that instructional plans are appropriate for meeting individual needs.

**Interactive Planning** Your goals for a unit or a lesson may be carefully drawn on paper and imagined in your head, but as you begin to implement your plans, you might need to make changes on the spot to promote learning for all students. For example, you might observe that one or more students are having difficulty learning a skill or concept. That's when interactive planning comes in. **Interactive planning** involves monitoring students' learning while you teach and adapting your plans in response to their needs.

You might say to yourself, "Isn't interactive planning just teaching?" The two certainly overlap, but interactive planning differs somewhat, in that it focuses on the way students are learning and making appropriate adjustments. Teachers check frequently with students to ensure that they are understanding the key ideas or can perform the necessary skills. When teachers monitor while they teach, it provides opportunities for them to reteach difficult concepts or skills, adjust the pacing of the lesson, decide to focus more on one of the key ideas and teach the others later, and to ensure that students master the critical material before moving on.

As Lampert and Clark (1990, p. 21) noted, "teaching is a complex act requiring the moment-by-moment adjustments of plans to fit continually changing and uncertain conditions." Thus, interactive planning involves the on-the-spot decisions you make as a teacher to respond to student needs and to ensure that learning takes place.

**Postplanning** Postplanning is follow-up planning, and frequently occurs at the end of a lesson. After a lesson, you might reflect on the way students performed, then use that information to guide your planning and assessment for subsequent instruction. For example, you might realize that you covered less material than you anticipated and need to adjust your plans for the next day, or you might realize that by providing a quick assessment, you can determine which critical pieces of the lesson need to be retaught or taught differently. If many students did not grasp what you were teaching, you might need to develop plans for reteaching the lesson in a different way.

When evaluating a lesson, you may also reflect on how you would teach it in the future or simply think, "When I teach that lesson next year, I'll be certain to make some changes." In other words, you evaluate what occurred and decide what to keep and what to leave out in the future.

Overall, postplanning involves thinking about and evaluating a lesson and determining how student needs can best be met in future lessons.

## Factors That Influence Planning

The Flow of the Planning Process Model includes four interrelated factors that influence planning: teacher, environment, student, and topic. These factors can have a strong impact on what you plan, how you plan, and even how much you plan. **Teacher-related factors** are those that pertain to you as a planner not only for your class as a whole, but also for students with special needs. **Environment-related factors** pertain to the context in which you teach and include state, local, and class-level factors. **Student-related factors** pertain to who your students are, how they learn, and how they respond to instruction, both academically and socially. **Topic-related factors** concern specifically what you are teaching. Table 7.1 presents examples of each of the four factors that influence planning.

What process did this teacher undertake in planning this geography lesson? What factors influenced this process?

---

## TABLE 7.1

### Four Factors That Influence Planning

---

**Teacher-Related Factors**

- Attitudes and beliefs about planning in general and motivation to do so
- Attitudes and beliefs specific to planning for students with special needs and motivation to do so
- Knowledge and skills in planning and making accommodations for students with special needs
- Knowledge of and experience and interest in the subject matter you are teaching
- Amount of planning time
- Confidence in planning and making adaptations

**Environment-Related Factors**

- State and school-district guidelines and policies regarding planning and curriculum
- School-level guidelines and policies regarding planning and curriculum
- Grade-level, department, or subject-area guidelines and policies regarding planning and curriculum
- State-adopted textbooks and available materials
- Access to specialists (i.e., reading resource specialists, special education teachers, school counselors)
- Scheduling of special classes: physical education, special education, ESL classes, music, and art

- Scheduling of special holidays, assemblies, and special activities
- Physical arrangement and condition of school and classroom

**Student-Related Factors**

- Class size
- Engagement and interest in the topic and tasks
- Motivation
- Learning strategy preferences
- Level of background knowledge
- Behavior patterns
- Acceptance of adaptations
- Language and cultural differences
- Difficulty with basic skills

**Topic-Related Factors**

- New or review material
- Prior knowledge of topic
- Interest level of topic
- Number and complexity of new concepts or skills introduced
- Clarity of topic presentation in curricular materials
- Importance of topic in relation to overall curriculum

---

### r e s e a r c h b r i e f

### Facilitators and Barriers to Planning Instruction for Students with Special Needs

Before 1990, the topic of general education teachers' planning for students with disabilities was restricted to research on the classroom teachers' role in the IEP process. Because larger numbers of students with disabilities are placed in general education settings for all or part of the school day, teachers require knowledge about how to plan and make adaptations for exceptional students.

We have learned a great deal about resources that facilitate planning for students with disabilities (Schumm & Vaughn, 1992a). Classroom teachers viewed fellow professionals (special education teachers, school-based curriculum specialists such as reading resource teachers, fellow teachers, department chairs, and guidance counselors) as those who help in the planning process. Budgetary factors (particularly the need for

larger classes) were identified as the greatest barriers. The need to cover curriculum objectives, access to equipment and materials, and lack of planning time were also identified as factors that inhibit planning.

---

Meeting the instructional needs of all your students takes careful advance planning (preplanning), adjustments during lessons to be certain that learning is taking place (interactive planning), and reflection and evaluation to improve instruction in the future (postplanning). The need for conscientious planning of all three types is particularly important when you teach diverse learners, including students with disabilities. The task might seem daunting, but it can be done. First, it can be accomplished by considering the reality of your situation: the teacher, student, environmental, and topic-related factors. It can also be accomplished by using planning procedures specifically designed to focus on individual needs within the framework of planning for the class as a whole. In the next sections, you'll read about procedures for long-term planning, unit planning, and lesson planning.

## Long-Term Planning

It is interesting to observe three or four teachers in the same school who teach the same grade (at the elementary level) or the same grade and subject (at the secondary level). Even in schools in which teachers use the same state-adopted textbooks and follow the same state or district curriculum objectives, you are likely to see differences, particularly in the ways teachers accommodate individual student needs. Many of these differences stem from the type of **long-term planning** (planning for the whole school year) teachers do to meet individual student needs. This section presents suggestions for ways to include individual student needs in your long-term preplanning, interactive planning, and postplanning for your class as a whole. Few travelers would start out on a cross-country trip without a map. Long-term planning is your map for the school year. Long-term preplanning is essential to helping you get the big picture in respect to curriculum and classroom management. It can help you set a plan for moving from unit to unit and developing a sense of continuity. Most important, it can help you set a framework for meeting the individual needs of your students throughout the year.

## Procedure for the Course Planning Routine

If you are an elementary teacher, you'll probably teach a number of subjects: language arts, reading, mathematics, science, social studies, and so on. If you are a secondary teacher, you'll need to prepare for one or more courses. In either case, it's important to develop a master plan for what you'll teach and how to teach it. Of course, you'll need to work within your planning parameters, but even so, you'll have many decisions to make for your own class.

The six-stage **Course Planning Routine,** developed by researchers at the University of Kansas (Lenz et al., 1993), is a guide for long-range planning for classrooms with diverse learners. This guide includes procedures for setting goals for the course, getting the course off on the right foot, monitoring and managing the course during the year, and closing the course. As an elementary teacher, you can use this routine in your planning for each subject. As a secondary teacher, you can use this routine for planning each course. In either case, the Course Planning Routine can help you get the big picture:

**Stage 1**—ReflActive Planning Process—consists of seven steps designed to help teachers think through an overview of the course. The steps are easy to remember because they're organized by the acronym **SMARTER** (Lenz et al., 1993, p. 14–15):

- *Select* the critical content outcomes and turn them into a set of 10 questions that everyone in the class will be able to answer at the end of the course.

- *Map* the organization of the critical content of the entire course and create a visual device that will help students see their progress in mastering course content.

- *Analyze* why the critical course content might be difficult to learn, based on quantity, complexity, interest, student background, relevance, organization, abstractness, and external conditions (e.g., calendar).

- *Reach* decisions about the types of routines, devices, or learning strategies that should be used throughout the course to address learning difficulties.

- *Teach* using these routines regularly throughout the year to inform students about the devices and strategies being used and to involve students in constructing the devices and strategies in explicit ways.

- *Evaluate* mastery of the critical course content and related processes for high achievers, average achievers, low achievers, and others.

- *Reevaluate* course decisions and revise plans for the next unit or for next year.

**Stage 2**—Community of Learners—guides teachers through a series of questions related to creating a community of learners in the classroom, one in which every student feels accepted as a full participant:

- How can I nurture the community of learners enrolled in this course so that connections among them are strengthened and students help each other learn?

- How can I include everyone enrolled in the course in the learning process, such that each person becomes an involved learner?

- How can I determine the strengths and resources of course participants to ensure that these can be contributed to the community?

● How can I circumvent and compensate for the limitations of course participants?

**Stage 3—Target Students**—helps teachers focus on individual needs by identifying four types of student: high-, average-, and low-achieving students and those with disabilities. (In some classes, identifying a student who speaks English as a second language may also be helpful.) The teacher keeps these target students in mind during all aspects of planning. In planning for diversity in the classroom, it's difficult—if not impossible—to plan for the needs of every single student for every single lesson. This is particularly true in high schools where teachers may instruct over 100 students in a day! Identifying target students is a practical, realistic technique that helps make teaching more sensitive to diversity.

**Stage 4—Course Launching**—involves developing a plan for getting the course under way. Launching involves a plan for

● developing rapport with students
● communicating course goals and expectations to students
● describing classroom routines and procedures
● generating enthusiasm and interest in the course

**Stage 5—Course Maintenance**—revisits the course map developed during Stage 1 periodically to make certain that everything is on track and to make any necessary revisions. At the beginning of the school year, it will be helpful to mark specific dates on your calendar for conducting a review of the course map.

**Stage 6—Course Closure**—serves as a course evaluation. The 10 questions outlined in the course map are once again revisited to determine how well all students have fared in learning the content. During this stage, the teacher and students also discuss issues related to the learning community and how well goals were achieved.

The Course Planning Routine can serve as your road map for a grading period, a semester, or an entire school year. Its strengths include a system for considering individual student needs through target students, planning for academic goals through 10 questions, and planning for social goals through questions about the community of learners. As with any planning, the Course Planning Routine takes time. But the payoff is having a clear idea of where you're going and how you're going to get there. Tips for Teachers 7.1 provides time-management suggestions.

## Tips for Teachers

### 7.1 Time Management for Teachers

As you begin to plan for a new school year, you may start wondering, "How am I going to get all of this done?" Time management for teachers is complex—so much to do and so little time. With careful planning and prioritizing, however, you can accomplish a great deal. Here are some tips:

1. Keep your radar out for time-management tips from other teachers. They know the job and can give you hints for getting things done.
2. Write to-do lists, and keep them short. Use the 80–20 rule suggested by Alan Lakein (1973). Twenty percent of the items on your list should yield 80 percent of the value. In a list of 10 items, identify 2 and have a plan for getting them done.

3. As you look at your to-do list, identify 5-minute tasks, 15-minute tasks, and 1-hour tasks (and try to figure out when they can be done). You'd be surprised at what you can accomplish during in-between times, with a little planning.
4. Set realistic goals. For example, you may not be able to contact every parent every week, but you can make a commitment to contacting five parents a week. Before you know it, you'll have contacted all the parents of students in your class.
5. Schedule time for contacting fellow professionals, for planning and coordinating. Say to yourself, "I'll contact two fellow professionals per week. This week I'll talk to the teacher of the gifted and talented students in my class and to the teacher of the special education students."

*(continued)*

## Tips for Teachers

### 7.1 Time Management for Teachers (continued)

6. Learn how to delegate. Can someone help you with all or part of a project? Perhaps a parent, paraprofessional, volunteer, or student can assist you with tasks.

7. Think about how technology can help. Keep your eye out for computer programs to help with your grading, planning, and so on.

8. Avoid the temptation to overplan. As a teacher, you will be interrupted by parents, administrators, and, naturally, by students. It is important to keep these interruptions in mind and to realize that they are part of the job.

9. Plan for long-term, monthly, weekly, and daily goals, but be prepared to change your plans. Be flexible with your plan when legitimate situations arise.

10. Schedule a time every day for conferences. Meet with certain students on Monday, others on Tuesday, still others on Wednesday, and so on.

11. Plan for 60-second lessons while students are engaged in seatwork.

12. Take note of students who arrive early or leave late, and meet with them during those times.

13. Once or twice a week, make an appointment for lunch with a student.

14. Schedule conference times, and have students sign up for a conference with you.

15. This is the tough part: schedule time for planning. The payoff for a short time spent planning is tremendous.

## An Example of the Course Planning Routine

Jeanette Robinson teaches a self-contained fifth-grade class in a suburban elementary school. Of the 24 students in Jeanette's class, 3 are students with learning disabilities who are mainstreamed into the class for science and social studies. Jeanette used the Course Planning Routine to plan her overall goals for teaching a semester-long course on earth science. Her questions were based on overall objectives presented in her textbook and in her district science curriculum guide. Figures 7.2 and 7.3 illustrate Jeanette's course organizer and course map for science instruction during the school year.

--- FIGURE 7.2 ---

### Course Organizer

**Name of Course:** _____ Earth Science

is about

Our planet, its place in space, how it changes naturally and due to pollution, and what we need to do to preserve it.

**Course Questions:**

1. What is the atmosphere?
2. How do storms form?
3. How do scientists predict weather changes?
4. What is the earth's crust?
5. What is the earth's surface made of?
6. What are sources of energy and how are these energy resources used?
7. What are the sources of air, water, and land pollution?
8. How does pollution affect natural resources?
9. What is the solar system and what objects can be found in space?
10. How has space been studied and what instruments are used to study it?

*Source:* Adapted from Vaughn, S., Schumm, J. S., Lenz, K., Schumaker, J., Deshler, D., Morocco, C., Gordon, S., Riley, M., Fuchs, L., & Fuchs, D. (1995). *Planning for academic diversity in America's classrooms: Windows on reality, research, change, and practice.* Lawrence, KS: University of Kansas Center for Research on Learning.

— FIGURE 7.3 —

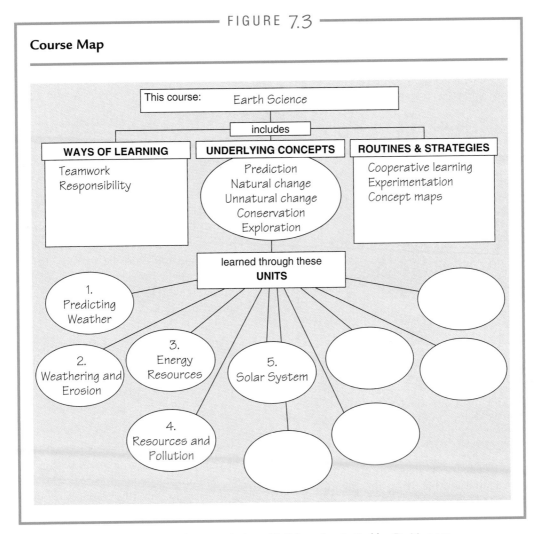

**Course Map**

*Source:* Adapted from Vaughn, S., Schumm, J. S., Lenz, K., Schumaker, J., Deshler, D., Morocco, C., Gordon, S., Riley, M., Fuchs, L., & Fuchs, D. (1995). *Planning for academic diversity in America's classrooms: Windows on reality, research, change, and practice.* Lawrence, KS: University of Kansas Center for Research on Learning.

## ● Unit Planning

After you establish the big picture for what you want to accomplish during the school year, the next step is to plan for units of study. An **instructional unit** is actually a series of lessons related to the same topic. For example, your school district's mathematics curriculum guide may require you to teach a series of lessons on measurement, which includes lessons on liquid measurement, distance, and so on. The length of the unit will depend on the topic. Some may last only a few days; others may last a month or more. In this section, you'll read about a unit-planning framework for planning for diverse student needs, the **planning pyramid** (Schumm et al., 1994).

## Procedure for the Unit Planning Pyramid

The unit planning pyramid is a framework or a way of thinking about planning instruction to enhance learning for all students. The pyramid is designed as a flexible tool that teachers can adjust to their personal style of planning and teaching. It involves careful identification of what needs to be taught and careful attention to individual students' needs to determine how the information will be taught.

**Degrees of Learning**    The primary component of the planning pyramid (see Figure 7.4), the **degrees of learning,** make up the body of the pyramid and will help you examine the content to be taught and

= FIGURE 7.4 =

**Planning Pyramid**

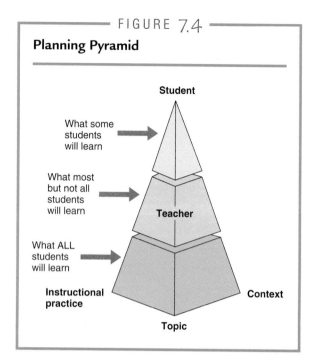

*Source:* Schumm, J. S., Vaughn, S., & Leavell, A. G. (1994, May). Planning Pyramid: A framework for planning for diverse students' needs during content area instruction. *The Reading Teacher, 47*(8), 608–615. Nancy Padak and Timothy Rasinski (Eds.). Copyright by the International Reading Association.

text or retain from a brief mention in class. The guiding question at this level is "What information will a *few* students learn?"

**Cautions and Comments**   A few cautions and comments about the planning pyramid:

- All students must have the opportunity to be presented with or exposed to the same information, although presentation of the information may vary somewhat according to a student's needs.

- All students must have equal access to information representing all levels of the pyramid.

- Students should not be assigned to a particular level of the pyramid on the basis of their ability; students who learn at the middle and top levels do so based on their interests, prior knowledge, or personal experience.

- Activities at the base of the pyramid should not be less stimulating (e.g., handouts, worksheets) than those at the other levels, nor should the upper levels be viewed as the only place for creative, fun activities.

prioritize concepts in an instructional unit. The degrees of learning are based on the premise that although all students are capable of learning, not all students will learn all the content covered. The three degrees of learning are the base of the pyramid, the middle level of the pyramid, and the top of the pyramid.

The base of the pyramid, considered the foundation of the lesson, consists of information that is essential for all students to learn. This section of the pyramid is directed by the question "What do I want *all* students to learn?"

The middle part of the pyramid represents information that is next in importance. This is information that *most* (but not all) students are expected to learn or grasp. This level of the pyramid includes supplementary facts and information about ideas and concepts presented at the base of the pyramid. The guiding question is "What do I want *most* students to learn?"

The top of the pyramid represents information that the teacher believes will enhance basic concepts and facts about the topic or subject. This type of information will be acquired only by a few students who have an added interest in and desire to learn more about the subject. It is information that the classroom teacher might not emphasize or elaborate on during a class but that students might read in a

**Deciding What Concepts to Teach**   After teachers have used the planning pyramid for a while, it is easier to determine what concepts belong at each degree of learning. Initially, teachers find it helpful to use a self-questioning process to determine what concepts to teach. Table 7.2 provides a list of questions you might ask to guide your thinking.

After you decide on the concepts to be taught, you can record them on the unit planning form (see Figure 7.5). This form also provides areas in which to record the unit title, materials and resources needed, instructional strategies and adaptations to be used, and evaluation or products that will serve as unit outcome measures.

## An Example of the Unit Planning Pyramid

Jeanette used the planning pyramid to structure a unit on weathering and erosion. She predicted that this would be a difficult unit for her students because they had little prior knowledge of this topic. She knew that it would be important for her to identify the key concepts she wanted students to learn and to predict adaptations necessary for special learners in her class. She liked the way the textbook presented the material and wanted to follow it closely. Because two of the students with learning

TABLE 7.2

## Questions to Guide Thinking about Concepts to Be Taught

**Questions Pertaining to the Topic**

- Is the material new or review?
- What prior knowledge do students have of this topic?
- How interesting is the topic to individual students?
- How many new concepts are introduced?
- How clearly are the concepts presented in the textbook?
- How important is this topic in the overall curriculum?

**Questions Pertaining to the Teacher**

- What prior knowledge do I have of this topic?
- How interesting is the topic to me?
- How much time do I have to plan for the lesson?
- What resources do I have available to me for this unit?

**Questions Pertaining to the Students**

- Will a language difference make comprehension of a particular concept difficult for a student?
- Is there some way to relate this concept to the cultural and linguistic backgrounds of my students?
- Will students with reading difficulties be able to function independently in learning the concepts from textbooks?
- Will there be students with high interest in or prior knowledge of these concepts?
- Will my students have the vocabulary they need to understand the concepts to be taught?
- What experiences have my students had that will relate to this concept?

*Source:* Schumm, J. S., Vaughn, S., & Leavell, A. G. (1994, May). Planning pyramid: A framework for planning for diverse students' needs during content area instruction. *The Reading Teacher*, 47(8), 608–615. Nancy Padak & Timothy Rasinski (Eds.). Copyright by the International Reading Association.

disabilities were nonreaders, however, she knew she would need to enlist a volunteer to make audiotapes of the chapters and to arrange cooperative learning groups for in-class reading of the text. Jeanette also planned to have in-class study time (with study buddies) before tests. To plan the weathering and erosion unit, Jeanette used the Unit Planning Form shown in Figure 7.6.

FIGURE 7.5

**Unit Planning Form**

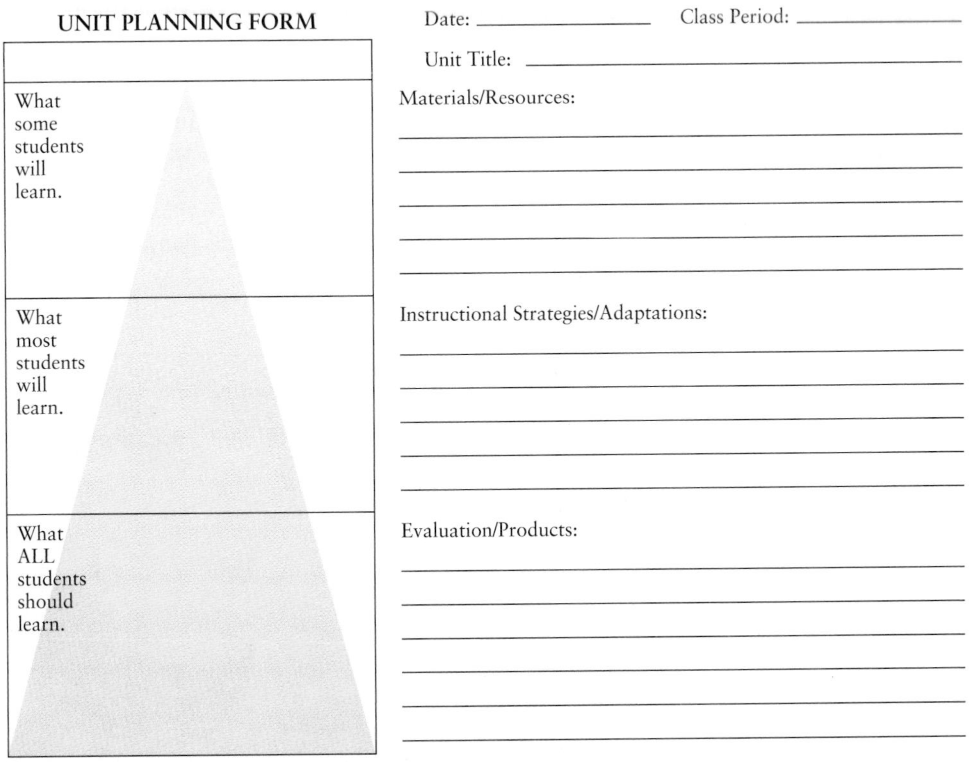

UNIT PLANNING FORM

Date: _____    Class Period: _____

Unit Title: _____

What some students will learn.

What most students will learn.

What ALL students should learn.

Materials/Resources:
_____
_____
_____
_____
_____

Instructional Strategies/Adaptations:
_____
_____
_____
_____

Evaluation/Products:
_____
_____
_____
_____
_____
_____

*Source:* Schumm, J. S., Vaughn, S., & Harris, J. (1995). *Collaborative planning for content area instruction.* Published by TEC. Reprinted with permission.

FIGURE 7.6

**Jeanette's Sample Unit Plan**

UNIT PLANNING FORM

Date: _Sept. 1–30_     Class Period: _1:30 – 2:30_

Unit Title: _Weathering and Erosion_

| What some students will learn. | • How Earth looked during Ice Age<br>• Disasters caused by sudden changes<br>• Geographic examples of slow and fast changes |
|---|---|
| What most students will learn. | • Compare and contrast weathering and erosion<br>• How humans cause physical and chemical weathering<br>• Basic types of rocks |
| What ALL students should learn. | • Basic components of Earth's surface<br>• Forces that change crust are weathering and erosion |

Materials/Resources:
Guest speaker on volcanoes
Video: erosion and weathering
Rock samples
Library books – disasters, volcanoes, etc.
Colored transparencies for lectures

Instructional Strategies/Adaptations:  Experiments!
Concept maps
Cooperative learning groups to learn material
    in textbook
Audiotape of chapter
Study buddies to prepare for quizzes and tests

Evaluation/Products:
Weekly quiz
Unit test
Learning logs (daily record of "What I learned")
Vocabulary flash

## Lesson Planning

Your overall plan for the school year is in place. Your plan for a unit of study is detailed. Now it's time to focus on a particular instructional session: the lesson. The earlier recommendation that you develop your own planning style is particularly important for lesson planning. As you consider your lesson-planning style, you'll want to think about how to plan to promote learning for all students. The lesson planning pyramid can help.

### Procedure for the Lesson Planning Pyramid

The lesson planning pyramid can be used for an individual lesson or to add depth and detail to the unit planning pyramid described earlier. The lesson planning pyramid does not necessitate a great deal of paperwork and contains most of the elements teachers think are necessary to plot out a lesson.

With the lesson planning pyramid, as with the unit version, you focus on identifying concepts to be taught by asking, "What do I want all, most, and some of the students to learn as a result of the lesson?" As you can see from Figure 7.7, the Lesson Planning Form also provides areas in which to

How could using unit and lesson planning pyramids help this teacher to adapt instructional activities for students with special needs? How should this teacher plan ways of grouping students for instruction?

FIGURE 7.7

**Lesson Planning Form**

Date: _____    Class Period: _____    Unit: _____

Lesson Objective(s): _____

_____

| Materials | Evaluation |
|---|---|
| | |

| In-Class Assignments | Homework Assignments |
|---|---|
| | |

**LESSON PLANNING FORM**

| Pyramid | Agenda |
|---|---|
| What some students will learn. | _____ |
| What most students will learn. | _____ |
| What ALL students should learn. | _____ |

*Source:* Schumm, J. S., Vaughn, S., & Harris, J. (1995). *Collaborative planning for content area instruction.* Published by TEC. Reprinted with permission.

record materials, evaluations, in-class assignments, and homework assignments. In addition, there is an agenda area on which to list activities that will occur during the lesson.

In lesson planning, it is important to think not only about the teacher, student, and topic, but also about the environment and the instructional strategies you will use. The questions in Table 7.3 can guide your thinking about the environment and instructional strategies.

## An Example of the Lesson Planning Pyramid

Jeanette used her Lesson Planning Form as a guide for her lesson plan for the science lesson on the earth's surface. This lesson included many new terms that she knew would be unfamiliar to her students. The vocabulary was important for students to learn

because it would be used throughout the unit. Her lesson plan included specific strategies for teaching the vocabulary and visuals to help the vocabulary come alive. Also, by having students write in learning logs, she could monitor what they were learning. She knew that while they were working on the learning logs, she would need to check in with students with writing difficulties to monitor their learning orally. Figure 7.8 shows Jeanette's plan.

## Monitoring Student Learning during the Lesson

As you read earlier in this chapter, interactive planning is planning that occurs during a lesson. When you recognize that students are not "getting it," you adjust or alter your plans to respond to student needs. Monitoring what students understand is critical for interactive planning. Monitoring helps you

=== TABLE 7.3 ===

**Questions to Guide Thinking about Environment and Instructional Strategies**

**Questions Pertaining to Environment**
- Are there any holidays or special events that are likely to distract students or alter instructional time?
- How will the class size affect my teaching of this concept?
- How well do my students work in small groups or pairs?

**Questions Pertaining to Instructional Strategies**
- What methods will I use to motivate students and to set a purpose for learning?
- What grouping pattern is most appropriate?

- What instructional strategies can I implement?
- What learning strategies do my students know (or need to learn) that will help them master these concepts?
- What in-class and homework assignments are appropriate for this lesson?
- Do some assignments need to be adapted for students with disabilities?
- How will I monitor student learning on an ongoing, informal basis?

*Source:* Schumm, J. S., Vaughn, S., & Leavell, A. G. (1994, May). Planning pyramid: A framework for planning for diverse students' needs during content area instruction. *The Reading Teacher, 47*(8), 608–615. Nancy Padak & Timothy Rasinski (Eds.). Copyright by the International Reading Association.

=== FIGURE 7.8 ===

**Jeannette's Sample Lesson Plan**

Date: Sept. 1     Class Period: 1:30 – 2:30     Unit: Weathering and Erosion

Lesson Objective(s): The students will describe components of the earth

| Materials | Evaluation |
|---|---|
| Colored transparencies<br>Rock samples | Learning logs<br>Oral summaries |

| In-Class Assignments | Homework Assignments |
|---|---|
| Write in learning log | Draw diagram of Earth's layers<br>Make vocabulary flash cards |

**LESSON PLANNING FORM**

| Pyramid | Agenda |
|---|---|
| What some students will learn. • Examples of 3 types of rocks | Introduce key vocab. using transparencies<br><br>Work in coop. groups to read chapter<br><br>Discuss chapter |
| What most students will learn. • Crust made of 3 types of rock • How rocks are formed | Show rock samples<br><br>Have students write in learning logs |
| What ALL students should learn. • Earth has 3 layers • Outer layer is where we live • Crust is constantly changing | Have several students read log entries aloud<br><br>Assign homework —<br>Recommend extra reading for students who want to learn more about rocks |

## making a Difference

### Using Lesson Reaction Sheets

Student monitoring provides an excellent opportunity for 60-second lessons. Lesson Reaction Sheets are one quick way to monitor students' understanding. After a lesson is completed, have your students write a brief reaction to it. Provide your students with the following questions:

## The 60-second Lesson

- What did you learn from this lesson?
- What was confusing about the lesson?
- What else would you like to know about the topic?

It should take students only a few minutes to write answers to these questions. You may need to find another time to ask these questions of students who have difficulty writing so that they can answer orally.

---

keep in touch with what students are learning and remain sensitive to the troubleshooting you must do when students experience difficulty. The most typical kinds of monitoring are to ask questions during class and to circulate around the room, checking in with students during individual or group seatwork. Some quick strategies for monitoring follow.

**Informal member checks** are frequent, quick checks to see whether students understand. For example, after Susan Moore taught her third graders a lesson about the four food groups, she asked for a "thumbs up" hand signal if they understood and "thumbs down" if they did not.

At frequent intervals during a lesson, you can ask students to summarize key points. This helps keep students on their toes while helping you keep tabs on what they are learning. Remember, good teachers ask questions of all students, including those with disabilities, and when needed prompt and nudge students toward the answer.

McTighe and Lyman (1988) described the **think–pair–share** method, which can be used during peer monitoring activities. This strategy yields high student involvement and verbal interaction. Students are first encouraged to think individually about a topic for 2 minutes. Then students pair up to discuss the topic. The teacher then signals the pairs of students to share their responses with the entire class. The think–pair–share method involves all students in active idea processing throughout the school day.

Class notes are the most tangible record of what students have learned during a lesson. Often, students with learning disabilities have a difficult time taking notes during class and thus have difficulty preparing for tests. One way to provide support is to have **collaborative open-note quizzes** (Schumm & Lopate, 1989). After completing a lecture, divide the students into small cooperative learning groups. Allow students some time to discuss the lecture and summarize key points. Students should also revise their notes, adding information from their fellow students. Then, give students questions about the lecture to answer as a group. Through sharing, students with learning problems are provided the opportunity to "fill in the gaps" of what they missed during a lesson and also to see examples of the way other students take notes.

## An Overview of Instructional Grouping

As you make your long-range, unit, and lesson plans, you'll want to plan for a variety of grouping patterns. At the beginning of the chapter, you read that Lisa uses a variety of grouping patterns: sometimes whole class, sometimes small groups, and sometimes pairs of students. Sometimes Lisa combines students with similar achievement levels; sometimes she mixes high- and low-level students. Part of Lisa's planning is to think about which grouping pattern seems most appropriate for each learning objective. Remember that grouping "can powerfully influence positively or negatively the levels of individual student engagement and hence academic progress" (Maheady, 1997, p. 325).

There is no easy answer to the question of how best to group students for instruction. Consequently, the issue of grouping has triggered vigorous debate among educators, parents, and students. Our experience is that almost everyone has an opinion based on personal experience as a teacher, parent, or student. Your personal experience has already helped you shape ideas about how grouping should occur in the school and classroom. In this section, you'll learn more about grouping from a historical standpoint, as well as current trends and issues associated with grouping students. The section also includes a description of various grouping configurations you might use in the classroom, as well as suggestions for implementing grouping patterns to promote successful learning for all students.

# TechTalk

## Computers and People with Special Needs

Teaching students with special needs and disabilities has undergone a revolution since the late 1970s through the introduction of adaptive computer technologies. Adaptive technology refers to the use of computers—both hardware and software—to help challenged individuals overcome a limiting condition in their lives. This can happen in many different ways. A vision-impaired student can have text read out loud

to her using special software and a sound card and speakers, a paralyzed individual can use a puff switch to activate a communications board or keyboard, or a mute individual can have words spoken to him.

Adaptive computer technologies involve the special modification and use of interface devices such as keyboards, mice, and touch screens. Output devices must also be adapted. In the case of a blind or visually limited individual, a printer can be redesigned to output raised braille letters, rather than print, and text output on a monitor can be magnified.

A good online source on adaptive input and output devices can be found at Vanderbilt University's Assistive Technology Viewer: http://natri.uky.edu.

An excellent introduction on adaptive technology that not only deals with technical issues, but also addresses questions about the appropriate use of computers for people with special needs is Arlene Brett and Eugene F. Provenzo, Jr.'s *Adaptive technology for special human needs* (Albany, NY: State University of New York Press, 1995). Also see Chapter 6, "Technology for Inclusion" in Eugene F. Provenzo, Jr., Arlene Brett, and Gary N. McCloskey's *Computers, curriculum, and cultural change: An introduction for teachers* (Mahwah, NJ: Lawrence Erlbaum Associates, 1998).

## Traditional Instructional Grouping

In the mid-1800s, preoccupation with improving the productivity of public education in the United States gave rise to "graded" schools. A teacher assigned to a specific grade could teach the entire class. The graded system spread widely across the United States, thus establishing the most durable form of grouping in our educational system: age-level grouping, or grades. Teachers quickly realized, however, that a single grade included a wide range of academic levels. As Berliner and Casanova note (1993, p. 6), teachers often resort to grouping by ability because of an "inescapable fact of life: students differ dramatically from one another."

**Homogeneous grouping,** or **same-ability grouping,** is the practice of putting students at approximately the same achievement level together for instruction. School-level ability grouping is called

> John Philbreck of the Quincy, Massachusetts, school system initiated the graded system in 1847. It is likely that Philbreck was influenced by Horace Mann's and Colonel Francis W. Parker's reports of the ordered curriculum they had observed in Prussia (Button & Provenzo, 1983).

**tracking.** At the school level, students might be assigned to a particular class. In an elementary school, for example, one teacher might be assigned all the high-achieving students, another teacher all the average-achieving students, and a third teacher all the low-achieving students. At the middle- or high-school level, high-achieving students might be assigned to accelerated courses, average-achieving students to regular courses, and low-achieving students to remedial courses. Students are assigned to tracks based on their grades, achievement test scores, and (in some cases) behavior. The idea of same-ability grouping is that the content and pacing of instruction can be better controlled to meet individual needs.

Although research on the effectiveness of same-ability grouping was inconsistent, reviewers of such literature generally recognized the positive impact of same-ability grouping, particularly for children with learning difficulties (Miller & Otto, 1930; Whipple,

> The first ability-grouped classes originated in 1862 in the St. Louis, Missouri, public schools, under the direction of superintendent William T. Harris (Otto, Wolf, & Eldrige, 1984).

1936). During the 1950s, the practice of **within-class same-ability grouping** for reading and mathematics began to take hold in elementary classes (Barr & Dreeben, 1991; Harris & Sipay, 1980). The goal of same-ability small groups is to reduce the range of abilities between group members so that the teacher can instruct students who are functioning on approximately the same level. For example, the reading and math groups in an elementary-school classroom might be based on similar student achievement (high, medium, or low) in each area. The teacher would pull one group at a time for instruction while the other groups focused on completing workbook assignments or silent readings. Within-class same-ability grouping for reading and mathematics was a dominant practice in elementary schools until recent years.

> The Joplin Plan, started in Joplin, Missouri (Floyd, 1954), involves regrouping students across grade levels. For example, all first-, second-, and third-grade students reading on the first-grade level would be moved to the same group during reading time.

## Current Issues in Instructional Grouping

Schooling in the United States is now in a phase in which educators are exploring new alternatives to traditional ways of organizing students for instruction (Barr, 1995). The current issues described here summarize trends about grouping. Points for you to consider about grouping for effective instruction are presented in Tips for Teachers 7.2.

**Current Issue #1: Use of Same-Ability Grouping, Especially for Reading and Math**   Although many critiques of inappropriate use of same-ability grouping within mixed-ability classes exist, particularly for older students (above grade 4), there is considerable evidence that same-ability grouping for reading and math can promote effective outcomes for students, particularly students with special needs (Vaughn, Hughes, Moody, & Elbaum, 2001). Briefly stated, criticisms of same-ability grouping have been raised, including the following (Oakes, 1992):

- Same-ability grouping can widen the gap between high and low achievers (Slavin, 1987).
- Same-ability grouping may restrict friendship choices (Hallinan & Sorensen, 1985).
- Although same-ability grouping may enhance the motivation and self-esteem of high-achieving students, it may lower the motivation and self-esteem of low-achieving students (Oakes et al., 1991).
- The quality of instruction in low-ability classes is frequently inferior. Emphasis in typical low-

ability classes is more on lower-level skills and discipline and less on higher-level thinking (Goodlad, 1984; Hiebert, 1983).

Many of these criticisms of same-ability groups, particularly in the early grades for reading and math, can be overcome if teachers implement the following:

- The best-quality instruction is provided to all students.
- Opportunities to engage in multiple grouping formats are provided, including same-ability small groups, mixed-ability small groups, pairs, and whole-class instruction.
- Teachers provide ongoing progress monitoring and regroup students regularly on the basis of their learning needs.
- Teachers provide opportunities for all members of the class to work together through the instructional day.

**r e s e a r c h  b r i e f**

### Students' Perceptions of Grouping

What do students think about grouping practices for reading instruction? Elbaum, Schumm, and Vaughn (1995) surveyed 549 elementary students (grades 3, 4, and 5), including 23 students with learning disabilities, to find out what students think. Results revealed that students at all levels of reading ability liked mixed-ability groups and mixed-ability pairs most (*mixed-ability* refers to arranging students by performance in the academic area in which they are grouped—thus, average-to-high achievers would be grouped with low achievers). Whole-class instruction received the next highest ratings. Same-ability groups and working alone were the least popular formats. Students in mixed-ability groups were perceived as getting more help from classmates, working more cooperatively, and making more progress in reading than those in same-ability groups. Same-ability groups were perceived to be desirable only for very poor readers.

**Current Issue #2: Students with Disabilities in General Education Settings**   Students with disabilities are spending more and more of their school day in general education settings. This movement toward inclusion broadens the range of student diversity in the classroom. Inclusion, coupled with the movement toward mixed-ability grouping discussed earlier, means that classroom teachers must learn new strategies and organizational procedures for meeting the needs of individual students.

# Tips for Teachers

## 7.2 Grouping for Effective Instruction: Points to Consider

The type of grouping that you use depends upon the purpose of instruction. Students can be grouped in mixed- or same-ability groups or pairs, provided whole-class instruction, or taught individually when needed.

| Group | Advantages | Sample Activities | Group Formation |
|---|---|---|---|
| Whole group | Engages students in shared learning experiences<br>Includes all students<br>Creates a community of knowledge that can be tapped in the future | Read-alouds<br>Shared writing<br>Introduction of new concepts<br>Class discussions<br>Modeling by teacher<br>Performances by individual or groups of students | All students assigned to the class participate |
| Small group (same ability) | Meets individual student needs<br>Maximizes opportunity for students to express what they know and to receive feedback<br>Provides opportunity for teacher to adjust pacing and assure mastery | Instruction provided by teacher or highly prepared paraprofessional<br>Instruction designed to meet the learning needs of the students in the group<br>Small group instruction in reading and math provided on an ongoing basis | Assigned to group of 3 to 8 students with similar knowledge and skills<br>Based on assessment or progress monitoring data<br>Students regrouped regularly to reflect needs |
| Small group (mixed ability) | Provides opportunities for students to work with all students<br>Teaches students to learn from and to teach their fellow students | Activities that allow students to practice and extend what they are learning<br>Activities that engage students in working with others<br>Activities that hold all students in the group accountable for learning | Reflects students' abilities or interests<br>Can be cooperative groups or student-led groups<br>Group composition changes regularly |
| Pairs/partner | Motivates students<br>Addresses social and academic needs | Peer tutoring<br>Activities to practice concepts<br>Shared projects | Cross-age pairs allows older students to tutor younger students<br>Same-age pairs allows students to co-teach<br>Progress monitoring data is used to assign students to pairs |
| One-on-one | Meets individual needs<br>Allows for more intensive instruction<br>Often used for students at risk or with disabilities<br>Allows access to the general education curriculum | Can be designed for a brief lesson, 1–5 minutes, or more extended time<br>Can be used to enhance learning in any area | Based on monitoring student progress |

*Source:* Adapted from Fountas, I. C., & Pinnell, G. S. (1996). *Guided reading: Good first teaching for all children.* Portsmouth, NH: Heinemann; Reutzel, D. R. (1999). Organizing literacy instruction: Effective grouping strategies and organizational plans. In L. B. Gambrell, L. M. Morrow, S. B. Newman, & M. Pressley (Eds.), *Best practices in literacy instruction* (pp. 271–291). New York: Guilford; *Second Grade Reading Academy.* Austin, Texas: Texas Education Leagency.

## Current Issue #3: A Critical Examination of "What's Best" for All Students

Those who oppose—or at least question—mixed-ability grouping do so out of concern for what will happen to students at the extremes of the ability spectrum. Two typical questions follow:

- Will mixed-ability grouping slow down the academic progress of gifted and high-achieving students?
- Can mixed-ability grouping enable teachers to provide the intensive, direct instruction needed by low-achieving students?

The answer to the first question is that there is no conclusive evidence about the effect of mixed- versus same-ability grouping for the academic success of gifted and high-achieving students. Indeed, an examination of the literature on grouping can be interpreted in very different ways. Allan (1991) concluded from such an examination that students who are gifted and high-achieving benefit from some form of same-ability grouping and that opportunities should be maintained for accelerated instruction of such students with their high-achieving peers. Allan concluded, "The strongest positive academic effects of grouping for gifted students result from either acceleration or classes that are specially designed for the gifted and use specially trained teachers and differentiated curriculum and methods" (p. 65). Slavin (1991) examined the same literature and determined that the evidence to support same-ability grouping for high achievers was sparse and that the modest academic benefits cannot compensate for maintaining an inequitable system. Slavin's conclusion is that students who are high achieving "will do well wherever they are" (p. 70).

Similarly, there is no clear-cut answer to the second question. There is little definitive evidence that ability grouping (including pull-out programs) positively affects the academic achievement of low-achieving students. "Nor—given the widespread practice of undifferentiated whole-class instruction in general education classrooms—is there much encouragement that low-achieving students in that setting will receive the intensive, direct instruction they need" (Baker & Zigmond, 1990; McIntosh et al., 1993). It is abundantly clear that the type of instruction needed to improve the basic skills of students who are low-achieving needs to be improved, regardless of the setting.

## Current Issue #4: Use of Multiple Grouping Formats

Research has not identified one "best" grouping pattern, in terms of academic and social benefits to students. However, research has suggested that smaller group sizes are associated with improved outcomes for students, especially for students with disabilities (Elbaum et al., 1999). Thus, teachers need to consider how they can provide very small groups (three students with one teacher) and one-on-one instruction for students at-risk and with disabilities since these grouping formats can be highly effective and necessary to assure progress for students with disabilities (Elbaum et al., 2000; Vaughn et al., n.d.).

Since very small group instruction cannot be provided all the time, teachers realize that using a variety of grouping formats is most appropriate for classrooms with a wide range of student diversity. These teachers are beginning to recognize that different grouping patterns are appropriate for different purposes.

The use of a variety of grouping patterns can be referred to as **multiple grouping formats.** As Table 7.4 demonstrates, when grouping students, you can think about different group sizes, composition, materials, purposes, and leadership. Principles for using multiple grouping formats include the following (Unsworth, 1984; Vaughn, Hughes, Moody, & Elbaum, 2001a):

- There are no permanent groups.
- Groups are designed to meet students' learning needs.
- Whole-class instruction is used but it is not the dominant grouping format.
- Groups vary and include very small groups (two or three students), larger groups (five to seven students), and still very large groups (seven to ten students).
- Students are taught to work in pairs, sometimes with students who have similar abilities and sometimes with students who have different abilities.
- Students are assigned to groups based on their learning needs, the purpose of instruction, and other goals as considered by the teacher.
- Students are occasionally provided instruction one-on-one from the teacher.
- Students are taught to work in small, cooperative groups as well as teacher-led groups.

## Current Issue #5: Opportunities for Students to Learn How to Work Together in Different Grouping Formats

Teachers may direct groups of students or may arrange for students to work together in a group. Teachers can group students for the purpose of working together to complete an assignment or project, to solve a problem, or to practice basic skills. It is unwise, however, to assume that students will automatically know how to work with each other. The current trend is not only to group students so that they can accomplish tasks together, but also to show students *how* to work together. Working collaboratively, students can learn such lessons as how to give and receive help, how to listen and respond to the ideas of others, and how to complete a task as a team. The teacher needs to structure group work, however, so that these valuable lessons are not lost.

In the upcoming sections, you'll read about different grouping patterns and how to implement them in your classroom. Particular emphasis is placed on

===== TABLE 7.4 =====

### Grouping Decisions

**Size**
- Individuals
- Pairs
- Small groups
- Half class
- Whole class

**Composition (placement in group determined by)**
- Adaptations
- Accommodation
- Technology
- Tools
- Ability
- Interests
- Skill levels
- Prior knowledge (content)
- Prior knowledge (strategies)
- Random
- Friendship
- Sex
- English proficiency
- Cultural background
- Behavior
- Teacher selection
- Student selection

- Standardized test scores
- Administrator preference
- Parent preference
- Previous success with group

**Materials**
- Teacher-chosen
- Student-chosen
- Same materials for all groups
- Different levels of different topics
- Different levels of similar topics
- Different materials and different activities—same level

**Purposes**
- Skill development
- Skill practice
- Projects
- Written assignments
- Reading assignments
- Problem solving
- Discussions

**Leadership**
- Teacher-led
- Student-led

*Source:* Adapted from Flood, J., Lapp, D., Flood, S., & Nagal, G. (1992). Am I allowed to group? Using flexible patterns for effective instruction. *The Reading Teacher, 45*(8), 608–616. James Baumann, (Ed.). Copyright by the International Reading Association.

how to meet the needs of students with disabilities in each grouping pattern. You will also learn to teach students how to work effectively in groups. Finally, you'll learn how to incorporate different grouping patterns as part of a flexible grouping plan.

## Planning for Multiple Grouping Structures

For multiple grouping structures to be successful, careful planning is essential. Without thoughtful planning, different grouping patterns sometimes don't occur. The temptation becomes not to group at all but instead to fall into the pattern of whole-class teaching followed by individual practice, a less than ideal pattern for meeting individual needs (Radencich & McKay, 1995; Schumm, Moody, & Vaughn, 2000; Taylor, Pearson, Clark, & Walpole, 1999). As you think about a lesson, keep grouping in mind by asking yourself the following questions:

- What is the best group size for teaching this lesson?
- What is the best group size for follow-up activities?
- What is the best composition of learners for each group with respect to student academic ability and work habits?
- What materials are needed for each group?

- Will the groups be teacher-led, student-led, or cooperative?
- What room arrangement is necessary for the grouping plan?
- When students move from one group to another, how can I ensure quick and smooth transitions?
- What issues related to students' behavior and social needs should I consider?

## ● Grouping Patterns

There are many ways to group students of varying abilities for instruction. This section describes different grouping patterns and includes guidelines for classroom implementation of these grouping arrangements. The discussions focus on ways to create student groups of different sizes (whole class, small group, pairs, and single student).

## Whole Class

**Whole-class grouping** is the pattern students have experienced most often. Indeed, whole class is the most frequently used grouping pattern. Whole classes can comprise students of same or mixed ability. Quite often, the decision whether to track students or group them by ability is a districtwide or schoolwide decision. You may or may not be part of that decision-making process. Even in a "same-ability" class, however, you'll quickly note that students in your class have a range of differences to which you, the teacher, need to attend.

Keeping the whole class together may be appropriate sometimes to accomplish the following:

- Build classroom community
- Establish classroom routines
- Introduce new units of study
- Introduce new skills and concepts
- Conduct whole-class discussions
- Develop common experiences
- Listen to guest speakers
- View educational videos

Many teachers like whole-class grouping because it makes planning fairly simple, with one instructional plan (including one set of instructional activities) for the whole group. Whole-class grouping also makes classroom management easier, in that teachers do not have to divide their time among different groups.

There are some drawbacks to using a whole-class grouping format. The primary problem is that it is more difficult to attend to individual needs during whole-class grouping. Students with learning difficulties are likely to try to fade into the woodwork and not participate fully in class activities (Brozo, 1990). The pace of instruction might be too fast for some students and too slow for others. Moreover, the content might be too difficult for some students and too easy for others. The planning pyramid discussed earlier in this chapter is particularly important to use in planning whole-group instruction. With whole-class grouping, it is important not only that you monitor what students are learning, but also that you think about necessary adaptations to ensure success for all students. For example, if whole-class instruction involves a reading assignment followed by a discussion, you'll need to plan adaptations, such as enabling students who are nonreaders to listen to an audiotape of the reading assignment.

## Small Groups

Small groups consist of three or more students. In this section, you'll read about same-ability small groups,

*Very small group instruction yields greater academic gains for students with disabilities than large-group instruction does (Elbaum et al., 1999; Simmerman & Swanson, 2001).*

mixed-ability small groups, and cooperative learning groups. Figures 7.9 and 7.10 provide examples of small-group instruction plan sheets.

### Same-Ability Small Groups

Students in same-ability groups are at approximately the same level (as determined by achievement tests, informal tests, or teacher judgment). Many teachers appreciate the benefits of same-ability grouping especially for early reading and math skills.

In Yvette Myers's fourth-grade class, for example, six students are reading below the third-grade level. Yvette finds it necessary to provide this group of students with explicit instruction in word study, fluency, and comprehension for 20 minutes each day. She also includes many other types of grouping patterns during the school day so that the students don't feel isolated from the class as a whole.

The pros and cons of same-ability groups were discussed earlier in this chapter. If you elect to use same-ability groups as part of your total grouping plan, Tips for Teachers 7.3 includes some suggestions for their most effective use.

**Mixed-Ability Small Groups**   Students in **mixed-ability groups** represent a wide range of levels. Group placement may be determined by many different criteria, from student interest to needed skill lessons. Mixed-ability groups are created for special purposes and are fluid, in that they tend to change throughout the school year and even throughout the school day. In fact, students can belong to more than one group at a time. Once the goals of the project are achieved, the groups are reorganized.

Mixed-ability groups can be organized for a variety of purposes, including the following:

- Conducting minilessons on an as-needed basis
- Completing a project
- Preparing a presentation for the class
- Completing a follow-up assignment
- Practicing new skills
- Discussing a reading assignment

Students can be grouped in a number of ways, some of which follow:

- *Interest.* Students with similar interests can be placed together in small groups. Teachers can determine student interests through surveys and group discussions and place students together for an assignment such as describing how a volcano works during science time. Interest groups tend to yield impressive products because students in the group are highly motivated.
- *Skills to be learned.* Several students who are experiencing difficulty with a particular skill, such as antonyms, may be placed in a small group. This may give them the extra time and support they need. If necessary, the teacher can intervene with this group to support acquisition of the needed skill. Once the skill is mastered by individual group members, they no longer need to be in this particular group.
- *English proficiency.* For students who need help understanding English, you can provide very necessary support by including in the group a bilingual classmate with greater proficiency and preteaching key vocabulary words and concepts before group work.

FIGURE 7.9

**Grouping Instruction Plan Sheet: Math**

Group Members:   Ae-hwa
                 Leila
                 Marco
                 Robert
                 Crystal

Instructional Focus:

1. Math race facts
2. Math kit-box A, problem #2

Group Members:   Juan
                 Carmela
                 Dheepa
                 Karla
                 Russell

Instructional Focus:

1. Design 3 math story problems

Group Members:   Lilly
                 Jose
                 Ui-jung
                 Mary

Instructional Focus:

1. Math tracks
2. Subtraction with regrouping #14–21

Group Members:   Stanley
                 Mark
                 June
                 Jennifer

Instructional Focus:

1. Word problems 4–6
2. Finish math puzzle

Group Members:   Sylvia
                 Tomeka
                 Derik
                 Kyle
                 Maria

Instructional Focus:

1. Math facts game
2. Group problem-solving solution

Note: Be sure to check individually with Tomeka and Mark to ensure they
understand subtraction with regrouping.

— FIGURE 7.10 —

**Instructional Reading Group Lesson Plan**

Week: _____      *Scheduled Time:* _____

*Students in Group:* _____

|  | **Phonological Awareness** ___ *Min. per day* | **Word Study & Spelling** ___ *Min. per day* | **Fluency** ___ *Min. per day* | **Comprehension** ___ *Min. per day* | **Writing** ___ *Min. per day* |
|---|---|---|---|---|---|
| Mon. | | | | | |
| Tues. | | | | | |
| Wed. | | | | | |
| Thurs. | | | | | |
| Fri. | | | | | |

# Tips for Teachers

## 7.3 Effective Grouping Strategies for Small Same-Ability Groups

1. Instead of having an arbitrary number of groups (for example, three groups), make sure that you have enough groups to handle individual differences.
2. Plan for appropriate pacing of instruction.
3. For students who have difficulty learning, plan to reteach concepts and skills, using different methods and explanations.
4. Keep student assignment to groups fluid so that students can be moved to more appropriate groups, as necessary.
5. Disband groups that have served their purpose.
6. Be flexible about the time spent with each group. A rigid schedule will not permit you to work with groups that need extra or reduced time.

7. Avoid using student membership in a same-ability group to determine involvement in other activities. For example, if students are in the "yellow" group for extra help in reading, don't put the "yellow" students together for science or social studies projects.
8. A good rule of thumb is to keep groups of students who need extra help small and to provide students with the intensity of instruction they need.

*Source:* Adapted from Good, T. L., & Brophy, J. E. (1994). *Looking in classrooms* (6th ed.). New York: HarperCollins. Copyright © 1994 by Allyn & Bacon. Reprinted by permission.

- *Level of basic skills.* Depending on the purpose of the group and the task to be completed, it may be helpful to group students who are better readers, writers, or mathematicians with students who may need assistance.
- *Prior knowledge.* Students can be grouped according to how much they already know about a topic. If you are teaching a lesson on pre-algebra, for example, you might want to develop mixed-ability groups of students who know a great deal about pre-algebra and students who are new to the topic.

Finally, two types of groups do not depend on students' knowledge or needs:

- *Student-selected.* The teacher may give students time to create their own small groups at specific times during the week. One instance of this type of grouping occurs when the teacher asks students to discuss with their classmates the books they read independently over the weekend.
- *Teacher assignment.* Teacher assignment to groups for special projects can be done to expose students to different classmates throughout the year.

The advantages of small mixed-ability groups are both social and academic. Socially, students learn how to work collaboratively, communicate effectively in groups, and give and receive help. Academically, students become more engaged in their learning and spend more time on-task.

The disadvantages mainly concern classroom management. Teachers can be in only one place at a time. When the class is divided into groups, the possibility for misbehavior increases. Therefore, guidelines for student responsibilities during small-group

activities need to be communicated clearly and reinforced consistently. The research conducted in cooperative learning groups has yielded classroom procedures for maximizing productivity in small mixed-ability groups. Those procedures are discussed in the next section.

## Cooperative Learning Groups

The purpose of this section is to provide an overview of cooperative learning. In **cooperative learning groups,** students work together toward a common goal, usually to help one another learn academic material (Slavin, 1991). Students not only help explain material to each other and provide mutual support, but also give group members multiple perspectives (Morrow & Smith, 1990). In cooperative learning groups, students perceive that the main goal of the group is that all students learn and that each member of the group is critical for group success. As the Research Brief indicates, research in cooperative learning has yielded positive outcomes.

> Of all recent education innovations, cooperative learning has undergone the most extensive research, including research on both academic and social outcomes for students of different grade levels, achievement levels, and cultural backgrounds (Slavin, 1991).

## research brief

### Cooperative Learning and Students with Disabilities

The benefits of cooperative learning for general education students are well documented in the research literature. Slavin (1991) synthesized the research in this area with the following highlights:

1. Cooperative learning is most successful when there are group goals coupled with individual accountability.
2. Achievement effects of cooperative learning have been positive for high-, average-, and low-achieving students across grade levels—elementary through high school.
3. Social effects of cooperative learning have been demonstrated in terms of improving self-esteem, intergroup relations, acceptance of students with disabilities, and attitudes toward school.

Goor and Schwenn (1993, p. 8) identified six key elements of cooperative learning:

● Teams are formed to maximize heterogeneity.
● Positive interdependence is structured through shared goals and rewards.
● Management systems are established to maximize group learning.
● The room is arranged to facilitate small-group activity.
● Students are taught skills necessary to cooperate and teach one another.
● The structure of each cooperative learning activity is chosen to match the goals of the lesson.

Cooperative groups consist of three to six students, with typically about four per group (Wilcox et al., 1987), and should include high, average, and low achievers (Slavin, 1987). Some teachers create permanent cooperative learning groups that are seated together for an entire school year. Other teachers keep the groups together for a grading period; still others do so for a single project.

To ensure full student participation, each member of a cooperative learning group is assigned a role. It is the teacher's responsibility to explain the roles thoroughly, including why each role is important. For example, one student can serve as timekeeper, another as quiet control, another as secretary or scribe, and still another as an encourager or "cheerleader."

While the cooperative learning groups are in session, it is the teacher's job to listen and observe how students work as a group. When necessary, the teacher models collaborative behaviors, such as how to give and receive help and how to ask what others think. It is also important to praise groups that are following guidelines and to redirect groups that are not. The teacher also needs to clarify directions or clear up any misconceptions students may have about the topic. As you can see, cooperative learning time is an active time for the teacher as well as for the students.

Many teachers are concerned about how to grade students for cooperative learning work. What happens if one student does all the work for the group?

What are the six key elements of effective cooperative learning? What are some special considerations for students with disabilities when working in cooperative learning groups?

Should everyone get the same grade? What happens if one group member does nothing? In determining a grade for the group product, it's probably best to have both an individual score and a group score. When making the cooperative learning assignment, announce a group goal and an individual goal. For example, you might be teaching a lesson on the layers of the earth. The group project might be to complete a drawing of the earth and its layers and to ensure that each group member can name the layers. The group goal is to complete the drawing and teach the names of the layers to group members. The individual goal (followed by a quiz) is to demonstrate knowledge of the layers. It is important for students to evaluate the group process as well as to earn a "grade" for a project. Evaluating the process makes students aware of the importance of working together and of the steps necessary for enhancing group dynamics.

Teachers need to ensure that students with disabilities are benefiting from cooperative learning groups, as the positive effects for these students is not as well established as it is for students without disabilities (Pomplun, 1997). Teachers can make special considerations for students with disabilities working in cooperative learning groups by considering the following (Gillies & Ashman, 2000; Goor & Schwenn, 1993; Pomplun, 1997):

● Students with disabilities may have difficulty monitoring their own learning, following directions, and using appropriate group social skills. Prepare students with disabilities for success in the group by explaining how to behave. Prepare other members of the group for how to respond and to support learning for all members of the group.
● Some students may have difficulty participating fully in groups when their basic skills in reading,

writing, and mathematics are not on a par with those of their peers. Establish procedures for how to complete the assigned work so that students maximize learning and are not penalized for what they cannot do.

● Make certain that the role you assign to a student with disabilities is appropriate for that student. For example, the job of recorder may be inappropriate for a student who cannot write, unless that student is allowed to tape record the session and then make an oral summary.

● For students who have difficulty staying on task, develop signals for keeping excess movement and noise to a minimum.

● Monitor student learning consistently to make certain that students are picking up on key concepts and not becoming more focused on group process than on learning the designated material.

● Students with disabilities may contribute less to the group and require more support. Provide students with group partners who can ensure that their partners participate and are provided the support needed. As the teacher, you may want to spend more time with this group to ensure that all students are working cooperatively.

● Students with disabilities who are placed in structured groups with clear guidelines are more likely to learn and make progress than are students in less structured or unstructured groups.

## Learning Partners in Pairs

Pairing occurs when students work together in groups of two, sometimes called **pairs**. Depending on the task, pairs can be either same- or mixed-ability. When two students of the same ability level are placed together for an assignment, they can offer each other support, corrective feedback, and praise. For example, two students who are at about the same level in mathematics might work together to solve word problems.

Pairing also can be effective when students of differing ability levels work together. When one student in such a pair acts as teacher to the other student, **peer tutoring** occurs (Cohen, Conway, & Gow, 1988). When peer tutoring involves a student with learning disabilities, that student can serve as either the tutor or the tutee of a general education student (Eiserman, 1988). An example of mixed-ability pairs might be a more able reader serving as partner to a less able reader to complete the reading of a science chapter.

When older students tutor younger students, we refer to this as **cross-age tutoring**. In these situations, students with disabilities benefit considerably more when they are in the role of the tutor rather than the tutee (Elbaum, Vaughn, Hughes, & Moody, 1999). For example, a sixth-grade student with disabilities could be paired with a second-grade student and serve as a reading tutor. Benefits of this method include

motivation to read (for the younger student) and application and reinforcement of previously learned language arts concepts (for the older student). Cross-age pairing has been shown "to boost the self-esteem of each of the buddies" (Morrice & Simmons, 1991, p. 573). Some suggested activities to use during cross-age pairing are creating big books, making cards and writing letters for holidays, and participating in science projects (Morrice & Simmons, 1991).

Pairs can also be based on friendships or interests or can be random. The important things to think about in planning for student pairing are the task to be completed and the kind of support your students need to complete that task.

Student pairing can be used for the following activities:

● Revising written assignments
● Practicing new skills
● Developing fluency in reading or computation
● Preparing for tests
● Completing reading assignments
● Solving problems
● Conducting library research
● Conducting science experiments
● Reflecting about stories or books read
● Practicing spelling words

Many teachers like to use student pairs because pairing provides students with additional support and helps them learn how to work as a team. Pairing involves minimal planning and is easily implemented in the classroom. Many students like pairing because it makes learning more fun and helps them feel less isolated. Furthermore, classwide peer pairing is a highly effective strategy for students with disabilities (Greenwood & Delquadri, 1995). Students like to give and receive help. As one third-grade student put it, "Two heads are better than one." One potential pitfall of student pairing is that students can get off task and spend more time socializing than working. Another problem is that a student who is asked to "tutor" another student may simply not know what to do, and both students may get frustrated. In some classrooms, higher-achieving students are asked too often to help their lower-achieving peers, and resentment occurs. Finally, some students may simply prefer to work alone. These problems can be minimized. Tips for Teachers 7.4 suggests ways to make the most of student pairs.

## One-on-One Instruction

Research indicates that general education teachers rarely make extensive individualized plans for students (Schumm & Vaughn, 1991), yet one-on-one instruction is a highly effective practice for students with learning problems (Elbaum et al., 2000). However, teachers do have one-to-one instructional encounters

# T i p s for T e a c h e r s

## 7.4   Making the Most of Working with Pairs

*Set procedures for peer tutoring, such as:*
1. Give everyone a chance to be a tutor—every student has something to share with a peer.
2. Give the tutor very specific suggestions about what to teach and how to teach it.
3. Keep tutoring sessions short for students with short attention spans.

*Set procedures for collaborative pairs, such as:*
1. Give specific guidelines about the responsibilities of each partner.
2. Hold each partner accountable for fulfilling responsibilities.

3. Give students the opportunity to work with a variety of partners.

*Set rules, such as:*
1. Talk only to your partner.
2. Talk only about your assignment (project).
3. Use a low voice.
4. Cooperate with your partner.
5. Try to do your best.

*Source:* Used by permission of Douglas and Lynn Fuchs, Vanderbilt University.

with students throughout the day. For example, while you are monitoring students as they complete seatwork, you may observe that one student doesn't understand. So you do some quick reteaching. During writing instruction, you may have one-to-one conferences with students about their writing. You may also take 30 seconds to check on understanding of key concepts with a target student. In yet another scenario, a student assigned to a special education resource room might be in your class for only 15 minutes of a language arts period. In such cases, you may want to consult with the special education teacher to plan activities for the best use of that 15 minutes each day. The advantage of one-to-one instruction is that you can zero in on a student's individual needs. The obvious disadvantage is finding the time to do it.

## Progress Monitoring

The key to successful grouping is to monitor student progress. While small-group instruction, cooperative learning, and pairs may be successful for many students, only by monitoring student progress can we detect when a student is not making adequate progress so that alternative instruction or grouping practices can be implemented.

How do you use the data from monitoring student progress to plan and group for appropriate instruction? Following are some suggestions:

- Examine established benchmarks for the students. These include grade-level expectations, benchmarks for high-stakes assessments, and goals from students' individual education programs.
- Look closely at the data from the progress monitoring (e.g., rate and accuracy of reading, success in math problem solving) to determine the next steps for students to progress toward established benchmarks.
- Identify instructional goals and plan instruction.
- Group students in ways that are most likely to meet instructional goals and their needs.
- Continuously monitor group and individual performance and regroup students to reflect their needs.

## s u m m a r y

- The Flow of the Planning Process Model indicates the sequence and relation between three types of planning (preplanning, interactive planning, and postplanning) and factors that influence planning (teacher, environment, topic, and student).
- In long-range planning, planning parameters such as state, district, and school guidelines for curriculum and instruction must be considered.

- The Course Planning Routine, a guide for long-range planning, includes procedures for setting goals for the course, getting the course off on the right foot, monitoring and managing the course during the year, and closing the course.
- The planning pyramid, a framework for unit and lesson planning, helps you examine the content to be taught and prioritize concepts to ensure learning for all students.

- Current trends in instructional grouping include a critical examination of homogeneous grouping, a movement toward inclusion of students with disabilities in general education settings, critical examination of "what's best" for all students, exploration of alternatives to ability grouping, and an emphasis on flexible grouping as well as on helping students learn how to work in various grouping patterns.
- A variety of group sizes—whole class, small group, pairs, and individual student—can be used for instruction. The decision about which size is most appropriate depends on student needs and the learning activity being planned.
- Students can be grouped in a number of ways, including by interests, skills to be learned, English proficiency, and prior knowledge.
- In cooperative learning groups, students work together toward a common goal, usually to help each other learn academic material. Students in cooperative learning groups perceive that the group's main goal is that all students learn and that each member of the group is critical for group success.

## key terms and concepts

collaborative open-note quizzes
cooperative learning groups
Course Planning Routine
cross-age pairing
degrees of learning
environment-related factors
Flow of the Planning Process Model
homogeneous grouping
informal member checks

instructional unit
interactive planning
long-term planning
mixed-ability groups
multiple grouping formats
pairs
peer tutoring
planning pyramid
postplanning
preplanning

same-ability grouping
SMARTER
student-related factors
teacher-related factors
think–pair–share
topic-related factors
tracking
whole-class grouping
within-class same-ability grouping

## think and apply

1. Now that you have read Chapter 7, reread the interview with Lisa. How does Lisa plan with Ellen, the special education teacher? How does she use a variety of grouping practices?
2. Use the Course Planning Routine to develop initial plans for a course you might teach. Compare your plans with those of a classmate who is teaching the same (or a similar) course.
3. Interview three classroom teachers to elicit their tips for time management. Probe for specific suggestions for finding time to meet the special needs of students either individually or in small groups. Share their tips with your classmates.
4. Teach a lesson based on the planning pyramid. Write a reflective statement about the lesson. What went well? What would you change? How did the lesson affect a student with special needs? An average-achieving student? A high-achieving student?
5. Use the planning pyramid to develop a unit plan and a plan for an individual lesson within that unit. Compare your plans with those of a classmate.
6. Imagine that you have been assigned to a task force to make a proposal about whether or not to keep tracking at your school. In preparation for the first meeting, you have been asked to draft a position statement explaining your stance on the issue. Develop a brief statement explaining your thoughts.
7. Describe an appropriate instructional activity that could be used with each of the following group sizes: whole class, small group, pair, individual.

## read more about it

1. Cohen, E. (1994). *Designing groupwork: Strategies for the heterogeneous classroom* (2nd ed.). New York: Teachers College Press.

*Comprehensive handbook to help make your students' small group work productive. Includes chapters on planning group work, preparing students for cooperation, setting expectations, and applications for group work in classrooms in which some students speak English as a second language.*

2. Johnson, D. W., & Johnson, R. T. (1991). *Learning together and alone: Cooperative, competitive, and individualistic learning* (3rd ed.). Boston: Allyn & Bacon.

   *Comprehensive overview of cooperative learning, with specific instructions for ways to implement different cooperative learning methods, such as Cooperative Integrated Reading and Composition (CIRC), Student Teams–Achievement Divisions (STAD), and Teams–Games–Tournaments (TGT).*

3. Moran, C., Stobbe, J., Baron, W., Miller, J., & Moir, E. (1992). *Keys to the classroom: A teacher's guide to the first month of school.* Newbury Park, CA: Corwin.

   *How do you get the school year off on the right foot? This teacher-friendly guide for elementary teachers provides specific suggestions for preparing the classroom, structuring routines, planning the first day, and activities for the first month. It also includes sample letters to parents, in both English and Spanish.*

4. Radencich, M. C., & McKay, L. J. (Eds.). (1995). *Flexible grouping for literacy in the elementary grades.* Boston: Allyn & Bacon.

   *Provides guidelines for planning and implementing flexible grouping for reading and writing instruction in elementary classrooms. Provides detailed descriptions of ways to implement a variety of grouping options.*

5. Slavin, R. E. (1990). *Cooperative learning: Theory, research, and practice.* Englewood Cliffs, NJ: Prentice-Hall.

   *A detailed manual for structuring cooperative and individualized learning. Includes a chapter on teachers' concerns about cooperative and individualized learning that is particularly helpful in considering students who are low and high achieving as well as students who are socially isolated and disruptive.*

6. Vaughn, S., Schumm, J. S., Lenz, K., Schumaker, J., Deshler, D., Morocco, C., Gordon, S., Riley, M., Fuchs, L., & Fuchs, D. (1995). *Planning for academic diversity in America's classrooms: Windows on reality, research, change, and practice.* Lawrence, KS: University of Kansas Center for Research on Learning.

   *This monograph reports findings from a series of investigations conducted by four research groups. Each group investigated general education teachers' planning for students with disabilities. The monograph includes practical suggestions for planning and implementing instruction for students with disabilities.*

7. Schumm, J. S., Vaughn, S., & Sobol, M. C. (1997). Are they getting it? How to monitor student understanding in inclusive classrooms. *Intervention in School and Clinic, 32*(3), 168–171.

   *This article provides a summary of 12 monitoring strategies gleaned from the professional literature. Particular emphasis is placed on specific things teachers can do to gather data about what and how students are learning.*

8. Nagel, G. K. (2001). *Effective grouping for literacy instruction.* Needham Heights, MA: Allyn & Bacon.

   *This book provides teachers with ideas about planning effective grouping. It presents educators' decision making about forming groups and setting tasks, especially for reading instruction. It introduces various types of group formats and group activities as a means to promoting literacy learning.*

9. Tomlinson, C. A. (2001). *How to differentiate instruction in mixed-ability classrooms.* Alexandria, VA: Association for Supervision and Curriculum Development.

   *The book provides teachers with a practical guide for how to differentiate instruction in ways that meet the special learning needs of students. Topics include how to plan differentiated lessons and how to differentiate content, process, and products.*

## suggested websites

**www.hcc.hawaii.edu/intranet/committees/FacDevCom/ guidebk/teachtip/lesspln1.htm**
This website provides an overview of the lesson planning process.

**www.okbu.edu/academics/natsci/ed/398/ lesson.htm**
This website provides tips for lesson planning.

**www.edu.gov.on.ca/cng/general/elemsec/speced/icp/iep.html**
This website provides an overview of IEPs (the definition, assessment/evaluation, etc.).

**www.clcrc.com/pages/cl.html**
This website provides the definition of cooperative learning, a rationale for using cooperative learning, and critical features of cooperative learning.

**www.nerel.org/sdrs/areas/issues/content/cntareas/math/ ma1group.htm**
This website introduces several different grouping practices.

**www.ed.gov/databases/ERIC_Digests/ed434435.html**
This website contains information about different grouping practices (peer tutoring, small grouping).

# Managing Student Behavior and Promoting Social Acceptance

**f o c u s | q u e s t i o n s**

1. What are some basic principles of classroom management?

2. What does it mean to establish a few clear rules with known consequences?

3. What procedures can you implement to decrease inappropriate behavior?

4. What mistaken behavioral goals do students have? How can teachers recognize these goals?

5. How can you establish a classroom climate that promotes appropriate behaviors and acceptance of all students?

6. How could you implement positive behavioral support and functional behavioral assessments in your school?

7. What are some examples of social skills intervention programs that can be used by classroom teachers?

8. What are the principles teachers can apply to enhance the self-concepts and social skills of their students?

9. What steps can you implement to teach self-management skills to your students?

10. How should teachers manage the behavior of students from diverse ethnic and socioeconomic backgrounds?

**i n t e r v i e w**

**Nina Zaragoza**

Nina Zaragoza, a third-grade teacher at Morningside Elementary School, asked to be placed in an inner-city school. She has spent her entire 20-year career teaching in different inner-city schools. A visit to Nina's classroom is a most rewarding experience. Students work in pairs, in small groups, alone, and sometimes with the class as a whole. The atmosphere of the classroom is much like that of a workshop. There is the healthy buzz of activity, without the noise of students who are lost or off-task. The students are not the only ones who are busy. Nina moves from student to student, from group to group, asking questions, listening, and teaching. She stops the entire group to teach a minilesson when she realizes they are all

**interview**

having difficulty with a particular concept. The students in Nina's classroom know the rules and routines and seem to be able to work without prodding from the teacher. During several interviews with Nina, she revealed what she considered the critical components to successful classroom management.

First, you have to teach that all students are valuable, contributing members to the classroom community and that it is everyone's job to be sure everyone is learning. This is not the usual "teacher is responsible for everyone" mentality. In my class, everyone is responsible for themselves and for everyone else. Second, students have to know that you care for and respect them. For some students, this is a difficult task because they have been told by many of the adults they have previously encountered that they are not worthwhile. Third, you need to establish a few rules and a lot of routines. What I mean by this is that the class needs to have some rules that we all agree on as important. We occasionally revisit these rules during our class meetings. But I don't like to have too many rules because then we don't follow any of them. Respect for others, following directions, and safety for self and others are the three basic rules I apply. The routines are the minute-

by-minute, day-by-day procedures for how the classroom runs. As much as possible, I turn routines over to the students so that I have as much of my time devoted to teaching as possible. For example, I never collect or pass out materials, take attendance, or other activities that the students can learn to do. Fourth, I have established consequences for inappropriate behavior. I do not get emotional or upset, just enforce the consequence. It saves me energy and is more effective for students. Fifth, and maybe the most important, I look and recognize what is going well. I praise and provide positive feedback to my students individually, in small groups, and to the class as a whole. I don't think teachers can ever be too positive. I also spend time teaching social skills to my class as a whole. In the beginning of the year, I teach interpersonal problem-solving skills that students apply during our class meetings. Teaching interpersonal social skills at the beginning of the year is time consuming, but I find it pays off because, over the year, I spend less and less time on it and students get more and more skillful. I have to add one more thing. I think a lot of behavior problems are a result of students being involved in "busy work" that is not productive. They get bored with what they are doing, so they start to bother their neighbors, and the next thing you know, there is a behavior problem.

# introduction

What are some of the principles Nina uses that allow her to spend so much of her time teaching and so little of her time managing student behavior? How did she establish in her classroom a community in which students work together and all students feel accepted and valued? How did she manage her classroom so that she supported students rather than continuously corrected behavior? The purpose of this chapter is to provide principles of managing student behavior, promoting social acceptance, and providing social support so that you will be prepared to create a classroom similar to Nina's. This chapter addresses several issues:

- An overview of the basic principles of managing student behavior
- Ways to establish a harmonious classroom climate

- Practices for providing social support
- Procedures for enhancing the acceptance of students with disabilities by peers and professionals
- Procedures for teaching social skills, enhancing self-esteem, and self-management
- Considerations of students' behavior, based on ethnicity and socioeconomic factors

## Basic Principles of Managing Student Behavior

Glen Nichols, a seventh-grade science teacher, felt frustrated. One of his science classes included several students with special needs, and he was interested in modifying his usual routine to ensure that they had an adequate opportunity to learn. He had spent considerable time preparing a science experiment for the laboratory, one he thought students would learn from and enjoy. He arranged the materials ahead of time, identified the key concepts he wanted to teach, and was optimistic that the lesson would go well. What happened? Glen described it this way:

> First of all, the students came to the lab and were more interested in who their lab partner would be than the topic. They seemed to have a more difficult time settling down than usual and talking seemed to occur during the entire session. There were a few students who seemed to follow the procedures and get something out of it, but for the most part I think it was a waste of my time.

Often, teachers need to change their own behavior in order to change the behavior of students in their classrooms (Hunter, 1982; Rosenshine & Stevens, 1986). Glen is a good example. He understood well the content he was teaching but was less able to manage student behaviors so that he could teach effectively. Glen is not alone. Not only do teachers identify classroom management as a cause of stress, but many also cite it as their reason for leaving the profession (Elam & Gallup, 1989; Fettler & Tokar, 1982). The following sections describe some guiding principles that might help you to establish more effective classroom management.

## Looking for the Positive

Told that he needed to look for positive behaviors, Glen threw up his hands and said, "There weren't any! The poor behavior far outweighed the good." But when Glen examined the videotape of his lesson and was asked to make a written list of student behaviors that he found acceptable, he noticed quite a few. "Actually, there were more students behaving appropriately than I thought."

Glen, like many teachers, got into the habit of noticing and calling attention to *misbehavior* instead of noticing appropriate behavior and providing positive reinforcement. He was asked to list the behaviors he most wanted to see in his students. He was then asked to look for and say something positive to students who were performing those behaviors.

In addition to focusing on negative rather than positive behavior, teachers tend to think they speak positively to students more often than they actually do. When someone counts the positive comments in the classroom, teachers are surprised at how few they actually made. McIntosh, Vaughn, Schumm,

Haager, and Lee (1993) found that even general education teachers who were identified as effective and accepting of students with special needs made very few positive statements during a lesson. You need to provide much more positive feedback than you think is necessary.

Positive feedback to students must be specific and must be presented immediately after you witness the target behaviors you want the students to continue (and other students to model). At the elementary level, teachers can comment on which students are displaying the desired behavior: "Mark, Jacob, and Cynthia are looking at me with their books open. I can tell they are ready. Who else knows what to do to show me they are ready?" At the secondary level, teachers can state the desired behavior and then ask students to summarize the request. For example, Glen could have said, "Today we are going to work in pairs in the lab. You can talk with your lab partner while you are conducting the experiment, but I do not want you to talk while I am preparing you for it, which will take about 15 minutes. You need to look at me and remain quiet during this time. Daniel, in your own words, what is the request?"

How effective is positive reinforcement with students in middle and high school? Because positive reinforcement is more effective with younger students than with older students, it is more useful at the elementary level than in middle school and least effective with high-school students (Forness, 1973; Stallings, 1975). This does *not* mean that you should not have a positive attitude and look for appropriate behavior with older students. All students like to be told when they are doing something right. They all like a classroom in which the atmosphere is positive and upbeat and a teacher they can count on to look for good things, not only bad behaviors. Table 8.1 provides a list of positive teacher comments to use in response to students' behaviors.

> Students do not always interpret teachers' positive recognition in the positive ways that teachers intend. For some students, receiving praise in front of their peers is embarrassing and therefore not rewarding (Grossman, 1995).

Several authors distinguish between positive feedback and encouragement (Dreikurs & Cassel, 1972; Dreikurs et al., 1982). The primary difference is that **positive feedback** often provides some judgment from the teacher about the appropriateness of the behavior, whereas *encouragement* recognizes the behavior but does not provide judgment from the teacher. An example of positive feedback is a teacher saying, "Shana is waiting in line quietly. Good job, Shana." An example of encouragement is to say,

— TABLE 8.1 —

### Positive Teacher Comments for Use in Response to Student Classroom Behaviors

| Student Behaviors | | Teacher Responses |
|---|---|---|
| *Appropriate/Desired* | *Inappropriate/Undesired* | |
| Sitting with bottoms flat on carpet | Kneeling up | "I'm glad so many people remember how to sit in Magic Five." |
| Raising hand to speak | Calling out a response | "It really helps me to know if you have something to say when you raise your hand." |
| Sitting inside the tape | Sitting outside the tape/leaning on the wall | "It's important to sit inside the tape because it helps you remember what you're supposed to be looking at and thinking about." |
| Looking in the direction of whoever is speaking | Talking to another person or playing with something | "It's so polite to look at someone when it's their turn to speak." |
| Walking quickly and quietly to desk | Running to desk or stepping on and over a chair. Yelling to friends while going to desks. | "I like how _____ went to her desk so quickly and got started. _____ did a great job walking quietly to his desk." |
| Working on the right assignment | Drawing instead of working on assignment | "People are working so hard on this assignment." |
| Using quiet voices | Yelling or talking too loudly | "It's so important to use quiet voices at our desks so we don't disturb our friends who are working." |
| Finding something appropriate to do when work is done | Wandering around the room when work is done or drawing or playing an inappropriate game | "_____ is a great thing to do when all your work is done. Good idea." |

*Source:* Carpenter, S. L., & McKee-Higgins, E. (1996). Behavior management in inclusive classrooms. *Remedial and Special Education, 17*(4), 200. Reprinted with permission.

"I'm sure that you know how to stand in line when we get ready for lunch." With encouragement, the focus is on the process (Dweck, Kamins, & Person, 1999), as in the following: "The ending of this paper is quite strong. Can you reread the ending and consider how to improve the introduction?" Both encouragement and positive feedback are effective procedures for noticing what is positive about the behavior of your students.

## Using Reinforcers to Encourage Positive Behavior

How do positive and negative reinforcement differ? **Positive reinforcement** is the presentation, following the target behavior, of a **stimulus** (a verbal response, a physical response, such as touching, or a tangible response, such as a reward) to maintain or increase the target behavior. **Negative reinforcement** is the removal of a stimulus to increase engagement in desirable behaviors. If a teacher rings a bell until the students are quiet, then the removal of the bell sound is a negative reinforcer for quieting student behavior. Because "negative" is often misinterpreted to mean "harmful," the implication is that positive reinforcement is good and negative reinforcement is bad, but this is not necessarily the case. However, although negative reinforcement can be effective, positive reinforcement is the best way to increase desirable student behaviors (see Tips for Teachers 8.1).

There are four ways in which reinforcers can be classified (Axelrod & Hall, 1999): **tangible reinforcers** (e.g., food, magazines, clothes, toys), **activity reinforcers** (e.g., free time, extra time on the computer, time to listen to a CD), **social reinforcers** (e.g., notes of congratulations, handshakes, positive notes home to parents), and **token reinforcers** (e.g., smiley

# Tips for Teachers

## 8.1          Suggestions for Positive Reinforcement

- Access to lunchroom snack machines (student supplies money)
- Attend school dances
- Attend school assemblies
- Be first in line (to anything)
- Be team captain
- Care for class pets
- Choose activity or game for class
- Class field trips
- Decorate the classroom
- Eat lunch in cafeteria rather than in classroom
- Extra portion at lunch
- Extra P. E., recess, or break time
- Free time to use specific equipment or supplies
- Give student a place to display work
- Have use of a school locker
- Help custodian
- Omit certain assignments
- Pass out papers
- Run errands

- Run film projector or video player for class
- Serve as class or office messenger or aide
- Sharpen class pencils
- Sit at teacher's desk for a specified period
- Sit by a friend
- Time with a favorite adult or peer
- Tutor in class, or with younger students
- Use of playground or P. E. equipment
- Use of class "walkman" or tape recorder
- Use of magic markers and/or art supplies
- Visit the principal (prearranged)
- Visit the school library (individual or group)
- Water class plants
- Work as a lunchroom server
- Write on chalkboard (regular or colored chalk)

*Source:* Rhode, G., Jenson, W. R., & Reavis, H. K. (1992). *The tough kid book: Practical classroom management strategies* (pp. 34, 36). Longmont, CO: Sopris West. All rights reserved. Reprinted with permission.

---

face stickers, stars, check marks). Table 8.2 provides a list of reinforcers teachers can use to increase appropriate behavior. In most classrooms, teachers do not have to use tangible reinforcers to maintain student behavior, though they may be necessary for students with severe behavior problems. Some teachers, however, particularly those who have students with emotional and behavioral problems in their classrooms, may need to establish a token system in which the tokens are exchanged for tangible and/or consumable rewards.

You might also consider these tips by Carpenter and McKee-Higgins (1996):

- Focus on instructional techniques to improve behavior.
- Motivate students by establishing a supportive atmosphere.
- Establish procedures that are dynamic in their response to students' changing behaviors.
- Encourage other teachers to use a positive approach.

Juanita Cowell is a middle-school teacher who has five students with special needs in her classroom. One of her students has emotional and behavioral

disorders and had difficulty staying on-task, not disrupting others, and raising his hand when he had something to say. Unfortunately, several students seemed to be learning his "bad" behavior instead of

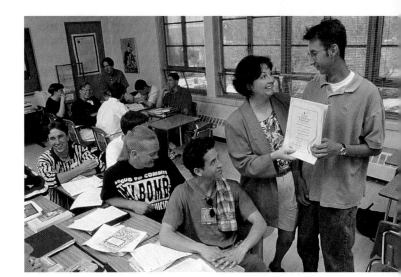

What reinforcer is being used? What other types of reinforcers could be used to enhance positive behavior? If this were your classroom, what reinforcers might you consider using?

--- TABLE 8.2 ---

## Reinforcers Teachers Can Use to Increase Appropriate Behavior

**Students Provide Self-Reinforcers**
- Students give themselves points for behaving well.
- Students say positive things to themselves. ("I'm working hard and doing well.")
- Students monitor their own behavior (see Making a Difference: The 60-Second Lesson on page 235).

**Adult Approval**
- Teacher provides verbal recognition that student is behaving appropriately. ("John, you are following directions on this assignment.")
- Teacher provides physical recognition of appropriate student behavior. Teacher moves around classroom, touching the shoulder of students who are behaving appropriately.
- Teacher informs parents or other professionals of students' appropriate behavior. This can be accomplished orally or with "good news" notes.

**Peer Recognition**
- Teacher informs other students of a student's appropriate behavior. ("The award for student of the day goes to the outstanding improvement in behavior demonstrated by [student's name].")
- Students can place in a special box the names of students who have demonstrated appropriate behavior. These names can be read at the end of the week.
- A designated period of time is allocated at the end of the class period (high school) or day (elementary school) to ask students to recognize their fellow classmates who have demonstrated outstanding behavior.

**Privileges**
- Students are awarded free time after displaying appropriate behavior.
- Students are allowed to serve in key classroom roles after demonstrating outstanding behavior.
- Students are awarded passes that they can trade for a night without homework.

**Activities**
- Students can perform an activity they like (e.g., drawing) after they complete the desired activity (e.g., the activity during that class period).
- Students can perform their tasks on the computer.
- Students can perform their tasks with a partner they select.

**Tokens**
- Tokens are items (e.g., chips, play money, points) that can be exchanged for something of value.
- Use tokens to reward groups or teams who are behaving appropriately.
- Allow groups or individuals to accumulate tokens they can "spend" on privileges, such as no homework or free time.

**Tangibles**
- Tangibles are rewards, objects that students want, but usually not objects they can consume (e.g., toys, pencils, erasers, paper, crayons).
- Tokens can be exchanged for tangible reinforcers.
- Tangible reinforcers can be used to reward the class for meeting a class goal.
- Tangible reinforcers may be needed to maintain the behavior of a student with severe behavior problems.

**Consumables**
- Consumables are rewards that students can eat (e.g., raisins, pieces of cereal, candy).
- Tokens can be exchanged for consumable reinforcers.
- Consumable reinforcers can be used to reward the class for meeting a class goal.
- Consumable reinforcers may be needed to maintain the behavior of a student with severe behavior problems.

---

his learning the good behavior of other students. Juanita had tried many of the reinforcers mentioned in Table 8.2 (such as adult, peer, and activity reinforcers, as well as privileges), and although the class had more good days than bad, she was still concerned about the behavior of several students. She decided to establish a **token system** (or token economy), whereby she would place a token in a glass bank. The token represented that the student was behaving appropriately at the following times:

- At the end of every period (usually about 50 minutes) if students followed rules during the period
- At the beginning of each new period if the students made a quiet transition to the new task

- For exceptional student behavior, such as ignoring another student's interfering behavior or helping a student who was distracted get back to work
- For successfully completing activities

She removed a token from the jar when rules were broken. The target student added up the tokens at the end of each day. If the student earned 10 tokens or more, a note was sent home. The number of tokens each day was recorded, and when the student reached 200 (approximately 10 days of good behavior), the student could exchange the tokens for a pizza party at lunch with two students of his choice. Juanita soon found that she could shake the jar as a signal to quiet down or as a warning that the student was about to lose a token.

Ayllon (1999) provides several points to consider when implementing a token system:

- Clearly identify the behavior(s) you want to change.
- Make the tokens readily available and easy to administer.
- Identify items, activities, or reinforcers that are highly rewarding for the student and that can be obtained by exchanging the tokens.
- Give regular opportunities to exchange the tokens.

## Establishing a Few Clear Rules with Known Consequences

Effective management of student behavior requires clearly specified guidelines and consequences when students do not follow those guidelines. *Guidelines* in the classroom consist of procedures and rules (Brophy, 1988). *Procedures* are classroom routines that occur at specified times and allow the classroom to run effectively. These procedures need to be taught to students and used consistently so that the classroom will run smoothly. Each teacher needs to establish procedures for record keeping (taking attendance, for example), passing out papers and materials, storing materials and books, collecting papers and materials, entering and leaving the room (alone and with the class), and making the transition between tasks.

*Rules* provide the structure for acceptable and unacceptable classroom behaviors. Instead of trying to develop a rule to govern every possible misbehavior, teachers should develop a few general rules that guide students in determining whether behavior is or is not acceptable. These rules should be based on the teacher's criteria for what constitutes a behavior problem (Emmer et al., 1989). Some teachers involve students in determining class rules and consequences. **Consequences** are the repercussions associated with appropriate (e.g., gaining a token in a token economy) and inappropriate behavior (e.g., losing a token). When students are involved in the development of the consequences, the teacher needs to play an active role. Students often want to establish consequences far harsher than those established by the teacher.

Examples of general rules follow:

- Raise your hand if you have something to contribute.
- Do not interfere with your fellow students' learning.
- Do not interfere with the teacher's instruction.

- Complete tasks and homework on time.
- Do not bring to school materials (e.g., toys, action figures) that interfere with your learning.

Some teachers show each new class the rules from the previous year and allow the current students to make changes.

Think about Nina's introductory comments. As you may recall, she indicated that she had few rules but many routines. She also stated that procedures and rules are not enough. The teacher and students need to know what the consequences are of not following a procedure or rule. Nina said that during her first year as a teacher, establishing consequences was difficult. She had a hard time anticipating the kinds of problems she would have and had limited experience in providing consequences for student behavior. She implemented a strategy in which consequences for breaking class rules were as closely related to the problem as possible. For example, students who interfered with the learning of others suffered the consequences of being removed from the group for a designated period of time.

Nina also established a system for classroom procedures. Every Friday, two students were selected to distribute and collect papers and materials during the following week. She identified these students by using a lottery system, with eligibility based on meeting weekly behavior goals. Also, so that students would understand what was expected of them, all students practiced procedures for transitions between centers, going to and from their classroom, and other routines. Rules were handled through the new token system she established. On Friday, she counted the number of tokens for the week, and students solved math problems about the number of tokens needed to win the prize.

## Helping Students to Change Inappropriate Behavior

What should a teacher do when focusing on positive behaviors does not change the negative behaviors? Three alternative techniques are ignoring on purpose, time out, and punishment. Effective procedures for implementing these techniques follow.

**Ignoring on Purpose**    The goal of **ignoring on purpose** or **planned ignoring** is to eliminate (extinguish) a student's undesirable behavior, which is being reinforced through attention (Hall & Hall, 1999). Many teachers and students unknowingly maintain the unwanted behaviors of students by attending to these behaviors. **Extinction** is the technical term for when teachers recognize that an undesirable behavior is being maintained by either their attention or the attention of fellow students and then plan to eliminate the attention. For example, a teacher might want to extinguish a student's behavior of shouting out. Having determined that telling the student to raise his hand provides the attention the student wants and therefore reinforces the student's shouting-out behavior, the teacher decides to ignore the student (with the intention of reducing the behavior through ignoring on purpose). Ignoring can be a very effective strategy to reduce undesirable behaviors but is harder to implement than most people think. Often, the teacher does not say anything but looks at the student, and that may be enough to reinforce the student's undesirable behavior.

Ignoring can be an effective means of decreasing undesirable behaviors. It is often slow, however, and can be impractical for many behaviors that occur in the classroom because the reinforcers for an undesirable behavior may not be completely under the teacher's control. Let's return to the example of the student who continually shouted out in class. If this student's behavior was reinforced not only by the attention of the teacher, but also by that of his classmates, then both teacher and classmates need to ignore the undesirable behavior.

Another characteristic of extinction as applied through ignoring is the rate at which the target behavior continues to occur. During extinction, the target behavior will increase in rate or intensity before decreasing. To be effective, this strategy requires patience and the ability to control reinforcement.

**Time Out**   Time out occurs when the student is removed from the opportunity to receive reinforcement. In the classroom, the student receives reinforcement from classmates, the teacher, and ideally the environment. When a student is removed from this setting, he or she is no longer able to receive these reinforcers. The underlying principle behind the successful use of time out is that the environment the student leaves must be reinforcing and the time-out environment must not. In busy classrooms and schools where there is little space, time out is often difficult to accomplish.

For example, a tenth-grade teacher asked students who were interfering with his lesson to sit in a chair in the back of his classroom. Laurence, a student with learning problems, was frequently asked to remove himself from the class lesson and sit in that chair. Because Laurence did not like geography and could sleep when he was in the chair, his behavior never really improved during class. The teacher moved the chair so that it was just outside the door. Laurence's desire to be with his classmates served as a motivator, and his behavior in class quickly improved.

The efficacy of time out is strongly influenced by environmental factors (Burke, 1992; Hall & Hall, 1999). If the environment the student is leaving is unrewarding, then time out is not an effective means of changing the student's behavior. Guidelines for implementing time out in the classroom are provided in Tips for Teachers 8.2.

> The record-keeping procedure for monitoring time out should include the student's full name, the date and times the student was placed in and removed from time out, the behavior that led to the use of time out, the context in which the behavior occurred (e.g., where, with whom), and the student's behavior during and after time out.

# Tips for Teachers

## 8.2   Guidelines for Implementing Time Out

1. Time out should be used as a last resort.
2. Time-out procedures should be discussed with school administrators and parents before implementation.
3. Students should be provided in advance with information about behaviors that will result in time out.
4. The amount of time the student is in time out should be brief (between 15 and 20 minutes).
5. The amount of time the student is in time out should be specified ahead of time.
6. The student should be told to go to time out. If the student does not comply, the teacher should unemotionally place the student in time out.

7. Time out should be implemented *immediately* following the inappropriate behavior.
8. Contingencies should be established in advance for the student who fails to comply with time-out rules.
9. Do not leave the time-out area unmonitored.
10. When time out is over, the student should join his or her classmates.
11. The teacher should look for ways to provide reinforcement for appropriate behavior after time out.

**Punishment**    Punishment is the opposite of reinforcement, in that it follows a behavior and decreases the strength of the behavior. In other words, it reduces the likelihood that the behavior will continue to occur. Although punishment often reduces the undesired behavior, it does not ensure that the desired behavior will occur (Axelrod & Hall, 1999). Instead of teaching students to do what the teacher wants them to do, punishment may simply teach them to avoid doing what the teacher does not want them to do. For example, a student who is punished for talking in class might stop talking but might not attend to his or her studies for the remainder of the day.

Following are some of the many significant arguments against the use of punishment:

- Punishment is often ineffective in the long run.
- Punishment often causes undesirable emotional side effects such as fear, aggression, and resentment.
- Punishment provides little information about what to do, teaching the individual only what *not* to do.
- The person who administers punishment is often associated with it and subsequently viewed as harsh or negative.
- Punishment frequently does not generalize across settings; therefore, it needs to be readministered.
- Fear of punishment often leads to escape behavior.

Unfortunately, despite the many arguments against the use of punishment, it is frequently used by parents and teachers. Why is punishment so frequently used? There are several reasons:

- Because teachers may be unfamiliar with the consequences of punishment
- Because teachers are unable to effectively implement a more positive approach
- Because it is often reinforcing to the person who administers it. When punishment rapidly changes the undesirable behavior, the person who implements the punishment is highly rewarded.

Punishment should be used as a last resort and when behaviors are harmful to a student or others. For example, Marleen Sugai decided to implement punishment with Latrene Jackson, whose fighting on the playground was harmful to others. Despite positive attempts to change her behavior, Latrene continued to attack others when they did not do what she wanted. Marleen implemented the following procedures, which are necessary to effective punishment:

- Tell the student ahead of time what the punishment will be for implementing the behavior.
- Deliver punishment immediately after the undesirable behavior (e.g., fighting).
- Consistently apply punishment when the behavior occurs.
- Unless a sharp decrease in the frequency and intensity of the behavior occurs, the punishment is ineffective and should be altered.
- Identify and reinforce the appropriate behaviors of the target student.

Table 8.3 provides a summary of behavioral techniques for increasing students' desirable behavior and decreasing undesirable behavior.

## Recognizing Students' Mistaken Goals

Rudolf Dreikurs, who was a follower of Alfred Adler and director of the Adler Institute, is well known for his contribution to understanding the classroom behavior of students (Dreikurs & Cassel, 1972; Dreikurs et al., 1982). He believed that all behavior is purposeful and that student behavior and misbehavior can be better dealt with by teachers if they better understood the purpose behind the behavior.

The following principles form the foundation of Dreikurs's approach to discipline:

- Students (like the rest of us) are social beings, and their behaviors are attempts to be liked and accepted.
- Students can control their own behavior.
- When students display inappropriate behavior, they do so because they have the **mistaken goal** that it will get them the recognition and acceptance they want.

Many students learn that they can garner the acceptance and recognition they need by behaving appropriately and completing school tasks. Other students do not feel capable or worthy of obtaining recognition in these ways; they attempt to obtain the acceptance and recognition they need by displaying inappropriate behavior and not completing their school tasks. Over time, they begin to feel that the only way to get recognition is through inappropriate behavior.

Dreikurs identified four mistaken goals that categorize the behavior of most students:

- Attention
- Power or control
- Revenge or getting even
- Display of inadequacy

---
TABLE 8.3
---

### Summary of Behavioral Techniques that Can Be Used to Increase and Decrease Students' Behaviors

| Procedures for Increasing Desirable Behaviors | Methods for Decreasing Undesirable Behaviors |
|---|---|
| • *Positive reinforcement:* The application of a pleasurable consequence following the display of a desirable behavior. Positive reinforcement increases the target behavior that it follows. Positive reinforcement can be social (e.g., a smile, pat on the back) or tangible (e.g., a sticker or food).<br>• *Negative reinforcement:* The removal, following a behavior, of an unpleasant consequence that increases the likelihood of that behavior being maintained or increased.<br>• *Contract:* An oral or written agreement between student and teacher that identifies the expected behavior and the consequences for exhibiting or not exhibiting that behavior. For example, the teacher and student write up the specific behavior to be demonstrated, how often it should occur, and the positive consequences of fulfilling the contract.<br>• *Premack principle:* The **Premack principle** provides the opportunity for behaviors (acceptable to both teachers and students) to serve as reinforcers for behaviors that teachers want, as well as other behaviors that are acceptable to teachers but less acceptable to students. | • *Extinction:* The removal of positive reinforcement. For example, when a student shouts in class and other students laugh at this behavior, that laughter can be a positive reinforcer for the shouting behavior. In such cases, the teacher may want to have a class meeting when the target student is not present and elicit the cooperation of classmates, asking them to help reduce or extinguish the shouting behavior by not laughing when the student shouts.<br>• *Punishment:* The application of an unpleasant or aversive consequence immediately following an undesirable behavior. In many cases, teachers think only of physical punishment. Other forms of punishment include any behavior that is extremely unpleasant or undesirable to the student and that reduces the occurrence of the student's target behavior. Sometimes staying after school or staying in the classroom during lunch is used as punishment. It is important for teachers to remember that a consequence is punishing only if it reduces the occurrence of the target behavior.<br>• *Time out:* The removal of a student from a positively reinforcing situation. Many teachers use time out ineffectively, removing students from classroom situations that are not positively reinforcing. Also, time out should be for a very specific period of time, not more than 15–20 minutes, and students should be told ahead of time when they will be allowed to return to the reinforcing situation. |

According to Dreikurs, the best way to determine a student's mistaken goal is to identify what the student is doing and how you feel about or react to the behavior. Table 8.4 provides a description of a student's mistaken goal, the student's behavior, and the teacher's reaction. Dreikurs indicates that the teacher's job is to identify the student's mistaken goal and to discuss it with him or her. Teachers also need to identify their own reaction to the student's behavior and how that might contribute to the student's mistaken goal. See Charles (1989) for further information on the application of Dreikurs's approach to classroom management.

---
TABLE 8.4
---

### Students' Mistaken Goals

| Student's Goal | Student's Behavior | Teacher's Feeling |
|---|---|---|
| Attention | Repeats aversive behavior | Annoyed |
| Power | Refuses to stop behavior | Threatened, loss of control |
| Revenge | Becomes hostile, tries to hurt others | Hurt |
| Exhibition of inadequacy | Refuses to participate or cooperate | Helpless, gives up |

How does the miscommunication between students with cultural and linguistic diversity and their teachers influence the way the teachers manage the behaviors of the students? What considerations will help the teachers cope more effectively with the behaviors of students with cultural and linguistic diversity?

## research brief

## Behavior Management Considerations in Culturally Diverse Classrooms

Educators tend to have low expectations of poor, African American, Native American, and Hispanic students (e.g., Cortes, 1978; Dusek & Joseph, 1983; Ford, 1992; MacLeod, 1987; Ogbu, 1990; Webb-Johnson et al., 1998).

> Beginning in preschool and continuing through their college careers, educators and education students tend to expect the European American middle-class students in their classes to do better academically than non-European American and poor students. In addition, they expect European American middle-class students to be more intelligent, even when students' achievement test scores, grades, and school histories would predict otherwise (Grossman, 1995, pp. 69–70).

It is likely that teachers also hold low expectations for individuals with disabilities, and these low expectations influence the extent to which the teachers interact with these students.

How might these low expectations influence the ways in which teachers manage the behavior of students? This question is particularly relevant because disproportionate numbers of students from minority groups are identified as needing special education,

although many of them remain in the general education classroom for all or part of the school day (Robertson et al., 1994). Although there is little information about ways in which teachers' attitudes might influence their treatment of the behavior problems of students in their classrooms, there is little doubt that lowered expectations for students do *not* yield positive benefits. Teachers are likely to expect the behavior of students from traditionally underrepresented groups to be worse and (in an attempt to stop problems before they get out of control) provide overcorrection for problems they would be willing to overlook in other students. African American males are particularly vulnerable to disproportionate discipline by educators (Townsend, 2000). The primary solution to the problem is awareness of prejudices and the subtle and not so subtle ways in which these prejudices might influence the way you manage the behavior of students in your classroom. Keep the following questions in your desk, and read and reflect on them frequently:

- What behaviors bother me as a teacher? Who is exhibiting these behaviors? Am I sure that *all* students who behave in these ways are treated in the same way?
- Who are the students I have the most difficulty managing? What socioeconomic, cultural, and linguistic background(s) do they represent? How does this affect my attitude?
- To what extent have I reached out and demonstrated genuine caring and concern to *all* students in my class?
- If students were asked to identify which students in the class I like best and least, what would they say? What does this say about me?
- How are students from traditionally underrepresented groups performing in my class? What behaviors do I demonstrate to promote their success?
- What steps am I taking to better engage all students in instruction and learning?

Teachers often misinterpret the behavior of minority students and thus respond inappropriately to their behavior (Irvine, 1991; Morgan, 1980). However, teachers' conceptions are subject to change (Trent et al., 1998). The miscommunications between minority students and their teachers may cause misunderstandings

FIGURE 8.1

## Implementation Checklist

If your intervention is not working, consider the following:

✔ Have you adequately identified and defined the target behavior?

✔ Have you selected the right kind of reinforcer? (What you decided on may not be reinforcing to the student.)

✔ Are you providing reinforcement soon enough?

✔ Are you providing too much reinforcement?

✔ Are you giving too little reinforcement?

✔ Are you reinforcing too often?

✔ Are you being consistent in your implementation of the intervention program?

✔ Have you made the intervention program more complicated than it needs to be?

✔ Are others involved following through (e.g., principal, parent, "buddy")?

✔ Is social reinforcement by peers outweighing your contracted reinforcement?

✔ Did you fail to give reinforcers promised or earned?

*Source:* Larrivee, B. (1992). *Strategies for effective classroom management: Creating a collaborative climate* (p. 259). Boston: Allyn & Bacon. Reprinted with permission.

that lead to discipline problems and ultimately discouragement on the part of the minority student. Following are cautions and considerations that should help you cope more effectively with the behavior of minority students. For a complete review of these issues, see Grossman (1995) and Townsend (2000).

- Behaviors that are acceptable and encouraged in home and community may be incompatible with behaviors at school. Students may not only receive conflicting messages about their behavior, but also be forced to choose between loyalty to home and community or to school. Teachers should avoid placing any student in this position by learning as much as they can about the expectations of all students' home and community and communicating acceptance of these practices. So informed, teachers can help students distinguish which behaviors are acceptable in which settings. For example, aggressive, emotionally charged behavior may be expected of African American males at home and in their community but be unacceptable in classrooms. Another example is the behavior of Hispanic students, many of whom are viewed by teachers as dependent, passive, and reticent about participating and responding to the teacher. Yet these behaviors are expected and nurtured in the Hispanic family and community.
- Behaviors that are indicative of problems in one group of students might not be so in another. For example, teachers may overlook signs of internalizing behaviors in African American students, who may express such behaviors differently. Also, teachers who know that Hispanic students might not ask for help may need to check frequently with these students to determine how they are proceeding. Finally, behaviors of some African American students may be viewed as aggressive and acting

out when their intention is merely to fit in and be recognized.

- Some behaviors that students exhibit may be wrongly attributed and interpreted by teachers who do not understand the students' culture or background. For example, some students who are limited speakers of English may fail to respond, make limited eye contact with the teacher, or appear defiant because they lack confidence. Some students from other cultures (e.g., Asian groups) are accustomed to clearly defined rules and regulations and may have difficulty interpreting more implicit rules.

If, after implementing the suggestions in this section, you are not satisfied with your students' progress in increasing desirable classroom behaviors and decreasing undesirable behaviors, ask yourself the questions shown in Figure 8.1.

 ## Establishing the Classroom Climate

You cannot control certain aspects of your classroom's climate. The condition of the building, the size of your classroom, the type of furniture, and the nature of the ventilation in your classroom are examples of important elements in your environment that affect you and your students but over which you are likely to have little or no control. However, you can attempt to optimize the environmental conditions you have and to utilize classroom space and seating arrangements (Levin & Nolan, 1991) in a way that is most likely to enhance students' learning. Consider the following questions as you think about seating arrangements:

- What grouping arrangement is used for students' seating? Are students arranged in small-group pods, individual seats, pairs, and so on?
- On the basis of the seating arrangement in my class, is any student not an obvious member of the group?
- To what extent is the seating arrangement contributing or reducing behavior problems of selected students?
- How often during the day does the seating arrangement change? For what reasons? Are any students not involved? If not, why not?

Perhaps an even more important factor than the physical arrangement of the room are the procedures that you, the teacher, implement to create a classroom climate that is respectful and accepting of all students.

## Creating a Learning Community

Reread the beginning of this chapter, with its focus on the third-grade teacher, Nina. What did she say that leads you to believe that establishing a classroom community was important to her? In a subsequent interview, Nina described how she establishes a classroom community:

> There are three things I emphasize. First, all students in the room are full members and participants in the community. It is all of our responsibility to assure that they are active, involved, and engaged. Second, everyone in the classroom has a role. These roles rotate but tend to focus on students' interests and expertise. Third, the class belongs to all of us (teachers and students), not just to me. I serve as the leader who is responsible for learning and [for] creating a classroom environment that promotes acceptance, but I engage all of the students in the process.

What are some things you can do to establish a classroom that fosters acceptance of all students? A list of guiding principles follows:

- *Students are children or adolescents first.* Teachers who remember this look beyond the visible and less obvious ways in which students differ and respect their common needs and goals—to be accepted, recognized, and valued members of the community. The classroom community is one of the most important places this needs to occur. An attitude that places children or adolescents first recognizes that students are more alike than different.
- *Focus on abilities.* To foster an accepting classroom climate, you must establish an environment in which teachers and students seek and use knowledge about the abilities and expertise of *all* class members. In Laureen Rankin's third-

grade class, a picture of each student was framed in a decorated star and hung in the classroom. Attached to each star were lists of self- and teacher-identified strengths or abilities. In addition, all students were encouraged to recognize their fellow students' abilities (which, when identified, were added to the appropriate star).

- *Celebrate diversity.* Diversity can be viewed by teachers as something to be tolerated, mildly accepted, or celebrated. *Celebrating diversity* means conveying to students the value of students who learn or behave differently, are physically challenged, speak other languages, or represent other cultural backgrounds. Sharon Andreaci, a sixth-grade teacher, was delighted that many of the students in her classroom spoke Spanish and represented the cultural backgrounds of several Hispanic groups (e.g., Cuban, Nicaraguan, Colombian, Mexican). She often asked students about their backgrounds and encouraged them to share their knowledge and practices with others in the classroom. For example, she routinely asked such questions as "Juan, how would you say that in Spanish? Ana, do you agree with Juan? Is there another way to say it in Spanish?"
- *Demonstrate high regard for all students.* Students know when teachers prefer particular students, even when teachers go out of their way to disguise this information. Demonstrating high regard for all students means treating each of them as the most important student in the class. Carlos Rivera, a ninth-grade science teacher, provides this advice:

Listen carefully and attentively to each student's responses, not just those of the brighter students. Look for ways to connect each student's response to what you are talking about now or in a previous lesson. Make eye contact with each student, do not always look at the brighter students. Be sure to call on each student at least every day. Get to know a few personal things about each student and check on them periodically.

> "I expect as much from the students with disabilities in my class as I do from each of my other students. I understand that their goals and expectations often have to be altered, but I set high expectations for them, and it surprises me and them how often they live up to those expectations."
> —A fifth-grade teacher

- *Provide opportunities for students to work in mixed-ability groups.* Students prefer, and benefit from, opportunities to work with their peers in groups that represent a range of abilities. Be sure that each group member plays a genuine role, in which he or she contributes to the group process. Particularly for students with disabilities, work to ensure that each student's role is active and linked to the group's success.

What instructional and management goals can be met through a class meeting format? How might class meetings increase students' stake in the day-to-day cohesion and operation of their classroom?

## Using Class Meetings

Joan McGinnis and Laura Prinstein are fifth-grade teachers who use **class meetings** to involve students in the management of their classes but who do not approach class meetings in the same way. Joan has a regularly scheduled Friday afternoon meeting. Laura calls class meetings when she needs them. She has one meeting some weeks, two meetings other weeks, and at times several weeks pass without a meeting. Laura uses class meetings to solve crises and to deal with immediate problems. Joan uses class meetings to prevent problems, identify potential or occurring problems, teach problem solving, and foster class responsibility for the cohesion and functioning of the classroom. Joan's application of class meetings is more likely to be effective in the long run (Nelson et al., 1993).

The format of the class meeting is much the same at both the elementary and secondary levels. Nelson and colleagues (1993) emphasize the importance of starting the class meeting by forming a circle so that everyone can see everyone else. The change in the seating structure of the classroom reminds students that this is a special time.

The first 10 minutes of the meeting are used for compliments and appreciations, which can be handled in several ways. Joan uses a recognition box, a decorated shoe box into which students and teachers place written recognitions of classmates or teachers who have done helpful or special things, such as helping a classmate, doing well on a paper, or ignoring someone who is bothering them. Recognitions also include personal information, such as winning a swim meet. When the class meeting starts, Joan brings the recognition box and passes it

around the circle. Each student selects one slip until all the slips have been removed from the box. Students take turns reading the recognitions. Joan often allows several minutes during which students can contribute recognitions they did not submit to the recognition box.

The second part of the class meeting—follow-up on prior solutions—takes approximately 15 minutes. During this time, problems that had been brought up at previous meetings are discussed and evaluated. Students and teachers share their perceptions in answer to the following questions:

- How frequently does the problem occur? More or less than before?
- How well are people implementing the selected solution? Is this still a problem? Is the solution effective?

The third part of the meeting—new problems—takes approximately 15 minutes and gives students and teachers an opportunity to identify problems and work with the group to identify potential solutions to the problems. Joan cautions that it is important not to let this part of the meeting turn into a gripe session and to be sure not to allow students to complain about a selected student. Joan teaches all her students how to solve problems and encourages them to use those skills.

The fourth part of the meeting—future plans—takes approximately 10 minutes. Joan describes this section of the meeting:

> I try to keep this part of the meeting very upbeat with an emphasis on future projects, school events, or field trips. I use this time to engage the students not just in the social plans of the class and school but also in my academic plans for the future weeks. If I have a special project planned, I use this time to introduce the new project to the students.

Joan has used class meetings for different grade levels, including middle and high school. She comments on these meetings:

> I feel that it is an essential aspect of a successful classroom. The students in my room are not only better behaved, they work more as a team. They take more responsibility for their own behavior as well as that of other students in the class. I think the benefits go way beyond classroom management and include academic gains as well. I guess you can tell I'm pretty enthusiastic about their function.

# TechTalk

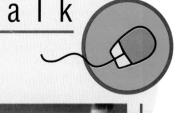

## Using Anchored Instruction to Promote Student Acceptance

Anchored instruction can be used to create a cooperative learning environment that promotes the social acceptance and peer interaction of students with special needs. During anchored instruction, students have opportunities to work together in small groups toward a common goal. In small groups, each student can contribute his or her unique knowledge and skills to accomplish a common goal. This cooperative learning environment promotes social and emotional benefits as well as academic benefits (Nastasi & Clements, 1991).

*The Adventures of Jasper Woodbury* is one of the most famous examples of an anchored instruction project. *The Adventures of Jasper Woodbury* consists of 12 videodisc-based adventures that focus on mathematical problem solving. There are four areas (complex trip planning, statistics and business plans, geometry, and algebra), and each area contains three adventures. Each adventure is designed to incorporate the standards recommended by the National Council of Teachers of Mathematics (NCTM): providing students with multiple opportunities for problem solving, reasoning, communication, and making connections to other areas such as science, social studies, literature, and history (NCTM, 1989, 1991). A preview of *The Adventures of Jasper Woodbury,* as well as ordering information, is available at http://peabody.vanderbilt.edu/projects/funded/jasper.

*Source:* Nastasi, B. K., & Clements, D. H. (1991). Research on cooperative learning: Implications for practice. *School Psychology Review, 20* (1), 110–131.

## Increasing Social Acceptance of Students with Disabilities and Exceptional Learners

Judith Warner, a veteran fifth-grade teacher, is well respected by her students, their parents, and her fellow teachers for the effective way she manages students' behavior. "I probably take advantage of Judith," said her school principal, "because I can always give her the students who are the biggest behavior problem and I know she will be successful with them." Judith indicates that the secret to her success is to establish a personal relationship with each student in her class. She says,

I spend the first month of class getting to know each of my students, what they are like, what they do outside of school, who is special to them at home and in their community, what their strengths are, and what makes them tick. I use this information to facilitate their adjustment to the classroom community and to establishing a

relationship with me that will influence our year together. Yes, you can say that each student learns very early in the year that I genuinely respect and care about each of them. When students are not behaving, I always assume initially that it is because they do not know that they are bothering me or another student. I pull them aside and tell them what they are doing and how it is affecting me or others. It usually works.

What are some of the things Judith does to ensure acceptance of all students in her classroom?

> Conveying acceptance of all students in the classroom is one of the teacher's most important roles.

● *All students are treated with respect.* Her classroom is not segmented into those who know and those who do not. She genuinely communicates respect for each student and expects students to communicate respect to each other.

- *The students are taught concern for each other.* The students in Judith's classroom learn quickly that they are responsible for themselves and for each other. The following are examples of the types of questions Judith asks her students during the day:

  "Jonathan doesn't know how to complete his writing project. Who is going to help him?"

  "There are several students who are not involved in the activity centers. Who should be involving them in their group?"

  "One of the groups is too noisy. What should they be doing?"

  "Is everyone ready to go to lunch? What do you need to do to ensure that everyone is ready?"

- *Students' abilities are pointed out.* Judith insists that when a negative statement is made about a student, something positive about that student must be said: "Yes, Myla (a student who uses a wheelchair) does slow us down going to lunch, but Myla is the class artist. She helps us, and we help her."

As a teacher, what is your role in promoting the social acceptance of students with disabilities? How will you model social acceptance for your students, and what other strategies will you use?

Conveying acceptance of all students in the classroom is an important role the classroom teacher can play. Serving as an advocate for all of your students with other professionals is another critical role. Students with special needs may be more likely than other students in your class to receive criticism from other professionals.

The classroom teacher needs to serve as advocate for the student, both in the classroom and with other professionals.

## Practices for Providing Positive Behavioral Support

In the previous sections, you were introduced to principles of behavior management that classroom teachers can use to improve the behavior of students and reduce behavior problems. In recent years, the principles of behavior management have been applied in various community settings (school, family) with supports to reduce problem behaviors and develop appropriate behaviors that lead to enhanced social relations and lifestyle (Horner et al., 1999–2000). This modification of behavior management principles is called **positive behavioral support**. Positive behavioral supports for students with disabilities is not just good practice, it's part of the law (IDEA, 1997).

### Positive Behavioral Support as Prevention

The focus of positive behavioral support is to develop individualized interventions that stress prevention of problem behaviors through effective educational programming to improve the individual's quality of life (Janney & Snell, 2000). Behavior is one way of communication and is often a product of a combination of the environment and the individual (Carr et al., 1994). Hence, positive behavioral support involves careful observation of circumstances and the purpose of the problem behavior. A significant number of negative behaviors can be dealt with by modifying the environment (e.g., who sits near a student, how a student is responded to). Positive behavioral support also emphasizes teaching appropriate behaviors to replace the inappropriate behavior in the target setting (Janney & Snell, 2000).

Juan is a fifth-grade student who has a physical and cognitive disability, poor social skills, and difficulty interacting with peers. He hits and gets into fights for no apparent reasons. A careful observation of Juan's interactions with peers and his behaviors suggested that hitting was Juan's way of saying, "Get off my back." He was very sensitive to teasing, and students learned that they could get him very mad very easily by teasing him. Juan was taught to say, "Get off my back" and walk away instead of hitting. He was also taught to recognize teasing and to not let the other students control his behavior. Furthermore, the students who were primarily associated with teasing Juan were taught to have fun in other ways. All the teachers in the school reminded Juan to use his words instead of his hands to communicate. He was taught other specific skills necessary for successful social interactions, such as joining a group and initiating and maintaining a conversation. All students were rewarded with tokens when Juan did not get into a fight or hit someone; thus, everyone was interested in seeing Juan's behavior improve. Teachers tried to pair Juan with other students during classroom activities to provide him with opportunities to practice his new skills.

In this case, Juan's behavior and the environment in which target behaviors occurred were observed. Once the causes, circumstances, and purposes of the behaviors were identified, the classroom teacher met with other teachers to discuss and enlist their help in providing Juan with the support he would need. The teachers also developed a list of specific social skills to teach him. Over time, Juan's problem behaviors decreased, his social skills improved, and he made friends with a few students.

Teachers can work in teams with other teachers, specialists, the parents, and often the student to prepare **behavior support plans**. These plans are written to describe the target problem behaviors and the ways the environment will change to improve the social behavior of the target student (Sugai et al., 2000).

For teachers, it may be helpful to think of behaviors as having one of the following purposes (Durand, 1990; Evans & Meyer, 1985; Janney & Snell, 2000):

- Getting attention
- Escape or avoidance
- Getting something tangible
- Self-regulation
- Play or entertainment

This way, they can consider the student's behavior and how the environment supports this behavior and can work with a team to identify a behavior support plan.

A few key elements should be part of any behavioral support plan (Horner et al., 1999–2000, pp. 209–211):

- *Element 1: Learn how the student perceives or experiences events in his or her environment.* Some disabilities, such as autism, obsessive-compulsive disorder, and attention deficit hyperac-

tivity disorder, influence the way the student understands and interprets events. Teachers may need to consider this when they consider the purpose of a student's behavior and how to adjust the environment for positive change.
- *Element 2: Invest in preventing occurrences of problem behavior.* The behavior support plan should also reflect consideration of ways to prevent problems. Problems are more likely to occur when students (a) do not have effective ways to move around, (b) do not have effective ways to communicate with others, (c) do not know the routines and schedule of the day, (d) have few choices about what they do and how long they do it, (e) participate in a limited number of activities, (f) interact with others rarely, and (g) do not receive positive attention or acknowledgement.
- *Element 3: Teaching is the most powerful behavior support strategy.* Students who have the skills to get what they want, interact with others, and engage in positive ways are less likely to continue to exhibit problems. Teach students the skills they need to be successful.
- *Element 4: Avoid rewarding problem behaviors.* Remember the previous presentation on ignoring on purpose or planned ignoring? Teachers often inadvertently reinforce inappropriate behaviors by providing students with attention for these behaviors. When students engage in disruptive or dangerous behaviors, other students and the teacher are often unaware that they are supporting the behaviors through their attention.
- *Element 5: Reward positive behaviors.* It is difficult to provide too much positive reinforcement, attention, and acknowledgment for desirable behaviors. Even though it might seem that you spend a lot of time telling students what they do right, acknowledging appropriate behavior, and sending home "good news" notes, it is very important to consider who gets the positive attention, when, and whether all students' positive behaviors are being supported.
- *Element 6: Know what to do in the most difficult situation.* An effective behavior support plan will provide guidance for what to do if the most dangerous and difficult situation arises. Considering how to act ahead of time will provide you with the confidence you need and the action plan necessary.

## Functional Behavioral Assessments

**Functional behavioral assessments** are a method of gathering data to design the most effective positive support plans and to monitor their progress. Figure 8.2 provides a description of the methods of functional behavioral assessment.

FIGURE 8.2

**Methods of Functional Behavioral Assessment (FBA)**

Functional behavioral assessment (FBA) is a systematic process for gathering information in order to determine the relationships between a person's problem behavior and aspects of their environment. Through FBA, it is possible to identify specific events that predict and maintain behavior and design a support plan that effectively addresses those variables. FBA methods can, and should, vary across circumstances but typically include *record reviews, interviews,* and *direct observation.*

| Method | Sample Sources/Tools | Examples/Products |
|---|---|---|
| Record reviews | Diagnostic/medical records, psychological reports, assessments from therapies, developmental profiles, social histories, previous behavior management plans, IEPs, ISPs, anecdotal records, incident reports, discipline referrals | Sammy's records contained: History of allergies and asthma Some effective educational strategies used in the past Patterns of discipline referrals |
| Structured interviews | People who know the individual well and represent a range of environments (the person, family members, teachers, friends, direct service providers, etc.) may be interviewed. Some interview tools: *Functional Assessment Interview, Student-Directed Functional Assessment Interview* (O'Neill et al., 1997) *Motivational Assessment Scale* (Durand & Crimmins, 1988) | Interviews of Delores's family, friends, and job coach addressed her preferences for "low-key" settings, difficulty with dramatic changes in routine, and beliefs that she is motivated to avoid demanding social circumstances |
| Direct observation | Observations should be conducted across a variety of times and circumstances. Some observation tools: *ABC (Antecedent-Behavior-Consequence) Recording Scatterplot* (Touchette, MacDonald, & Langer, 1985) *Frequency Measures across Conditions* | Scatterplot data indicates that Ben's biting is most likely when he is getting ready to leave in the morning and immediately after lunch. |

FBA methods range from highly precise and systematic to relatively informal. Particular tools and strategies should be selected based on the circumstances, individuals involved, and goals of intervention. The goal of FBA, regardless of which methods are used, is to answer certain questions:

1. Under what circumstances is the behavior most/least likely to occur (e.g., when, where, with whom)?
2. What outcomes does the behavior produce (i.e., what does the person get or avoid through his or her behavior)?

To answer these questions, the information gathered must be analyzed and summarized. Hypothesis (or summary) statements describe the specific patterns identified through the

*Source: Methods of Functional Behavior Assessment.* Positive Behavioral Interventions and Support Technical Assistance Center; Behavioral Research and Training; 5262 University of Oregon; Eugene, OR 97403-5262; PBIS@oregon.uoregon.edu

## Preventing Violence

Perhaps one of the most pervasive concerns in education is what educators can do to prevent individual or schoolwide violence. The fear of school violence is now a national concern. There is increasing evidence that effective behavioral supports and functional behavioral assessments (see above) may be the most effective tools for improving the school climate and reducing violence. A systemwide ap-

proach to reducing school violence is needed and requires the following considerations (Skiba & Peterson, 2000; Sprague & Walker, 2000):

- Conflict resolution and social instruction
- Classroom strategies for disruptive behavior
- Parent involvement
- Early warning signs and screening for extreme behavior problems

FBA and, if supported by the data, provide a foundation for intervention. A hypothesis statement must describe the behavior and surrounding conditions and be clear, comprehensive, and unbiased to be useful. Example: "When Steven finishes his work early, he makes noises and destroys his materials. His behavior prompts his supervisor to initiate an alternative activity."

### Frequently Asked Questions

1. *When and why should a functional behavioral assessment be completed?* An FBA may be initiated when a person's behavior interferes with performance, progress, and/or participation within typical daily routines and environments. It is completed for the purpose of designing an effective intervention that will allow the person with challenging behavior to be successful across all circumstances.

2. *Who should do a functional behavioral assessment (e.g., what qualifications are needed)?* It is important to have individuals who are experienced and skilled in FBA, competent in promoting collaboration, and proficient in designing effective positive behavioral support strategies involved in the process. Such individuals may come from varying backgrounds (e.g., applied behavioral analysis, school psychology).

3. *Are there shortcuts (e.g., one-page forms) for conducting FBAs?* Yes and no. A variety of tools are available for data collection and synthesis. In many cases, an informal or abbreviated approach can lead to reasonable interventions. However, in other circumstances, a more comprehensive and systematic process is required. An appropriate FBA is one that is matched to the circumstances and leads to an effective behavioral support plan.

4. *What is the difference between functional behavioral assessment and functional analysis?* Functional behavioral assessment is a broad term referring to the information gathering and hypothesis development process. It can involve a variety of methods, including functional analysis. Functional analysis is a rigorous experimental procedure in which hypotheses are tested by manipulating antecedents and consequences to see what impact they have on behavior. Whereas functional analysis may be useful in some circumstances, it is not always necessary or appropriate.

### Other Resources

Demchak, M., & Bossert, K. W. (1996). *Assessing problem behaviors.* Innovations (No. 4). Washington, D.C.: American Association on Mental Retardation.

Foster-Johnson, L., & Dunlap, G. (1993). Using functional assessment to develop effective, individualized interventions for challenging behaviors. *Teaching Exceptional Children, 25,* 44–50.

O'Neill, R. E., Horner, R. H., Albin, R. W., Sprague, J. R., Storey, K., Newton, J. S. (1997). *Functional assessment and program development for problem behavior: A practical handbook.* Pacific Grove, CA: Brooks/Cole.

Repp, A. C., & Horner, R. H. (Eds). (1999). *Functional analysis of problem behavior: From effective assessment to effective support.* Belmont, CA: Wadsworth Publishing.

- Schoolwide and districtwide data systems
- Crisis and security planning
- Schoolwide discipline and behavioral planning
- Functional assessment and individual behavioral plans
- Design, use, and supervision of school space
- School administrators who are accessible and interested in positive behavioral support

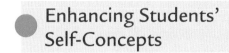

## Enhancing Students' Self-Concepts

Ask parents what they most want for their children, and a frequent response is that they want their children to be happy. They want their children to like themselves and be proud of what they do and who they are. This section of the chapter identifies procedures that teachers can implement to enhance self-concept and social skills.

How do you feel about yourself? Do you think you are a valuable person, worthy of love and appreciation from others? Do you think you have friends and are liked by others? Do you think you do well in school and are likely to succeed? How do you feel about the way you look? What about your ability to play sports? Your answers to these questions provide insight into your self-concept. Individuals with positive self-concepts generally feel as though they are worthwhile and deserve the respect, recognition, and appreciation of others. They have positive feelings about themselves in multiple settings, including at school, with friends, and with family. They generally like the way they look and who they are.

> Individuals with positive self-concepts feel worthwhile, competent, and deserving of others' respect and caring.

What about students who are disabled, at risk, or exceptional? What are their self-concepts like? Because these students are not a homogeneous group, no general statements can be made about their self-concept. But because individuals who are at risk or disabled often receive more negative feedback than other students do, their self-concepts probably are poorer, on the average, than those of other students (Haager & Vaughn, 1995).

Following are some of the ways in which teachers can enhance the self-concepts of students with disabilities:

- Hold all students to high standards, and then provide the encouragement and support to meet those standards (Canfield & Wells, 1994). Teachers often have lower expectations for students who demonstrate learning and behavior problems than for other students. These lowered expectations, however unintentional, limit the opportunities available to these students as compared to those for whom we have high standards.
- Discover students' talents, abilities, or interests, and recognize them personally. Every student in the classroom can be an expert on something. Be sure to find out what expertise every student in your classroom possesses. Remember, students with disabilities who excel in an extracurricular activity such as sports or music demonstrate levels of self-concept similar to those of academically average students (Kloomok & Cosden, 1994).
- Provide opportunities for students who do not succeed academically to succeed in other ways. One parent described it this way:

  The best thing that happened to my son is swimming. He joined a swim team when he was 6, and all his friends know he has won many swimming

awards. No matter how discouraged he is about school, he has one area in which he is successful.

- Recognize students' difficulties with learning, and explain their problems to them in a way they can understand. Sometimes, teachers and parents try to protect students and do not explain to them why they are having problems in school. An honest explanation (that they have attention problems, learning problems, physical problems, etc.) often helps students understand why some things are more difficult for them than for other students. The explanation should help the student understand that we are all different from each other in many ways, and this is one way in which the student is different from others. Group counseling can be an effective process for improving the self-concept of middle-school students with disabilities (Elbaum & Vaughn, 2001).
- Remember the important role you play in influencing students' self-concepts (both negatively and positively). Teachers exert an enormous influence on the self-perceptions of students, even students whom you feel pay too little attention to you. Students know (much better than you might imagine) what you think and how you feel about them (Babad et al., 1991).

## Teaching Social and Self-Management Skills

Have you ever met someone who seems to know the right thing to say and do, no matter what the situation might be? We often watch these people with envy as they move from person to person, always seemingly at ease. We refer to them as demonstrating good social skills or demonstrating social competence. **Social competence** is defined as "those responses, which within a given situation, prove effective, or in other words, maximize the probability of producing, maintaining, or enhancing positive effects for the interactor" (Foster & Ritchey, 1979, p. 26) and, it should be added, while causing no harm to others. Social skills allow one to adapt and respond to the expectations of society. Social competence is a process that begins at birth and continues throughout life. Many students with disabilities have difficulties with social skills (see Figure 8.3).

### Interpersonal Problem Solving

**Interpersonal problem solving** is an important skill for many students to learn, particularly students with special needs. The goal of interpersonal problem solving is to teach students to identify their problems, their goals, and a wide range of alternative strategies for effectively solving their problems. Some students learn to problem solve with little assistance from adults, but

FIGURE 8.3

### Examples of Social Skill Deficits

- Deficits in social perception and social cognition that inhibit students' abilities to interact with others
- Lack of consequential thinking
- Difficulty expressing feelings
- Difficulty in feeling empathy for others
- Difficulty delaying gratification (impulsive)
- Inappropriate grooming and hygiene
- Failure to understand and fulfill the role of listener
- Inability to take the perspective of another
- Less time spent looking and smiling at a conversational partner

- Unwilling to act in a social situation to influence the outcome
- Less likely to request clarification when given ambiguous or incomplete information
- Lack of self-confidence and tendency to portray learned helplessness behaviors
- Aggressive or antisocial behaviors
- Tendency to talk more or less than non-LD peers
- More likely to approach teacher and ask inappropriate questions
- Less proficient in interpersonal problem solving
- Less proficient in planning for the future

many students, particularly those with special needs, must be taught the skills for interpersonal problem solving. Interpersonal problem solving has been used successfully with different groups, including adult psychiatric patients (Platt & Spivack, 1972), preschoolers (Ridley & Vaughn, 1982), kindergarteners (Shure & Spivack, 1978), children with mental retardation (Vaughn et al., 1983), children with learning disabilities (Vaughn et al., 1988, 1991), and aggressive children (Vaughn et al., 1984). It is valuable for teachers to remember that self-initiated and peer-initiated assistance is often more valued than support provided by the teacher (Pavri & Monda-Amaya, 2000).

Four components appear in most interpersonal problem-solving programs (Spivack et al., 1976): problem identification, generation of alternative solutions, identification and evaluation of consequences, and solution implementation. For example, an interpersonal problem-solving program was implemented with students who had been identified as having serious emotional and behavioral disorders (Amish et al., 1988). The intervention was taught once a week for approximately 40 minutes, for a total of 15 weeks. Students who participated in the program improved their interpersonal problem-solving skills and were able to generate more alternatives to interviewing and role-playing measures. The following steps were taught:

1. Say what the problem is and how you feel.
2. Decide on a goal.
3. Stop and think before you decide what to do.
4. Think of many possible solutions to the problem.
5. Think about what will happen next (after each possible solution).
6. When you find a good solution, try it.

A sample worksheet for recording interpersonal problems and identifying procedures for addressing them is provided in Figure 8.4.

Vaughn and colleagues (McIntosh, Vaughn, & Bennerson, 1995; Vaughn & Lancelotta, 1990; Vaughn et al., 1988a, 1991) have developed the

FAST and SLAM strategies as part of an overall interpersonal problem-solving program. The purpose of **FAST** is to teach students to consider problems, identify alternatives, and evaluate consequences to their interpersonal problems. A description of the FAST strategy (see Figure 8.5) follows:

*Step 1. Freeze and think.* Students are taught to identify the problem. They are encouraged to view the problem from their own perspective as well as that of the other student.

*Step 2. Alternatives.* Students are taught to generate many possible alternative solutions to each problem. Students learn to categorize the solutions to ensure that they represent many different types.

FIGURE 8.4

### Problem Log

? What is the problem?
Describe it (who is involved, where did it happen, and what happened?).

? What do you want to happen?

? What did you do or say to solve the problem?

? Did your choice solve the problem?

? How well did it work?

| 1 | 2 | 3 | 4 | 5 |
|---|---|---|---|---|
| Poorly | Not so well | Okay | Good | Great |

*Source:* Goldstein, A. P. (1999). *The Prepare Curriculum: Teaching prosocial competencies* (2nd ed.). Champaign, IL: Research Press. Copyright 1999 by A. P. Goldstein. Reprinted by permission.

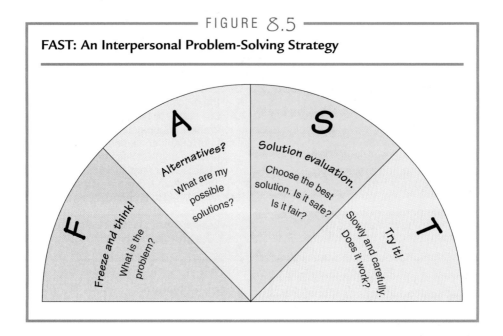

FIGURE 8.5

**FAST: An Interpersonal Problem-Solving Strategy**

*Step 3. Solution evaluation.* Students select several of the most feasible alternatives generated in step 2 and evaluate the likely consequences if the alternatives were implemented. Students also select an alternative that is safe and fair. The goal is to teach students to identify solutions that are effective in the long run.

*Step 4. Try it.* Students rehearse and implement the solution and evaluate its effectiveness. If that solution is not effective, students go back to step 2.

Figure 8.6 presents an activity sheet for implementing FAST in your classroom.

FIGURE 8.6

**Activity Sheet for Use with the FAST Strategy**

This activity sheet can be used to give students written practice in using the FAST strategy.

You are in the cafeteria. Another student keeps bugging you. He hits you, pokes you, tries to steal your food, and will not stop bullying you. You start to get angry. What would you do? Use FAST to help you solve the problem.

1. **Freeze and think.** What is the problem?
2. **Alternatives.** What are your possible solutions?
3. **Solution evaluation.** Choose the best one. Remember: safe and fair; works in the long run.
4. **Try it.** Do you think this will work?

*Source:* Bos, C. S., & Vaughn, S. (1998). *Strategies for teaching students with learning and behavior problems* (4th ed., p. 395). Boston: Allyn & Bacon. Reprinted with permission.

The purpose of **SLAM** (see Figure 8.7) is to develop a strategy, compatible with FAST, that would teach students to accept and respond appropriately to negative feedback from others. This is how SLAM works:

*Step 1. Stop.* Students are taught to stop what they are doing and take a breath when someone gives them negative feedback. Through role-play and rehearsal, teacher and students identify the typical response to negative feedback—saying something negative or stopping work. This step teaches students to stop, take a breath, and simply listen.

*Step 2. Look.* Teaches students that the best thing to do when someone is giving them negative feedback is to stop what they are doing and look at the other person. Sometimes stu-

FIGURE 8.7

**The SLAM Mnemonic to Aid in Accepting Negative Feedback SLAM Strategy**

| **S** | **L** | **A** | **M** |
|---|---|---|---|
| **STOP** | **LOOK** | **ASK** | **MAKE** |
| Stop whatever you are doing. | Look the person in the eyes. | Ask the person a question to clarify what he or she means. | Make an appropriate response to the person. |

*Source:* Council for Exceptional Children, McIntosh, R., Vaughn, S., & Bennerson, D. (1995). FAST social skills with a SLAM and a rap. *Teaching Exceptional Children, 28,* 37–41.

---
FIGURE 8.8
---

**The ASSET Method for Teaching Social Skills to Secondary Students**

Each social skill is taught by implementing the following nine-step procedure:

**Step 1**    *Review.* Previously learned skills are reviewed and homework is evaluated and integrated.

**Step 2**    *Explain.* The skill that is the focus of the lesson is explained and discussed.

**Step 3**    *Rationale.* A rationale for why the skill is important and why the students need to learn it is provided.

**Step 4**    *Example.* Examples of situations in which the skill can be used are provided. These examples relate directly to the experiences and interests of the students.

**Step 5**    *Examined.* A skills sheet that lists the component skills (refer to text for list of skills for following directions) is provided to each student.

**Step 6**    *Model.* Through videotapes that can be purchased with the curriculum, or as implemented by the teacher, the skills are demonstrated and modeled.

**Step 7**    *Verbal Rehearsal.* The procedure of verbally stating the components of each skill so that they can be learned by the student is implemented. The students practice saying the skill components and play games and engage in activities that teach them the skills.

**Step 8**    *Behavioral Rehearsal.* Students practice performing each subskill and overall skill, and demonstrate proficiency.

**Step 9**    *Homework.* Designed to enhance generalization, homework provides students with directed activities that allow them to practice the subskills and skills outside the classroom.

---

dents look down or away when they are given negative feedback.

*Step 3. Ask.* Teaches students to ask questions to clarify what the other person means. Often, students feel as though they do not deserve the negative feedback that teachers or parents give them. Instead of saying, "I didn't do that," students are taught to ask questions for clarification before they respond.

*Step 4. Make.* Teaches students to make an appropriate response to the other person. Students role-play these responses, which include agreeing with the other person, agreeing to stop the behavior, or explaining their point of view.

## Example of a Social Skills Program for Adolescents

The purpose of **ASSET** is to develop the social skills of adolescents with special needs who demonstrate difficulties in social functioning (Hazel et al., 1982). The program also has been used successfully in regular classrooms.

ASSET provides a comprehensive social skills training program that emphasizes the following eight fundamental skills:

- Giving positive feedback
- Giving negative feedback
- Accepting negative feedback
- Resisting peer pressure

- Negotiation skills
- Personal problem solving
- Following directions
- Conducting conversations

Figure 8.8 provides a description of the steps in the ASSET program. The Leader's Guide (Hazel et al., 1982) from the ASSET program provides instructions for running the groups and teaching the skills. Eight teaching sessions are provided on videotapes that demonstrate the skills. Program materials include skill sheets, home notes, and criterion checklists.

Teachers might want to implement the specific approaches to social skills instruction identified in this section of the chapter and to use some or all of the social skills materials described in Tips for Teachers 8.3.

## Principles for Conducting Social Skills Training

There are several principles of social skills training that generalize across social skills programs (Vaughn & La Greca, 1993):

1. *Use principles of effective instruction.* These principles include the following:
   - Obtain a student's commitment to learn the targeted social skill.
   - Assess social skills and target skills appropriate for the students with whom you are working.

# Tips for Teachers

## 8.3 Instructional Materials to Enhance Students' Social Skills

Anderson, J. (1981). *Thinking, changing, rearranging: Improving self-esteem in young people.* Eugene, OR: Timberline Press.

*Intended for students age 10 and older, the activities in this book examine students' cognitions as related to social interaction.*

Bash, M. A. S., & Camp, B. W. (1985). *Think aloud: Increasing social and cognitive skills: A problem-solving program for children.* Champaign, IL: Research Press.

*Developed for elementary students, this program is organized into three sections for grades 1 through 6. Students are taught how to think through and successfully deal with social conflicts.*

Canfield, J., & Wells, H. C. (1994). *100 ways to enhance self-concept in the classroom* (2nd ed.). Boston, MA: Allyn & Bacon.

*Provides 100 strategies to help teachers build a positive classroom community and promote the growth of their students. Particularly useful are the references for instructional books, videotapes, and organizations.*

Cautela, J. R., & Groden, J. (1978). *Relaxation: A comprehensive manual for adults, children, and children with special needs.* Champaign, IL: Research Press.

*Provides different techniques for teaching relaxation training.*

Elardo, P., & Cooper, M. (1977). *Aware: Activities for social development.* Menlo Park, CA: Addison Wesley.

*Provides specific exercises (e.g., games, role-play activities) to develop social competence in elementary students.*

Gerald, M., & Eyman, W. (1981). *Thinking straight and talking sense.* New York: Institute for Rational Living.

*This workbook, designed for students in the sixth grade and above, helps students examine the cognitions behind their behavior.*

Goldstein, A. P., & Glick, B. (1987). *Aggression replacement training: A comprehensive intervention for aggressive youth.* Champaign, IL: Research Press.

*This multifaceted program includes activities to help students improve their behavior, affect, and cognitions.*

Goldstein, A. P., Sprafkin, R. P., Gershaw, N. J., & Klein, P. (1980). *Skillstreaming the adolescent: A structured*

learning approach to teaching prosocial skills. Champaign, IL: Research Press.

*Provides explicit methods for enhancing the social skills of adolescents. The inclusion of a transcript from a skills training session is particularly illustrative and helps to crystallize the procedures necessary for effective instruction.*

Jackson, N. F. (1983). *Getting along with others: Teaching social effectiveness to children.* Champaign, IL: Research Press.

*This program, designed for elementary students, provides guides, exercises, and lessons targeted to develop skills in cooperating, accepting feedback, responding to criticism, dealing with peer pressure, and reacting to harassment.*

Mannix, D. (1993). *Social skills activities for special children.* West Nyack, NY: Center for Applied Research in Education.

*This workbook provides 142 lessons and accompanying activity sheets that teachers can reproduce and use with their students. The activities focus on skills, both in the classroom and at home.*

McGinnis, E., Goldstein, A. P., Sprafkin, R. P., & Gershaw, N. J. (1984). *Skillstreaming the elementary school child: A guide for teaching prosocial skills.* Champaign, IL: Research Press.

*Based on the skillstreaming model, this book provides instruction and activities for teaching social skills to elementary-age students.*

Vaughn, S., Levine, L., & Ridley, C. (1986). *PALS: Problem-solving and affective learning strategies.* Chicago: Science Research Associates.

*This skills training program targets students between 4 and 8 years of age. A teacher's guide outlines recommended activities, which are designed for small-group and whole-class instruction.*

Walker, H. M., McConnell, S., Holmes, S., Todis, B., Walker, J., & Golden, N. (1983). *The Walker social skills curriculum: The Accepts program.* Austin, TX: PRO-ED.

*A tool for teachers to help students with disabilities make the transition into less restrictive settings. Association with classmates and coping strategies are some of the topics covered.*

- Explain the targeted social skills to students and demonstrate and model appropriate uses of the skills.
- Identify the steps in implementing the social skill and provide adequate time to rehearse the skill.
- Allow students to role-play the implementation of the social skill in controlled and natural settings.

- Teach students to monitor and evaluate their use of and progress in implementing the targeted social skill.

2. *Involve peers in the training program for low social status students.* Students who do and do not demonstrate social skills problems need to be included in the training. Why? Because when social skills programs target only students with social skills difficulties, the changes those stu-

dents make in their behavior are not noticed by students of higher social status (Bierman & Furman, 1984; Vaughn et al., 1988a). Thus, despite positive changes in their social behavior, targeted students are often still rated by their peers as undesirable social partners. For example, Vaughn et al. (1988a) found that popular students who were involved in social skills training with students who were low in popularity were more likely to increase their acceptance of the low-social-status students than were popular students who were not involved in the training.

3. *Teach for transfer of learning and generalization.* As with other skills (e.g., learning strategies), social skills training programs often effectively increase students' social skills within the context of social skills training but do not effectively generalize the skills to other settings (Berler et al., 1982; Vaughn & Ridley, 1983). Program plans for teaching generalization have been developed (Vaughn et al., 1986) and include such strategies as varying the setting, the trainer, the materials, the task, and the cues. The extent to which these components of generalization are built into the training will increase the likelihood that the learned social skills will generalize to other settings. Michelson and Mannarino (1986) provide a summary of strategies for promoting generalization of social skills. These strategies include the following:

- Teach social behaviors that will be supported naturally in the setting.
- Teach alternative response patterns, not just pat phrases.
- Teach students to adapt the procedures of the social skill taught so that it becomes their own.
- Rehearse skills in a variety of settings.
- Use natural and logical consequences to maintain the target skills.
- Use peers as change agents.

## making a Difference

### Encouraging Self-Monitoring

**Purpose:** To have students monitor their own behavior during an activity.

**Procedure:**

1. Clearly write the directions for the activity on the chalkboard, overhead projector, or writing pad so that all students can see them.
2. Explain the following to your students: "While you are working on this project I want you to monitor how

## research brief

### Why Has Social Skills Training Not Been More Effective for Students with Disabilities?

Although many students with disabilities have social skills difficulties, social skills interventions have not been as effective as you might think. Why? According to several meta-analyses of the research literature (e.g., Forness & Kavale, 1999; Gresham, Sugai, & Horner, 2001), social skills training has not yielded overall very positive outcomes or improved social competence or been associated with generalized changes in social behavior because (1) the social skills interventions do not last long enough, (2) they often do not occur over a long period of time, (3) they do not provide sufficient opportunities to practice the new behaviors within classroom settings, and (4) the newly taught social behaviors may be competing with other behaviors the student exhibits that are receiving reinforcement.

## Teaching Self-Management Skills

The purpose of teaching students **self-management** skills is that such skills enable them to be more aware of their own behaviors and to govern the reinforcers for their behaviors. Furthermore, teaching students self-management skills enables them to depend less on the teacher. You might recall, from the basic principles of managing student behavior introduced earlier in this chapter, that much of the responsibility for targeting behavior, identifying reinforcers, and implementing a behavior-change plan rested with the teachers. Self-management skills require that

## The 60-second **Lesson**

well you are following the directions I have provided. Every 10 minutes, I will say stop, and I want you to give yourself a rating from 1 to 5. Five means you are following the directions and working all the time, 4 means you are mostly following the directions and working, 3 means sometimes you do and sometimes you don't, 2 means you are more frequently not following directions and working, and 1 means you have done very little since the last time we stopped."

3. At the end of the activity period, ask students to report their scores.

students learn some principles of behavior management and then implement the selected reinforcers. Self-management requires a more active role from the student and a more collaborative role from the teacher.

Margarite Rabinsky is a fourth-grade teacher whose student, Eduardo Cora, is not completing assignments. Although Margarite worked closely with Eduardo to ensure that the assignments were not too difficult and that Eduardo understood how to complete them, he was still unsuccessful at turning in completed assignments on time. Deciding to involve Eduardo in a self-management plan, Margarite implemented the following steps for developing a self-management plan with a student:

**Step 1.** *Teacher and student identify and agree on the behavior to be changed.* Margarite and Eduardo agreed on the behavior to change and put it in writing (see Figure 8.9).

**Step 2.** *Identify when and where the behavior most frequently occurs.* Margarite stated, "First, let's think about what classes it occurs in most, and then let's think about whether there are certain days when it occurs." Eduardo volunteered that he started the week off pretty well and then felt he got worse on Thursday and Friday. Margarite indicated that she did not think he had difficulty with math, since he most frequently turned in his math work but seemed to have trouble with social studies and science. Eduardo agreed, and they summarized this on the form shown in Figure 8.9.

**Step 3.** *Establish realistic goals for changing the behavior.* Margarite and Eduardo discussed his behavior and then established the goals listed in Figure 8.9.

**Step 4.** *Identify a time line showing how long the behavior-change plan will be in effect.* Because neither Margarite nor Eduardo had done this before, they decided to meet for five minutes every Friday to review the progress for the week and to have a longer meeting in three weeks to determine how effective the program had been.

**Step 5.** *Identify reinforcers and consequences.* Margarite and Eduardo reexamined their goals and discussed what reinforcers should be provided if Eduardo met the goals. They also discussed consequences if the goals were not met. These reinforcers and consequences were written into the plan in Figure 8.9.

**Step 6.** *Self-evaluate the success of the program each day.* Margarite explained to Eduardo that he would be responsible, at the end of each day, for writing a brief evaluation of how effective the plan was for that day. These steps were implemented by the teacher, who observed a noticeable change in Eduardo's behavior after one week. After two weeks Eduardo's behavior was more like the behavior of other students in the class. Though Eduardo would still have bad days they were far less frequent.

---

FIGURE 8.9

---

**Self-Management Plan**

**Name:** _____ Eduardo Cora _____

**Target Behavior:** Submit completed assignments to teacher on time or meet with teacher before assignment is due to agree on alternative date and time.

**When Behavior Occurs:** Mostly on Thursdays and Fridays.

**Where Behavior Occurs:** Social Studies and Science.

**Goals:**

1. Eduardo will write down assignments and due dates in a separate assignment book for each subject.
2. Eduardo will look at each assignment and be sure that he knows how to complete it. Eduardo will ask questions, as necessary.
3. Eduardo will tell the teacher ahead of time if an assignment is going to be late.

**Timeline:** Meet each Friday to review the progress on the plan, and then revise the plan in 3 weeks.

**Reinforcer:** Eduardo will receive 15 minutes of extra time to work on the computer each day his assignments are completed.

**Evaluation:** Eduardo will write a brief description of the program's success.

## s u m m a r y

- Teachers need to continually monitor how their perspectives, attitudes, beliefs, expectations, and experiences influence the ways in which they interpret the behaviors of their students.
- Often, teachers first need to change their own behavior in order to change the behavior of their students.
- Teachers tend to focus on negative student behaviors and to estimate that they praise students *more* than they actually do.
- Positive reinforcement is the most significant means of increasing desirable student behaviors.
- Reinforcers can be intangible (e.g., verbal praise) or tangible (e.g., food, tokens), and supplied from a variety of sources (e.g., adults, peers, self).
- The effective management of student behavior requires the implementation of guidelines, procedures, and rules in the classroom as well as the specification of consequences for nonadherence.
- Additional techniques for decreasing undesirable student behaviors include ignoring on purpose, time out, and punishment.

- The learning environment itself can help students maintain appropriate behavior in the classroom.
- Positive behavioral supports are required by law for students with disabilities.
- Functional behavioral assessments provide the means to develop and monitor the most effective positive support plans.
- Social competence is a multifaceted construct. Many instructional programs (e.g., FAST, ASSET) aimed at improving students' social skills are available to teachers.
- Principles for effectively conducting social skills training include principles of effective instruction, involving peers in the training, and teaching for transfer of learning and generalization.
- Procedures for teaching students self-management skills that will enable them to govern and reinforce their own behavior are described.
- Considerations for teachers regarding behavior management for students from diverse ethnic and socioeconomic backgrounds are provided.

## k e y   t e r m s   a n d   c o n c e p t s

activity reinforcers
ASSET
behavioral support plans
class meetings
consequences
extinction
FAST
functional behavior assessments
ignoring on purpose

interpersonal problem solving
mistaken goal
negative reinforcement
planned ignoring
positive behavioral support
positive feedback
positive reinforcement
Premack principle
punishment

self-management
SLAM
social competence
social reinforcers
stimulus
tangible reinforcers
time out
token reinforcers
token system

## t h i n k   a n d   a p p l y

1. Nina Zaragoza identified several key principles of effective classroom management. On a sheet of paper, list the principles of effective classroom management she followed. Now add several others to the list, based on information provided in this chapter and your own experience. Rank these principles according to their importance to you. As you continue reading, return to your list of classroom management principles and see whether there are any you would rewrite or reorder.

2. This chapter provides several suggestions for developing forms and describes forms that have already been developed. For example, in the section of the chapter on time out, a set of procedures for effectively monitoring time out is provided. The procedures (e.g., student's name, date, and time student was placed in time out) could be used to develop a record form for time out. Develop and copy the forms you think will be helpful to you as a teacher. Keep them in your portfolio. As you read each chapter, develop additional forms.

3. Many teachers identify classroom management as the issue they are most concerned about prior to teaching, and practicing teachers identify it as the issue with which they have the most difficulty. Interview five practicing teachers and ask the following questions:
   a. What classroom management strategies do you find most useful?
   b. What aspects of classroom management do you wish you knew more about?
   c. What advice about classroom management would you offer?

4. Identify the key elements of a positive behavioral support plan. Interview the teachers who work with students with severe disabilities. Ask them how they include each of the elements in the positive behavioral support plan.

5. This chapter provided several practices teachers can implement to enhance the self-concept of students. Think about your own experiences as a student, the teachers who enhanced your self-concept, and those who affected your self-concept negatively. What did these two types of teachers say and do? How do your experiences compare with this chapter's recommendations for enhancing students' self-concepts?

6. Return to the Research Brief entitled "Behavior Management Considerations in Culturally Diverse Classrooms." Think about the questions posed (e.g., What behaviors bother you as a teacher? Who is performing these behaviors? Are you sure that *all* students who perform these behaviors are treated in the same way?). What additional questions might be important to add to this list? On the basis of your experiences as a student and as a teacher, why are these questions important?

## read more about it

1. Branden, N. (1987). *How to raise your self-esteem.* New York: Bantam.

   *Provides a sequenced approach to better understanding your self-esteem and methods you can apply to improve your self-esteem and that of others. The author provides a practical step-by-step sequence to improving self-esteem.*

2. Canfield, J., & Wells, H. C. (1994). *100 ways to enhance self-concept in the classroom.* Boston: Allyn & Bacon.

   *Packed with ideas about what teachers can do in the classroom to positively affect the self-concept of their students. The activities are divided into seven sections: getting started, my strengths, who am I?, accepting my body, where am I going?, the language of self, and relationships with others.*

3. Dreikurs, R., & Stoltz, V. (1964). *Children: The challenge.* New York: Dutton.

   *Though almost 40 years old, this book continues to provide teachers and parents with guidance for better understanding and coping with children's behavior problems. The major principles of understanding why children do what they do and how the reactions of teachers and parents affect behavior are very informative.*

4. Dreikurs, R., Grunwald, B., & Pepper, F. (1982). *Maintaining sanity in the classroom.* New York: Harper & Row.

   *This book provides teachers with guidance for better understanding and coping with children's behavior problems in the classroom. The major principles of understanding why children do what they do and how the reactions of teachers affect behavior are very informative. In addition, it addresses ways in which teachers can replace punishment of bad behavior with lessons for children on how to discipline themselves.*

5. Grossman, H. (1995). *Special education in a diverse society.* Boston: Allyn & Bacon.

   *Provides excellent materials regarding ways in which socioeconomic status, gender, and cultural and linguistic background are likely to affect the behavior of students. Describes what teachers can do to be sensitive to these issues as they develop behavior-management strategies.*

6. Kaufman, J. M., Mostert, M. P., Trent, S. C., & Hallahan, D. P. (1998). *Managing classroom behavior: A reflective case-based approach.* Boston: Allyn & Bacon.

   *Through 16 cases, teachers are led through an empirical approach to analyzing behavior problems.*

7. Larrivee, B. (1992). *Strategies for effective classroom management.* Boston: Allyn & Bacon.

   *This two-part training package consists of a Leader's Guide and a Teacher's Handbook that provide practical strategies and procedures for effectively managing behavior in the classroom. The format is an alternative to traditional textbooks, with multiple examples and forms to help teachers implement the suggested practices.*

8. Nelson, J., Lott, L., & Glenn, H. S. (1993). *Positive discipline in the classroom.* Rocklin, CA: Prima.

   *An easy-to-read book written more like a trade book than a textbook. The major principles in the book are related to positive discipline strategies and illustrated with examples and suggestions for application.*

9. Janney, R., & Snell, M. E. (2000). *Behavioral support*. Baltimore, MD: Brookes.

   *A practical guide to positive behavioral support that addresses assumptions about behavioral problems, individual behavior support plans, teaching social interaction and self-management, and the classroom community.*

10. Axelrod, S., & Hall, R. V. (1999). *Behavior modification: Basic principles.* Austin, TX: PRO-ED.

    *This booklet is written specifically for teachers to improve their understanding and guide their practice regarding such behavior modification practices as reinforcers, schedules for reinforcement, decreasing behavior, modeling and imitation, and behavioral changes.*

11. Nelson, J., Lott, L., & Glenn, H. S. (2000). *Positive discipline in the classroom: Developing mutual respect, cooperation, and responsibility in your classroom.* Roseville, CA: Prima.

    *This book provides a practical guide for creating a classroom climate that enhances academic learning and fosters cooperation and mutual respect in children. It contains various strategies that teachers can use for improving children's positive behaviors and social skills (e.g., use of encouragement, use of class meetings).*

12. Shoop, L. L., & Wright, D. (1999). *Classroom warm-ups: Activities that improve the climate for learning and discussion.* San Jose, CA: Resource.

    *This book helps teachers build a comfortable and confident learning environment for their students. It provides activities that improve the classroom climate and do not consume extensive classroom time. The emphasis is on establishing a positive classroom environment while allowing plenty of time for instruction.*

## suggested websites

**www.pbis.org**
This website provides research-based information on the implementation of positive behavioral supports and interventions. This center is funded in part through the Office of Special Education Programs.

**www.ccbd.net**
This website describes the efforts of the Council for Children with Behavioral Disorders of the Council for Exceptional Children.

**www.BehaviorAdvisor.com**
This website provides advice on behavior management from Dr. Mac.

**www.usoc.k12.ut.us/sars/Upi/behavior_management.htm**
This website provides several links related to behavior management (e.g., positive behavior support, supporting students with challenging behavior).

**www.ldonline.org/ld_indepth/teaching_techniques/ strategies.html#anchor1001355**
This website provides several useful links to material on social skills training.

**www.ldonline.org/ld_indepth/social_skills/ soc-skills.html**
This website provides several useful links to material on social skills (teacher's roles in social skills, fostering social competence, etc.).

**http://cpt.fsu.edu/tree/JUSTEN.html**
This website introduces various behavior management strategies.

**www.familyeducation.com/whatworks/item/front/ 0,2551,1-16209-4481-3,00.html**
This website introduces one activity targeted toward improving social skills.

**www.vaxxine.com/socialskill/programdescription.html**
This website introduces several classwide social skills programs.

**www.feat.org/autism/social_skills.htm**
This website contains a variety of research studies on social skills training for students with autism.

**http://cases.coedu.usf.edu/CECComp/ CEC%20Competencies.htm**
This website contains a variety of case studies on behavior management and social skills training.

**www.ldonline.org/ld_indepth/special_education/ cecp_behavior.html**
This website provides information about behavior management plans (functional behavior analysis).

**http://ici2.umn.edu/preschoolbehavior**
This website introduces a project designed to enable school districts to become more self-sufficient in serving preschoolers with disabilities with challenging behavior.

# Collaborating and Coordinating with Other Professionals and Family

# chapter | outline

# inter view

### Angela and Todd Hammond

# focus | questions

1. What is collaboration? Describe two collaboration models that can be used in schools. What components of these models make them effective?

2. What is cooperative teaching, or co-teaching? What parts of co-teaching are necessary to make it effective? How might it be used to provide an educational program for students with disabilities?

3. What are the issues and dilemmas to consider when implementing collaboration models?

4. To communicate effectively with parents and professionals, what skills does a teacher need? Can you identify some good and bad examples of communication with parents and professionals?

5. Why is family adjustment an important factor for students with disabilities? How might teachers assist in the family adjustment of their students?

6. Working effectively with parents requires several skills. What are they? What techniques presented in this chapter might you use to more effectively communicate with parents?

Angela and Todd Hammond are the parents of three children. Their middle child is 11 years old and was born with spina bifida. Spina bifida is a neural tube defect that results in varying degrees of paralysis.

Angela relayed the following story:

> When Nick was born, I was overwhelmed with grief. I had no idea if Nick would ever walk, and due to hydrocephalus (fluid on the brain), I didn't know how well he would learn. As he grew, we learned he would walk with braces, which was a huge relief. As a toddler, he seemed to learn as well

as his brother, so I wasn't as worried about his intelligence. When he entered kindergarten, the Individuals with Disabilities Education Act (IDEA) was in effect, so he was entitled to a free appropriate education in our neighborhood school. I was really happy that Nick could go to school with his brother, and he wasn't in a special program; he was fully included. Until third grade, Nick didn't seem to need a special program or special materials. He did, however, receive occupational and physical therapy at school. I learned that these were related services that he was entitled to. Once Nick entered third grade, he started having academic difficulties. He had a lot of trouble with math—he could memorize but couldn't apply it—and he was very slow as well as sloppy in writing. His teacher kept telling us that Nick was easily distracted and lazy. She felt that he just wasn't trying. All year, Nick was punished for not finishing his homework and for being disorganized. We thought his teacher knew best. It was a rough year, and it seemed like he was always in trouble.

At the end of third grade, we attended a spina bifida conference and attended a session on learning difficulties in children with spina bifida. We learned that many of Nick's learning problems were a result of his condition. We felt awful that we had not been sensitive to things that were beyond his control. We also learned about family advocacy groups that train advocates to attend the individual educational plan (IEP) with your family. As a result, fourth grade was a very different experience. We asked for a referral for an evaluation of Nick's academic function. After the evaluation, it was determined that Nick did have learning disabilities that made him eligible for special services. The next step was to hold a meeting and develop an IEP that tells the teachers and other school staff what special programs and related services your child needs. The meeting was a little

intimidating. There were a lot of people there—the occupational and physical therapist, the principal, his teacher, his Dad and I, the exceptional student specialist, and an advocate from Family Network on Disabilities that we had invited. The advocate and ESE specialist were very helpful in identifying academic accommodations for Nick. For example, the ESE specialist recommended a laptop to facilitate Nick's writing. The principal initially told us he didn't have the money to provide it, but the advocate explained that it was necessary to support and maintain Nick's full inclusion in the regular classroom. The team agreed, and it was written into the IEP. I never would have known what to ask for on my own or even that I had a right to ask for it. Having an advocate with us helped a lot. The team identified further goals, such as organization skills, and placed him in a study skills class. At the end of the meeting I felt excited that Nick would have his needs met and proud that I had learned to advocate for my son. His teacher feels much better now that she has a support facilitator to help her meet Nick's needs in the classroom. Now that I have become knowledgeable about this educational process, I really feel part of the team.

## i n t r o d u c t i o n

Sally Mynor had just completed her first year of teaching. When asked about her thoughts about her first year, she said, "I didn't realize how much time I would spend interacting with other teachers and parents. I guess during my student teaching, my lead teacher took care of all of that." As a classsroom teacher, your primary responsibility is instructing your students. However, planning and instruction are only part of your job. Increasingly, teachers are required to work with other professionals and parents and need skills to collaborate and communicate effectively. Teachers may also be asked to supervise one or more paraprofessionals in their classroom. The increasing diversity in our classrooms, including second language learners, students with disabilities, and students who are gifted, requires collaboration with other professionals and parents. The chapter begins with suggestions for working with other professionals and continues with guidelines and practices for working with the parents of your students.

## Working with Other Professionals

Whether you are an elementary or secondary teacher, you can expect to work with the special education teacher, the counselor, and other teachers (O'Shea & O'Shea, 1997). You might also work with the school psychologist or nurse, the Title I teacher, the ESL teacher, the teacher of gifted students, and an inclusion specialist. You might have students in your class who need specialized services from the speech and language teacher or the occupational or physical therapist. Most of your ongoing collaboration, however, will be with the special education teacher, the school counselor, and the students' parents.

Your interaction with some professionals might be limited to an occasional phone call, a brief meeting, or an IEP staffing. In other cases, your working relationship might be more involved. Working with other professionals can be rewarding and can provide the opportunity to learn from others who have different training and experiences. It can also be

---

## TABLE 9.1

### Qualities of Collaborative Professionals

- Realize that goals are often complex and that the success of achieving these goals requires joint effort. Everyone's effort is needed to solve problems and make schools more effective in meeting the needs of all students.
- Recognize the creativity that occurs when people work together to solve common problems. Collaborative professionals realize that working together makes the problem more manageable and often yields more effective and creative solutions.
- Enjoy the social aspect of problem solving with others. Collaborative professionals respect the other members of the group even when they do not always agree with them. They are able to express their point of view without hostility or put-downs toward others in the group.
- Recognize and value the benefits from working collaboratively. Collaborative professionals realize that many ideas and experiences could not be developed independently; thus, they value the work of the group.
- Be interested in reflecting on and changing their own practices. Collaborative professionals are willing to consider alternative instructional practices and to think about suggestions and comments that arise during collaboration.

---

*Source:* Adapted from Pugach, M. C., & Johnson, L. J. (1995). *Collaborative practitioners, collaborative schools.* Denver, CO: Love.

demanding. In identifying myths and misunderstandings about professional collaboration, Friend (2000) pointed out that collaboration does not come naturally to everyone. Because the professional preparation of teachers focuses primarily on working with students, working with adults can be new territory—and can take skill, practice, and patience.

Regardless of the intensity or duration of the working relationship, the qualities of collaborative professionals described in Table 9.1 should be applied.

Different ways in which general education teachers might work with other professionals include consultation, collaboration, and co-teaching:

- *Consultation.* Friend and Cook (2000) define consultation as, "a voluntary process in which one professional assists another to address a problem concerning a third party" (p. 73). For example, a special education teacher might consult with you in how to develop a behavior management plan for a child with a behavior disorder who is included in your classroom.

- *Collaboration.* According to Friend and Cook (2000), "Interpersonal **collaboration** is a style for direct interaction between at least two co-equal parties voluntarily engaged in shared decision making as they work toward a common goal" (p. 6). Collaboration describes the interaction that is occurring: People are working together as equal partners in shared problem solving. For example, you might collaborate with a special education teacher to develop a long-range plan for teaching mathematics to a child with learning disabilities in your class.

- *Co-teaching.* Cook and Friend (1995) define co-teaching as "two or more professionals jointly deliver[ing] substantive instruction to a diverse, or blended, group of students in a single physical space" (p. 1). For example, if you are teaching a mathematics lesson in your classroom, you might work with a special education teacher to divide students into two teacher-led groups for guided practice sessions.

In general, teachers prefer the term "collaboration" over "consultation" even though both terms refer to ways one or more teachers work together (Arguelles, Schumm, & Vaughn, 1996). The term "collaboration" implies that all teachers are professionals with a certain area of expertise. "Consultation" implies that one teacher is the "expert" and the other is the recipient of that expertise. As Olivia Plant, a special education teacher, put it, "I like the term *collaboration,* because that is what we really do—two heads are better than one!"

Aside from using consultation and collaboration models, general and special education teachers can work together to enhance instruction for students with disabilities through co-planning and co-teaching. As you may recall, Chapter 1 introduced the concept of cooperative teaching. The key aspects of cooperative teaching include long-range co-planning, lesson co-planning, lesson co-teaching, and grading.

What are some models and procedures for consultation, collaboration, co-planning and co-teaching? The following sections describe various ways in which you can work with other professionals to provide the best learning opportunities for all students. In addition, Tips for Teachers 9.1 provides specific suggestions for working with paraprofessionals.

## A Consultation Model

Collaboration in the Schools (West et al., 1988) is a consultation model outlining procedures for the special education teacher to work as a consultant to

# Tips for Teachers

## 9.1   Working with Paraprofessionals

Jamie DeFraites is a first-grade teacher in New Orleans with 22 children in her class. Her multicultural classroom of 22 students includes 11 Vietnamese children and 2 Hispanic students who are English language learners. Jamie explains, "I love my class and was actually asked to loop to second grade—so I'll have the same students next year!"

Jamie is fortunate enough to work with two paraprofessionals, who join her classroom at different times during the day. Here are Jamie's tips for working with paraprofessionals:

1. It's important to have mutual respect and trust. I let the paraprofessionals know how fortunate I feel to have additional adults in the classroom and how important their job is in helping all students learn. I also thank them every chance I get—in the presence of the principal, parents, and students.
2. At the beginning of the year, I talk with the paraprofessionals individually about their interests and skills and try to match their duties with their strengths. Both paraprofessionals are bilingual (one in Vietnamese and one in Spanish), so assisting me with parent communication is very important. One of the paraprofessionals is very creative and helps me design learning centers. The other is very interested in math and helps me with review and extra practice for students with challenges in that area.
3. Each of the paraprofessionals is anxious to learn new skills and strategies. It is worth my time to explain instructional strategies to them so that they

can do more than grade papers—they can actually interact with children in small groups or individually. It took me a long time to learn to teach—I'm still learning. I don't assume that the paraprofessionals automatically know how to teach. If I can share some of my training, the payoff is big for my students.
4. At the beginning of the year, we also clarify roles, responsibilities, classroom routines, and expectations for student learning and behavior. Spending that time in planning and communicating is time well spent. We're on the same page.
5. The paraprofessionals both work with several other teachers, so their time in my class is very limited. We have to make each minute count. Their tasks have to be well defined. I also plan a backup—what to do when there is nothing to do.
6. Finally, I encourage the paraprofessionals to get additional professional training. I let them know about workshops and other opportunities to learn. They more they learn, the more my students benefit!

Jamie admits that she would like to have a regular planning time with the paraprofessionals. As she says, "Often, we have to plan on the run." Also, her school district does not require periodic feedback or performance review sessions. This is something Jamie definitely recommends. "Fortunately, I have not run into problems with either paraprofessional, but if I did, it would be a good idea to have a system for giving feedback in a systematic way."

general education teachers and help them successfully include students with disabilities in their classes. The underlying principle of the **consultation model** is that it is

An interactive process that enables people with diverse expertise to generate creative solutions to mutually defined problems. The major outcome of collaborative consultation is to provide comprehensive and effective programs for students with special needs within the most appropriate context, thereby enabling them to achieve maximum constructive interaction with their nonhandicapped peers (Idol et al., 1986, p. 1).

West and Idol (1990) cite three reasons for using consultation models for students with disabilities in the schools:

1. *Prevention.* Many of the expenses of assessing and placing students with disabilities in special education can be eliminated through the use of effective consultation models.
2. *Effective schools.* Collaborative planning and problem solving promote the collegial relationships associated with effective schools.
3. *Coordinated instruction.* Consultation models can provide opportunities to coordinate instruction between special and general education and

to exchange knowledge about effective practices for enhancing instruction.

Collaboration in the Schools is based on a six-stage consultation process that a team of professionals completes. Typically, the team includes the professionals who have primary responsibility for the student's educational program, often the general education and special education teachers.

*Stage 1. Goal/Entry.* The team discusses roles, objectives, responsibilities, and expectations. Topics include the role of each member of the team, what is expected (e.g., number of meetings, implementation tactics), the type of paperwork to be maintained and who will do it, and the responsibilities of each team member.

*Stage 2. Problem Identification.* The student is identified, and the specific nature and extent of the problem is defined. Each member of the team receives a written copy of the problem description, which helps the group stay focused on the problem at hand.

*Stage 3. Intervention of Recommendations.* The team brainstorms potential interventions and predicts outcomes. In this stage, the team can discuss possible alternatives and their consequences before recommendations are prioritized and selected. Team members decide how, and by whom, recommendations will be implemented. They develop objectives to specify the intervention details, the procedures, and the means for determining whether the problem has been solved.

*Stage 4. Implementation of Recommendations.* The intervention plan is implemented. The individuals responsible for the implementation keep notes on the effects so that they can report back to the team.

*Stage 5. Evaluation.* The team completes an evaluation of the intervention, which includes any data collected, evidence from the student's work, and reports from persons who implemented the intervention. The evaluation includes a report on the impacts on the student, the consultants, and the context in which the intervention is occurring.

*Stage 6. Redesign.* Evaluation informs the revision process. The intervention is continued, redesigned, or discontinued on the basis of the evaluation, and the process begins again with Stage 2, problem identification.

Figure 9.1 presents a consultation problem-solving worksheet to use in conjunction with this consultation process. The team completes a worksheet for each member, and each member takes notes on the progress of his or her role in the intervention.

Consultation is increasingly used in schools and districts throughout the United States. The **Mainstream Assistance Team (MAT)** (Fuchs et al., 1990), for example, was designed as a prescriptive approach to problem solving, in which a specialist (e.g., the special education teacher) serves as consultant and the classroom teacher as the consultee. The MAT method follows four common problem-solving steps:

- Problem identification
- Problem analysis
- Plan implementation
- Problem evaluation

The team works with a list of preidentified potential interventions to facilitate the process and save time. Research indicates that both special and general education teachers are satisfied with the concept, process, and outcomes of the MAT program.

## A Collaboration Model

The **Peer Collaboration Model** (Johnson & Pugach, 1991; Pugach & Johnson, 1995) was developed to help classroom teachers solve problems by providing time and structure to do so. The model was designed for teachers to work with one or two other teachers. By engaging in a structured conversation about a specific problem, teachers can increase their awareness of the problem and develop potential solutions.

According to Johnson and Pugach (1991), 86 percent of the teachers who participated in peer collaboration indicated that the problems that they worked on were eliminated and referral rates for special programs were reduced.

How might you participate in peer collaboration? Collaboration may occur at varying levels of teacher and school involvement. For example, Michelle Canner is a high-school English teacher who has several students with learning disabilities in her classes. These same students are also in Jonathan Wood's social studies classes and Maria Rodriguez's science classes. The special education teacher and these three teachers established a collaborative team to meet the needs of the target students more effectively. At a middle school, the special education teacher and the speech and language teacher work cooperatively with the general education teachers to develop strategies for facilitating vocabulary and concept learning of target students.

FIGURE 9.1

**Consultation Problem-Solving Worksheet**

Collaborative Team Member Name and Position:

_____

Team Member's Responsibilities Include:

a) _____

b) _____

c) _____

d) _____

_____

Target Student's Name: _____

Problem Behavior Student Is Exhibiting: _____

_____

_____

Potential Interventions and Consequences Include:

a) _____

b) _____

c) _____

d) _____

Implemented Intervention: _____

Procedures Include: _____

_____

Team Members Involved and Their Responsibilities: __

_____

_____

Summary Evaluation of the Intervention: _____

_____

Future Interventions/Objectives: _____

---

Procedures for peer collaboration include the following five steps (Friend & Cook, 2000; Hudson & Glomb, 1997):

1. *Initiation or facilitation.* Each participant takes a role as either an **initiator,** the teacher with the problem to be addressed, or **facilitator,** the teacher who guides his or her peer through the process and helps to generate solutions.
2. *Clarifying questions.* The initiator states the problem, and the facilitator asks questions that clarify the problem.
3. *Summarization.* The team takes time to examine and summarize the problem. The format for summarizing the problem includes (a) establishing the pattern of behavior, (b) acknowledging the teacher's feelings about the problem, and (c) identifying aspects of the classroom and school

environments that the teacher can modify (Pugach & Johnson, 1995).
4. *Interventions and predictions.* The team tries to develop at least three interventions for the problem and to predict the likely outcomes of each one.
5. *Evaluation.* The team develops an evaluation plan that includes strategies for keeping track of the intervention, recording the student's progress, and meeting on an ongoing basis.

## Resources Needed for Collaboration

Time is the most precious and necessary resource for effective collaboration. Unless time is built into teachers' and other professionals' schedules and work-

Factors to be considered in implementing consultation and collaboration models include systematic and ongoing staff development, administrative support, and flexible scheduling (West & Idol, 1990).

loads, collaboration simply does not occur regularly. Also, if the special education teacher is going to work collaboratively with the social studies teacher, both need to have a planning period at the same time. What are some ways in which planning time can be arranged?

- Administrators designate a common time for collaborating professionals (e.g., all fourth-grade teachers who are members of the same team).
- School boards pay professionals for one extra time period each week that is used for collaboration or for meeting parents.
- School districts provide early dismissal for students one day a week so that team members have a common planning time.
- Teachers schedule brief but focused planning periods with each other as necessary.

Participants must be familiar with the procedures for collaborating. Having a regular time to meet to collaborate is the first step. Knowing what to do with that time is the next step. Which collaboration model does the school use, and what are the designated procedures? What paperwork is required, and how should it be completed and submitted? All teachers involved in collaboration should participate in an ori-

What are the hallmarks of the peer collaboration model? What steps should these teachers follow in planning and problem solving to achieve a successful peer collaboration?

entation that addresses basic questions about their roles and responsibilities.

Space for meeting is another necessary resource. In some schools, overcrowding is such a problem that classroom space is never available for meetings with colleagues. Designated meeting rooms or other conference space may be needed for collaboration to occur.

# TechTalk

## Collaboration and Computers

Through the use of computer software, teachers can collaborate with school personnel in other cities, states, and even different countries. Synchronous collaboration occurs when the individuals involved interact at the same time (Collis & Heeren, 1993). *Aspects* is an example of a computer program that enables the user to engage in synchronous collaboration. This computer program allows its users to open and work on the same file(s). Changes made to the file by one user will appear on the screens of all of the current participants. In this manner, users can work together, simultaneously changing text files and drawing files of a shared document. *Aspects* is available from Group Logic (telephone 1-800-476-8781).

The importance and value of collaboration are underscored throughout this chapter. Technological advancements such as *Aspects* provide teachers with greater opportunities and increased flexibility in collaboration.

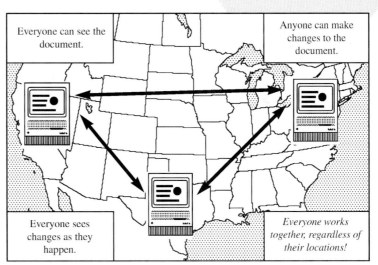

Courtesy of Group Logic Inc.

## Teachers' Perceptions of Collaboration

A team of researchers at the University of Miami interviewed general and special educators at 69 schools across the state of Florida (see Arguelles, Schumm, & Vaughn, 1996, for a technical report). These schools participated in a statewide pilot program designed to encourage more participation of students with disabilities in the general education classroom. An analysis of interview transcripts indicated that collaboration is worth the effort in terms of impact on students; however, an investment of time and energy is needed to make collaborative arrangements work (Schumm, Hughes, & Arguelles, 2001). The most commonly voiced suggestions included the need for communication about expectations for students, common planning time, ongoing support from administrators, professional development, mutual respect for roles and responsibilities, and above all flexibility and a sense of humor.

## Co-Planning

In **long-range co-planning,** the general education and special education teachers broadly plan their overall goals and desired outcomes for the class and for specific students with disabilities in the class. This co-planning of broad goals occurs quarterly (or more frequently if necessary). This planning fits in with the IEP of each student with disabilities.

In **lesson co-planning,** the general education and special education teachers plan specific lessons and desired outcomes for the week (Vaughn, Schumm, & Arguelles, 1997). The teachers decide who will take the lead in the lesson, who will ensure that target students' needs are met, and who will provide individual or small-group instruction. A form for daily co-planning is provided in Figure 9.2.

The planning pyramid (Chapter 7) is another excellent tool for co-planning. Schumm, Vaughn, and Harris (1997) report that when teachers use the planning pyramid together, they develop a common mindset about what all students will learn. They also can identify potential trouble spots and identify accommodations for students who may need them. Ruth Rogge, a special education teacher, adapted the planning pyramid lesson plan sheet for her weekly meetings with general education teachers (see Figure 9.3).

Joyce Duryea, a special education teacher, has a set day and time for co-planning with each teacher. Meetings take place during the school day while students are in other classes, such as Spanish, art, or music. "We discuss the planning for the following week and how we can best work together," explains Joyce.

---

FIGURE 9.2

### Co-Teaching Daily Lesson Plans

General Educator _____     Special Educator _____

| Date | What are you going to teach? | Which co-teaching technique will you use? | What are the specific tasks of both teachers? | What materials are needed? | How will you evaluate learning? | Information about students who need follow-up work |
|------|------|------|------|------|------|------|
| | | | | | | |
| | | | | | | |
| | | | | | | |
| | | | | | | |
| | | | | | | |

*Source:* Vaughn, S., Schumm, J. S., & Arguelles, M. E. (1997). The ABCDEs of co-teaching. *Teaching Exceptional Children, 30*(2), p. 7. Reprinted with permission.

───────── FIGURE 9.3 ─────────

**Planning Pyramid**

Week of: _____

General Educator:_____ Special Educator: _____

| | General Educator | Special Educator |
|---|---|---|
| Monday | | |
| Tuesday | | |
| Wednesday | | |
| Thursday | | |
| Friday | | |

Week of: _____ Grade Teacher: _____ Subject: _____

Objectives: _____

_____

**Materials/In-Class Assignments**

Monday _____

Tuesday _____

Wednesday _____

Thursday _____

Friday _____

**Homework Assignments**

Monday _____

Tuesday _____

Wednesday _____

Thursday _____

Friday _____

Evaluation: _____

_____

| Pyramid | Agenda |
|---|---|
| | 1. _____ |
| | 2. _____ |
| | 3. _____ |
| | 4. _____ |
| | 5. _____ |
| | 6. _____ |
| | 7. _____ |
| | Monday _____ |
| | Tuesday _____ |
| | Wednesday _____ |
| | Thursday _____ |
| | Friday _____ |

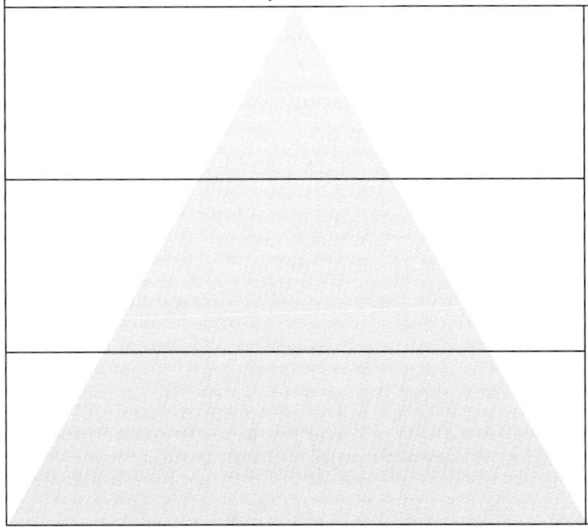

*Source:* Ruth Rogge, Silver Ridge Elementary, Broward County, Florida. Used with permission.

Once a month, she and the other teachers go over the goals and objectives from the students' IEPs and discuss whether they are meeting goals or whether they need to switch over to another goal if the students have accomplished the one previously established. As Joyce puts it, "We discuss each student's progress in depth."

Patty Weiss, a general education teacher in an inclusion classroom, has set up a planning routine with her special partner, Bethany Karlstein. Patty and Bethany meet once a week to develop general ideas for lesson plans and decide who is going to take the lead for planning and instruction. They work on their assignments individually and email each other daily to solidify plans and work out details. As Patty says, "We'd love to meet for an hour or so every day, but we can't. Technology has helped us to communicate on a regular basis. Now we both feel we have our act together."

## Co-Teaching

For **lesson co-teaching**, the special education and general education teachers are both in the classroom during the same lesson, and both participate in the instruction (Bauwens & Hourcade, 1995). Because lessons are co-planned, the specific roles and responsibilities of each teacher are decided ahead of time. Sometimes the general education teacher works with the class as a whole, and the special education teacher adapts assignments for special needs students, accommodating their learning needs or working with small groups of students. At other times, the class is divided into groups, and each teacher works with a different group. Sometimes the special education teacher takes the lead in providing instruction to the class while the general education teacher moves from student to student, conducting individual lessons or conferences. The roles of both teachers vary according to the goals of the lessons and the needs of the students. Table 9.2 provides an overview of different models of co-teaching.

Joyce, a special education teacher in an inclusive setting, explains her role this way:

> I work in three general education classrooms, and in each classroom I do something different. Teachers differ in the extent to which they are willing to share control of their classrooms. Ruby, a second-grade teacher, prefers that I take the lead role when I'm in her class, and she likes to provide me support. Tiffany, the fifth-grade teacher, likes to

## TABLE 9.2

### Co-Teaching Models

| Model | Grouping Arrangement | Teacher Roles | Description |
|---|---|---|---|
| A | Individual students, pairs, or small groups | 1 lead teacher 1 teacher "teaching on purpose" | One teacher takes primary responsibility for the overall lesson. The second teacher provides one- to five-minute minilessons for students who need additional help. |
| B | 2 heterogeneous groups | 2 teachers— same content | In this model, both teachers teach the same content to small groups. This format works well when complex new information is presented or when students need smaller groups to promote clarifying questions or discussion. |
| C | 2 homogeneous groups | 2 teachers— different content | Students are placed in groups based on instructional needs. One group might focus on review and additional practice; a second group might engage in extension activities. |
| D | Multiple groups | 2 teachers— content may vary | This model includes multiple groups—some teacher-led, some student-led. This model includes reading groups and learning centers in which learners are engaged in a variety of activities. |
| E | Whole class | 2 teachers— teaching together | Teachers divide up the agenda for teaching a lesson. Teachers share responsibility for lecturing, demonstrating, modeling note taking, and providing strategies for learning content. |

*Source:* Adapted from Vaughn, S., Schumm, J. S., & Arguelles, M. E. (1997). The ABCDEs of co-teaching. *Teaching Exceptional Children, 30*(2), 4–10.

share control through either co-teaching or alternating the role of lead teacher. Lupita, on the other hand, prefers to maintain the lead role in her class.

**Cooperative teaching** requires that both teachers work with all students. When general education and special education teachers co-teach in the same classroom, the goals of the instruction and the needs of all students are the responsibility of both teachers.

## Co-Assessment

Grading is an important consideration when students with disabilities are in general education classrooms. Often the special education co-teacher makes adaptations to homework, assignments, and tests. How do these modifications affect the way students are graded? To what extent should students' motivation affect their grades? What about their persistence and their ability? How can these qualities be measured? These issues need to be openly discussed by teachers who have students with disabilities in their classrooms.

The questions about assessment are often easier for elementary teachers to answer than for middle-

and high-school teachers. At the elementary level, teachers often consider a student's ability and then assign a grade based on the extent to which the student's progress matches his or her ability. At the middle- and high-school levels, however, student performance is often assessed on the basis of established standards. Grading procedures for students with disabilities are often an IEP item, and grading guidelines are written and agreed upon during the development of the IEP. This means that students with special needs who are included in general education classrooms often do poorly in these classes. Even when students do their best, their grades are often in the failure range. Students with disabilities need grades that reflect more than the extent to which their performance compares with that of other students in the class. They need encouragement and reinforcement for their work and effort and reasonable accommodations in assessment and grading. Sample criteria for grading a special education student are provided in Figure 9.4.

---

═══════════ FIGURE 9.4 ═══════════

**Sample of Criteria for Grading a Special Education Student**

The following procedures could be jointly developed by the school, student, and parent when specifying grading options.

**Tests**
- Administer tests orally, with questions and answers.
- A teacher, other student, or resource teacher reads the regular test to the student. (Please give the resource teacher at least one day's notice.)
- Administer the regular test using open book, class notes, or both.
- Modify the modality of tests, written or oral, such as multiple choice instead of essay questions.
- Redo the test if the student does not pass.
- Lower the criterion for passing.

**In-Class Assignments**
- Give regular assignments with lower criteria for passing.
- Shorten the regular assignment (e.g., half the questions).
- Grade assignments as "complete" rather than with a letter grade.
- Modify the set of questions students will answer.
- Pair the student with another student for help.
- Require the student to give oral answers to a teacher.

- Redo assignments if incorrect.
- Give credit for appropriate behaviors not normally graded, such as taking notes.

**Homework**
- Same options as "In-Class Assignments."

**Class Participation, Behavior, and Effort**
- Same expectations as for other class members, but special education students may need extra encouragement and frequent feedback from teacher.
- Focus on a specific study skill or behavior deficit by giving a Pass/No Pass each day for that behavior (examples: coming prepared to class with correct materials, or volunteering answers during class discussions).

**Other Considerations**
- Give extra credit for projects that the student or teacher suggests.
- Have a student aide tape the reading assignments or read aloud to the student.
- Set expectations for attendance.

---

*Source:* Gersten, R., Vaughn, S., & Brengelman, S. V. (1996). *Communicating student learning,* T. R. Guskey (ed.), p. 52. Alexandria, VA: Association for Supervision and Curriculum Development.

## Co-Teaching: Students and Parents Speak Out

What do students and parents think about co-teaching? Gerber and Popp (1999) conducted focus group interviews with students and their parents to learn about their perceptions of co-teaching. Elementary, middle-school, and high-school students with and without disabilities and their parents participated in the group interviews. Overall, parents and students were enthusiastic about co-teaching. Perceived benefits included improved academic understanding and self-esteem. Some suggestions for improvement were offered. Students recommended better coordination between teachers to avoid confusing students. Parents requested more information about the implementation of co-teaching in their children's classes and (a minority position) alternative placements when co-teaching didn't seem to be working out.

## Collaboration Issues and Dilemmas

At some time, most general education teachers will work with special education personnel in consultation, collaboration, or cooperative teaching roles. Following is a description of issues and dilemmas that frequently occur. Perhaps by considering these issues now, you will be able to work more effectively in future collaborative situations.

What is involved in co-planning, co-teaching, and co-assessment? What are some issues that might arise in collaborations between classroom teachers and special education teachers?

**Concerns about Cooperative Teaching**  When asked to co-teach, teachers often express concerns about the effectiveness of their teaching (Salend et al., 1997). Some teachers feel out of place in another teacher's classroom and find it difficult to determine how much control to take. It is important for teachers to reach the point at which they can recognize skill differences and strengths with regard to their teaching partners (Salend et al., 1997).

**Student Ownership**  When students with special needs are placed in general education classrooms for all or part of the day, both general education and special education teachers are responsible for their education. It is not uncommon, however, for teachers to claim "ownership" of or responsibility for some students and not others. Effective programs for all students require teacher attitudes that say, "All students are members of the learning community in my classroom, and I welcome them all."

**Individual versus Class Focus**  Research confirms that for the most part, general education teachers at all grade levels plan instruction for the class as a whole rather than for individual learning needs (McIntosh et al., 1993; Schumm et al., 1995a). This approach to planning reflects the need to cover the content for a subject area. Special education teachers, on the other hand, focus on meeting students' individual needs. Neither perspective is inherently better than the other (Glatthorn, 1990), but the difference can lead to conflict. Teachers need to understand and respect each other's perspectives (Salend et al., 1997). Sallie Gotch, an elementary special education teacher, puts it this way:

> I am a special education teacher, and so the direction of my interest is always with the individual student and how the educational setting can be altered to meet his or her needs. During the last few years, I have been working in a cooperative teaching situation with general education teachers, and I realize that I've needed to adjust my perspective if I am to work effectively with them. When they think about planning, they think about the class as a whole. I have to work cooperatively to think about meeting the needs of individual students without slowing the progress of the class as a whole.

**Content versus Accommodation**  When classroom teachers discuss planning and instruction, one of the most consistent themes is content coverage (Schumm et al., 1995a; Vaughn & Schumm, 1994). Classroom teachers feel they must cover more content to meet local and state guidelines and to ensure that students are prepared for the next grade level. Teachers acknowledge that this need often conflicts with some students' knowledge acquisition but feel obliged to continue teaching new material (Schumm et al., 1995a). Judy Schloss, a seventh-grade science teacher, puts it this way: "I know that when I complete a science unit, some of the students understand the main concepts and others do not, but I do not have time to reteach. We just move on to new material." As a result of such moving on, many students, particularly students with learning problems, are introduced to a lot of material but learn little about any of it. As Ed Glover, a ninth-grade social studies teacher, says, "If I waited until the students got it, we would never be able to cover all the material."

The issue of content coverage directly influences the instruction of students with special learning needs in general education classrooms. You can imagine the difficulty you might have if you felt pressured to cover extensive amounts of content and at the same time felt pulled to meet the needs of individual students who failed to learn the material. Many teachers learn to make adaptations and accommodations that will help all students learn, even if the content coverage and pace are reduced.

**Real World versus Student's World**   Some general education teachers think that treating all students fairly means treating them "the same." Making adaptations in homework or tests is perceived as providing undue advantage for some students. Furthermore, some general education teachers define their mission as preparing all students for the real world, where, they believe, accommodations and adaptations will not be made. Other general education teachers know that the best way to prepare students for the real world is to have an opportunity to be successful in their present world. Maria Pino, a secondary social studies teacher, explains, "My first responsibility is to help students feel successful in their present world—the world of the classroom. Making accommodations helps them feel that success. I also explain to them that employers are required by law to make reasonable adaptions for individuals with disabilities." Successful collaborative teams emphasize the importance of establishing a community of teachers and learners who share and learn together (Salend et al., 1997).

This section covered several of the issues involved in collaboration and cooperative teaching, such as concerns about cooperative teaching, student ownership, focus on individuals versus the class, content versus accommodation, and the real world versus the student's world. The next section addresses ways to communicate effectively with professionals and parents.

> In a working alliance, all professionals are invested in a common goal, centered on the student. All members of a working alliance feel that they are working together as a team to enhance the student's educational and social development.

## Critical Communication Skills

Some teachers communicate effectively with parents and other professionals with seemingly little effort. They seem to have acquired the skills to listen effectively and express their point of view. Jacob Levitz, an eighth-grade English teacher, conveys an accepting attitude and is able to make parents feel at ease and willing to disclose information. He is also able to express his views in ways that make parents *want* to listen.

The following sections and Tips for Teachers 9.2 describe basic principles for communicating with parents, teachers, and other professionals.

### Acceptance

People know when you accept them and are interested in their point of view. Acceptance by the teacher is critical to parental and professional participation in the student's program. Lucia Corzo, a third-grade teacher, has been working with parents and professionals for 12 years. Despite expected frustrations and disappointments, she communicates her care and concern to the parents and professionals with whom she interacts and always manages to find the few minutes necessary to meet with them. She says, "Parents have a great deal to teach me about their child. They have spent a lot of time with their child and have seen patterns of behavior that can help me as a teacher. Also, if I can get the parent on my team, we can work together to solve problems."

### Listening

Your willingness to genuinely listen to parents and professionals is important to your ability to learn and to work effectively with others. **Effective listening** is more than waiting politely for someone to finish before you speak. You must hear the message the other person is sending, and must often ask questions to clarify that you truly understand what others are saying. Effective listening involves the following elements:

- *Listening for the real content in the message.* The **real content** in the message is the main idea or the key information the person wants to convey.
- *Listening for the feelings in the message.* As you listen, consider what the message conveys about the person's feelings about the issue.
- *Restating content and reflecting feelings.* After the person has talked for a while, consider all that he or she has said. Then either ask a question to clarify what you know or restate the main idea to verify that what you heard is correct.
- *Allowing the speaker to confirm or correct your perception.* Give the speaker a chance to correct any misunderstanding you may have or to say more.

# Tips for Teachers

## 9.2 Facilitating Effective Communication with Parents and Professionals

1. Indicate respect for parents' knowledge and understanding of their child.
2. Demonstrate respect for the diverse languages and cultures parents and their children represent.
3. Introduce parents to other members of the education team in a way that sets the tone for acceptance.
4. Give parents an opportunity to speak and be heard.
5. Represent the parents to other professionals and ensure that a language of acceptance is used by all professionals and parents.
6. Even when you are busy, take the time to let parents and professionals know that you value them, and that you are simply unable to meet with them at *this* time.
7. Avoid giving advice unless it is requested. This does not mean that you can never give suggestions; however, suggestions should be given with the expectation that the person may or may not choose to implement them.
8. Avoid providing false reassurances to colleagues or parents. Reassurances may make them and you feel better in the short run but are harmful in the long run. When things do not work out as you predicted, everyone can become disappointed and potentially lose trust.
9. Ask specific questions. Unfocused questions make a consistent, purposeful conversation difficult to conduct.
10. Avoid changing topics too often; you must monitor the topic and direct others to return to it.
11. Avoid interrupting others or being interrupted. Interruptions disturb conversation and make effective collaboration difficult.
12. Avoid using clichés. A cliché as a response to a problem situation makes the other person feel as though you are trivializing the problem.
13. Respond to colleagues and parents in ways that attend to both the content of their message and their feelings.
14. Avoid jumping too quickly to a solution. Listening carefully and fully to the message will help you get at the root of the problem.

---

An example of a special education teacher listening effectively to a parent is provided in Figure 9.5.

## Questioning

Questions, an important part of the communication process, can have multiple purposes. Questions can be used not only to teach, to establish relationships, to inquire, and to investigate, but also to bully or intimidate. As teachers work with parents and professionals, they need to consider the questions they ask, to ensure that they set a tone of acceptance.

Knowing which types of questions to ask helps you obtain the information you need. Questions can be open or closed. An **open question** allows a full range of responses (often beginning with "How," "What," or "Tell me about," for example) and discourages short "yes" or "no" answers. Following are several examples of open-ended questions:

- How do you explain the change in your son's behavior?
- What suggestions do you have about how I might help Mark get a better grade in social studies?
- Tell me your opinion about ways I might adjust my math instruction for Juan.
- How does what I've said about Tanika relate to her behavior at home?

- What do you suggest?
- How would you describe Gilbert's behavior?

Antoinette Spinelli, a seventh-grade science teacher, was concerned about Naomi, who was not paying attention in class, seemed sleepy and uninterested, and was not completing assignments. She called Naomi's mother, explained the behavior, and let Naomi's mother give her point of view.

**Antoinette (teacher):** Naomi has not been paying attention in class and has generally seemed tired and disinterested. What do you think might be happening?

**Tracey (parent):** Well, I don't know. Maybe she just isn't that interested in science. I don't know why.

**Antoinette:** Well, the reason I'm concerned is that her behavior in class has gotten worse in the last few weeks, and I wonder if you might be able to help me understand.

**Tracey:** Maybe it's because there have been so many people in the house the last few weeks. My family is visiting, and they were supposed to only stay one week and now they are starting on their third week. We really don't have room for all of them, so Naomi's had to give

─── FIGURE 9.5 ───

**Effective Listening: An Example**

Anna Martinez is the mother of Michael, a student with spina bifida and learning problems who has been placed full-time in a fifth-grade classroom. Michael's special education teacher, Joyce, works with him in the general education classroom for part of the school day. Anna made an appointment to meet with Joyce about her son's progress. Their conversation models effective listening.

**Anna:** (parent) I'm worried about Michael in this new program. I liked it better last year when I knew he was being pulled out of class and getting the help he needed. He seems to have a lot more work, and he complains about homework.

**Joyce:** (teacher) Let me see if I understand the problem. First, you are concerned about his progress in this new program, and second, Michael seems to have too much work. Is this right? Is there anything else you are concerned about?

**Anna:** Well, I can't help him with the work because I don't read English that well. He needs help when he comes home, and it can't be from me.

**Joyce:** The homework he is getting is too hard for him, and there isn't someone to help him at home.

**Anna:** That's right. He's going to flunk if he does not do his work, yet I can't help him with it, and we are both very worried about it.

**Joyce:** What if I met with Michael at the end of every day to ensure that he knows how to do his homework by himself. I could also meet with him in the morning before school to make sure he completes it and to help with what he doesn't know. How does that sound?

**Anna:** I would like to try that. That sounds good.

**Joyce:** Now let's get back to his placement this year. You indicated some concern about his being in the fifth-grade class all day.

**Anna:** No, it was really the homework in the class. If we solve that, it will be okay.

**Joyce:** Well, let's give this plan a try.

---

up her room. Maybe I need to make sure she is sleeping well enough.

The teacher's questions gave the parent a chance to consider the relationship between her child's behavior and what was occurring at home. This parent was able to identify a change in the household that might be related to her child's poor performance. The parent and teacher were able to identify a possible solution and felt better about their working relationship.

## Staying Focused

Staying focused in your communication and keeping others focused is an important skill that contributes to successful collaboration. One thing you can do when someone has difficulty keeping to the topic is redirect them, saying, for example, "Go back to talking about Katelyn. You were providing some suggestions for note-taking skills that might be helpful to her." Another thing you can do is remind them of the purpose of the meeting (for instance, "Jackie, let's stick to talking about content-area reading instruction"). Sometimes parents have so many problems of their own that they want to spend their time with you discussing their issues (including such personal problems as financial or marital difficulties) rather than the student's. When this occurs, a good

strategy is to have ready a referral list for specialized assistance. It is your responsibility to remind parents that you cannot assist them with *these* problems and to suggest others who can.

 ## Working with Parents

School systems have expended considerable effort to involve parents in their child's educational program. The rationale is that parent involvement is related to their child's adjustment in the educational setting, as well as to academic achievement (Hughes, 1995). Also, both federal laws and state regulations require parental involvement for students with disabilities (refer to Chapter 1 for a review). This section discusses family adjustment and the roles parents can play in supporting their children's education. Chapter 10 provides additional suggestions for working with parents of diverse linguistic and cultural backgrounds. Chapter 11 offers hints for working with parents of students who are identified as gifted or who are potentially at risk of school failure.

### Family Adjustment

Much of what has been written about **family adjustment** to having a child with disabilities addresses

How does the family's response to having a child with disabilities affect the child's learning and development? How can teachers help in family adjustment? How can teachers promote effective parental involvement?

family reaction to children with severe disabilities, mental retardation, or physical disabilities (Turnbull & Turnbull, 1990). Considerably less attention has been paid to how families adjust to having family members with learning disabilities, communication problems, attention problems, emotional or behavioral problems, and multiple risks (Hanson & Carta, 1996). This occurs because the more obvious or severe disabilities, such as mental retardation or physical disabilities, are apparent before children start school, whereas other problems, such as learning and behavior disorders, are often not identified until children are older (age 3 and older). Although many parents are aware long before diagnosis that their child is different, they continue to hope that their observations are incorrect or that their child will outgrow the problem.

Families with children with disabilities have two critical features (Alper, Schloss, & Schloss, 1994):

● The entire family needs resources and support.
● The needs and roles of the student with disabilities and family members evolve over time.

From a systems perspective, the family is an important force in the student's learning and development. For this reason, many mental health and social work professionals recommend an integrated approach to working with students with disabilities.

The following principles of support should be considered: provide opportunities for positive caregiving transactions, focus on individual and family strengths, encourage informal sources of support, provide comprehensive and coordinated services across a broad spectrum, and deliver flexible services (Hanson & Carta, 1996). In an integrated approach, all family members and other important caretakers are involved in some way.

Simpson (1982) suggests that the needs of parents of children with disabilities fall into five broad categories:

1. *Information exchange.* Parents need conferences, program and classroom information, progress reports, interpretations of their child's academic and social needs, and informal feedback about their child. Teachers can rarely provide too much information to parents (particularly parents of children with special needs, who are already aware of their child's differences).

2. *Consumer and advocacy information.* Parents of students with disabilities sign seemingly endless numbers of forms and permissions. Be sure to summarize for parents not only the purpose of the forms, but also what the parents are agreeing to by providing their signature. Advocacy for students with disabilities and their families is a lifelong process that includes self-advocacy, social support advocacy, interpersonal advocacy, and legal advocacy (Alper, Schloss, & Schloss, 1994).

3. *Home/community program implementation.* Parents want to assist their children at home and also to involve them in appropriate community activities. How can you help? Provide helpful information. If possible, ask other professionals or community resource people to offer a program to all parents on these topics. Work with other teachers to develop an informational handout or brochure, and provide it in the languages parents read.

4. *Counseling, therapy, and consultation.* When parents request information about support groups, counseling, therapy, and other consultation services, what should you do? First, identify the information sources available from your school or school district, and keep them handy in a folder. Second, ask the school counselor or principal what procedures you should follow.

5. *Parent-coordinated service programs.* Parents need to be able to provide services to and receive services from other parents through advisory councils, parent-to-parent participation, advocacy, and other options. In a study reported by Simpson (1988), the services most widely requested by parents were program information and informal feedback.

## Parents and Homework

Often, parents are so interested in helping their child that they get deeply involved in assisting with schoolwork at home. Homework (or *home learning,* as some schools systems refer to it) gives parents a daily idea of your curriculum and instruction. Many parents want to help but do not know what to do. It is your responsibility to provide parents with guidance so that they can help their child as effectively as possible. Here are some suggestions for providing that guidance.

**Establishing a Homework Policy**   Start the school year with a written policy statement that begins with a rationale for assigning homework. According to Epstein and Becker (1982), teachers assign homework for a number of reasons:

- Practice (to help students strengthen skills learned in class)
- Participation (to increase involvement with learning activities)
- Personal development (to build a sense of responsibility and time-management skills)
- Parent–child relations (to increase involvement in home-learning activities)
- Policy (to conform to school and district mandates)
- Public relations (to communicate to parents what students are learning in school)
- Punishment (to correct misbehavior in school)

As you might expect, using homework for punishment is not particularly effective and can be counterproductive besides. It is important to communicate why you think homework is important and what positive outcomes it might have for students.

What guidance can teachers provide to parents so that they can help with their child's homework assignment?

Your policy statement should also include a set of expectations: what you expect of the student, what you expect of the parent, and what both the parent and the student can expect of you. Whenever possible, involve parents in developing the policy statement.

Tips for Teachers 9.3 is an outline of issues to address in your policy statement.

## Tips for Teachers

### 9.3   Communicating Homework Policy

**What You Expect of the Student**
- Record homework assignments on an assignment sheet or in an assignment notebook.
- Complete homework assignments in a neat and timely manner.

**What You Expect of the Parent**
- Assist the student in setting up a homework center.
- Assist the student in determining a regular homework schedule.
- Monitor and assist as necessary in the completion of homework.
- Write a note if confused about the assignment.

**What the Parent and Student Can Expect of You**
- Create homework assignments that are meaningful and provide for independent practice of skills taught in class or enrichment of content covered in class.
- Write homework assignments on board daily.
- Provide parents with a general homework schedule (e.g., Monday night, math and spelling; Tuesday night, math and composition).
- Provide a system for reporting missing or late homework to parents and students.
- Grade homework in a timely fashion and provide feedback to students.

One suggestion is to send home biweekly progress reports. By taking 30 minutes every other week to complete a progress form, you can eliminate problems that arise when parents are uninformed about the student's progress. Secondary students value homework adaptations that allow them to participate successfully (Nelson et al., 1998).

**Encouraging Student Independence**    Parents are often unsure about how much or how little they should help with special projects such as term papers, book reports, and science fair projects. Parents' resources for providing assistance vary widely. Your policy statement should clarify expectations, such as arranging transportation to the public library and access to a typewriter or word processor for term papers. When a major project is assigned, let parents know the purpose of the assignment, its components, the due dates, and precisely when and how their assistance may be needed. A special project checklist and contract (see Figure 9.6) will help to clarify the responsibilities of the teacher, parents, and students for the completion of long-term assignments.

## Parents as Teachers

Free or inexpensive brochures about parents as teachers are available from various professional organizations. These brochures can be sent home as report card or progress report inserts, and bibliographies and other helpful resources can be sent home during the school year. In addition, websites are available to parents to assist with a wide array of home learning activities (see the website suggestions at the end of this chapter).

## research brief

### Parental Involvement in Literacy Instruction

Hughes, Vaughn, and Schumm (1999) conducted a study of Hispanic parents of children with learning disabilities to determine their involvement in literacy instruction. The study addressed the types of reading and writing activities practiced in the home and parents' perceptions of the desirability and feasibility of different reading and writing activities.

The Hispanic parents involved in this study reported that they regularly provided their children with different reading and writing activities at home. The most frequent activities involved parents reading to children and children reading to parents. Parents emphasized reading activities more than writing activities. The writing activities in which parents and children did

engage included writing related to homework assignments, writing letters to relatives, or writing lists.

In telephone interviews to determine what reading and writing activities they thought were desirable and feasible to do at home, parents indicated that many suggested activities were desirable and that before the interview they had not thought of doing so many activities. They also indicated, however, that many activities were not feasible to do at home because their children had difficulties with reading and writing and they (the parents) did not know how to help their children with these difficulties.

Parents identified the following activities as helpful to them:

- More communication with the teacher about reading and writing activities they could do at home
- Further information about how to do the reading and writing activities with their children, since their children had trouble learning to read and write
- Providing information to the parents both orally and in writing in the parents' first language (Spanish)

The goal of helping students with homework and providing an academic support system at home is to enable them to develop independent study skills. For this to happen, parents and teachers need to work cooperatively.

What happens when students with special needs fall behind their same-age peers and parents want to help? Particularly for students with disabilities, it is rarely a good idea for an untrained parent to become the child's tutor. This does not mean that the parent should not help with homework, coach the child for a spelling test, or assist with a school project. Providing assistance and serving as a tutor are two different roles, however. Our use of the term **tutoring** refers to a systematic plan for supplementing the student's educational program. Ask parents who are providing their own home tutoring to consider the suggestions provided in Figure 9.7.

## Planned and Unplanned Parent Conferences

The opportunity for a planned conference with parents occurs often. This conference could be part of the multidisciplinary team meeting, part of an annual parent–student meeting, or a specific meeting scheduled because of an academic or behavioral problem. Figure 9.8 is a sample letter teachers can send to parents to confirm a planned meeting.

With a planned conference, the teacher is able to prepare materials and provide background knowledge.

———— FIGURE 9.6 ————

## Special Project Checklist

**Step**                                                                      ***Date Done***

☐   1. Decide on a project theme.                                             _____

☐   2. Have theme approved by a teacher.                                      _____

   ***Theme:*** _____

☐   3. Make a list of what needs to be done and the order in which the tasks should be completed.
       (List, then number each task.)

☐   4. Decide who is going to do what. (Initial each task.)

☐   5. Set deadlines for completion of each task. (Write in the dates.)

| *Task* | *Date Due* | *Date Done* | *Person Responsible* |
|--------|-----------|------------|---------------------|
|        |           |            |                     |
|        |           |            |                     |
|        |           |            |                     |
|        |           |            |                     |

☐   6. Make a list of materials needed to do the project.

☐   7. Make a projected budget. (Write the estimated cost of each item.)

| *Item* | *Cost* |
|--------|--------|
|        |        |
|        |        |
|        |        |

☐   8. Send away for resource materials needed.

| **Resource Material** | **Date Requested** | **Date Received** |
|-----------------------|--------------------|--------------------|
|                       |                    |                    |

☐   9. Contact community resources.

| **Community Resource** | **Date Contacted** |
|------------------------|--------------------|
|                        |                    |

☐   10. Visit the library.

| **Purpose of Visit** | **Date of Visit** |
|----------------------|-------------------|
|                      |                   |

☐   11. Complete the project ON TIME.

**Date Handed In:** _____   **Year:** _____

*Source:* This Special Project report is an excerpt from *How to help your child with homework* by Margarite
C. Radencich, Ph.D., and Jeanne Shay Schumm, Ph.D. Copyright © 1988. Reprinted with permission
of Free Spirit Publishing Inc., Minneapolis, Minn.; (800) 735-7323. All rights reserved.

═══════════════ FIGURE 9.7 ═══════════════

**Tips for Tutors**

1. Have specific, realistic goals developed *with* the classroom teacher or the special education teacher.

2. Begin and end each tutoring session with an activity that is fun and with which the child is successful.

3. Keep the tutoring session brief—not more than 15 minutes for students up to grade 6, and not more than 30 minutes for older students.

4. Work on small segments of material at a time.

5. Use creative, novel ways of reviewing and teaching new material.

6. Prevent the student from making mistakes. If the student does not know the answer, give it.

7. Keep a tutoring log in which you record a couple of sentences about what you did and how the student performed.

8. Provide encouragement and support. No one learns more by being "corrected" more.

9. Practice the activities in fun ways that prevent boredom.

10. Work should be challenging but not so difficult that there is not considerable opportunity for success.

11. Tutor at the same time and in the same place, so that the student develops an expectation set for what will happen. Do not extend the designated time.

12. If you are frustrated or your interactions with your child are strained or stressful during the tutoring, stop. Your relationship with your child is much more important than what you can teach him or her during the tutoring session.

To prepare for a planned conference, teachers should do the following:

1. Review the student's materials, grades, and work progress.
2. Meet with and learn the perspectives of other professionals who also work with the student.
3. Review the student's folder, portfolio, and previous assessment information.
4. Obtain samples of the student's most recent work.
5. Make an outline of topics to discuss.

What happens when conferences are unplanned? Sometimes, at the end of the day, as students line up to go home, you notice a parent waiting by the door to speak with you. There is little question that unplanned conferences with parents will occur (Turnbull & Turnbull, 1990). Often, parents who come to school to talk with the teacher do so because they are concerned about something they have seen or heard. Their source of information might be their own child, who might not have told the story accurately. The guidelines in Tips for Teachers 9.4 will help you work effectively with parents in such situations.

## Forms of School-to-Home Communication

Communicating with parents must be an ongoing part of your routine as a teacher. Communication with all parents is important, but it is particularly important with parents of students with special needs.

What are some ways to communicate? Letters, notes, calendars, newsletters, phone calls, websites, and email are but a few described in this section.

There are many letters you can send home to all parents. In the beginning of the year, it is a nice idea to send home with students a note that introduces you and provides a means for parents to contact you (see Figure 9.9).

─────────── FIGURE 9.8 ───────────

**Sample Note for Parent Conference**

It's a Date

Dear Parent of _____,
    Thank you for your response to my request for a meeting about your child. Your appointment has been set for _____ (time) on _____ (day), _____ (date).
    I have set aside _____ minutes for our visit. If you will be bringing any guests, please let me know in advance. If this time is no longer convenient, please let me know.

Looking forward to seeing you,

_____
Teacher's Name

# Tips for Teachers

## 9.4   Working toward Effective Parent Conferences

1. *Listen until they are finished.* As difficult as it may be to hear them out, particularly when the statements they are making are inaccurate, the best way to begin the meeting is to allow them to say everything that is on their minds. Chances are they have thought for a long time about what to say and have even rehearsed it. Listening does not mean that you agree. Let them finish.

2. *Take notes.* Write down key phrases the parent says, summarize key points, and jot down notes of things you want to remember to tell them. While you are doing this, be sure to maintain eye contact and composure. Your getting upset increases the likelihood of the parent growing more upset.

3. *Summarize their major concerns.* As was stated previously, good communication includes effective summarization of the speaker's words and their meaning. Your summary shows parents not only that you have been listening, but also that you care about what they say.

4. *State your position calmly.* After you have listened thoroughly and let parents know that you understand their key points, state your position calmly and succinctly. If parents have inaccurate information, now is the time to provide accurate information. Be sure that they understand your point of view. Speak calmly while stating your position and addressing their concerns.

5. *Come to closure.* Getting to closure differs according to the situation. Sometimes, for example, you hear a parent's concern and quickly find a solution. "Oh, Mrs. Garcia, Lucy can stay in during lunch while she is sick. That is no problem. Just be sure she remembers to bring her own lunch." At other times, an issue needs to be negotiated. "Well, Mrs. Garcia, I do not think that Lucy has too much homework. The main reason it takes her so long is that she does not work on her math homework during the time allotted at school. Let's first set up a plan to increase her working on math at school."

You might also want to send home a letter or bulletin (see Figure 9.10) before any long break (one week or more) to alert parents to activities they can do with their children to reinforce learning while they are out of school or to introduce a new unit of study, such as measurement or space. Remember, parents want to receive notification of things that are going well, progress reports, your expectations of their child, materials the child needs, problems (early on), and general ideas of how to help their child learn.

Another letter that many parents appreciate is a progress report for the year. Joyce (a special education teacher) and the classroom teachers with whom she works send the letter shown in Figure 9.11 to parents of children with disabilities who are included full-time in general education classes.

--- FIGURE 9.9 ---

**Sample Beginning of School Year Letter**

Dear Parents:

The purpose of this letter is to welcome you and your child to my classroom. I have taught at West Elementary School for four years and at two other schools in this school district before moving to West Elementary. I am confident that this school year will be an interesting and productive one for your child and me.

You are welcome to visit the classroom; however, I would appreciate receiving notice ahead of time to be sure your visit will not be interrupted. Feel free to call me at 544-1257 and leave a message. I will return your call as quickly as possible. I look forward to meeting you in person in the near future.

Sincerely,

Julia Anderson, 4th-grade teacher

FIGURE 9.10

**Parent Bulletin**

Name: _____     Date: _____

Subject: _____

_____

_____

**You can help at home by:** _____

_____

FIGURE 9.11

**Year-End Progress Report**

Dear Parents and Guardians:

We thank you all for your cooperation and support this school year. As the school year ends, we always ask parents how they feel the special education program met the needs of their children. We hope you have been satisfied with the results.

Following are your child's scores from the beginning of the year and from the end of the year. Please feel free to call one of us at 555-0000 and leave a message. We will return your call as soon as we can.

| | Beginning Scores | End-of-Year Scores |
|---|---|---|
| Reading Comprehension | _____ | _____ |
| Word Recognition | _____ | _____ |
| Math Computation | _____ | _____ |
| Math Application | _____ | _____ |

Thank you,

*Joyce Duryea, Special Education Teacher*
*Maggie Lowe, Classroom Teacher*

Suggestions or Comments:

_____

_____

_____

_____

_____

Send a note to a parent. "Good news" notes (see the 60-Second Lesson) have been used to communicate effectively regarding academic and behavioral progress of students (Kelly, 1990). There are many different types of notes; you can create some of your own. It is also possible to use notes written by the student and structured by the teacher to send home to parents. An example of a student note is provided in Figure 9.12.

Teachers also use weekly and monthly calendars to communicate key information and to record homework assignments. You can fill in events on a calendar and then copy and distribute it to students to take home. A fourth-grade teacher who regularly sends home a weekly calendar reports that it takes her about 10 minutes to do. Alternatively, you

and the special education teachers you work with might decide that providing parents with a weekly list of accomplishments (see Figure 9.13) will help a student.

Another option, newsletters, can be written by the teacher or by students. The purpose of a newsletter is to keep parents informed of what is happening in the classroom. Newsletters should not target the poor performance or behavior of a particular student. If your newsletter recognizes student accomplishments, be careful not to name certain students repeatedly while never mentioning others.

Phone calls are an important and often effective means of communicating with parents. Make a list each week of several parents you want to contact with positive reports. Allow three to five minutes

## making a Difference

# The 60-second Lesson

### Reinforcing Parent Involvement through Positive Feedback about the Child

When you keep a supply of photocopied notes on hand, sending feedback to parents takes only a minute.

# GOOD NEWS!

**Name** _____

**Date** _____

_____
_____
_____
_____

Sincerely,

_____

— FIGURE 9.12 —

**My Behavior Can't Be Beat**

How I worked at school: _____

_____

How I got along with friends: _____

_____

What I tried for the first time: _____

_____

How I helped others: _____

_____

My most amazing deed: _____

_____

_____
Student's Name

for each call, and make one call at the end of each day. Be sure to keep a phone log of parents contacted by phone during the year.

More and more teachers are beginning to communicate with parents via electronic means. Working parents often cannot come to school for meetings during the day, so email communication is becoming more popular. Using email is great for providing par-

ents with updates and clarifying questions about homework and other activities. Of course, major concerns and dilemmas should be resolved in face-to-face meetings or by phone. It is also important to communicate to parents your availability and guidelines for using email. Spending your evenings or afternoons answering 30 emails might not be the best use of your time. In addition to email, many schools now have

—————— FIGURE 9.13 ——————

**Mechanical Genius's Accomplishment Sheet**

Name _____

Week of _____

Teacher's Signature _____

| Subject | Monday | Tuesday | Wednesday | Thursday | Friday |
|---------|--------|---------|-----------|----------|--------|
| _____ | _____ | _____ | _____ | _____ | _____ |
| _____ | _____ | _____ | _____ | _____ | _____ |
| _____ | _____ | _____ | _____ | _____ | _____ |
| _____ | _____ | _____ | _____ | _____ | _____ |
| _____ | _____ | _____ | _____ | _____ | _____ |
| _____ | _____ | _____ | _____ | _____ | _____ |
| _____ | _____ | _____ | _____ | _____ | _____ |
| _____ | _____ | _____ | _____ | _____ | _____ |
| _____ | _____ | _____ | _____ | _____ | _____ |
| _____ | _____ | _____ | _____ | _____ | _____ |

websites that provide information about calendar, major events, and homework tips. Maria Pino, an ESL teacher, recently remarked, "At first I was scared to death of developing a web page. Now I'm a pro. It's the best way to get information out to parents."

In using electronic communication, keep in mind that not all parents may have access to computers, so other modes of communication need to be made available too.

## summary

- Teachers' ability to collaborate with significant people in a student's life (e.g., special education teacher, psychologist, parent) is a vital skill, growing in importance to general education teachers whose classrooms include increasingly diverse students.
- Collaboration may take many different forms. For example, one common form allows for the

special education teacher to serve as a consultant, assisting general education teachers who are instructing students with special needs. Such consultation programs usually involve a collaborative team of parents, general and special education teachers, and other people who contribute to a student's educational program.

- This chapter describes the six steps upon which one consultation program is based: (1) goal/entry, (2) problem identification, (3) intervention of recommendations, (4) implementation of recommendations, (5) evaluation, and (6) redesign.

- Peer collaboration involves the regular participation of two or three teachers in structured conversations so that each teacher assists and receives assistance from the other teachers regarding planning, problem solving, and instructing.

- For any collaboration model to be effective, several criteria must be in place, including (1) time to co-plan, (2) knowledge of the procedures involved in the particular model, and (3) a location where participants can meet.

- Effective collaboration also requires particular skills, such as (1) effective listening, (2) appropriate questioning, and (3) focus. Procedures for communicating with other school personnel and parents are delineated in this chapter. collaboration

## key terms and concepts

consultation model
cooperative teaching
effective listening
facilitator
family adjustment
initiator

lesson co-planning
lesson co-teaching
long-range co-planning
Mainstream Assistance
Team (MAT)
open question

Peer Collaboration
Model
real content
tutoring

## think and apply

1. How did the teachers in the opening interview help Sheena's parent feel at ease and become more willing to cooperate? Trace Sheena's parent's adjustment to having a child with disabilities. What events contributed to this adjustment?

2. With a partner from your class and using the Consultation Problem-Solving Worksheet (see Figure 9.1) as a guide, work through the six stages of the consultation process outlined in this chapter. Be sure to target a student, define the nature of the problem, and generate as many practices for effective implementation as you can. As you work through the problem-solving worksheet, make a list of your questions (then keep the list in your portfolio). As you read through the book, answer your questions.

3. This chapter's "Collaboration Issues and Dilemmas" section lists four issues you might need to consider if you are involved in a consultation or cooperative teaching model with another professional. Write your current feelings about each issue (student ownership, individual versus class focus, content versus accommodation, and real

world versus student's world). What knowledge and experiences might support your perspectives? What knowledge and experiences might cause you to change your views?

4. Consider the five qualities of effective collaborators (see Table 9.1). To what extent do you feel you have displayed these qualities in past collaborative efforts? Select one quality to improve and monitor over a designated time period (e.g., one month), and then evaluate your progress.

5. Have you ever had a conversation during which you did not feel connected? Think about what the other person(s) did and what you did. Using the principles of effective listening identified in this chapter, make a checklist of things you should consider during a conversation.

6. Make a list of the ways you want to ensure that you are working effectively with parents. What are some of the materials and resources you need to do your job effectively? Contact parent and professional organizations for information about parent involvement.

# read more about it

1. Anderson, W., Chitwood, S., & Hayden, D. (1997). *Negotiating the special education maze: A guide for parents and teachers* (3rd ed.). Kensington, MD: Woodbine House.

   *A valuable resource for parents and professionals about terminology, legal issues, and procedures for better understanding special education.*

2. Cramer, S. F. (1998). *Collaboration: A success strategy for special educators.* Boston: Allyn & Bacon.

   *This text is designed to assist teachers who are learning how to collaborate in ways that facilitate their becoming curious, self-motivated learners. Topics address improving the school climate through collaboration, legislative influences on collaboration, intrapersonal and interpersonal characteristics for successful collaboration, appraising your school as a context for collaboration, designing and evaluating a design for change, and improving collaboration with parents and family members.*

3. Friend, M., & Cook, L. (2000). *Interactions: Collaboration skills for school professionals* (3rd ed.). New York: Addison Wesley Longman.

   *A practical orientation to developing and using knowledge and skills with which to work effectively with other professionals. Procedures for team building, team meetings, conferences with parents, co-teaching, and problem-solving formats are provided.*

4. Jordan, A. (1994). *Skills in collaborative classroom consultation.* New York: Routledge.

   *An application of collaboration skills as a tool for creating change in educational practice. Topics include collaborative consultation in context; alternative school delivery models; consulting skills; contracting; assessment and feedback; developing action plans; difficult consulting situations; working with parents, administrators, and service professionals; drawing on the resources of the school; and classroom consultation.*

5. Kelly, M. (1990). *School–home notes: Promoting children's classroom success.* New York: Guilford Press.

   *A resource for teachers interested in examples of "good news" notes. Includes many examples of uses of these notes, as well as procedures for using them to increase academic achievement and appropriate behavior in the classroom.*

6. Pugach, M. C., & Johnson, L. J. (1995). *Collaborative practitioners, collaborative schools.* Denver, CO: Love.

   *An orientation to teaching by working collaboratively with others. Teaches adults to form a community of learners and to grow professionally. Includes descriptions of teamwork approaches, communication skills, group work, problem solving, and team teaching.*

7. Risko, V. J., & Bromley, K. (Eds.) (2000). *Collaboration for diverse learners: Viewpoints and pactices.* Newark, DE: International Reading Association.

   *This book contains 21 chapters addressing a variety of topics related to building collaborative relationships to support student learning, particularly in the area of reading instruction. Topics include collaboration among professions, communication with parents of diverse cultural and linguistic backgrounds, and resources for collaboration, including technology.*

# suggested websites

**www.ldonline.org/ld_indepth/teaching_techniques/ tec_coteaching.html**
This website provides suggestions for successful co-teaching.

**www.ldonline.org/ld_indepth/teaching_techniques/ dld_ecologies.html**
This website describes a variety of issues and provides resources on inclusion.

**www.libertycornercomputing.com/sri/Inclusion.html**
This website provides a variety of sources for inclusion.

**www.uni.edu/coe/inclusion/index.html**
This website provides a variety of sources on inclusion (e.g., philosophy, legal requirements, teaching strategies, etc.).

**www.sherm.com**
This website introduces consulting and training for successful inclusion.

**www.weac.org/resource/june96/speced.htm**
This website provides an overview of inclusion (definition, legal issues, etc.).

**www.uni.edu/coe/inclusion**
This website provides a brief definition of co-teaching and relevant citations.

**www.usoe.k12.ut.us/sars/Upi/collaboration.htm**
This website contains several useful links related to collaboration (e.g., professional supporting team, inclusion supporting team, etc.).

**www.projectchoices.org/faq.htm**
This website contains answers to FAQs (frequently asked questions) about inclusion.

# Teaching Culturally and Linguistically Diverse Students

chapter

10

# chapter | outline

# focus | questions

1. How are the demographics of our schools changing?

2. What is the relationship between the macroculture and the microcultures of culturally and linguistically diverse students?

3. As a classroom teacher, how can you learn about your culture and your students' cultures and communities?

4. What is multicultural education?

5. As a classroom teacher, how can you incorporate multicultural education and culturally relevant teaching into your curriculum?

6. What are five factors that affect second language acquisition, and how do they relate one to another?

7. What are the characteristics of African American Vernacular English (AAVE), and how can you facilitate learning for students who use AAVE?

8. As a classroom teacher, how can you promote second language acquisition in your classroom?

9. What accommodations can you make for students who are in the process of acquiring English as a second language?

# inter view

## Co-Teachers at Mission Way School

Gloria Rodriguez is a fifth-grade bilingual education teacher who co-teaches with Lidia Romo, a fourth-grade bilingual education teacher at Mission Way Elementary School in southwest Arizona. Maria Chavez is the English as a second language (ESL) teacher for this K–5 elementary school. Most students at Mission Way speak Spanish or Spanish and Yaqui, a Native American language, as their first language(s). Although over 85 percent of these students qualify for free lunch, they come from culturally rich communities such as the Mexican American barrios and the Yaqui Reservation.

Two years ago, with the support of the principal, Gloria and Lidia decided to co-teach. They made this decision for several important reasons. First, by co-teaching, they offer broader cultural and linguistic expertise. Gloria, whose background is Mexican American, grew up in the local barrios, attended a local university, and has been teaching at Mission Way for five years. In contrast, Lidia grew up on the Yaqui Reservation, went to a university in northern Arizona, and has been teaching for three years at Mission Way. She has a rich knowledge of the Yaqui ways.

Second, by co-teaching, they believe that they increase their ability to effectively use their approach to multicultural education. This approach, which uses the culture and community as the foundation on which learning and curriculum are built, provides students with the opportunity to learn about and respect their cultural and linguistic heritages. At the same time, the students are learning English and how to assimilate into the mainstream of American life.

Third, by co-teaching, Gloria and Lidia are able to group students flexibly while many of them make the transition from their first language(s) to English. As in other learning, not all students are ready to make the transition at the same time or at the same rate. The teachers believe that flexibility is important for students to succeed at becoming competent English speakers, readers, and writers. Lidia comments,

> The transition from first language to second language is one of the most complex aspects of bilingual education that we deal with. We often have a good sense for when students are ready to make this transition, but our curriculum and grouping don't allow us to meet the students' needs. Team teaching with Gloria helps me better meet the needs of the students and make adjustments tailored to them.

Another reason that Gloria and Lidia decided to team teach is that it seems to give them more time to integrate the family and communities into the school and their classroom. Gloria comments,

Fourth and fifth grades are often times when students are beginning to be pressured to join gangs. We feel that one reason our students are not as likely to join gangs is because they have a strong sense of respect for their own cultures. We feel that combining our cultural expertise and engaging the students in thematic units built on their cultures serve as a deterrent to joining gangs.

In contrast to Gloria and Lidia, the ESL teacher, Maria, grew up in Puerto Rico and New York City. She attended college in Puerto Rico and then taught for several years in a New York public school serving a Puerto Rican community. She started teaching ESL at Mission Way two years ago, when her husband was transferred to the Southwest. Maria has found that although both she and Gloria are considered Latinos or Hispanics, their cultural roots and heritage are different, in much the same way that New Englanders differ from Southerners and Midwesterners.

In her teaching, Maria works to broaden the students' knowledge of various cultures to include not only different Latino and Native American cultures, but also European American, African American, and Asian American cultures. In teaching ESL, Maria goes into the classroom or sometimes works with small groups of students in her resource room. On a regular basis, new students are enrolled in Mission Way who speak no English and have limited academic skills in their first language. Maria, whose job is to provide intensive support to these students and their teachers, sees herself also as a resource for the other teachers. She comments,

> I feel like one of my major job roles is that of a school-wide resource. I switch lunch periods during the week so that I have the opportunity to eat with different teachers and find out their needs and offer help. One of my concerns is how to be of assistance to more teachers. I think communication and time are the keys.

# introduction

Clearly, the cultural and linguistic diversity of Mission Way adds to the richness of the school community and the complexity of teaching. But compared to schools whose students come from many different cultural and linguistic backgrounds, Mission Way is relatively homogeneous.

This chapter focuses on the growing diversity of schools and students in the United States. It also presents the key concepts associated with multicultural education, linguistic diversity, second language learning, and bilingual education. Finally, it discusses instructional strategies for educating students who are culturally and linguistically diverse. As you read this chapter, think about how the ideas presented by

Gloria, Lidia, and Maria create schools and classrooms that facilitate the successful education of culturally and linguistically diverse students.

## Diversity in Classrooms and Schools

The United States is one of the most culturally diverse nations in the world. A Mexican immigrant commented, "Before I came to America I had dreams of life here. I thought about tall Anglos, big buildings, and houses with lawns. I was surprised when I arrived to see so many kinds of people—Black people, Asians. I found people from Korea and Cambodia and Mexico. In California I found not just America, I found the world" (Olsen, 1988). This diversity continues to increase as new immigrants relocate in the United States. From 1995 to 2000, the population of Latino Americans rose from 22 million to 34 million, and the Asian American population rose from 7 million to 10 million. It is anticipated that this growth in immigration will continue in the upcoming years.

Minorities constitute the majority of public school students in more than 20 of the country's largest school systems, including those of Miami, Philadelphia, Baltimore, and Los Angeles. Although many of these students do well in school, a substantial number of students come from homes in which families live in poverty and parents are unemployed or underemployed, have little education and few technical skills, and are not fluent in English (Berliner & Biddle, 1995). Furthermore, education practice often does not provide a good match with the students' cultures and the curriculum (Jordan, 1985; Ovando & Collier, 1998). Tips for Teachers 10.1 has suggestions to help teachers learn about students' home communities.

The average achievement of African Americans, Native Americans, and Latino Americans is consistently lower than that of middle- and upper-class European Americans at every grade level (National Center for Educational Statistics, 2000). The dropout rates and the grade retention rates are also higher for these groups of students. African Americans also have high dropout rates, with inner-city youth dropping out at a rate of 80 percent. The dropout rates for Asian Pacific Americans are lower, but when only Asian Pacific American students from developing countries are considered, the rate is high (Grossman, 1995).

A disproportionately high percentage of African Americans, Latino Americans, and Native Americans

> Over 2 million people in the United States are Native Americans, representing over 500 tribal groups and speaking more than 200 languages. The largest tribes are Cherokee and Navajo. The largest populations of Native Americans are in California, Arizona, New Mexico, and Oklahoma.

## Tips for Teachers

### 10.1   Learning about the Funds of Knowledge in Students' Home Communities

Teachers may begin their teaching careers in schools in which the students' home communities are neither their home community nor similar to their home communities. Following are some ideas that help teachers learn about the students' home communities:

- Learn about students' cultural backgrounds. Learn how the culture views the role of teachers and schools and the role of parents in relation to schools.
- Locate at least one person in the community who can serve as your cultural guide or informant. This can often be a fellow staff member. Develop a relationship in which that person teaches you about the culture and community.
- Be a learner in the classroom. Discuss with students your interest in learning about their cultures, including community activities. Information that can help guide your learning includes jobs of parents, their special skills and knowledge, special interests of students (at home and in the community), community activities, special occasions and holidays, family structure, and family responsibilities and relationships.
- If it is appropriate and within school policy, visit students' homes and talk with parents and other family members. This is an ideal opportunity to learn more about the students, the households, and culture, including interests of the family, the role of the extended family, the way in which jobs are shared, and the ways in which literacy is used in the home.

have been identified as having learning disabilities, mild mental retardation, and emotional or behavioral disorders (Drew et al., 1996). In contrast, a disproportionately low percentage of students from these cultural groups have been identified as gifted and talented (VanTassel-Baska et al., 1991).

The reasons for these students' limited success in school are complex and interrelated, but several factors should be considered (Stephen et al., 1993). First, role models from minority groups are often limited in school, in that many teachers are European Americans and limited mentor programs are available for these students to connect with leaders in their communities. Second, discrimination against students from minority groups continues in assessment for and placement in advanced and gifted programs. Third, curriculum and educational practice are often not culturally responsive, with limited integration of information about different cultural groups into the curriculum (Erickson & Mohatt, 1982). Fourth, teaching styles might not match the learning styles of students from diverse cultures (Ladson-Billings, 1995). Fifth, a greater proportion of students from minority groups live in poverty and their poverty levels are lower than that of European Americans (Banks, 1996). Furthermore, the number of children in poverty in the United States continues to rise, and the proportion of children in poverty is well above that in most European countries (Banks, 1997a; Berliner & Biddle, 1995).

## Understanding Diverse Cultures

The United States is composed of a shared core culture and many subcultures (Banks, 1997a). Students in our schools are influenced by this core culture, sometimes referred to as the **macroculture.** The United States is such a complex and diverse nation that its core culture is somewhat difficult to describe, but Banks and Banks (1995) suggest the following key components:

- Equality of opportunities for individuals in the society
- Individualism and the notion that individual success is more important than the family, community, and the nation-state
- Social mobility through individual effort and hard work
- Individualistic attitudes toward values and behaviors
- Belief in the nation's superiority
- Orientation toward materialism and exploitation of the natural environment

At the same time, students are influenced by their home cultures, or **microcultures.** Microcultures are often based on such factors as national origin, ethnicity, socioeconomic class, religion, gender, age, and disability (Gollnick & Chinn, 1990). Even geographical areas of the country (e.g., New England,

Appalachia) can be considered microcultures because of differences in customs and mores.

Sometimes the core values of the macroculture and microcultures are relatively similar, but in other cases the microculture values are quite different from those of the core culture (Banks, 1997a). For example, the emphasis on individuality is generally not as important in African American, Latino American, and Native American ethnic communities as it is in the European American macroculture. Instead, these communities place more importance on group and family values (Hale-Benson, 1986; Ramirez & Castaneda, 1974; Swisher & Deyhle, 1992). Hence, cooperative learning may be a better match than competitive learning for students from these ethnic backgrounds. In fact, cooperative learning activities that support equal status contact between majority and minority groups in pursuit of common goals have been shown to increase cross-ethnic friendships in classrooms (e.g., Kagan et al., 1985; Oishi et al., 1983). Another example of differences between the macroculture and various microcultures in the United States is the value given to personalized knowledge (i.e., knowledge that results from firsthand observation). Although the macroculture values knowledge based on objectivity, and educational institutions emphasize abstract out-of-context knowledge, research on women's ways of knowing suggests that women value personalized knowledge (Belenky et al., 1986; Gilligan, 1982; Maher, 1987). Similarly, Ramirez and Castaneda (1974) found that Mexican American students who were socialized within traditional Latino cultures also responded positively to knowledge presented in a personalized or story format.

When the core values in the macroculture and microculture are relatively different, teachers can help students understand and mediate differences between the cultures. To act as mediators, teachers need to learn about and incorporate the various microcultures and home communities into school life and the curriculum. For example, Luis Moll and his colleagues (e.g., Gonzales et al., 1995; Moll & Greenberg, 1990) have been working as participants and researchers in Tucson's barrio schools for a number of years. Moll's research and ethnographic methods of study provide strategies for teachers to integrate the home and school communities by building on the **funds of knowledge** found in the home community (see Tips for Teachers 10.1).

Learning about the funds of knowledge in the students' home community can help teachers to not overgeneralize characteristics that are often attributed to different cultural groups.

## Cultural Characteristics

In learning about cultural influences, there is a tendency to make generalizations based on common beliefs about a culture. As Lynch and Hanson (1992) note, however, "Culture is only one of the characteristics that determine individuals' and families' attitudes, values, beliefs, and ways of behaving. . . . Assuming that culture-specific information . . . applies to all individuals from the cultural group is not only inaccurate but also dangerous—it can lead to stereotyping that diminishes rather than enhances cross-cultural competence" (p. 44). Still, having some knowledge of students' **cultural characteristics** serves as a starting point for understanding individual students' behaviors and learning styles.

Knowledge of cultural characteristics can keep teachers from misinterpreting students' actions. One example is the learning style of some Native American groups. Teachers typically encourage students to attempt tasks publicly or to answer questions, even though they are unsure of what to say or do, but the traditional learning styles of some Native American groups encourage learning privately and gaining competence before performing publicly. Learners repeatedly watch an activity and review it in their heads before attempting any kind of public performance (Appleton, 1983; Longstreet, 1978). For example, after watching a medicine man, an apprentice will collect a plant for a specific remedy. If the selection is not correct, the medicine man more than likely will walk to the correct plant and show and explain some characteristics that make it the appropriate plant. The same rich style of watching, modeling, and explaining is used for jewelry making, weaving, and classroom learning.

Werner and Begishe (1968) capture this contrast in learning by comparing the European American philosophy "If at first you don't succeed, try, try, again" to the Native American philosophy "If at first you don't think, and think again, don't bother trying." A teacher of Native American students comments, "The Indian students seem to need time to think about things before they take action on their assignment. It is almost like they have to make sure they can do it before they try. . . . If I didn't know better, I could interpret this as they just do not care about doing their assignments" (Swisher & Deyhle, 1992, p. 82).

Díaz-Rico and Weed (1995) suggest that teachers should learn about their students' cultural characteristics to understand the students' actions and help them to integrate the home and school cultures. Following are general areas and questions that teachers can use to guide their inquiry:

- *Time:* How do students perceive time? How is timeliness regarded in their cultures?

What is involved in the process of mediating among diverse cultures? What environmental and instructional measures can teachers take to help diverse students mediate between the microcultures of their homes and communities and the macrocultures of their nation and school?

- *Space:* What personal distance do students use in interactions with other students and with adults? How does the culture determine the space allotted to boys and girls?
- *Dress and food:* How does dress differ for age, gender, and social class? What clothing and accessories are considered acceptable? What foods are typical?
- *Rituals and ceremonies:* What rituals do students use to show respect? What celebrations do students observe, and for what reasons? How and where do parents expect to be greeted when visiting the class?
- *Work:* What types of work are students expected to perform in the home and community, and at what age? To what extent are students expected to work together?
- *Leisure:* What are the purposes for play? What typical activities are done for enjoyment in the home and community?
- *Gender roles:* What tasks are performed by boys? By girls? What expectations do parents and students hold for boys' and girls' achievements, and how do these differ by subject areas?
- *Status:* What resources (e.g., study area and materials, study assistance from parents and siblings) are available at home and in the community? What power do parents have to obtain information about the school and to influence educational choices?
- *Goals:* What kinds of work are considered prestigious or desirable? What role does education play in achieving occupational goals? What education level do the family and student desire for the student?
- *Education:* What methods for teaching and learning are used in the home (e.g., modeling and

imitation, didactic stories and proverbs, direct verbal instruction)?

- *Communication:* What roles do verbal and non-verbal language play in learning and teaching? What roles do conventions such as silence, questions, rhetorical questions, and discourse style play in communication? What types of literature (e.g., newspapers, books) are used in the home, and in what language(s) are they written? How is writing used in the home (e.g., letters, lists, notes), and in what language(s)?
- *Interaction:* What roles do cooperation and competition play in learning? How are children expected to interact with teachers?

Common characteristics in a culture can serve initially to guide teacher inquiry. For example, Kitano (1973) and Cheng (1991) note several characteristics of Asian cultures that may help to explain parents' expectations and students' actions:

- Students are to be quiet and obedient, not calling attention to themselves in a group.
- Didactic methods of learning are common. Teachers are to teach by demonstrating or transmitting knowledge, skills, and strategies. Students are to study and learn.
- Teachers are to be respected and generally not to be challenged.
- In school, students respond when they have something important to share and do not engage easily in free discussion and brainstorming.

On the basis of these characteristics, a teacher would understand why students from Laos or Vietnam would not consider raising their hands and asking for clarification when a teacher is lecturing (Bliatout et al., 1988) or would not want to be singled out for attention or praise by teachers (Furey, 1986).

In many Native American cultures, the role of time is viewed differently from the European and Asian concepts of time. The time to begin is when people arrive for the gathering. Work is oriented toward the common good of the community rather than personal recognition and fame, and a deep respect for knowledge and wisdom of elders is evident (Pepper, 1976; Swisher & Deyhle, 1992). The role of silence is important, in that it communicates respect and thoughtfulness. Being comfortable with silence helped the counselor in the following scenario establish trust and rapport.

Norman, a Paiute youth from Reno, Nevada, had an agonizing decision to make. At the age of 18, he had graduated from the Indian Youth Training Program in Tucson, Arizona, and was free to return home to live. Living at home would possibly jeopardize the hard-won habits of diligence and self-control that he had learned away from the home community, in which he had been arrested for ju-venile delinquency. As the counselor in Norman's group home, I knew he could possibly benefit by talking over his decision. After school, I entered his room and sat on the chair by his bed, indicating that I was available to help him talk through his dilemma. One-half hour of total silence elapsed. After thirty minutes he began to speak. Silence rather than language had achieved the rapport I sought (Díaz-Rico & Weed, 1995, p. 246).

In African American cultures, interaction is more informal, with greater spontaneity and general participation in discussion rather than the more focused question-and-answer format (Ratleff, 1989). In studying a small African American community in the rural Carolinas, Heath (1983) noted that young children in "Trackton" were encouraged to use spontaneous verbal play, rich with metaphors and similes. The use of multiple modes of communication, particularly nonverbal expressions, plays an important role in understanding the meaning of the message.

In many Latin American cultures, the family and community are strongly valued, and time is more flexible. For example, "Adela, a Mexican-American first-grade girl, arrived at school about 20 minutes late every day. Her teacher was at first irritated and gradually exasperated. In a parent conference, Adela's mother explained that braiding her daughter's hair each morning was an important time for the two of them to be together. This family time presented a value conflict with the school's time norm" (Díaz-Rico & Weed, 1995, p. 231). Just as family and community are valued, *interdependence* (rather than independence) is viewed as a strength. Decisions are made as a group, and those who are successful have responsibilities for others. Classrooms that foster learning through cooperation may help students extend their predisposition for interdependence (Banks, 1997c; Díaz-Rico & Weed, 1995; Ovando & Collier, 1998).

Ogbu (1978, 1992) has suggested that some cultural groups seem to cross cultural boundaries more easily than other groups. The case for this idea is built on the information presented in the Research Brief.

> Terminology for racial and ethnic groups changes, reflecting both cultural and political decisions and historical development (Nieto, 1996). Using the current preferred terms when referring to groups is important.

## research brief

### Crossing Cultural Boundaries

Teachers often ask why some cultural groups seem to cross cultural boundaries and succeed in school more easily than others do. On the basis of his comparative research, John Ogbu (1978, 1992) has put forth one explanation. In his work, he classified cultural groups as autonomous minorities, immigrant or voluntary minorities, and castelike or involuntary minorities.

- *Autonomous minorities* are considered minorities in a numerical sense; they include Jews, Mormons, and the Amish. In the United States, there are no non-White autonomous minorities.
- *Immigrant or voluntary minorities* are people who have moved to the new society or culture more or less voluntarily because they desire greater economic opportunities and political freedom. The Chinese and Punjabi Indians are representative examples in the United States.
- *Castelike or involuntary minorities* are people who were brought to the United States or conquered against their will. Examples in the United States are African Americans, Native Americans, early Mexican Americans in the Southwest, and Native Hawaiians.

Ogbu (1992) suggests that voluntary groups experience initial (but not lingering) problems in school because of language and cultural differences. The involuntary minorities, on the other hand, usually experience greater, more persistent difficulties learning in school. This difficulty for involuntary minorities appears related to several factors:

- **Cultural inversion,** or the tendency to regard certain forms of behavior, events, symbols, and meanings as inappropriate because they are characteristic of European American culture.
- A *collective identity,* in opposition to the social identity of the dominant group, develops as the involuntary minorities are treated as subordinates by European Americans in economic, political, social, psychological, cultural, and language domains.

Hence, in an effort to retain their own identity and roots, students from involuntary minorities may be more oppositional and less motivated to learn in school. Ogbu (1992) explains, "They fear that by learning the White cultural frame of reference, they will cease to act like minorities and lose their identity as minorities and their sense of community and self-worth" (p. 10). In contrast, because voluntary minorities do not feel the need to protect their cultural identity, they do not perceive learning the attitudes and behaviors required for school success as threatening to their own culture, language, and identities. Instead they interpret such learning as *additive,* that is, adding to what they already have (Chung, 1992).

It is important to note that these are generalized types that include groups who may more appropriately "fit" a different type. For example, Cubans who fled Cuba during the 1960s were an involuntary minority, yet many acculturated and became quite successful in the Miami community.

Cummins (1992) suggests that academic success of students from involuntary minority groups is related to the extent that schools reflect the following:

- Minority students' language and culture are incorporated into the school program.
- Minority community participation is encouraged as an integral component of children's education.
- Instruction (pedagogy) is used to motivate students to use language actively to generate their own knowledge.
- Professionals involved in student testing (assessment) become advocates for minority students by focusing primarily on ways in which students' academic difficulties are a function of interactions with and within the school context, instead of locating the problem within the students (p. 5).

Do not assume that cultural characteristics are common to all members of a cultural group. Rather, these characteristics serve as a starting point in your education about the cultural diversity of the students you teach. They also provide rich opportunities for students to learn about their cultural backgrounds.

## Assessment of Students with Cultural and Linguistic Differences

Although progress has been made in many areas of teaching students with cultural and linguistic differences, the one area that still is in need of development is assessment (Hurley & Tinajero, 2001). The issue of assessment is particularly controversial with respect to high-stakes standardized tests. Such tests may be culturally incompatible for some students and may be linguistically impossible for students who have not reached a level of English academic language development consistent with the examination (Fradd & Lee, 2001). The development of reliable and valid measures for students with a wide range of cultural and linguistic differences has yet to be seen. Also, the controversy about how best to include students with such differences in large-scale, high-stakes tests will rage on for some time.

Jerry Baumann is a middle-school social studies teacher. Jerry has taken a number of courses on teaching English to speakers of other languages but admits that, as a mainstream teacher, he is not an expert in meeting the needs of students who are not native speakers of English.

> At the beginning of the school year, I had several of my eighth-graders who were not paying attention in class and who were starting to become a behavior problem. I quickly realized that English was not their first language and that they were having difficulty with the academic language of the classroom. The ESL specialist and reading resource specialist in our school were terrific. I referred Pablo, Walter, Jorge, and Manuel to them for assessment.

The specialists were able to give me information about their levels of English language development and reading levels. They also gave me suggestions for accommodations to make in assignments and tests. The four boys have calmed down in class. What they needed was sensitivity, structure, and support. They got it, and we're all doing fine!

Jerry started using learning journals, concept and vocabulary maps, and portfolio assessment for the four boys. Using the alternative assessment forms took extra time but in the long run proved to be worth it. Jerry began to realize what the boys knew and what they could do.

 ## Multicultural Education

**Multicultural education** is "an idea, an educational reform movement, and a process whose major goal is to change the structure of educational institutions so that male and female students, exceptional students, and students who are members of diverse racial, ethnic, and cultural groups will have an equal chance to achieve academically in school" (Banks, 1997a, p. 1). Multicultural education is closely linked to cultural diversity (Yee, 1991) and fosters pride in minority cultures, assists students in developing new insights into their cultures, reduces prejudice and stereotyping, and promotes intercultural understanding (Rubalcava, 1991). In the fullest sense, multicultural education is a total rethinking of the way we conduct schooling in a diverse society within a democratic, civic framework (Lessow-Hurley, 1996).

### Dimensions of Multicultural Education

Multicultural education is much more than a curriculum focused on learning about diverse cultures based on such parameters as gender, ethnicity, and race. It is a thread running through the total curriculum, not a subject to be taught (Tiedt & Tiedt, 1995). Banks (1997c) suggests that multicultural education has four dimensions: content integration, knowledge construction, an equity pedagogy, and an empowering school culture.

**Content Integration** **Content integration** focuses on using examples and content from a variety of cultures and groups to illustrate concepts, principles, generalizations, and theories. Ethnic and cultural content is infused into the subject areas in a natural, logical way (Banks, 1997a). For example, you can teach students about traditional dress and celebrations in many different cultures by discussing different holidays, the dress worn, and the reasons for the holidays and traditional dress. As a follow-up activity, students can interview their parents and other family members to learn about traditional dress and holidays celebrated by their families.

**Knowledge Construction** **Knowledge construction** refers to students learning about how implicit cultural assumptions, frames of reference, perspectives, and biases influence the ways in which knowledge is constructed. For example, the discovery of America by Europeans has two very different frames of reference when presented from the perspectives of the Native Americans and the Europeans. Similarly, the power of the mind over the body is viewed differently by Asian and European cultures.

**Equity Pedagogy** With an **equity pedagogy**, the teacher attends to different teaching and learning styles and modifies teaching to facilitate the academic achievement of students from diverse cultures. Adjusting the learning process so that Native American students can learn in private or encouraging the use of cooperative learning can accommodate cultural differences and promote academic learning.

**Empowering School Culture** An **empowering school culture** promotes gender, racial, and social-class equity. Establishing such a culture entails examining the school culture for biases and prejudices, developing strategies to alleviate them, and replacing them with opportunities that promote positive self-esteem for all students. An initial step in creating an empowering school culture is to have the staff share, learn about, and respect their own diversity.

A school's staff can learn about their school community through many of the activities used to help students learn about each other, such as sharing information about heritage, birthplace, family, traditional foods, and hobbies. For example, Stan Williams, the principal at an urban elementary school, takes time each year at the initial full-staff meeting for the staff to interview each other about their families, cultural backgrounds, areas of educational expertise, traditional foods, and hobbies. Then each interviewer uses the information garnered to introduce the interviewee to at least two other staff members. In the past, Stan has also displayed staff photos and profiles in the staff lounge. Stan comments, "When we take time [for] this activity, the staff immediately begins to learn about each other and find common interests that are fostered throughout the school year. It helps to create a sense of equality across all staff jobs (e.g., teachers, paraprofessionals, office staff, building maintenance staff)."

To implement multicultural education and integrate these four

> Multicultural education grew out of the civil rights movement of the 1960s, which called for curriculum reform to reflect the experiences, histories, cultures, and views of African Americans and other groups. Early responses included recognition of ethnic holidays and high-school courses such as "Black Studies."

dimensions successfully, multicultural education should be conceptualized as much more than a curriculum or a subject to teach. Several leaders in the field have suggested that viewing the school as a social system and studying and reforming the major variables is necessary to create a learning environment in which students have an equal chance for school success (e.g., Banks, 1997a; Grant & Sleeter, 1993; Ladson-Billings, 1995; Nieto, 1994; Ogbu, 1992). Banks (1981, 1997a) suggests that the following aspects of the school as a social system need to be considered:

- School policy and politics
- School staff: attitudes, perceptions, and actions
- School culture and hidden curriculum
- Formalized curriculum and course of study
- Assessment and testing procedures
- Instructional materials
- Learning styles for the school
- Teaching styles and strategies
- Language and dialects of the school
- Counseling program
- Community participation and input

As you study the schools in which you teach as social systems and teaching and learning communities, consider these variables and determine the degree to which they foster the overarching goals of multicultural education, that is, to create a learning community in which students have not only equal opportunities for academic success, but also an understanding of and respect for diversity.

## Desired Student Outcomes

Given these dimensions of multicultural education and its overall goals, what are some desired student outcomes that lead to these goals? Tiedt and Tiedt (1995) suggest that students should be able to do the following:

- Identify a strong sense of self-esteem and express the need and right of others to similar feelings of self-esteem
- Describe their own cultures, recognizing the influences that have shaped their thinking and behavior
- Identify racial, ethnic, and religious groups represented in our pluralistic society
- Identify needs and concerns universal to people of all cultures and compare cultural variations
- Recognize, understand, and critique examples of stereotypic thinking and social inequities in real life and literature and develop solutions for altering their status
- Discuss special gender-, ethnic-, age-, and disability-related concerns
- Inquire multiculturally as they engage in broad thematic studies related to any field of study

How can school culture empower all students to succeed? What student outcomes lead to the goal of creating a learning community in which students understand and respect diversity and have equal opportunity for academic success?

Clearly, these outcomes call for learning curricula that highlight cultural diversity. The next section discusses curricula for multicultural education.

## Multicultural Curricula

Banks (1997b) suggests that since multicultural education was introduced in the 1960s, curricular approaches to multicultural education have evolved, based on the degree to which diversity plays a central role in the curriculum. Banks (1997b) identifies four approaches: contributions, additive, transformation, and social action (see Table 10.1).

**Contributions Approach**   The **contributions approach** is characterized by the insertion of ethnic heroes and discrete cultural artifacts into the curriculum—adding culturally diverse inventors and their inventions to a thematic unit on inventions, for example.

This approach is the easiest to use but has several serious limitations. First, because the heroes are usually presented in isolation, students do not gain an overall understanding of the role of ethnic and cultural groups in the United States. Second, this approach does not address issues such as oppression and discrimination. Instead, it reinforces the Horatio Alger myth in that ethnic heroes are presented with little attention paid to how they became heroes despite the barriers they encountered.

**Additive Approach**   The **additive approach** is characterized by the addition of content, concepts, themes, and perspectives without changing the basic structure of the curriculum. Typical examples are adding books about different groups to the literature sets (e.g., Mildred Taylor's *Roll of Thunder, Hear My Cry*), adding a unit on Native Americans to an American history course, and adding a course on ethnic or gender

═══ TABLE 10.1 ═══

## Approaches for the Integration of Multicultural Content

| Approach | Description | Examples | Strengths | Problems |
|---|---|---|---|---|
| Contributions | Heroes, cultural components, holidays, and other discrete elements related to ethnic groups are added to the curriculum on special days, occasions, and celebrations. | • Famous Mexican Americans are studied only during the week of Cinco de Mayo (May 5). African Americans are studied during Black History Month in February but rarely during the rest of the year.<br>• Ethnic foods are studied in the first grade with little attention devoted to the cultures in which the foods are embedded. | • Provides a quick and relatively easy way to put ethnic content into the curriculum.<br>• Gives ethnic heroes visibility in the curriculum alongside mainstream heroes.<br>• Is a popular approach among teachers and educators. | • Results in a superficial understanding of ethnic cultures.<br>• Focuses on the lifestyles and artifacts of ethnic groups and reinforces stereotypes and misconceptions.<br>• Mainstream criteria are used to select heroes and cultural elements for inclusion in the curriculum. |
| Additive | This approach consists of the addition of content, concepts, themes, and perspectives to the curriculum without changing its structure. | • Adding the book *The Color Purple* to a literature unit without reconceptualizing the unit or giving the students the background knowledge to understand the book.<br>• Adding a unit on the Japanese American internment to a U.S. history course without treating the Japanese in any other unit.<br>• Leaving the core curriculum intact but adding an ethnic studies course, as an elective, that focuses on a specific ethnic group. | • Makes it possible to add ethnic content to the curriculum without changing its structure, which requires substantial curriculum changes and staff development.<br>• Can be implemented within the existing curriculum structure. | • Reinforces the idea that ethnic history and culture are not integral parts of U.S. mainstream culture.<br>• Students view ethnic groups from Anglocentric and Eurocentric perspectives.<br>• Fails to help students understand how the dominant culture and ethnic cultures are interconnected and interrelated. |

*Source:* Banks, J. A. (1997). Approaches to multicultural curriculum reform. In J. A. Banks (Ed.), *Multicultural education: Issues and perspectives* (3rd ed., pp. 244–245). Boston: Allyn & Bacon.

studies to a high school curriculum. This approach offers better integration of multicultural perspectives than the contributions approach but does not result in a restructured curriculum. For example, including a unit on the Plains Indians in a U.S. history class will increase students' understanding of Native Americans but not as clearly as will transforming the curriculum so that the movement to the West is viewed as both an expansion (from a European perspective) and an invasion (from a Native American perspective).

**Transformation Approach**     In the **transformation approach,** the basic core of the curriculum is changed and the focus is on viewing events, concepts, and

| Approach | Description | Examples | Strengths | Problems |
|---|---|---|---|---|
| Transformation | The basic goals, structure, and nature of the curriculum are changed to enable students to view concepts, events, issues, problems, and themes from the perspectives of diverse cultural, ethnic, and racial groups. | • A unit on the American Revolution describes the meaning of the revolution to Anglo revolutionaries, Anglo loyalists, African Americans, Indians, and the British.<br>• A unit on 20th-century U.S. literature includes works by William Faulkner, Joyce Carol Oates, Langston Hughes, N. Scott Momaday, Saul Bellow, Maxine Hong Kingston, Rudolfo A. Anaya, and Piri Thomas. | • Enables students to understand the complex ways in which diverse racial and cultural groups participated in the formation of U.S. society and culture.<br>• Helps to reduce racial and ethnic encapsulation.<br>• Enables diverse ethnic, racial, and religious groups to see their cultures, ethos, and perspectives in the school curriculum.<br>• Gives students a balanced view of the nature and development of U.S. culture and society.<br>• Helps to empower victimized racial, ethnic, and cultural groups. | • The implementation of this approach requires substantial curriculum revision, in-service training, and the identification and development of materials written from the perspectives of various racial and cultural groups.<br>• Staff development for the institutionalization of this approach must be continual and ongoing. |
| Social Action | In this approach, students identify important social problems and issues, gather pertinent data, clarify their values on the issues, make decisions, and take reflective actions to help resolve the issue or problem. | • A class studies prejudice and discrimination in their school and decides to take actions to improve race relations in the school.<br>• A class studies the treatment of ethnic groups in a local newspaper and writes a letter to the newspaper publisher suggesting ways that the treatment of ethnic groups in the newspapers should be improved. | • Enables students to improve their thinking, value analysis, decision-making, and social-action skills.<br>• Enables students to improve their data-gathering skills.<br>• Helps students to develop a sense of political efficacy.<br>• Helps students to improve their skills to work in groups. | • Requires a considerable amount of curriculum planning and materials identification.<br>• May be longer in duration than more traditional teaching units.<br>• May focus on problems and issues considered controversial by some members of the school staff and citizens of the community.<br>• Students may be able to take few meaningful actions that contribute to the resolution of the social issue or problem. |

themes from multiple perspectives based on diversity. Banks (1997b) suggests that

> When studying U.S. history, language, music, arts, science, and mathematics, the emphasis should not be on the ways that various ethnic and cultural groups have contributed to mainstream U.S. society and culture. The emphasis rather, should be on

how the common U.S. culture and society emerged from a complex synthesis and interaction of the diverse cultural elements that originated within the various cultural, racial, ethnic, and religious groups that make up the U.S. society (page 204).

In developing multicultural units, it is important to identify the key concept and generalizations associated with that concept. Specific activities can then be planned so that students have the evidence to draw the generalizations and understand the key concept. Table 10.2 provides an example of a unit for high-school students on the key concept of social protest.

**Social Action Approach** The **social action approach** incorporates all the elements of the transformation approach and also includes a cultural critique. Teaching units that use this approach incorporate a problem-solving process in which stu-

---

TABLE 10.2

### Key Ideas and Activities for a Unit on Social Protest

---

**Key Ideas**

*Key Concept:* Social protest

*Key Generalization:* When individuals and groups are victims of oppression and discrimination, they tend to protest against their situation in various ways.

*Intermediate-Level Generalization:* Throughout their experiences in the United States, ethnic minorities have resisted discrimination and oppression in various ways.

*Low-Level Generalization:* Mexican Americans have resisted Anglo discrimination and oppression since Anglo-Americans conquered and occupied the Southwest.

**Activities**

1. To give the students a general overview of Mexican-American history, show them a videotape, such as *Mexican People and Culture*, a videotape in *The Hispanic Culture Series* distributed by Zenqer Video. After showing the videotape, ask the students to discuss the questions:
   a. What major problems have Mexican Americans experienced in the United States?
   b. What actions have been taken by Mexican-American individuals and groups to eliminate the discrimination they have experienced?

2. Ask a group of students to prepare reports that reveal the ways in which the following men led organized resistance to Anglo Americans in the 1800s:
   Juan N. Cortina
   Juan Jose Herrera
   Juan Patron
   The class should discuss these men when the reports are presented. A good reference for this activity is Rodolfo Acuña, *Occupied America: A History of Chicanos*, 3rd ed.

3. Ask a group of students to prepare a report to be presented in class that describes Chicano involvement in strikes and unions between 1900 and 1940. When this report is presented, the students should discuss ways in which strikes and union activities were forms of organized resistance.

4. Ask the students to research the goals, tactics, and strategies used by the following Mexican-American civil rights groups: Order of the Sons of America, League of United Latin-American Citizens, the Community Service Organization, the American G. I. Forum, Federal Alliance of Free Cities, and Crusade for Justice. Ask the students to write several generalizations about the activities of these groups.

5. Ask the students to research the following questions:
   a. How is the "Chicano" movement similar to other Mexican-American protest movements?
   b. How are its goals and strategies different?
   c. When did the movement emerge?
   d. What long-range effects do you think the movement will have? Why?

6. Ask the students to read and dramatize the epic poem of the Chicano movement, *I Am Joaquin*, by Rodolfo Gonzales.

7. Ask the students questions that will enable them to summarize and generalize about how Mexican Americans have resisted Anglo discrimination and oppression in both the past and in contemporary American society.

8. Conclude the unit by viewing and discussing the film *I Am Joaquin*, distributed by El Teatro Campesino, San Juan Bautista, CA.

---

*Source:* Banks, J. A. (1997). *Teaching strategies for ethnic studies* (6th ed., pp. 518–519). Boston: Allyn & Bacon.

dents make decisions and take actions related to the concept, issue, or problem being studied, following these steps:

1. Identify the problem or question (e.g., discrimination in our school).
2. Collect data related to the problem or question (e.g., what discrimination is, what causes discrimination, what examples are evident in our school).
3. Conduct a value inquiry and analysis (i.e., students examine and reflect on their values, attitudes, and beliefs related to discrimination).
4. Make decisions and establish a plan of social action based on a synthesis of the knowledge obtained in step 2 and the values identified in step 3.

Robinson (1993) describes how a class of African-American middle-school students in Dallas used the social action approach. The important problem they identified was that their school was surrounded by liquor stores. Investigating further, they found that the city's zoning regulations made some areas dry but that their school was in a wet area. Further investigation revealed that schools serving white upper-middle-class stu-

dents were located in dry areas, whereas schools in poor communities were in wet areas. The students, assisted by their teacher, planned a strategy for exposing this inequity. By using mathematics, literacy, and social and political skills, the students proved their points with reports, editorials, charts, maps, and graphs. In this case, the curriculum and the students' learning became a form of cultural critique and social action.

As a teacher, you will undoubtedly use all four approaches to multicultural education, with the goal of primarily employing the transformational and social action approaches. Tips for Teachers 10.2 presents general strategies for integrating content about cultural groups into the school curriculum, and Tech Talk describes how to create a community video using videography. The curriculum should incorporate opportunities to foster student achievement and cultural competence as well as help students recognize, understand, and critique current social inequities (Ladson-Billings, 1995).

> Concern with gender equity in textbook publishing is an example of transformation and social action approaches in education. In 1972, Scott Foresman was the first to publish curriculum guidelines for recognizing women's achievement, treating girls and boys equally, and avoiding sex-role stereotypes and sexist language.

# Tips for Teachers

## 10.2  Guidelines for Teaching Multicultural Content

- Take time to learn about your culture(s) and how it influences your beliefs and actions. Be sensitive to your attitudes and behaviors.
- To teach cultural content you need knowledge of cultural groups. Read books that survey the histories of cultural groups in the United States. (See Read More about It for suggested books.)
- Make sure that your room conveys positive images of various cultural groups (through bulletin boards, posters, literature, software, and so on).
- Plan time in which you and your students can learn about each other's cultural backgrounds. (See Read More about It for reference books.)
- Be culturally conscious in selecting teaching materials. If the materials you use include stereotypes or present only one perspective, point out the limitation to the students.

- Use trade books, films, videotapes, and recordings to supplement the textbook and to present more varied perspectives.
- Use literature to enrich students' understanding of cultural pluralism.
- Be sensitive to the development levels of your students when you select concepts, content, and activities. Use concrete, specific concepts and activities for students in early elementary grades. As students develop, focus on more abstract concepts and problem solving.
- Use cooperative learning and group work to promote integration.
- Make sure that not only classroom activities but also schoolwide activities (such as plays, sports, and clubs) are culturally integrated.

# Tech Talk

## Using Multimedia and Videography to Create Community Connections

Creating multimedia and videography presentations can integrate multicultural education and the resources of students' home communities into the curriculum. Such activities provide students with opportunities to learn new technology skills and celebrate their home communities and cultures.

Even as simple a process as having students videotape typical scenes in their neighborhood and interview respected members of the community presents opportunities for planning, developing storyboards, writing, and scheduling and conducting interviews. If editing equipment is available, students can learn simple editing skills by piecing together the segments of videotape as they construct the community video.

Multimedia production, or hypermedia, as it is sometimes called, allows students to use a variety of resources from their community to create a presentation that shares what they have learned in an interactive way. Sources can include not only video, but also audio for music and interviews, photographs and drawings that can be scanned in, and text such as newspaper headlines and maps. All these information sources can be included in a multimedia format. Software programs such as Hypercard, HyperStudio, or Linkway enable young people to create hypermedia programs with buttons and links that allow the user to experience the material in his or her own unique way.

Constructing a community media product provides many opportunities to learn about the community's "funds of knowledge" and the people the community considers to be experts. These funds of knowledge can extend across many contexts, including home life, traditions and celebrations, work, art, and politics. For example, an upper elementary class might decide to focus on home life, traditions, and celebrations. A high-school American government class might select a political subject such as "illegal immigrants" and make connections to the many elements of this issue such as home countries, labor opportunities, or health, education, and welfare issues.

Media activities can provide ideal opportunities for students to learn basic videography and computer skills, such as using a camera and external microphones for interviews. By using a storyboard to draw and describe the different parts of the media presentation, students can plan and visualize the end prod-

## Linguistic Diversity and Second Language Acquisition

Linguistic diversity is not new in the United States, with its rich history of immigration. Today, as in the past, many students live in homes in which the language spoken is not English. This trend is increasing rather than decreasing. According to the 2000 U.S. Census, a total of 45 million Americans spoke a language other than English at home, an increase from 32 million in 1992.

José is a good example of such a student. At the age of 4, he immigrated with his parents and three siblings from a rural community in Mexico to an urban Spanish-speaking community in Texas. His parents spoke only Spanish when they arrived. Although he has some exposure to English and his father is taking a night course to learn English, José entered school at age 5 with Spanish as his first language and only a limited knowledge of his second language, English. This same scenario is true of children who immigrate from Central and South American countries, Asian and Pacific Island countries, and Eastern European countries. The U.S. Department of Education estimates that of the 40 million students in public and private schools, over 2 million are English language learners (Díaz-Rico & Weed, 1995; Ovando & Collier, 1998).

The implications of this demography are that a growing number of students who enter school in the United States learn English as a second language in school. The teacher's knowledge of second language acquisition and general instructional guidelines can help make school a success for students like José.

uct before they begin to construct it. Community media production also provides natural opportunities for meaningful language arts, art, and social studies activities. For example, students learn about their communities and cultural traditions, as well as who the good sources of this information are in the community. Students write the interviews and practice their interviewing skills with each other. In many communities the arts, including dance, visual arts, theater and drama, and traditional dress, play an important role. As students construct their presentation, they can learn to integrate scenes from the arts with their interviews for greater interest and to provide pictures of what is being described.

The completed media presentation can be shared in many ways. Copies can be placed in school and local libraries and in the classroom, and a special showing for parents and the community can be held at the school. It is also possible to utilize the World Wide Web for more resources and for further dissemination of their work. Students can create their own website with internal or external links to related information by using any one of several software packages that allow beginner-level graphic hypermedia production such as Claris Homepage, Front Page, or PageMill just by learning to write HTML code. Access to an Internet service provider (ISP) is required to work online.

Resources to help you plan a community media presentation include the following:

1. Gross, L. S., & Ward, L. W. (1991). *Electronic moviemaking.* Belmont, CA: Wadsworth. Describes how to make a movie, including preproduction activi-

ties (such as developing scripts and storyboards), production activities, and postproduction activities (such as editing).

2. Jonassen, D., Peck, K., and Wilson, B. (1999) *Learning with technology: A constructivist perspective.* Upper Saddle River, NJ: Merrill. Provides a constructionist perspective for technology-mediated learning environments as well as practical information about affordable and accessible "mind tools."

3. Male, M. (1997). *Technology for inclusion: Meeting the special needs of all students.* Boston: Allyn & Bacon. This book includes a vision for teachers, advice on increasing student/teacher productivity, and information about access to tools and materials available.

4. Valmont, W. J. (1995). *Creating videos for school use.* Boston: Allyn & Bacon. Written for teachers; explains use of videos in schools; provides many examples of how to use video in class and how to teach basic videography skills.

5. Wigginton, E. (Ed.) *The Foxfire series.* New York: Doubleday. An English teacher in an Appalachian community helped students publish their oral histories, starting with *The Foxfire book* in 1972. Information about the Foxfire Teacher Networks is available from Foxfire Teacher Outreach, P.O. Box 541, Mountain City, GA 30562.

6. Zimmerman, W. (1988). *Instant oral biographies: How to tape record, video or film your life stories.* New York: Guarionex Press. Written for students in upper elementary and middle schools; describes how to make oral histories and includes sample forms.

## Framework for Second Language Acquisition

Ellis (Ellis, R., 1985, 1994) provides a framework for second language acquisition that can guide you in making accommodations for students whose first language is not English. Ellis suggests that five interrelated factors govern the acquisition of a second language. Figure 10.1 depicts the relationship among these factors.

**Situational Factors**   **Situational factors** are related to the context or the situation (i.e., the learning environments) in which the second language learning occurs. Students learn the second language in multiple learning environments—from relatives, friends, and neighbors who speak English; through ESL or bilingual education programs at school; and from peers in the classroom and on the playground.

Environments such as these can provide both formal teaching and more natural opportunities to acquire language. When José's uncle explains the concept "scientist" in Spanish and then pairs it with English, he is providing formal instruction. On the other hand, the instruction is much more natural when José and his uncle converse about what happened in school and his uncle provides José with words in English when José is searching for the English word. One goal of both bilingual education and English as a Second Language (ESL) instruction is to create environments that are nonthreatening and in which students are willing to take risks and play

Students whose first language is not English and who are not fluent in English are sometimes referred to as English language learners (ELL).

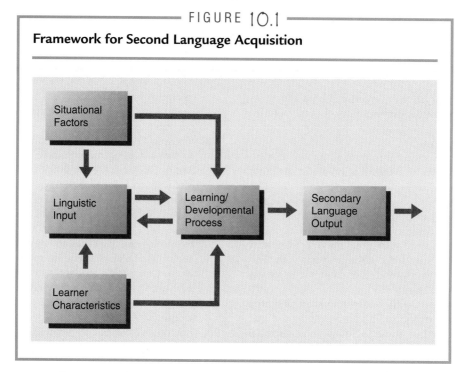

FIGURE 10.1

**Framework for Second Language Acquisition**

*Source:* Adapted from Ellis, R. (1985). *Understanding second language acquisition.* Oxford: Oxford University Press.

with the language (Ovando & Collier, 1998; Vaughn & Gersten, 1998). Maria, the ESL teacher interviewed at the beginning of this chapter, encourages students to play with the language by experimenting with sounds, words, and syntactic construction. She makes these opportunities for discovery by encouraging experimentation.

Another situational factor that promotes second language acquisition is an environment in which the students' first language and culture are respected and valued. The research consistently demonstrates that valuing students' first language is an important factor for student success (Carter & Chatfield, 1986; Lucas et al., 1990; Thomas & Collier, 1997). One important aspect of valuing the students' language is to learn about their community's funds of knowledge and language (refer to Tips for Teachers 10.1).

**Linguistic Input**   **Linguistic input** refers to input received when reading or listening to a second language. Comprehensible input is a key factor for success (Krashen, 1985). Input is made more comprehensible by a number of strategies, including the following:

● Selecting a topic of conversation that is familiar to students
● Creating a context for what is being discussed
● Using simpler sentence construction

● Repeating important phrases
● Incorporating the students' first language into the instruction
● Emphasizing key words to promote comprehensible input

When teaching linguistically diverse students, it is important to consider the linguistic input. Tips for Teachers 10.3 presents guidelines and ideas for making input more comprehensible.

**Learner Characteristics**   The third factor affecting second language acquisition or output is **learner characteristics.** Relevant learner characteristics include the age at which students learn a second language, their aptitude for learning language, their purposes and degree of motivation for learning the second language, their self-confidence in language learning, and their learning strategies.

Another important variable is the degree of acquisition of proficiency in the first language. Cummins (1991), in a review of research, concluded that the better developed the students' proficiency and conceptual foundation in

Assessment used in screening for proficiency in English includes the Bilingual Syntax Measure (Burt et al., 1980), the IDEA Oral Language Proficiency Test (Ballard & Tighe, 1987), and the Language Assessment Scales (De Avila & Duncan, 1986).

# Tips for Teachers

## 10.3 Guidelines for Making Input More Comprehensible for Second Language Learners

- Begin teaching new concepts by working from the students' current knowledge and incorporating the funds of knowledge from the students' community.
- Use demonstrations and gestures to augment oral communication.
- To the degree possible, create the context in which the concepts occur. For example, when teaching about shellfish, visit an aquarium, watch a film, display shells in the classroom.
- Discuss connections between the concepts being taught and the students' home cultures.

- Encourage students to share the new vocabulary in their first language and incorporate the first language into instruction.
- If students share a common first language, pair more proficient second language learners with less proficient peers, and encourage students to discuss what they are learning.
- Highlight key words and phrases by repeating them and writing them.
- Use simple sentence constructions, particularly to present a new or difficult concept.

the first language, the more likely they were to develop similarly high levels of proficiency and conceptual ability in the second language. He has referred to this as the **common underlying proficiency,** using the analogy of an iceberg to explain this hypothesis and relationship between first and second language acquisition (see Figure 10.2) and why proficiency in the first language complements proficiency in the second language (Cummins, 1981).

As shown in Figure 10.2, both languages have separate surface features, represented by separate

icebergs. Below the surface and less visible, however, is the underlying proficiency common to both languages.

No matter which language the person is using, the thoughts that accompany the talking, reading, writing, and listening come from the same language core. One implication of this analogy is that individuals who are **balanced bilinguals** have an advantage over monolingual individuals in that they have greater cognitive flexibility and a greater understanding of language (see the Research Brief that follows).

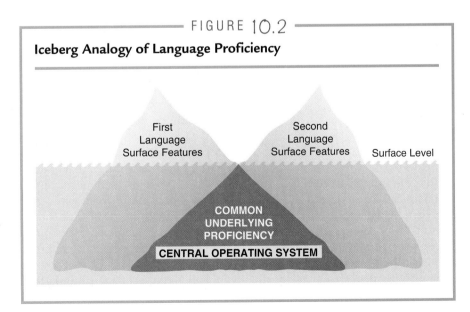

FIGURE 10.2

**Iceberg Analogy of Language Proficiency**

First Language Surface Features

Second Language Surface Features

Surface Level

COMMON UNDERLYING PROFICIENCY

CENTRAL OPERATING SYSTEM

*Source:* Adapted from Cummins, J. (1981). *Bilingualism and minority language children.* Ontario: Ontario Institute for Studies in Education.

## r e s e a r c h b r i e f

### Relationship of Bilingualism to Cognitive Development and Learning

From the early nineteenth century to approximately the 1960s, the dominant belief was that bilingualism was detrimental to cognitive development and academic learning. Diaz (1983) summarized the research performed before 1962, which built the case for bilingualism as a "language handicap." Researchers found that bilingual children had more limited vocabularies, more deficient articulation, and more grammatical errors than monolingual students. One interpretation was that bilingualism caused "linguistic confusion," which affected students' cognitive ability and academic performance. This research overall had many flaws. Bilingual and monolingual groups were not matched for other important variables such as socioeconomic status, for example, and tests for intellectual functioning and learning of bilingual students generally were conducted in English, not in the first or more dominant language.

In 1962, Peal and Lambert published the study that is now considered the turning point in the history of the relationship between bilingualism and cognition. This research broke new territory in two respects: It overcame many methodological deficiencies, and it found that bilingualism has cognitive advantages over monolingualism. Peal and Lambert concluded that bilingualism provides greater cognitive flexibility, greater ability to think more abstractly, and greater ability in concept formation.

Subsequent research has shown that higher degrees of bilingualism are correlated with increased cognitive abilities in such areas as creativity, knowledge of how language works (*metalinguistics*), concept formation, and cognitive flexibility (Galambos & Goldin-Meadow, 1990; Nieto, 1992; Orando & Collier, 1998; Skutnabb-Kangas, 1981).

**The Learning and Developmental Process**   The fourth factor addresses the **learning and developmental process** of second language acquisition and learning. Cummins (1984) suggested that students generally acquire competency in the **basic interpersonal communication skills (BICS)** before becoming competent with **cognitive academic language proficiency (CALP)**. The BICS, or **social language**, are the conversational competencies we develop with a second language—the greetings and small talk between peers, which generally do not require much cognitive effort or social problem solving. The CALP, or **academic language**, by contrast, refers to the more cognitively demanding language skills required for the new learning that occurs in school. In general, BICS develop in a second language before CALP. Cummins (1981) suggested that it takes one to two years to develop BICS but five to seven years to develop competence in CALP.

Although these guidelines have been shown to vary widely, depending on situational factors, linguistic input, and learner characteristics, they do have implications for teachers in general education classrooms. You might assume that because students can converse easily with you in their second language, they are ready to learn new concepts, strategies, and skills in the second language. This is not necessarily the case. For example, when Hoang Hy Vinh entered Sarah Miles's third-grade class, Sarah immediately noticed that he conversed easily with other students and with her. Vinh had immigrated from Vietnam two years before and had begun learning English through the school's ESL program. His parents, who take English in a night course, feel that learning English is important for their economic and personal success in America. Still, Vietnamese is the primary language spoken in the home.

As Sarah got to know Vinh, she realized that although his conversational skills were strong enough for him to be comfortable in the classroom community, he was not yet proficient in academic tasks such as reading and writing in English. She also found that for him to learn new concepts in social studies and science, she needed to provide lots of context. Sarah incorporated an extended segment on farming communities into a thematic unit on California, for example, because Vinh and several other students came from other Asian and Mexican farming communities. From the school and public libraries, she checked out books and magazines about farming and rural life in Vietnam, Mexico, and other Asian countries. The students also visited a California market, as well as Asian and Mexican food markets. They compared the foods from the markets and learned how those foods were grown in the three communities. For Vinh and other students from other cultures who were in the process of acquiring English as a second language, providing the link to their cultures helped to give them a context in which to build both their language and cognitive skills. This is an example of the **context-embedded communication and instruction** that Cummins (1981) and others (Chamot & O'Malley, 1994; Gersten & Jiménez, 1998; Reyes & Bos, 1998; Ruiz, Garcia, & Figueroa, 1996) recommend as facilitating second language learning. A good teacher incorporates both social

> Giving students the opportunity to discuss a new concept in their first language helps to promote content learning for second language learners.

(BICS) and academic (CALP) language into every lesson (Ovando & Collier, 1998).

**Secondary Language Output**   The fifth factor in the framework (Figure 10.1) is **secondary language output.** Students may understand a language (listening and reading) but not be proficient in producing the language (speaking and writing). An important part of developing speaking proficiency is the opportunity to engage in meaningful oral exchanges (in the classroom and the community) and to experiment with oral and written language in nonthreatening environments. Swain (1986) emphasized that not only **comprehensible input** but also opportunities for students to develop **comprehensible output** by oral practice with the language are important for acquisition of a second language. Feedback from listeners and from self-monitoring enables second language speakers to develop and fine-tune their oral language.

Also important in a consideration of secondary language output is that receptive language skills typically develop before expressive language skills. It has been well documented that second language learners experience a **silent or nonverbal period** (Ervin-Tripp, 1974; Hakuta, 1974), during which they are absorbing information and language that they cannot demonstrate or do not yet feel comfortable demon-

strating (Coelho, 1994). For example, Hakuta (1974) observed a 5-year-old Japanese girl, noting that it took from her arrival in October until the following April for her to begin speaking English. During the intervening period, she attended kindergarten and played with neighborhood English-speaking friends but did not speak English.

## Language Variation and Dialect

**Language variation,** which refers to the fact that language varies from place to place and from group to group, usually relates to the characteristics of groups of people (such as geographical region, social class, ethnic and cultural backgrounds, age, and gender). **Dialect** generally refers to language variations associated with a regional or social group of people. All English speakers use a dialect or variation of the English language. Think for a moment. Do you use the term "pop," "soda," "soda pop," "tonic," or some other term to label this popular type of drink? The answer depends on your dialect, which most likely relates to where you live and your cultural background. Dialect is also affected by age; for example, use of the term "icebox" rather than "refrigerator" is more evident in older people who grew up in times when iceboxes were used.

Language variation or dialects vary in several ways. Regional dialects tend to be distinguished by pronunciation and vocabulary features, whereas social and cultural dialects show variation not only in these areas, but also in grammatical usage. Dialects also reflect conversation patterns. In a good, satisfying conversation in some speech communities, for example, speakers overlap one another's talk. In other communities, the listener waits for a break to enter a conversation, and the speaker is likely to stop talking when someone else starts speaking.

**African American Vernacular English (AAVE)** is a dialect used by some African Americans. It is the most prevalent native English vernacular dialect in the United States. (The word "vernacular" is included in the term to avoid the stereotype that all African Americans speak AAVE.) Estimates based on socioeconomic demographics show that about three-fourths of African Americans speak AAVE. As with any other language or dialect, there is great language variation among speakers of AAVE.

Because of African Americans' historical status as an oppressed and involuntary minority, there has been a tendency to consider AAVE not as a valid language system, but rather as random errors (Labov et al., 1968). Like any other language, however, AAVE has an internally consistent linguistic infrastructure and set of grammar rules. Table 10.3 presents some common grammatical contrasts between AAVE and Standard American English. In teaching

According to Ellis's framework for second language acquisition, what five factors will influence this student's acquisition of English? What kinds of instructional activities for second language acquisition might you recommend for this student, based on effectiveness research?

TABLE 10.3

## Grammatical Contrasts between African American Vernacular English and Standard American English

| AAVE Grammatical Structure | SAE Grammatical Structure |
|---|---|
| **Possessive -'s**<br>Nonobligatory word where word position expresses possession.<br>  Get *mother* coat.<br>  It be *mother's*. | Obligatory regardless of position.<br><br>  Get *mother's* coat.<br>  It's *mother's*. |
| **Plural -s**<br>Nonobligatory with numerical quantifier.<br>  He got ten *dollar*.<br>  Look at the cats. | Obligatory regardless of numerical quantifier.<br>  He has ten *dollars*.<br>  Look at the cats. |
| **Regular past -ed**<br>Nonobligatory; reduced as consonant cluster.<br>  Yesterday, I *walk* to school. | Obligatory.<br>  Yesterday, I *walked* to school. |
| **Irregular past**<br>Case by case, some verbs inflected, others not.<br>  I *see* him last week. | All irregular verbs inflected.<br>  I *saw* him last week. |
| **Regular present tense third person singular -s**<br>Nonobligatory.<br>  She *eat* too much. | Obligatory.<br>  She *eats* too much. |
| **Irregular present tense third person singular -s**<br>Nonobligatory.<br>  He *do* my job. | Obligatory.<br>  He *does* my job. |
| **Indefinite an**<br>Use of indefinite *a*.<br>  He rode in *a* airplane. | Use of indefinite *an*.<br>  He rode in *an* airplane. |
| **Pronouns**<br>Pronominal apposition: pronoun immediately follows noun.<br>  Momma *she* mad. She . . . | Pronoun used elsewhere in sentence or in other sentence; not in apposition.<br>  Momma is mad. *She* . . . |
| **Future tense**<br>More frequent use of *be going to* (gonna).<br>  I *be going to* dance tonight.<br>  I *gonna* dance tonight.<br>Omit *will* preceding *be*.<br>  I *be* home later. | More frequent use of *will*.<br>  I *will* dance tonight.<br>  I *am going to* dance tonight.<br>Obligatory use of *will*.<br>  I *will* (I'll) *be* home later. |

about diversity, it is important that students study dialects and learn that AAVE is a linguistic system. In teaching Standard American English to students who speak AAVE, it is important to help them understand the systematic differences between the standard and vernacular forms. You can do so by using many of the strategies recommended for second language acquisition.

## Historical Perspective on ESL Instruction and Bilingual Education

Bilingual education and English as a Second Language (ESL) instruction or teaching English to speakers of other languages (ESOL) for culturally and linguistically diverse students have evolved through the years. Figure 10.3 shows the chronology of this evolution in the United States.

| AAVE Grammatical Structure | SAE Grammatical Structure |
|---|---|
| **Negation**<br>Triple negative.<br>   *Nobody don't never* like me. | Absence of triple negative.<br>   *No* one ever likes me. |
| **Modals**<br>Double modals for such forms as *might, could,*<br>and *should.*<br>   I *might could* go. | Single modal use.<br><br>   I *might be able to* go. |
| **Questions**<br>Same form for direct and indirect.<br>   What *it is*?<br>   Do you know what *it is*? | Different forms for direct and indirect.<br>   What *is it*?<br>   Do you know what *it is*? |
| **Relative pronouns**<br>Nonobligatory in most cases.<br>   He the one stole it.<br>   It the one you like. | Nonobligatory with *that* only.<br>   He's the one *who* stole it.<br>   It's the one (that) you like. |
| **Conditional *if***<br>Use of *do* for conditional *if*.<br>   I ask *did* she go. | Use of *if*.<br>   I asked *if* she went. |
| **Perfect construction**<br>*Been* used for action in the distant past.<br>   He *been* gone. | *Been* not used.<br>   He left a long time ago. |
| **Copula**<br>Nonobligatory when contractible.<br><br>   He sick. | Obligatory in contractible and<br>noncontractible forms.<br>   He's sick. |
| **Habitual or general state**<br>Marked with uninflected *be*.<br>   She *be* workin'. | Nonuse of *be*; verb inflected.<br>   She's working now. |

*Source:* Owens, Jr., R. E. (1995). *Language disorders: A functional approach to assessment and intervention* (2nd ed., pp. A-8–A-9). Boston: Allyn & Bacon. Reprinted with permission.

What is interesting about this chronology is the way bilingualism has been tied to assimilation into American culture and therefore linked to political policy. Bilingualism in our schools and communities dates back to the early colonies. It was common among both the working and educated classes that many official documents were published in German and French as well as English. By the late 1800s, however, language restrictions were being placed on schools. Under strong political pressures to assimilate immigrants, bilingual education was virtually eradicated by the 1930s. After World War II, students from minority cultures were described as "culturally deprived" and "linguistically disabled."

In the early 1960s, however, bilingual education was reborn in Dade County, Florida, as Cuban

========================= FIGURE 10.3 =========================

**Recent Developments in Second Language and Bilingual Education in the United States**

| | |
|---|---|
| **Before 1914** Many community schools existed to teach a specific language, such as German. Saturday classes were common. | **1981** Senator S. I. Hayakawa first introduced a constitutional amendment to declare English the official language of the United States. (It was defeated.) |
| **1918** World War I brought about reactions against Germany and a resurgence of patriotic feeling; use of "English only" in schools was legislated in many states. | **1981** *Castenada* v. *Pickard* established a framework for determining whether school districts are in compliance with *Lau* v. *Nichols* decision. The framework for compliance included: |
| **1945** World War II led to realization of need for knowledge of foreign languages; teaching of foreign languages in schools was encouraged. | Theory—Is the program based on sound theory? Implementation—Does the district have an implementation plan? Results—What kinds of results does the district have for implementing the program? |
| **1958** Soviet launching of *Sputnik* shocked U.S. leaders, who then funded schools' efforts to promote key subject areas, including foreign languages. | **1984** California voters passed a bill to publish ballots and other election material in English only. |
| **1963** Dade County, Florida, initiated bilingual programs for Spanish-speaking Cuban children coming to Miami. | **1985** U.S. Secretary of Education William Bennett spoke out against federal bilingual education programs. |
| **1964** Civil Rights Act forbade language-based discrimination. | **1994** Reauthorization of the Bilingual Education Act (Title VII of the Improving American Schools Act, formerly Elementary and Secondary Education Act). In this reauthorization, bilingualism was reconceptualized as a valuable national resource. Bilingual programs are no longer defined by types: maintenance, transitional, and immersion. |
| **1968** Bilingual Education Act: Title VII of the Elementary and Secondary Education Act promoted bilingual programs in the schools. | |
| **1971** Massachusetts Bilingual Education Act: A law mandating bilingual education for non-English-speaking children; Massachusetts was the first state; other states followed. | |
| **1974** Bilingual Education Reform Act: Updated the 1968 law; mandated language instruction; added study of history and culture in bilingual programs. | **1994** Reauthorization of Improving American Schools Act resulted in language minority students being eligible to receive Title I services, even if the source of disadvantage is determined to be language. |
| **1974** U.S. Supreme Court decision in *Lau* v. *Nichols* gave non-English-speaking students the legal right to instruction that enables them to participate in education process, and to bilingual instruction, as part of "equal educational opportunity." | **1998** The California state legislature passed the English for the Children Initiative that restricts the programs in which ELL students can participate, including the number of years to several years only and the types of programs to ESL programs. |
| **1975** The U.S. Department of Education developed guidelines that specified approaches, methods, and procedures for educating students with limited proficiency in English. These Lau Remedies were not enacted. | |

*Source:* Adapted from Tiedt, P. L., & Tiedt, I. M. (1995). *Multicultural teaching: A handbook of activities, information, and resources* (p. 4). Boston: Allyn & Bacon.

immigrants requested bilingual schooling for their children. Programs were developed throughout the United States, under the authority of the Bilingual Education Act passed (as Title VII of the Elementary and Secondary Education Act) in 1968. Based on the law, suits were brought to ensure better services for students with cultural and linguistic diversities. The most noted case is *Lau* v. *Nichols*, in which the

U.S. Supreme Court ruled that equal treatment is not merely providing students with the same facilities, textbooks, teachers, and curriculum when students do not understand English.

Bilingual education may be justified as (1) the best way to attain the maximum cognitive development of English language learner (ELL) students, (2) a means of achieving equal educational opportunity,

(3) a means of easing the transition into the dominant language and culture, (4) an approach to educational reform, (5) a means of promoting positive interethnic relations, and (6) a wise economic investment to help ELL students to become maximally productive in adult life for the benefit of themselves and society (Baca & Cervantes, 1998).

Although the Bilingual Education Act and the Civil Rights Act and their rules and regulations have promoted equal access and bilingual education, political developments have moved the country back toward an assimilation philosophy. For example, in 1981, Senator S. I. Hayakawa introduced a constitutional amendment to declare English the official language of the United States. This amendment was defeated, but a growing number of states have passed what has been referred to as "English-only" legislation. More recent legislation has moved to restrict the type and length of programs for ELL students, such as the English for the Children Initiative passed in 1998 by the California state legislature. This legislation limits the number of years ELL students can participate in programs and does not support programs that promote maintenance of the first language along with development of English.

## Instructional Guidelines and Accommodations for Culturally and Linguistically Diverse Students

As a teacher, you will have students from many cultures and students who are in the process of acquiring English as a second language or second dialect. You may or may not be familiar with the culture and language of these students. Moreover, their parents' views about schooling and the roles and responsibilities of parents and teachers (Rodríguez-Brown, 2001) as well as their own experience in schools in the United States and elsewhere may be very different from your own. It will be your responsibility to help all students to feel comfortable in your class and to learn and to reach out to parents in culturally sensitive ways.

To promote learning, you should incorporate their language and culture into the curriculum, demonstrate that you value their culture and language, have high expectations for these students, and make accommodations so that they can learn successfully.

# Tips for Teachers

## 10.4   Working with Parents from Diverse Cultural and Linguistic Backgrounds

Most parents want the very best for their children. However, some teachers may think that parents are not interested in their child's education because they do not get involved in school functions, parent conferences, or helping their child with homework. There are many reasons parents do not get involved in traditional ways. Some parents do not feel comfortable in schools and are fearful of discrimination and disrespect. Others are not comfortable with the English language in either speaking or writing. Others may come from cultures where the teacher has the responsibility of formal schooling and parents customarily do not get involved. Still others may have been educated in another system or might not have had the opportunity for schooling at all.

Here are some general suggestions for teachers in working with parents from diverse cultural and linguistic backgrounds:

- Take a look at your own cultural background, and try to get in touch with your own experiences with schooling and parent involvement.

- Learn as much as you can about the cultural backgrounds of your students.
- Be inviting and welcoming. For beginners, learn the correct pronunciation of the child's first name and of the family name, and learn a few words of the child's native language.
- When preparing your classroom and curriculum, make certain that the heritage of your students is reflected.
- Explore the best ways to communicate with your parents.
- Do not talk down to parents; provide them with the respect you would expect as a parent.
- Enlist the support of a translator.
- Encourage parents to bring a translator or person who can provide support to parent conferences.
- Do your best to provide written communication in the parents' native language.
- Interview parents to determine how they can be a resource at home or at school. All parents have time, treasure, or talent to share in large or small ways.

Research into the characteristics of effective teachers of students with cultural and linguistic diversities (Chamot, 1998; Garcia, 1991; Gersten et al., 1998; Ladson-Billings, 1995; Tikunoff, 1983) indicates that such teachers:

● Have high expectations of their students and believe that all students are capable of academic success
● See themselves as members of the community and see teaching as a way to give back to the community
● Display confidence in their ability to be successful with students who are culturally and linguistically diverse
● Communicate clearly, pace lessons appropriately, involve students in decisions, monitor students' progress, and provide immediate feedback
● Through culturally relevant teaching, integrate the students' native language and dialect, culture, and community into classroom activities to make input more relevant and comprehensible, to build trust and self-esteem, and to promote cultural diversity and cultural pluralism
● Use curriculum and teaching strategies that promote coherence, relevance, progression, and continuity
● Structure opportunities for students to use English
● Challenge their students and teach higher-order thinking

As you will learn from the next section, schools have developed specific programs to promote second language acquisition.

## Programs for Promoting Second Language Acquisition

Two broad categories of programs have been used in schools in the United States to promote second language acquisition: English as a second language (ESL) instruction and bilingual education. English as a second language generally has as its goal the acquisition of English, whereas the goal of bilingual education is to promote bilingualism or proficiency in both the first and second languages.

**Instruction in English as a Second Language**
**English as a Second Language (ESL) instruction** uses English to teach students English as a second language, with limited emphasis on maintaining or developing proficiency in the student's first language. Instruction may be given during a specified instructional time (with students receiving the rest of their instruction in general education classrooms), or it

Based on research findings, higher degrees of bilingualism are correlated with students' increased cognitive development and learning. What kinds of instructional practices and strategies can teachers implement to promote bilingualism?

may be integrated into content-area instruction (as is the case with Sheltered English). **Sheltered English** is a type of ESL instruction in which the goal is to teach English language skills at the same time that students are learning content-area knowledge (Chamot & O'Malley, 1994; Northcutt & Watson, 1986). Sheltered English techniques that you can use as a classroom teacher include the following:

● Increase wait time.
● Respond to the message, not to the correctness of the pronunciation or grammar.
● Simplify your language.
● Don't force reluctant students to speak.
● Demonstrate the concept; use manipulatives.
● Make use of all senses.
● Pair or group native speakers together.
● Adapt the materials, don't water down the curriculum.
● Learn as much as you can about the language and culture of your students.
● Build on students' prior knowledge.
● Bring students' home language and culture into the classroom and curriculum (Chamot, 1998; Gersten et al., 1998; Reyes & Bos, 1998; Sullivan, 1992; Towell & Wink, 1993).

Schools often use the ESL model when the non-English-speaking students are from several language groups or there are too few students from a common language group to support a bilingual education model. Many educators suggest that students should be encouraged to continue to develop proficiency in their first language even if it is not formally supported through bilingual education (e.g., Baker, 1993; Cummins, 1989; Ovando & Collier, 1998). To promote this, teachers can do the following:

> Research indicates that academic and linguistic skills developed in a student's first language usually transfer easily to the second language (Lanauze & Snow, 1989).

- Encourage students to use their first language around school.
- Provide opportunities for students from the same language group to communicate with one another in their first language (e.g., in cooperative learning groups, during informal discussions).
- Recruit people who can tutor students in the first language.
- Provide, in classrooms and the school library, books written in various languages.
- Incorporate greetings and information in various languages in newsletters and other official school communications (Cummins, 1989).

The ESL teacher is usually considered a resource teacher in that he or she works daily, or at least several times a week, with groups of students or whole classes of students for a specified instructional time. In addition, the ESL teacher is usually responsible for assessing the students' language proficiency in English and, depending on the language, in their first language.

When Maria, the ESL teacher interviewed at the beginning of this chapter, was asked about her job and what she believed would make her most effective, she said,

> I feel fairly comfortable teaching the ESL students. I use a model that requires active learning on the part of the students with lots of use of gestures, demonstrations, and playing with language integrated into the instruction. I also build the students' culture into the instruction, and I encourage the students to use an inquiry model to learn more about their cultures and share them with the other class members. My greatest concern is my ability to serve as a resource for the classroom and bilingual teachers in the school. One way that I feel that I am more effective with classroom teachers is that I am doing more co-teaching. This allows me to demonstrate ESL techniques to the teachers, and I work with the teachers to plan ESL lessons that are relevant to the content being taught in class.

**Bilingual Education**    **Bilingual education** students usually spend the entire day in classrooms designated as *bilingual classrooms*. These students are learning English and may be receiving content instruction in their first language, in English, or in both, according to their level of development in English. Frequently, bilingual education approaches are described as *transitional* or *maintenance*, depending on the degree to which the first language is developed and maintained.

The focus of **transitional bilingual education** is to help students shift from the home language to the dominant language. These programs initially provide content-area instruction in students' native language along with ESL instruction. Students transfer from these programs as soon as they are deemed sufficiently proficient in English to receive all academic instruction in English (Baca & Cervantes, 1998). The time taken for this transition from the students' first language to English varies, depending on the program (Ramirez & Merino, 1990). In programs in which literacy is taught in the first language, with other content taught in English, students may make the transition in two to three years. In other transition programs, at least 40 percent of the instruction is in the first language—including reading, language arts, math, and sometimes social studies or science—and students usually remain in the programs through fifth or sixth grade (Ramirez, 1992).

> When biliteracy is encouraged in second language learners, literacy skills transfer from one language to the other (Lanauze & Snow, 1989).

**Maintenance bilingual education** fosters the students' first language and strengthens their sense of cultural identity while teaching the second language and culture. Maintenance programs typically provide native language content-area instruction throughout the elementary grades, with the amount of native language instruction decreasing as students progress through the program. This model values bilingualism and sees the learning of a second language as a positive addition for the students' cognitive development and life success. This model also places a strong emphasis on incorporating the students' culture and heritage into the instruction. A particularly compelling use of the maintenance bilingual model is in the education of Native Americans (Díaz-Rico & Weed, 1995) in which the goal is to increase the number of speakers of Native American languages and preserve the cultural and linguistic heritage (Reyhner, 1992).

Recently, **two-way bilingual programs** have become an option for students learning English as a second language. In two-way programs, half the students

# T i p s  f o r  T e a c h e r s

## 10.5    Using Cognates

Cognates are words in different languages that sound alike (homophones) or that look alike (homographs) and have roughly or exactly the same meaning. Cognates are very helpful when learning a new language because they make the process a little friendlier. We can say that cognates are "good friends." For example, words that end in *-ción* in Spanish tend to have cognates that end in *-tion* in English; *nación* means "nation," and *constitución* means "constitution."

Here are some exact Spanish/English homographs:

| | |
|---|---|
| atlas | atlas |
| popular | popular |
| hospital | hospital |
| metal | metal |
| fatal | fatal |
| hotel | hotel |
| actor | actor |

There are many more words that, although not spelled exactly the same, are still understandable:

| | |
|---|---|
| ácido | acid |
| alfabeto | alphabet |
| igual | equal |
| familia | family |
| plástico | plastic |

With all of these words looking and sounding alike, you wonder why you don't speak four or five languages. This seems like a breeze, right? Wrong! Beware of *false cognates,* or "false friends." The term was first used by Koessler and Derocquigny in their 1928 book *Les faux amis ou les trahisons du vocabulaire anglais.* The title itself contains a false cognate and a true cognate: *trahisons* is not "treason" but "betrayal," and *vocabulaire* is "vocabulary."

Here are some common Spanish/English false cognates:

- *Introducir* means to introduce into, to bring in, to place; to introduce friends, you will need to use *presentar.*
- You will be very embarrassed if you use *embarazada* in the wrong context; it means pregnant, as in "with child." Try *avergonzada/o* for embarrassed instead.
- *Delito* is not delightful; it is a crime. Use *delicia* or *encanto.*

Here are some tips on using cognates in a multicultural or foreign language classroom:

- Take advantage of the students' prior knowledge of language.
- Ask questions like "Does that sound/look like a word in Spanish/English?"
- Use the cognates in different contexts to facilitate understanding.
- Point out the homographic cognates to LEP students.
- Allow the students to repeat and get used to the homophonic cognates (*peace—paz, pleasure—placer*).
- Use words with the same roots to aid in learning others (*appear, disappear—aparecer, desaparecer*).
- Make generalizations about grammatical differences and similarities between the languages.
- Get the students to talk about words and language so that they are more aware of what they know.
- Create a wall of cognates and/or false cognates.
- Use cognates to introduce science lessons (e.g., biology prefixes and roots such as *epi, dermis, itis, geo,* and *lympho*).
- Use cognates to introduce lessons about (language) history, such as words that came into English during the Norman period (French and Latin terms) or Germanic (Anglo-Saxon terms) and the difference between synonyms; *insane/crazy, autumn/fall.*

*Source:* Manuel Bello. Used with permission.

---

are native speakers of English, and the other half speak another language, usually Spanish. Instruction is in English half the time and in Spanish the other half. The goal is for all students to become fully bilingual and biliterate. Although the number of programs in the United States is limited, estimated at under 200 (Willis, 1994), the long-term results from early established programs are promising (Collier, 1989; Crawford, 1995; Thomas & Collier, 1997), with most of the native English and Spanish speakers bilingual and attending college, even though students were

from poor, working-class backgrounds. Results also indicate that the native English speakers have positive attitudes toward multicultural issues and are more sensitive toward students learning a second language.

When Gloria and Lidia, the bilingual education teachers team teaching at Mission Way, were asked about their model of bilingual education, they described it as best fitting the transition model, with a relatively late transition to English (fourth to fifth grade). One of the reasons Gloria and Lidia chose to team teach was to better meet the needs of their students as they made the transition from skill and content instruction in Spanish to English. Gloria said,

> During grades four and five, we transition the language of instruction to almost exclusively English. For us, the exception is reading and writing. In our literature-based reading program and writer's workshop, we continue to encourage the students to read some literature written in Spanish and to write some compositions in Spanish, although most instruction is in English. We also discuss the literature in Spanish. In this way, students do not lose those Spanish literacy skills that they have developed in the bilingual programs. We feel that this is important not only for them to stay connected to their home community, but also because being bilingual and biliterate are highly desired job skills.

## research brief

### Science for All

Differences in science achievement among students of diverse cultural and linguistic groups have prompted action in many sectors. Science reform documents stress that scientific inquiry is central to science instruction. Educators have focused their efforts on promoting scientific inquiry as both science content and a way to teach and learn science.

In response to this need, Dr. Okhee Lee of the University of Miami has conducted research to promote science learning and literacy development of elementary school students since the early 1990s. By taking into account the diversity of the student body in South Florida schools, Dr. Lee has been able to work with learners from different cultural and linguistic backgrounds.

Dr. Lee initially focused on the following questions:

- What is effective instructional scaffolding that considers students' cultural and linguistic experiences and the nature of science along the teacher-explicit to student-exploratory continuum?
- What are trends in science learning and achievement, particularly with a focus on scientific inquiry, and literacy development with culturally and linguistically diverse elementary students?
- How do state and district policies influence science instruction?

The project Science for All began as an exploratory study to examine the interrelationship of language development, science knowledge, and cognitive strategies as students engaged in three science tasks: tornado, lever, and sinking/floating. From these humble beginnings, the study expanded to address cultural congruence in science instruction with linguistically diverse students and subsequently to examine how fourth-

grade elementary teachers who shared the languages and cultures of their students made science meaningful and relevant on the basis of shared understandings.

Over the years, the research program has expanded in size and scope. From a small-scale exploratory study outside the classroom to a classroom study with a selected number of fourth-grade teachers, Science for All has grown to a program involving third-, fourth-, and fifth-grade teachers at 12 elementary schools in two school districts in two states.

The expanded program covers units on measurement and matter (grade 3), the water cycle and weather (grade 4), and ecosystems and the solar system (grade 5). The topics were selected to follow a logical sequence of instruction from basic skills and concepts to increasingly global systems. The units are organized to move from structured, teacher-explicit lessons to more open-ended projects that encourage student exploration.

From the beginning, Dr. Lee was interested in maintaining a sense of cultural and instructional congruence in her study; this was very important, since the first six schools she worked with represented a wide spectrum of ethnic and cultural backgrounds. Two schools had predominantly bilingual Spanish speakers, two had predominantly bilingual Haitian Creole speakers, and two had predominantly monolingual English speakers.

From the onset, teacher input was crucial for maintaining cultural congruence. The teachers were encouraged to engage in a discourse that takes into account the cultural values and beliefs of their students as these relate to science. To accomplish this, the teachers used artifacts, examples, and analogies that were congruent with the students in their class.

A crucial component of instructional congruence was for the teachers to relate academic subjects to the students' prior knowledge and experiences within their specific cultural contexts and utilize the students' cultural funds of knowledge to promote learning and achievement. Instructional congruence, then, is a process for using students' languages and cultures to mediate their understanding of the nature of science.

Observations in the schools show that students from diverse backgrounds bring their cultural knowledge and experience to the classroom. To date, the results suggest that promoting inquiry with elementary students from diverse languages and cultures requires sustained assistance over a long period of time.

So far, the results are very encouraging. There were significant achievement gains in both science concepts and inquiry for all three language groups. Total scores as well as subset scores for concepts and inquiry indicate comparable growth in both.

*Source:* Manuel Bello. Used with permission.

## making a Difference

### Teaching a Concept to Second Language Learners

When students do not understand a concept, use one or more of the following strategies:

- Draw a picture.

## The 60-second Lesson

- Have students with the same first language explain it in that language.
- Reexplain, but simplify the language.
- Demonstrate it.
- Provide examples and, if necessary, nonexamples (i.e., use of nonexamples is typical language used in teaching concepts).

## Promoting Language Learning during Content Instruction

Students who are acquiring English as a second language are focusing their attention not only on learning content and vocabulary, but also on learning English. Richard-Amato (1996) described the following stages of second language development related to learning in content classes:

- *Low-beginning:* Students depend on gestures, facial expressions, objects, pictures, a phrase dictionary, and often a translator to understand or be understood. Occasionally, students comprehend words or phrases.
- *Mid-beginning:* Students begin to comprehend more, but only when the speaker provides gestural clues, speaks slowly, and uses concrete referents and repetitions. Students speak seldomly and haltingly, show some recognition of written segments, and may be able to write short utterances.
- *High-beginning to low-intermediate:* Students comprehend more, but with difficulty. Students speak in an attempt to meet basic needs but remain hesitant and make frequent errors in grammar, vocabulary, and pronunciation. Students can read very simple text and can write a little (but writing is very restricted in grammatical structure and vocabulary).
- *Mid-intermediate:* Students may experience a dramatic increase in vocabulary recognition, but idioms and more advanced vocabulary remain difficult. Students often know what they want to say but grope for acceptable words and phrases. Errors in grammar, vocabulary, and pronunciation are frequent. Students can read text that is

more difficult but still concrete and can write with greater ease than before.

- *High-intermediate to low-advanced:* Students begin to comprehend substantial parts of normal conversation but often require repetitions, particularly with academic discourse. Students are gaining confidence in speaking ability; errors are common but less frequent. Students can read and write text that contains more complex vocabulary and structures than before but experience difficulty with abstract language.
- *Mid-advanced:* Students comprehend much conversational and academic discourse spoken at normal rates but sometimes require repetition. Speech is more fluent, and meaning is generally clear, but occasional errors occur. Students read and write with less difficulty materials commensurate with their cognitive development but demonstrate some problems in grasping intended meaning.
- *High-advanced:* Students comprehend normal conversation and academic discourse with little difficulty. Most idioms are understood. Students speak fluently in most situations with few errors. Students read and write both concrete and abstract materials and are able to manipulate the language with relative ease (Richard-Amato & Snow, 1992).

On the basis of this progression of second language development, Richard-Amato and Snow (1992) have developed strategies for general classroom teachers to use in teaching content (see Tips for Teachers 10.6). The *CALLA Handbook: Implementing the Cognitive Academic Language Learning Approach* (Chamot & O'Malley, 1994) also focuses on strategies for teaching second language acquisition

# Tips for Teachers

## 10.6 Teaching Strategies for Promoting Content and Second Language Learning in General Education Classes

**Beginning to Mid-Intermediate Proficiency Level**

- Provide a supportive environment in which help is readily available to second language learners.
- Establish consistent patterns and routines in the classroom.
- Use gestures, visuals, and demonstrations to present concepts.
- Connect content to students' home cultures.
- Simplify grammar and vocabulary.
- Slow the pace of presentation, enunciate clearly, and emphasize key concepts through gesture, facial expression, intonation, and repetition.
- Record your lectures or talks on tape, and make them available for students.
- Make copies of your notes, or have another student take notes, so that second language learners can concentrate on listening.
- Build in redundancy by restating the concept in a simpler form, providing examples, and giving direct definitions.
- Extend wait time so that second language learners have time to volunteer.

- Avoid forcing second language learners to speak.
- Arrange cooperative learning so that students with the same first language work together.
- Encourage students to use their second language in informal conversations.
- Whenever possible, use tutors who speak the native language of the second language learners.
- Alter criteria for grading.

**High-Intermediate to Advanced Proficiency Level**

- Add contextual support to your lesson (e.g., advance organizer, study guides, glossaries, videos/films).
- Take into account the linguistic demands of the content.
- Provide opportunities for students to write in the content area.
- Provide opportunities for second language learners to practice critical thinking skills.
- Coach second language learners in appropriate learning strategies for mastering content.

within content areas. In addition, it simultaneously teaches learning strategies such as those presented in Chapter 15.

Although planning for culturally and linguistically diverse students takes some creative thinking

and modifications of the curriculum, these students will broaden both your horizons and those of the class. In your planning, be sure to provide ample time for students to engage in meaningful conversations about topics related to language and culture.

## summary

- The demographics of our nation and schools are changing, and the number of students with cultural and linguistic diversities is increasing.
- In U.S. schools, the number of students whose first language is not English is increasing substantially.
- The macroculture represents the dominant culture of the United States; the microcultures represent the students' home cultures. Teachers can help students understand and mediate the macroculture.

- Learning about your students' home cultures and communities and integrating those cultures and communities into the curriculum is important.
- The goal of multicultural education is to change the structure of schools so that students from different cultural groups have an equal chance to achieve in school.
- Dimensions of multicultural education include content integration, knowledge construction, equity pedagogy, and an empowering school culture.

- Four basic approaches to multicultural education include the contributions, additive, transformation, and social action approaches.
- Five elements that affect second language acquisition are situational factors, linguistic input, learner characteristics, the learning and developmental process, and second language output.
- In considering language proficiency it is important to consider both the basic interpersonal communication skills or social language (BICS) and cognitive academic language performance or academic language (CALP).
- Language varies from place to place and from group to group and includes dialects such as African American Vernacular English (AAVE).
- English as a Second Language instruction and bilingual education are two types of programs for educating second language learners.
- A number of strategies facilitate learning for students who are second language and dialect learners.

# key terms and concepts

academic language
additive approach
African American Vernacular
   English (AAVE)
balanced bilinguals
basic interpersonal communication
   skills (BICS)
bilingual education
cognitive academic language
   proficiency (CALP)
common underlying
   proficiency
comprehensible input
comprehensible output
content integration

context-embedded communication
   and instruction
contributions approach
cultural characteristics
cultural inversion
dialect
empowering school culture
equity pedagogy
English as a Second Language
   (ESL) instruction
funds of knowledge
knowledge construction
language variation
learner characteristics
learning and developmental process

linguistic input
macroculture
maintenance bilingual
   education
microcultures
multicultural education
secondary language output
Sheltered English
silent or nonverbal period
situational factors
social action approach
social language
transformation approach
transitional bilingual education
two-way bilingual programs

# think and apply

1. Now that you have read Chapter 10, think about the interview with bilingual teachers Gloria Rodriguez and Lidia Romo and with ESL teacher Maria Chavez. What questions do you have for them about strategies for working with students who are culturally and linguistically diverse? Make a list of the questions and then ask them of an ESL or bilingual education teacher.

2. Visit a school known for its positive emphasis on multicultural education. Watch for evidence of cultural integration and an empowering school culture. Observe a lesson to see how the teacher builds upon the students' cultural diversity.

3. To learn more about your own cultural background, answer the questions posed in the "Cultural Characteristics" section or partner with a fellow student and interview each other.

4. Select a unit you have taught or plan to teach. Review it for its focus on multicultural perspectives. Then, using one of the four approaches to multicultural education (contribution, additive, transformation, social action), modify the unit to include a stronger multicultural emphasis.

5. Select a unit you have taught or plan to teach, and review it to determine how you would modify it for second language or dialect learners.

# read  more  about  it

1. Agar, M. H. (1996). (2nd ed.). *The professional stranger: An informal introduction to ethnography.* Orlando, FL: Academic Press.

   *A very readable book that provides information on strategies for learning about the home environment.*

2. Anstrom, K. (1998). *Preparing secondary education teachers to work with English language learners.* National Council of Bilingual Education. Washington, DC.

   *Provides practical strategies for making mainstream instruction accessible to linguistically and culturally diverse students.*

3. Banks, J. A. (1997). *Teaching strategies for ethnic studies* (6th ed.). Boston: Allyn & Bacon.

   *An overview of ethnic studies for Native Americans, African Americans, European Americans, Hispanic Americans, and Asian Americans. This is an excellent resource for videotapes, films, children's literature, and trade books highlighting different ethnic groups.*

4. Banks, J. A., and Banks, C. A. M. (Eds.) (1995). *Handbook of research on multicultural education.* New York: Macmillan.

   *A reference work in which scholars report on multicultural education from a variety of disciplines and fields. A valuable resource for teachers.*

5. Block, C. C., & Zinke, J. A. (1995). *Creating a culturally enriched curriculum for grades K–6.* Boston: Allyn & Bacon.

   *Provides activities and short units on different aspects of multicultural education. For each activity, children's literature (rated for difficulty) is provided.*

6. Chamot, A. U., & O'Malley, J. M. (1994). *The CALLA handbook: Implementing the cognitive academic language learning approach.* Reading, MA: Addison-Wesley.

   *Middle- and high-school curriculum for English language learners that integrates teaching ESL, learning strategies, and higher-order thinking.*

7. Delpit, L. (1996). *Other people's children: Cultural conflict in the classroom.* New York: The New York Press.

   *A collection of essays about effective ways to teach children from diverse racial, ethnic, and cultural groups.*

8. Diamond, B. J., & Moore, M. A. (1995). *Multicultural literacy.* White Plains, NY: Longman.

   *This is an excellent resource for teachers interested in using multicultural literature and reading and writing experiences in the classroom. The book also includes excellent sections on using technology and working with parents from diverse backgrounds.*

9. Díaz-Rico, L., & Weed, K. Z. (2002). (2nd ed.). *The crosscultural, language, and academic development handbook: A complete K–12 reference guide.* Boston: Allyn & Bacon.

   *A very readable book about second language acquisition, bilingual education, culture and cultural diversity, and language policies, with many ideas for teaching.*

10. Fradd, S. H., & Klinger, J. (Eds.). (1995). *Classroom inclusion strategies for students learning English.* San Antonio, TX: Communication Skill Builders.

    *A practical, how-to book for the teacher with a multicultural classroom. It includes lesson plans, projects, activities, explanations, graphic organizers, and a lot of practical advice for teachers.*

11. Gersten, R. M., & Jimenez, R. T. (Eds.). (1998). *Promoting learning for culturally and linguistically diverse students.* Belmont, CA: Wadsworth.

    *A readable book that provides strategies for classroom teachers to use in teaching English language learners.*

12. Ladson-Billings, G. (1997). *The dreamkeepers: Successful teachers of African American children.* San Francisco: Jossey-Bass.

    *Tells the stories of teachers who are successfully educating African American students.*

13. Meinbach, A., & Kassenhoff, M. K. (1994). *Memories of the night.* Torrance, CA: Frank Schaffer Publications.

    *An excellent resource for teachers in planning a unit on the Holocaust.*

14. Noel, J. (2000). *Notable selections in multicultural education.* Guilford, CT: Dushkin/McGraw-Hill.

    *An outstanding selection of essays and excerpts from important books dealing with multicultural issues. The book is organized by themes and includes writers with a wide range of philosophical and theoretical perspectives.*

15. Ovando, C. J., & Collier, V. P. (1998). *Bilingual and ESL classrooms: Teaching in multicultural contexts* (2nd ed.). Boston: McGraw-Hill.

    *Provides an overview of bilingual education and ESL that includes teaching strategies.*

16. Reyhner, J. (Ed.). (1992). *Teaching American Indian students*. Norman, OK: University of Oklahoma.

    *Readings on strategies for teaching Native American students.*

17. Ruiz, N. T., Garcia, E., & Figueroa, R. A. (1996). *The OLE curriculum guide: Creating optimal learning environments for students from diverse backgrounds in special and general education*. Sacramento, CA: California Department of Education, Specialized Programs Branch.

    *Early literacy curriculum for teaching English language learners that incorporates a sociocultural perspective and includes such teaching components as interactive journals, writers' workshops, literature study, and shared reading.*

18. Siccone, F. (1995). *Celebrating diversity: Building self-esteem in today's multicultural classrooms*. Boston: Allyn & Bacon.

    *Provides many multicultural activities to promote self-worth and confidence in students (grades K–8).*

19. Sleeter, C. E., & Grant, C. A. (1999). *Making choices for multicultural education: Five approaches to race, class, and gender* (3rd ed.). New York: Merrill.

    *Critically examines five alternative models of multicultural education that are used in American schools and classrooms today.*

20. Spangenberg-Urbschat, K., & Pritchard, R. (Eds.). (1994). *Kids come in all languages: Reading instruction for ESL students*. Newark, DE: International Reading Association.

    *Presents practical strategies for teaching ESL students.*

21. Soto, L. D. (1997). *Language, culture, and power: Bilingual families and the struggle for quality education*. Albany, NY: State University of New York Press.

    *Documents the story of a Puerto Rican community as they struggle to get quality education for their children.*

22. Tiedt, P. L., & Tiedt, I. M. (1998). *Multicultural teaching: A handbook of activities, information, and resources* (5th ed.). Boston: Allyn & Bacon.

    *Presents general strategies for multicultural education in addition to topical activities and units.*

## suggested websites

**http://coe.sdsu.edu/people/jmora**
This is Dr. Mora's Cross-cultural Language & Academic Development (CLAD) website. It is a very informative and easy to surf site that is designed to be a "comprehensive resource on the philosophy, methods and public policy issues in educating language minority students." This site has access to lectures, articles, model lessons plans for teachers, and many useful links to related sites.

**www.ed.gov/free**
More than 30 federal agencies have made "hundreds of federally supported education resources available at this site." It includes incredible links to museum sites that include activities for students at all levels and has foreign languages and cultural awareness components.

**http://thegateway.org**
This is the Gateway to Educational Materials, and it is "the key to one-stop, any-stop access to high quality lesson plans, curriculum units and other educational resources on the Internet!" This site allows you to be as broad and as specific as you want to be to fulfill your needs. From free, detailed lesson plans for a bilingual unit on animals to web activities on geography and culture, it is a great resource for busy teachers.

**www.everythingesl.net**
This website includes lesson plans for classroom teachers, general teaching suggestions, and a wealth of resources to help your ESL student feel welcome and to help you teach your ESL student in effective ways.

**www.ed.gov/offices/OBEMLA**
This is the website of the U.S. Department of Education, Office of Bilingual Education and Minority Languages Affairs (OBEMLA). This site has information about federal programs and can clarify questions about the law and different government studies and pilot programs.

**www.splcenter.org**
This is the website of the Southern Poverty Law Center, a "nonprofit organization that combats hate, intolerance and discrimination through education and litigation." The center provides resources for educators to help teach about these issues.

**www.cudenver.edu/~mryder/itc_data/postmodern.html**
This is the website of the School of Education in the University of Colorado at Denver. It is very easy to navigate and has extensive sources for writers in the field of critical pedagogy, cultural studies, and contemporary philosophy.

**www.nmci.org**
This is the website of the National MultiCultural Institute. Since 1983, the institute has been a leader in the field of diversity training and education. On this site, you will find publications and "resource materials that include trainer manuals, books on cross-cultural mental health and videos."

**http://members.aol.com/lacillo/multicultural.html**
"This site will provide you with information about different cultures and some of the issues facing multicultural counseling." The site helps you focus on many elements of multicultural issues, including "gender, socioeconomic status, age, race, religion, ethnic heritage, and sexual orientation."

**http://falcon.jmu.edu/~ramseyil/multipub.htm**
This site brings together resources for parents, teachers, students and librarians. It includes links, reviews, and activities for students of all ages. It has lesson plans for teachers and a multitude of ideas for the classroom.

# Teaching Students Who Are at Risk and Students Who Are Gifted and Talented

# chapter | outline

# focus | questions

1. What conditions place students at risk? Are there conditions over which you as a teacher have some control? What are your responsibilities regarding conditions over which you have no control?

2. What programs are available to provide educational support for students at risk?

3. What are the key components of different definitions of gifted and talented? How can these definitions affect who receives special services and who does not?

4. How can you identify students who are gifted and talented in your classroom and refer them for special programs?

5. How can you create a positive, productive learning environment for students in your classroom who represent a wide range of academic and social needs?

# inter view

**Lawanzer Ellis**

Lawanzer Ellis is a fourth-grade teacher in Miami, Florida. Students at her school are among the most ethnically and linguistically diverse in Miaimi Dade County Public Schools. The school qualifies as a Title I school, so it receives additional federal funds to assist children in high-poverty areas. Of the 34 students assigned to Lawanzer this year, 17 were identified by the school district as qualifying for special services for the gifted and talented. To simplify scheduling, the principal decided to place all fourth-grade gifted and talented students in one general education classroom. Two days a week, the 17 students go to a resource room to work with a teacher trained in gifted education. On those two days, Lawanzer teaches the other 17 children—a group representing a wide range of achievement levels.

Lawanzer has succeeded in creating a classroom climate that enables all her students to get excited about learning and to feel affirmed about themselves as learners. She attributes her success to four factors:

This classroom seems to work for a number of reasons. First, I think that the physical appearance and arrangement of the classroom sets the tone for learning. The classroom really is set up as a workplace, with work stations or centers all around the room. The writing center, the computer center, and the art center are used every day. Even though it is almost the end of the school year, my class is still very neat and well ordered. That's because the students take responsibility for their work environment very seriously. The students have helped me plan bulletin boards and centers all year long. I really believe that they feel a sense of ownership about the classroom.

A second reason that things have gone well this year is that every student feels good about his or her own gifts and talents. Sometimes this is really difficult for me to accomplish. I work hard to recognize everyone as being special and as having something important to contribute to our classroom community.

A third reason is that I have high expectations for all my students, and I communicate those expectations to my students and to their parents. Mostly I expect everyone to do his or her best and to stay on task. I give very detailed instructions about what to do and how to do it. We don't have much wasted time around here. Don't get me wrong, I don't over-pressure them. But I do expect them to work hard. I know each student's strengths and areas of need very, very well. They know that they can get help if they need it.

Finally, things go well around here because I'm a good planner. Some teachers get frustrated because the gifted kids get pulled out and miss so much of what is taught in the regular class. I just plan carefully. Other teachers get upset because the gifted teacher is off doing her own thing—I'm lucky we plan together. Some teachers never know what to do to keep the gifted kids busy—they finish their work so fast. Look around this room—there's always something to learn around here. It just takes coordination and planning.

# introduction

Lawanzer Ellis is a "planful" teacher. She knows her students and realizes the importance of a well-structured learning environment. She also realizes that a child's learning environment extends beyond her own classroom. Thus, having learned to think about each student's whole day, she plans with the Title I teacher and gifted resource teacher, communicates with parents regularly, and draws from community agencies to provide resources for her students. As Lawanzer puts it, "Some teachers teach to the middle. That won't work in my class. There is no middle. I teach to my children because the range of their needs is so wide." Her careful planning has enabled her to circumvent some of the potential pitfalls of a classroom with a full range of academic diversity, including students identified as gifted and talented as well as students who are potentially at risk of school failure.

Lawanzer is concerned about the academic and social progress of all of her students. She finds, as do many teachers, that planning for and teaching students with extraordinary potential for high performance (either academically or creatively) or students who have exceptional talent in specific areas (e.g., music, leadership, art) pose special challenges. She finds that children who experience family poverty and live in neighborhoods where they are in daily contact with drugs and violence have special needs as well. Providing for the needs of all students can be difficult, but as Lawanzer Ellis has demonstrated, with careful planning, it can be done! The chapter begins with background information about students who are at risk of school failure and students who are gifted and talented. The chapter ends with ideas to help you meet the instructional needs of all children in your classroom.

# Defining Students at Risk

Every September 3 million 6-year-olds enter our nation's first grades. Most enter confident of doing well in school, highly motivated, and eager to learn. Just 9 months later, many of these bright, enthusiastic youngsters have learned a hard lesson: they have failed first grade (Madden, Slavin, Karweit, Dolan, & Wasik, 1991).

Many young people in our nation are led to believe, in some cases early on, that success in school is beyond their reach. Students who struggle to learn to read, write, compute, or master concepts in the content areas can get discouraged in the world of school and eventually squeak by without mastering basic skills, or drop out.

The faces of students at risk are many, and the reasons for their lack of success in school are varied. Who are students at risk?

They are students like LeeAnn, who is in fourth grade and doesn't know the alphabet or letter sounds. She still reads on a preprimer level. LeeAnn is the youngest of five children of a single mother. Because the mother works at night, LeeAnn spends evenings with her older siblings. LeeAnn said to her teacher, "Maybe if my mom could afford *Hooked on Phonics,* I could learn to read."

They are students like Henry, who is in fifth grade, reads on a first-grade level, and has never had a grade higher than a D on a test. Henry goes to an urban school in which over 90 percent of the students qualify for free or reduced-price lunch. The school is overcrowded. Henry's class has 35 students. At the end of the school year, Henry told his teacher, "I'm just tired of having a dumb brain."

They are students like Ryan, who is in seventh grade and is failing three out of six subjects. Ryan's older brother and sister are excellent students, and both parents are college graduates. His teachers have identified Ryan as a gifted learner, but he doesn't seem to care about school and simply doesn't try. Ryan is candid about his position: "I can do the work if I want to. But I don't want to."

They are students like Javier, who is in eighth grade and whose achievement test scores in reading and mathematics are extraordinarily low. Javier has attended more than a dozen schools. His parents, migrant workers, must move frequently to make a living. As Javier says, "I'd just like to stay put for a while."

The situations of LeeAnn, Henry, Ryan, and Javier are different, as are their reasons for having difficulty in school. What they do have in common is that they are all at risk of school failure.

The term "at risk" came into being on publication of the report *A Nation at Risk* by the National Commission on Excellence in Education (Gardner, 1983). This report indicated that quality of education in the United States was low and that large numbers of students were in jeopardy of leaving school without the skills they need to help the United States compete in a world market. The commission's report set off a rush of educational reform and made the term "at risk" part of everyday vocabulary. There are some who argue that the term now serves as a negative label and who would prefer a more upbeat term, such as "students at promise."

Before the 1980s, terms such as "educationally disadvantaged" and "culturally deprived" were commonly used to describe students at risk.

Slavin, Karweit, and Madden (1989) define **students at risk** by four areas that serve as qualifications for at-risk status: remediation, retention, dropping out, and substandard basic skills. Figure 11.1 shows the history of legislation that addresses the needs of students at risk.

## Remediation

**Remediation** refers to additional instruction for students who do not demonstrate competency in basic skills in reading, writing, and mathematics at an expected rate. A third-grade student who reads at kindergarten level might need remediation in letter and word recognition, for example. Or a high-school student who cannot add two-digit numbers might need remediation.

## Retention

The practice of having a student repeat a grade level because of low academic performance is referred to as **retention.** For example, a third-grader who has not mastered the school district's reading and writing competencies may be required to repeat third grade, and a seventh-grader who has received a failing grade in most academic subjects may be required to repeat seventh grade.

Retention policies vary considerably across the nation. Some school districts have lenient policies based on research indicating that retention does not have significant positive effects on student achievement and may even be harmful to students (Holmes & Matthews, 1984). Other school districts have more stringent criteria for passing from one grade to the next and contend that "social promotion" is an indication of lowered academic standards.

══════════ FIGURE 11.1 ══════════

## Selected Federal Laws for Equal Educational Opportunity for Students at Risk

| | |
|---|---|
| **1954** | School Milk Program Act extended National School Lunch Act of 1946 to address basic needs of children in poverty. |
| **1954** | U.S. Supreme Court decision in *Brown* v. *Board of Education of Topeka, Kansas,* led to laws requiring racial integration of schools to achieve equal educational opportunity. |
| **1964** | Economic Opportunities Act first provided federal funding for Head Start and other programs for students at risk. |
| **1965** | Public Law 89–313 funded educational support for children in hospitals and institutions. |
| **1965** | Elementary and Secondary Education Act (ESEA) established Title I programs for low-income learners, dropouts, vocational students, preschoolers, bilingual learners, and children of immigrant workers; provided funding for preservice and inservice teacher training for Title I programs; and defined *accountability.* |
| **1966** | National Upward Bound program established for low-income high-school students who show potential for completing a post-secondary degree. |
| **1968** | Bilingual Education Act (Title VII) amended the Elementary and Secondary Education Act to require states to provide bilingual education programs. |
| **1969** | Public Law 91–230 recognized learning disabilities and giftedness as special-education categories. |
| **1970** | Drug Abuse Education Act provided first federal funding for anti-drug-abuse programs in schools. |
| **1972** | Women's Educational Equity Act (Title IX) amended the Elementary and Secondary Education Act to outlaw sex discrimination in schools. |

| | |
|---|---|
| **1972** | Public Law 92–424 amended the Elementary and Secondary Education Act to extend Head Start programs to children with disabilities. |
| **1974** | Juvenile Justice and Delinquency Prevention Act included federal funds for educational and school programs. |
| **1975** | Indian Self-Determination and Education Assistance Act extended the Indian Education Act of 1972 and gave Native Americans more control over their education. |
| **1975** | Indochina Migration and Refugee Assistance Act extended educational and other programs of the Migration and Refugee Assistance Act of 1962 to immigrants displaced by the Vietnam War. |
| **1981** | Education Improvement and Consolidation Act (ECIA) incorporated and amended key provisions of the Elementary and Secondary Education Act, renamed Title I programs as Chapter 1 programs, and gave states more control over funding the programs using one federal block grant. |
| **1984** | Public Law 98–377 added new science and mathematics programs, established magnet schools, and mandated equal access to public schools. |
| **1987** | Stewart B. McKinney Homeless Assistance Act was enacted in part to provide for educational needs of homeless children. |
| **1988** | The Hawkins-Stafford School Improvement Amendments made Chapter 1 schools more accountable for student achievement. |
| **1994** | As in 1984, public law continued federal funding for Head Start and Follow Through programs. |
| **1995** | Improving America's Schools Act (IASA) amended key provisions of the Elementary and Secondary Education Act, renamed Chapter 1 programs as Title I programs. |

## Dropping Out

Students who do not complete high school are **dropouts.** Students who drop out of high school have limited employment opportunities and find it difficult to compete for well-paid jobs. Typically, dropouts possess only low-level academic skills that limit employability, reduce opportunities for advancement, and reduce readiness for additional training (Rumberger, 1987). Lack of educational training and job preparation results in higher unemployment rates and lower pay among dropouts. The majority of individuals on welfare and in prison have not obtained a high-school degree (National Education Goals Panel, 1994).

## Substandard Basic Skills

**Substandard basic skills** exist when individuals cannot read, write, or compute at levels necessary to perform in the workplace. Functional illiteracy and innumeracy inhibit citizens from becoming productive at work and at home in performing basic living tasks. Increasingly, substandard skills in using computers in-

Why do students drop out of school? How does dropping out place students at further risk? What are some characteristics of successful dropout-prevention programs?

hibits adults from securing satisfying employment in an increasingly technologically oriented job market.

## Conditions That Place Students at Risk

In the 1930s and 1940s, educational researchers, psychologists, and physicians began to recognize that academic difficulties can be caused by a number of factors—social, psychological, physiological, and educational. A **multiple causation theory** emerged, suggesting that although some students may be at risk because of one primary condition, multiple conditions quite often interact to compound learning challenges. The theory applies to all areas of academic achievement and helps explain why students are at risk of failure in school.

Multiple conditions interact for most at-risk students. The bottom line is that these students have a hard time learning to read, write, and compute. Frymier (1992, p. 258) put it this way: "Children who hurt, hurt all over. . . . Risk is pervasive. If a student is at risk in one area, that student is very likely to be at risk in every other area. The question then becomes, 'What are teachers and others in the schools doing to help students who are at risk?' "

The National Dropout Prevention Center at Clemson University (www.dropoutprevention.org) serves as a clearinghouse for research on students at risk for dropping out of school and for research-based strategies for preventing students from leaving

school. The center recognizes that there is no one reason why students drop out. Many of the reasons are identified in upcoming sections. As a classroom teacher, you must recognize that some factors are conditions over which you as a classroom teacher have no control. For example, it is beyond your scope to change your students' economic level or living conditions. As Taylor, Harris, and Pearson (1988, p. 24) observed, "There is rarely a single causal factor for learning problems; even if teachers can identify a cause, eliminating the cause may be difficult, if not impossible." What teachers can do is be aware of conditions that explain why a student is at risk and "make the learning experience rich and rewarding in spite of the underlying cause." You can also be alert to other family, health and safety, and school conditions that potentially can put students at risk.

## Family Conditions

There is no doubt that what happens in the home affects students' success or failure at school. Unsettling circumstances at home can affect student motivation and concentration both in and out of class. Sometimes these circumstances are temporary; at other times, they are an ongoing part of the student's life. Home conditions that can potentially affect student academic performance include family poverty and family instability (Frymier, 1992).

**Family Poverty**   Students whose families live in poverty often come to school without their basic needs of food, clothing, shelter, and health care being met. As Crosby (1993, p. 604) expressed it, "We certainly don't need a great deal of research to determine that a child of poverty is at risk and that poverty is harmful to one's mental and physical well being." The facts about poverty have been reported by the Children's Defense Fund (www.childrensdefense.org). They are staggering:

- Over 12 million children in the United States (one out of every six) come from families living below the poverty level.
- In 2000, 15.4 million students received free or reduced lunch support.
- In 1999, 9.3 million children received food stamps.

# Tech Talk

## Improving Computer Equity

One of the realities of computers is that they are expensive. A home computer is simply not in the budget for many students from low-income families. Many schools in low-income areas, where additional money for computers (often donated by parent organizations) is not available, have fewer computers than schools in high-income areas.

Data also suggest that in schools with large numbers of at-risk students, computers are likely to be used for drill in basic skills, whereas in wealthier schools, computers are more likely to be used to teach programming (Maddux et al., 1992). In the twenty-first century, students without basic computer skills will be at a tremendous disadvantage in terms of employability. Thus, issues of **computer equity**—equal access to computers in the home and in the school—are a real concern (Maddux et al., 1992).

Here are some suggestions for improving computer equity:

- Structure opportunities for computer access before and after school. Consider starting a computer club.
- Include instruction in word processing, database management, spreadsheet usage, and computer programming, as well as opportunities to use software to improve basic skills.
- Select software that encourages problem solving and higher-order thinking.
- Select software that helps make connections between basic skills and real-life situations.

---

Poverty knows no racial or ethnic boundaries. Although the greatest subgroup of poor children is white, the proportion of members of minority groups who are poor is higher. Poverty also knows no geographic limits. Approximately 60 percent of poor students live in suburban or rural areas, and over 25 percent of children in urban areas are living at or below the poverty level (Council for Exceptional Children, 1991).

The limitations poverty places on families are likely to affect students' performance in school. Families often cannot afford educational materials, home computers, and extended vacations or day trips that broaden horizons. Students may have extended work responsibilities, such as caring for siblings or contributing to the family income. A student's level of poverty does not automatically determine success or failure in school (Au, 1993), but disproportionate numbers of students from low-income families are less successful in school and eventually drop out (Kortering et al., 1992).

> The poverty rate among Native Americans (25.9 percent) is nearly twice the national average, according to the Bureau of Indian Affairs.

**Family Instability**   Most families experience changes from time to time, but some changes in families are potentially hazardous to students' emotional and physical well-being and to their progress in school.

One of the most common jolts to family stability is divorce. Approximately 40 percent of students will experience parental divorce during their school years (Quay & Werry, 1986). Divorce can cause students to become depressed and angry and can affect their desire to achieve in school (Wallerstein & Blakeslee, 1989). In addition to its emotional impact, a divorce also causes inevitable changes in the home routine. For example, after a divorce, children may have two homes instead of one, which can disrupt homework and study patterns, as well as such basic routines as getting dressed and ready for school.

Family mobility also can have a negative effect on schooling. Children of migrant workers who move from region to region face a multitude of problems. Regular attendance in school is limited, and students who might qualify for special services are not in one school long enough to go through the identification process. Another dilemma migrant students face is that if they are needed to help support the family, they must drop out (Prewitt-Diaz et al., 1990).

The National Coalition for the Homeless estimates that 57 percent of children who are homeless do not attend school (Rafferty & Rollins, 1989).

Lack of a permanent place to live is also a risk factor, with increasing numbers of students who are homeless. It is difficult to gauge exactly how many school-age children are homeless, but it is estimated that on any given day, approximately 100,000 children in the United States are homeless (Sherman, 1994). The fastest-growing segment of the homeless population (nearly 40 percent) is families with children (National Coalition for the Homeless, 1999).

Many other situations can cause family instability. Although the educational impact (both short-term and long-term) of family instability varies from student to student, it is important that you, as a teacher, create a classroom atmosphere that is a safe haven from the unpredictable circumstances that affect your students' lives.

## Risks to Health and Safety

Every day, we hear and read about risks to the health and safety of young people at home and at school. Consider the following statistics (Stevens & Price, 1992, p. 18):

- Some 350,000 newborns each year are exposed prenatally to drugs, including alcohol.
- Some 3 million to 4 million children have been exposed to damaging levels of lead.
- The incidence of pediatric infection with human immunodeficiency virus has risen dramatically, affecting some 15,000 to 30,000 children.
- Of the 37,000 babies born each year who weigh less than 3½ pounds and live long enough to leave the hospital, many will face substantial learning problems as a result of prematurity and medical intervention.

Millions of young people face risks that not only inhibit learning, but also can be life threatening or can compromise normal growth and development. Poor nutrition, lack of adequate rest, lack of access to health care, exposure to harmful substances, and exposure to sexually transmitted diseases contribute to students' health problems. Stories about safety issues are equally sobering. We hear about child abuse and neglect, school shootings, and domestic and neighborhood violence. Consider these U.S. statistics from the Children's Defense Fund (2001):

- Over 9 million children are not covered by health insurance.
- Nearly 900,000 preschoolers have elevated levels of lead in their blood.

- The numbers of children who witness some form of family violence are in the millions.
- In 1997, one of three high school students reported being offered an illegal drug while at school.
- Ten children die from gun violence each day.

It is imperative that you, as a classroom teacher, become familiar with your school district's procedures for student health and safety. School districts have policies and procedures for reporting cases of child abuse or neglect, and you must be responsible for knowing them. Certainly, you would not want to accuse a parent or guardian unfairly; nonetheless, failure to report cases of suspected or confirmed abuse or neglect is a crime in some states. Similarly, you need to become familiar with your school's procedures for school safety in the case of an emergency.

National tragedies continue to challenge our community and our teachers in how best to help students cope with safety issues that are beyond most of our experience. Well-publicized shootings at schools have undermined students' feelings of safety. We can only begin to imagine the impact of our national tragedy of September 11, 2001. Organizations such

This student is in a school-based after-school program. What risk factors can before-school and after-school programs address?

as the Council for Exceptional Children (www.cec.sped.org) provide updated resources to general and special education teachers for helping students through crises and trying times.

Children who experience threats to their health, safety, and basic well-being are at risk of having academic and socioemotional problems at school, but appropriate assessment, instruction, and administrative planning can be provided. As Stevens and Price (1992, p. 23) wrote, "Strategies exist that schools can use to ameliorate the effects of the conditions described here and to give these children real opportunities to be successful learners."

## At-Risk Schools

Some students are enrolled in schools that are ill-equipped, overcrowded, and in desperate need of renovation. Some teachers are not prepared to deal with students' individual needs or suffer from burnout. Just as individual students can be at risk of school failure, so can schools be at risk when they do not provide an environment for learning. According to Waxman (1991, p. 5), at-risk schools:

- Alienate students and teachers
- Provide low standards and a low quality of education
- Have lower expectations for some students
- Have high student noncompletion rates for students
- Are unresponsive to students
- Have high truancy and disciplinary problems
- Do not adequately prepare students for the future

At-risk schools also fail to ensure students' freedom from violence. The National School Safety Center reported the following data (Greenbaum, 1989):

- More than 28,000 students are physically attacked in secondary-schools each month.
- Over 5,000 secondary school teachers are physically attacked each month.
- Approximately 8 percent of urban middle- and high-school students skip school at least one day a month because they are afraid to go to school.

As classroom teachers become more involved in the task of restructuring and revitalizing the American educational system, they are shifting their outlook from children who have failed to learn to children we have failed to teach (Johnston & Allington, 1991). You, too, can assume the responsibility of becoming aware of programs available for at-risk students in your district and school and creating a positive, productive learning environment in your own classroom. Professional collaboration should be part of this process.

## Prevalence of Students at Risk

Indicators of prevalence of students at risk are students in need of remediation, retention rates, dropout rates, and indicators of substandard basic skills (literacy rates). Although data about these indicators are often reported in different ways by different states and school systems, we do know that the numbers of students at risk, particularly for minority students, are still far larger than is desirable.

Large numbers of students in the United States are in need of remediation. The most recent National Assessment of Education Progress (http://nces.ed.gov/nationsreportcard/naepdata/) indicated that among the fourth-graders tested, 31 percent tested below a basic level in mathematics and 37 percent tested below a basic level in reading.

Because of the wide range of state and school district policies on student promotion, precise numbers of students who were not promoted are particularly difficult to attain. In fact, the U.S. Department of Education does not routinely collect this information. However, there is some evidence that the numbers of students who are retained is high (Darling-Hammond, 1997). The American Federation of Teachers has estimated that more than half of high school students in urban school districts have been retained at least one grade (Feldman, 1997).

School systems across the country have different systems for counting the number of students who leave school. In some districts, for example, marriage, death, entering college early, going to vocational school, entering the army, or taking a job qualifies as dropping out. Therefore, a specific definition and the precise number of dropouts due to academic failure are difficult to determine. In 1994, the dropout rate was estimated at 11 percent of 18- to 24-year-olds who dropped out of high school (National Center for Educational Statistics, 2000).

According to the National Education Goals Panel (1994), almost half the adults in the United States have substandard basic skills. They read, write, and compute at levels below those regarded as necessary for working in high-performance workplaces. It is estimated that 23 million adults are functionally illiterate (Thornburg et al., 1991). A survey of companies in the United States revealed that three out of four employers report a shortage of qualified workers (National Literacy Summit, 2000).

# Identifying Students at Risk

As a classroom teacher, you will have students who are at risk enrolled in your class. How will you recognize these students? Knapp and Turnbull (1991) argue against holding stereotypic notions about what to assume or expect of students at risk. For example, students who are at risk are not all from low-income families. The common characteristic of students at risk is that they are not achieving in school as they should be. Be aware of the following warning signals:

- *Poor academic performance.* Poor performance on standardized tests, failing grades on tests and assignments, and general difficulty in achieving competency in reading, writing, and mathematics are direct indicators that a student is having difficulty learning.
- *Counterproductive attitudes and behavior.* Some students do not value what they are learning, have a history of failure, and believe that they will be unsuccessful. Students who do not believe in themselves or do not see the purpose in schooling are not motivated to learn or achieve in school. Motivation problems can lead to distractibility, inattentiveness, no participation, and misbehavior.
- *Excessive absenteeism.* Students who are chronically tardy or absent may want to avoid school because they are not successful. For them, school is associated with failure.

# Programs for Students at Risk

Because a wide range of students with many different needs are at risk, a variety of programs and service-delivery models are needed to meet those needs. School districts across the country are developing programs to meet the needs of students at risk. Some programs are financed through federal funds, others by state or local governments or through private businesses and foundations. Programs for students at risk are both school-based and community-based, with most taking the forms of **compensatory education** (instruction designed to compensate for prior lack of educational opportunities), and intervention or prevention programs.

## Compensatory Education

Schools with concentrations of students from low-income and immigrant families qualify for additional federal funding under Title I of the Elementary and Secondary Education Act (ESEA). **Title I** (formerly known as Chapter I), the core of the 1965 Elementary and Secondary Education Act, provides funding for compensatory education for the neediest children in the United States, with funds used for additional teachers, paraprofessionals, and instructional materials for qualified students. The intent of the act is to provide local school systems that enroll large numbers of poor children with resources for intensive instruction in reading, writing, and mathematics. Most federal funds for compensatory education have been allocated to elementary schools.

> Congress allocates over 7 billion dollars a year to Title I of the Elementary and Secondary Education Act. Ninety percent of the school districts in the country receive Title I funds.

An important provision of Title I is the "supplement, not supplant" requirement (Miller, 1991); that is, Title I funds are designed to enhance existing programs, not to replace them. The purpose of the funding is to provide something extra that would not normally be part of students' regular instruction. That something extra can be materials, lower student-to-teacher ratios, or additional time spent in intensive, direct instruction.

Today, implementation of Title I programs emphasizes coordination between Title I specialists and general education teachers of both procedural and instructional matters. If students in your class are assigned to a specialist for remedial services in reading, writing, or mathematics, your collaboration with the specialist will make a big difference for the children you teach.

Compensatory education takes many forms; the most common are pull-out programs and in-class programs. In elementary schools, compensatory education services often are delivered in a resource room. Such services are called **pull-out programs** because children are literally pulled out of their general education classroom for supplemental instruction in basic skills. In middle schools and high schools, students who need special help in reading, writing, or mathematics are typically placed in a "remedial" class during regular school periods. **In-class programs** are housed in the general education classroom and are designed to address the stigma attached to attending remedial classes. In this case, a reading or math specialist collaborates by planning for individual student needs, suggesting instructional adaptations,

> Once a school qualifies for Title I funding, any low-achieving student in that school, regardless of socioeconomic status, is entitled to compensatory education. Identification of children for services within schools is based not on family income, but on academic achievement.

and demonstrating instructional strategies. Guidelines for working with pull-out and in-class programs will be discussed in the instructional guidelines section of this chapter. Other compensatory programs include add-on programs, schoolwide programs, and tracking.

**Add-on Programs**   Services provided in time slots that are typically not allocated to regular instruction are called **add-on programs.** They include before- or after-school programs, year-round schools, and weekend or summer programs. Most public school–sponsored add-on programs are located at the school site. The benefits of add-on programs are that the general education curriculum and routines remain intact and the amount of instructional time is extended.

Bonnie Kohl is an eighth-grade teacher who has been assigned to direct the after-school study hall, "The Homework Club." The goal of the Homework Club is to support students as they complete their homework and develop reading and math skills through recreational reading, games, and computers. When Bonnie agreed to take on this responsibility, she set up a system for regular communication with teachers to learn their systems for assigning homework. She also communicated with parents so that they would understand and support the Homework Club.

An example of a secondary-level add-on program is Upward Bound, a federally funded program that serves at-risk high-school students whose parents have not attended college. Students attend Upward Bound sessions at a sponsoring college or university during the school year, then live on campus during the summer. Their sessions include classes in basic skills (reading, writing, mathematics), study skills, enrichment in content areas, tutoring, and counseling—personal, academic, and career.

**Schoolwide Programs**   When the number of children qualifying for compensatory services is very high, **schoolwide programs** may be the answer. In schools in which more than 75 percent of the students are from low-income families, Title I funding can be used to improve instruction on a schoolwide basis (U.S. Department of Education, 1992). The advantage of schoolwide programs is that children are not singled out for special services.

For example, Tucker Elementary School in Coconut Grove, Florida, has a schoolwide program. Over 90 percent of the students receive free or reduced-price lunch, and for a variety of reasons, the number of students potentially at risk is high. Therefore, the faculty and administration decided to use their Title I funding to reduce class size and to purchase supplies for all classes, giving all classes the benefit of Title I funding.

**Tracking**   The practice of placing students with similar needs together for extended periods of the school day is called **tracking.** Students may be assigned to classes on the basis of achievement test scores. At the middle-school or high-school level, low-achieving students may be placed together in basic or remedial tracks in a number of subject areas. The perceived advantage of tracking is that it better serves students by reducing the range of academic diversity so that low achievers receive remediation and high achievers are not slowed down. The disadvantages of tracking are well documented (see Research Brief).

## research brief

### Negative Effects of Tracking

Research (Oakes, 1985, 1990) has suggested that students placed in low tracks have limited access to information and are likely to be exposed to a limited curriculum. Also, the quality of instruction in low-track classes is generally inferior because teachers spend instructional time on discipline, use methods and materials that do not foster higher-order or critical thinking, and often speak in demeaning ways to students. Students often suffer from lowered self-esteem and become increasingly disinterested in academics and other school-related activities.

Tracking also tends to reinforce social inequality. Low-income and minority students are overrepresented in lower tracks, thus stratifying the educational system by class and race. Placement of students in tracks tends to become permanent. A student labeled as low-achieving is likely to wear that label throughout the school experience.

## Early Intervention Programs

Research on programs for students at risk has indicated that the most fruitful time to provide remediation is during the preprimary and early primary grades (Kennedy, Birman, & Demaline, 1986). The trend is to implement **early intervention programs.** Two early intervention programs, Reading Recovery and Success for All, have received a great deal of national exposure for their success in early prevention of failure in reading. The premise of both programs is that early, intensive intervention, although costly, saves the higher cost of later remediation, retention, and dropouts.

**Reading Recovery** Reading Recovery is an early intervention program based on the work of Marie Clay of New Zealand (Clay, 1985; Pinnell, Fried, & Estice, 1990). The first extensive Reading Recovery program in the United States was launched at Ohio State University, but school districts throughout the country now implement this program (Pinnell, 1990). Reading Recovery involves individual tutoring of low-achieving first-grade students for 30 minutes a day. Students continue with the program until they are reading at a level comparable to average-achieving students in their class or until they have completed a certain number of tutoring sessions. Teachers who have received training in Reading Recovery procedures conduct the tutoring sessions with eight or so students a day. Lessons involve both reading and writing activities. The reading books are storybooks that one could find in the library, but are carefully selected for their natural language and predictable text.

A typical session involves the following activities:

1. child rereading a familiar book
2. teacher analyzing the reading by keeping a running record
3. letter identification activities, if necessary
4. child writing a story, with emphasis on hearing the sounds of words
5. putting together a cut-up story
6. child becoming acquainted with and reading a new book

Reading Recovery is not a packaged program in that very few materials are required—participants need only pencil, paper, and books with good stories that are appropriate for the students' reading level. Reading Recovery's success is based on the teacher (Pinnell, 1990), who commits to intensive teacher development to learn how to conduct ongoing assessment of student needs during the tutoring sessions and how to respond appropriately to those needs.

**Success for All** The Center for Research on Effective Schooling for Disadvantaged Students, housed at Johns Hopkins University, sponsors Success for All (Madden et al., 1991), a program being adopted in schools across the United States. Success for All targets children in grades K–3 and involves a high degree of collaboration between remedial and

Success for All has been considered an effective early reading intervention program for struggling readers. What critical components of this program seem to relate to improved reading outcomes?

general educators and parents. The program includes the following components:

● A family-support team (including a social worker and a parent liaison)
● Reading tutoring for students with particular problems, for as long as necessary
● An innovative curriculum that integrates reading and writing instruction in meaningful contexts
● Regrouping of students across grades for reading instruction

All students in Success for All participate in a 90-minute instructional reading period, during which time additional tutors participate to reduce class size. During reading periods students go from their grade-level classes to a reading group of 10 to 20 students who read at about the same level. For example, a beginning Grade 2 class might include students from first, second, or third grades—all reading at approximately a Grade 2 level. The curriculum, which is consistent in both general education classes and in individual tutoring sessions, includes instruction in phonics, reading comprehension, and listening comprehension. Typical tutoring sessions include reading of familiar stories, drill on letter sounds, reading of stories with controlled vocabulary, and writing activities.

Slavin and his colleagues have adapted the reading and mathematics programs developed for Success for All into a program called Roots and Wings. Roots and Wings adds guidelines for an integrated approach to other content areas, such as science and social studies. Roots and Wings has two objectives.

The first (the *roots*) is to guarantee that every child, regardless of family background or disability, will successfully complete elementary school, achieving the highest standards in basic skills such as reading and writing, as well as in mathematics, science, history, and geography. The program's second objective (the *wings*) is to engage students in activities that enable them to apply everything they learn so that they can see the usefulness and interconnectedness of knowledge (Slavin, Madden, Dolan, & Wasik, 1994).

During a 90-minute integrated learning period (called *WorldLab*), students work in cooperative learning groups to learn about a particular theme in science and social studies topics. A variety of materials (e.g., videos and newspapers) and instructional activities (e.g., role playing, field trips, experiments) are used. The emphasis is on making the learning true to life. For example, one Roots and Wings class studied the Chesapeake Bay, its history, geography, and related scientific issues such as pollution, tides, and wildlife. Then the class visited the bay and drafted letters to legislators about preserving the estuary.

## Full-Service Schools

The conditions that place students at risk are so pervasive that schools alone cannot alleviate or compensate for the problems that interfere with student success. One way in which school districts have tackled this challenge is by establishing full-service schools. A **full-service school** serves as a hub for educational, psychological, physical, financial, social, and health-related services for a community (Dryfoos, 1994). The school houses health centers, social service and employment agencies, and adult education organizations. Mobile health care units and other such temporary services can be brought on site and advertised to the community. Full-service schools can also organize services for basic family needs, including distribution of food and clothing, child care, and transportation. At a single facility, families can have dental work, workshops on parenting skills, financial counseling, and crisis management.

Frequently, low-income families have difficulty finding transportation from one agency to another, have limited access to telephones during work hours, and do not have the luxury of taking a day off from work to take family members to the doctor. Full-service schools provide for the integration and coordination of health, educational, and social services. By making access to these services more convenient for parents, many of the barriers that keep students from learning can be overcome.

Funding for full-service schools is often multifaceted, with support coming from federal, state, and local sources. Businesses, church groups, and private foundations also are frequently involved in funding personnel (such as nurses or social workers), donating equipment, underwriting special events or programs, or to enlisting and training volunteers.

##  Defining Giftedness

Defining **giftedness** is a task that has challenged parents, educators, theoreticians, and researchers for decades (Borland, 1989). Some definitions assume that intelligence is innate and fixed; in other words, you are born with a certain capacity for learning. Other definitions assume that intelligence can be developed and shaped by a nurturing environment. Some definitions are based on the notion that intelligence is a **unidimensional trait**; others assume that intelligence is characterized by **multidimensional traits.**

Traditional definitions of giftedness, which tend to emphasize the stability of intelligence, underlie the practice of gauging student eligibility for gifted programs strictly on scores on an intelligence (IQ) test. For example, a student might need to achieve a cutoff score of 130 on an IQ test such as the Wechsler Intelligence Scale–Revised to be eligible for a school district gifted program. This practice is still common in some areas of the country despite the fact that IQ tests (which emphasize language and logical skills) are inappropriate (culturally and linguistically) for some students and are not designed to identify extraordinary ability in many areas (e.g., art, music, leadership).

Although Congress has approved a definition for talented youth, no single definition is endorsed uniformly in the 50 states (Stephens & Karnes, 2000). Nonetheless, definitions are important because they determine how giftedness is to be measured, what programs will be offered, and ultimately who will receive services. This section presents both federal and alternative definitions of gifted and talented, as well as information about prevalence of gifted and talented students in the United States.

## Federal Definitions of Gifted and Talented

In the early 1970s, under the administration of U.S. Commissioner of Education Sydney Marland, a task force was formed to study educational services for the gifted. The report of the task force, the Marland Report, brought attention to the inadequacies of educational services and to the resentment of such programs among some school personnel (Feldhusen et al., 1989). Perhaps the most significant contribution of the Marland task force was a definition of the gifted that offered a broadened view of who might be available for special services. This definition (Marland, 1972) has been criticized for its lack of specificity and inability to translate easily into practice (especially in respect to identification of students), but its spirit of defining giftedness beyond IQ test performance is important:

> Gifted and Talented children are those identified by professionally qualified persons who by virtue of outstanding abilities, are capable of high performance. These are children who require differentiated educational programs and/or services beyond those normally provided by the regular school program in order to realize their contribution to self and society. Children capable of high performance include those with demonstrated achievement and . . . potential ability in the following areas:
> - general intellectual ability
> - specific academic aptitude
> - creative or productive thinking
> - leadership ability
> - visual or performing arts
> - psychomotor ability

This definition was modified in 1978 (eliminating psychomotor ability) and again in 1988. The 1988 definition is as follows:

> The term "gifted and talented students" means children and youth who give evidence of high performance capability in areas such as intellectual, creative, artistic, or leadership capacity, or in specific academic fields, and who require services or activities not ordinarily provided by the school in order to fully develop such capabilities" (P.L. 100–297, Title IV, Sec. 4103. Definitions).

The 1994 definition was included in a U.S. Department of Education report entitled *National Excellence: A Case for Developing America's Talent.* This definition differs from previous definitions in that it does not used the term "gifted" and recognizes the potential for the presence of talent among children and youth across all cultural and socioeconomic groups.

> Children and youth with outstanding talent perform or show the potential for performing at remarkably high levels of accomplishment when compared with others of their age, experience, or environment.
>
> These children and youth exhibit high performance capability in intellectual, creative and/or artistic areas, possess an unusual leadership capacity, or excel in specific academic fields. They require services or activities not ordinarily provided by the schools.
>
> Outstanding talents are present in children and youth from all cultural groups, across all economic strata, and in all areas of human endeavor (p. 26).

**research brief**

## Definitions of Gifted and Talented: The Story across Our 50 States

Stephens and Karnes (2000) conducted a content analysis of state definitions of gifted and talented. What they found was that a wide array of definitions is in use. At least five states have not adopted definitions and assign that responsibility to local school districts. Most states use some form of the 1978 definition. At the time of their investigation, only one state, Wisconsin, was using the 1994 definition.

## Alternative Definitions of Gifted and Talented

Some definitions of giftedness make a distinction between being *gifted* (i.e., having extraordinary intellectual ability and creativity) and being *talented* (i.e., having exceptional skills and ability in a specific area such as art, music, science, and language) (e.g., Cohn, 1981; Gagne, 1991). The following is an example of such a definition:

> In general, giftedness is characterized by above average intellectual ability, which may be accompanied by superior academic achievement and creative capability. Talented individuals, in contrast, excel in one or more specific areas of endeavor: drama, art, music, leadership, and so on (Lewis & Doorlag, 1995, p. 447).

How are giftedness and talent defined? How does the theory of multiple intelligence overcome the limitations of assessment procedures that identify students who are gifted on the basis of IQ?

More recent, although not uniformly adopted, definitions of giftedness also include a reference to commitment to task (i.e., motivation and task completion). The idea is that gifted behavior is an interaction among ability, creativity, and task commitment (Renzulli & Delcourt, 1986). The following is an example:

> Giftedness refers to cognitive (intellectual) superiority (not necessarily of genius caliber), creativity, and motivation in combination and of sufficient magnitude to set the child apart from the vast majority of age-mates and make it possible for him or her to contribute something of particular value to society and to be identified for special services (Gallagher, 1993).

## Multiple Intelligence

In his book *Frames of Mind* (1983), Howard Gardner proposes the theory of **multiple intelligence.** Gardner suggests that human beings are capable of exhibiting intelligence in seven domains: linguistic, logical–mathematical, spatial, musical, bodily–kinesthetic, interpersonal (i.e., discerning and responding to the needs of others), and intrapersonal. In 1995, Gardner identified an eighth intelligence, the naturalistic, which consists of the "human ability to discriminate among living things (plants and animals) as well as sensitivity to other features of the natural world" (Checkley, 1997). Traditional intelligence tests tap only linguistic and logical–mathematical intelligence. Gardner advocates a revamping of assessment procedures to evaluate all eight areas in ways that are sensitive to culture, age, gender, and social class (Checkley 1997; Gardner & Hatch 1989). Assessment needs to investigate skills that are needed to survive in society, not skills associated with the ability to succeed in a school setting. Gardner explains that the idea of intelligence is steered by the values of the learner's culture (Reiff, 1997). Therefore, the theory of multiple intelligence when applied to learning can be implemented not only by each school individually, but also by teachers who need to plan, teach, and assess students "based upon the learner's individual needs and intelligences" (Reiff, 1997). The main tenet of Gardner's theory to remember when planning educational programs is the responsibility to help all students realize and enhance their potential and strengths by showing children joy and interest in learning while helping them with the mastery of skills and curriculum (Campbell, 1997). Gardner's theory has experienced a great deal of popularity among parents and teachers. The impact of this theory on national policy may emerge in the future (Stephens & Karnes, 2000).

# Characteristics of Students Who Are Gifted and Talented

Consider the following quotation:

> Of all the students you are teaching in a given class, which group do you think will probably learn the least this year? It may surprise you to find that in a class that has a range of abilities (and which class doesn't?), it is the most able, rather than the least able, who will learn less new material than any other group (Winebrenner, 1992, p. 1).

How can this occur?

Think about Henry, a fifth-grade student who knows all the spelling words at the beginning of the week. He gets a grade of 100 percent on the spelling test, but has he learned anything?

Think about Mina, a sixth-grade student who is a voracious reader and is particularly interested in astronomy. She skims the chapter in her general science textbook, quickly gets its gist, and realizes that the content is basic and boring. The class lecture does not go beyond answering the end-of-chapter questions. Mina does not have the opportunity to share what she really knows and "tunes out" during class discussion. She gets a grade of 70 percent on a chapter test because she simply doesn't care about "proving" what she knows.

Think about Caroline, an eighth-grade student who has known all about the eight parts of speech since third grade. Even if she had forgotten the eight parts of speech in third grade, it wouldn't have mattered because they were also taught in fourth, fifth, sixth, and seventh grades. She gets a grade of 100 percent on a grammar unit test, but has she learned anything?

Think about Thaddeus. Thaddeus loves to draw and does so constantly at home and at school. Unfortunately, he would rather draw than do anything else, and his teacher frequently reprimands him for "doodling" rather than completing assignments. The once-a-week art class does not provide Thaddeus with the instruction he needs to develop his talent.

You've got the picture. Frequently, students who are gifted or talented and other high-achieving students already know the material being covered in the general curriculum. Can you imagine spending seven hours a day, five days a week, school year after school year, reviewing information you already know? Can you imagine having genuine artistic talent and not having the opportunity to develop that talent or to share it with others?

There are two common (and conflicting) misconceptions about individuals who are gifted (Hallahan & Kauffman, 1991). One is that gifted individuals are intellectually advanced but physically, socially, and emotionally behind. The other misconception is that gifted individuals are "superhuman" and exceptional in every way. The longitudinal research initiated by Terman starting in the 1920s has made a major contribution to dispelling these misconceptions. The reality is that gifted individuals are human beings with special gifts in certain areas—areas that differ considerably depending on the individual.

As a classroom teacher, you'll need to get beyond these misconceptions and stereotypes to recognize the characteristics of students with extraordinary gifts and talents so that you can help identify students for special services and provide appropriate instruction for gifted students who are members of your class. This section describes the cognitive and affective characteristics of the intellectually gifted and creatively gifted or talented.

## Intellectually Gifted

Students who are **intellectually gifted** are exceptional learners. They tend to excel both in the classroom and on standardized tests, but they are not homogeneous in their thinking strategies. Some are *convergent thinkers* who approach tasks in a sequenced, linear fashion. Others are *divergent thinkers* who employ creativity and innovation to express ideas. Concrete thinkers exhibit a wealth of specific information, whereas abstract thinkers have the ability to understand complex ideas and create mental structures of concepts that may be vague to their understanding (Berger, 1994).

Students who are intellectually gifted usually respond more quickly and appropriately to questions than their peers. Given several alternatives, these students will usually select the best course of action, the preferred outcome, or the most accurate response. They are usually very curious and ask numerous questions about the topic or subject under discussion. During discussions and in their writing, the intellectually gifted demonstrate the ability to make applications and abstractions from their knowledge. They tend to perform in a goal-related manner and can clearly define the final goal or outcome of an activity or project.

There are downsides to these seemingly desirable student behaviors in general education classrooms. The gifted student's insatiable curiosity can interfere with the teacher's lesson, taking the lesson off track and in directions far beyond the other students' level of understanding. Gifted students' high

verbal ability can lead to domination of class discussions. Usually understanding general principles, gifted students may become impatient when the teacher focuses on specific steps or details in a procedure for the benefit of other students in the class. They may become frustrated or bored when others are not able to understand a concept quickly. Intellectually gifted students sometimes focus on their personal educational goals and ignore those set by the teacher, thus causing misperceptions that the child is stubborn or self-centered (Tuttle et al., 1988).

## Creatively Gifted or Talented

**Creatively gifted or talented** students display their unique abilities within the framework of the visual or performing arts. They demonstrate a superior ability to express ideas through various forms of communication (drawing, music, singing, writing, and acting). Significant factors in talent development are early and ongoing parental support, early commitment followed by intense and continuous work in the specific area, opportunities for interaction with a peer group of similar interests and abilities, opportunities for out-of-school learning, and motivation to be superior at a talent (Durden & Tangherlini, 1993).

Students with artistic talent are enthusiastic about expressing themselves and enjoy participating in art activities that allow incorporation of different media. They display unusual and creative solutions to artistic challenges. Students with musical ability display a lifelong interest in music and look for opportunities to listen to and create music. They can hear small differences in musical tones and can remember and reproduce these tones easily and accurately. Students with dramatic talent effectively incorporate gestures, facial expressions, body language, and voice to communicate feelings and to express meaning. They can hold the attention of others when they tell a story or perform. Students who are talented writers are able to make their point clearly and to revise and edit without losing the essence of their ideas (Renzulli & Smith, 1979).

Talented students who don't have an outlet for their gifts can run into problems in the general education class. They can become totally focused on their area of interest and exclude the tasks set forth in the curriculum. Teachers of talented students need to find ways to incorporate these students' interests and talents into the daily routines.

Figure 11.2 provides an overview of characteristics of gifted and talented students. As you can see, some characteristics relate to academic factors, while others refer to social and emotional factors, and some characteristics are positive, whereas others are

═══════════════════ FIGURE 11.2 ═══════════════════

**Characteristics of Gifted and Talented Students**

✔ Advanced vocabulary for chronological age

✔ Outstanding memory; possesses lots of information

✔ Curious; asks endless questions ("why?" "and then what?")

✔ Has many interests, hobbies, and collections

✔ May have a "passionate interest" that has lasted for many years (example: dinosaurs)

✔ Intense; gets totally absorbed in activities and thoughts

✔ Strongly motivated to do things of interest; may be unwilling to work on other activities

✔ Operates on higher levels of thinking than same-age peers; is comfortable with abstract thinking

✔ Perceives subtle cause-and-effect relationships

✔ Prefers complex and challenging tasks to "basic" work

✔ May be able to "track" two or more things simultaneously (example: daydreams and a teacher's words)

✔ Catches on quickly, then resists doing work, or works in a sloppy, careless manner

✔ Comes up with "better ways" for doing things; suggests them to peers, teachers, and other adults

✔ Sensitive to beauty and other people's feelings and emotions

✔ Advanced sense of justice and fairness

✔ Aware of global issues that are uninteresting to many age-level peers

✔ Sophisticated sense of humor; may be "class clown"

*Source:* Excerpted from *Teaching gifted kids in the regular classroom* by Susan Winebrenner. Copyright © 1992. Used with permission from Free Spirit Publishing Inc., Minneapolis, Minn. (800) 735-7323. All rights reserved.

negative. Note that not all gifted or talented students demonstrate every one of these characteristics.

As you might expect, there is a wide range of individual differences in the physical, academic, social, and behavioral traits of students who are gifted.

## The Invisible Gifted

In the late 1970s, Congresswoman Shirley Chisholm brought the issue of underrepresentation of minority students in gifted and talented programs in schools in the United States to the attention of Congress and the general public. Chisholm argued that traditional methods for recognizing the unique gifts and talents of individuals are inappropriate for minority populations. Since that time, others have continued to recognize underidentified groups—or, as Davis and Rimm (1989, p. 277) put it, the **invisible gifted.**

The unfortunate consequence of being among the "invisible" is that such students are not identified for special services and tend to become underachievers. **Underachievers** are individuals with high academic or creative potential but low academic or creative performance. These students are a source of frustration for parents and teachers because they fail to "live up" to their ability. Underachievement can be caused by a number of different factors in the home, school, or community, and we have much to learn from research about these factors (Reis & McCoach, 2000). Students who are underachievers often exhibit low self-esteem, poor work habits, and negative attitudes toward academic tasks.

Who are the invisible gifted? Some of the most frequently cited groups are the following:

● *Minorities.* Students who are members of cultural or linguistic minorities have been underrepresented among programs for the gifted and talented. This underrepresentation is frequently attributed to assessment tools and procedures that are largely insensitive to diverse cultural values and abilities or to tests developed on norming populations that do not include minorities (Ford, 1998; Masten, 1981).

● *Disabled.* Students with physical or learning disabilities are among the invisible gifted. Quite often, parents and teachers attend more to the educational and social implications of students' disabilities than to their unique cognitive and creative gifts.

● *Females.* Although the gap between numbers of girls and boys identified for gifted programs has narrowed over the years, at least two lingering concerns remain. First, girls tend to score lower than boys on mathematical ability assessments. Second, the early achievement of girls who have been identified as gifted appears to diminish during adolescence and beyond.

Another group that is of particular interest to many general education teachers is that of high-achieving students who are not identified for special programs. Frequently, teachers will notice a child with extraordinary talents and abilities who might not meet state or school district criteria to qualify for a special program. It becomes the general education teacher's responsibility to provide such children with the support, encouragement, and stimulation they need to feel productive and successful.

The predicament of how best to identify giftedness among historically marginalized groups continues to perplex school districts throughout the United States. Similarly, research examining how best to provide programs for members of these populations is in its infancy. Therefore, it is imperative that classroom teachers not only keep abreast of current trends and developments, but also continue to recognize the special gifts and talents of all students and find opportunities to strengthen and develop those gifts in a nurturing classroom environment.

What determines the number of individuals in the student population who are identified as academically or creatively exceptional? What groups tend to be underidentified and why?

## Prevalence of Giftedness

The number of individuals in the population of students who are identified as either academically or creatively exceptional depends largely on which definition of giftedness is used to identify students for special services. Perhaps the simplest (and most restrictive) way of determining prevalence is through students' scores on standardized intelligence tests. With this approach, students who score highest on the test (roughly 3–5 percent) are identified for gifted education services (Davis & Rimm, 1989).

The U.S. Department of Education accumulates records of the number of students enrolled in both public and private schools across the nation. These records, which are compiled each year at the National Center for Educational Statistics, include the number of students participating in programs for the gifted and talented. As of August 1995, approximately 6 percent of the public school population and 5 percent of the private school population received special services.

> The number of students receiving services as gifted or talented is second only to one other exceptionality: learning disabilities (Ysseldyke & Algozzine, 1990).

## Identifying Students Who Are Gifted and Talented

Some have argued that multiple measures of giftedness should be used to identify students who are gifted and talented, primarily because intelligence tests are inappropriate for students with cultural and linguistic differences and because such tests cannot gauge such areas as artistic talent and leadership skills. The **talent pool approach** developed by Renzulli and Reis (1991) is a frequently used procedure that represents this more inclusive point of view. Using both test and nontest criteria, 15–20 percent of the school population qualifies for special services. The broadened criteria included in the talent pool approach avoid the danger of overlooking students with exceptional talents and abilities who might not be identified solely through a single intelligence test or teacher nominations.

According to a survey of state educational consultants (Adderholdt-Elliot et al., 1991), most states currently employ multiple measures to identify students who are gifted and talented. These measures can include tests of individual and group academic prowess and creativity, as well as samples of student work. Teachers (past and present), parents, peers, school counselors, and principals may also complete rating scales and checklists about the candidates (Davis & Rimm, 1989). These data sources typically are compiled and reviewed by a screening committee to determine eligibility, after which the results are discussed with the student's parents (Gearheart et al., 1993).

Although general education teachers generally are not responsible for determining a student's eligibility for gifted programs, teachers play an important role in the identification process. What is the role of the general education teacher? Mike Hamasaki, a beginning fourth-grade teacher, learned about his role

> Rear Admiral H. G. Rickover, the first commander of the nuclear submarine *Nautilus* during the Cold War, said that identifying and educating talented youth was in the national interest because the United States needed highly skilled workers to compete with the Soviet Union.

═══════ FIGURE 11.3 ═══════

## Nomination Form for Gifted Education

Student's Name _____ Grade _____

Teacher's Name _____ Date _____

1. In what areas do you feel this student has special talents or abilities?

2. What makes you feel that this student's educational needs are not being met in the general education classroom?

3. Has this student had any problems in your class as a result of high ability? Explain.

4. Describe briefly the student's work habits.

5. Rate the student's academic levels in various school subjects on a 1 to 5 scale (1 = low, 5 = high):

   Language Arts _____

   Math              _____

   Art                _____

   Music           _____

   Social Studies _____

   Science        _____

6. What is the student's most outstanding academic area? If possible, include sample of exceptional work.

7. What are the student's major interests, activities, and hobbies?

8. Describe this student's involvement in any special projects.

9. List any particular traits that you feel differentiate this student from others of the same age.

10. List any additional information about this student that you feel is relevant to potential placement in a gifted program.

---

in the identification process during the first open house of the school year. Mike describes it this way:

> Open house went really well. Parents of all but three of my students showed up. I especially enjoyed circulating around the room and talking with parents as they looked over their kid's work. My only trouble was that two different sets of parents cornered me. In both cases, the parents thought that their children were bored and not challenged enough in my class. They wanted their children tested for giftedness. Their children are bright, but I'm not certain that they're "gifted." At least two other children in my class seem to have more outstanding vocabularies and catch on to new ideas more quickly. I'm not sure what the process is for getting them tested, but I promised the parents that I'd find out.

The next day, Mike met with the school guidance counselor, Maria Plaza, who provided an orientation to the school district's referral process. Mike learned that in his district, nominations could be initiated by teachers or parents. In either case, he would be responsible for completing several checklists, providing exam-

ples of representative work, and attending a school-based referral meeting for each of the nominated students. Maria gave Mike a sample of the nomination form used by their school district (see Figure 11.3). Maria Plaza also gave Mike the following suggestions:

● *Realize that teachers are on the front line.* Parents frequently come to the teacher first. The parents of other children who could possibly qualify for special services might not speak out in their behalf. In such cases, it is the teacher's responsibility to document observations and initiate the referral. In fact, teacher nomination is the most frequent pathway to student referral (Davis & Rimm, 1989).

● *Understand state and school district criteria.* Guidelines for qualification for programs for the gifted and talented differ from place to place. It is important to find out what the guidelines are and then to be constantly on the lookout for students who might meet those guidelines.

● *Document student behavior.* If you think one of your students has the potential to qualify for special services, gather information to document your impressions. Documentation can include samples of student work and anecdotal records of student performance in class. Present the documentation to the person who is responsible at your school for initiating the referral process.

- *Go beyond academic performance.* Your state and school district's definition of giftedness and identification criteria provide structure for observing your students. Nonetheless, in considering students for referral, do not limit yourself to grades and achievement test scores. Traditional measures of performance might not be sensitive to the potential of students who are culturally different, who have not had the experiential and economic advantages of other students, or who are not motivated to complete tasks that seem boring or repetitive. Develop a sensitivity to students who think critically and creatively, have powerful concentration, and have large vocabularies.

- *Listen to parents.* Parents have the opportunity to observe their children in environments other than the classroom. They see their children during play and in community-related activities and witness involvement in academic and creative activities beyond the more restrictive setting of the classroom. The information parents gather about their children is information that might not be readily apparent to the classroom teacher and is

extraordinarily valuable in the referral process. A common myth—that *all* parents think their children are gifted and entitled to special services—is not the case (Feldhusen et al., 1989). Many parents do take action, however, when they believe the school is not meeting their child's educational needs (Feldhusen et al., 1989).

- *Understand the politics.* Identification of students for programs for the gifted and talented is not without controversy. Some argue that identification procedures are elitist and favor teachers' children or the children of parents in a position of power in the community. Some say that identification procedures are biased toward students from minority populations; others contend that minority students are underrepresented. It is important that you understand the politics involved but that you do not let the politics inhibit your judgment about what is fair and appropriate for your students.

Mike's situation is not unusual. Frequently, teachers learn about the referral process only when the need arises and often must network with other professionals to learn what to do and how to do it. As you might expect, the referral process for gifted and talented students varies from state to state and even from district to district within a state. Tips for Teachers 11.1 outlines generic steps in the referral process.

# Tips for Teachers

## 11.1   Referral Process for Gifted and Talented

The referral process for gifted and talented will vary among states and communities, but in general, these are the steps taken to qualify a student for a program.

*Screening:* The process of screening is the initial identification of students who demonstrate unusual ability. Students can be screened using one or more of the following criteria:

- Academic achievement, as indicated by standardized test scores or coursework grades
- Unusual creative output in artistic, literary, scientific, or mathematic endeavors
- Very rapid learning rate or unusually insightful conclusions
- Multiple nominations from teachers or staff who perceive unusual talent
- Parental reports of unusual developmental behavior, such as early reading and verbal precocity or evidence of mechanical aptitude
- Outstanding academic, creative, or leadership abilities—self-reported or reported by peers or adults

*Referral:* School contact person or guidance counselor submits referrals to the district office responsible for exceptional student education. The following items usually are submitted as part of the referral packet:

- Standardized test scores
- Copy of academic transcript
- Referral forms or checklists
- Student questionnaire providing information on nonacademic performance

After the completed referrals are submitted to the district teacher or advisor coordinating the program, the district arranges for psychological evaluation of the student.

*Determining Eligibility:* If district criteria are met, the student is recommended for placement, and an education plan is developed.

*Source:* Jeanne Bergeron, University of Miami. Used with permission.

## Programs for Students Who Are Gifted and Talented

As was discussed earlier, individual states and school districts vary tremendously in their policies toward education of gifted individuals. Similarly, individual states and school districts offer a wide array of service-delivery models for education of these students. Although there are many possible combinations and variations, programs can be classified by approach to the content of instruction and by administrative arrangement (Hallahan & Kauffman, 1991).

### Approaches to Content of Instruction

As you might recall, the earliest procedure for educating gifted students was to accelerate them quickly through the grades. Since those early years, gifted education programs in the United States have varied in their emphasis on acceleration or enrichment. In some cases, programs in general education have elected to incorporate elements of both. Research concerning effective practices with gifted and talented students (Coleman & Gallagher, 1995; Ormrod, 1995) corresponds with the strategies Lawanzer Ellis uses in her general education classroom. Lawanzer's class is an appropriate learning environment for all students, including those who are gifted and talented.

Lawanzer's approach to teaching is as a facilitator of learning, rather than a disseminator of knowledge. She extends learning beyond the textbook and insists on high standards for everyone in her class, including herself. She also realizes that excellence for all students does not necessarily mean that all students are doing the same thing. Her ideas for classroom strategies and adaptations are provided in Tips for Teachers 11.2.

**Acceleration** Gallagher and Gallagher (1994) make a distinction between two types of acceleration. **Student acceleration** is the rapid movement of students through their years of schooling. An example of this type of acceleration is the 16-year-old who has been admitted to medical school. Student acceleration can be accomplished through home schooling, grade skipping, college courses in high school, or early admission to college.

**Content acceleration,** by contrast, is the practice of rapid movement through the curriculum "to speed up the delivery of content, to deliver more content, to examine content in greater depth, or to deal with more complex and higher levels of subject matter" (Feldhusen et al., 1989, p. 106). An example of content acceleration is a fifth-grade student learning introductory algebra in a fifth-grade class. In short, content acceleration is the process of providing students with advanced work beyond their current grade placement or age.

# Tips for Teachers

## 11.2 Classroom Strategies and Adaptations for Gifted Students

Research concerning effective practices with gifted and talented students (Coleman & Gallagher, 1995; Ormrod, 1995; Van Tassel-Baska, 1992) corresponds with the strategies that Lawanzer Ellis uses in her general education classroom. Lawanzer's class is an appropriate learning environment for all students, including those who are gifted and talented. Lawanzer's approach to teaching is as a facilitator of learning, rather than a disseminator of knowledge. She extends learning beyond the textbook and insists on high standards for everyone in her class, including herself. She also realizes that excellence for all students does not necessarily mean all students are doing the same thing.

Several strategies and adaptations are incorporated into the daily activities to ensure that all students maximize their potential. The strategies that Lawanzer uses include:

- An exploratory, interdisciplinary curriculum
- Emphasis on thinking strategies, problem solving, creative solutions, and decision making within the context of specific subject areas
- Open-ended, self-paced assignments
- Students setting their own high, yet realistic, outcomes for assignments that vary in complexity for each student
- Centers where students select topics and work together on projects that require several types or levels of skills
- Interest-group assignments that enable gifted students to work together
- Use of outside resources to help students develop their talents

*Source:* Jeanne Bergeron, University of Miami. Used with permission.

**Enrichment**    The intent of **enrichment** is to provide students with supplementary learning opportunities that help them branch beyond the basic curriculum presented in the general classroom. Enrichment activities offer students the opportunity to explore topics in depth or breadth and can include extended reading, creative research and art projects, community service projects, and field trips. For example, if your class is studying the environment, gifted students might be assigned enrichment activities such as writing poetry about the environment, developing position statements about environmental policies, or planning a service project for cleaning debris from a local river bank. Enrichment can also include material that is of a higher level of complexity (sophistication) or material that is of high interest (novelty) (Gallagher, 1998).

## making a Difference

### Instant Enrichment

During Writer's Workshop in her fourth-grade class, Lawanzer Ellis is giving a whole-class lesson on how to edit. As she explains how writing is marked for deletion, insertion, paragraph indentation, and the like, she writes some symbols and examples on the board. Lawanzer mentions that even authors of books and magazine articles have their work improved through the help of professional editors and that professional editors use similar marks. Robert, an intellectually gifted high achiever who is very interested in creative writing, looks up from the limerick he has been drafting. On his own, he has already practiced applying carets to insert words in his poem. Now he wants to know more about editorial marks and the work of professional editors. Lawanzer acknowledges him before his urgent arm waving and enthusiastic bouncing in place disrupt the lesson.

> **Robert:**  Are the ways you are showing us to edit our work the same as professional editors?
>
> **Lawanzer:**  Professional editors have a much more complex system for marking changes. We're just looking at a few of the most common ways.

Robert points to the symbols on the board.

> **Robert:**  Are those the right ones? How many marks are there? Is there a mark for every kind of change you could think of?
>
> **Lawanzer:**  I don't know.
>
> **Robert:**  Does everyone use the same marks? In that case, it would be like a language. Is it like the periodic table? Everyone in the whole world knows that He stands for helium.

## Administrative Arrangements

School districts throughout the nation have devised a full range of administrative arrangements for the education of the gifted and talented. As a general education teacher, you may be involved in referring students for participation in a variety of special programs, as well as in planning collaboratively with other professionals when the students you teach are placed in gifted programs housed in your school. The general administrative arrangements for programs are resource, self-contained, and inclusion.

**Resource Programs**    In *resource programs*, students are grouped homogeneously with other gifted and talented students for part of their educational program. The most frequently used resource model at the elementary level is the pull-out program, in

## The 60-second **Lesson**

Lawanzer heads for the reference dictionary. Other students are beginning to respond to Robert with groans and stray remarks ("What's a periodic table?" "That's what we need here—helium, for balloons.") Lawanzer knows the dictionary has a page on editors' and proofreaders' marks.

> **Lawanzer:**  Class, let's think about what Robert said just now. If all professional editors everywhere used the same marks for editing, would that be like a language?

Some students answer yes, others no, but small discussions start up in the room. To students answering yes, Lawanzer asks, "Why?" To those answering no, she asks, "Why not?" Meanwhile, she places the dictionary on Robert's desk and speaks quietly to him, one-on-one:

> **Lawanzer:**  I think you'll find the answers to some of your questions in here, Robert. I see you're already using editorial marks in your poetry— good for you. I wonder if you would mind preparing a poster that shows *all* the editorial marks, for students who are interested. We could keep it in the Writing Workshop.

Lawanzer moves back to the front of the class, leaving Robert dazzled with possibilities and therefore temporarily content. She calls on students to answer Robert's question, accepts the first answer suggesting that editorial marks are like a language for editors, and moves on. Amazingly, only a minute has passed, but she has managed to take advantage of an opportunity to provide enrichment for both Robert and his classmates while still accomplishing her instructional goals. She has ideas for following up with Robert, such as helping him set up communication with a professional editor on the Internet.

which students are "pulled out" of the general education program for several hours, usually once or twice per week, for special services. In some elementary schools, pull-out services are provided at the individual school site by a resident teacher of the gifted. In some cases, an itinerant teacher services a number of elementary schools; in other cases, students from several schools are transported to a gifted center for the resource program.

Resource programs at the elementary and secondary level can also include weekend, after-school, and summer programs for gifted and talented students. Workshops, institutes, and individualized mentoring or supervised independent study programs may be sponsored by local or state educational agencies and are frequently centered on a particular theme or academic or artistic area.

**Self-Contained Programs**   *Self-contained programs* are those in which homogeneous groups of gifted and talented students receive all their instruction. In some areas of the country, individual elementary schools place students who have been identified for special services in a self-contained class for gifted students. At the secondary level, gifted students are placed in an honors track and assigned to classes composed primarily of children with exceptional academic abilities. Many large school districts designate specific elementary and secondary schools as centers (or **magnet schools**) for the education of gifted and talented students. Students from throughout the district who are identified as gifted or talented are assigned to the target school, which frequently focuses on a theme (such as performing arts or particular academic subjects). In a few states, gifted and talented high-school students are invited to attend full-time residential programs at sites that are much like college campuses (Kollott, 1991).

**Inclusion Programs**   Many states and school districts have inclusionary models in which children of all achievement levels are educated in heterogeneous general education classrooms. Inclusion programs may be instituted by default (because of a lack of funding for special programs) or by design (out of recognition of the benefits, for all students, of learning in mixed-ability groups). *Inclusion by default* is simply the placement of gifted and talented students in general education classrooms, with no systematic plan for attending to their special needs or for helping teachers with ways to develop expertise in working effectively with these students. *Inclusion by design* represents a comprehensive districtwide or schoolwide effort to meet the needs of gifted and talented students in general education settings. In such cases, general education teachers may receive extra training through professional development workshops. Usually, they are assisted with their planning through collaboration with a gifted education specialist and may co-teach with a gifted education specialist in the general education classroom for all or part of the school day.

One approach to inclusion is called cluster grouping (Winebrenner & Devlin, 1998). With **cluster grouping,** a group of five to eight students qualifying for services as gifted or talented are placed together in a general education classroom. Ideally, the classroom teacher is provided with specific training in how to provide for the needs of these students and is given support from a specialist in gifted education. This arrangement provides precocious students with the opportunity to interact on an ongoing basis with other children who need challenges in learning.

Another approach to inclusionary schooling is the **schoolwide enrichment model,** in which a large portion of the school population is given the opportunity to participate in enrichment activities (Olenckak & Renzulli, 1989; Renzulli & Reis, 1991). School personnel engage in ongoing assessment of student abilities, interests, and needs to identify individual "talent pool" students who would profit by engaging in more advanced independent research and art enrichment activities. This pool includes up to 15 percent more students than would normally be serviced by gifted programs (Renzulli & Reis, 1991). Enrichment activities include research projects, learning study and research skills, individual and small-group problem solving, and communication skills (Renzulli & Reis, 1991). When appropriate, these activities are incorporated into the general education curriculum. As you might expect, staff development is necessary to get the schoolwide enrichment model up and running. The model also requires ongoing attention to program implementation and evaluation by a schoolwide enrichment team.

## ● Instructional Guidelines and Accommodations

This chapter includes descriptions of students with a wide range of academic and social needs. Both students who are at risk of school failure and students who are gifted and talented can easily be ignored in the general education classroom. But how can the general education teacher meet this range of needs? As Feldhusen (1998) wrote, a one-size-fits-all mentality will not work:

> It is undesirable to identify some students as "gifted" and the rest as "ungifted." All students at all ages have relative talent strengths, and schools should help students identify and understand their own special abilities. Those whose

talents are at levels exceptionally higher than those of their peers should have access to instructional resources and activities that are commensurate with their talents (p. 738).

Similarly, students who are potentially at risk for school failure need access to instructional resources and activities. So, once again, how can the general education teacher meet this range of needs? The academic chapters in this textbook provide you with specific suggestions for differentiating instruction in various subject areas. You might also want to follow the following guidelines that Lawanzer Ellis uses in her classroom: communicating high expectations, creating a positive classroom climate, assessing students' prior knowledge, enhancing motivation, using authentic learning tasks, and promoting inquiry and independent learning.

## Communicating High Expectations

Remind yourself that all students are capable learners, and keep your expectations high. For students to be able to accomplish what you expect, you must communicate your expectations clearly, explicitly, and repeatedly. Be especially definite about your expectations in the following areas:

- Classroom rules and routines
- Students' roles and responsibilities
- What they will learn
- Following directions for completing assignments
- Quantity and quality of process and product

You communicate your expectations to students daily through ongoing conversations and lessons. Research has indicated that many teachers have fewer instructional encounters and more disciplinary ones with low-achieving students than with students'

higher-achieving peers. Teachers also have a tendency to talk down to low achievers. These practices must be avoided. You can show students that you respect them by treating them equitably. Tips for Teachers 11.3, based on the work of Good and Brophy (1994), provides hints for avoiding bias in your interactions with low-achieving students.

## Creating a Positive Classroom Climate

Teachers who are successful in working with a wide range of academic and social needs develop a classroom atmosphere that is both compassionate and productive. Three key factors are critical to creating such a climate: caring, order, and coordination.

Communicate that you care about each of your students and want them to be successful. One way to show that you care is to get to know your students' names the first day of class. After that, keep trying to learn as much as possible about each student's interests, strengths, and learning challenges. Some teachers find it helpful to keep a log with a page for each student and to record notes about the student and how best to teach him or her. By identifying their interests, you can engage students in personally meaningful ways. By knowing their strengths, you can give each student the opportunity to be an expert and to share expertise with classmates.

The second factor, order, is important because students cannot learn when the classroom is chaotic and the rules change daily. Whether you prefer an active classroom in which students talk and interact with each other to accomplish tasks or a quiet classroom with students working individually at their desks, you can be a successful teacher. The key point is that you need to let students know routines, boundaries, and expectations.

# Tips for Teachers

## 11.3   Treating Low-Achieving Students Equitably

- Give all students ample time to answer questions.
- Call on low-achieving students as often as you call on other students.
- Avoid constantly calling on other students to correct errors made by lower-achieving students.
- Give all students the opportunity to answer difficult and higher-order questions.
- Give lower-achieving students as informative feedback about their answers as you would other students.

- Accept the ideas of all students and respect their ideas as valuable.
- Interact with low-achieving students on instructional matters as frequently as with other students.
- Avoid differentiating curriculum, materials, and instructional methods to the degree that these accommodations publicly reinforce the idea that students are low-achieving.

An orderly, businesslike classroom environment that focuses on productivity is especially helpful to students at risk. Knapp, Turnbull, & Shields (1990) explain that classroom environments that enable students to learn have the following common characteristics:

- Minimal disruptions
- Pacing of instruction appropriate for the topic and for students
- Consistent classroom routines
- Regular systems for giving feedback to students
- Systematic ways to keep students accountable for their work
- Planning of instructional assignments and tasks appropriate for students' level of learning

To further facilitate order in the classroom, plan for the unexpected. In your weekly planning, include activities for what to do when there is nothing to do. In other words, plan meaningful learning tasks for all students who finish their work early. At the beginning of each week, communicate your plan to your students. Many students who excel academically will finish their work early, and you need to be prepared for this. The activities can be related to what you have planned and can also focus on holidays, birthdays of famous individuals, and historical events. Also, make certain that students always have a library book for personal reading, as well as writing projects in progress that they can work on between other activities.

Sometimes students are reluctant to complete additional activities because they are "just extra work" or because they "don't count for a grade." When assignments are purposeful, meaningful, and challenging, these complaints are likely to diminish. Moreover, teachers whose classrooms are productive workplaces expect students to be actively engaged in learning tasks. Finally, to create a positive classroom climate, you must be prepared to coordinate your own planning with the school's administrative arrangement for meeting the needs of students who are at risk and students who are gifted and talented. As described earlier in this chapter, the administrative arrangements can be quite diverse. You will need to coordinate with administrators and other professionals (e.g., Title I reading and math specialists, gifted education specialists) to make this all happen. Tips for Teachers 11.4 includes suggestions for working with specialists in your school. The most typical administrative arrangements are pull-out and in-class models.

**Pull-Out Models**    The advantage to pull-out models for gifted or remedial students is that students can receive more individual instruction in small-group settings with students with similar needs. Disadvantages develop when a lack of coordination of instruction exists between resource room and general education settings, when transitioning between settings is inefficient, and when pull-out programs interfere with a student's sense of belonging and peer relations.

It is important to communicate with gifted education and remedial reading, writing, and mathematics teachers to know how best to work with the

---

# Tips for Teachers

## 11.4    Working with Reading, Writing, and Mathematics Specialists in Your School

- Initiate contact early in the school year and schedule regular meetings throughout the year to discuss students' needs, plan instruction, and evaluate the program.
- Become familiar with each other's programs (philosophy, curriculum, instructional procedures, and materials).
- Discuss roles and decide on responsibilities. Clarify who will teach what skills, and how. Who will be accountable for grades and reporting to administrators and parents?
- Clarify procedures for placing students with the specialist and for making decisions to terminate student eligibility for special services.

- Discuss ways to support students in Title I classes. How can you reinforce each other's efforts?
- Start an information exchange, sharing with each other teaching tips and ideas that might be appropriate for specific children.
- Plan to attend conferences and professional workshops together, and discuss ways to incorporate new ideas into your program.
- Develop a system for handling irregularities in the schedule. What happens when one teacher is absent? How can you keep each other informed about special events, such as guest speakers and field trips?

students who most need help. Walp and Walmsley (1989) suggest that both procedural and instructional congruence between general education and specialized programs must occur. **Procedural congruence** is needed to improve communication between classroom and specialized teachers, and time must be allocated for this to happen. For example, both teachers must have a common understanding of schedules and procedures.

One of the biggest issues related to elementary pull-out classes is indeed a procedural issue: movement from the general education classroom to the resource room and back. Transition from class to class takes time—not only to physically move from class to class, but also for students to "close up" one activity in one room and "settle into" activity in another room. Over a period of years, this loss of instructional time can add up to staggering numbers. Make certain that your plan includes your ideas for the following procedures:

- Moving from one room to the next
- Communicating student absences to the specialist
- Entering a room and settling into new activities
- Closing up activities
- Consequences for students' not following procedures

**Instructional congruence** at the elementary level is necessary to decide what type of instruction is most appropriate for an individual student. Does the student need extra practice in skills or acceleration activities taught in the general education classroom or a totally different approach? At both elementary and secondary levels, instructional congruence is important to ensure that general education teachers are aware of the student's current level of functioning and how best to make instructional accommodations for the student in the general education setting.

**In-Class Programs**   Because of the problems inherent in pull-out programs and the stigma that middle-school and high-school students often attach to remedial classes, many schools offer in-class programs as an alternative. As the name implies, the primary setting for in-class programs, sometimes called *pull-in or inclusion* programs, is the general education classroom. The classroom teacher and specialist collaborate by planning for individual student needs, suggesting instructional adaptations, and demonstrating instructional strategies. Specialists can offer in-class tutoring that reinforces what the classroom teacher has presented. Specialists also can offer small-group instruction to children with special needs while the general classroom teacher is working with other students.

Lisa Parker is a third-grade teacher in a Title I elementary school. When the school administrator instituted a pull-in program for Title I, some teachers, including Lisa, were resistant to the idea of having another teacher in their class. Classroom teachers felt that they would lose autonomy in planning and instruction, and specialists were concerned about moving from class to class instead of working in their own resource room.

Collaborative planning time and administrative support for this change were in place, however. Lisa realized that the new arrangement would give her the opportunity to learn more about her students and their needs. She and the Title I teacher, Denise Pressman, made a commitment to planning and decided that they were going to make the most of having two adults in the room for the 90-minute reading and language arts period. Denise and Lisa agreed to divide the class into two groups for reading instruction every day for 45 minutes and that Denise would pull in individuals or small groups of students as necessary. Lisa and Denise also planned where in the room the groups would meet and how groups would begin and end (to avoid disruptions). Both teachers became enthusiastic supporters of the pull-in program, as did the students. As one student said, "It's great to have two teachers. You can get more help and the teachers come up with more ideas. Two heads are better than one!"

## Enhancing Motivation

Keeping students motivated and willing to learn can be challenging. You are the one who can provide the structure and strategies to make students willing to be actively involved in learning. But how can you get low-achieving students to focus less on their inability to learn and more on effort? How can you get students to value learning enough to be willing to invest the effort it might take to complete a learning task? How can you keep students with unusual academic or artistic talent motivated to perform at a level consistent with their potential? Tips for Teachers 11.5 provides suggestions for improving motivation.

Keep in mind that different students are likely to become motivated in different ways. Some students might be motivated by a pat on the back or a smile, others might like completing a project and then showing it to classmates, others might be encouraged to learn through group work, still others might become more engaged in hands-on learning. Try to attend to each of your students and note what seems to work best for each one.

Sometimes, rewards such as food, extra time on the computer, or working with a friend may be appropriate. When you do give rewards, reward *improvement*, emphasizing the student's hard work and

# Tips for Teachers

## 11.5    Helping Students Improve Motivation to Learn

- *Create an orderly, safe learning community.* Avoid practices that tend to isolate, stigmatize, or disfavor at-risk students.
- *Set clear purposes for learning.* Let students know their academic mission and the importance of what they are learning.
- *Have high present expectations for academic achievement,* allowing students gradually to develop high expectations for future achievement.
- *Choose tasks and materials at an appropriate level of difficulty* so that students can be successful without too much or too little effort.
- *Encourage and reward effort and improvement,* making students feel special when they are high achievers. Explain how effort contributed to their success.
- *Base assessment of student performance on improvement.*
- *Provide a comfortable atmosphere* in which students are not afraid to take risks or ask for help.

- *Give immediate substantive feedback* to reinforce the idea that completing assignments and participating in class are important.
- *Attribute students' successes and failures to effort and perseverance (or lack thereof) and other intrinsic qualities that students can control.* Teach students to make appropriate attributions in explaining their successes and failures.
- *Develop activities that call for individual effort or cooperation rather than competition.* Enable every student to feel like a winner.
- *Integrate into curriculum and instruction opportunities for students to build self-esteem and a sense of what they can accomplish.*
- *Present lessons and assign learning activities that are fun.* Develop interesting ways for students to apply basic skills instruction.

effort and why the accomplishment is important. In addition, make a clear connection between the reward and the accomplishment, and make certain that the reward is something the student values (McIntyre, 1992). For example, after students learn in math class how to make change, you might decide to award a certificate to take home. When you award the certificate, you might say, "Todd, I know how hard you worked to learn how to make change. You completed six homework assignments and participated in our practice activities with money in class. Making change is an important skill to know—not only as a worker, but also as a customer. You'll know that you're not being shortchanged by a cashier."

Students can be motivated to learn through the type of praise you offer for effort and for a job well done. Brophy (1981) suggests that praise is effective when it is:

- For a specific accomplishment
- Specific about the aspects of the accomplishment that were particularly well done
- Guided to help students appreciate their task-related behavior
- Focused on particularly difficult tasks
- Acknowledged that the student's effort led to the success
- Recognized that this success can lead to success with similar tasks in the future

Another important way to motivate students is to involve them in setting their own learning goals,

which helps them become more independent. For example, a student who is learning multiplication tables might set goals for mastering each table in a certain period of time.

## Using Authentic Learning Tasks

When is learning authentic? **Authentic learning** takes place when students can do the following:

- Construct meaning by connecting new information to what they already know and have experienced
- Recognize the value of what they are learning (beyond grades and success in school)
- Connect what they learn in school to the "real world"

Newmann and Wehlage (1992–1993) identified five standards of instruction for authentic learning: higher-order thinking, depth of knowledge, connectedness to the world beyond the classroom, substantive conversation, and social support for student achievement.

**Higher-Order Thinking**    One common stereotype about students who are low achievers and students at risk is that their thinking is basic and concrete. Most students at risk are able learners, however, and are capable of higher-order thinking. **Higher-order thinking** involves problem solving, decision making, creative thinking, critical thinking, and investigation.

How does this authentic learning activity stimulate higher-order thinking and provide social support for student learning? How will these students' learning connect to the world beyond the classroom?

Instructional methods for at-risk students should not be limited to mindless recitation, skill, and drill. Make certain that students have opportunities to apply skills to solve real-life problems, make decisions, or complete meaningful projects. For example, after a lesson on angles, you might ask the students, "How might our classroom look if there were no right angles?" Students might draw diagrams to demonstrate their answers.

**Depth of Knowledge**   In most school systems, teachers are under pressure to cover content. This pressure impels teachers to increase the pace of instruction and, frequently, to move on to the next topic before all students have understood it or (because they lack depth of knowledge) been able to successfully apply what they have learned to new situations. Rapid pacing can be especially devastating for students at risk. Through planning, you can help students acquire depth of knowledge and still keep a reasonable pace of instruction.

**Connectedness to the World beyond the Classroom**   Learning becomes meaningful when it is connected to reality—to the world beyond the classroom. You can help students make connections by making links between their own worlds and what they are learning and by providing opportunities to expand their worlds through rich examples and direct experiences.

Students come to school with knowledge about their own language,

culture, communities, and customs. Take the time to get to know your students and then design instructional tasks and select examples that are meaningful to them and apply to real-life situations in their own worlds. For example, reading materials that reflect students' interests, experiences, and background help them to realize that their culture and heritage are to be valued.

For secondary students in particular, learning must be relevant to their future. Poor academic performance and dropping out of school can result when students do not see the relevance of what they are learning to their occupational goals (Natriello, McDill, & Pallas, 1990). Two ways to connect the worlds of school and work are to bring in guest speakers from the community who represent various occupations, and to develop apprenticeship programs in local businesses.

Clearly, people remember and learn best what they experience directly. Direct experiences can help students broaden their world and transfer their learning. In 1969, Edgar Dale proposed what is now considered a classic model for providing direct experiences in the classroom. Figure 11.4 presents Dale's **cone of experience,** which classifies experience on a scale from concrete to abstract and from action to observation to representation.

Direct experiences such as some examples in Dale's cone of experience can be difficult to engineer. Fantasy, role-playing, and simulation can help. For example, elementary students can create a pretend grocery store in the classroom to learn about money

How do field trips such as this museum tour enhance the students' education? What other strategies can be used to provide meaningful direct experiences for students?

FIGURE 11.4

**Dale's Cone of Experience**

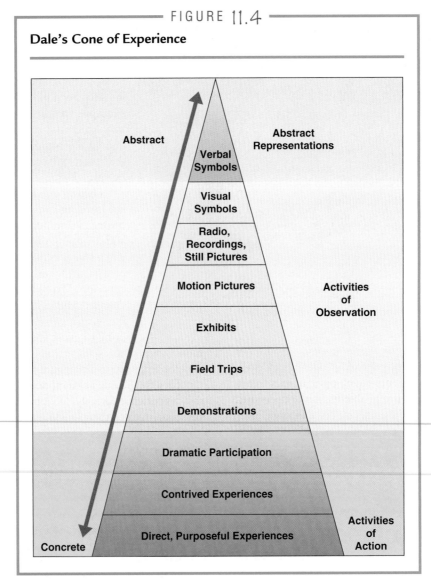

*Source:* Dale, E. (1969). *Audio-visual methods in teaching* (1st ed.). Copyright © 1969. Reprinted with permission of Wadsworth, an imprint of Wadsworth Group, a division of Thomson Learning. Fax (800) 730-2215.

and product labels. High-school students might assume the roles of historical figures deciding what to do at turning points in history. Involvement in contemporary real-life problems also can help build interest in learning. For example, science or social studies classes might become interested in local environmental or social issues.

## Assessing Prior Knowledge

When you begin a new unit or topic, it is important to find out what your students already know and what they need to learn. Finding out what students know will help you plan accommodation and support systems for students who have less prior knowledge and to identify acceleration or enrichment activities for students with more prior knowledge.

Some of your students will have exceptionally large vocabularies, will process a wide information base, and will remember skills and concepts taught in previous grades. When appropriate, pretests or mastery tests can be used to permit students to test out of previously learned material (Treffinger, 1982). Pretests can be administered to the whole class or to volunteers who are willing to take the risk to test out.

One way to assess prior knowledge (a way that takes little preplanning) is "most difficult first" (Winebrenner, 1992). In a list of tasks organized by relative difficulty, identify the most difficult tasks and have students who are willing to take the challenge do them first. Allow students who demonstrate mastery to go on to a self-selected task. Students who are gifted or high achieving frequently get bored

## making a Difference

### Helping Students Make Book Choices

Library visits are prime time for 60-Second Lessons on research skills or for just incidental enrichment of vocabulary and concepts as students browse through the stacks. While students search for books, you have the opportunity to circulate and meet with them individually. Students who are poor or reluctant readers frequently have a tough time choosing books. The following procedure is one way to help students find books:

1. Identify a topic of interest to the student (you may have to do some probing to get an area of interest or

## The 60-second Lesson

genre: "What is your favorite TV show?" "What new skills would you like to learn?" "Where would you like to go for your dream vacation?").

2. Find three or four books on the topic.
3. Read a few lines from each book.
4. Have the student select one of the books.
5. Make a point to follow up to see whether the student has started reading the book, and schedule a "book talk."

---

with undue repetition and practice. "Most difficult first" can help to circumvent this problem.

Renzulli, Smith, and Reis (1982) suggest that general education teachers work cooperatively with teachers in gifted programs to compact the general education curriculum for gifted students. **Curriculum compacting** provides students with the opportunity to demonstrate what they already know about a subject. Teachers can then eliminate content that is repetitive or review for students, replacing it with advanced learning experiences.

> Curriculum compacting strategies include allowing students to identify content they already know or to "test out" of a unit and move on to more advanced or more in-depth materials for that unit.

### Promoting Inquiry and Independent Learning

Many students like—and indeed crave—**independent learning.** Students who learn how to work independently not only gain a great deal of knowledge and personal satisfaction by exploring topics in breadth and depth, but also develop strategies for inquiry and knowledge acquisition that will help them become lifelong learners.

Winebrenner (1992) offered some general procedural tips for teachers and students working on individual activities. Specific planning for independent learning can be tricky and should include behavioral guidelines for students (see Tips for Teachers 11.6). Also worth noting are routines that some general

---

## Tips for Teachers

### 11.6   Working Conditions for Alternative Activities

1. Stay "on task" at all times with the alternative activities you have chosen.
2. Don't interrupt the teacher while he or she is teaching.
3. When you need help, and the teacher is busy, ask someone else who is also working on the alternative activities.
4. If no one else can help you, continue to try the activity yourself until the teacher is available, or move on to another activity until the teacher is free.
5. Use "6-inch voices" (voices that can be heard no more than 6 inches away) for talking to each other about the alternative activities.

6. Never brag about your opportunities to work on the alternative activities.
7. If you must go in and out of the room, do so soundlessly.
8. If you are going to work in another location, stay on task there, and follow the directions of the adult in charge.
9. Don't bother anyone else.
10. Don't call attention to yourself.

*Source:* Excerpted from *Teaching gifted kids in the regular classroom* by Susan Winebrenner. Copyright © 1992. Used with permission from Free Spirit Publishing Inc., Minneapolis, MN; (800) 735-7323. All rights reserved.

FIGURE 11.5

## Self-Management Sheet

Student's Name   Manny Garcia                                        Grade   3

Teacher's Name   Gail Hargrave                                       Date   03/22/96

**Textbook:** Mathematics and You

| Page | Instructions | Complete | Required Correct | If Not |
|------|-------------|----------|------------------|--------|
| 98   | Read Sec. A | Evens 2–22 | 9 | Odds 1–21 |
| 100  | See teacher | Evens 2–16 | 6 | Odds 1–15 |
| 101  | Read Carefully | 10–15 | 4 | 1–9 |

education teachers have found effective for independent learning.

Gail Hargrave, a third-grade teacher, has found that several of her students need to work ahead in mathematics. With the help of a self-management sheet (see Figure 11.5), Gail structures independent activities to promote acceleration through the curriculum. This self-pacing of instruction allows students to move ahead independently but also makes provisions for instructional episodes as well.

Fifth-grade teacher Marina Alvarez likes to provide her students with opportunities for more extensive independent library and scientific research or art projects for independent study. Marina's experience with such projects has taught her that students should be held accountable for a product and should have the opportunity to share their product with an audience (either peers or an audience beyond the classroom). She has also learned that although some students are able to set personal goals and accomplish tasks autonomously, others need more guidance and structure, especially with particularly ambitious projects. Marina uses a project planning sheet (see Figure 11.6) and a research paper checklist (see Figure 11.7) as formats for initiating planning of independent projects.

In thinking about independent assignments, consider the needs of gifted and talented students. There is a great deal of pressure on gifted students to earn good grades for all their work, but the criteria that are used to assign grades to gifted students are often unclear. Often, students are not only given a more rigorous curriculum or extra assignments as part of a gifted program, but also evaluated by a more rigorous grading system. This may cause gifted students to resent their participation in advanced work, and

they may request to be excused from such assignments. They might not see the advantages of working harder on extra assignments for the grades they receive (Hoctor & Kaplan, 1989). Tips for Teachers 11.7 suggests effective grading strategies for gifted students (Winebrenner, 1992).

One suggestion for avoiding these negative feelings is to formally evaluate students on grade-level assignments only. Enrichment activities should not be graded at all; they should serve as an opportunity for students to explore topics of interest and share what they have learned with their classmates (Winebrenner, 1992). If a student wants credit for an enrichment activity, "credit may be earned for staying on task with alternate activities, adhering to the working conditions, persisting with frustrating tasks, or sharing what was learned with the class" (Winebrenner, 1992, p. 112). Another grading strategy for gifted students is to give them an incentive to participate in more challenging tasks; for example, you could tell them that "the lowest grade their work can earn is a B, assuming that they complete the terms of the contract they negotiate with the teacher" (Winebrenner, 1992, p. 112). Teachers can also use alternative or holistic methods of assessment, leading students to develop the ability to evaluate their own work according to a set of predetermined criteria. The teacher can discuss with students the objectives they must meet in an assignment in order to earn a B and those required to earn an A.

Research has shown that some parents of gifted students feel that they had not received adequate information about the standards used to determine their children's grades (Collins & Goldinher, 1984). Whatever grading methods you decide upon, it is important to discuss your rationale for grading with the parents.

—— FIGURE 11.6 ——

## Project Planning Sheet

---

1. Decide on a project theme.                                **Date Done** _____

2. Have the theme approved by your teacher.                  **Date Done** _____

**Theme:** _____

3. Make a list of things you need to do to complete your project. Rank them in the order they should be completed.

   **Will Need Help With:**                          **Who Will Help Me:**



4. Set deadlines for finishing each part of your project. Write the deadline dates on your calendar.

   **Task**                    **Date Due**        **Date Done**          **Person Responsible**



5. Make a list of materials you will need. Estimate how much they will cost.

   **Item**                                        **Cost**



6. Send away for resource materials.

   **Resource Material**                           **Date Requested**     **Date Received**



7. Contact community resources.

   **Community Resource**                          **Date Contacted**     **Result(s)**



8. Visit the library.

   **Purpose of Visit**                            **Date of Visit**



9. Complete your project on schedule.

   **Date Turned In:** _____           **Grade:** _____

*Source:* Excerpted from *School power: Strategies for succeeding in school* by Jeanne Shay Schumm, Ph.D., and Marguerite Radencich, Ph.D. Copyright © 1992. Used with permission from Free Spirit Publishing Inc., Minneapolis, MN; (800) 735-7323. All rights reserved.

FIGURE 11.7

**Research Paper Checklist**

**Assignment:** To write a term paper on _____

**Due Date:** _____

**Requirements:**

My paper will need:                                  It should be:

_____  title page                                 _____  typed

_____  table of contents                          _____  doublespaced

_____  bibliography                               _____  handwritten OK

_____  graphics

What kind of graphics? _____

| Steps | Date Due | Date Done |
|---|---|---|
| _____  1. Choose a topic. | _____ | _____ |
| _____  2. Write a thesis sentence. Have it approved by the teacher. | _____ | _____ |
| _____  3. Do library research. *Sources:* | _____ | _____ |
| _____  4. Contact community resources for information. *Names of resources:* | _____ | _____ |
| _____  5. Write letter to request information from national sources. *Wrote letter to:* | _____ | _____ |
| _____  6. Take notes. *Took notes from these sources:* | _____ | _____ |
| _____  7. Make a writing plan. | _____ | _____ |
| _____  8. Write a rough draft. | _____ | _____ |
| _____  9. Revise and edit rough draft; make corrections. | _____ | _____ |
| _____  10. Write the final draft. | _____ | _____ |
| _____  11. Turn the final draft in on time. | _____ | _____ |

*Source:* Excerpted from *School power: Strategies for succeeding in school* by Jeanne Shay Schumm, Ph.D., and Marguerite Radencich, Ph.D. Copyright © 1992. Used with permission from Free Spirit Publishing Inc., Minneapolis, MN; (800) 735-7323. All rights reserved.

# Tips for Teachers

## 11.7 Grading Strategies for Gifted Students

1. Formally evaluate grade-level assignments but not enrichment activity products. Treat enrichment activities as opportunities to explore personal interests.
2. Give credit for learning behavior associated with an enrichment activity, such as staying on task, adhering to alternative working condition rules, persisting with frustrating tasks, or sharing what was learned with classmates.

3. Provide incentives for undertaking more challenging learning tasks on a contractual basis by offering an automatic high minimum grade if the terms of the contract are met.
4. Use alternative holistic methods of assessment that include student's self-evaluation on the basis of predetermined criteria.

## Teaching Thinking Skills

Throughout the school day, opportunities exist for teaching students processes for thinking. Here's an example. Lawanzer Ellis, the teacher interviewed at the beginning of the chapter, was annoyed that her students were writing on their desks, essentially defacing school property. She presented the problem to the class (including a discussion about school property and how that property was funded through local taxes) and asked them to brainstorm about the situation. The discussion continued, addressing issues related to graffiti and litter on public buildings and highways.

After some deliberation, the class came up with a solution: to put a wide strip of masking tape around the perimeter of their desks and write on the tape, not on the desk itself. The students further refined their idea, deciding to call the strips of tape "reference borders" and to use these borders to record frequently misspelled words and ideas that students wanted to remember. Soon realizing that the reference borders could serve as opportunities to cheat on tests, the students set up class rules for use and misuse of reference borders. The ideas worked. There was a real problem, and the class worked together to solve it.

It is important that you, as a teacher, structure activities that help students get beyond simple memorization of facts or mastery of skills, enabling them to think critically and creatively and helping them identify and solve problems. Thinking skills are important for all students. We live in an information age. All students must learn how to access information, evaluate it, and make decisions about or act upon that information. Students must also have opportunities to create new products, come up with fresh ideas, and synthesize the ideas of others in an innovative way. For students with exceptional talent for higher-level thinking, this aspect of education is vital (Davis & Rimm, 1989).

As Lawanzer's experience indicates, thinking skills can be taught indirectly. Throughout the school day and in all subject areas, you can initiate critical thinking and problem solving related to subject matter or to issues in and beyond the classroom. You can also increase students' awareness of and appreciation for creative people and creative ideas by talking about them and—most important—by involving students in creative activities.

In recent years, emphasis on thinking and problem-solving skills has increased. Although a detailed description of curriculum in this area is beyond the scope of this chapter, Table 11.1 lists the components that are typically included in a thinking skills curriculum.

You can teach these skills directly, using a curriculum specifically designed to focus on creative or critical thinking or problem solving. (For information

Why might this and similar activities engage a student who is gifted? What kinds of instructional strategies and learning activities can be vital to students with exceptional talent for higher-level thinking?

═══════════ TABLE 11.1 ═══════════

**List of Core Thinking Skills**

| Skill | Description |
|---|---|
| Analyzing | Examining the parts of an idea or task, organizing the parts and seeing relationships among the parts |
| Synthesizing | The process of creating a new thought, idea, or product after analysis |
| Evaluating | Judging a thought, idea, or product by subjecting it to a set of predetermined criteria |
| Recalling | Remembering specific words, facts, or other information after sensory input |
| Translating | Transforming information coming in through the senses into one's own words |
| Interpreting | Recognizing and giving meaning to information (thoughts, ideas, concepts, etc.) |
| Extrapolating | Using present or past information, experiences, and so on to predict future or sequential events |
| Applying Information | Using information to accomplish a task, solve a problem, or create additional or new knowledge |
| Classifying | Categorizing and labeling objects, ideas, phenomena, and so on, according to similar characteristics; the ability to differentiate examples from nonexamples |
| Defining | Identifying words, phrases, or expressions that connote the essential nature of a person, thing, and so on |
| Describing | Using words or graphic symbols to express the characteristics of a given thing or experience |
| Identifying the Main Idea | Deciding the central theme or notion presented by or connected with a given experience or story line, speech, or paragraph |
| Drawing Conclusions | Deciding on an appropriate consequence or reasoned judgment based upon prior examination of one or more related propositions taken as premises |
| Identifying | Examining characteristics of an object, idea, or phenomenon, recognizing which label best fits the datum, and so labeling it |
| Justifying | Using facts, principles, theories, and passages to support one's answers or ideas |
| Recalling Details | Remembering specific facts, words, and information |
| Seeing Relationships | Recognizing how one variable or set of variables is related to others |
| Sequencing | Recognizing the chronology of happenings, operations, and so on |
| Explaining | Using words, concepts, or other information to make an idea clear and understandable |
| Summarizing | Covering the main points of an idea in a presentation, article, speech, and so on |
| Imagining | Forming a mental picture of something not presently available to the senses |
| Cause and Effect | Recognizing how one or more variables has a direct or indirect effect upon other variables |
| Inferring | Making logical guesses; concluding from examination of ideas or relationships among things, experiences, and so on |
| Comparing | Identifying similarities between two or more things |
| Contrasting | Identifying differences between two or more things |
| Elaborating | Expanding on an idea by adding details, examples, or relevant information |
| Hypothesizing | A formal prediction based on reference to facts and other information |
| Observing | Noticing the attributes of things |

*Source:* Hannemann, C. (1995). *List of thinking skills.* Unpublished manuscript. Reprinted with permission.

about a number of commercial thinking skills programs, see the Read More about It section of this chapter.) In selecting a commercial program, you might want to consider the following:

- Make certain that you have adequate training for implementing the program.
- Evaluate whether the program is attractive, enjoyable, and appropriate for your students.

- Determine whether the skills taught seem applicable to real-life situations.
- Decide whether the program's content seems worthwhile in light of everything you need to teach during the school year.

## Involving Other Adults

Lawanzer Ellis knows that she is not alone in the classroom. She knows that people in the community are willing to help, but she also knows that she has to be the catalyst—she has to be the one to generate support from parents, volunteers, and community leaders. As Lawanzer puts it, "If you don't ask, you don't get."

**Parent Involvement**   The assumption that parents of students at risk do not care about their children's progress in school and are not capable of making substantive contributions to their children's education is unwarranted. Increasingly, school personnel are not only exploring ways to involve parents in making decisions about their children's education, but also providing parents with resources for promoting learning in the home (e.g., Come & Fredericks, 1995). The process of involving parents can be difficult. Some parents do not have a phone, and many cannot take time away from work to come to school. Some parents might be illiterate or might not know English. And because of cultural differences or lack of personal success as a student, schools and teachers intimidate some parents. Don't assume that parents who don't attend school functions or respond to your notes do not care. Many parents want to help but are not sure what they can do.

Terry Bradford has been particularly effective in involving parents in her classroom. Terry teaches third grade at an inner-city school with many students from low-income families. Many of her students are children of single, teenage mothers. Two of her students live in foster homes, and grandparents are raising three others. Terry describes her parent-involvement program as follows:

Each year I identify three or four parents who are willing to serve on a parent committee. The role of the parent committee is to help me brainstorm about topics for parent workshops, ways of getting information home, and ways of involving parents as volunteers. Parents know their neighbors and know their community much better than I do. They are the experts.

I work with my students to develop a monthly newsletter for parents. The newsletter contains headlines about what we are studying in class. I try to make sure that *every* student's name is mentioned at least once in the newsletter. Also, the newsletter includes a homework and special events calendar for the month. It also includes a list of ways that parents can get involved, developed by the parent committee. Some of the ideas are things that working parents can do at home to help out the class—for example, preparing materials for art projects. This all takes a great deal of work and planning, but it pays off.

**Volunteer Programs**   Another growing area of community–school partnering is the use of volunteers (Pinnell & Fountas, 1997; Schumm & Schumm, 1999; Wasik, 1998). Volunteer tutors can offer students a service that is sometimes difficult for classroom teachers to provide: sustained one-on-one assistance with academics. As Tips for Teachers 11.8 indicates, however, volunteer tutors need training and monitoring. A volunteer might know how to read but not how to teach someone to read.

## Tips for Teachers

### 11.8   Working with Volunteers

- *Decide why you need volunteers.* Possible jobs include clerical tasks, working with individual students, reading aloud to students, and planning and implementing special events.
- *Conduct a volunteer-recruitment campaign.* Begin by contacting your school or district volunteer coordinator, or try a sign-up table at school events and PTA meetings. Also, contact local retirement communities, and check high schools and universities, especially those that require students to complete service learning hours.

- *Train volunteers in their roles and responsibilities.* Include where to find equipment and materials, what school rules to enforce, and how to report to you when they will be absent.
- *Have a system for monitoring volunteers.* Make certain that volunteers feel comfortable with their duties and have no questions or concerns.
- *Have a plan for recognizing and thanking volunteers.* You and your students might plan a party or send a thank-you letter. Be sure to let volunteers know that their time and energy are appreciated.

**Mentoring programs** are volunteer efforts that structure partnerships between a student and an adult who can offer guidance and support. In some mentoring programs, adults from the community provide general guidance for students who need to talk with a positive role model for staying in school or for achieving a successful career. In other programs, students who are going through a personal or academic crisis are paired with someone who has overcome a similar difficulty. In Dade County, Florida, the Committee of 100 is a community group of successful African American males who volunteer to mentor students at risk in the public schools. Members of the committee visit the schools and meet one-on-one with students to listen, talk, and encourage.

Students at risk also benefit from participating in volunteer activities. By helping someone else, students learn responsibility and compassion. Cross-age tutoring, which involves pairing an older student (tutor) with a younger student (learner), is one of the most popular ways to involve students in volunteer activities. The tutor typically receives training in tutoring basics (developing rapport, conducting a tu-

toring session, giving positive feedback) and in tutoring techniques (how to read aloud to a learner, how to respond to the learner's writing, how to help learners solve math problems).

**Business–School Partnerships**    Private corporations are becoming more responsive to the needs of communities through sponsorship of school programs and activities. Business involvement comes in many forms. The Pizza Hut Book-It program, a reading incentive program, and grants from IBM and Apple for computer equipment are examples. On the local level, many businesses are making large commitments to schools through Adopt-A-School programs. In such cases, businesses make financial contributions, organize apprenticeship programs (in which students spend time working at the business), or recruit volunteers for the school from among their personnel.

You might want to apply for a corporate-sponsored grant or to solicit funds for a specific project or piece of equipment for your class. In arranging a business sponsorship, you should first clear your request with your school principal.

## summary

- The conditions that place students at risk vary and include family conditions (such as poverty and instability), risks to health and safety, and at-risk schools.

- A variety of local, state, and federal programs (including Title I) are available to provide funding for educating students at risk.

- Federal compensatory education programs are designed to compensate for the negative effects that poverty and adverse social conditions may have on academic performance.

- The way in which students are identified for special services for the gifted or talented depends largely on the definition used and the measures employed, consistent with the definition.

- Definitions have varied throughout the history of gifted education in the United States, and continue to differ from state to state and even school district to school district.

- Not all students identified as gifted or talented exhibit the same characteristics. A wide range of extraordinary characteristics exists, with marked

individual differences in respect to physical, academic, social, and behavioral traits.

- Multiple intelligence is the theory that human beings are capable of exhibiting intelligence in eight domains: linguistic, logical–mathematic, spatial, musical, bodily–kinesthetic, interpersonal (i.e., discerning and responding to the needs of others), intrapersonal (i.e., having detailed and accurate self-knowledge), and naturalistic (i.e., differentiating between living things and accurate knowledge of the natural world).

- Planning for students who are high achieving, gifted, and talented should include both acceleration activities (i.e., opportunities to advance through the curriculum at an appropriate rate) and enrichment activities (e.g., experiments, independent projects, or field trips).

- As a classroom teacher, your responsibilities toward students who are gifted and talented lie primarily in referral and in providing adequate instruction for such students in the classroom.

- Many of the instructional guidelines and accommodations for students at risk and for gifted and talented students represent quality teaching for all students. Those that are particularly important for students at risk include communicating high expectations, creating a positive classroom climate, enhancing motivation, using authentic learning tasks, assessing prior knowledge, promoting inquiry and independent learning, teaching thinking skills, and involving other adults.

# key terms and concepts

add-on programs
authentic learning
cluster grouping
compensatory education
computer equity
cone of experience
content acceleration
creatively gifted or talented
curriculum compacting
dropouts
early intervention programs
enrichment
full-service school

giftedness
higher-order thinking
independent learning
in-class programs
instructional congruence
intellectually gifted
invisible gifted
magnet schools
mentoring programs
multidimensional traits
multiple causation theory
multiple intelligence
procedural congruence

pull-out programs
remediation
retention
schoolwide enrichment model
schoolwide programs
student acceleration
students at risk
substandard basic skills
talent pool approach
Title I
tracking
underachievers
unidimensional trait

# think and apply

1. Interview Title I teachers involved in pull-out and pull-in programs. Ask them to identify the strengths and weaknesses of the two service-delivery models and explain how the particular model was determined in their situation.

2. After reading about tracking, think about your own position on the subject and draft a position paper providing a rationale for your stance.

3. Interview a teacher of the gifted in your school district. Ask about state and school-district definitions of gifted and talented, identification and assessment procedures, and the predominant service delivery models.

4. You have read about enrichment and acceleration approaches to gifted education. What do you think are the pros and cons of each? Be prepared to discuss the pros and cons with your classmates.

5. For your content area, plan a lesson that focuses on authentic learning.

6. Using the updated version of Dale's cone of experience, identify learning activities in your content area for each segment of the cone.

7. Using the unit planning pyramid form, plan a unit that you are going to teach and include acceleration opportunities for students who have mastered the material previously and students who might need remediation.

8. Using the lesson planning pyramid form, plan a lesson that you are going to teach to provide enrichment opportunities for students who need to expand their understanding of the topic and students who might need remediation.

9. Work with a fellow student to role-play the following situation: An irate parent requests a conference with you. The parent's complaint is that his child is bored and is simply not getting enough academic stimulation in your class. What is your response?

# read more about it

## Students at Risk

1. Anthony, P., & Jacobson, S. L. (1992). *Helping at-risk students: What are the educational and financial costs?* Newbury Park, CA: Corwin Press.

   *Includes descriptions of federal and state programs and policies for students at risk, including students from low-income families, students with limited English proficiency, and Native American students.*

2. Barn, R. D., & Parrett, W. H. (1995). *Hope at last for at-risk youth.* Boston: Allyn & Bacon.

   *Describes school-based programs and strategies that have proven effective for different grade levels.*

3. Dryfoos, J. G. (1998). *Full-service schools: A revolution in health and social services for children, youth, and families.* San Francisco: Jossey-Bass.

   *A comprehensive overview of full-service schools. Includes descriptions of how full-service schools are organized, funded, and staffed.*

4. Harman, M. (1994). *Inspiring active learning: A handbook for teachers.* Alexandria, VA: Association for Supervision and Curriculum Development.

   *A dynamic book that provides specific suggestions for actively involving students in learning. Suggestions that are particularly helpful for students at risk include strategies for raising student motivation, organizing the classroom, producing meaningful learning, and stimulating thinking.*

5. Hiebert, E. H., & Taylor, B. M. (Eds.). (1994). *Getting reading right from the start.* Boston: Allyn & Bacon.

   *Includes descriptions of effective early intervention programs for teaching reading to students at risk, including Reading Recovery, Success for All, and others.*

6. Johnson, L. A. (1993). *My posse don't do homework.* New York: St. Martin's Press.

   *One teacher's success story about working with high-school students at risk of school failure.*

7. Sherman, A. (1994). *Wasting America's future: The Children's Defense Fund report on the costs of child poverty.* Boston: Beacon Press.

   *A brief but powerful summary of the state of poverty in the United States.*

## Gifted and Talented Students

1. Chaffee, J. (2000). *Thinking critically* (6th ed.). Boston: Houghton Mifflin.

   *Describes methods of teaching students to think critically, with particular emphasis on applying problem-solving skills to real-life situations.*

2. Colangelo, N., & Davis, G. A. (1996). *Handbook of gifted education* (2nd ed.). Boston: Allyn & Bacon.

   *In this book, designed primarily as a scholarly handbook, with chapters written by thirty-seven experts in the field of gifted education, the sections on instructional models and practices and on creativity and thinking skills are of particular interest to practitioners.*

3. DeBono, E. (1986). *CoRT thinking teacher's notes.* New York: Pergamon Press.

   *Describes CoRT (Cognitive Research Trust), a system for direct teaching of thinking skills in gifted or general education classrooms. Includes lessons in three areas: basic thinking skills, creative thinking, and critical and interactive thinking.*

4. Gallagher, J. J., & Gallagher, S. A. (1994). *Teaching the gifted child* (4th ed.). Boston: Allyn & Bacon.

   *This comprehensive book provides detailed information about curriculum and instruction for gifted and talented students, including specific suggestions for modifying content in mathematics, science, social studies, language arts, and visual and performing arts.*

5. Gardner, H. (1993). *Frames of mind* (10th ed.). New York: Basic Books.

   *Presentation of Gardner's theory of multiple intelligence. Includes a description of the seven types of intelligence, as well as an introduction to applications of this model.*

6. Hannemann, C. E., & Potter, R. L. (1993). *Brainstorm 1000, 2000, 3000: Cooperative learning case studies in critical thinking.* Austin, TX: Steck-Vaughn.

   *A curriculum for direct teaching of critical thinking skills for middle-school students. Combines teaching of critical thinking with cooperative learning.*

7. Micklus, S. (1986). *OM program handbook.* Glassboro, NJ: OM Association.

   *Describes the Odyssey of the Mind, a creative problem-solving program for students in grades K–12 that emphasizes teamwork and communication skills as students work collaboratively to solve short- and long-term problems.*

8. Parke, B. N. (1989). *Gifted students in regular classrooms.* Boston: Allyn & Bacon.

   *Contains practical suggestions for adjusting the pace and varying the depth of learning, accommodating interests, and modifying the curriculum. Includes suggestions for program planning and classroom management as they pertain to students who are gifted and talented.*

9. Schmitz, C. C., & Galbraith, J. (1985). *Managing the social and emotional needs of the gifted.* Minneapolis, MN: Free Spirit Publishing.

   *A practical guide to coping positively, for teachers and parents of gifted students.*

10. Winebrenner, S. (2000). *Teaching gifted kids in the regular classroom.* Minneapolis, MN: Free Spirit Publishing.

    *This compact book provides numerous practice suggestions for general education teachers. The forms for learning contracts and suggestions for classroom activities are particularly helpful.*

# suggested websites

**www.ciera.org**
This is the website for the Center for the Improvement for Early Reading Achievement, a research group focused on prevention of early reading failure.

**www.reading.org**
The International Reading Association provides publications and conference sessions to assist Title I teachers.

**www.teleport.com/~rkaltwas/tag**
This is the website for the Association for the Gifted (TAG), a division of the Council for Exceptional Children.

**www.aagc.org/index.html**
This is the website for the American Association for Gifted Children at Duke University.

**www.gifted.uconn.edu**
This is the website for the Neag Center for Gifted Education and Talent Development. The Neag Center is a collaborative effort of several universities (including University of Connecticut, Stanford University, and University of Virginia) as well as public and private schools, and other key stakeholders (e.g., parent groups, private consultants, professional organizations).

**www.ri.net/gifted_talented/parents.html**
This website is a clearinghouse for thousands of websites related to gifted education.

**www.eskimo.com/~user/kids.html**
A website for gifted students and their parents that provides general information and resources.

**www.teachergrants.org**
This website provides teachers with suggestions and resources for writing grants to support innovative classroom projects.

# Facilitating Reading

## chapter | outline

## focus | questions

1. What are current trends and issues in reading instruction, particularly for struggling readers, and how might they affect your planning for reading instruction in your classroom?

2. What factors that influence reading might you encounter among the students you teach?

3. What are the components of reading instruction and how would you vary instruction for a beginning and advanced reader?

4. What are principles of effective reading instruction for struggling readers?

5. What guidelines and teaching strategies can you implement for students who have difficulty with phonological awareness, letter–sound correspondence, and the alphabetic principle?

6. What guidelines and teaching strategies can you use to help your students identify words when they are reading?

7. What are some activities you can use to help your students become more fluent readers?

8. What strategies can you teach to help improve students' comprehension before, during, and after they read?

9. How has technology affected reading in our society and the way you teach reading?

# inter view

### Ines Lezcano

Ines Lezcano is a third-grade teacher at Flamingo Elementary School in Miami, Florida. Of the 29 students in her inclusion classroom, eight of these students are originally speakers of languages other than English but have transitioned into speaking, reading, and writing in English. Four are children with learning disabilities (LD) and are in her class full time. Ines works with the ESL teacher, Maria Huerra, who has taught her many ESL strategies that she uses in class. These include a strong focus on teaching vocabulary and demonstrating new concepts and processes. Ines has found that these assist many of the students in her class, including the students with LD. Ines also works with the special education teacher, Joyce Duryea, to plan for the reading and writing instruction of these four students. Joyce, whose responsibilities are to co-teach lessons and to make necessary adaptations for the students with LD, comes to Ines's class each day during the reading and language arts block for 30 minutes.

Ines considers herself to have a balanced approach to teaching reading (defined and described later in this chapter). Her undergraduate training focused on balanced reading instruction and whole language, and her principal has encouraged teachers to implement reading programs in which the students read various types of texts and for various purposes. However, the principal also encourages the teachers to teach the word recognition and comprehension skills that students need to be successful readers. Ines uses the basal reading program to guide her teaching and also ties her teaching to Florida's state language arts standards and the third-grade-level expectations. These grade-level expectations will eventually become the basis for state assessments. In addition to the basal reading materials, she uses trade books, literature text sets, magazines, newspapers, computer-assisted instruction, and the Internet. She encourages the students to read lots of literature from different genres and cultures and to tie their reading to their cultural backgrounds. She regularly reads aloud to the students. Ines talks about ways in which her reading program meets the needs of special learners.

I've been teaching culturally and linguistically diverse students since I began teaching and have always collaborated with the ESL teacher. Maria regularly provides me with lots of new resources and ideas for supporting the students who have transitioned to reading in English. For the last two years, I have also been an inclusion classroom. Even though I received a lot of support from Joyce, I was still concerned about whether or not the academic needs of the students with LD could be met in my classroom. What I've learned is that it can be done, but I've had to rethink my teaching style—especially for reading. For my students who have reading skills that are substantially below those of the other students in my class, I keep on having to think, "How can I meet their needs and still keep things going for everyone else in the classroom?" I've figured out how to do this through multilevel activities, adaptations during whole-group activities, and small-group instruction.

Multilevel activities are just great. They are activities that all of my students can plug into, whatever their skill level in reading. They are activities designed so that everyone can learn and everyone can succeed. My favorite multilevel activity is classwide peer tutoring. During classwide peer tutoring, everyone is reading to a partner. I like it because the students really get involved and learn how to give each other help with their reading. I also teach comprehension strategies such as finding the main idea or making a story map as multilevel activities. I teach the whole class the strategy and then have the students work in groups and practice using text that is appropriate for their reading levels.

When I do give whole-class assignments in reading that I think are going to be hard for the students with reading problems, particularly with recognizing the words, that's when I have to plan for adaptations. For example, sometimes we read a story from the basal reader. I have a listening station set up in my room so that my lowest readers can listen to an audiotape of the story. Volunteer readers make the audiotapes of the stories from the fifth-grade class. It's important to keep in mind how to give kids the support they need to do well.

Most of my students are pretty solid with their word-recognition skills, but I do have a few that need intensive instruction in sight words and phonics. I can hit these areas through multilevel activities such as making words and small-group instruction using a program that teaches them how to decode multisyllabic words. But some kids, including the ones with LD, just need more. Joyce typically meets with these students in small groups or sometimes individually. She sets up a program for each student, and for the students with LD, she uses their IEPs. We're monitoring their progress and really starting to see some growth.

The reading [and] language arts block is my favorite time of the day. It's fun to see my students get excited about reading. It is also rewarding to watch their progress and to see how much more fluent and competent they're becoming as readers. It's a challenge to think about what each one needs, but I'm getting better at observing them and thinking of ways to help them become independent learners. I feel that during reading [and] language arts time I'm giving them the tools they need to be successful learners in all of their subjects.

# introduction

Ines takes a multipronged and balanced approach to meeting the needs of culturally and lingistically diverse students and special learners during reading instruction. She has always collaborated with other teachers, and in her two years as an inclusion teacher, she has learned to value the help and support of Joyce, the special education teacher. She is always on the lookout for strategies, instructional materials, and computer-assisted instruction that can make all students successful learners. Ines has also developed ways to observe students' progress in reading on an ongoing basis and respond to their individual needs. This chapter focuses on what general education teachers can do to provide effective instruction for students who struggle with learning to read.

## Current Trends in Reading and Reading Instruction

The goal of reading instruction is to provide students with the skills, strategies, and knowledge to read fluently and to understand and construct meaning from text for purposes of enjoyment and learning whether reading a book, magazine, sign, pamphlet, e-mail message, or information on the Internet. Reading is considered by many to be the most important area of education, and proficiency in reading is becoming even more critical in our technological society (National Reading Panel, 2000). Skill in reading is a prerequisite for many of the learning activities in content-area classes such as social studies, science, and vocational education and for successful employment and daily living.

In the last decade, growing emphasis has been placed on teaching students to read. Concern was raised in the early 1990s by students' performance on the National Assessment of Educational Progress, on which 40 percent of fourth-graders were reading below the basic level, with performance by culturally and linguistically diverse students and students in poverty of particular concern (Donahue, Voelkl, Campbell, & Mazzeo, 1999). On the basis of these concerns and a growing body of research on beginning reading and teaching beginning reading to struggling readers (e.g., Adams, 1990; Lyon, 1999),

state and national initiatives were enacted to improve the reading performance of students. For example, both California and Texas instituted statewide reading initiatives in the mid-1990s that focused on teaching beginning reading. Emphasis was placed on using research-based practices and highlighted the importance of teaching phonological awareness and the alphabetic principles as important components to early reading instruction. At the national level, the National Research Council established a Committee on the Prevention of Reading Difficulties in Young Children that in 1998 published the report *Preventing Reading Difficulties in Young Children* (Snow et al., 1998). This report also stressed the importance of a balanced approach to teaching early reading, including the important role of phonological awareness and phonics instruction. This was reiterated by a report prepared by the National Reading Panel (a panel charged by Congress to assess the research-based knowledge in teaching reading: *Teaching Children to Read: An Evidence-Based Assessment of the Scientific Research Literature on Reading and Its Implications for Reading Instruction* (National Reading Panel, 2000). This report also supported the critical role that repeated reading plays in the development of reading fluency and the importance of teaching reading comprehension strategies, vocabulary, and text structure.

> Many teachers and researchers recommend a balance in reading programs. The International Reading Association now has a special-interest group called Balanced Reading Instruction.

Whether you become an elementary teacher, become a language arts teacher in middle or high school, or teach a content such as social studies, science, or vocational education, several overarching concepts will be important to you to employ when supporting students in reading.

1. *Reading is a skilled and strategic process in which learning to decode and read words accurately and rapidly is an essential feature.* Reading requires a variety of thinking skills and strategies, including those for recognizing words, sometimes called **decoding** or **word identification.** Reading entails using your attention, perception, memory, and retrieval processes so that you can automatically identify or decode words. You use selective attention and perception coupled with your knowledge of the letter–sound relationships

and context to help you automatically recognize the words. As students become proficient readers, they recognize most words with little effort on their part. But as students are learning to read or when readers encounter unknown words, they use their knowledge of the **alphabetic principle** (how speech relates to print), **phonological awareness** skills such as segmenting and blending sounds and patterns (e.g., -*at*, -*ight*, prefixes, suffixes, syllables), and their decoding strategies (e.g., phonic analysis, structural analysis, context) to assist in decoding. When students have difficulty identifying words, they also have difficulty with **fluency** (reading quickly and smoothly) because so much effort is spent just on figuring out the words. When decoding is fluent, then effort can be focused on comprehension. Therefore, one goal of reading instruction is to teach phonological awareness, the alphabetic principle, decoding, and fluency so that students decode quickly and effortlessly and attention can focus on comprehension.

2. *Reading entails understanding and constructing meaning from text and is dependent on active engagement and interpretation by the reader.* Reading also entails skills and strategies for understanding or constructing meaning from text (**reading comprehension**) and for monitoring understanding (**comprehension monitoring**). Understanding is influenced both by the text and by the readers' prior knowledge (Anderson & Pearson, 1984). When readers read, the author does not simply convey ideas to the readers but stimulates readers to actively engage in such comprehension strategies as *predicting* to make hypotheses about the meaning, *summarizing* to put the major points in the text into their own words, *questioning* to promote and check for understanding, and *clarifying* when concepts are not clear. Effective readers regularly monitor their comprehension to determine whether they understand what they are reading. When they are not sure, they might decide to employ "fix-up" strategies such as rereading or reading on for further clarification, or they might decide not to worry about the confusion, depend-

ing on the purpose for reading. Hence, a second goal of reading instruction is to teach comprehension and comprehension-monitoring strategies.

3. *Reading is a socially mediated language-learning activity.* Because reading is a mode of communication, learning to read, like learning to listen, speak, and write, is socially mediated (Vygotsky, 1978). When students and teachers talk about what they are reading, they share what they already know about the topic and integrate their knowledge with that of the text. When students and teachers talk about the reading process, they share the strategies they use to decode words and construct meaning, sometimes referred to as **instructional conversations** (Tharp et al., 1999). Therefore, a goal of reading instruction is to use a social context in which to engage students in discussions about what they are reading and the reading process.

## Learning Difficulties in the Process of Reading

Because reading is a complex process, there are many areas of potential difficulties. As Figure 12.1 indicates, a variety of interrelated factors influence whether students experience success in learning how to read. Stanovich (1986) refers to this combination of factors as **reciprocal causation**—essentially a domino effect, in which an initial factor leads to a second factor, to a third, and so on. For example, children who are not read to during their preschool years might not have

What happens as these students read? What processes are involved that students with disabilities might find difficult?

FIGURE 12.1

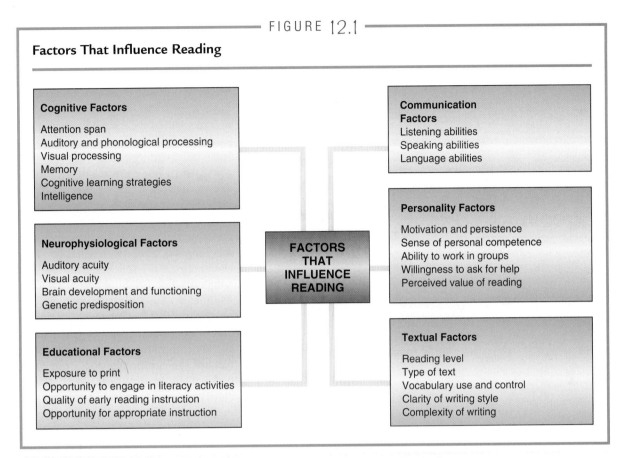

**Factors That Influence Reading**

**Cognitive Factors**

Attention span
Auditory and phonological processing
Visual processing
Memory
Cognitive learning strategies
Intelligence

**Neurophysiological Factors**

Auditory acuity
Visual acuity
Brain development and functioning
Genetic predisposition

**Educational Factors**

Exposure to print
Opportunity to engage in literacy activities
Quality of early reading instruction
Opportunity for appropriate instruction

**FACTORS THAT INFLUENCE READING**

**Communication Factors**
Listening abilities
Speaking abilities
Language abilities

**Personality Factors**

Motivation and persistence
Sense of personal competence
Ability to work in groups
Willingness to ask for help
Perceived value of reading

**Textual Factors**

Reading level
Type of text
Vocabulary use and control
Clarity of writing style
Complexity of writing

*Sources:* Stanovich, 1986; McCormick, 1995; Taylor, Harris, & Pearson, 1988; Johnston & Allington, 1991; Hiebert & Taylor, 1994.

the opportunity to become familiar with books and how print and sounds relate to one another, which may lead to greater challenges in learning how to read, which may lead to limited motivation to read, which may result in the child not choosing to read and thus having less opportunity to practice reading skills and less opportunity to develop new concepts and vocabulary through reading. As a classroom teacher, you must be sensitive to the factors that influence reading and to the individual needs of your students in their attempts to tackle this complex process.

## Components of Reading Instruction

Components of an effective and efficient reading program are depicted in Figure 12.2. Depending on the student's level of development and needs, you will want to emphasize certain components. Yet at the same time, it is important to integrate these components to obtain a balanced approach to teaching reading. For example, Stephanie is a third-grader with a specific reading disability who receives reading instruction in her classroom and also works with the

special education teacher on reading. She reads at a beginning level and is able to recognize only about 30 words. When she comes to a word she does not recognize, she sometimes attempts to sound out the word. However, she has difficulty remembering common letter–sound relationships. She also struggles blending the sounds so she can generate a word that is close enough to the correct word that she can figure it out. Her reading instruction focuses primarily on building phonological awareness, letter–sound relationships, decoding strategies, and fluent word identification. However, her instructional program also includes repeated and partner reading of instructional level **decodable books** (i.e., books that primarily use words that reflect the phonic and word patterns she has already learned) to build fluency. She also listens to and discusses a wide variety of literature and content-area materials with her classmates to support her development of vocabulary and comprehension. It is important that Stephanie pair reading and writing activities so that as she builds reading decoding skills, she works simultaneously on spelling (see Chapter 13). Similarly, as she develops an

FIGURE 12.2

**Components of Reading and Reading Instruction**

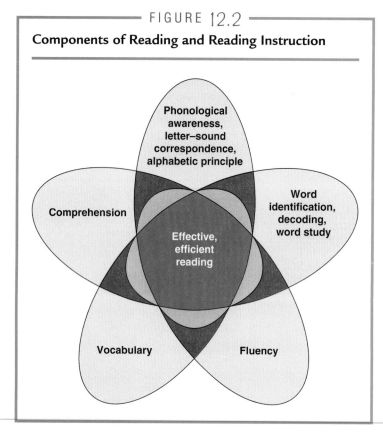

Phonological awareness, letter–sound correspondence, alphabetic principle

Comprehension

Word identification, decoding, word study

Effective, efficient reading

Vocabulary

Fluency

*Source:* Bos, C. S., & Vaughn, S. (2002). *Strategies for teaching students with learning and behavior problems* (5th ed., p. 118). Copyright © 2002 by Allyn & Bacon. Reprinted by permission.

who works with Manuel and a group of six students on building their vocabulary, comprehension, and advanced decoding skills. To build both decoding of multisyllabic words and vocabulary, they have learned to identify and separate prefixes, suffixes, and endings in words using the DISSECT strategy. They also learn the meaning of these affixes and of root words. For example, if the word is "construction," they make a "struct" web with words such as "destruction," "construct," "reconstruction," and "deconstruct." (You will find more ideas for teaching vocabulary in Chapter 15 in the sections on teaching content-area subjects.) For teaching comprehension, Manuel and his classmates have been working with Ms. Gonzalez and the special education teacher to learn to use collaborative strategic reading (CSR). It teaches the comprehension strategies of previewing, questioning, summarizing, clarifying, and comprehension monitoring. The students work in collaborative learning groups, and they have been using social studies content. Next semester, the special education teacher will work with the social studies teacher, Mr. Trent, and Manuel and his classmates will use CSR two to three days a week. Like Stephanie, Manuel's reading program is balanced in that it contains various components of reading depending on his needs: word identification, vocabulary development, and comprehension.

understanding of different types of text and genres (e.g., narratives such as folktales, adventure stories, and mysteries and expositions such as descriptions, comparisons/contrasts, persuasions), it is also important that she explore writing in different genres and different types of texts (see Chapter 13).

Manuel, another student, is an eighth-grader who is reading at approximately the fourth-grade level. He entered school speaking both Spanish and English. He struggled with learning to read in Spanish because of his limited vocabulary knowledge and comprehension skills (e.g., getting the main idea, comprehension monitoring). He began reading in English during third grade and continued to struggle with vocabulary knowledge and comprehension and also had difficulty with decoding in English because its letter–sound relationships are not as regular as those in Spanish. As an eighth-grader, he is taking English/language arts from Ms. Gonzalez,

These students are using newspapers to find words with prefixes and suffixes. How might you use newspapers to teach skills in your classroom?

## Effective Reading Instruction for Struggling Readers

It is important that you, as a classroom teacher, provide effective reading instruction and support for all your students, including those that struggle with reading. Features include the following:

- Establishing an environment to promote reading
- Using appropriate and ongoing assessment so that you know the students' reading level and what skills and strategies your students have mastered and need to develop
- Providing intensive instruction
- Obtaining early intervention when needed

Collaborating with the reading specialist, special education teacher, and grade-level team members will be important for implementing effective instruction.

### Establishing an Environment to Promote Reading

Research has documented the importance of the opportunity to engage in reading and to read with others for building vocabulary and reading skills (Cunningham & Stanovich, 1991; Stanovich & Siegel, 1994). Jane Saunders, a second-grade teacher in a culturally and lingistically diverse school, has a room that reflects a **print-rich environment.** When her second-graders walk into the classroom on the first day of school, they feel right at home. There are curtains on the windows, a basket for writing supplies at the center of each cluster of four student desks, and a reading center with a couch and carpet for informal reading. The writing center has materials for making books. The library center is well stocked with reading materials (e.g., newspapers, magazines, catalogs, brochures) and organized with books color-coded according to genre and reading levels. The word study center has lots of activities and games for making words using difference phonics elements, spelling patterns, and common prefixes and suffixes. The listening station has books on tape that can be used for reading along or for repeated reading to build fluency.

The social environment for reading is also critical. Jane plans times when students can engage in recreational reading. She also models reading by reading aloud to students daily and talking about the books with the students. She uses echo and choral reading so that students have more opportunities to practice their newly learned reading skills. Parents, grandparents, school personnel, and community leaders frequently visit Jane's class to read to students and to listen to students read. Reading is valued, reading is emphasized—reading happens!

### Using Appropriate and Ongoing Assessment

Assessment includes formal and high-stakes assessments that are becoming more prevalent in schools as accountability for learning to read moves to the forefront of educational reform (e.g., the California Reading Initiative, Texas Reading Initiative, Reading Excellence Act). When matched to state standards or benchmarks in reading, these assessments can provide helpful information in determining what reading skills the students have developed. Although they are one source of information, it is important to remember that for struggling readers, these assessments can be particularly difficult and might not provide a good picture of their reading. Furthermore, standardized tests tend to focus on the "product" of reading and ignore salient factors that influence success or failure in literacy development (see Figure 12.1).

Informal reading inventories and curriculum-based measurement are means for monitoring ongoing student progress. Using **informal reading inventories,** students read lists of words and passages that are leveled by grade and retell or answer comprehension questions about the passages they have read. As a teacher, not only can you determine the independent, instructional, and frustration reading levels of the students, you can also gain insight into the decoding and comprehension strategies the students use when reading. Typical criteria used for determining reading level are as follows:

|  | Word Recognition | Comprehension |
|---|---|---|
| **Independent** | 95–100% | 90% and above |
| **Instructional** | 90–95% | 75–90% |
| **Frustration** | Below 90% | Below 75% |

The **independent reading level** is characterized by the students reading on their own without support from others. The **instructional reading level** is the level at which instruction should occur. At this level, students are challenged by the reading and still need some support (e.g., preteaching words the students do not recognize automatically, teaching new vocabulary, making predictions about the story). At the **frustration reading level,** the material is too difficult for the students to read even with assistance (Gunning, 1998). Students can read at their frustration level depending on the purpose and their interest. These guidelines, however, do provide a means for increasing the likelihood that students are reading materials that are appropriate.

## making a **Difference** through **Action Teaching**

## Reading Activities for All Learners

### Phonological Awareness Songs

**Objective:** To teach sound matching, isolation, blending and segmentation.

**Grades:** Kindergarten to third grade.

**Materials:** Song sheets or poster with words to songs.

**Teaching Procedure:**

1. For younger students, the singing and rhyming may occur only as a listening activity.
2. For older students, words and letters could be added using song sheets or posters with words to the songs.

#### Yopp-Ivers Song Sheet

### Sound Matching Activity

(To the tune of "Jimmy Crack Corn and I Don't Care")

| | |
|---|---|
| **Teacher:** | Who has an /m/ word to share with us? |
| | Who has an /m/ word to share with us? |
| | Who has an /m/ word to share with us? |
| | It must start with the /m/ sound. |
| **Child:** | Man is a word that starts with /m/. |
| | Man is a word that starts with /m/. |
| | Man is a word that starts with /m/. |
| | Man starts with the /m/ sound. |

### Sound Isolation Activity

(To the tune of "Old MacDonald Had a Farm")
What's the sound that starts these words:
Turtle, time, and teeth? (wait for a response)
T is the sound that starts these words:
Turtle, time, and teeth.
with a /t/, /t/ here, and a /t/, /t/ there,
Here a /t/, there a /t/, everywhere a /t/, /t/.
T is the sound that starts these words:
Turtle, time, and teeth.
(This can be used with medial and final sounds as well.)

### Blending Activity

(To the tune of "If You're Happy and You Know It, Clap Your Hands")
If you think you know this word, shout it out!
If you think you know this word, shout it out!
If you think you know this word,
Then tell me what you've heard,
If you think you know this word, shout it out!
(Sound out a word slowly such as /m/-/a/-/n/ and have students blend the sounds to make a word.)

### Segmentation Activity

(To the tune of "Twinkle, Twinkle, Little Star")
Listen, listen
To my word
Then tell me all the sounds you heard: cape
(slowly)
/k/ is one sound
/a/ is two
/p/ is last in cape
It's true.
Thanks for listening
To my words
And telling all the sounds you heard!

*Source:* Yopp, H. (1992). Developing phonemic awareness in young children. *The Reading Teacher, 45,* 696–703.

### Sound Magic Game

**Objective:** To improve phonological awareness of beginning, medial, and ending sounds.

**Grades:** Primary.

**Materials:** List of one-syllable words.

**Teaching Procedure:**

1. Decide whether you want to play Sound Magic with the whole class or with small groups of students.
2. Place all participating students in a circle.
3. Begin by introducing a one-syllable word.
4. Explain that you play the game by moving the word around the circle from person to person. To move the word, you make a new word by changing the beginning, middle, or end sound and say the new word out loud. For example, you might start out with the word "sit." The first child might form the new word "hit," the next child "hat," the next child "mat," and so on.
5. If a child can't think of a word in a reasonable period of time, the child can pass.
6. Keep going until there are three passes in a row.
7. Start again with a new word and with the next child.
8. The object of the game is to make new words out of one word and to break the group's record.

### Compound Concentration

**Objective:** To give the students practice in identifying compound words and to illustrate how words may be combined to form compound words.

**Grades:** Intermediate and secondary

**Materials:** 36 index cards (3" × 5") on which the two parts of 18 compound words have been written. Make sure each part can only be joined with one other part.

**Teaching Procedure:** Explain the game. Have the students shuffle the cards and place them face down in six rows with six cards each. Each player takes a turn at turning over two cards. The student then decides whether the two words make a compound word. If they do not, the cards are again turned face down and the next player takes a turn. If the words make a compound word, the player gets the two cards and turns over two more cards. The student continues playing until two cards are turned over that do not make a compound word. The game is over when all the cards are matched. The player with the most cards wins.

**Adaptations:** Students can match synonyms, antonyms, prefixes, suffixes, initial or final consonants, categories, and sight words.

*Source:* Bos, C. S., & Vaughn, S. (1994). *Strategies for teaching students with learning and behavior problems* (3rd ed.). Boston: Allyn & Bacon.

## How Short Can You Make It?

**Objective:** To improve summarizing skills.

**Grades:** Intermediate grades and above.

**Materials:** Any reading material.

**Teaching Procedure:**
1. Decide whether to play this game as a whole class or small group activity.
2. Have students read a sentence or paragraph aloud or silently.
3. Give students time to think how to reduce the sentence or paragraph to its most important ideas, write down their reduction, and make edits as needed.
4. Have students "bid" on how short they can make it. For example, one student might say, "I can reduce it to six words"; another might say, "I can reduce it to four words."
5. The lowest bidder then reads his or her reduction. If the group agrees that it maintains all key ideas, then the lowest bidder gets to conduct the next round of bidding. If not, then necessary revisions are made and the teacher runs the next round of bidding.

## WH-Game

**Objective:** To provide students practice in answering who, what, when, where, why, and how questions.

**Grades:** All grades.

**Materials:** (1) Generic gameboard, spinner or die, and markers. (2) WH cards: cards with "WH-Game" written on one side and one of these written on the other: Who, What, When, Where, Why, How. (3) Sets of story and article cards: copies of short stories and

articles mounted on cards. There should be one set for each player. Select topics of interest for the students' age level.

**Teaching Procedure:** Explain the game to students or have them read the directions. First, the players set up the game. Next, they select a set of story or article cards. All players read the card and place it face down. Each player then takes a turn by throwing the die or spinning and selecting a WH card. The player must make up a question using the WH word and answer it correctly to move his or her marker the indicated number of spaces. If another player questions the validity of a player's question or answer, the players may look at the story or article card. Otherwise, these cards should remain face down during play. After 10 questions have been asked using one Story or Article card, another set is selected. The students read this card, and the game continues. The first player to arrive at the finish wins.

**Adaptations:** Students may also work in pairs, with one person on the team making up the question and the other person answering it.

*Source:* Bos, C. S., & Vaughn, S. (1994). *Strategies for teaching students with learning and behavior problems* (3rd ed.). Boston: Allyn & Bacon.

## Comp Checks

**Objective:** To help students learn to monitor their own comprehension.

**Grades:** All grades.

**Materials:** Paper strips (2" × 8"). Assigned reading.

**Teaching Procedure:**
1. As you prepare a reading assignment, think about the characteristics of the text, your purpose for having students read the assignment, and your goals for learning about students' response to the text.
2. Identify key comprehension monitoring goals. For example, you might want to know during a social studies reading assignment when a student is bored or confused, when a student thinks an idea is important, and when a student encounters a surprising new fact.
3. Brainstorm with students to create a code. For example, Bored = ^, Confused = ?, Important idea = *, Surprising fact = !
4. While students read, have them record page numbers and codes on paper strips.
5. After reading, focus the discussion on what students found to be boring, confusing, new, and surprising.

Curriculum-based measurement (CBM) is another means of measuring students' progress and highlights the close tie between curriculum and student performance. It uses frequent samplings from the curriculum materials to assess the students' academic performance (e.g., Deno, 1985). CBM has been used successfully in general education classrooms to increase word recognition, reading fluency, and reading comprehension (e.g., Fuchs et al., 1994, 2000; Mathes et al., 1998). For example, to assess reading comprehension, students read passages at their instructional level and complete a maze task. For this task, the first sentence is left intact, but thereafter, every seventh word is deleted. Students select from three choices the one semantically correct word that fills in the blank. Tech Talk describes how the computer has aided in the use of CBM, allowing teachers and students to see progress, set goals, and make timely instructional decisions. This type of measurement provides ongoing data for making instructional decisions by considering (a) how performance is affected by changing the instructional level, (b) the rate of learning (as reflected by changes in the slope of the trend line) compared to the goal, and (c) the variability in the consistency of the performance.

## Providing Intensive Instruction

For students with special learning needs in reading, whole-class instruction can be treacherous. Therefore, it is important to find ways to provide instruction that is both appropriate for meeting individual students' needs and intensive enough for progress to occur. Research has demonstrated that a substantial number of students who are identified as initially having difficulty learning to read can profit from intensive small-group instruction (Elbaum et al., 2000; Lou et al., 1996; O'Connor, 2000) or working as pairs in structured peer tutoring formats (Elbaum et al., 2000; Walberg, 1984). Reading instruction is appropriate and intensive when:

- Students have a clear understanding of teacher expectations and the goals of instruction.
- The reader's instructional reading level and needs match the instruction provided.
- Instruction is explicit and direct in the skills and strategies the reader needs to become proficient and more independent.
- Students are grouped appropriately, which includes ability-level grouping.

# Tech Talk

### Computerized Curriculum-Based Measurement

Lynn and Doug Fuchs and their colleagues at Vanderbilt University have been working with classroom teachers for a number of years on developing strategies for improving the academic performance of students with learning and behavior problems in the general education elementary classroom (e.g., Fuchs et al., 1994, 2000; Phillips et al., 1993, 1995). They have utilized a computer-based, curriculum-based measurement system (CBM) (Peabody/Vanderbilt University, 615-343-4782) to provide teachers and students with feedback on student performance. Each week, students work at the computer, taking assessments in reading that take about three to five minutes, depending on the grade level. Every 2 weeks the students and teachers receive computer-generated performance feedback on individual students, and each teacher receives a class report. Students are taught to ask themselves such questions as:

- Are my scores going up?
- Are my boxes getting darker?
- Which skills can I work harder on next time to get darker boxes?

Teacher interviews indicated that when 19 to 20 teachers compared their instruction before participation in the curriculum-based assessment (paired with peer tutoring), they reported that the model not only increased their students' academic performance but also improved students' maintenance of skills and test-taking skills (Phillips et al., 1995).

- Instruction includes frequent opportunities for responding with feedback with ongoing progress monitoring.
- Teachers and peers support the students when necessary.

Teachers frequently ask, "What skills do I teach?" and "How do I decide what students to put in a particular skill group?" Tips for Teachers 12.1 provides some suggestions (Vaughn et al., 2001a).

## Obtaining Early Intervention

Early intervention programs address students' reading difficulties as soon as they become apparent. At Roma McCormick's school, where she is the reading specialist, kindergarteners who are not making adequate progress by the second semester of kindergarten and first-graders are enrolled in the school's literacy support programs. These programs provide supplemental small-group and some one-on-one instruction in which students are grouped by level and needs. The programs emphasize teaching phonological awareness, letter–sound correspondences, decoding skills and word recognition, fluent reading, and vocabulary and oral language development. For grades 2 through 5, Roma asks teachers early in the school year to identify any students who are having difficulty with grade-level reading material. Roma confers with teachers to decide how to meet the needs of individual students in the general education classroom and in supplemental programs if appropriate.

## Strategies for Teaching Phonological Awareness, Letter–Sound Correspondence, and the Alphabetic Principle

Ms. Ramirez, the kindergarten teacher, partners with Ms. Harry, special education teacher, to assist the students who are having the most difficulty learning letter–sound correspondence, separating words by syllables, and blending and segmenting phonemes. With these kindergarteners, the teachers work on reinforcing with each letter–sound, for example "b," *ball*, /b/, and having the students participate in phonological awareness games and activities in which they count the number of syllables in words, count the sounds in simple words (e.g., *me* and *sit*), and create word families (e.g., *-it, sit, mit, bit, fit, hit*). At first, they had the students only listen when working on these phonological awareness activities. Now they are using letters to demonstrate how the syllables and sounds are related to print.

Ms. Harry also works with a small group of six students in Ms. Wenske's first grade who are having difficulty learning to read. Ms. Harry engages these students in such activities as listening and clapping the number of sounds in words to help them segment the sounds; saying each sound in a word slowly and then "saying them fast" to practice blending, and when spelling having them say the word, then say the sounds, then say the first sound and write it, then say the first two sounds and write the second sound, and so on until they have spelled the word.

---

# Tips for Teachers

## 12.1    Flexible Grouping Strategies for Reading Instruction

- At the beginning of the school year, decide on the critical skills and strategies you want all students to learn by the end of the school year. Make a checklist of these skills, and place the list in each student's assessment portfolio. Keep a master list in your planbook or gradebook.
- Base skills and strategies on your textbook series, school district curricular guides, and your own goals for reading and writing instruction.
- Schedule a regular time to meet with skill groups. Skill lessons can be whole-class, small-group, or for individual students, depending on student needs.

- Keep the membership of skill groups flexible. You may have a permanent group of low achievers that you meet with regularly, but include them as members of other groups as well.
- Do not limit skill and strategy lessons to low-achieving students only. Average and high-achieving students also need this instruction.
- Focus on a few skills or strategies each week, allowing some time in your schedule to teach skill lessons based on student requests and needs that arise from your daily observation of student work.
- Keep a record of the skill lessons you teach and which students participate in each lesson.

These teachers are directly teaching phonological awareness, letter–sound relationships, and the alphabetic principle, all of which are associated with successful reading and spelling (Adams, 1990; Blachman, 2000; National Reading Panel, 2000; Snow et al., 1998). Blending and segmenting individual phonemes have been one of the most consistent predictors of difficulties in learning to read, and children who struggle with these skills are likely to be among the poorest readers and most likely to be identified as having a learning/reading disability (e.g., Blachman, 1997; Foorman et al., 1998; Torgesen & Burgess, 1998; Velluntino et al., 1996). Hence, the first- and second-grade teachers are working with students to help prevent or lessen later reading disabilities.

> Children who develop phonological awareness early in life begin to read earlier, read more books, and develop a larger vocabulary and store of knowledge than other children. Stanovich (1986) calls this the "Matthew Effect" in reading, based on Matthew 25:29 (commonly known as the Bible's "rich get richer" passage).

## Teaching Phonological Awareness

If phonological awareness is so important, how does it develop and how can it be taught? Phonological awareness is knowing and demonstrating that spoken language can be broken down into smaller units (words, syllables, phonemes), which can be manipulated within an alphabetic system or orthography. Phonological awareness includes the following skills:

- **Rhyming** (identifying similarities and differences in word endings)
- **Alliteration** (identifying similarities and differences in word beginnings)
- **Blending** (putting syllables or sounds together to form words)
- **Segmenting** (dividing words into syllables and sounds)
- **Manipulating** (deleting, adding, and substituting syllables and sounds)

In general, children's awareness of the phonological structure of the English language develops from larger units of sounds (e.g., words in a sentence, syllables in a word) to smaller units (e.g., **phonemes**, or individual speech sounds in a word). Table 12.1 presents a continuum for the development of phonological awareness with examples. Skills such as rhyming and alliteration develop earlier, whereas skills such as blending and segmenting and sound manipulation

— TABLE 12.1 —

### Phonological Awareness Continuum

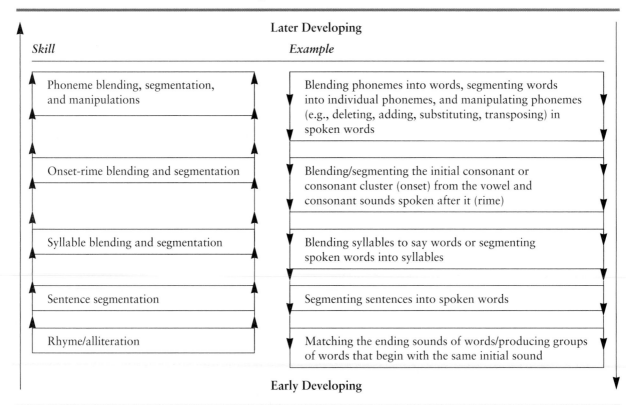

| Skill | Example |
|---|---|
| **Later Developing** | |
| Phoneme blending, segmentation, and manipulations | Blending phonemes into words, segmenting words into individual phonemes, and manipulating phonemes (e.g., deleting, adding, substituting, transposing) in spoken words |
| Onset-rime blending and segmentation | Blending/segmenting the initial consonant or consonant cluster (onset) from the vowel and consonant sounds spoken after it (rime) |
| Syllable blending and segmentation | Blending syllables to say words or segmenting spoken words into syllables |
| Sentence segmentation | Segmenting sentences into spoken words |
| Rhyme/alliteration | Matching the ending sounds of words/producing groups of words that begin with the same initial sound |
| **Early Developing** | |

*Source:* Adapted from *First Grade Teacher Reading Academy* (Austin: University of Texas, Texas Center for Reading and Language Arts, 2000).

develop later. Activities that focus on individual sounds in words are **phonemic awareness**. *It is these more advanced skills of phoneme blending, segmenting, and manipulation that are most related to success in learning to read* (Stanovich, 1992; Torgesen, Wagner, & Rashotte, 1994).

To teach rhyming and alliteration, use books that are based on rhyme and alliteration, such as *There's a Wocket in My Pocket* (Seuss, 1974) and *Each Peach Pear Plum* (Ahlberg & Ahlberg, 1979). You can have students create, say, and listen/look for rhymes, alliterations, and "silly sayings." To build blending and segmenting skills, you might want to use the Elkonin procedure (Elkonin, 1973). As a phonological task, students listen to a word and push a marker, block, or other small object into a printed square for each sound they hear (see the first row in Figure 12.3). As students gain knowledge about the letter–sound relationships, students can push or write letters in the boxes (see the second row in Figure 12.3). This is one way in which an oral language activity can be made more visible and kinesthetic. Other ways are tapping one finger to the thumb for each sound and watching your mouth in a mirror, feeling the facial movements by placing your fingers on your cheeks, and concentrating on how your mouth changes when different sounds are made.

What are the characteristics of a good phonics program? How can phonics instruction be enhanced through strategies for teaching phonemic awareness?

General guidelines for teaching phonological awareness activities include the following (Bos and Vaughn, 2002):

- Consider the students' levels of development and tasks that need to be mastered.
- Model each activity.
- Use manipulative and movement to make auditory/oral tasks more visible.
- Move from less to more difficult tasks considering level of development (syllables, onset-rimes, phonemes), phoneme position (initial, final, medial), number of sounds in a word (*cat* is easier than *split*), and phonological features of the words (e.g., continuing consonants such as /m/, /n/, /s/ are easier than stops or clipped sounds such as /t/, /b/, /d/).
- Provide feedback and opportunities for practice and review.
- Make learning fun!

A number of programs and resources are available for teaching phonological awareness and the alphabetic principle (see Tips for Teachers 12.2 for a selected list), and a number of sources provide lists of children's books focused on different aspects of phonological awareness (Coldwell, 1997; Optiz, 1998; Perfect, 2000; Yopp, 1992).

## Teaching Letter–Sound Correspondence and the Alphabetic Principle

As students learn letter–sound correspondences and to blend, segment, and manipulate sounds, it is important that they associate speech with

---

=== FIGURE 12.3 ===

**Using the Elkonin Procedure to Support Phonemic Awareness and the Alphabetic Principle**

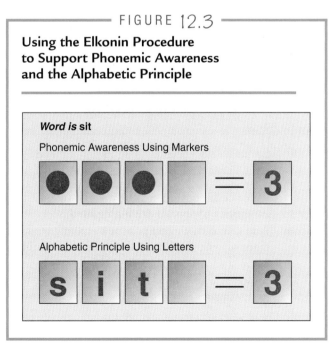

*Source:* Bos, C. S., & Vaughn, S. (2002). *Strategies for teaching students with learning and behavior problems* (5th ed., p. 121). Copyright © 2002 by Allyn & Bacon. Reprinted by permission.

# Tips for Teachers

## 12.2 Selected Programs and Resources for Teaching Phonological Awareness

*Ladders to Literacy: A Kindergarten Activity Book* by O'Connor, R., Notari-Syverson, A., and Vadasy, P. F., 1998, Baltimore, MD: Paul H. Brookes.

*Phonemic Awareness in Young Children: A Classroom Curriculum* by Adams, M. J., Foorman, B. G., Lundberg, I., and Beeler, T., 1998, Baltimore, MD: Paul H. Brookes.

*Phonological Awareness and Primary Phonics* by Gunning, T. G., 2000, Boston: Allyn & Bacon.

*Phonological Awareness Training for Reading* by Torgesen, J. K., and Bryant, B. R., 1994, Austin, TX: PRO-ED.

*Road to the Code: A Program of Early Literacy Activities to Develop Phonological Awareness* by Blachman, B. A., Ball, E. W., Black, R., and Tangel, D. M., 2000, Baltimore, MD: Paul H. Brookes.

*The Phonological Awareness Book* by Robertson, C., and Salter, W., 1995, East Moline, IL: LinguiSystems.

*Sounds Abound* by Catts, H., and Olsen, T., 1993, East Moline: IL: LinguiSystems.

*The Lindamood Phoneme Sequencing Program for Reading, Spelling, and Speech* by Lindamood, P. A., and Lindamood, P., 1998, Austin, TX: PRO-ED.

*The Sounds Abound Program: Teaching Phonological Awareness in the Classroom* (formerly *Sound Start*) by Lechner, O., and Podhajski, B., 1998, East Moline, IL: LinguiSystems.

*A Basic Guide to Understanding, Assessing, and Teaching Phonological Awareness* by Torgesen, J. K., and Mathes, P. G., 2000, Austin, TX: PRO-ED.

*Source:* Bos, C. S., & Vaughn, S. (2002). *Strategies for teaching students with learning and behavior problems* (5th ed., p. 123). Boston: Allyn & Bacon.

---

print (Chard & Dickson, 1999; Smith, 1998; Torgesen, 1999), thereby teaching the alphabetic principle (understanding that the sequence of letters in written words represents the sequence of sounds in spoken words). A number of programs have been developed to teach letter–sound correspondences and decoding to struggling readers using systematic approaches that introduce the letter–sound relationships and how to decode words, such as *Alphabet Phonics* (Cox, 1992), *Corrective Reading* (Engelmann et al., 1999), *Lindamood Phoneme Sequencing Program for Reading, Spelling, and Speech* (Lindamood & Lindamood, 1998), *Phonic Remedial Reading Lessons* (Kirk et al., 1985), *Wilson Reading System* (Wilson, 1996), and *Word Detectives: Benchmark Word Identification Program for Beginning Readers* (Gaskins, 1996). These programs have similar features of instruction that include the following:

● Teach a core set of frequently used consonants and short vowel sounds that represent clear sounds and nonreversible letter forms (e.g., /a/, /i/, /d/, /f/, /g/, /h/, /l/, /n/, /p/, /s/, /t/).

● Begin immediately to blend and segment the sounds to read and spell the words and read the words in **decodable text** (i.e., text in which most of the words are composed of letter–sound correspondences that have been taught).

● Separate the introduction of letter–sounds with similar auditory or visual features (e.g., /e/ and /i/, /m/ and /n/, /b/ and /d/).

● Use a consistent key word to assist students in hearing and remembering the sound (e.g., *b, ball,* /b/).

● Teach that some letters can represent more than one sound. For each letter, first teach the most frequent sound and then teach other sounds (e.g., /c/ in *cat*, then /s/ in *city*; /g/ in *gate*, then /j/ in *gem*).

● Teach that different letters can make the same sound, such as the /s/ in *sit* and *city*.

● Teach that sounds can be represented by a single letter or a combination of letters (e.g., /a/ in *make* and *rain*, /sh/ in *fish*) and may be represented in boxes with a dotted line.

| f | i | s | h |
|---|---|---|---|

● Color-code consonant and vowel so that the two categories of sounds are highlighted.

● Add a kinesthetic component by having students trace or write the letter as they say the sound.

● Have students use mirrors and feel their mouths to see and feel how sounds are different (Bos and Vaughn, 2002).

Teaching letter–sound correspondences is a key element in understanding the alphabetic principle and learning to decode and spell unknown words. However, programs that focus too much on teaching letter–sound relationships and not enough on putting them to use are likely to be ineffective. Through modeling and discussion, students need to understand that the purpose for learning these relationships is to apply them to their reading and writing activities (National Reading Panel, 2000).

 ## Strategies for Teaching Word Identification

Reading words quickly and easily is one key to successful reading (Ehri, 1998; Gough, 1996). Successful readers identify words fluently and, if a word is unknown, have effective decoding strategies to decipher the word. Therefore, it is important that students develop a sight word vocabulary (i.e., the words that students recognize without conscious effort) and decoding strategies to support them when they encounter an unknown word.

## Teaching Sight Words

A **sight word** is a word for which the student can recognize the pronunciation and meaning automatically. In reading words by sight, the words are processed quickly and accessed from information in memory. LaBerge and Samuels (1974) argue that it is important for students to develop **automaticity** (quick word recognition) so that they can focus on comprehension. Some students have difficulty with automatic recognition of words in print, particularly with **high-frequency words**—words such as *the, you, and,* and *was*—that serve as the basic glue of our language. According to Fry, Fountoukidis, and Polk (1985), about 50 percent of written language contains 100 high-frequency words, such as those presented in Table 12.2.

You can select words to teach on the basis of the materials the students are reading, words the students are having difficulty learning, key vocabulary from content-area textbooks, or high-frequency words from graded word lists. Consider

─ TABLE 12.2 ─

### The Instant (Sight) Words

| The First 100 Words (approximately first grade) | | | | The Second 100 Words (approximately second grade) | | | |
|---|---|---|---|---|---|---|---|
| *Group 1a* | *Group 1b* | *Group 1c* | *Group 1d* | *Group 2a* | *Group 2b* | *Group 2c* | *Group 2d* |
| the | he | go | who | saw | big | may | ran |
| a | I | see | an | home | where | let | five |
| is | they | then | there | soon | am | use | read |
| you | one | us | she | stand | ball | these | over |
| to | good | no | new | box | morning | right | such |
| and | me | him | said | upon | live | present | way |
| we | about | by | did | first | four | tell | too |
| that | had | was | boy | came | last | next | shall |
| in | if | come | three | girl | color | please | own |
| not | some | get | down | house | away | leave | most |
| for | up | or | work | find | red | hand | sure |
| at | her | two | put | because | friend | more | thing |
| with | do | man | were | made | pretty | why | only |
| it | when | little | before | could | eat | better | near |
| on | so | has | just | book | want | under | than |
| can | my | them | long | look | year | while | open |
| will | very | how | here | mother | white | should | kind |
| are | all | like | other | run | got | never | must |
| of | would | our | old | school | play | each | high |
| this | any | what | take | people | found | best | far |
| your | been | know | cat | night | left | another | both |
| as | out | make | again | into | men | seem | end |
| but | there | which | give | say | bring | tree | also |
| be | from | much | after | think | wish | name | until |
| have | day | his | many | back | black | dear | call |

*Source:* Reprinted by permission of Edward Fry, author.

two factors: usefulness (words that occur most frequently) and ease of learning (Gunning, 2000). The words *the, of, and, a, to, in, is, you, that,* and *it* account for more than 20 percent of the words that students will encounter. Nouns and words with distinctive shape are generally easier to learn. Use the following guidelines for teaching sight words, particularly those that are less predictable on the basis of phonics and spelling patterns (e.g., *was, want, come*) (Bos & Vaughn, 2002; Cunningham, 2000a; Gunning, 2000):

- Teach the most frequently occurring words.
- Check to see that students understand the meaning, particularly if the students have limited language, have a specific language disability, or are English language learners.
- Introduce these new words before students encounter them in text.
- Limit the number of words introduced in a single lesson.
- Reinforce the association by adding a kinesthetic component such as tracing, copying, and writing from memory.
- Introduce visually similar words (e.g., *where* and *were, was* and *saw*) in separate lessons to avoid confusion.
- When students confuse visually similar words (e.g., *what* for *when*), highlight the differences.
- Provide multiple opportunities, including games and computer-assisted instruction, for the students to read the words in text and as single words until they "automatically" recognize the words.
- Review words that have been previously taught, particularly if the students miscall them when reading text.

## Teaching Decoding Strategies for Identifying Words

What decoding or word identification strategies do readers employ to decode words they do not know automatically? Research on teaching struggling readers, including those with specific reading disabilities, would suggest that six strategies are helpful in teaching these students to decode words (see Figure 12.4).

**Phonic Analysis** *Identify and blend letter–sound correspondences into words.* This is referred to as *phonic analysis* or *phonics.* This strategy builds on the alphabetic principle and assumes that the students have basic levels of phonological awareness and knowledge of some letter–sound correspondences. Students with reading difficulties need systematic word-identification instruction including phonics instruction (see the Research Brief for per-

---

### FIGURE 12.4

## Strategies for Decoding Unknown Words

- *Phonic Analysis:* Identify and blend letter–sound correspondences into words.
- *Onset-Rime:* Use common spelling patterns (onset-rimes) to decode words by blending the initial sound(s) with the spelling pattern or by using analogy.
- *Structural Analysis and Syllabication:* Use knowledge of word structures such as compound word, root words, suffixes, prefixes, and inflectional endings and syllable types to decode multisyllabic words and assist with meaning.
- *Syntax and Context:* Use knowledge of word order (syntax) and context (semantics) to support the pronunciation and confirm word meaning.
- *Use Other Resources:* Use other resources such as asking someone or using a dictionary.

---

spectives on phonics instruction). Consider the following guidelines for phonics instruction:

- Build on a child's foundation of phonological awareness and rich concept of how print functions.
- Use direct and systematic instruction, as follows:
  - Begin with simple VC (*in*) and CVC (*pet*) words, and then move to more complex sound patterns, e.g., CCVC (*slim*), CVCC (*duck*), CVCe (*make*).
  - Demonstrate and have the students point to each letter–sound as they say the sound, and then have them sweep their fingers under the word when they "say it fast."
  - Provide practice with feedback.
- Integrate phonics instruction into a balanced reading program.
- Teach only the the most salient and needed patterns (e.g., silent *e*).
- Develop automatic word recognition so that students can devote their attention to comprehension, not identifying words.

### r e s e a r c h b r i e f

### Perspectives on Phonics Instruction

Several comprehensive reviews of research conducted during the 1990s consistently supported the importance of teaching phonics, particularly to struggling readers: *Beginning to Read: Thinking and Learning about Print* (Adams,1990), *Preventing Reading Difficulties in Young Children* (Snow et al., 1998), *Teaching Children to*

*Read: An Evidence-Based Assessment of the Scientific Research Literature on Reading and Its Implications for Reading Instruction* (National Reading Panel, 2000). These reviews are considered the most comprehensive summaries of the topic since Jeanne Chall's 1967 classic, *Learning to Read: The Great Debate.* In respect to phonics instruction, the reviews make the following recommendations:

- Systematic phonics instruction results in significant benefits in decoding and spelling for students in kindergarten through sixth grade.
- Synthetic phonics instruction (i.e., teaching students explicitly to convert letters into sounds and then blend the sounds to form recognizable words) was particularly effective for students with reading/learning disabilities and students from low socioeconomic status.
- Although conventional wisdom has suggested that kindergarten children might not be ready for phonics instruction, this assumption was not supported by the research.
- Invented spellings should be encouraged, in that they help students develop the necessary phonological awareness skills for reading and spelling. Students should also be taught to transition to conventional spellings.
- Teaching of some phonics rules and generalizations can be helpful if they bring attention to spelling patterns. But learning rules is no substitute for practicing with spelling patterns.
- Teaching of onsets-rimes and the blending and segmenting of sounds is particularly important to build decoding and spelling skills.
- Teachers need to be flexible in their phonics instruction to adapt to the strengths and needs of individual students.
- Systematic phonics is only one component, but a necessary one, of a total reading program.

**Onset-Rime** *Use common spelling patterns to decode words by blending.* One salient feature of the English language is the use of spelling patterns, also referred to as **onset-rimes,** *phonograms,* or *word families.* When using spelling patterns to decode an unknown word, the students segment the word between the onset (/bl/ in the word *blend*) and the rime (-*end*) and then blend the onset and rime to make the word (*blend*). Figure 12.5 presents a list of 37 common rimes that make almost 500 words (Wylie & Durrell, 1970). Guidelines for teaching onset-rimes follow the same guidelines as those suggested for teaching phonic analysis except that the word is segmented at the level of onset-rime rather than at the phoneme level.

**Structural Analysis and Syllabication** *Use knowledge of word structures such as compound word, root words, suffixes, prefixes, and inflectional*

---

FIGURE 12.5

**Common Spelling Onset-Rimes from Primary Grade Texts**

| | | | | |
|---|---|---|---|---|
| -ack | -ail | -ain | -ake | -ale |
| -ame | -an | -ank | -ap | -ash |
| -at | -ate | -aw | -ay | |
| | -ell | -est | | |
| -eat | | | | |
| -ice | -ick | -ide | -ight | -ill |
| -in | -ine | -ing | -ink | -ip |
| -ir | | | | |
| -ock | -oke | -op | -ore | -or |
| -uck | -ug | -ump | -unk | |

---

*endings and syllabication to decode multisyllabic words.* Between third and seventh grades, children learn from 3,000 to 26,000 words, most of them being multisyllabic words encountered through reading and only a limited number taught directly (Wysocki & Jenkins, 1987). Teach students **structural analysis,** in which they analyze words for compound words, root words, prefixes, suffixes, and inflectional endings, because (a) it provides students with ways to segment longer, multisyllabic words into decodable (and meaningful) parts and (b) it assists students in determining the meaning of words (Henry, 1997). For example, the word *unbelievable* can be segmented into three parts: *un–believe–able.* Not only does chunking make this word easier to decode, it also tells us about the meaning. In the case of *unbelievable, un-* means "not," and *-able* means "is or can be." Hence, *unbelievable* means something that it not to be believed. When teaching students to divide words into meaning parts, begin with analyzing compound words. Teach high-frequency prefixes (e.g., *re-, pre-, un-*), suffixes (e.g., *-er/-or, -ly, -tion/-ion,-ness, -ful*), and inflection endings (e.g., *-s, -es, -ing, -ed*). Ideas and guidelines for teaching and reinforcing structural analysis include the following:

- Teach the meanings along with recognition of the meaning parts.
- Explain and demonstrate how may "big words" are just "smaller words" with prefixes, suffixes, and endings.
- Ask students to decode words they do not know by covering all but one part of the word and having them identify it, then uncovering the next part and identifying it, and so on.
- Make a class or student dictionary that has each word part, its meaning, and several example words.
- Use a word map to demonstrate how one root word can make a cadre of related words (see Figure 12.6).

FIGURE 12.6

**Root Word Map of Friend**

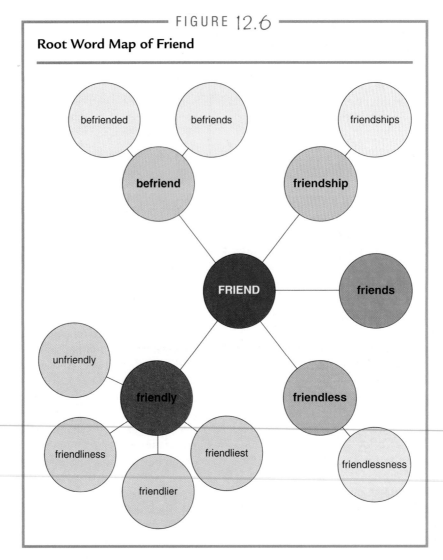

Dividing words by common syllable types, or **syllabication,** can also provide struggling readers with clues for decoding multisyllabic words. A high percentage of more than 600,000 words of English can be categorized as one of six syllable types or a combination of different syllable types (Carreker, 1999). By providing examples, lead students to discover the six types and how to apply them when decoding unknown words. The six types are are follows:

| Type | Description/Examples |
|---|---|
| Closed (CVC) | Ends in at least one consonant; vowel is short.<br>*bed, lost, and, magnet, dap-* in dapple, *hos-* in hostel |
| Open (CV) | Ends in one vowel; vowel is long.<br>*me, mo-* in moment, *ti-* in tiger, *ta-* in table |
| Vowel-consonant-e (CVCe) | Ends in one long vowel, one consonant, and a final *e* that is silent.<br>*name, slope, five, -pite* in despite, *-pete* in compete |

| Type | Description/Examples |
|---|---|
| Vowel team (CVVC) | Uses two adjacent vowels. Sounds of vowel teams vary.<br>*rain, sweet, -geal* in congeal, *train-* in trainer, *bea-* in beagle |
| R-controlled (CV+r) | Vowel is followed by /r/, and vowel pronunciation is affected by /r/.<br>*fern, burn, car, forge, charter* |
| Consonant-le (-C+le) | Unaccented final syllable with a consonant plus /l/ and silent *e*.<br>*-dle* in candle, *-tle* in little, *-zle* in puzzle. |

**Syntax and Semantics** *Use knowledge of word order (syntax) and context (semantics) to support the pronunciation and confirm word meaning.* Whereas students with reading difficulties often over-rely on syntax and context to decode an unknown word (Briggs et al., 1984), good readers use syntax and context for cross-checking their pronunciation and monitoring comprehension (Share & Stanovich, 1995; Torgesen, 1999). This is evident when students reread a word, phrase, or sentence because "it doesn't make sense." Key questions that students can ask are the following:

- Does that sound right here?
- Does that make sense?

## Techniques for Teaching Decoding and Sight Words

A number of programs and strategies have been developed for teaching decoding strategies and sight words. The techniques of making words, word sorting, and using word walls have been used by many elementary teachers. The DISSECT strategy has been used by middle- and high-school teachers to assist students in decoding multisyllabic words. The sight word association procedure provides a means for students to practice words until they automatically recognize them.

**Making Words, Word Sorting, and Using Word Walls** A number of activities can be developed around making words, word sorts, and word walls. Available resource books include the following:

- T. Gunning, *Building Words: A Resource Manual for Teaching Word Analysis and Spelling Strategies*, Boston: Allyn & Bacon, 2001.
- P. Cunningham and D. Hall, *Making Words* and *Making Big Words*, Parsippany, NY: Good Apple, 1994.
- M. Henry, *Patterns for Success in Reading and Spelling: A Multisensory Approach to Teaching Phonics and Word Analysis*, Austin, TX: PRO-ED, 1996.
- P. Cunningham, *Phonics They Use: Words for Reading and Writing*, 3rd ed., New York: Longman, 2000.
- P. Cunningham, *Systematic Sequential Phonics They Use: For Beginning Readers of Any Age*, Greensboro, NC: Carson-Dellosa, 2000.
- K. Ganske, *Word Journeys: Assessment-Guided Phonics, Spelling, and Vocabulary Instruction*, New York: Guilford Press, 2000.
- D. Bear, M. Invernizzi, S. Templeton, and F. Johnston, *Words Their Way: Word Study for Phonics, Vocabulary, and Spelling Instruction*, Upper Saddle River, NJ: Merrill, 2000.

**Making words** is one technique that was initially developed for students in the primary grades to de-velop sensitivity to manipulating sounds and building decoding strategies (Cunningham, 2000b; Cunningham and Hall, 1994), but it can also be used with upper-elementary or middle-school students who need to work on common spelling patterns, prefixes, and suffixes. It was adapted for struggling readers by Schumm and Vaughn (1995). Making words provides opportunities to construct words using magnetic letters, letter tiles, or laminated letters to see how words are affected. For example, the teacher might start with the sounds /s/, /t/, /r/, /n/, and /a/ and ask the students to do the following:

**Teacher:** What two sounds make the word "at"?

Now add a letter sound to the beginning to make the word "sat."

Remove the /s/. What one sound would you add to the beginning to make the word "rat"?

Now listen. We're going to make a three-letter word. Take off the /t/ sound at the end of the word. Now add the one sound that will make the word "ran."

Using a specific set of letters (e.g., *a, c, h, r, s, t*), students make approximately 15 words beginning with two-letter words (e.g., *at*) and progressing to three-, four-, and five-letter words (e.g., *tar, cart, star, cash*) until the final "mystery word" is made (e.g., *scratch*). Students complete a three-step process that includes making words, word sorting, and making words quickly to build fluency (see Figure 12.7). The whole sequence (including distribution of materials) takes about 30 minutes.

Using a **word wall** can reinforce students learning to recognize and spell words. The word wall (Cunningham, 1995) is a large, permanent bulletin board to which words are added each week and grouped in alphabetical order. When a new word is added, the teacher and students talk about its meaning, use the word in a sentence, and determine whether its spelling follows a regular or irregular pattern. The words remain on the word wall throughout the school year. Students can use these words to help them spell words they are writing and eventually learn to read and spell the words through repeated practice. Cunningham (2000a) suggests that some students might need portable word walls, especially if they move from classroom to resource room. A portable word wall is a file folder with one square for each letter of the alphabet. Each week, the five new word wall words are added to the wall and to the student's folder.

**Using the DISSECT Strategy** As students become more advanced in their reading, they begin to use structural analysis (e.g., compound words, prefixes, and suffixes) and syllabication to identify

━━━━━━━━━━━ FIGURE 12.7 ━━━━━━━━━━━

**Steps in Making Words**

**STEP 1.** **Making Words Slowly (about 15 minutes)**

Students make 12 to 15 words, using a set of individual laminated letters. The teacher guides students through the lesson by directing them to spell words with their letters. The last word includes all the letters a student has been given that day. For example, a student might be given the letters "eudhnrt." The teacher would direct them to spell words such as *red, Ted, Ned, her, hut, rut,* and *under.* The final word would be *thunder.* After the students spell the words with their own letters, the teacher or a student shows the correct spelling, using large letters and a sentence strip chart in the front of the room. Students correct their own work.

**STEP 2.** **Word Sorting (about 10 minutes)**

The teacher puts up on the sentence strip board word cards with all the words spelled that day. Students are then asked how some of the words are alike. A volunteer sorts the words on the sentence strip board by putting all like words together (e.g., *fat, rat, sat*). The other students in the class then guess why those words are grouped together, which helps students focus on word patterns.

**STEP 3.** **Making Words Quickly (about 2 minutes)**

Students write as many words as they can using the day's letters, writing the words in a making words log. Students take 1 minute to write the date and the day's letters at the top of the page; when the teacher says, "Go," they write words for 2 minutes. This activity helps build fluency. Because each lesson starts with easy words and ends with more difficult words, all students in the class can participate.

---

multisyllabic words. Lenz, Schumaker, Deshler, and Beals (1984) developed a strategy for secondary students with learning disabilities to approach multisyllable words in a strategic way. This strategy, known by the acronym **DISSECT**, includes the following steps:

- *D*iscover the word's context.
- *I*solate the prefix. Students look at the beginning of the word to see whether the initial letters of the word match a prefix they know. If they do recognize a prefix, they isolate it, e.g., pre/heat. If students do not recognize a prefix, they proceed to step 3.
- *S*eparate the suffix. Students look at the end of the word to see whether the letters match a suffix they know. If they do recognize a suffix, they separate it; if not, they go on to the next step.
- *S*ay the stem.
- *E*xamine the stem. Students dissect the stem into easy-to-pronounce parts, two or three letters at a time. When they can pronounce the whole word, students reread the whole sentence to check their understanding. If students still cannot figure out the word, they go on to the last steps.
- *C*heck with someone.
- *T*ry the dictionary.

DISSECT can be taught to your whole class. Students can then practice using the strategy in small groups or pairs. You may also want to put the steps for DISSECT on a poster in front of your room and remind students regularly about the steps.

In the upper-elementary grades, middle school, and high school, reading instruction focuses more on comprehension and reading for learning in the content areas. Even so, it is not unusual for students who decode at a third-grade level or below to be members of heterogeneous classes. What can you do when only a few students are nonreaders? Tips for Teachers 12.3 presents some other strategies for teaching older students to read.

**The Sight Word Association Procedure** The sight word association procedure (SWAP) (Bradley, 1975) is a way to help students associate spoken words with their printed forms. SWAP can be used individually, with pairs of students, or with small groups. Working as reading partners or directed by the teacher, students follow these steps:

1. Select four to six words, and introduce each word as you do with the word wall.
2. Flash the words to the student, one card at a time for five seconds, with you or the reading partner saying the word twice.
3. Shuffle the cards, and have the student read each word. Provide corrective feedback by verifying the correctly identified words, giving the correct word for any word miscalled, and saying the word if the student does not respond in five seconds.
4. Present all the words again, using the same format given in step 2.
5. Have the student identify each word, using the same format as in step 3. Repeat this step at

## Tips for Teachers

### 12.3    Strategies in Reading Instruction for Older Students

- *Be an advocate for nonreaders.* As a content-area teacher you might not be able to teach these students to decode, but you can be an advocate for them as individuals and for nonreaders collectively.
- *Work collaboratively with other professionals in the school.* What resources are available to help you teach and for students to receive additional help?
- *Work out a plan for what you can reasonably do in your classroom.* Communicate the plan to administrators, other professionals, parents, and students, and follow it regularly.

- *Include in your plan ways to provide support for students to complete reading assignments and tests by using audiotaping, parent support, or peer support.* Work out a way to have assignments and tests read aloud to students if they cannot read them on their own.
- *Find out about and build on the strengths of nonreaders.* Make certain that in your class they have an opportunity to share their gifts and talents with classmates.

---

least two more times or until the student can automatically recognize all the words.

6. After initially teaching the words, review them for several days to see whether the student remembers the words.

7. If the student has difficulty recognizing a word after the seventh exposure to it, switch from a recall task to a recognition task. To do this, place several word cards on the table and have the learner point to each word as you say it. If the student still has difficulty with the words, use a different technique, such as writing the word in a sentence on

the back of the card or having the student draw a picture representing the word on the back of the card. Figure 12.8 provides a record sheet that can be used in monitoring student progress.

## Strategies for Helping Students Develop Fluency

Fluency is the ability to read a text quickly, accurately, and with expression (Richards, 2000; Zutell & Rasinski, 1991). Students are fluent in reading

---

FIGURE 12.8

**Sight Word Association Procedures (SWAP) Record Sheet**

✔ Correct
0 Incorrect

| Words | Initial Teaching | | | | | Retention | | | Comments |
|---|---|---|---|---|---|---|---|---|---|
| | 1 | 2 | 3 | 4 | 5 | 1 | 2 | 3 | |
| | | | | | | | | | |
| | | | | | | | | | |
| | | | | | | | | | |
| | | | | | | | | | |
| | | | | | | | | | |

*Source:* Bos, C. S., & Vaughn, S. (1994). *Strategies for teaching students with learning and behavior problems* (3rd ed., p. 140). Boston: Allyn & Bacon.

when they can recognize printed words quickly and effortlessly (LaBerge & Samuels, 1974) and are therefore able to focus more of their attention on comprehension. Since struggling readers often take longer and require more exposures to automatically recognize and rapidly recall words than do normally reading students (Ehri & Wilce, 1983), it is important that fluency instruction provide multiple opportunities for practice. Use the suggestions in this section to help students become more fluent readers.

## Reading Aloud

Reading aloud to children and previewing a book are not only a means for developing an enjoyment of literature and reading, but also an avenue for modeling and building fluent reading (Reutzel & Hollingsworth, 1993; Trelease, 1995). Reading aloud and previewing the book promote reading fluency in a number of ways:

- *Reading aloud models fluent reading.* For younger children, **big books** (books with large pictures and words that can be seen by the whole class) are ideal because they allow you to point to the text while reading and use the pictures to create more interest in the story.
- *Students can become familiar with the story.* Reading aloud gives you the opportunity to preview the book (discuss with the students the content of the story and to introduce difficult vocabulary).
- *Students can listen to and discuss books that may be too difficult for them to read.* Struggling readers may have listening comprehension that is several years more advanced than their reading comprehension due to difficulties with word recognition. This allow them access to more advanced books and literature.
- *Less adept older readers can read books to young children and serve as cross-age tutors.*

## Repeated Reading

Children have a natural tendency to enjoy hearing familiar stories over and over again. Eventually, as you sit with them and read a book, they automatically begin to read along with you. Children become so familiar with the text that their memory helps them become fluent readers. **Repeated reading** consists of reading short, meaningful passages several times until a satisfactory level of fluency is reached. The general format for this reading procedure is to have the students repeatedly read short passages (50–200 words long) that are at the students' instructional to independent reading levels (90–100 percent word recognition) until they reach a fluent reading rate.

As discussed in Chapter 2, the reading rate is most frequently measured by the words correct per minute (WCPM) and through observations of phrasing, smoothness, and pace. Having students read for one minute and then counting the total number of words read minus the incorrect words (e.g., mispronunciations, substitutions, omissions, and words pronounced after a hesitation of more than three seconds) provides the WCPM. Guidelines (words correct per minute) for reading fluency for grades 2 through 5 (Hasbrouck & Tindal, 1992) are as follows:

| Grade | Fall | Winter | Spring |
| --- | --- | --- | --- |
| 2 | 50–85 | 80–100 | 95–125 |
| 3 | 80–105 | 95–125 | 115–140 |
| 4 | 100–125 | 110–135 | 120–144 |
| 5 | 105–126 | 120–145 | 130–151 |

For example, Jeff, a fourth-grade student with an instructional level at second grade read the second-grade passage on whales at the rate of 25 words per minute. He and his teacher set a goal of Jeff reading the passage at 55 words per minute. It took him five repeated readings to reach this goal, and he graphed his progress. If you are measuring fluency across passages such as depicted in the graph in Figure 2.4, page 47, increases of one to two WCPM per week are realistic goals (e.g., from 25 WCPM to 27 WCPM) (Fuchs et al., 1993).

Students reading below grade level who have used repeated reading have consistently demonstrated gains in both fluency and reading comprehension (Mastropieri et al., 1999; Meyer & Felton, 1999; National Reading Panel, 2000). From these reviews of research, several instructional guidelines for using repeated reading are apparent:

- Consistently using repeated reading with poor readers increases reading speed, accuracy, expression, and comprehension.
- Text materials should be at the students' independent to instruction reading levels (90–100 percent word recognition).
- Passages should be read at least three to five times.
- Multiple reading of phrases may also improve fluency.
- For students with more significant reading problems, do the following:
  - Provide more adult guidance during reading.
  - Use more decodable texts as reading materials.
  - Practice on words and phrases from the text before reading the text.
  - Use shorter passages.
  - Model expressive reading.
- Use short, frequent sessions of fluency practice (10–15 minutes).
- Have students set goals and record progress.

You can incorporate repeated reading into whole-class or small-group routines. You can also pair students to read to each other. Tech Talk provides ideas for using technology to support repeated reading.

# TechTalk

## Using Technology to Build Reading Fluency

### Using Tape-Recorded Books

Using tape-recorded books or passages allows students to practice reading multiple times. Use good-quality recording tape and recorder. Audiotape a book, speaking in a slow conversational rate with expression.

- Allow 10 seconds of blank tape before recording.
- Remind students of any strategies you want them to use (e.g., "Remember to use your finger or a marker as a guide.").
- Use a signal to cue turning the page.

- For a new page, announce each page number.
- Direct students to put their finger on the first word on the page.

Label each side of the tape by the title of the book and page numbers covered. Store the books with their tapes in clear plastic bags.

### Keeping Student Records

Have each student make a reading folder. Staple forms inside the folder (see the form). In this way, both the teacher and the student have a record of the student's reading.

| Name of Book | Author | Dates | Read with | | | | Discussed with | |
|---|---|---|---|---|---|---|---|---|
| | | | Self | Tape | Student | Teacher | Student | Teacher |
| | | | | | | | | |
| | | | | | | | | |
| | | | | | | | | |

### Computer-Based Reading Practice

Computer software provides another avenue for children to repeatedly read books using the computer. Computer programs such as *Living Book Series* (The Learning Company 1-800-852-2255), *Read Naturally* (Read Naturally, 1-800-788-4085), and *Start-to-Finish Books* (Don Johnston, 1-800-999-4660) provide opportunities for students to listen to books being read, to read along with the computer, and to record their own reading of the book. Reading software provides flexibility; the text can be read in sentences or phrases, or the students can highlight individual words and have them pronounced. Many of these programs have assessment tools that allow teachers to measure students' progress and easily change reading speed so students can practice reading accuracy. Some pronounce words in both English and Spanish.

### Using Taped Books at Home to Support English-Language Learners

In the *Dog Gone Good Reading Project,* first-grade teachers provided additional opportunities for linguistically diverse students to repeatedly read books by audiotaping books and having students listen to them and read along at home (Koskinen et al., 1999). In preparing the tapes, the books were read twice, first at a slow but expressive "read-along" rate and then at a faster rate, more typical of fluent oral reading. Simple

tape recorders were provided and students were taught how to use the taped books. Notes went home reminding the children and their parents to read the books two or three times every day. While this technique promoted literacy for all students, it was particularly helpful for students who were learning to read in English but had limited access to English role models and books in English.

### Using Voicemail to Support Summer Reading

Struggling readers usually do not choose reading as a recreational activity during the summer. Ann Willman, a reading specialist, used her school voicemail to promote summer reading (Willman, 1999). She sent home books with the students along with directions on how to use the school voicemail. The students practiced reading a book until they were comfortable. Then she asked the students, with the assistance of their parents, to call her voicemail and read the book to her for three minutes or to summarize the book. She called backed to compliment the students. Ann also invited parents to leave a message about how the process was going. Parents noted that it made their "sometimes reluctant reader more amenable to reading during vacation" (p. 788).

*Source:* Adapted from Bos, C. S., & Vaughn, S. (2002). *Strategies for teaching students with learning and behavior problems* (5th ed.). Boston: Allyn & Bacon.

## Classwide Peer Tutoring

In **classwide peer tutoring (CWPT)**, students of different reading levels are paired, one average or high reader with one low reader. The reading material for the tutoring sessions can be a basal reader, trade book, or magazines; what is important is that the less able reader in the pair can read it easily. During CWPT sessions, which last approximately 30 minutes, the pairs work through a sequence of structured activities in which partners read orally, share story retelling, and summarize what was read. Students earn points as they work through the series of activities. When reading, first the stronger reader reads aloud to serve as a model, and then the other reader reads. Teach students how to be both tutors/listeners and tutees/readers and provide role-play practice and feedback. For the tutors, give guidelines for how they should correct errors during oral reading (e.g., point out the word, pronounce the word, and have the tutee say the word) and the questions they should ask when the students have finished reading (e.g., What is the story about? What is happening in the story now? What do you think will happen next?). Also assist the students in giving positive feedback.

CWPT has been researched extensively in various school settings (e.g., Delquardi et al., 1986; Fuchs et al., 1993, 2000; Mathes & Babyak, 2001; Mathes et al., 1994, 1998; Vaughn et al., 1998). Results indicate that when the procedure is implemented consistently (3 times a week over a period of 16 weeks), the amount of reading practice time increases substantially, and students of all ability levels improve in fluency and comprehension.

## ● Strategies for Improving Reading Comprehension

Understanding is the ultimate goal of reading. For many students, however, reading the words is not enough to make understanding happen. Students with reading difficulties need to learn specific ways to get ready for reading, to understand what they're reading while they read it, and to summarize and reflect about what they have read. In other words, many struggling readers need **comprehension strategies** to use before, during, and after reading. Students also need to learn strategies for dealing with both *narrative* and *expository* text (stories and informational writing, respectively) and to monitor their comprehension (comprehension monitoring). Consequently, instruction should include the direct teaching (e.g., Mastroprieri & Scruggs, 1997; Swanson, 1999; Gersten et al., 2001) of the following:

- *Activating background knowledge:* thinking about what you already know about the topic and how your knowledge relates to what you are reading
- *Predicting:* making predictions about what is going to happen or what will be learned from reading the text
- *Generating and answering questions:* asking and answering relevant questions that promote understanding such as who, what, when, where, why, and how questions
- *Clarifying:* clarifying unclear concepts or vocabulary
- *Summarizing:* determining the main ideas and important concepts related to the main idea
- *Using text structure:* using knowledge of different text structures (e.g., narrative, expositive) as a framework for comprehension
- *Comprehension monitoring:* checking for understanding and using fix-up strategies (e.g., rereading, clarifying a concept) to facilitate comprehension

Each of the teaching techniques in this section focuses on teaching comprehension strategies and comprehension monitoring and can be used with a variety of texts.

## K–W–L Strategy

K–W–L is a strategy to help students become actively engaged in comprehension before, during, and after reading (Ogle, 1986). The **K–W–L strategy** is based on research that underscores the importance of activating prior knowledge before reading (e.g., Anderson, 1977; Anderson et al., 1985) and consists of three basic steps:

- Accessing what I **K**now
- Determining what I **W**ant to learn
- Recalling what I **L**earned

During the know step, teachers and students engage in a discussion about what they already know about a topic, such as volcanoes. During the want-to-learn step, teachers and students describe what they hope to learn from reading about the topic. Finally, during the learned stage, teachers and students discuss what they learned and what information the passage did not provide. As with many reading comprehension strategies, K–W–L can also be used as a listening comprehension strategy before and after lectures. Ogle (1989) added a fourth column, "what we still want to know." Schmidt (1999) referred to it as K–W–L–Q with the "Q" representing more questions. Figure 12.9 shows a K–W–L–Q worksheet you can use to help students learn this strategy.

───── FIGURE 12.9 ─────

**K–W–L–Q Chart for Pond and Pond Life**

All about Ponds (K–W–L–Q)

| *What We Know* | *What We Want to Know* | *What We Learned* | *More Questions We Have* |
| --- | --- | --- | --- |
| Contains water | How does the pond get its water? | Underground springs and rain | Why do ponds die? |
| Smaller than a lake | Why are ponds green and muddy? | Algae and other plants make it green | What happens to a pond in winter? |
| Fish | What fish live in the pond? | Blue gill, trout, bass, catfish | How do algae help or hurt a pond? |
| Ducks | What insects live on the pond? | Dragonflies, mosquitoes, water fleas | |
| Frogs | | | |
| Muddy | | | |
| Algae | | | |
| Insects on top | | | |

*Source:* Adapted from Schmidt, P. R. (1999). KWLQ: Inquiry and Literacy Learning in Science, *The Reading Teacher, 52,* 789–792.

## Question–Answer Relationships Strategy

Teachers' manuals and students' workbooks, readers, and textbooks contain many comprehension questions. There are different kinds of questions that can be asked about reading and different ways of classifying these questions. Pearson and Johnson (1978) developed a way to classify questions on the basis of the relationship between the question and the location of its answer. From this classification system, a strategy for teaching students how to answer different types of questions was also developed. This strategy, called the **question–answer relationships (QAR) strategy** (Raphael, 1982, 1984, 1986), helps students realize that when answering questions, they need to not only consider the text and their prior knowledge, but also use strategic behavior to adjust the use of each of these sources.

The four question–answer relationships are based on the source of information and the types of reasoning involved:

1. *Right there.* Words used to create the question and words used for the answer are in the same sentence.
2. *Think and search.* The answer is in the text, but words used to create the question and those used for an appropriate answer are not in the same sentence.
3. *Author and me.* The answer is implied in the author's language, style, and tone.
4. *On my own.* The answer is found not in the text but in one's head on the basis of personal experience.

Teaching QAR involves having students learn to differentiate first between the two sources of infor-

mation and then between the four question–answer relationships. Students also learn how to identify the type of questions they are trying to answer. Figure 12.10 presents a cue card students can use during instruction.

Adapted from Raphael (1986), the following are procedures for introducing the QAR strategy to students:

1. The first day, introduce students to the concept of question–answer relationships using the two major source categories. Read several short passages to demonstrate the relationships. Provide practice by asking students to identify the type of QAR, the answer to the question, and the strategy they used for finding the answer. The progression for teaching should be from highly supportive to independent:

   *Most supportive:* Provide text, questions, answers, QAR label for each question, and reasons the label is appropriate.

   *Most independent:* Have students generate their own questions, QAR labels, and reasons for their choices.

2. When students have a clear picture of the difference between "in my head" and "in the book," teach the next level of differentiation for each of the major categories. First, work on "in the book," then go to "in my head." The key distinction between the two "in my head" subcategories is "whether or not the reader needs to read the text for the questions to make sense" (Raphael, 1986, p. 519).

3. When students can use the QAR strategy effectively in short passages, gradually increase the length of the passages and the variety of reading materials. Review the strategy, model its use on

──────── FIGURE 12.10 ────────

### Question–Answer Relationships (QARs)

| IN THE BOOK QARS | IN MY HEAD QARS |
|---|---|

**Right There**

The answer is in the text, usually easy to find. The words used to make up the question and words used to answer the question are **Right There** in the same sentence.

**Author and You**

The answer is not in the story. You need to think about what you already know, what the author tells you in the text, and how it fits together.

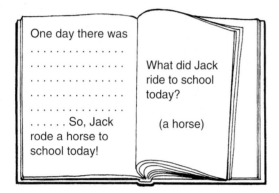

**Think and Search (Putting It Together)**

The answer is in the story, but you need to put together different story parts to find it. Words for the question and words for the answer are not found in the same sentence. They come from different parts of the text.

**On My Own**

The answer is not in the story. You can even answer the question without reading the story. You need to use your own experience.

*Source:* Adapted from Raphael, T. E. (1986). Teaching question–answer relationships, revisited, *The Reading Teacher, 39*(6), 519. Copyright by the International Reading Association.

the first question, and then have students use the strategy on the rest of the questions.

4. When students are proficient, use expanded or alternative QAR activities:
   • Have students work in pairs or cooperative learning groups, using QAR to answer comprehension questions.
   • Ask students to write stories with questions. Have other students determine the answer

to each question and what kind of question it is.
   • Play a detective game in which students answer questions in their search for clues to solve the case, and cite the source for their evidence.
   • Divide students into teams, and have the teacher read a short passage, followed by questions. The teams earn points by answering questions and determining the QAR labels.

## Story Retelling

**Story retelling** actively involves students in the reconstruction of stories they have read or heard. Retelling stories not only enhances comprehension but also has the following benefits (Morrow, 1985; Pellegrini & Galda, 1982):

- Students acquire a sense of story structure.
- Recall of details is enhanced.
- Oral language and vocabulary are improved.
- Peer interaction and student involvement are promoted.

It is important to establish conditions that make students willing and eager to participate in a story retelling session. The following guidelines are helpful:

- Select a story your students would enjoy having you read to them. Read to them with enthusiasm and animation.
- Explain why it is important to share stories with friends.
- Model the retelling process. Be sure to include a description of characters and setting, key plot elements, and ending. Using the acronym STORE (Bos, 1987) can assist students in retelling:

  *Setting:* Who, what, when, where

  *Trouble:* What is the trouble that the main character(s) needs to solve?

  *Order of action:* What action(s) does the main character(s) take to solve the problem?

  *Resolution:* What was the outcome (resolution) for each action? How does the main character(s) react and feel?

  *End:* What happened in the end?

- Help students find stories to share and assist them with retelling as needed. Use STORE as a guide for retelling.

- Provide a variety of audiences, such as younger children from other classes or parents, so that students can get plenty of practice.

## Collaborative Strategic Reading

**Collaborative strategic reading** (CSR) is a multicomponent learning strategy that combines essential reading comprehension strategies that have been demonstrated as effective in improving students' understanding of text (Palincsar, 1986; Rosenshine & Meister, 1994) with cooperative learning groups or paired learning. CSR takes advantage of the growing knowledge base that youngsters need to be taught specific strategies to enhance their understanding of text but should not be overwhelmed with so many strategies that they are unable to decide which ones to use. CSR is based on reciprocal teaching (Palinscar & Brown, 1984) and teaches four strategies using the following steps: preview (i.e., predicting), click and clunk (i.e., questioning and clarifying), get the gist (i.e., summarization), and wrap-up (i.e., summarization). Preview is used only before reading the text, and wrap-up only after reading the entire text. Figure 12.11 presents the four CSR steps with key questions the students can ask as they complete the process.

**Previewing**    The goals of previewing are for students to (a) learn as much about the passage as they can in two to three minutes, (b) activate their background knowledge about the topic, (c) make predictions about what they will read, and (d) pique their interest in the topic and engage them in active reading. In previewing, teach the students to check out the headings, key words, pictures, tables, graphs, and other key information.

**Click and Clunk**    Students "click and clunk" while reading each section of the text. "Clicks" reference to the portions of the text that make sense, and "clunks" are the portions in which comprehension isn't clear (e.g., students do not know the meaning of a word). Clicking and clunking is designed to assist students in monitoring their comprehension and to employ fix-up strategies to clarify their understanding. Clunk cards read as follows:

- Reread the sentence and look for ideas that help you understand the word.
- Reread the sentence leaving out the "clunk." What word makes sense?
- Reread the sentences before and after the sentence with the "clunk."

What strategies might these students use to increase their reading comprehension? How can they learn those strategies? Why are strategies such as questioning and story retelling helpful to students with reading difficulties?

─── FIGURE 12.11 ───

## CSR's Plan for Strategic Reading

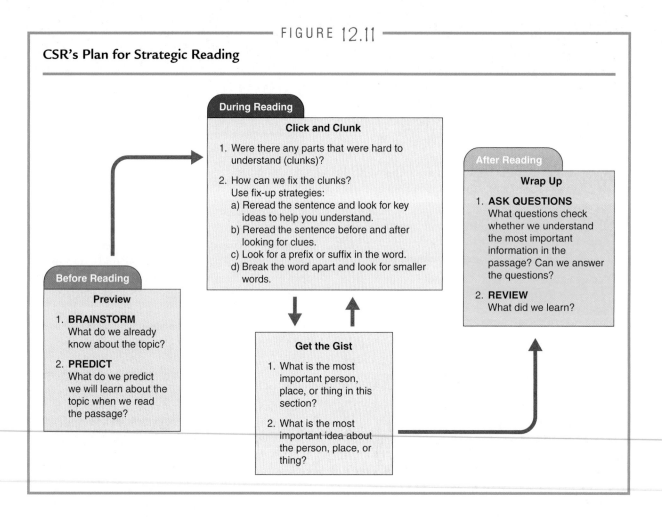

**During Reading**

**Click and Clunk**

1. Were there any parts that were hard to understand (clunks)?

2. How can we fix the clunks?
   Use fix-up strategies:
   a) Reread the sentence and look for key ideas to help you understand.
   b) Reread the sentence before and after looking for clues.
   c) Look for a prefix or suffix in the word.
   d) Break the word apart and look for smaller words.

**After Reading**

**Wrap Up**

1. **ASK QUESTIONS**
   What questions check whether we understand the most important information in the passage? Can we answer the questions?

2. **REVIEW**
   What did we learn?

**Before Reading**

**Preview**

1. **BRAINSTORM**
   What do we already know about the topic?

2. **PREDICT**
   What do we predict we will learn about the topic when we read the passage?

**Get the Gist**

1. What is the most important person, place, or thing in this section?

2. What is the most important idea about the person, place, or thing?

---

- Look for prefixes or suffixes in the word.
- Break the word apart and look for smaller words you know.

**Getting the Gist**    Students learn to get the gist (get the main idea) by reading each section and then asking and answering in their own words and in 10 words or less:

- Who or what is it about?
- What is most important about the who or what?

Teach the students to restate in 10 words or less the most important point as a way of making sure they understood what they read. Students repeat the second and third steps for each paragraph or section of the passage.

**Wrap Up**    In the wrap-up step, students formulate questions and answers about the key ideas from the entire passage and discuss what they have learned. The goal is to improve students' knowledge, understanding, and memory for what they read. For students with learning and language disabilities, it may be necessary to explicitly teach them to ask questions using the WH + How questions (*What?, When?, Where?,*

*Why?,* and *How?*). Students can use the gists they have generated for the different sections to think about the most important information in the whole passage.

**Cooperative Learning Groups**    Once students have developed proficiency in applying the comprehension strategies through teacher-led activities, the students learn to use CSR in peer-led cooperative learning groups of about four or five students (Johnson & Johnson, 1989). Typical roles used during CSR include the following:

- *Leader:* Leads the group by saying what to read and what strategy to use next
- *Clunk expert:* Reminds students to use clunk strategies to figure out a difficult word or concept
- *Announcer:* Calls on different members to read and share ideas
- *Encourager:* Watches the group and gives encouragement and feedback
- *Reporter:* During the whole class wrap-up, reports to the class the important ideas learned and favorite questions
- *Time keeper:* Keeps time and lets the group know when it is time to move on

Roles should change on a regular basis. After wrapping up in their cooperative groups, a whole class wrap-up is completed to give the teacher and groups the opportunity to report and to discuss the content.

CSR has been used in diverse classrooms including those containing students with reading problems and students learning English as another language to help students read content area materials more efficiently and effectively (Klingner & Vaughn, 1998, 2000; Klingner, Vaughn, & Schumm, 1998; Vaughn & Klingner, 1999; Vaughn, Klingner, & Bryant, 2001). Tiffany Royal, a fifth-grade inclusion teacher notes, "What I like best is that my students learn how to understand what they read while they improve their vocabulary. Also it helps on our standardized achiement tests."

## summary

- In the last decade, national, state, and local initiatives have emphasized balanced approaches to teaching reading and the use of research-based strategies for teaching students how to read.
- Students' success with learning to read is influenced by a number of factors that are student-based factors and environmental-based factors.
- Effective reading instruction for struggling readers is composed of several areas (phonological awareness, letter–sound correspondence, alphabetic principle, word identification, fluency, vocabulary, and comprehension) that teachers balance on the basis of the students' current reading levels and needs and the purposes of instruction.
- In planning and using effective reading instruction for struggling readers, teachers should establish an environment that promotes reading, use appropriate and ongoing assessment, provide intensive instruction, and obtain early intervention.
- Students, especially struggling readers, need systematic instruction in phonological awareness, letter–sound correspondence, and decoding strategies, including phonics instruction. This instruction includes modeling and guided practice with feedback in context and with words in isolation.

- Research has indicated the importance of phonological awareness in learning to read. Teaching phonological awareness is the foundation for phonics instruction.
- Some students have difficulty automatically recognizing words in print and need specific instruction with sight words.
- Students are fluent in reading when they can recognize printed words quickly and effortlessly. Using repeated reading, reading aloud to students, and classwide peer tutoring promotes reading fluency. Fluency instruction should be integrated with instruction in word identification and comprehension.
- The ultimate goal of reading is understanding. Research has demonstrated that for many struggling readers teaching reading comprehension strategies, text structures, and comprehension monitoring is critical for successful comprehension. Students frequently need to learn specific ways to get ready for reading, to activate understanding during reading, and to summarize and reflect about what they have read.

## key terms and concepts

alliteration
alphabetic principle
automaticity
big books
blending
classwide peer tutoring
   (CWPT)
collaborative strategic
   reading (CSR)
comprehension strategies

comprehension
   monitoring
curriculum-based measurement
   (CBM)
decodable books
decodable text
decoding
DISSECT
fluency
frustration reading level

high-frequency words
independent reading
   level
informal reading
   inventory
instrumental
   conversations
instructional reading
   level
K–W–L strategy

| | | |
|---|---|---|
| making words | print-rich environment | sight word |
| manipulating | question–answer relationships | sight word association procedure |
| onset-rime | (QAR) strategy | (SWAP) |
| phonemes | reading comprehension | story retelling |
| phonemic awareness | reciprocal causation | structural analysis |
| phonic analysis | repeated reading | syllabication |
| phonics | rhyming | word identification |
| phonological awareness | segmenting | word wall |

# think and apply

1. Now that you have read Chapter 12, reread the interview with Ines. What strategies does she use to teach phonological awareness, letter–sound correspondence, word identification, fluency, and comprehension to her third-grade students? What procedures does she use that you would or would not incorporate into your own reading program?

2. Think about your own experience learning to read. What instructional strategies were most helpful in learning to read? What were least helpful?

3. Think about several students you have taught or are currently teaching who are struggling with reading. Which are the factors that are influencing their learning? What components of the reading process pose the most problems for each student? How have you integrated the components to meet their needs?

4. Plan a whole-class lesson to teach phonological awareness or reading comprehension. Describe the follow-up activities, including the instructional grouping formats you plan to use to reinforce learning and meet individual student needs. Describe how you will monitor progress.

5. Plan a small-group or paired learning activity to teach word identification or fluency. Describe how you will monitor student progress.

6. Interview three teachers about how they plan their reading and language arts programs. Specifically, ask about how they plan for diverse students including students with reading/learning disabilities.

# read more about it

1. Bos, C. S., & Vaughn, S. (2002). *Strategies for teaching students with learning and behavior problems* (5th ed.). Boston: Allyn & Bacon.
   *Provides many strategies for teaching reading to struggling readers.*

2. Cunningham, P., & Allington, R. (2001). *Classrooms that work: They can all read and write* (2nd ed.). New York: HarperCollins.
   *An excellent resource for planning effective, multilevel reading instruction in diverse classrooms.*

3. Cunningham, P. M. (2000). *Phonics they use: Words for reading and writing* (3rd ed.). New York: Longman.
   *Provides instructional ideas and strategies for teaching decoding skills and word identification.*

4. Fry, E. B., Fountoukidis, D. L., & Polk, J. K. (1985). *The new reading teacher's book of lists.* Englewood Cliffs, NJ: Prentice Hall.

   *Provides numerous lists related to reading including lists of high frequency words, onset-rimes, antonyms, and idioms.*

5. Gunning, T. G. (1998). *Assessing and correcting reading and writing difficulties.* Boston: Allyn & Bacon.
   *Provides ideas and strategies for assessing and teaching struggling readers.*

6. Morrow, L. M. (1997). *Literacy development in the early years: Helping children read and write* (3rd ed.). Boston: Allyn & Bacon.
   *An excellent tool for planning reading programs for preschool through the primary grades.*

7. National Reading Panel. (2000). *Teaching children to read: An evidence-based assessment of the scientific research literature on reading and its implications for reading instruction.* Bethesda, MD: National Institutes of Health, National Institute of Child Health and Human Development.

*Reviews the research on teaching reading. Executive summary available on-line: http://www.nationalreadingpanel.org.*

8. Pinnell, G. S., & Fountas, I. C. (1998). *Word matters: Teaching phonics and spelling in the reading/writing classroom.* Portsmouth, NH: Heinemann.

   *A comprehensive tool for teaching phonics and spelling. Includes reproducible sheets for use in mini-lessons and in writing workshops.*

9. Tierney, R. J., & Readence, J. E. (2000). *Reading strategies and practices: A compendium* (5th ed.). Boston: Allyn & Bacon.

   *A collection of detailed strategies for phonological awareness, word identification, fluency, and comprehension. Includes underlying research as well as cautions and comments.*

10. Klingner, J. K., Vaughn, S., Dimino, J., Schumm, J. S., & Bryant, D. (2001). *From clunk to click: Collaborative strategic reading.* Longmont, CO: Sopris West.

    *A teacher activity guide that describes collaborative strategic reading as a means to enhance comprehension. Activities for classroom use are provided.*

## suggested websites

**www.NationalReadingPanel.org**
This website is for the National Reading Panel and provides a current review of the research on teaching reading.

**www.reading.org**
This website is for the International Reading Association and provides a wide variety of resources for teaching reading.

**www.interdys.org**
This website is for the International Dyslexia Association and provides resources for teaching individuals with reading disabilities.

**www.ncld.org**
This website is for the National Center for Learning Disabilities and provides resources related to reading and other learning disabilities.

**www.ciera.org**
This website is for the Center for Improvement of Early Reading Achievement and provides resources for teaching early reading.

**www.texasreading.org**
This website is for the Texas Center for Reading and Language Arts at the University of Texas at Austin and provides a variety of resources and links for teaching reading.

**http://cars.uth.tmc.edu**
This website is for the Center for Academic and Reading Skills at the University of Texas–Houston Health Science Center and the University of Houston and provides resources on the assessment and teaching of reading.

**www.ed.arizona.edu/rimes2000**
This website is at the University of Arizona and provides resources for teaching early reading and spelling.

**www.ldonline.org/ld_indepth/reading/ldrp_chard_guidelines.html**
This website provides information on phonics and word recognition instruction in early reading programs.

**www.ldresources.com/readwrite/readingtolearn.html**
This website provides an overview of learning to read, including phonological awareness and word identification.

**www.ldonline.org/ld_indepth/reading/teaching_children_to_read.html**
This website contains information on the alphabetic principle, phonemic awareness, and phonics.

**www.ldonline.org/ld_indepth/reading/torgeson_catchthem.html**
This website contains information on identification and assessment of reading difficulties with a focus on phonemic awareness.

**www.ldonline.org/ld_indepth/teaching_techniques/cld_hownow.html**
This website introduces phoneme awareness activities for collaborative classrooms.

**www.successforall.net**
This website provides information about the Success for All Program, including effective practice research.

**www.ala.org**
This is the website of the American Library Association and provides recommendations for books for children including reluctant and struggling readers.

**www.ncte.org**
This is the website for the National Council of Teachers of English and includes numerous resources on teaching literature and children's literature.

**www.ldonline.org/ld_indepth/teaching_techniques/collab_reading.html**
This website introduces Collaborative Strategic Reading to improve reading comprehension and fluency.

**www.dk.com**
This website features programs that build reading comprehension and vocabulary.

# Facilitating Writing

# chapter | outline

# focus | questions

1. What are current trends in writing curriculum and instruction, and how might they affect your planning for writing instruction in your classroom?

2. What are areas of potential difficulty in writing for students with disabilities?

3. What are principles of effective writing instruction for all learners?

4. What strategies can you implement for students who have difficulties with composition?

5. What strategies can you implement for students who have difficulties writing stories?

6. What strategies can you implement for students who have difficulties with informational writing?

7. What strategies can you implement to help all students develop spelling skills?

8. What strategies can you implement to help all students develop handwriting skills?

# inter view

**Gina Terry**

Gina Terry is a fourth-grade teacher at South Miami Heights Elementary in Miami, Florida. The special education teacher, Galia Pennecamp, is assigned full time to Gina's inclusion classroom of 32 students, 12 of whom are students with learning disabilities.

In Florida, all fourth-grade students are required to take a statewide writing assessment test, *Florida Writes*. Here's what Gina says about writing instruction:

> When I first heard about the *Florida Writes* test, I panicked. I really didn't learn too much about writing instruction in my undergraduate program. Even when I was in elementary school, we didn't write

much and what I remember about it wasn't too motivating. All I remember is a lot of red ink! I kept wondering, "How am I going to prepare them for this test—and keep it fun?"

Two events in my life helped change my attitude about writing. The first is that Nina Zaragoza, a professor at Florida International University, taught a workshop about writing at our school. While she was giving the workshop, she talked about different stages of writing—brainstorming, drafting, editing, and publishing—but frankly, I didn't think my students would have the patience for all that. Nina agreed to spend a day in my class to show me how to get it going. I was amazed—the students were excited about writing for the first time. They really felt like authors and started taking pride in their written work. Nina showed me that it could be done. The students with problems in writing didn't necessarily publish as much as some other children, but they worked hard on their stories. It was not unusual for students to say, "Can we write today?" They actually asked to write! Best of all, Nina taught me how to build spelling, handwriting, and composition skills required by the school district curriculum objectives into the students' real writing. I began to realize that students could spend more time on their writing, less time on worksheets. Through whole-class and small-group minilessons, they could still learn their basic language arts skills. Galia, my special education partner, is most helpful here. While students write their books and stories, she zeros in on the students with learning disabilities and gives them the support they need to feel successful as authors.

The second event that changed my mind about writing was attending the Zelda Glazer Writing Workshop sponsored by Dade County Public Schools and the University of Miami. Each school in Dade County is allowed to nominate one teacher . . . to go to this week-long summer event. During that week I learned strategies to spark student writing even more. Probably the most helpful thing I learned was how to give students feedback about their writing in positive, constructive ways.

We do what we call Writing Workshop in our class three or four times a week. You should see it—it really looks like a writer's studio. The children are busy brainstorming about stories with their friends, drafting, editing each other's drafts, or working in the publishing center making covers or illustrating their books. Their favorite time is when we share stories together as a whole class.

You should also know that writing is not limited to Writing Workshop time. Writing is integrated with our thematic units and with the literature that we read together and individually. Each student has a personal journal and makes daily entries in the journal. Each student also has a pen pal. My college roommate teaches fourth grade in Ohio, so we send letters to our Ohio pen pals every other week. It's safe to say that we write all day long.

# intro duction

Like many teachers, Gina has discovered that writing instruction can be dynamic and exciting. Throughout the country, students are beginning to realize that they are authors—writing to real audiences for real purposes. Recently, for example, one of the authors of this book met Sara, a second-grader, who asked, "What do you do?" When told, "I am a writer," Sara said, "I am an author too. I've written six books." Her mother proudly concurred. Sara's six books are part of the family's home library and will be saved to share with Sara's children and grandchildren some day. They are a family treasure. This chapter focuses on ways to bring the joy of writing to all students.

## Current Trends in Writing Curriculum and Instruction

Gina's experience is similar to that of many teachers over the past decade. She has become increasingly aware of the research-based practices that accelerate student progress in writing including the following:

- Movement toward a student-centered model of writing instruction
- The importance of early writing experiences
- Greater allotment of time to writing instruction
- Teaching the mechanics of communicating effectively through writing

## A Student-Centered Model of Writing Instruction

In recent years, the growing trend has been toward a **student-centered model** of instruction for writing. The emphasis in this model is on giving students ample opportunity to find personal meaning in what they write. Rather than being taught in isolation, as they are in more traditional models, skills are part of connected, meaningful experiences in communication. The work of Donald Graves (1983, 1994) has provided a major contribution to the understanding of writing as a student-centered activity. His observations of children as they write reveal that even young children go through an **authoring cycle** of prewriting, composing (drafting), and postwriting (revising, editing, and publishing). Graves and others (Atwell, 1987; Calkins, 1991; Hansen, 1985; Routman, 1991) have provided educators with procedures for implementing this authoring cycle in the classroom and for helping students and teachers realize the importance of authorship and audience. Charles Schwartz teaches eighth-grade language arts using a student-centered model. Charles integrates reading, writing, speaking, and listening activities in his language arts program. To document students' progress in writing, Charles uses writing samples, self- and peer evaluations, and teacher-observation checklists. His classroom looks like a writer's workshop; daily, students are busy prewriting, writing, postwriting, and thinking of new and creative ways to share their work in the classroom and beyond. Charles says that his role is to serve as a writing coach, providing not only encouragement, but also direct skills instruction.

Although the student-centered model promotes creativity and student productivity, critics claim that teaching of skills is incidental, inconsistent, and not intensive enough for students with problems in learning to write. This chapter provides specific suggestions for making a student-centered model work for all students in your classroom by ensuring that the mechanics of writing are an essential feature of instruction.

Should children be encouraged to write before they can read or spell? Why or why not?

## Early Writing Experiences

Until recently, traditional thinking was that students needed to learn to read before they could learn to write. As a matter of fact, not only was writing instruction delayed until students learned to read, but composition was not encouraged until students learned to form letters and spell in a conventional manner. The work of Read (1971) and Chomsky (1979) indicates that reading and writing develop si-

multaneously and that children's **invented spelling** (i.e., their early attempts to spell in their own way) can reveal a great deal about their phonological awareness. Therefore, the current trend is to encourage students as early as possible to write. Even if they can't form conventional letters or spell standard English, it is important to try to get their ideas down in any way possible: pictures, scribbling, pretend letters, or invented spelling. These early forms of writing create a natural sequence for learning to write and should be encouraged.

> Two-, three-, and four-year-olds scribble and sometimes mix their scribble with letters and pictures. For young writers scribble has meaning (Heald-Taylor, 1984).

## More Instructional Time for Writing

In response to national concern about the quality of writing among students in the United States, the amount of time allotted to writing instruction has increased in recent years (Graham et al., 1991). Fifteen years ago, when Alice Newell started teaching eleventh-grade English, she gave her students one writing assignment every other week. At the end of the year, students had to spend about one month writing a research paper on some aspect of U.S. history. When Alice's school district mandated daily writing assignments, she was upset—daily assignments, when she was overwhelmed by having to grade *weekly* assignments for her 135 students? Since that time, Alice has learned that students can be taught to provide constructive peer review of each other's writing. She has learned also that although students write daily, they might work on the same piece (revising, editing, etc.) for several days—or several weeks. And she has learned that the teacher does not need to be the only audience for student work; there are other ways for students to share what they have written.

The trend toward allotting more time to writing extends to other content areas at all grade levels. For example, secondary teachers are assigning both informal (e.g., journals, diaries) and formal (e.g., essays, reflection papers) writing in their classes (Ellis, E. S., 1994; Healy & Barr, 1991).

## Teaching the Mechanics of Writing

Teachers realize what research has demonstrated, students need to know the mechanics of writing if they are going to communicate effectively with others. Thus, whereas earlier instruction in writing often focused too much on the mechanics and too little on conveying meaning, many worry that recent movements in writing are focusing too much on the meaning and too little on the mechanics. Effective teachers know that both are essential elements to successful writing and are best taught in an integrated fashion. For example, Mrs. Zakibe knows that she must ensure that students understand the rules of language including capitalization, punctuation, and spelling as well as the value of a well-organized story structure.

When teachers implement effective intervention approaches that use both the conventions of teaching writing, such as capitalization, punctuation, and sentence structure, and strategies for improving written expression, such as planning and composing, the results are quite positive (Gersten & Baker, in press).

Remember the following critical points about teaching conventions (Fearn & Farnan, 1998):

- Attention to conventions does not disrupt the flow of writing but is part of the discipline of writing.
- Focus on the conventions of writing does not inhibit growth in writing but facilitates it.
- Even very young children can learn simple conventions and perform them automatically.

- Students with disabilities need to have about 20 percent of their instructional time in writing address the use and application of the conventions of writing.

 ## Teaching Writing as a Process

Think about some of your recent experiences as a writer. Perhaps you were writing a research paper for school. You might have been writing a letter or an e-mail message to a friend. Maybe you were carefully crafting a letter of application for a job. Think about the process. To compose, you needed to do the following:

- Formulate your message in your head.
- Organize your ideas in a logical fashion.
- Think about the reader and how he or she might understand and react to the message.
- Choose words carefully to make the flow of language, the syntax, smooth.
- Select individual words to convey your meaning succinctly.
- Attend to your spelling, capitalization, and punctuation.
- Consider the appearance of the final product (the legibility of your handwriting, typing, or word processing).

Writing is a complex process. Difficulties can occur at any point in the process. Tips for Teachers 13.1 offers general guidelines for teaching writing to students who have difficulty.

## Writing Is an Interactive Process

Writers use the sounds, grammar, and meaning of our language system to **encode** and to communicate a message to the reader. And in writing, as in reading, students may have problems with any aspect of the language system—with using language interactively and with using it fluently. In addition, students may have problems with the physical act of writing. For example, Grant Ellsworth, a fifth-grader with learning disabilities, loves to tell stories, especially about fishing with his father, but is reluctant when asked to write them. Grant is a poor speller and for some reason cannot get the hang of capitalization and punctuation rules. In addition, his handwriting is illegible, and he hasn't learned to use a keyboard. Writing a single sentence takes Grant so long that he

# Tips for Teachers

## 13.1    Guidelines for Teaching Writing to Students with Disabilities

1. *Allocate adequate time for writing.* Adequate time is a necessary criterion for improving the writing skills of special learners. Students need a minimum of 30 minutes a day for writing.

2. *Provide a range of writing tasks.* Students should select topics and write about what they know. After students' skills improve, the range of writing tasks should broaden to include problem solving, writing games, and other assignments.

3. *Create a social climate that promotes and encourages writing.* Teachers set the tone through acceptance and encouragement. Conferences between students, students and teachers, and students and other people in the school are conducted to provide constructive feedback and audiences with whom to share writing.

4. *Integrate writing with other academic subjects.* Writing can be integrated with every subject. Use writing as a means of expression in content areas such as social studies and science.

5. *Focus on the processes central to writing.* These processes include prewriting activities, writing, and rewriting activities.

6. *Focus on composing, and attend to spelling and punctuation after the writing is complete.* Mechanics interfere with some students' ability to get ideas down on paper successfully. Focus first on basic elements to facilitate the writing process.

7. *Teach characteristics of good writing.* Implicit knowledge about writing needs to be made explicit. For example, discuss different genres and their characteristics.

8. *Teach skills that aid composing.* Skills include conferencing, brainstorming, sentence writing, and evaluating the effectiveness of the written piece.

9. *Ask students to identify goals for improving their writing.* Students can set realistic goals regarding their progress in writing. Goals can focus on prewriting, writing, and rewriting. Students and teacher can provide feedback on how well the goals are realized.

10. *Avoid using instructional practices that do not improve writing.* Such practices include grammar instruction, diagramming sentences, and overemphasis on students' errors.

*Source:* Graham, S., & Harris, K. R. (1988). Instructional recommendations for teaching writing to exceptional students, *Exceptional Children, 54*(6), 506–512. Copyright 1988 by the Council for Exceptional Children. Reprinted with permission.

---

soon loses his story and its intended meaning. Even though Grant can tell stories in a most entertaining way, he cannot get them on paper.

## Writing Is a Strategic Process

Because writing is such a complex task, successful writers need a strategy or plan to communicate ideas clearly. It is important to have systematic procedures for being successful and productive at each stage of the authoring cycle. Students, especially those with learning and behavior problems, often have difficulty not only planning their writing, but also monitoring and regulating themselves while they write. Since the 1980s, researchers have worked to develop ways to teach students to become strategic writers (Englert, Berry, & Dunsmore, 2001; Graham et al., 1991). The good news is that we have made more progress in written expression for students with disabilities than in any other academic area (Vaughn, Gersten, & Chard, 2000). This includes students with disabilities who are bilingual (Echevarria & Graves, 1998; Graves, Valles, & Rueda, 2000). Students may find a checklist like the one in Tips for Teachers 13.2 helpful for monitoring their writing.

## Writing Is an Active Attempt to Convey Meaning

The purpose of writing is to communicate a message. If you ask a student with good writing skills, "What is writing?," the response might be, "Writing is communication of thoughts and ideas" or "Writing is sharing a good story." Some students, however, assume that the purpose of writing is only to conform to the conventions of writing (Graham et al., 1991). Asked the same question, students with writing problems might respond, "Writing is spelling all the words right" or "Writing is making a very neat paper."

How can students arrive at such a misconception about writing? Consider the example of Jim Reed, a seventh-grade student with learning disabilities who

## Tips for Teachers

### 13.2 Helping Students to Monitor Their Writing

_____ I found a quiet place to work.

_____ I set up a schedule for when I would work on this paper.

_____ I read or listened to the teacher's directions carefully.

_____ I thought about who would read my paper.

_____ I thought about what I wanted my paper to accomplish.

_____ I started planning my paper before I actually started writing it.

_____ I tried to remember everything I already knew about the topic before I started to write.

_____ I got all the information I needed before starting to write.

_____ I organized my information before starting to write.

_____ I thought about the reader as I wrote.

_____ I thought about what I wanted to accomplish as I wrote.

_____ I continued to develop my plans as I wrote.

_____ I revised the first draft of my paper.

_____ I checked what I wrote to make sure that the reader would understand it.

_____ I checked to make sure that I accomplished my goals.

_____ I reread my paper before turning it in.

_____ I asked other students, the teacher, or my parents when I needed help.

_____ I rewarded myself when I finished my paper.

*Source:* Harris, K. R., & Graham, S. (1992). *Helping young writers master the craft: Strategy instruction and self-regulation in the writing process.* Boston: Brookline Books. Reprinted by permission.

has been assigned to the special education resource room since third grade. In all that time, the focus of his instruction in writing has been on mechanics: spelling, capitalization, and punctuation. He has had worksheet after worksheet for more than four years and still can't get it right. Jim's case is not unusual. In an examination of writing instruction in 10 urban schools, Christenson, Thurlow, Ysseldyke, and McVicar (1989) found that the majority of writing instruction for students with learning disabilities was related to mechanics rather than to composing for genuine audiences.

### Writing Is a Process of Constructing Meaning

When a writer composes, he or she needs to keep potential readers in mind. Readers need to have background information and specific links (such as examples and definitions of new terms) to help them connect the new information with what they already know. In short, the writer needs to take responsibility for helping readers to construct meaning. Stu-

dents with writing difficulties might not understand the role of audience or potential readers or how to help readers construct meaning by providing background knowledge and using predictable story or informational writing structures. For example, Terry Macinello wrote a story about a recent trip but did not indicate where or why he went on his trip and gave only sketchy details of one event. In his narrative, which had no distinguishable beginning, middle, or end, he referred to family members without letting the reader know who they were. Terry doesn't realize that when he writes a story, it is for someone to read and that he needs to fill in some gaps so that readers can understand and enjoy his story.

### research brief

### Effectiveness of the Writing Process with Students with Learning Disabilities

How do students with disabilities progress as writers? Zaragoza and Vaughn (1992) conducted three year-long case studies (with students identified as gifted, low-achieving, and learning disabled) in which they examined the students' progress in writing and writing-related skills (e.g., capitalization, spelling, punctuation). Single case studies have revealed that students in all achievement groups benefit from participating in the writing process. For example, one student with learning disabilities was very hesitant about writing. He asked for constant teacher assistance and would not write unless a teacher worked closely with him. He wrote slowly and neatly, even on first drafts. His first piece of writing was untitled and incomplete. He was insecure about working with other students and never volunteered to share his writing. His piece, entitled "Disneyworld," demonstrated an understanding that you can write down what you really think. He included his own dog in a Disneyworld theme ("Goofy is a dog I like to play with but Goofy is not better than my dog.") The other students loved this story, and asked him to read it over and over.

Subsequently, he frequently volunteered to share his writing with the class. He had a flair for good endings and became the class expert on developing endings. For example, in "The Spooky Halloween," he ended with "Halloween is nothing to play with." "Freddy Is in My Room" ended with "Give it up." This student and many others demonstrated gains on standardized writing measures, as well as increased confidence and skills in their daily writing.

## Writing Is a Socially Mediated Language-Learning Activity

To become more proficient writers, students must have social interaction with others to move forward (Vygotsky, 1978). Students who have experienced failure in learning to write may be reluctant to share their writing with teachers and peers because they are embarrassed about their lack of skill in writing mechanics. It is important, however, that students have the opportunity not only to share their writing, but also to have that sharing focus on the intended meaning rather than on how many words are misspelled. It is also important for young writers to have time to talk with the teacher about composing strategies (Bereiter & Scardamalia, 1982).

*Shared writing* (writing with a teacher, student partner, or group of students) can help some reluctant writers get started and feel more confident about authorship (Mather & Lackowicz, 1992).

## Strategies for Establishing an Environment That Promotes Writing

From what you have already read about current trends and effective writing instruction, you can imagine the importance of planning the environment in which writing is taught. You may recall that Gina (a general education teacher) and her teaching partner Galia (a special education teacher) have created a classroom environment that encourages students to write. Gina and Galia have learned that the classroom's physical and social environment both need to be considered when you establish a writing community.

### Physical Environment

As they planned the physical arrangement of their classroom at the beginning of the year, Gina and Galia had a vision of creating a writer's studio. According to Graves (1983, 1994), the classroom setting should create a work atmosphere similar to that of a studio, which promotes independence and in which students can easily interact. Gina and Galia felt that structuring their classroom as a studio was especially important for students who had already experienced failure in writing. The message they wanted to convey from day one was "This is a place for writers, and all of us are writers. Enjoy!"

A publishing center is set up for making books. Writing materials and supplies are plentiful and readily available to students. At the beginning of the year, Gina and Galia explain guidelines for using materials in responsible ways. In addition to individual writing folders for ongoing writing projects, each student has an assessment portfolio that serves as a record of his or her progress in writing. Individual folders and portfolios are located in a permanent place in the classroom, ready for student or parent conferences. Gina and Galia wanted the room arranged so that students could work together or individually. They planned spaces for writing conferences of small groups of students, teacher and student, and student and student.

They also realized that many students with disabilities would benefit from having technology and tools readily available to facilitate their writing. For this reason, the following tools and technologies were available in their classroom:

- Portable word processor
- Computer

- Slantboard
- Paper with raised lines, highlighted lines, etc.
- Adaptive grip for pencil or pen
- Word cards/word book/key words in a file
- Pocket dictionary
- Pocket thesaurus
- Electronic talking dictionary/thesaurus
- Voice recognition software
- Keyboard with easy access
- Key guard
- Alternative keyboard
- Mouth stick/head pointer with alternate or standard keyboard
- Head mouse/head master with onscreen keyboard
- Switch with scanner

## Social Environment

Realizing that for students to write well, an environment of mutual trust and respect is essential, Gina and Galia have posted the writing workshop's student guidelines (see Figure 13.1) in their classroom. Writers must also be able to depend on the predictability of the classroom structure. Most important, Gina and Galia have read that the tone for writing is set by what the teacher does (Graves, 1983). The guidelines these teachers follow to establish a social environment for a productive writing community are presented in Tips for Teachers 13.3.

---

FIGURE 13.1

**Writing Workshop**

---

### Writing Workshop

1. Write three first drafts.
2. Pick one draft to publish.
3. Self-edit your draft.
4. Have a friend edit your draft.
5. Take your draft to an adult to edit.
6. Publish your draft.
7. Read over your final copy and make corrections.
8. Give a friend your final copy to make corrections.
9. Give an adult your final copy to make corrections.
10. Put your final copy in a cover.
11. Share, help others, go back to step 1.

### Our Rights

- We have the right to use the things in our classroom.
- We have the right to receive caring from our teachers.
- We have the right to be listened to by our teachers and friends.
- We have the right to call our families in cases of emergency.
- We have the right to be decision makers in our classroom.

### Our Responsibilities

- We have the responsibility to encourage and be caring toward our friends and teachers.
- We have the responsibility to treat all things in our classroom carefully.
- We have the responsibility to participate in all activities and help our community to become strong and positive.
- We have the responsibility to help others to meet their responsibilities successfully.

### Classroom Rules

- We try our best.
- We listen and look when others talk.
- We are kind and helpful to others.
- We help others remember the rules.

### Rewards

- We feel proud.
- We have parties and free time.
- We call, tell, write our family.

### Consequences

- We feel sad and disappointed.
- We lose parties and free time.
- We call, tell, write our family.

---

*Source:* Zaragoza, N., & Vaughn, S. (1995). *Writing Workshop Manual.* Unpublished manuscript.

# Tips for Teachers

## 13.3 Establishing a Social Environment for Productive Writing

1. *Write every day for at least 30 minutes.* Students need time to think, write, discuss, rewrite, confer, revise, talk, read, and write some more. Good writing takes time.
2. *Encourage students to develop areas of expertise.* At first, students will write broadly about what they know. With encouragement, however, they can become class experts in a particular area, subject, or writing form. Take the time to help students discover their own writing "turf."
3. *Model the writing process.* Write with students in the classroom. Using an overhead or easel, teachers may share how they compose.
4. *Share writing.* Include in the writing time an opportunity for the whole class to meet to read their writing to others and to exchange comments and questions.
5. *Read to the students.* Share and discuss books, poems, and other readings. Young authors can learn from the writing of others.
6. *Expand the writing community outside the classroom.* Place books published by your students in the library so that other students can use them and so that students can share their writing with other classes. Encourage authors from other classrooms to visit and read their writing.
7. *Develop students' capacity to evaluate their own work.* Students need to develop their own goals and document their progress toward them. By conferring with the teacher, they will learn methods for evaluating their own work.
8. *Slow the pace.* Graves (1985) says, "Teachers need to slow down so kids can hurry up." When teachers ask questions, they need to be patient, giving students time to answer.

## Strategies for Conducting a Writing Workshop

If you were to visit Gina and Galia's classroom during their writing workshop, the first thing you would notice would be variety of activities. Some students would be working individually on a writing project; others would be working in small groups or pairs, generating ideas for a book or putting the final touches on a story. You would also observe that the teachers are very busy. You might see Gina **conferencing** with a student or Galia teaching a minilesson on punctuation to a small group. You would discover that students often choose their own topics but also have expectations that they will provide writing products that reflect a broad range of writing formats (e.g., letter to a pen pal, story biography, persuasive argument). Also, students often have two or three writing projects in progress at a time. Some students have even elected to co-author with a classmate. You would also note that amid all this activity, there is routine. Students seem to know exactly what to do and how to get help if they need it.

What is involved in the writing process? In **prewriting,** a writer collects information about a topic by observing, remembering, interviewing, and reading. In **composing** (or **drafting**), the author attempts to get ideas on paper in the form of a draft. The drafting process tells the author what he or she knows or does not know. In **postwriting,** the author revises, edits, and publishes the work. During **revising,** the fo-

cus is on meaning; points are explored further, ideas are elaborated, and further connections are made. When the author is satisfied with the content, **editing** takes place as the author reviews the piece line by line to determine that each word is necessary. Punctuation, spelling, and other mechanical processes are checked. The final element is **publishing.** If the author considers the piece a good one, it is published.

Students with writing problems differ in the degree to which components of the writing process are difficult for them (Stires, 1983; Zaragoza & Vaughn,

What characteristics of a learning environment promote writing? How can teacher and students effectively conduct a writing workshop?

## making a Difference

## through Action Teaching

### Writing Activities for All Learners

**Interview a Classmate**

**Objective:** To give students practice in developing and using questions as a means for obtaining more information for the piece they are writing

**Grades:** Adapted for all levels

**Materials:** Writing materials and a writing topic, a list of possible questions, a tape recorder (optional)

**Teaching Procedures:** Using the format of a radio or television interview, demonstrate and role-play "mock" interviews with sport, movie, music, and political celebrities. Give the students opportunities to play both roles.

Discuss what types of questions allow the interviewee to give elaborate responses (e.g., open questions), and what types of questions do not allow the interviewee to give a very expanded answer (e.g., closed questions). Practice asking open questions.

Use a piece that you are writing as an example, and discuss whom you might interview to obtain more information. For example, "In writing a piece about what it might be like to go to the New York World's Fair in 1964, I might interview my grandfather, who was there, to obtain more information."

Ask the students to select an appropriate person to interview for their writing piece and to write possible questions. In pairs, the students refine their questions for the actual interview. The students then conduct the interviews and later discuss how information from the interview assisted them in writing their piece.

*Source:* Bos, C. S., & Vaughn, S. (1994). *Strategies for teaching students with learning and behavior problems* (3rd ed., pp. 252–253). Boston: Allyn & Bacon.

**Flashwriting**

**Objective:** To improve writing fluency

**Grades:** Intermediate and above

**Materials:** Paper and pencil; timer

**Teaching Procedures:**
1. Give students 1 or 2 minutes to think of a topic.
2. Start the timer and give students 5 to 10 minutes to flashwrite about the topic.

3. The goal is to keep writing about the topic. If ideas don't come, just write, "I can't think of what to write," until an idea pops up.
4. At the end of the designated time, have pairs of students share their writing.
5. Have the pairs circle key ideas that might be worth developing during extended writing periods.

**Sentence Stretching**

**Objective:** To help students learn to elaborate simple sentences

**Grades:** Intermediate, middle school

**Materials:** Paper and pencil

**Teaching Procedures:**
1. On the board, write a simple sentence of two to four words—for example, "The king fell."
2. Have students expand the sentence by adding words and phrases.
3. If you choose, have students illustrate their expanded sentences and share with the class.

**Up in the Air for a Topic**

**Objective:** To provide support to students with problems with topic selection

**Grades:** Primary and intermediate

**Materials:** Poster with suggestions for topic selection; paper and pencil

**Teaching Procedures:**
1. During writing workshop, discuss topic selection and ask students what they do when they are "stuck" for a topic.
2. Present the following suggestions on a poster:
   - Check your folder and reread your idea list.
   - Ask a friend to help you brainstorm ideas.
   - Listen to others' ideas.
   - Write about what you know: your experiences.
   - Write a make-believe story.
   - Write about a special interest or hobby.
   - Write about how to do something.
   - Think about how you got your last idea.
3. Model or solicit examples for each suggestion, add students' other suggestions, and post the chart in

1992). Many students with writing problems experience significant difficulty in editing and writing final copies because they have difficulty with mechanics. These students often produce well-developed stories that are hard to read because of the mechanical errors. Other students with writing problems have difficulty organizing during the composing stage and need to re-

think the sequencing during revision. Following are descriptions of each of the elements of the writing process.

## Prewriting: Getting Started

"What should I write about?" As a teacher, it's easy to say, "Write about what you did during your sum-

the room for students to consult whenever they are "stuck" for a topic.

*Source:* Bos, C. S., & Vaughn, S. (1994). *Strategies for teaching students with learning and behavior problems* (3rd ed., p. 221). Boston: Allyn & Bacon.

### Finding the Topic by Using the Goldilocks Rule

**Objective:** To help students brainstorm for expository writing topics

**Grades:** Intermediate and above

**Materials:** Timer, paper, and pencil

**Teaching Procedures:**
1. Describe the "Goldilocks procedure."
   - Brainstorm as many ideas as possible in five minutes.
   - Write down all ideas. Don't stop to read or judge them.
   - Stop when timer goes off.
   - Organize ideas into categories with the Goldilocks Rule:
     Too broad
     Too narrow
     Just right
   - Choose a topic from the Just Right category.
2. Model the use of the Goldilocks procedure.
3. Try out the procedure as a whole-class activity.
4. Have students try out the procedure independently and then share their topics in small groups.

*Source:* Schumm, J. S., & Radencich, M. (1992). *School power.* Minneapolis: Free Spirit Publishing.

### Tell It Again

**Objective:** To help students learn story elements

**Grades:** Primary, intermediate

**Materials:** Paper, pencil, crayons, markers

**Teaching Procedures:** Story retellings are a good way to determine which elements of a story are familiar (and unfamiliar) to your students. To help students "Tell It Again," follow these steps:

1. Provide a story for your students. It might be a story you read, that they read independently or with a partner, or a story they hear on TV or on a video.

2. Decide on a retelling format. Students can retell the story by drawing pictures of major events (making a wordless picture book), rewriting and illustrating the story, dramatizing the story, or by orally retelling the story to you or to a friend.

3. Keep tabs on the story elements your students include in their retellings. If a story element (such as setting, character, plot) is missing, provide instruction (either individually, in small groups, or with the class as a whole) about one element at a time. Monitor that element in subsequent retelling assignments.

### The RAFT Technique

**Objective:** To help students learn to vary their writing in respect to writer's role, audience, format, and topic

**Grades:** Intermediate and above

**Materials:** Paper and pencil

**Teaching Procedures:** The RAFT technique was developed by Santa (1988) to help secondary students write in the content areas. RAFT provides a framework for thinking about how to write for different purposes by varying the writer's role, audience, format, and topic. Here's how to teach it:

1. Explain the components of RAFT:
   *Role of the writer.* Who are you? A professor? A volcano? An ancient Egyptian?
   *Audience.* Who will be your reader? A friend? A famous athlete? A lawyer?
   *Format.* What form will your writing take? A brochure? A letter? A newspaper article?
   *Topic.* What topic have you chosen? Hazards of smoking? Need for gun control? How cheese is made?

2. Write R–A–F–T on the board or on a transparency. Brainstorm with students about possible roles, audiences, formats, and topics. Following is an example:
   **R**—Role = a liver
   **A**—Audience = alcoholic
   **F**—Format = script for TV commercial
   **T**—Topic = the ill effects of drinking

3. Have students work in cooperative groups to generate other RAFT ideas.

4. Have students work independently to complete a RAFT assignment.

mer vacation," but Graves (1983) emphasizes that the key to engaging students as writers is to have them select topics. Saying to students, "Just write about anything," isn't enough. Students want to select topics but don't know how (Zaragoza & Vaughn, 1995a). The following section shows how to help students approach topic selection.

**Selecting Topics**   Give each student (and yourself) a piece of paper. Say to them, "You know lots of things about yourself, about your family, and about your friends. You have hobbies and activities that you like to do. You have stories about things that have happened to you and to people you know. You have lots of things to share with others. I want you to make a

One way to model brainstorming for a topic is to use an overhead projector. On the transparency write a list of things you do very well—in which you're an expert. Then select one item from the list to write about. Have your students develop their own "expert list" and add it to their writing folder (Routman, 1991).

list of things you would like to share with others through writing. Do not put them in any specific order—just write them down as you think of them. You will not have to write on all of these topics. The purpose of this exercise is to think of as many topics as you can. I will give you about 10 minutes. Begin." For older students, teachers might want to talk about the different genres of writing, including personal biography, persuasion, sarcasm, humor, narrative story, and reporting, as a means to facilitate topic generation.

Model the process by writing as many topics as you can think of during the assigned time. When time is up, tell the students to pick a partner and share their topics. They may add any new topics they think of at this time. Then share your list with the entire group and comment on topics you are looking forward to writing about. Ask for volunteers to read their topic lists to the entire group. Have students select the three topics they are most interested in writing about and place their topic lists in their writing folders as resources for future writing. Finally, ask students to select one of their top three topics and begin writing.

Teachers may want to hold students accountable for writing in multiple genres. For example, you might say, "During this six-week period, I need you to submit a completed composition in each of the following areas: story, opinion, and expository factual report on a topic of interest."

**Problems in Topic Selection**   Maintaining a supply of writing topics is difficult for some students. When students tell you stories, ask them whether the story generates a topic they might want to write about. When students read or you read to them, ask whether the reading has given them ideas for their own writing. If they were going to write the end of the story, how would they do it? If they were going to continue this story, what would happen? If they were going to add characters to the story, what type of characters would they add? Would they change the setting?

Some students want to repeat the same topic. Students with writing problems may find security in repeating a topic or theme in their writing. Before suggesting that students change topics, check whether their stories are changing in other ways (through development of vocabulary, concept, story, or character). Students may be learn-

ing a great deal about writing, even though the topic is the same.

**Planning**   Prewriting also includes developing a plan for writing. Planning for writing includes the following steps:

1. *Identify the intended audience.* To make a writing project meaningful, it is important that the writer identify the audience. Who will be the reader? The audience might be family, friends, businesspeople, politicians, teachers, potential employers—or one's self.
2. *State a purpose for writing.* The purpose for writing may be to inform, entertain, or persuade. An example of a purpose statement might be "I am writing this story about my imaginary pet shark Gums to entertain my friends."
3. *Decide on a format.* Before writing begins, it's good to have a general idea of how the piece will be structured. Although the structure may change during drafting and revision, it's good to have an initial road map at the prewriting stage.

Graham, Harris, and their colleagues (e.g., De La Paz & Graham, 1997; Sexton, Harris, & Graham, 1998; Troia, Graham, & Harris, 2000) have successfully taught students with learning disabilities to use the following strategy with improvements in their composition:

1. Think, "Who will read this, and why am I writing it?"
2. Plan what to say using the acronym TREE (note Topic sentence, note Reasons, Examine reasons, note Ending).
3. Write and say more.

Some students are limited in text-organization skills because they have difficulty categorizing ideas

What are the stages of the writing process? What are some effective strategies for teaching each stage to students?

related to a specific topic, providing advance orga-nizers for the topic, and relating and extending ideas about the topic (Englert & Raphael, 1988). As you teach the thought that goes into a piece of writing, you can model your own thinking as you move from topic selection to planning for audience, purpose, and format to drafting. During whole-class sharing time, you can also encourage students to tell how they gen-erated topics and planned for their own writing.

## Composing

The purpose of the composing stage is to develop an initial draft that will be refined later. Some teachers call this a *sloppy copy*. Many students with learning and behavior problems think of a topic and, without much planning, begin writing. Composing is also difficult for students who lack fluency in the me-chanics of writing or in the physical act of writing. During composing, it is important that you assume the role of coach and encourage students to concen-trate on getting their ideas on paper (Graham, 1992).

## Revising and Editing

The purpose of revision is to make certain that the meaning is clear and that the message can be un-derstood by others. Editing focuses mainly on me-

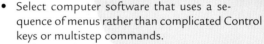

### Using Personal Computers for Word Processing

Word processing on personal computers holds great promise not only for students with writing disabili-ties, but also for students who have problems with composing, spelling, or handwriting. Using word-processing software, students can revise and edit text more easily and can publish a neat, legible final prod-uct. Reviewing research on the use of computers by students with writing disabilities, Majsterek (1990) observed that research in this area is in its infancy and has yielded mixed findings. Nonetheless, on the basis of the current research, Majsterek made the following initial recommendations about using computers with students with writing disabilities:

- Select computer software that emphasizes a proc-ess approach to writing (i.e., prewriting, compos-ing, revising, editing, publishing). Examples are *Kidspiration* (Inspiration Software, Inc., at www. inspiration.com), *Hollywood High* (Scholastic at

www.scholastic.com), and *The Writing Workshop* (Milliken Publish-ing at www.millikenpub.com).
- Select computer software that uses a se-quence of menus rather than complicated Control keys or multistep commands.
- Make certain that students are familiar with the writing process before you introduce them to computer software.
- Review the software manual and either adapt for students with reading problems or develop cue sheets to simplify procedures.
- Keep in mind that for many students, concurrently learning keyboarding, machine skills, and writing software commands can be a demanding task. Teach basic keyboarding and machine skills be-fore you introduce writing-process software.
- Keep a balance between writing with and without a word processor so that students will work on handwriting, spelling, and composition skills in both modes.

Courtesy of The Learning Company.

Courtesy of Knowledge Adventure.

chanics, such as proofreading. After the students and teacher are happy with the content, it is time to finalize correction of spelling, capitalization, punctuation, and language. During editing, students circle words whose spelling they are not sure of, put boxes where they are unsure of punctuation, and underline sentences in which they feel the language may not be correct. Students are not expected to correct all errors but are expected to correct known errors. Revising and editing are difficult tasks for all writers, especially beginning writers and students for whom writing is difficult. Getting the entire message down on paper the first time is difficult enough; making changes so that the piece is at its best and can be understood by others is a most formidable task.

Most students with learning and behavior problems have difficulty revising and editing. Teachers often find it best initially to let students move to publication without much revision, then gradually show them the benefits of revision and editing.

**The AOK Strategy**    The **AOK strategy**, which stands for "all OK" (Schumm, 1987), is a way to help students learn to read and reread for different purposes during revision and editing: for meaning, paragraphs, sentences, words, and neatness. For students with learning and behavior problems, concentrate on one aspect of the AOK strategy at a time and build gradually. The strategy consists of evaluating five areas, as follows:

> *Revising,* which means attending to meaning, is an ongoing process. You need to tell your students that they may need to revise once, twice, or more until they feel that their intended meaning is expressed clearly and completely.

- **MOK** (Is the meaning OK?) This stage involves reading for revision, to determine whether the message is communicated to the reader. After "MOKing," many authors need to obtain more information or to confer with others to find out what parts of the piece are going over well and what parts need additional work. It is also at this stage that some authors abandon the piece and start again with a new idea.

- **POK** (Is each paragraph OK?) "POKing" is reading to see whether paragraphs are logically organized and made up of sentences that are all related to each other.

- **SOK** (Is each sentence OK?) "SOKing" is reading to determine whether sentences are well constructed and punctuated correctly.

- **WOK** (Is each word OK?) "WOKing" is reading to determine whether words are spelled, capitalized, and used correctly.

- **NOK** (Is the neatness OK?) "NOKing," the final stage, refers to getting the piece ready for publication.

The AOK strategy can be adapted to meet curriculum objectives at any grade level (see Table 13.1).

Adolescents with disabilities (Wong, Butler, Ficzere, & Kuperis, 1997) can learn procedures such as compare, diagnose, and operate to assist them during the revision process (De La Paz, Swanson, & Graham, 1998). When teachers model, demonstrate, and provide feedback using the following procedure, students' revisions and writing improve.

**Global Concerns**

1. Compare and Diagnose. Read your writing and consider the following:
   - Ignores the obvious point against my idea
   - Too few ideas
   - Part of the essay doesn't belong with the rest
   - Part of the essay is not in the right order

2. Tactic Operations
   - Rewrite
   - Delete
   - Add
   - Move

3. Compare
   - Reread the paper and highlight problems

4. Diagnose and Operate
   - This doesn't sound right
   - This isn't what I intended to say
   - This is an incomplete idea
   - This part is not clear

The problem is _____

The following suggestions are designed to assist students in removing the mechanical barriers from their writing (Isaacson & Gleason, 1997):

- Have students dictate their story to improve the flow of their writing.

- Provide students with a list of key words and difficult-to-spell words to assist with writing and editing.

- Promote peer collaboration in editing.

---

## TABLE 13.1

### AOK Sample Questions

| First Grade | Sixth Grade |
|---|---|
| **MOK** (Is the meaning OK?)<br>1. Did I say what I wanted to say?<br>2. Does it make sense?<br>3. Are my facts correct? | **MOK** (Is the meaning OK?)<br>1. Are ideas expressed clearly?<br>2. Are ideas expressed concisely?<br>3. Are ideas expressed completely?<br>4. Are ideas expressed correctly? |
| | **POK** (Is each paragraph OK?)<br>1. Is each paragraph indented?<br>2. Do paragraphs consist of sentences related to one topic sentence?<br>3. Is each paragraph connected logically with paragraphs that come before and after? |
| **SOK** (Is each sentence OK?)<br>1. Is there a period or question mark at the end of each sentence?<br>2. Is the first word capitalized?<br>3. Does each sentence make sense? | **SOK** (Is each sentence OK?)<br>1. Is there a period, question mark, or exclamation mark at the end of each sentence?<br>2. Is the first word capitalized?<br>3. Does each sentence make sense?<br>4. Does each sentence express a complete thought?<br>5. Is the sentence a fragment or a run-on?<br>6. Do the subject and verb agree?<br>7. Are commas used correctly?<br>8. Are direct quotations capitalized and punctuated correctly? |
| **WOK** (Is each word OK?)<br>1. Is each word spelled correctly?<br>2. Are the names of people capitalized? | **WOK** (Is each word OK?)<br>1. Is each word spelled correctly?<br>2. Is each word capitalized correctly?<br>3. Is each word correct the way it is used in the sentence?<br>4. Are slang words used?<br>5. Are pronoun referents clear?<br>6. Are any words overused?<br>7. Is each word the BEST word or could a more effective synonym be substituted? |
| **NOK** (Is the neatness OK?)<br>1. Are the size and shape of each letter OK?<br>2. Are words and letters spaced correctly?<br>3. Are the margins even?<br>4. Is the heading correct? | **NOK** (Is the neatness OK?)<br>1. Are the size, shape, and slant of letters OK?<br>2. Are words and letters spaced correctly?<br>3. Are the margins even?<br>4. Is the format correct? |

*Source:* Schumm, J. S. (1987). A-OK: A reading for revision strategy. *Reading: Exploration and Discovery, 10*(1), 26–34.

**Peer Editing** In addition to revising and editing their own work, students can serve as editors for the work of their peers. This **peer editing** can work several ways. One way is to have students edit their own work first and then ask a friend to edit it. Another way is to establish a class editor who is responsible for reading the material and finding mechanical errors. The role of class editor can rotate so that every student has an opportunity to serve in that capacity.

It is important that students not be too critical while revising and editing each other's work. You can communicate that the purpose of revising and editing is to support the author in developing a finished piece. You can also model acceptable ways to give feedback.

## Publishing

Not all student writing is published; often only one in five or six pieces is published. *Publishing* means preparing a piece so that others can read it. Publication is often in the form of books with cardboard bindings decorated with contact paper or scraps of wallpaper. Books can include a picture of the author, a description of the author, and a list of books published by the author. Young children writing short pieces may publish every two weeks; older students who spend more time composing and revising publish less frequently.

Publishing is a way to confirm a student's hard work and share the piece with others. Publishing is also a way to involve others in school and at home with the students' writing. It is important for all students to publish, not just the best authors.

## Sharing

Sharing work with others is important during all stages of the writing process. The author's chair (Graves & Hansen, 1983) is a formal opportunity to share writing. When Romain, a student who recently moved from Haiti to the United States, signed up for author's chair early in the school year, Galia and Gina were surprised. Romain, the most reluctant writer in their class, was also extremely self-conscious about not being able to spell. During author's chair, Romain sat on a special stool in a circle of peers and read his letter to an imaginary pen pal in Haiti. He described life in Miami and ended with a wish: "I hope that you are happy and have enough food to eat." It turned out that most of Romain's story wasn't written at all—he held a paper in front of him and made up the letter as he spoke. But because Romain got a positive response from his audience about how well he communicated his ideas, he was encouraged to become a writer. The author's chair experience was his launching point.

Teachers often need to set rules for students' behavior when a classmate is sharing work in the author's chair. Such rules might include raising one's hand, asking a question, making a positive comment, and giving feedback when asked. A simple but powerful framework for students to give each other feedback about their writing is called **TAG** (Zaragoza, 1987):

> **T**ell what you like.
> **A**sk questions.
> **G**ive suggestions.

After an author has read his or her writing, the author leads the class in a TAG session, asking class members the three questions "What did you like?," "Do you have any questions?," and "Do you have any suggestions?" Three or four responses are usually allowed for each question. TAG sessions give authors valuable feedback about their writing as well as a chance to lead a class discussion.

**Conferencing** The heart of the writing workshop—the student–teacher writing conference—is ongoing. The student comes to the writing conference prepared to read his or her piece, to describe problem areas, and to respond to questions. Students know that the teacher will listen and respond and that they will be asked challenging questions about their work. Questions should be carefully selected, with enough time allotted for the student to respond. Even though you may see many problems with the piece of writing, try to focus on only one or two specific areas. Some key points about conferencing with students are presented in Tips for Teachers 13.4.

> In addition to student–teacher writing conferences, students can learn (with some preparation) to have writing conferences with each other. Guidelines for giving and receiving feedback need to be clearly defined.

**Teaching Writing Skills** A question frequently asked about writing workshop is "When do I teach skills?" This question is especially important for teachers whose students have poor writing skills to be-

# Tips for Teachers

## 13.4    Guidelines for Conducting a Writing Conference

### Big Principles of a Writing Conference

1. *Follow the student's lead during the conference.* Avoid imposing your ideas about the topic or the way you would write the story.

2. *Listen to and accept what the student says.* When you talk more than the writer does during conferences, you are being too directive.

3. *Ask questions the students can answer.*

4. *Make conferences frequent and brief.* Although conferences can range from 30 seconds to 10 minutes, most last 2 to 3 minutes.

5. *Listen to what students have written and tell them what you hear.* Nancy Atwell (1985) suggests that students should retain the right to reject the teacher's advice.

### Suggestions to Compliment Writing

1. I like the way your paper began in this way . . .

2. I like the part where . . .

3. I like the way you explained . . .

4. I like the order you used in your paper because . . .

5. I like the details you used to describe . . .

6. I like the way you used dialogue to make your story sound real. In particular, this section . . .

7. I like the action and describing the words you used in your writing, such as . . .

8. I like the facts you used, such as . . .

9. I like the way the paper ended because . . .

10. I like the mood of your writing because it made me feel . . .

### Questions and Suggestions to Improve Writing

1. I got confused in the part about . . .

2. Could you add an example to the part about . . .

3. Could you add more to this _____ part because . . .

4. Do you think your order would make more sense if you . . .

5. Do you think you could leave this part out because . . .

6. Could you use a different word for _____ because . . .

7. Is this _____ paragraph on one topic?

8. Could you write a beginning sentence to "grab" your readers?

9. What happens in the end?

10. Can you think of another word for "said"?

---

gin with. Prolific writing without help from a teacher will not lead to improvement (Graham, 1992).

Skills lessons can be taught to the class as a whole and then in small groups composed of students who need additional knowledge and practices with a specified skill. Skills lessons, or minilessons, should be brief (15–20 minutes), and the topics for these lessons should be based on the students' needs. Ideas for topics can come from your observations of student writing, requests for help, and data from writing conferences. After teaching a skill and providing ample opportunities to practice it, help students to generalize and apply the skill in their daily writing. As Graham (1992, p. 140) recommended for students with writing problems, skills are best taught in the context of "real" writing and have the most impact when they bring the greatest rewards in writing improvement.

##  Strategies for Teaching Narrative Writing

In the elementary grades and in middle school, students typically practice **narrative writing** (writing stories). For many students, story writing is not a problem. Through hearing and reading stories, they have learned the basic elements of a story and can incorporate those elements into their own storytelling and writing. According to Montague and Graves (1993), students with writing problems may be aware of story elements but may not incorporate them into their writing in a systematic way. Students with writing problems may also exhibit the following problems when they compose stories:

- Lack of organization
- Lack of unity and coherence

- Lack of character development
- Incomplete use of story elements

Story webbing and direct instruction on the development of story elements are effective ways to address these difficulties.

## Using Story Webs to Plan

**Story webs,** or *maps*, were originally developed as visual displays to help students understand the structure of the stories they read (Beck & McKeown, 1981; Bos, 1987; Idol, 1987). Stories are composed of predictable elements and have a characteristic narrative structure or story grammar. Elements of stories include the setting, characters, a problem statement, the goal, the event sequence or episodes, and the res-

olution or ending (Mandler & Johnson, 1977; Stein & Glenn, 1979). Using story webs such as the one shown in Figure 13.2, students can trace these elements when they read, plan, or write a story.

You can conduct minilessons on webbing with your whole class or just with students who need help with story planning. To introduce the story web, first talk about its components and model its use in planning a story. You might want to have students work together in small, mixed-ability groups to plan a group story.

## Instruction in Story Development

As was previously stated, some students might include a story element, such as a main character, in their stories but fail to develop the element fully.

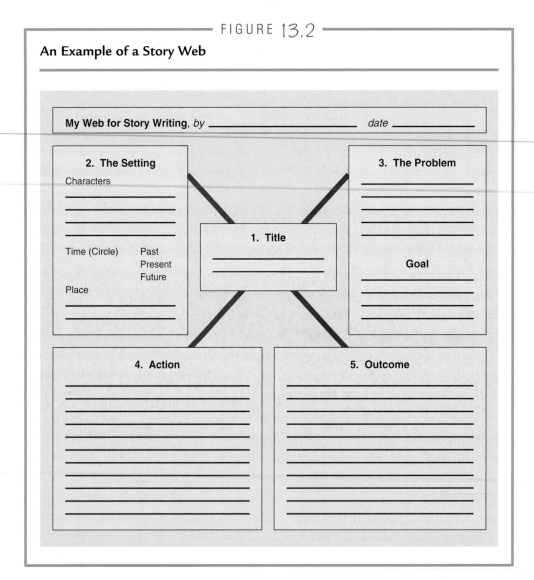

=== FIGURE 13.2 ===

**An Example of a Story Web**

**My Web for Story Writing,** *by* _____ *date* _____

**2. The Setting**
Characters
_____
_____
_____

Time (Circle)    Past
                Present
                Future
Place
_____

**1. Title**
_____

**3. The Problem**
_____
_____
_____
_____

Goal
_____
_____

**4. Action**
_____
_____
_____
_____
_____
_____
_____
_____
_____

**5. Outcome**
_____
_____
_____
_____
_____
_____
_____
_____
_____

*Source:* Zipprich, M. (1995). Teaching web-making as a guided planning tool to improve student narrative writing. *Remedial and Special Education, 16*(1), 3–15, 52. Copyright © 1995 by PRO-ED, Inc. Reprinted by permission.

# Tips for Teachers

## 13.5  Teaching Characterization in Story Development

1. In discussing stories students have read or heard, talk about how authors develop characters.
2. Provide explicit instruction in character development by conducting minilessons on describing physical appearance, speech, actions, thoughts, and emotions.
3. Have students brainstorm examples of vivid words for physical appearance, speech, actions, thoughts, and emotions.
4. Teach students to evaluate character development in their own stories and to use feedback to improve their writing.
5. Provide a cue sheet to help students monitor character development as they plan and write.

*Source:* Adapted from Leavell, A., & Ioannides, A. (1993). Using character development to improve story writing. *Teaching Exceptional Children, 25,* 41–45.

Leavell and Ioannides (1993) provided some recommendations for helping students improve character development in their stories (see Tips for Teachers 13.5). Graves and Hauge (1993) developed the cue sheet shown in Figure 13.3 to help students improve their story writing.

## FIGURE 13.3

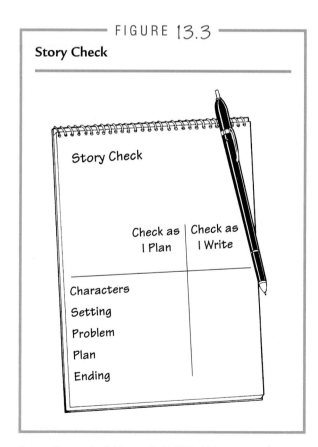

### Story Check

*Source:* Graves, A., & Hauge, R. (1993). Using cues and prompts to improve story writing. *Teaching Exceptional Children, 25*(4), 38–45. Copyright 1993 by the Council for Exceptional Children.

## Strategies for Teaching Expository Writing

**Expository writing,** or informational writing, once reserved for middle and upper grades, is now being included in the curriculum for even very young students. Expository writing poses particular problems to students with writing problems who may be unaware of the purpose of informational writing (Englert et al., 1988). Graham and Harris (1989) reported that the informational writing of students with learning disabilities often contains irrelevant information and inappropriate conclusions.

### Paragraph Writing

Students with writing problems often have difficulty developing coherent, logical paragraphs. The **PLEASE strategy** (Welch, 1992; Welch & Link, 1989) was developed to provide students with a step-by-step procedure for paragraph writing:

Pick the topic, audience, and paragraph type (cause/effect, compare/contrast, etc.).
List information about the topic.
Evaluate whether the list is complete and also determine how to order items in the list.
Activate your writing by starting with a topic sentence.
Supply supporting or detail sentences, using items from the list.
End with a strong concluding sentence, and evaluate the paragraph by revising and editing.

### Essay Writing

As students mature and move through the grades, they must progress from writing paragraphs to writing well-developed essays. Graham and Harris (1989) developed a three-step strategy for helping students learn to write essays:

Step 1. Think about the audience and purpose for writing the essay.
Step 2. Plan the essay, using the **TREE method:**
Write a Topic sentence.
Think of Reasons to support the topic sentence.
Examine your reasons.
Think of an Ending or conclusion.
Step 3. Write the essay.

Typically, essays written to persuade or convince others are included in school curricula and state writing-assessment tests. Atwell (1987) suggests the following procedure for helping students learn to write persuasive essays:

1. *Make a list of arguments.* State your arguments in positive terms. Be convincing.
2. *Start with a purpose statement,* and explain why you are presenting the argument.
3. *Organize the list of arguments* into points to be made.
4. *Write one paragraph to elaborate each point.*
5. *Use transition words (e.g., moreover, in addition)* to aid coherence and logic.
6. *End with a strong closing statement* that summarizes the argument and suggests future action.

## Research Paper Writing

As students progress through the grades, summarizing information in the form of a research paper is a common assignment. Korinek and Bulls (1996) offer a strategy to help students get organized for what can be a cumbersome task—not just for students with disabilities, but for any student with organizational problems or who has difficulty with long-range, multiphase assignments. The mnemonic **SCORE A** (the goal for a grade) is used to identify the steps:

Select a topic.
Create categories.
Obtain reference tools.
Read and take notes.
Evenly organize the information using notecards.
Apply writing process steps (i.e., prewriting, drafting, etc.).

## Strategies for Helping All Students Acquire Spelling Skills

Even in the age of computers and word processors with spell-check programs, learning how to spell is important. If a writer is bogged down with the spelling of even commonly used words, progress in writing is stymied. Many students with reading and learning disabilities are poor spellers (Johnson & Myklebust, 1967). Spelling, like reading, involves phonological awareness. Research by Gentry (1982) on the stages of spelling development clearly points to the role of phonological awareness in learning to spell standard English (see Figure 13.4). Without specific instruction, some students (because of their problems with phonological awareness) can easily get stuck in the early stages of spelling development. You will discover also that even very good readers can be poor spellers (Carpenter & Miller, 1982; Frith, 1980). The English language contains many irregular forms and is not as regular phonemically as other written languages, such as Spanish. Irregularities can stump even the most phonemically aware.

Spelling instruction is important for all students, but the students in your class are likely to differ in terms of their stages of development, the types of errors they make, and what they need to learn in spelling to become more fluent writers. What instructional methods can you use to teach all your students to spell?

## Traditional Spelling Instruction

Mary Jacobs uses a traditional spelling-instruction model in her third-grade class. All students in the class have the same third-grade spelling book. Each lesson in the speller focuses on a particular pattern (e.g., long vowels, short vowels, vowel plus *r*, prefixes). On Monday, Mary gives a spelling pretest on the 15 new words, and for homework, students write (five times) each word they missed. On Tuesday and Wednesday nights, students are assigned exercises in the spelling book. On Thursday night, they write one sentence for each word on the list. On Friday during class, Mary gives students a spelling test on the 15 words. Some teachers vary this traditional pattern by selecting words from the

─── FIGURE 13.4 ───

**Characteristics of Learners in Five Stages of Development**

**Stage 1: Precommunicative Spelling**

- Uses scribbles, letter-like forms, letters, and sometimes numbers to represent a message.

- May write from left to right, right to left, top to bottom, or randomly on the page.

- Shows no understanding of phoneme–grapheme correspondences.

- May repeat a few letters again and again or use most of the letters of the alphabet.

- Frequently mixes upper- and lowercase letters but shows a preference for uppercase letters.

**Stage 2: Semiphonetic Spelling**

- Becomes aware of the alphabetic principle that letters are used to represent sounds.

- Uses abbreviated one-, two-, or three-letter spelling to represent an entire word.

- Uses letter–name strategy to spell words (e.g., U for you).

**Stage 3: Phonetic Spelling**

- Represents all essential sound features of a word in spelling.

- Develops particular spellings for long and short vowels, plural and past tense markers, and other aspects of spelling.

- Chooses letters on the basis of sound, without regard for English letter sequences or other conventions.

**Stage 4: Transitional Spelling**

- Adheres to basic conventions of English orthography.

- Begins to use morphological and visual information in addition to phonetic information.

- May include all appropriate letters in a word but reverse some of them.

- Uses alternate spellings for the same sound in different words, but only partially understands the conditions governing their use.

- Uses a high percentage of correctly spelled words.

**Stage 5: Correct Spelling**

- Applies the basic rules of the English orthographic system.

- Extends knowledge of word structure, including the spelling of affixes, contractions, compound words, and homonyms.

- Demonstrates growing accuracy in using silent consonants and doubling consonants before adding suffixes.

- Recognizes when a word doesn't "look right" and can consider alternate spellings for the same sound.

- Learns irregular spelling patterns.

- Learns consonant and vowel alternations, and other morphological structures.

- Knows how to spell a large number of words.

*Source:* Genry, J. R. (1982). An analysis for developmental spelling in GYNS at WRK. *The Reading Teacher, 36,* 192–200. Copyright by the International Reading Association.

basal reader or from the current science or social studies unit.

## Spelling Instruction for Students with Difficulties in Learning How to Spell

How appropriate is the traditional approach for classrooms that include students of different academic levels? Many students who are good spellers know all the words at the beginning of the week and so have no real challenge. For students with learning difficulties, 15 words may be too many to learn, feedback about their errors may be ineffective, and the amount of practice insufficient. In addition, traditional spelling instruction does not teach for transfer to new situations. Students often learn words from their speller, get 100 percent on the test, but misspell those same words in their compositions. Tips for Teachers 13.6 provides language you can use to improve spelling.

# Tips for Teachers

## 13.6 Providing Instructional Feedback to Help Students Spell Correctly

### Prompts to Help Students Notice Errors

Check to see if that looks/sounds right.

There is a word spelled incorrectly on this line.

You're nearly right with this word.

Try it another way that goes with the rule.

You've almost got it spelled right.

The vowel needs to be changed.

### Prompts to Help Students Fix Errors

What do you hear first? Next? Last?

What word starts with those letters?

Do you think it looks/sounds like _____?

What does an *e* do at the end of a word?

What do you know that might help?

What could you try?

You said _____. Does that make sense?

(Repeat what child said). Can you think of a better way to say _____?

### Prompts to Help Students Find Errors

Find the part that's not right.

Look carefully to see what's wrong.

You noticed something was wrong.

Where is the part that's not right?

### Prompts to Help Students Write Words

You have only one letter to change.

That sounds right, but does it look right?

One more letter will make it right.

It starts like that. Now check the last part.

Did you write all the sounds you hear?

Did you write a vowel for each syllable?

What do you hear first? Next? Last?

It starts (ends) like _____.

There's a silent letter in that word.

You wrote all the sounds you hear. Now look at what you wrote—Think!

*Source:* Adapted from Fountas, I. C., & Pinnell, G. S. (1998). *Word matters: Teaching phonics and spelling in the reading/writing classroom.* Portsmouth, N.H.: Heinemann; Fountas, I. C., & Pinnell, G. S. (1996). *Guided reading: Good first teaching for all children.* Portsmouth, N.H.: Heinemann; and Fry, E. B., Kress, J. E., & Fountoukidis, D. L. (1993). *The reading teacher's book of lists.* New York: The Center for Applied Research in Education.

## research brief

### Spelling Instruction for Students with Disabilities

Gordon, Vaughn, and Schumm (1993), in a search for empirically based instructional practices for improving the spelling skills of students with learning disabilities, reviewed 15 studies on spelling acquisition, in which the research focused on students with learning disabilities. Findings from the studies can be grouped into six areas of instructional practice:

- Error imitation and modeling
- Unit size
- Modality
- Computer-assisted instruction (CAI)
- Peer tutoring
- Study techniques

*Error Imitation and Modeling.* Students with learning disabilities need to compare each incorrectly spelled word with the correct spelling. The teacher copies the incorrect spelling and then writes the word correctly, calling attention to features in the word that will help students remember the correct spelling.

*Unit Size.*    Students with learning disabilities tend to become overloaded and have difficulty when they have to study several words at once. These students can learn to spell if the unit size of their assigned list is reduced to three words a day and if effective instruction is offered for those three words.

*Modality.*    When studying words, students with learning disabilities learned equally by (1) writing the words, (2) arranging and tracing letter shapes or tiles, and (3) typing the words at a computer. Most students preferred to practice their spelling words at a computer.

*Computer-Assisted Instruction (CAI).*    Computer-assisted instruction (CAI) has been shown to be effective in improving the spelling skills of students with learning disabilities. CAI software programs for spelling improvement often emphasize awareness of word structure and spelling strategies and make use of time delay, voice simulation, and sound effects.

*Peer Tutoring.*    A teacher's individual help is preferable, but structured peer tutoring can be a viable alternative. In a study conducted by Harper and colleagues (1991), daily peer tutoring was extended classwide by using a team game format. Tutored by their peers, students with learning disabilities achieved 100 percent mastery of their weekly spelling words.

*Study Techniques.*    Study techniques provide a format and a standard procedure that help students with learning disabilities organize their study of spelling.

Meredith Millan is a third-grade teacher whose three students with learning disabilities are in a pull-out program for special education services. Meredith and the special education teacher have agreed that Meredith will assign students their weekly spelling words. Meredith has worked hard to integrate spelling instruction into her ongoing writing program. She likes the idea of having weekly spelling tests but knows that the range of student spelling levels in her class is too broad for all students to benefit from having the same words and the same number of words to learn. The following section describes the way Meredith has structured her spelling program.

**Selecting Words**    Meredith teaches spelling words that correspond with the phonics rules she is teaching in reading. For example, if she is teaching students the VCe rule, by which the first vowel says its name, as part of word study, she also uses VCe words for spelling. This is connecting reading and spelling rules and capitalizes on the patterns of language (Carreker, 1999). This procedure can be used for older students as well. If students are progressing beyond rule-based instruction in reading, then spelling words can be selected from their writing errors or key words needed in their social studies and science instruction.

Each student in Meredith's class has a spelling log, a running list of words. At the beginning of the week, students select words from the log for the Friday spelling test and write the words on their homework sheet. Meredith and each student agree in advance on the number of words. Some students have five or six words, others as many as 20. Meredith also assigns all students two to three words from the thematic unit they are studying at the time. Words that students misspell are taken from the edited drafts of their compositions. During a writing conference, Meredith not only discusses the words a student should add to his or her spelling log, but also asks, "Are there other words you really would like to learn to spell?" and adds them to the log.

**Providing Instruction and Practice**    Meredith provides spelling instruction and practice in four ways: through minilessons, student pairs, parental involvement, and collaboration with the special education teacher. Each week, Meredith provides minilessons on spelling patterns. For example, she noticed that about 20 students were using *-ing* words in their writing and spelling them incorrectly. Meredith met with this group for two weeks, gave them minilessons on adding *-ing,* and included *-ing* words on their spelling tests.

Early in the school year, Meredith figured out that 10 of her students needed more practice preparing for spelling tests. She decided to have these students work in pairs and taught them the following spelling strategy (Graham & Freeman, 1986):

1. Say the word.
2. Write and say the word.
3. Check the word.
4. Trace and say the word.
5. Write the word from memory.
6. Check the word.
7. If incorrect, repeat steps 1–5.

The pairs meet for 15 minutes, three times a week, usually while other students are composing during writing workshop. Meredith involves parents in the spelling program in two ways. First, at the beginning of the year, she writes parents a letter about the spelling program and ways in which parents can help their child study for spelling tests. Second, she invites parents to add one or two words to the spelling list each week. Parents observe their children's writing at home and can pick up on important misspellings.

Two of the students with learning disabilities, Kara and Mitchell, need additional help learning their words. In collaboration with Meredith, the special education teacher helps Kara and Mitchell learn and maintain new words by using individualized, multisensory methods.

**Keeping Track of Student Progress** All students take their Friday spelling test during the same class period. Because it is not possible to give 36 students individual spelling tests based on the words in their spelling logs, Meredith pairs the students to test each other. Students follow these strict guidelines during the test period:

- You can talk only to your partner and only about the test.
- You cannot give or receive information about how to spell words.
- You must take your test in ink—no erasing allowed.

Meredith monitors the test process, collects and grades papers, and adds words missed to next week's spelling list.

## Principles of Effective Spelling Instruction

The following sections describe principles of effective spelling instruction that Meredith observes. Any approach that is used with students who have spelling problems should include these principles.

**Teaching Spelling Patterns** Cunningham and Cunningham (1992) have written that the human brain remembers patterns of words better than rules. In other words, teaching students common **spelling patterns** may be more advantageous than teaching them rules. According to Graham and Miller (1979), students should have frequent exposures to common word patterns such as base words, prefixes, suffixes, consonants, consonant blends, digraphs, and vowel sound–symbol associations.

**Teaching in Small Units** Teach students with spelling problems three words a day rather than four or five. In one study, students with learning disabilities who were assigned three words a day performed better than a control group of students with learning disabilities who were assigned four or five words (Bryant et al., 1981).

**Providing Sufficient Practice and Feedback** Give students opportunities to practice words each day, with feedback. Many teachers do this by having students work with spelling partners who ask them words and provide immediate feedback. Try the following procedure for self-correction and practice:

1. Fold a paper into five columns, and write the correctly spelled words in the first column.
2. The student studies one word, folds the column back, and writes the word in the second column. The student then checks his or her spelling against the correctly spelled word in column one.
3. After folding columns 1 and 2 back, the student writes the word in the third column. When the word is spelled correctly three times, the student moves on to the next word. The student continues until each word is spelled correctly from memory three times in a row.

**Selecting Appropriate Words** The most important strategy for teaching spelling is to make sure that students know how to read the word and already know its meaning. Selection of spelling words should be based on students' existing vocabularies.

**Maintaining Previously Learned Words** For students to be able to remember how to spell words, you must frequently assign (for review) words they've already learned, along with new words. Previously learned words must be reviewed frequently to be maintained.

**Teaching for Transfer of Learning** After spelling words have been mastered, provide opportunities for students to see and use the words in different contexts.

**Motivating Students to Spell Correctly** Using games and activities, selecting meaningful words, and providing examples of the use and need for correct spelling are strategies that help motivate students and give them a positive attitude about spelling (Graham & Miller, 1979).

**Including Dictionary Training** Dictionary training (which includes alphabetizing, identifying target words, and locating the correct definition when several are provided) should be developed as part of the spelling program.

## Strategies for Helping All Students Develop Handwriting Skills

Before typewriters, legible handwriting was a must. Even though we now have typewriters and computers, learning how to write legibly is still a must for students who are physically able. For most students, learning how to write legibly and fluently is a key to success in school.

What strategies work with students who have difficulty learning to spell? How can you help students who have difficulty with handwriting?

## Traditional Handwriting Instruction

In traditional handwriting instruction in the United States, students learn **manuscript writing** (printing) in the early grades and move to **cursive writing** (script) in third grade (Hodges, 1991). Clare Whiting teaches handwriting as a whole-class activity. To plan her lessons, she uses a commercial handwriting program that includes individual student booklets and extra worksheets to serve as models. As a third-grade teacher, Clare begins the school year by reviewing manuscript writing, then introduces the cursive alphabet after the first grading period. Clare assigns grades on the basis of her judgment of the legibility of students' handwriting.

Critics of traditional handwriting instruction say that spending valuable class time on developing legible handwriting is time not well spent, and that time could be better spent teaching students to keyboard. Some critics maintain that handwriting should be taught during composition rather than whole-class instruction (Graves, 1994). Others argue against teaching two handwriting systems, some arguing for manuscript and others for cursive (see Table 13.2). Frose (1981) proposed that both systems be maintained, students deciding individually which form is most comfortable for them. The controversy over manuscript and cursive handwriting adds to the problems of students who have difficulties learning to write. In general, manuscript should be taught early on and maintained. Students who can make the transition to cursive should have the opportunity to do so.

## Students with Difficulty in Handwriting

Students with dysgraphia have severe problems learning to write. Hamstra-Bletz and Blote (1993) define dysgraphia as follows:

*Dysgraphia* is a written-language disorder that concerns the mechanical writing skill. It manifests itself in poor writing performance in children of at least average intelligence who do not have a distinct neurological disability and/or an overt perceptual-motor handicap. . . . Furthermore, dysgraphia is regarded as a disability that can or cannot occur in the presence of other disabilities, like dyslexia or dyscalculia (p. 690).

Poor handwriting, whether of students with dysgraphia or others, may include any of the following characteristics:

- Poor letter formation
- Letters that are too large, too small, or inconsistent in size
- Incorrect use of capital and lowercase letters
- Letters that are crowded and cramped
- Inconsistent spacing between letters
- Incorrect alignment (letters do not rest on a base line)
- Incorrect or inconsistent slant of cursive letters
- Lack of fluency in writing

Fortunately, with direct instruction and regular practice, most of these problems can be handled and corrected.

=== TABLE 13.2 ===

**Manuscript versus Cursive**

**Manuscript**

1. It more closely resembles print and facilitates learning to read.
2. It is easier for young children to learn.
3. It is more legible than cursive.
4. Many students write manuscript at the same rate as cursive and this rate can be significantly influenced through direct instruction.
5. It is better for students with learning disabilities to learn one writing process well than to attempt to learn two.

**Cursive**

1. Many students want to learn to write cursive.
2. Many students write cursive faster.
3. Many adults object to students using manuscript beyond the primary grades.

*Source:* Bos, C. S., & Vaughn, S. (1994). *Strategies for teaching students with learning and behavior problems* (3rd ed., p. 245). Boston: Allyn & Bacon.

## Principles for Effective Handwriting Instruction

It is important to address handwriting problems for several reasons. For one thing, they are associated with reduced interest in writing and thus influence written expression. Also, students with handwriting difficulties spell worse than those without handwriting problems even when spelling interventions are provided (Berninger et al., 1998).

The following instructional principles (Hagin, 1983) are suggested for any effective handwriting program:

- Use direct instruction.
- Use individualized instruction.
- Use a variety of techniques and methods, matching the students' individual needs.
- Teach handwriting frequently, several times a week.
- Teach brief handwriting lessons within the context of students' writing.
- Teach handwriting skills separately and then encourage students to use them.
- Have students evaluate their own handwriting and, when appropriate, the handwriting of others.
- Present your handwriting as a model for the students to follow.
- Teach handwriting not as only a visual task or a motor task, but as both.

To teach handwriting, you must focus on two major components—legibility and fluency—that can be improved when students have correct posture, pencil grip, and paper position:

- *Posture.* Hips touch the back of the chair and feet rest on the floor. The torso leans forward slightly in a straight line. Both forearms rest on the desk, with elbows slightly extended.
- *Pencil grip.* The pencil is held lightly between the thumb and first two fingers, about one inch above the point. The first finger rests on top of the pencil. The end of the pencil points toward the shoulder.
- *Paper position.* For manuscript writing, the paper is held straight in front of the writer, and the nonwriting hand holds the paper in place. For cursive writing, the paper is slanted counterclockwise for a right-hander and clockwise for a left-hander.

**Legibility** Legibility is the most important goal of handwriting, and incorrect letter formation is the most frequent obstacle to reaching that goal. Graham and Miller (1980) suggest the following procedures for teaching letter formation:

- Point out critical attributes by comparing and contrasting letters.

- Use physical prompts and cues—move the student's hand, or provide indicators such as arrows or colored dots.
- Provide specific reinforcement for letters or parts of letters that are formed correctly and corrective feedback for letters that need work.
- Teach self-verbalization (saying aloud the letter formation and then saying it to oneself while writing).

Hanover (1983) provided a system for teaching cursive writing based on the similarities of letters or letter families. Because students learn letters in groups with similar strokes, learning to write letters is easier. Letter families in the **Hanover method** (Hanover, 1983) are shown here in the order recommended for teaching them:

| | |
|---|---|
| e family: | e, l, h, f, b, k |
| handle family: | b, o, v, w |
| hump-shaped family: | n, s, y |
| c family: | c, a, d, o, q, g |
| hump family: | n, m, v, y, x |
| back-tail family: | f, q |
| front-tail family: | g, p, y, z |

One of the most effective ways to develop legibility is to provide a **moving model.** Modeling how to form letters and words is more helpful to students than simply having them copy letters and words (Wright & Wright, 1980). To provide a moving model, sit next to the student. As you form a letter or word, talk the student through the motions you are making. If the child writes with a different hand than you, have another child, a volunteer, or another teacher who writes with that hand provide the model. If you decide to have whole-class handwriting lessons, first provide a model by using the chalkboard or overhead projector; then circulate around the room, providing an individual moving model for students who seem to need the extra support.

**Fluency** After students begin to master basic letter forms and their writing becomes more legible, the next goal is to learn to write quickly and with ease. Tom Reynolds helps students in his class improve their fluency through timed writings and journal writing.

Tom has three students in his fifth-grade class who have improved the legibility of their writing considerably during the school year but who still need to learn to write more quickly. He decided to group the three students together for timed writings. (In a timed writing, students copy a 50-word passage and record the number of minutes the process takes.) When the group met for the first time, Tom showed them how to conduct a timed writing and keep records. For each student, he set up a folder with a collection of passages and a chart for recording progress. During this first meeting, Tom also explained that the idea is to work toward personal improvement, not to compete, and he talked about ways in which they could encourage each other. In time, the students could see that each was becoming a more fluent writer.

The daily 15-minute journal-writing activity Tom plans for all his students is a good way to enhance fluency. Because students know that their journals will not be graded for spelling or handwriting, they take risks and write more. Tom encourages students to evaluate their own journal writing. Tom makes certain that students with fluency problems evaluate how much they write.

At the beginning of the year, Tom talked with the first-grade teacher, Helen Byers, and they decided to initiate a dialogue journal activity (Atwell, 1984; Bode, 1989; Gambrell, 1985). A **dialogue journal** is actually an ongoing written conversation between two students (or in some cases between a student and an adult). Each of Tom's fifth-graders was paired with one of Helen's first-graders. Once a week, the fifth-graders visit the first-grade class and tell or read aloud a story to their first-grade partners. Then the pairs spend some time writing in a dialogue journal.

## summary

- In recent years, the growing trend has been toward a student-centered model of instruction for English and the language arts.
- Reading and writing develop simultaneously, and children's invented spelling can reveal a great deal about their phonological awareness. Thus, a current trend is to encourage students to write as early as possible.
- In response to national concern about the quality of writing among students in the United States, the amount of time allotted to writing instruction has increased.
- As a process, writing (like reading) is (1) interactive, (2) strategic, (3) an active attempt to convey meaning, (4) constructing meaning, and (5) socially mediated.
- Writing is a complex process with many areas of potential difficulty for students. In addition to extra time for writing, students who have difficulty need direct instruction in composing, spelling, and handwriting.
- The elements of the authoring cycle include prewriting, composing, revising, editing, and publishing.

- Skills lessons can be taught in conjunction with students' ongoing writing, using flexible grouping practices. The topics of skills lessons can be based on observations of student writing, requests for help, and data collected from writing conferences.
- Although students with writing problems may be aware of the elements of a story, they do not necessarily incorporate these elements into their writing. Students need direct instruction in narrative writing.
- Students need instruction in expository writing, including typical informational writing patterns and strategic planning for composing informational text.
- Spelling is an important tool for writers. Effective instruction for students with spelling problems includes teaching spelling patterns, teaching in small units, providing feedback and practice, selecting appropriate words, and maintaining previously learned words.
- Because handwriting is still necessary for success in school, students need specific instruction in how to write legibly and fluently.

## key terms and concepts

| | | |
|---|---|---|
| AOK strategy | expository writing | prewriting |
| authoring cycle | Hanover method | publishing |
| composing | invented spelling | revising |
| conferencing | manuscript writing | SCORE A |
| cursive writing | moving model | spelling patterns |
| dialogue journal | narrative writing | story webs |
| drafting | peer editing | student-centered model |
| editing | PLEASE strategy | TAG |
| encode | postwriting | TREE method |

# think and apply

1. Now that you have read Chapter 13, reread the interview with Gina. What strategies does she use to teach writing to her students? What changes might you make to her writing program?

2. What are the pros and cons of competency and student-centered models of writing instruction? Which is most consistent with your own way of thinking about teaching writing?

3. Think about your own experience in developing your writing skills. What instructional methods and procedures were most helpful? Least helpful?

4. Develop a personal writing portfolio to share with your students. In your portfolio include samples of your own writing from different phases of the authoring cycle. If possible, include some samples of your writing (and perhaps pictures of yourself) as a child. The portfolio will demonstrate to your students that you are a writer and will illustrate your own progress as a writer.

5. Interview 10 students from several grade levels to get their perceptions of writing. Ask them, "What is a writer?" and "Are you a writer?" Also ask them, "What kinds of writing do you do at school?," "What kinds of writing do you do at home?," and "What kinds of writing have taught you the most?"

6. If you were conducting a writing workshop in your classroom, how would you identify students who need minilessons? How would you keep track of what students are learning?

7. Plan the following activities: story writing, informational writing, spelling, and handwriting minilessons.

8. Make a list of all the tools and technologies you might use to make accommodations and adaptations for students with disabilities who have difficulties writing.

# read more about it

1. Atwell, N. (1987). *In the middle: Writing, reading, and learning with adolescents.* Portsmouth, NH: Boynton/Cook.

   *A middle-school teacher's inspirational, informative story about initiating writing and reading workshops in the classroom.*

2. Bright, R. (1995). *Writing instruction in the intermediate grades: What is said, what is done, what is understood.* Newark, DE: International Reading Association.

   *What do intermediate students think about the writing process? Here are some insights that have direct implication for instruction, drawn from observational studies.*

3. Fearn, L., & Farnan, N. (1998). *Writing effectively: Helping children master the conventions of writing.* Boston: Allyn & Bacon.

   *Trouble with capitalization, punctuation or grammar? Here's a set of lesson plans that can help.*

4. Fulk, B. M., & Stormont-Spurgin, M. (1995). Fourteen spelling strategies for students with learning disabilities. *Intervention in School and Clinic, 31,* 16–20.

   *A summary of research-based strategies for effective spelling instruction.*

5. Graves, D. H. (1983). *Writing: Teachers and children at work.* Portsmouth, NH: Heinemann.

   *A classic introduction to the writing process, with suggestions for implementing the writing process in the classroom.*

6. Graves, D. H. (1994). *A fresh look at writing.* Portsmouth, NH: Heinemann.

   *An excellent resource for implementing the writing process, with sections on using portfolios to assess writing, engaging parents in the writing process, and introducing students to different genres.*

7. Moffett, J., & Wagner, B. J. (1992). *Student-centered language arts, K–12* (4th ed.). Portsmouth, NH: Boynton/Cook.

   *Nine objectives for discourse and specific instructional suggestions for helping students learn to send and receive oral and written messages.*

8. Routman, R. (1991). *Invitations: Changing as teachers and learners K–12.* Portsmouth, NH: Heinemann.

   *A comprehensive guide to whole-language teaching, with excellent chapters on setting authentic contexts, journal writing, and spelling instruction. A chapter on students with learning disabilities includes case studies and suggestions for reading and writing instruction.*

9. Tompkin, G. E. (2000). *Teaching writing: Balancing process and product* (3rd ed.). Upper Saddle River, NJ: Prentice Hall.

*This book provides teachers with strategies designed to teach students in grades K–8 to use the writing process to improve their writing. The book contains strategies for a variety of types of writing (journal writing, letter writing, biographical writing, expository writing, narrative writing, poetry writing, and persuasive writing).*

10. Bear, D. R., Invernizzi, M., Templeton, S., & Johnston, F. (2000). *Words their way: Word study for phonics,* vocabulary, and spelling instruction (2nd ed.). Upper Saddle River, NJ: Prentice-Hall.

*This book provides word study activities, organized by developmental spelling stage. It contains the resources to teach students who speak Spanish, such as an examination of spelling in Spanish and a list of the Spanish names for all the sort and activity pictures in the text.*

# suggested websites

www.ldonline.org/ld_indepth/writing/isaacson_obstacles.html

This website introduces eight methods that teachers can use to help students deal with the spelling/writing obstacle: collaboration, precuing, word books, asking the teacher, invented spelling, peer collaboration, self-checking, and computer-assisted writing.

www.ldonline.org/ld_indepth/writing/isaacson_assessment.html

This website provides simple ways to assess writing skills of students with learning disabilities.

www.ldonline.org/ld_indepth/writing/harris_writing.html

This website introduces some strategies to help students with learning disabilities compose writing pieces.

www.ldonline.org/ld_indepth/writing/ERIC_E590.html

This website contains information on effective strategies for writing and also contains other useful links related to writing instruction.

www.interdys.org/parents_.stm#spelling

This website provides an overview of information on spelling difficulties and strategies.

www.edbydesign.com/parentres.html

This website contains practical resources for spelling and writing.

www.ldonline.org/ld_indepth/technology/tech_writing.html

This website provides information on using technology to enhance the writing process of students with LD.

www.nexus.edu.au/associations/nationallit/strat_spelling.htm

This website provides several strategies for spelling.

www.ed.sturt.flinders.edu.au/DLT/2000/Motor%20Dev/strategy.htm

This website provides strategies to promote handwriting.

# Helping All Students
# Succeed in Mathematics

# chapter | outline

# focus | questions

1. What are some of the reasons students with learning problems have difficulty with traditional mathematics curricula?

2. What are the recommended changes to traditional mathematics curricula and the implications of such changes for students with learning problems?

3. Which factors, in addition to knowledge of mathematics, can affect students' mathematical ability?

4. What curriculum resources are especially helpful for students with learning problems?

5. How can teachers check that students understand the meaning of a mathematical operation and not just the answer to the problem?

# inter view

## One Student's Experience

Paul is a freshman at the University of Miami, but unlike most freshman, he is 21 years old, not 18. Since Paul was very little, his parents have known he was not like the other children in the family or other children they knew. He was extraordinary in many ways and had problems in other ways. These problems were apparent when Paul started school. Although few subjects were easy for him, all subjects were easier than math.

Through elementary and high school, Paul received poor grades in mathematics, but not because of a lack of effort on his part. Paul says, "No matter how much I studied, I just did not get it. When I say I can't do math, I mean it's not that I'm not trying, it's that it just really doesn't make any sense to me." Paul also recalls that teachers made few accommodations to help him improve his mathematical abilities. He explains it this way, "I was mainstreamed in a public school and there were 29 other students in the class. I think the attitude toward students, especially students with learning disabilities, is 'Why should I change my teaching style just for you?'" In addition, Paul characterizes his teachers in elementary and high school as "unknowledgeable about learning disabilities" and therefore unsure about how to accommodate their instructional practices and class assignments to better meet his particular learning needs. Paul describes his years in school this way: "It's like somebody saying we are going to make you do this even though you don't

know how, you can't do it, and they are going to make you do it. It was so hard and frustrating all of the time."

In high school, Paul began to advocate for himself and seek out assistance with his courses, but again he describes the school as being uninformed: "I felt I had to fight every day in high school to get what I needed. And a lot of that was because I am LD; the school thought it was an excuse and never understood what the label really means."

Paul's experiences with mathematics have been so negative that he currently goes to great strides to exclude math from his life. "I don't take math. I switched my major so I won't have to take math. Math is just not a part of my life." As a student with learning disabilities, what advice would Paul give teachers? "The reason a student is coming to you with a problem and saying that they're LD is not because they want to give you more problems in your life, it's because they want you to help them."

## introduction

The purpose of this chapter is to introduce procedures for effectively instructing students like Paul who have extraordinary problems learning mathematics.

Think about how you felt about mathematics instruction. Was it a subject you looked forward to, or did you dread it? What do you think were some of the factors that influenced how you felt about mathematics instruction? Surely, the teachers you had and the way mathematics was taught had a great deal of influence on how you feel about the subject today. Unfortunately, far too few students consider mathematics an exciting subject (Mercer et al., 1994), and many students with disabilities perform poorly in mathematics because of low expectations for success and poor instruction (Jones, Wilson, & Bhojwani, 1997).

## Current Trends in Mathematics Curriculum and Instruction

A central topic in education is mathematics instruction. This issue has been paramount for students with learning difficulties. There is growing national concern that students across all achievement groups are not faring well in mathematics, compared with students in countries such as Belgium, Canada, England, Finland, Hungary, Japan, New Zealand, Scotland, and Sweden. Some think that the mathematics performance of students in the United States is related to the way in which mathematics is taught.

Mathematics instruction has been in a state of change over the past 30 years, with considerable emphasis on mathematical literacy through helping students construct knowledge (Goldman, Hasselbring, & The Cognition Group, 1997). Perhaps the most influential advocate for mathematics instructional practices is the National Council of Teachers of Mathematics (NCTM). In 1989, this group set curriculum standards for the development and implementation of mathematics curricula (National Council of Teachers of Mathematics, 1989). Since that time, NCTM has created professional standards in 1991, assessment standards in 1995, and most recently, a set of standards that builds on the three previous standards documents, published in 2000. These Principles and Standards for School Mathematics are summarized in Figure 14.1.

Think about your own mathematics instruction when you were in school. Was the emphasis on worksheets and learning computation, or was it on problem solving and activities? Math educators

━━━━━━━━ FIGURE 14.1 ━━━━━━━━

## NCTM Standards 2000

Instructional programs for prekindergarten through grade 12 in the following areas should enable all students to use the following concepts:

1. Number and operations
   - Understand numbers, ways of representing numbers, relationships among numbers, and number systems
   - Understand meanings of operations and how they relate to one another
   - Compute fluently and make reasonable estimates

2. Algebra
   - Understand patterns, relations, and functions
   - Represent and analyze mathematical solutions and structures using algebraic symbols
   - Use mathematical models to represent and understand quantitative relationships
   - Analyze change in various contexts

3. Geometry
   - Analyze characteristics and properties of two and three-dimensional geometric shapes, and develop mathematical arguments about geometric relationships
   - Specify locations and describe spatial relationships using coordinate geometry and other representational systems
   - Apply transformations and use symmetry to analyze mathematical situations
   - Use visualization, spatial reasoning, and geometric modeling to solve problems

4. Measurement
   - Understand measurable attributes of objects and the units, systems, and processes of measurement
   - Apply appropriate techniques, tools, and formulas to determine measurements

5. Data analysis and probability
   - Formulate questions that can be addressed with data and collect, organize, and display relevant data to answer them
   - Select and use appropriate statistical methods to analyze data
   - Develop and evaluate inferences and predictions that are based on data
   - Understand and apply basic concepts of probability

6. Problem solving
   - Build new mathematical knowledge through problem solving
   - Solve problems that arise in mathematics and in other contexts
   - Apply and adapt a variety of appropriate strategies to solve problems
   - Monitor and reflect on the process of mathematical problem solving

7. Reasoning and proof
   - Recognize reasoning and proof as fundamental aspects of mathematics
   - Make and investigate mathematical conjectures
   - Develop and evaluate mathematical arguments and proofs
   - Select and use various types of reasoning and methods of proof

8. Communication
   - Organize and consolidate their mathematical thinking through communication
   - Communicate their mathematical thinking coherently and clearly to peers, teachers, and others
   - Analyze and evaluate the mathematical thinking and strategies of others
   - Use the language of mathematics to express mathematical ideas precisely

9. Connections
   - Recognize and use connections among mathematical ideas
   - Understand how mathematical ideas interconnect and build on one another to produce a coherent whole
   - Recognize and apply mathematics in contexts outside of mathematics

10. Representation
    - Create and use representations to organize, record, and communicate mathematical ideas
    - Select, apply, and translate among mathematical representations to solve problems
    - Use representations to model and interpret physical, social, and mathematical phenomena

*Source:* National Council of Teachers of Mathematics. (2000) Principles and standards for school mathematics. Available on-line at www.nctm.org/standards/. Copyright © 2000 by the National Council of Teachers of Mathematics. Reprinted with permission. All rights reserved.

FIGURE 14.2

**The National Council of Teachers of Mathematics Recommendations**

★ Do not alter curricular goals to differentiate students; change the type and speed of instruction.

★ Make mathematics education student-oriented, not an authoritarian model that is teacher-focused.

★ Encourage students to explore, verbalize ideas, and understand that mathematics is part of their life.

★ Provide opportunities on a daily basis for students to apply mathematics and to work problems that are related to their daily lives. Relate what they are learning to real-life experiences.

★ Teach mathematics so that students understand when they can estimate an answer and when they need to compute an exact answer.

★ Teach problem solving, computer application, and use of calculators to all students.

★ Teach students to understand probability, data analysis, and statistics as they relate to daily decision making, model building, operations, research, and application to computers.

★ Shift from relying primarily on paper-and-pencil activities to use of calculators, computers, and other applied materials.

suggest that the emphasis in mathematics instruction should be on problem solving and activity-based learning. The argument made by many math educators is that too much time has been spent in the mathematics curricula on skill and drill and too little time on teaching students to think and discover mathematically (Romberg, 1993). The goal is to increase the emphasis on teaching students to solve problems effectively.

The National Research Council (NRC) has conducted an examination of U.S. mathematics education from kindergarten through graduate study. This joint activity was conducted by the Mathematical Sciences Education Board, Board on Mathematical Sciences, Committee on the Mathematical Sciences in the Year 2000, and National Research Council. The extensive report resulting from the work of these committees not only outlines problems in mathematics education, but also charts a course for remedying them. The suggestions that relate to students with learning and behavior problems are presented in Figure 14.2.

Despite this plea for additional emphasis on problem solving, computation is still an essential component of the mathematics curriculum. Some feel that students with learning problems potentially have the most to lose as the curriculum shifts away from computation and toward an emphasis on problem solving and teaching students to think mathematically (Hofmeister, 1993). Others fear that the standards may be too vague to provide the explicit instruction that students with disabilities often need (Miller & Mercer, 1997). The concern is that because students with learning problems need to learn basic math facts and because a lack of knowledge

of these facts is a common impediment to learning higher-level math, students with learning problems may learn neither math computation nor higher-order mathematics.

Students with learning problems are slower, but not necessarily less accurate, when it comes to doing and learning math facts (Garnett, 1992). When you teach mathematics in your classroom, consider that students with learning problems may need more time and additional practice to learn math facts and mathematics computations because they often lack the "automatization" to perform math computation effectively and efficiently (Garnett & Fleischner, 1983). It will be important for you to monitor their progress in these areas because they are less likely than the other students in your classroom to learn these skills incidentally through the process of problem solving (Cawley, Parmar, Yan, & Miller, 1996).

## ● Difficulties in Learning Mathematics

Not surprisingly, students with behavior disorders, mental retardation, learning disabilities, and attention problems typically score below their same-aged peers on measures of math achievement (Scruggs & Mastropieri, 1986; Zentall & Smith, 1993). Some of their difficulties in mathematics relate to understanding the problem. In other instances, they lack the computation skills to adequately complete the problem. Interestingly, not all of their difficulties in mathematics relate to their knowledge of math; some relate to motivation and other factors (Ginsburg, 1997).

## r e s e a r c h b r i e f

### Mathematics and Memory

There is increasing evidence that students who display mathematics difficulties do so because of their poor use of working memory to execute or retrieve information that would aid in solving problems (Geary et al., 1991). A primary factor that contributes to an early learning problem in mathematics is difficulty in the retrieval of basic information from long-term memory (Goldman et al., 1988; Svenson & Broquist, 1975). The reason students continue to use counting strategies beyond the point at which they are helpful is that they are unable to retrieve basic facts from long-term memory. This difficulty in memory inhibits their progress in mathematics. What is unknown is the extent to which students have difficulty learning the information and therefore never storing it in long-term memory or whether students have difficulty accessing the information. Children with mathematics difficulties also appear to have relatively poor working memory resources, which may lead to frequent use of verbal counting strategies that in turn may lead to computational errors.

### Influences on Mathematics Ability

According to Kosc (1981), four variables—cognitive, educational, and personality factors and neuropsychological patterns—influence the mathematics ability of all students.

What kinds of difficulties in mathematics do students with disabilities have? How can teachers help students with these kinds of difficulties?

**Cognitive Factors**   Intelligence, cognitive ability, distractibility, maintaining and sustaining attention, as well as cognitive learning strategies, influence students' thinking and therefore their skills in math.

**Educational Factors**   Learning is influenced directly by the quality and amount of instructional intervention across the range of areas of mathematics (e.g., computation, measurement, time, and problem solving).

**Personality Factors**   Persistence, self-concept, and attitudes toward mathematics influence students' motivation and performance. As with all learning, the extent to which we are interested in a topic and motivated to learn influences our performance. Many math educators are convinced that students' judgments about math relay the message that "you have to be a genius to do it" and that such judgments stem, at least in part, from faulty instruction (Mtetwa & Garofalo, 1989).

**Neuropsychological Patterns**   Perception, memory, and neurological trauma influence students' abilities to effectively solve mathematical problems. Students with learning problems often have difficulty with spatial relationships, distance, size, using a number line, and sequencing. These difficulties interfere with such math skills as measurement, estimation, problem solving, and geometry. Students with special learning needs also display memory problems that interfere with their progress in math (Geary et al., 1991). You can assist students with memory problems by reducing the amount of new information they are required to learn and by giving them opportunities to verbalize and demonstrate the new material. In addition to these four variables, recent research based on analysis of twin pairs reveals that for many students, mathematics disabilities are heritable (Alarcon, DeFries, Light, & Pennington, 1997).

After you consider these factors, it is not difficult to determine why many students with learning and behavior problems would have difficulty with mathematics. Although most students with learning and behavior problems have average or above-average intelligence, they often demonstrate difficulties in cognitive functioning that influence their learning. Furthermore, they are often characterized as passive learners who are less likely than other students to actively use their cognitive abilities. Because the focus of much of their everyday math instruction has been on computation, largely on activities that require students to complete problems and turn in worksheets, these students have had many negative experiences with math. They have had few opportunities to engage in problem solving or learning the language and reasoning of mathematics. Most of these students have had few opportunities to apply computation skills to the problems of daily life.

## Developmental Arithmetic Disorder

Students with **developmental arithmetic disorder** have significant difficulties learning arithmetic—difficulties that are unexpected given the students' overall cognitive functioning and academic performance in other subject areas. For example, Paul, the student introduced at the beginning of this chapter, demonstrated a significant arithmetic disorder. His performance in arithmetic was unexpectedly low, given his overall cognitive performance. His difficulty in mathematics was also long lasting, not related to an area of mathematics or a particular teacher. Good teaching is likely to help students with developmental arithmetic disorder but probably not enough to ensure grade-level performance.

## Nonverbal Math Difficulties

Johnson and Myklebust (1967) were the first to introduce the notion of **nonverbal math disabilities.** They were referring to a small group of students who displayed good reading and verbal expression but extreme difficulty with mathematics. Other problems associated with students who display nonverbal mathematics problems include the following:

- Social immaturity
- Disorientation
- Deficits in visual, motor, and self-help skills
- Problems estimating distance and time

Research supporting the social deficits associated with individuals who have good reading and poor math skills has been confirmed by others (Badian & Ghublikian, 1983; Rourke, 1993).

Saje, a third-grade student who read at grade level but had difficulties in mathematics, was really a puzzle to his teacher. She could not figure out why, despite Saje's high verbal expression and good vocabulary, he continually mixed up old and new rules. He not only had problems in math, but also was frequently inattentive and disorganized and

According to a survey of teachers of students with learning disabilities conducted by McLeod and Armstrong (1982), these mathematics deficits were most often reported: upper-level skills of division of whole numbers; basic operations involving fractions, decimals, and percent fraction terminology; and multiplication of whole numbers.

avoided responsibility. No matter how often she reminded Saje to keep his math paper neat, the papers he turned in had frayed edges, had numbers all over the place (instead of problems written in neat columns), and were covered with eraser marks and holes. She asked the special education teacher how to help Saje. The special education teacher worked with Saje, administered some tests, and explained to Saje's classroom teacher that he had a nonverbal math difficulty.

Although math would always be challenging for Saje, she could do some things to help him. First, she taught only one mathematical principle at a time until Saje became masterful and fluent with that principle. Second, she used word games, songs, and other verbal activities to enhance instruction. Third, she devised organizational aids such as graph paper with large boxes to write numbers. Finally, she provided Saje with devices such as computers and tape recorders as alternatives to pencil and paper.

##  Effective Math Instruction for All Learners

Students display poor math performance for several reasons. The one that can be most readily corrected is the inappropriate or inadequate instruction in mathematics that many students receive. Many professionals believe that the math difficulties of students with learning problems are compounded by ineffective instruction (e.g., Carnine, 1991; Cawley et al., 1987). Most teachers know the simple algorithms for solving mathematics computation problems but do not know alternative algorithms. Few teachers have procedures for using concrete approaches and manipulatives to teach computation. Figure 14.3 provides a summary of guidelines for adequate math instruction.

---
FIGURE 14.3

**Summary of Guidelines for Adequate Math Instruction**

---

1. Select appropriate, comprehensive math content.
2. Select goals that establish high expectations.
3. Provide systematic and explicit instruction.
4. Teach students to understand math concepts.
5. Monitor the progress of students.
6. Teach to mastery.
7. Promote a positive attitude toward math.
8. Teach students to generalize the math skills they learn.

As a general education teacher, you will also need to be prepared to meet the instructional needs of students who are mathematically gifted. As you read in Chapter 11, there is a debate about whether to accelerate the pacing of instruction for gifted students or to provide differentiated instruction. Johnson (2000) indicated that most experts recommend a combined approach. Tips for Teachers 14.1 provides some suggestions for meeting the needs of mathematically gifted students.

## Tips for Teachers

### 14.1    Instructional Practices for Gifted Students in the General Education Classroom

- Give preassessments so that students who already know the material do not have to repeat it but may be provided with instruction and activities that are meaningful. In the elementary grades, gifted learners still need to know their basic facts. If they do not, don't hold them back from other, more complex tasks, but continue to work concurrently on the basics.
- Create assessments that allow for differences in understanding, creativity, and accomplishment; give students a chance to show what they have learned. Ask students to explain their reasoning both orally and in writing.
- Choose textbooks that provide more enriched opportunities. Unfortunately, curriculum in this country is mainly driven by textbooks, which are used about 80 percent of the time (Lockwood, 1992). Math textbooks often repeat topics from year to year in the grades prior to algebra. Since most textbooks are written for the general population, they are not always appropriate for the gifted. Several series that hold promise for gifted learners have been developed recently under grants from the National Science Foundation; they emphasize constructivist learning and include concepts beyond the basics.
- Use multiple resources. No single text will adequately meet the needs of these learners.
- Be flexible in your expectations about pacing for different students. While some may be mastering basic skills, others may work on more advanced problems.
- Use inquiry-based, discovery learning approaches that emphasize open-ended problems with multiple solutions or multiple paths to solutions. Allow students to design their own ways to find the answers to complex questions. Gifted students may discover more than you thought was possible.
- Use lots of higher-level questions in justification and discussion of problems. Ask "why" and "what if" questions.
- Provide units, activities, or problems that extend beyond the normal curriculum. Offer challenging mathematical recreations such as puzzles and games.

- Provide AP level courses in calculus, statistics, and computer science, or encourage prepared students to take classes at local colleges if the supply of courses at the high school has been exhausted.
- Differentiate assignments. It is not appropriate to give more problems of the same type to gifted students. You might give students a choice of a regular assignment; a different, more challenging one; or a task that is tailored to interests.
- Expect high-level products (e.g., writing, proofs, projects, solutions to challenging problems).
- Provide opportunities to participate in contests such as Mathematical Olympiads for the Elementary School (grades 4–6), Math Counts (grades 7–8), and the American Junior High School Mathematics Exam (grades 7–8) or the American High School Mathematics Exam (grades 9–12). Give feedback to students on their solutions. After the contests, use some of the problems as the basis for classroom discussions.
- Provide access to male and female mentors who represent diverse linguistic and cultural groups. They may be within the school system, volunteers from the community, or experts who agree to respond to questions by email. Bring speakers into the classroom to explain how math has opened doors in their professions and careers.
- Provide some activities that can be done independently or in groups based on student choice. Be aware that if gifted students always work independently, they are gaining no more than they could do at home. They also need appropriate instruction, interaction with other gifted students, and regular feedback from the teacher.
- Provide useful concrete experiences. Even though gifted learners may be capable of abstraction and may move from concrete to abstract more rapidly, they still benefit from the use of manipulatives and "hands-on" activities.

*Source:* Johnson, D. T. (2000, April). Teaching mathematics to gifted students in a mixed-ability classroom. *ERIC Digest E594* (ERIC Document Reproduction Service No. ED441302). Reprinted by permission of the author.

## Evaluating Mathematics Curricula

Traditional math curricula have not worked very well for students with learning problems, for the following reasons (Blankenship, 1984; Carnine, 1990):

1. *Students have difficulty reading the information provided.* Because the reading vocabulary is too difficult and the reading level is too high, students with math difficulties are able to learn very little by reading their math books. All the information in the book must be taught directly to them. Max Diamond, a tenth-grade math teacher, assigned several pages of reading in the math textbook as homework. Realizing that several of his students would not be able to read and understand the text adequately, Max had these pages read into a tape recorder and made the tapes and recorders available to all students in his class.

2. *Math concepts are often presented poorly.* Multiple concepts are introduced at one time, and information is often presented in a scattered fashion. For this reason, Dawn McQueen reorganizes the information in the math text so that she can teach computation skills to mastery rather than skipping around teaching many new ideas in two weeks. Dawn introduces only one concept at a time, teaching that concept until *all* students in her class (not just those with learning problems) learn it. Then she moves on to the next concept. Although Dawn follows a sequence of pages different from that presented in the book, she believes that her efforts are worthwhile because her students seem to understand better.

3. *There are insufficient problems covering any one concept or operation and too few opportunities for application of knowledge learned.* The problems are not presented in enough different situations for students to learn and transfer what they know. Janice Kauffman, a sixth-grade teacher, addresses this problem by developing her own supportive materials to supplement the book. She also provides practice with problem solving, reasoning, and real-life application that helps students transfer their knowledge to real-life settings.

4. *Students often do not have the necessary prerequisite skills assumed by the text (and so the next level is too difficult).* As Margaret Gardner plans each math unit she teaches, she spends considerable time considering the prerequisite skills students need to master the concept or operation she is teaching. After identifying these prerequisite skills, she tells students directly that she is looking to see whether they know them. She prepares activities and exercises so that she

knows which students do and which do not possess the skills they need to move on to the next math concept or operation.

5. *The pages and organizational format of the text vary considerably and make learning from the text difficult.* Linda Saumell, having recognized this problem, walks students through the text section by section, explaining the format to them.

Considering this mismatch between most mathematics curricula and the learning needs of all students, particularly students with learning problems, teachers need to adapt traditional math curricula to best meet the learning needs of students in their classrooms.

**research brief**

### Secondary Students with Math Difficulties

Jones, Wilson, and Bhojwani (1997) conducted a review of research-based investigations of mathematics for students with LD. They recognized that the research base was not well developed and that more investigation in best practices for secondary students with difficulty in learning mathematics is necessary. Nonetheless, they were able to identify suggestions for teachers working with older students who have experienced years of challenge and frustration in learning math:

- Provide explicit instruction.
- Provide clear and a sufficient number of examples; most commercial materials fall short in this area.
- Give real-life applications for students.
- Provide ample opportunities to be successful.
- Use cooperative learning activities, but include individual accountability as a key component.

### Adapting Basal Materials for Students with Special Needs

Teachers need to do several things to adapt basal materials. One is to select appropriate math content. There is considerable concern that poor math content is a result of the **spiral curriculum**, which occurs when the same skills (e.g., mathematics skills) are woven into every year of school and students continually "relearn" the same skills in the same area. Jason, an eighth-grade student, said it this way: "It seems every year we start with multiplication and then go to division and then we learn something about fractions and then we stop. Then the next year, we do it all over again." One approach to teaching mathematics, the Corrective Mathematics Program (Englemann & Carnine, 1982), is designed to avoid the problems of the spiral curriculum and provide satisfactory pacing of instruction.

Teachers can also use instructional design principles to assist students with learning problems in acquiring proficiency in mathematics. These design principles include (1) teaching big ideas, (2) making strategies conspicuous, (3) using instructional time efficiently, (4) making instruction on strategies clear and explicit, and (5) providing appropriate practice and review (Carnine, 1997).

A key aspect of selecting the appropriate curriculum is that it be comprehensive. Gary Lancelotta reflected, "I know my curriculum should be more comprehensive than just the facts and computation, but I'm not sure what else I should teach. Also, the students seem to really need the time to learn computation." Working on other skills in mathematics does not mean that computation is left behind; in fact, computation can often be enhanced while other components of math are taught. Students need to be taught and involved in a full range of mathematics skills that include basic facts, computation, word problems, operations, problem solving, mathematical reasoning, time, measurement, fractions, and math application.

> Students who select their own math goals improve their performance on math tasks over time more than those students whose math goals are assigned to them by a teacher (Fuchs et al., 1988).

## Using Curricular Programs for Students with Math Difficulties

Other than the basal curriculum books, math workbooks, and the curriculum guidebooks published by many state departments of education, what curriculum resources are available to teachers? This section provides brief descriptions of some resources that are helpful for students who have difficulty learning math.

**Project Math**    Project Math is a math curriculum designed specifically for students with mild disabilities (Cawley et al., 1976). The program—which includes work on sets, patterns, numbers, operations, fractions, geometry, measurement, and lab activities—has eliminated many problems commonly associated with typical math curricula. Project Math reduces the reading level, provides a direct link between assessment and instruction, establishes procedures that encourage teaching to mastery, and provides for individualized instruction.

**DISTAR Arithmetic Program**    DISTAR Arithmetic Program stresses direct instruction through a highly sequenced format that provides immediate feedback to students (Englemann & Carnine, 1972,

1975, 1976). The DISTAR arithmetic kits come with a detailed teacher's guide, workbooks, teaching book, and take-home sheets for homework and parent involvement. The entire program is based on behavioral principles of learning and provides explicit instructions for the teacher.

**Computational Arithmetic Program**    Computational Arithmetic Program provides 314 worksheets for teaching basic math skills to students in grades 1 through 6 (Smith & Lovitt, 1982).

**Corrective Mathematics Program**    Corrective Mathematics Program provides remedial math for students in grades 3 through 12. This math program requires only minimal reading skills (Englemann & Carnine, 1982).

**NCTM Navigation Series**    NCTM Navigation Series is a series of graded and topical books with CD-ROMs published by NCTM. The books focus on activities for teaching algebra, geometry, numbers and operations, and the like, based on the NCTM principles and standards. The books can be ordered through the NCTM website at www.nctm.org.

> Computer-assisted instruction is a sound way to provide large amounts of effective practice for students with learning problems, particularly in automating math skills (Okolo, 1992). Instructional computer games can improve the basic skill and automaticity of students with learning disabilities.

**Real-Life Math Program**    Real-Life Math Program focuses on teaching students with learning difficulties the mathematics skills they need for daily living (Schwartz, 1977). The content for teaching functional math includes consumer skills, homemaking skills, health care, auto care, home care, and vocational needs. The focus is on older students, ages 13 to 18, who need to learn appropriate math skills for daily life.

**Touch Math**    Touch Math is a program for teaching students math skills through math strategies that include touch-point, count-on, count-off, and count-by strategies (Bullock, 1991). Touch math focuses on teaching the basic math facts in addition, subtraction, multiplication, and division.

**Key Math Teach and Practice**    Key Math Teach and Practice is designed to provide remedial practice in and diagnosis of math difficulties (Connolly, 1985). Materials include a teacher's guide, a student progress chart, and a sequence chart, as well as activities and worksheets.

**ETA/Cuisenaire**    ETA/Cuisenaire provides a variety of supplemental mathematics materials. This company specializes in math manipulatives that emphasize learning principles through hands-on learning. One of their earliest products is the Cuisenaire rods. Cuisenaire rods come in various lengths and colors and can be used to represent numbers. Students with disabilities can be taught to use Cuisenaire rods as manipulatives to facilitate their successful understanding of word problems. The understanding then generalizes to similar problems when the rods are not used (Marsh & Cooke, 1996).

## Establishing Appropriate Goals

Goals can be selected by the teacher, student, or both together. Expectations for meeting the goals should be clearly established. There is growing support for the premise that the goals and expectations teachers set for students with learning problems are too low. They need to challenge students and provide support so that students can meet the challenges.

Marie Fernandez realized that she often responded to students' low self-image by setting goals too low for them. Several of the students with learning problems in her class would indicate that the work was too difficult or that there was too much work, and she would respond without considering what they could do if they set goals jointly.

**Student Goal Setting and Self-Monitoring** In the goal-setting process, students are asked to set realistic goals for how much work they can complete and how many problems they can solve. Students can also set computational fluency goals. Students who set their own goals outperform students who do not.

Strategies designed to teach students to instruct themselves and monitor their own progress have been shown to work well with students who have difficulty learning mathematics. Leon and Pepe (1983) used the following sequence to teach students how to teach themselves:

1. *The teacher models and verbalizes the procedure for the student.* For example, the teacher might say, "First I read the numbers out loud and estimate how much it will be. Let's see—86 plus 22 is going to be more than 100, but not much more. Now I start on the right and add the column. Now I add the column on the left. The total is 108."
2. *The teacher guides the student through the verbalization of the problem computation and solves the problem with the student.* Thanks to the teacher's prompts and guidance, the student does not have to work through the verbalization alone. When the student has difficulty, the teacher fills in.
3. *The student verbalizes the procedure independently while the teacher monitors the student's progress.* In this step, the verbalization should be done almost solely by the student, with minimal support and assistance from the teacher.
4. *The student whispers the procedure to himself or herself.* Now the teacher lets the student work independently. When a new mathematical concept or procedure is introduced or the student is having difficulty, the teacher and the student return to step 1.

**Cooperative Instructional Practices** Peer tutoring is an extremely effective way for students with arithmetic problems to learn computation skills (Beirne-Smith, 1991) and problem-solving skills (Allsopp, 1997). Peer tutoring is effective not only for the student who is tutored, but also for the student who does the tutoring. Remember that students with mathematical difficulties frequently receive help from their classmates, and be sure to provide them with opportunities to be the tutor as well. Teaching not only helps enhance their self-concept, but also helps them learn a great deal.

Cooperative learning occurs when the teacher divides the class into small groups (ordinarily three or four students per group), usually not based on ability, and asks these groups to work together to solve problems. Maheady, Harper, and Sacca (1988) conducted a cooperative-learning math instruction program for ninth- and tenth-grade students with mild disabilities. The study showed that students who participated in the cooperative teams performed better in mathematics and received higher grades than those who did not.

Slavin, Madden, and Leavey (1984) designed **Team-Assisted Individualization,** in which individualized instruction is provided in a cooperative learning model. Each of the four or five students in the heterogeneous learning team is assigned individualized mathematics material at his or her own level. Students on the same team help each other with problems and also manage checking and record keeping for the individualized math materials. Students work independently, but teachers teach skills to groups of students who are at the same level by pulling them from various teams.

## Providing Appropriate Instruction

Christenson, Ysseldyke, and Thurlow (1989) discussed four elements that contribute to systematic and explicit instruction:

- A teaching routine that includes demonstration–prompt–practice enhances a student's outcome (see Tips for Teachers 14.2).
- Explicit instruction that not only involves highly organized step-by-step presentations related to the specific target skill, but also provides information about why learning this skill facilitates student learning.

## Tips for Teachers

### 14.2    Strategies for Cueing Students during Feedback

Ferrara (1987) provides the following hint-sequence scheme for cueing students when giving them feedback.

1. *Give simple negative feedback.* In this case the student is told that the solution is not quite right and is encouraged to try again.
2. *Refresh working memory.* Repeat parts of the problem verbatim and discuss the known quantities.
3. *Use numerals as memory aids.* Ask students to write down the quantities they know, based on information provided in the text.

4. *Provide a transfer hint.* Ask students to think about a similar problem they have done. Students provide the example of the similar problem.
5. *Provide a demonstration and rationale.* Provide all the information to solve the problem and an explanation or rationale for it.
6. *Give a strategic-orientation hint.* Encourage the students to apply the information they have just learned to other types of problems.

---

- Assurance that students understand the directions and the task demands. Periodic checks are necessary to determine whether students understand the directions, and the teacher must monitor students' progress.
- The systematic use of learning principles. This refers to maintaining and using positive reinforcement, providing varied practice, and ensuring motivation.

In their review of intervention studies in mathematics for students with learning disabilities, Mastropieri, Scruggs, and Shiah (1991) identify three major types of interventions. One is behavioral, the second is cognitive, and the third is alternative instructional delivery systems (including cooperative learning, computer-assisted instruction, and interactive video disks). According to the authors, "Although these interventions seem varied, the general perspective on mathematics instruction—involving direct teacher explanations, strategy instruction, relevant practice with worksheets, peers, or computer-assisted instruction, direct measurement, and feedback and reinforcement—represents a view of instruction that is currently well supported in special education" (p. 97). These principles are also effective for adolescents with learning disabilities (Maccini & Hughes, 1997).

> Students who were taught to do mathematical word problem solving on the computer made substantial gains in mathematics word problem solving and enjoyed working on the computer (Shiah et al., 1994). Students also felt that the pictorial information assisted them in solving the word problems.

**Math Manipulatives**    Learning the language of mathematics is an important skill for all students. Peterson, Mercer, and O'Shea (1988) examined the effectiveness of a three-stage teaching sequence on students' abilities to learn place value. The sequence included going from concrete to semiconcrete and then to abstract teaching strategies. In the *concrete* stage, the mathematical concept was taught by using manipulative objects such as pegs. In the *semiconcrete* stage, pictorial representations were used for instruction. In the *abstract* stage, only numbers were used. Students who used this three-step process for learning

What procedures can teachers develop for using concrete approaches and manipulatives in mathematics instruction? What instructional strategies work for helping students move from the concrete to the abstract?

## Tips for Teachers

### 14.3  Helping Students Move from Concrete to Abstract Learning

1. *Concrete.* Provide manipulative and interactive opportunities to integrate the new mathematical concept. Encourage students to use both oral and written language to relate to the new mathematical vocabulary and concept.
2. *Pictorial.* Represent the mathematics problem with pictures. Provide the problem and have students interpret it and draw pictures to represent it.
3. *Linking.* Encourage students to talk about what they have learned and to explain it to others. By recording or demonstrating what they have learned

in meaningful ways, they can link their language to the mathematical algorithm.
4. *Symbolic.* Have students demonstrate knowledge about the symbols by talking about them and demonstrating through drawing, pointing, or replicating the meaning of the symbol or algorithm.
5. *Abstract.* Have students teach the steps for computing or problem solving with alternative solutions, and then solve problems in new and creative ways without using concrete or pictorial representation.

---

place values significantly outperformed a control group. Tips for Teachers 14.3 shows another way to help students move from the concrete to the abstract.

The most important thing for you to remember as a teacher is to begin with the concrete and then move to the abstract when you are teaching new math concepts or when a student is having difficulty learning a math concept. Because all students have had opportunities to interact with objects, the process makes sense to them. By using examples from the manipulation to develop problems and to write them numerically, you bridge the gap between the abstractness of mathematics and students' needs to learn the information concretely.

**Teaching for Comprehension**  Teach students to understand math concepts. Most instruction is provided to ensure that the answer is correct, the math computation has been accurately completed, or the math fact is memorized. Additional emphasis on ensuring that students understand the math process needs to be included in the math curriculum. Jan Hughes, a third-grade teacher, continually asked students to say in their own words what she had just said. During math problem solving, she often asked students to work in groups of three to write story problems that went along with an operation she had just taught. She continually thought about ways to make the mathematics she was teaching "real" to students.

The following section describes ways to check for comprehension in math instruction.

**Checking for Comprehension: The Case of Trinette**
Be certain that students understand the *meaning* of an operation, not just the answer. Students who have memorized the facts by rote often operate with little understanding of what they are doing. For example,

Trinette was asked to write the answer to the following math problem:

$$3 \times 2 =$$

Answering correctly, she wrote 6. But when Trinette's teacher asked her to illustrate the problem with pictures of flowers, this is what Trinette drew:

Trinette demonstrated that she did not understand the problem, although she had successfully memorized the answer and her facts.

The following drawing illustrates how rows of chips can be used to illustrate multiplication. For example, ask, "How many fours make twenty?" "Fours are placed on the board _____ times."

$$4 \times \text{_____} = 20$$

Other ways to check for comprehension include having students "talk aloud" what is involved in solving a problem. Instead of letting them merely *read* the problem, ask them to *explain* what it means. For example, 63 – 27 could mean that someone had 63 pieces of gum and gave 27 pieces to a friend. Another strategy is to have one student explain the process to another student by using block manipulatives. For example, 24 + 31 is the same as adding 4 one-block pieces to 1 one-block piece and 2 ten-block pieces to 3 ten-block pieces. Some teachers use vocalization or have students close their eyes and use noises to illustrate operations. To illustrate multiplication, for example, the teacher and student might tap to indicate groups of six.

**Constant Time Delay Procedure**   Constant time delay is a procedure for teaching math facts that provides for the systematic introduction of teacher assistance. This nearly errorless technique employs a controlling prompt to ensure the successful performance of the student (Gast et al., 1988; Stevens & Schuster, 1988). In general, the procedure involves presentation of a stimulus (e.g., a word or math fact), after which the student is allowed a specific amount of time (e.g., three seconds) to provide the correct answer (e.g., read the word or answer the fact). If the student does not respond within the time allowed, a controlling prompt (typically a teacher modeling the correct response) is provided. The controlling prompt is a cue that ensures that the student will respond correctly (e.g., the word name or the answer to the problem is modeled). The student then repeats the teacher's model. Although correct responses before and after the prompt are reinforced, only correct responses given before the prompt count toward the criterion. The effectiveness of the constant time delay procedure has been demonstrated with a variety of academic skills, students, and instructional arrangements (Mattingly & Bott, 1990; Schuster et al., 1990; Stevens & Schuster, 1987; Wolery et al., 1991).

**Correction and Feedback**   Immediate correction and feedback are essential to the success of students with math difficulties. Saying, "Orlando, the first six problems are correct, and then the third row is all wrong. Please redo them," is an example of insufficient feedback. Teachers often tell students which problems are correct and which are wrong and hope that this feedback is adequate. For students with learning problems, it is not. They need more sustained interaction to help them acquire not only the skills for identifying what they did wrong, but also the procedures for how to do it differently. The teacher must analyze the problem and also obtain sufficient information from the student to determine why the problem was not done correctly. A better model for correction and feedback follows: "Orlando, point to the problems you think are correct. Think about each problem before you point." (The teacher positively reinforces Orlando as he points to problems that are right.) "Yes, those are all correct. You did an excellent job with those. You started on the right, added them correctly, carried numbers when you needed to." When students are first learning a math concept or operation, teachers need to provide a great deal of assistance to ensure that students perform correctly. Over time, teachers need to systematically reduce the amount of help they give students.

## Providing Practice

Practice is important if students are to exhibit high levels of accuracy consistently and across multiple problem types. **Mastery** occurs when students meet expectations for accuracy and speed in different types of problems. In operations, mastery refers to the ability to use multiple algorithms to solve an operation so that students truly learn (rather than memorize). Denise, a ninth-grade student, expresses her frustration this way: "I never seem to be able to really learn anything. Just when I feel like I'm starting to get it, we move on to a different thing. I wish I could just stay with something until I really get it."

**Counting by Numbers**   Students are taught to "count by" numbers, beginning with 2, 10, and 5, then 3, 4, 6, 7, 8, and 9 (Lloyd et al., 1981). This is done by group counting, singing the numbers in sequence, writing the numbers, erasing some numbers in the sequence and having students fill them in, and having students work on worksheets with the count-by sequences.

After students have learned to count by numbers, they can apply the strategy to multiplication by using the following steps:

1. Point to the number you can count by.
2. Make hash marks to represent the other number.
3. When you count by the number, point to each of the hash marks. The last number said when you reach the end of the hash marks is the answer to the problem.

**Games**   Games can be an important way for students to learn mathematics skills. Larson and Slaughter (1984) provide the following suggestions for using games in mathematics instruction:

1. *Choose games that reinforce present instruction.* Be sure that the selected game reinforces much of what students already know.

# Tips for Teachers

## 14.4   Promoting Positive Attitudes toward Math

1. Involve students in setting attainable goals that are challenging and require their participation and effort.

2. Provide opportunities for success. Failure should be infrequent.

3. Use progress charts that students can maintain to keep track of their progress, with the process of charting their progress serving as reinforcement.

4. Discuss the relevance of math to real-life situations. Remind and demonstrate that math is useful and necessary for success in the real world.

5. Model an enthusiastic, positive attitude toward mathematics and its application.

6. Give students positive reinforcement for their efforts and progress.

7. Link students' efforts to their achievement. Remind students that they performed the task well because they worked hard, persisted, reread, rethought, visualized, modeled, and so on.

*Source:* Adapted from Mercer, C. D., & Mercer, A. R. (1993). *Teaching students with learning problems* (4th ed.). New York: Merrill/Macmillan.

---

2. *Consider the complexity of the game* so that students do not spend more time learning the game's procedures and rules than they spend learning the math-related material.

3. *Foresee potential problems associated with games,* such as disruptive behavior and shouting out.

4. *Provide an answer key if an adult is not available.*

5. *Play at least one round of the game with students* to ensure that they understand the rules and procedures and are acquiring the mathematics skills desired.

6. *Use aides or parent helpers to monitor the games.*

## Monitoring and Communicating Progress

Carefully and systematically monitor the progress of students, checking their academic work frequently. More is involved in the monitoring process than simply determining whether students are doing the problem correctly or incorrectly. Effective math instruction involves checking students' work frequently and providing feedback. Student progress needs to be assessed, and if students are not progressing adequately, procedures should be altered.

Students in Alex Chinn's fifth-grade class were asked to complete a worksheet to practice a new skill he had taught them for using dollar signs and decimal points in subtraction problems. Alex told the students to complete only the first problem. After they completed the problem, they were to consider whether the answer made sense and whether dollar signs and decimal points were used correctly. If so, they were to place a C next to the problem. If they were not sure whether the problem was correct, they were to mark

it with a ?; and if they thought the problem was wrong, they were to use a star (*). Alex moved quickly from student to student, checking the first problem and providing them with feedback and reinforcement: "Jacob, you were right, you did have the problem correct. Maxine, what are you unsure about? Now, look at it again. What do you think? Yes, that's right, it's correct. Beth, let's do this problem together."

**Being a Model in Math**   Most of the time, a positive attitude toward math comes from effective instruction and the interest the teacher shows in mathematics. Tips for Teachers 14.4 offers suggestions for promoting positive attitudes toward math.

## Strategies for Helping All Students Acquire Basic Math Skills

Mathematics instruction used to focus on the acquisition of the basic math skills, saving problem solving for later in the math curriculum. We now realize that teaching basic skills and problem solving must be coordinated from the beginning of math instruction.

Key components of basic math skills include the following:

● Prenumber
● Numeration
● Place value
● Fractions

These skills and related subcomponents are presented next.

## Prenumber Skills

Many students with learning problems come to school without certain basic prenumber skills necessary for initial success in mathematics. Sonya Perez, a first-grade teacher, described Malcolm in this way: "When he came to my class, he knew how to count to 10, but he didn't know what he was doing. He didn't know what the numbers meant. As far as he knew, he could have been saying his ABCs." She realized that he first needed to learn one-to-one correspondence.

**One-to-One Correspondence**    One-to-one correspondence occurs when the student understands that each object corresponds to another object. For example, when a student puts out cereal bowls for himself, his sister, and his mother, he learns that each bowl represents one person. Early humans used one-to-one correspondence to keep track of their accounts. For example, a man might put a rock in a bucket to represent each bag of grain he gave to a neighbor. The following activities can be used to teach one-to-one correspondence:

1. *Use everyday events to teach one-to-one correspondence.* Allow students with difficulties in this area to pass out materials. "Allison, please get one pair of scissors for each student in your group. Naja, you need to have a chair for each member of your group. How many chairs are there? How many more do you need?"
2. *Use objects to work with small groups of students who need help with one-to-one correspondence.* Give each student 10 small blocks. Place 3 blocks in the center. Say, "I want you to place a block next to each one in the center. As you place a block, I want you to say the number. I will do the first one, and then you do what I did."
3. *Give students a set of cards with pictures on each card.* Ask students to put the correct number of objects (e.g., pegs) on top of each number card. Reverse the task by giving objects to students and asking them to put the correct picture card next to the objects.

**Classification**    Classification, the ability to group or sort objects based on one or more common properties, is an important prenumber skill because it focuses students, making them attend to the common properties of objects and reduce large numbers of objects to smaller groups. Classification can be by size, color, shape, texture, or design. Fortunately, most students are naturally interested in sorting and think that activities related to this prenumber skill are fun. Examples of such activities follow:

1. Provide students with a bag of miscellaneous articles that vary in size, shape, and color. Ask students to sort the articles any way they like into an empty egg carton or empty plastic containers. After they finish, ask them to tell you the rules for sorting their articles. After they have had a chance to listen to others, give them a chance to sort the articles again and to explain their rules for sorting.
2. Provide students with an empty egg carton and a box of small articles. Ask students to sort the articles by a single property, such as color. Now ask them whether there is another way in which they might be able to sort the articles. For example, ask them to consider size, texture, and so on.
3. Ask students to work in small groups, and provide them with a bag of articles. Ask one student to sort several of the articles by a property. Then ask other students in the group to guess the property that qualifies the articles for the group.
4. Use pictures for sorting tasks. Good pictures include ones that represent animals, foods, plants, and toys.
5. Board games and bingo games can be played by sorting or classifying shapes, colors, and pictures.

**Seriation**    Seriation, the ability to rank objects according to the degree to which they possess a certain common characteristic, is similar to classification in that it depends on the recognition of common attributes of objects but differs from classification in that the order in which objects are placed depends on the extent to which each object possesses the attribute. For example, seriation can occur by length, height, color, or weight. Sample activities for teaching seriation follow:

1. Give students a long piece of string. Ask them to cut the pieces into various lengths. Now ask them to put the lengths in order from shortest to longest. Now ask students to work in groups of three. Using those same piles of string, create one long seriation, from shortest to longest. Continue to ask students to work in different groups and sort the string sizes.
2. Ask students to work in groups of eight. In these groups, ask them to put themselves in order from shortest to tallest. Now ask them to put themselves in order from longest to shortest hair. Continue asking students to put themselves in seriation based on different attributes.
3. Using a peg with various sizes of rings, put the rings on the peg from largest to smallest.
4. Fill jars of the same size with different amounts of sand or water and ask students to put them in order.

## Working with Numeration

Numeration is the understanding of numbers and their manipulations. Do not assume that because students can count or identify numbers, they understand the value and the meaning of the numbers. This is a mistake that many teachers and parents make. Understanding numerals is an extremely important basic concept, one that throws many children into mathematical confusion early. A good example is Michelle, whose early experiences with math were positive. She learned to say, read, and write numbers with little or no difficulty. In first and second grade, she began to work with math addition and subtraction facts and did these problems easily. When Michelle was asked to do problems that involved addition with regrouping, however, her lack of knowledge of numerals and their meaning became quickly evident. Following are examples of the way Michelle did some problems:

Why is extra practice in estimation and other basic math skills important for students with math difficulties? How can instruction in those skills be modified for students with learning problems?

$$27 + 15 = 312$$

$$49 + 36 = 715$$

As you can see from Michelle's answers, she remembered her math facts but did not understand what the numbers meant.

Understanding numeration and place value is necessary for progress in computation. Like Michelle, many students fail to make adequate progress in math because they do not understand the meaning of the numerals and the place value with which they are working. For example, students who understand the meaning of the numerals 25 and 17 would be less likely to make the following conceptual error:

$$25 - 17 = 12$$

**Estimating**   Many students with learning difficulties in math do not have a sense of how much a certain amount really is—what it means to have five dollars, for example, or how many eggs are in a dozen or about what 15 and 15, added together, should equal. These students cannot check their answers to determine how far off they are because they do not have a good idea of what an answer that makes sense would be.

Estimating is something that can be done throughout the day and throughout the curriculum. For example, start the day by asking students to estimate how many children are absent. Estimation can be included in subject matters as well. You can use estimation in science, social studies, and even with art projects.

Students who do not understand the real meaning of numerals have difficulty applying computation to everyday problems. For example, when Michelle's teacher posed the following problem, Michelle did not understand how to begin to find the answer: "Let's pretend that you had three one-dollar bills and you were going to McDonald's to buy lunch. Let's pretend that your hamburger costs 89 cents, your French fries cost 74 cents, and your medium-sized Coke costs 69 cents. How much money would you have left to spend?"

Mistakes occur when students attempt problems that are entirely too difficult for them or when they do not understand the idea behind the problem. In such cases, the solutions students provide are totally unreasonable, given the problem. One of the best ways to help students who demonstrate this problem is to continually ask them to think about the problem and estimate what their answer probably will be. When students are taught to consider what a reasonable answer should be, they are better able to catch their mistakes. These problems are particularly severe for students with disabilities who demonstrate low understanding of mathematical problems and the meaning of numbers (Lucangeli, Coi, & Bosco, 1997).

**Understanding Regrouping**   Regrouping errors are less likely to occur when students understand numeration. Following are examples of regrouping errors:

$$39 + 27 = 516$$

$$56 - 18 = 42$$

$$41 - 24 = 23$$

Examine the errors students make and use the information to provide instruction.

**Understanding Zero** Students need to understand that zero is a number and means more than "nothing." In the number 30, for example, students need to understand that the number zero is a placeholder. In the number 306, students need to understand that there are 0 tens and that zero is serving as a placeholder.

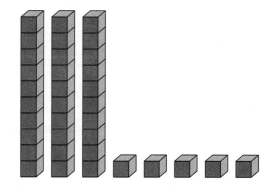

## Understanding Place Value

Before students can understand place value, they must understand numeration. Students who know the meaning of numbers will have far less difficulty understanding place value. For example, if a student knows what 56 actually means, then when someone talks about the tens place equaling 50, the student will not be confused. When someone talks about the ones place equaling 6 ones, the student will understand what is meant.

**Grouping by Ones and Tens** To teach grouping, start with manipulatives (buttons, sticks, and blocks are useful), then pictures, and then numbers. Ask students to practice grouping by ones and tens. Students can also develop a table to record their answers, as follows:

| Hundreds | Tens | Ones | Numerals |
|----------|------|------|----------|
| 1 | 3 | 1 | 131 |
| 1 | 2 | 3 | 123 |
| 1 | 4 | 5 | 145 |

Use "ten blocks" and "single blocks" to represent numerals. For example, 35 can be represented as follows:

**Naming Tens** Teach students to identify numerals by the number of tens. For example, six tens is 60, four tens is 40, eight tens is 80, and so on. Give students opportunities to count by tens and then name the number. For example, "Count by tens three times." "10, 20, 30." "Count by tens seven times." "10, 20, 30, 40, 50, 60, 70." Also, give students opportunities to draw picture diagrams that represent the place values of tens and ones and to identify the number.

**Place Value beyond Two Digits** When students can accurately group and identify numbers at the two-digit level, introduce them to three- and four-digit numbers. It is a good idea to be certain that students have mastered the concept of two-digit place value before you introduce numerals and place value. Give students plenty of opportunity to group, orally name, and sequence three- and four-digit place values.

Because place value is a skill taught during the primary grades, older students who have not adequately learned the skill will have difficulty with computation and word problems and may have little opportunity to learn place value. Many of the games and activities designed to teach place value are aimed at young children and are less appropriate for older students. Tips for Teachers 14.5 provides sources of numbers that may be useful for teaching place value to older students.

## Tips for Teachers

### 14.5 Sources of Numbers for Teaching Place Value to Older Students

- An odometer
- Numbers from students' science or social studies texts
- Numbers from school population (e.g., number of freshmen, sophomores, juniors, seniors, and so on)
- Population data from town, county, state, or country
- Financial data page from the newspaper

# TechTalk

## Video Discs and CD-ROMs Help Teach Fractions

Kelly, Carnine, Gersten, and Grossen (1987) compared interactive video disc programs with traditional basal mathematics programs for teaching fractions to students and found that the interactive video programs outscored basal programs on both the posttest and the maintenance checks. The researchers ascribed the success of interactive video discs to the following attributes:

1. They systematically reviewed previously taught skills.
2. There were discrimination practices among the different strategies.
3. Numerous examples were provided.
4. The terms *numerator* and *denominator* were taught separately.
5. The programs explicitly taught different strategies for problem solving.

Interactive computer applications also help students visualize information, which fosters problem solving. Shiah, Mastropieri, Scruggs, and Fulk (1994) taught students with learning disabilities to do mathematical word-problem solving on the computer. Students made substantial gains and reported that the pictorial information helped them with word problems.

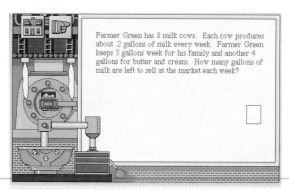

Farmer Green has 8 milk cows. Each cow produces about 2 gallons of milk every week. Farmer Green keeps 3 gallons week for his family and another 4 gallons for butter and cream. How many gallons of milk are left to sell at the market each week?

Form *Stickybear's Mathtown* by Optimum Resource, Inc.

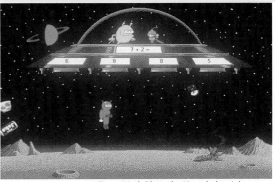

From *Math Blaster* by Knowledge Adventure.

## Learning Fractions

Although often thought of as one of the more difficult mathematical skills, fractions are actually introduced early in the mathematics curriculum. Children between the ages of 3 and 5 discover fractions when they begin to cook. "Pour in 1/2 cup of milk and 1/3 cup of raisins" is often a youngster's introduction to fractions. Sharing—as in "Give half of your cookie to your sister"—is also a good way for children to discover fractions.

The teaching of fractions, mirroring that of other computations, proceeds from concrete to abstract. Many manipulative aids can be used to teach

fractions: colored rods, cardboard strips and squares, blocks, fractional circle wheels, cooking utensils such as measuring cups and spoons, and any unit divider (e.g., egg cartons and muffin pans).

Students with learning problems are unlikely to learn fractions, however, unless they are taught directly and systematically (Kelly et al., 1990). Such teaching includes the following:

● *Systematic practice in discrimination among different problem types.* Students with learning disabilities and behavior problems often confuse algorithms when they compute fractions. For example, they learn to compute the denominator and then use this procedure when adding, subtracting, multiplying, and dividing.

- *Separation of confusing elements and terminology.* Because much of the language of learning fractions is unfamiliar and confusing, students are more likely to learn fractions successfully when the language and concepts are clearly explained and illustrated.
- *Use of a wide range of elements to illustrate each concept.* Students have a difficult time generalizing beyond the number of examples provided by the teacher; thus, by providing many different examples you help students understand.

The teaching sequence for fractions, which ensures that each student can do certain work, follows:

1. *Manipulates concrete models.* Refers to student's success at using fraction blocks and pegs and using instruments that require understanding of fractions (such as measuring cups, spoons, and rulers).
2. *Matches fractional models* (e.g., matching halves, thirds, and fourths).
3. *Points to fractional model when name is stated by another* (e.g., the teacher says, "half," and the student selects a model of "half" from several distracters).
4. *Names fractional units when selected by another* (e.g., the teacher points to a fractional unit such as a "fourth," and the student names it).
5. *Draws diagrams or uses manipulatives to represent fractional units* (e.g., the teacher says or writes fractional units such as "whole," "half," and "third," and the student uses manipulative drawings to represent these units).
6. *Writes fraction names when given fractional drawings.*
7. *Uses fractions to solve problems* (e.g., 1/2 cup of sugar in a bowl).

## Strategies for Helping All Learners Acquire and Use Computation Skills

The emphasis on problem solving from NCTM (1989) does not mean that students do not need to learn math computation. In fact, students will be unsuccessful problem solvers if they spend too little time on math computation. You can help students with special needs, who often have difficulty with math computation.

### Assessment

The first step in a successful instructional program is to gather sufficient knowledge about students' performance so that instruction is best suited to meet student needs. Assessment strategies can include portfolios that represent a collection of student work, criterion-referenced tests that demonstrate students' knowledge relative to a scope and sequence in mathematics, curriculum-based measurement that relates students' performance to the school system curriculum, and error analysis that requires the study of student performance and interpretation of the pattern of errors made (Bryant & Rivera, 1997).

## Patterns of Common Computation Errors

The computation errors that students make fit certain patterns. Rourke (1993) identifies common types of mechanical arithmetic errors, described in the following sections. Tips for Teachers 14.6 has suggestions for helping students learn computational techniques.

**Spatial Organization**  Mistakes in spatial organization are those that occur because students misalign numbers in columns. These mistakes can occur when students copy problems incorrectly or as they solve problems. One way to help students correct misaligned numbers is to tell them to draw vertical lines through their numbers to ensure that ones, tens, and hundreds are all in the right place. Another way to help is to provide graph paper with large squares so that students can write the numbers in boxes and more easily align them.

**Visual Detail**  Mistakes involving **visual detail** occur when students misread one aspect of the arithmetic problem—misreading a minus sign as a plus sign, for example, or disregarding a dollar sign. Because many of the problems that occur in mathematics can easily be corrected by the student, teach students to stop and reread the problem and their answers before they go to the next problem to be sure that they neither misread nor omitted something.

**Procedural Error**  Procedural error occurs when students misapply a procedure from one arithmetic operation to another. For example, a student learns that $5 \times 5 = 25$ and misapplies this information to a problem in which 5 and 5 should be added.

**Failure to Shift Operations**  A failure to shift operations occurs when students fail to move to one operation after completing another operation. For example, when the problem involves both subtraction and addition, the student fails to move to addition after completing the subtraction portion of the problem. To help students who demonstrate this

# T i p s   for   T e a c h e r s

## 14.6   Teaching Students Computational Strategies

1. *Use doubles.* Students know that 2 + 2 = 4, 3 + 3 = 6, and 5 + 5 = 10. With this basic information, they can easily compute related facts. For example, if 3 + 3 = 6 what is 3 + 4? Yes, it is one more.

2. *Count-on.* Students do not need to resort to counting from 1 to solve math facts. They can learn to count on from the largest numeral in an addition fact. For example, 8 + 3 means counting on 3 more from 8, for a sum of 11. Students learn to count on 3 more from 8: "9, 10, 11." The answer is the last number they say after they have counted on the correct number. Students can use this same principle for subtraction. For example, when asked to solve the following problem:

   8 – 3 =

   they now count backward from eight, "7, 6, 5." Again, the last number is the answer.

3. *Use the commutative idea.* With addition and multiplication, the order of the numbers does not matter—it always yields the same answer. For example, 3 + 4 = 7 and 4 + 3 = 7. With multiplication this is also true: 4 × 6 = 24 and 6 × 4 = 24. Give students many opportunities to use this principle, to be sure they understand and apply it.

4. *Think one more or one less than a known fact.* When students know a math fact, teach them that they

also know related math facts. For example, Guido knew that 6 + 7 = 13. When he was faced with the problem 6 + 8 = _____, he panicked. When his teacher told him that 8 is one more than 7, thus the answer is one more than 6 + 7 = 13, he was able to solve the problem quickly. Pictures such as the following can help to illustrate the principle:

5 + 5 = 10

5 + 6 =

5 + 4 =

5. *Using tens.* Students can learn that 10 + any single-digit number merely changes the 0 in the 10 to the number they are adding to it, as in the following examples:

   10 + 4 = 14
   10 + 8 = 18

6. *Using nines.* There are two strategies students can apply to addition facts that involve nines. First,

---

problem, ask them to reread the problem and tell you whether more than one operation is involved. Ask them to identify the types of operations involved and to provide an example of each one. Ask them to tell you how they will monitor their process and to determine how they will ensure accuracy in switching from one operation to the next.

**Motoric Problems**   Mistakes resulting from **motoric problems** can occur when the students' writing is so difficult to read that it leads to errors in arithmetic. Many students with learning problems demonstrate such poor writing ability that it interferes with their ability to successfully perform arithmetic computations. These students have difficulty not only writing their numbers, but also reading them. They

often mistake their fives for threes, their twos for threes, and so on. Thus, their calculations may be accurate, according to their interpretation of the number, but the answers are wrong because they have mistaken the number.

**Memory Problems**   Mistakes resulting from **memory problems** occur when students forget or misremember a fact that leads to an error in arithmetic calculation. As a teacher, you can help students with learning problems by providing them with adequate time and frequent opportunities to rehearse and learn arithmetic facts.

**Difficulty with Zero**   Difficulty with zero can lead to mistakes that occur when students do not under-

they can think of the 9 as a 10 and then subtract 1 from the answer. In the following example, the student is taught to "think" of the 9 as a 10:

$$9 \\ +6$$     think     $$10 \\ +6 \\ \hline 16 - 1 = 15$$

Second, students can think that whenever there is a 9 in an addition problem, the answer in the ones column is always one less than the number they are adding to the 9. For example:

$$9 \\ +4 \\ \hline 13$$     $$8 \\ +9 \\ \hline 17$$     $$9 \\ +6 \\ \hline 15$$

7. *Counting by twos, threes, fours, fives, and tens.* Beginning with 10, teach students to count by the number. This may be done with individual students or with a small group. It is sometimes helpful to develop a rhythm to the counting sequence:

10-20-30-40-50-60-70-80-90-100

After students can count by tens to 100, ask them to count aloud by 10 from two points other than 10 and 100. For example, "Count aloud from 20 to 80." After students have learned to count by tens, they should be taught to count by fives and then by twos, threes, and fours. Being able to count by multiples helps in addition, multiplication, and division. Multiplication facts can be taught by interpreting 3 × 4 as counting by threes four times. Division facts, such as 8 divided by 2, can be interpreted as "How many times do you count by twos before you reach 8?"

8. *Relationship between addition and subtraction, and multiplication and division.* After students learn addition facts, they can be shown the relationship between the addition fact and subtraction. For example, students who know 7 + 6 = 13 can learn the relationships between the known addition fact and the subtraction fact, 13 − 7 = _____. Whenever possible, reinforce this principle as students are working, "You know 8 + 4 = 12, so 12 − 4 = must be _____." Give students known facts and ask them to form subtraction problems. These sample relationships can be used to teach multiplication and division facts.

*Source:* Adapted from Thornton, C. A., & Toohey, M. A. (1985). Basic math facts: Guidelines for teaching and learning. *Learning Disabilities Focus, 1,* 44–57; and Thornton, C. A., Tucker, B. F., Dossey, J. A., & Brazik, E. F. (1983). *Teaching mathematics to children with special needs.* Menlo Park, CA: Addison-Wesley.

stand the multiple meanings and uses of zero. Many students with learning problems learn that zero means nothing and never really understand that zero is a number or the role of zero as a placeholder. The best way to help students who have difficulty with zero is to ensure that they understand how zero can be used as a placeholder. You can teach a minilesson to a small group of students who demonstrate difficulty with this concept, to facilitate their understanding and adequate use of zero.

## Computation and Calculators

There is a preponderance of evidence that calculators assist in the acquisition of mathematics achievement for students with learning problems.

Reviews of the calculator research have drawn the following conclusions:

1. Calculators for instructional purposes do not impede the acquisition of basic skills. In fact, calculators can increase skill acquisition.
2. The advantages of using calculators are more obvious for problems that include computation rather than for problem solving.
3. Students who use calculators on criterion tests produce higher achievement scores than students who do not.
4. Studies indicate that students do not develop a negative attitude toward math because of calculator use. In fact, calculators improve students' attitudes toward mathematics.

What is the most appropriate use of calculators in math instruction? When and how are calculators especially helpful for students with disabilities?

5. It is appropriate to introduce calculators at the same time that the paper-and-pencil methods are taught.
6. Students can develop their own complex problems and then solve them with use of the calculator. This also serves to increase their self-concept about math skills.

# Strategies for Helping All Students Develop Problem-Solving Skills

Another component of effective math instruction is problem solving, which has several unifying components that include the following:

● A mathematics knowledge base
● An application of knowledge to new and unfamiliar situations
● An ability to actively engage in thinking processes and apply this knowledge base to problems

Problem solving is increasingly visible in mathematics textbooks and curricula in regular education. Few programs are designed to instruct students with learning problems in problem solving (Cawley et al., 1987; Geary, 1993), although recently approaches to applying hypermedia to teaching mathematics problem solving to students with disabilities have been implemented (Babbitt & Miller, 1996). Secondary students with learning problems often

## research brief

### Math Problem Solving

Hofmeister (1989) provides a summary of the research on math problem solving:

● Problem-solving skills can and should be taught.
● Some generalization of problem-solving skills should be planned for and systematically taught. This generalization is most likely to occur across problems without a domain. Transfer across domains will depend on the similarity of the problem.
● It may be unreasonable to expect the majority of specific problem-solving strategies in one domain, such as ratio-based word problems, to transfer to another domain, such as geometry proofs.
● The development of practical problem-solving skills will require a considerable investment of time and explicitly taught strategies and practices.
● Teaching of problem-solving strategies should be integrated with the teaching of other content in the domain, such as computational and factual knowledge.

By providing a good mathematics knowledge base, students learn the strategies for developing problem-solving skills.

demonstrate extreme difficulty in problem solving because of the poor instruction they have received (Cawley et al., 1987). Students with disabilities have difficulty with problem representation, require additional time to acquire math problem-solving strategies, and need booster sessions to maintain learning (Montague & Applegate, 1993; Rivera et al., 1998).

## Problem-Solving Strategies

Mercer and Miller (1992) have developed a procedure called FAST DRAW to teach the concrete–representational–abstract teaching principle advocated in mathematics instruction. The Strategic Math Series is the name of their program. Following is an explanation of the **FAST DRAW** strategy:

> **F**ind what you're solving for.
>
> **A**sk yourself, "What are the parts of the problem?"
>
> **S**et up the numbers.
>
> **T**ie down the sign.
>
> **D**iscover the sign.
>
> **R**ead the problem.
>
> **A**nswer or draw a conceptual representation of the problem, using lines and tallies, and check.
>
> **W**rite the answer.

At the secondary level, Montague and Bos (1986) provided instruction in word-problem solving for six students. Five of the six students improved after the cognitive strategy training. Subsequent work in cognitive problem solving has yielded positive outcomes for students with learning problems (Montague, 1992). Their strategy included an eight-step process, as follows:

1. Read the problem aloud.
2. Paraphrase the problem.
3. Visualize what the problem is about.
4. State the problem in your own words.
5. Hypothesize.
6. Estimate.
7. Calculate.
8. Self-check.

Hutchinson (1993) also implemented a strategy for teaching adolescents with learning problems to solve algebra word problems. She taught them to ask themselves questions (self-question), to think aloud, to provide guided practice, and to use graphs to monitor their progress. Students displayed increased abilities to solve problems and transferred their skills to other settings. The self-questions Hutchinson used included the following:

1. Have I read and understood the sentence?
2. Do I have the whole picture, a representation, for this problem?
3. Have I written the representation on the work-sheet?

In summary, when teaching story problems to students with learning and behavior difficulties, keep the following guidelines in mind (Bos & Vaughn, 2002):

- Be certain the students can perform the arithmetic computation before introducing the computation in story problems.
- Develop a range of story problems that contain the type of problem you want students to learn to solve.
- Instruct with one type of problem until mastery is attained.
- Teach students to read through the word problem and visualize the situation. Ask them to read the story aloud and tell what it is about.
- Ask students to reread the story, this time to get the facts.
- Identify the key question. In the beginning stages of problem solving, students should write the key question so that it can be referred to when computation is complete.
- Identify extraneous information. Tell students to note that this information will not be used.
- Reread the story problem and attempt to state the situation in a mathematical sentence. The teacher plays an important role in this step by asking the students questions and guiding them in formulating the arithmetic problem.
- Tell students to write the arithmetic problem and compute the answer. Students can compute some problems in their heads without completing this step.
- Tell students to reread the key questions and be sure they have completed the problem correctly.
- Ask students whether their answer is likely, based on their estimate.

# Tips for Teachers

## 14.7 Designing Math Problem-Solving Activities for Students with Learning Difficulties

1. Begin problem solving as part of the initial mathematics program. Do not wait.

2. Make problem solving the reason for computation.

3. Develop a long-term perspective on the development of programs to teach problem solving.

4. Conduct problem solving as a multimodel activity.

5. Assist students with what they cannot do so that they can solve problems. If a student cannot read the problem, rewrite it. If the computation is too complex, make it simpler.

6. Ask students to write their own problems and to modify existing problems.

7. Differentiate between process and knowledge.

8. Prepare problems in such a way that students must act upon the information. Prepare a set of problems in which all problems have the same questions.

9. Use familiar subject matter as the content for the problems.

10. Monitor progress and modify problems to fit the students' weaknesses and progress.

*Source:* Adapted from Cawley, J. F., Miller, J. H., & School, B. A. (1987). A brief inquiry of arithmetic word-problem-solving among learning disabled secondary students. *Learning Disabilities Focus, 2*(2), 87–93.

Tips for Teachers 14.7 should be helpful as you design and implement problem-solving activities for students with learning problems.

## Designing Math Problem-Solving Activities for Students with Special Needs

What should teachers consider when they design math problem-solving activities for students with special needs? To what extent will these designs benefit other students? The instructional practices that we recommend for teaching problem solving will benefit all students.

## Integrating Math Problem Solving into the Curriculum

Problem solving does not have to occur only during math time. It is an interesting and fun activity to integrate into the rest of the curriculum. Math story problems are especially easy to integrate into the reading curriculum. How? Take stories that children are reading or books that you are reading to the entire class, and change the stories so that they include numbers and problems the students need to answer.

For example, Joan Lindquist asked students the following questions about a story they were reading

in class: "How many friends has Marcia told us about? How many friends does Linda have? Altogether, how many friends do they have? How many more friends does Linda have than Marcia?" Teachers can also add information to the stories and then ask children to solve word problems based on the additional information provided. It is also educational and fun to ask students to work in pairs to write their own word problems from the stories they are reading. Then have them read their word problems to the entire class so that the class can solve them.

Word problems can be easily integrated into the social studies curriculum also. When dates are discussed, ask students to compute how many years ago the event occurred. Ask students word problems about the age of central figures in the social studies lesson. Add numbers and information to the lesson and construct word problems. Cawley (1984) identifies the integration of math into other content areas as an important means of promoting generalization of math concepts.

Return to the interview at the beginning of this chapter, where you met Paul, a college student with learning disabilities who had extreme difficulty with math. What questions would you want to ask him? If Paul were in your class, how would you implement the suggestions in this chapter to ensure that his experiences in mathematics would be as positive as possible? Remember, you *can* make a difference in students' lives.

making a
# Difference

through **Action Teaching**

## Mathematics Activities for All Learners

### Cake for Four—No, Make That Six!

**Objective:** Developing students' concept of fractions by having them partition an object into equal parts.

**Grades:** Second through fourth grade (possibly higher)

**Materials:** For each student: (1) a 6-inch paper circle; (2) five strips of construction paper, 1/4 inch wide by 8 inches long, in a contrasting color to the paper circle; and (3) eight Teddy Grahams (or other small cookies), placed in a small sandwich bag.

**Teaching Procedures:**

1. Students move desks together so that each has a partner with whom to compare his or her work. Materials are distributed. Teacher introduces the lesson as a *Let's Pretend* activity in which students will learn that when they eat a piece of cake that has been divided into equal parts, they are eating a fraction of the cake.

2. Students are asked to imagine that they have just helped bake their favorite kind of cake for supper. To feed the four people in their pretend family, they need to divide the cake into four equal pieces. They are asked to think of the paper circle on their desk as the top of the cake, and to show the teacher (and their partners) how—using the strips of paper—they would divide the cake into four equal parts. When each student has successfully demonstrated this partitioning task, they are asked what fraction of the whole cake each piece is, and how that fraction is written.

3. Next, students are asked to imagine that their grandmother and grandfather have arrived unexpectedly and have accepted the family's invitation to stay for supper. Now, because students certainly want to share the cake with the grandparents also, into how many pieces will they divide it?

    The teacher makes sure that each student shows six equal portions and understands that each piece of cake is now 1/6 of the whole—just enough for the six people at the dinner table.

4. Before the cake is served, however, Uncle Bob and Aunt Doris arrive! Now the cake will be divided into how many equal pieces?

5. Finally, the time comes to decorate the cake with the Teddy Grahams, cut it, and serve it. (As a reward for all their good thinking, students now get to eat the decorations, 1/8 at a time!)

Students enjoy the story associated with this activity, and they enjoy comparing their partitioned cakes with those of their peers. (This is a good example of cooperative learning.) They especially enjoy eating their cookies at the end of this activity.

*Source:* Bos, C. S., & Vaughn, S. (1998). *Strategies for teaching students with learning and behavior problems* (4th ed.). Boston: Allyn & Bacon.

### Bingo Clock Reading

**Objective:** To give students practice in associating the time on a clock face, its written form on a game board, and its spoken form.

**Grades:** Primary

**Materials:** (1) Cards that show times on a standard clock; (2) large game boards with 16 squares and with times written at the bottom of each square; (3) 16 "clock" chips (made by placing gummed labels on game-board chips and drawing a clock on the face of the label); (4) markers.

**Teaching Procedure:**

A caller holds up a clock face. Players must decide whether the time shown by that clock is on their game board. If it is, players place a marker in the square that contains the written form. The winner is the first person who completes a row in any direction and reads the time in each winning square.

*Source:* Bos, C. S., & Vaughn, S. (1998). *Strategies for teaching students with learning and behavior problems* (4th ed.). Boston: Allyn & Bacon.

### Slap It!!!

**Objective:** To provide practice in responding quickly to math.

**Grades:** Second through eighth grade

**Materials:** A set of 4-inch by 6-inch cards on which the answers to math facts are written. Cards can be established as answers to addition, subtraction, multiplication, or division facts.

**Teaching Procedures:**

1. Students and teacher stand around a small table (preferably round), and teacher shows students the cards, each with a number (the answer to a math fact). Teacher spreads the cards (approximately 10) on the table, with the number side up.

2. Students are told to keep both hands on the table until the teacher says, "Go." Students who lift either hand prior to the "go" signal are eliminated from that round of competition.

3. The teacher says a computation problem, followed by the word *go.* For example, "6 × 7 = (go)."

4. Students slap the card that has the correct answer. The first hand on the card gets to keep the card. The student with the most cards gets to be the teacher.

*(continued)*

making a **Difference** through **Action Teaching**

## Mathematics Activities for All Learners *(continued)*

**Adaptations:**
1. Teachers can use the same game with word problems.
2. Teachers can use more than one computation during the game.

### Measurement

**Objective:** To reinforce understanding of perimeter and area.

**Grades:** Third grade and above

**Materials:** 1-inch graph paper, scissors, teacher-made table worksheet.

**Teaching Procedures:**
1. Have students cut out squares of graph paper of different sizes: a 1-inch square, a 2-inch square, a 3-inch square, a 4-inch square, and a 5-inch square.
2. Measure the number of small squares in each large cutout square, and complete the following table:

| edges | 1 | 2 | 3 | 4 | 5 | 6 |
|-----------|---|---|---|---|---|---|
| perimeter |   |   |   |   |   |   |
| area      |   |   |   |   |   |   |

3. Ask, "What happens to the perimeter and area each time the edges are doubled?"
4. Have students experiment with different-size squares and then complete the table.

*Source:* Reprinted with permission of the publisher, Teaching K–8, Norwalk, CT 06854. From the April 1993 issue of *Teaching K–8.*

### Subtraction with Money

**Objective:** To introduce the concept of subtraction of three-digit numbers with regrouping, using play money.

**Grades:** Third grade and above

**Materials:** Play money (20 one-dollar bills, 20 dimes, and 20 pennies for each student), place-value board for each student.

**Teaching Procedures:**
1. Review 100 pennies = 1 dollar
   10 pennies = 1 dime
   10 dimes = 1 dollar
2. Write example on the board: $5.36
   −1.27
3. Student makes $5.36 on place-value board.
4. Teacher begins questioning, "You have 6 pennies, you have to give me 7 pennies. Do you have enough pennies?" "Can you trade something?" "That's right. 1 dime = 10 pennies. Take 1 dime from your dimes place and trade it for 10 pennies from your bank. Put the 10 pennies in the pennies place." "Now, how many pennies do you have?" "Can you take 7 pennies away? How many are left?" (Teacher writes 9 in the ones column.) "Can you take 1 dollar away? How many are left?" (Teacher writes 3 in the hundreds place.)
5. Give students ample guided practice with one trade before giving them independent practice in pairs. Encourage students to self-question while completing each step.

**Modifications:** When students become proficient in subtracting with one trade, provide examples of problems involving two trades.

## summary

- The current trend in mathematics instruction is to emphasize effective problem solving and to promote positive attitudes toward a broad view of mathematics with less emphasis on rote memorization.
- Difficulties in mathematical problem solving may originate from cognitive factors, educational factors, personality factors, and neuropsychological patterns.
- Several curriculum resources are available to teachers of students who have difficulty learning math.
- Teachers tend to lower their expectations of students who have difficulty in mathematics, but lower expectations do not solve the problem.

Instead, teachers should instruct students to develop their own goals, help them develop joint (teacher-student) goals, and then provide the type of instruction that will maximize students' strengths.

- Appropriate and specific feedback can help students better understand their mistakes in mathe-

matics, promote student self-monitoring, and boost student self-concept.

- Just as basic skills must be mastered before higher-order problems can be taught and understood, mathematics instruction should begin at a concrete level and gradually move to increasingly abstract levels.

## key terms and concepts

classification
Computational Arithmetic
      Program
constant time delay
Corrective Mathematics
      Program
developmental arithmetic
      disorder
difficulty with zero
DISTAR Arithmetic
      Program

failure to shift operations
FAST DRAW
Key Math Teach and
      Practice
mastery
memory problems
motoric problems
NCTM Navigation Series
nonverbal math
      disabilities
one-to-one correspondence

procedural error
Project Math
Real-Life Math
      Program
seriation
spiral curriculum
Team-Assisted
      Individualization
Touch Math
visual detail

## think and apply

1. Reread Paul's description, at the beginning of the chapter, of his experience with math. Think of three things you would do if Paul were a student in your elementary math class. Be sure to consider how you might motivate Paul, what your attitude toward Paul would be, and what instructional practices you would consider implementing.

2. Make a copy of the NCTM standards (Figure 14.1). Show them to three special education teachers and ask for their opinions of the application of these standards to the special education students they teach. Be sure to ask them to identify the types of needs their students have and the extent to which the needs of their students relate to the requirements of the guidelines.

3. Contact two publishing companies that provide educational materials for students with special needs (e.g., www.proedinc.com, www.

etacuisenarie.com), and ask them to send you a copy of their materials catalog. In the catalog, examine the materials designed to teach mathematics to students with special needs. Consider the following questions: (a) Are more materials available to teach language arts or mathematics? (b) Of the materials available to teach mathematics, what proportion is designed for elementary students and what proportion is designed for secondary students? (c) Make a list of the skills that the materials indicate they cover. What skills are frequently not included?

4. A considerable amount of software is available for instruction in mathematics. Identify two software programs that you think would be effective for teaching mathematics to young children (ages 5–8). Identify two software programs that you think would be effective for teaching mathematics to intermediate-age children (ages 9–12).

# read more about it

1. Bley, N. S., & Thornton, C. A. (2001). *Teaching mathematics to students with learning disabilities* (4th ed.). Austin, TX: PRO-ED.

   *Describes the relationship between learning disabilities and mathematical performance, discusses different areas in mathematics (e.g., money and time, number and place value), describes the most common errors made in each area by students with learning disabilities, and provides instructional techniques for improving students' mathematical performance in each area.*

2. Cawley, J. F., Fitzmaurice-Hayes, A. M., & Shaw, R. A. (1988). *Mathematics for the mildly handicapped.* Boston: Allyn & Bacon.

   *Aims at developing a long-term, comprehensive curriculum for teaching mathematics to students with mild disabilities. Emphasis is on determining which area of mathematics to teach and when and for how long to teach this component.*

3. Cuevas, G., & Driscoll, M. (Eds.). (1993). *Reaching all students with mathematics.* Reston, VA: National Council of Teachers of Mathematics.

   *Discusses current trends in mathematics instruction, emphasizing ways to capitalize on increasingly diverse classrooms, and describes recent programs aimed at improving the mathematics instruction and outcome performance of special student populations.*

4. Helton, S. M. (1991). *Math activities for every month of the school year.* West Nyack, NY: Simon & Schuster.

   *Activities (appropriate for grades 3–6) for 12 basic math concepts are related to events (e.g., holidays, seasonal changes) in a particular month. Includes ideas for classroom displays, as well as reproducible activity sheets.*

5. Higgins, K., & Boone, R. (Eds.). (1997) *Technology for students with learning disabilities: Educational applications.* Austin, TX: PRO-ED.

   *Addresses the application of various technologies to the education of students with learning disabilities. Topics include instruction on multiplication performance for students with LD and using hypermedia to improve problem-solving skills. Includes a CD-ROM*

   *version of the original text, which provides enhancements through digital editing.*

6. Bryant, D. P., & Cox, J. (1999). Mathematics interventions for students with learning disabilities (219–259). In W. M. Bender (Ed.), *Professional issues in learning disabilities: Practical strategies and relevant research findings.* Austin, TX: PRO-ED.

   *This chapter provides a detailed description of intervention research in mathematics that addresses the special learning needs of students with learning disabilities. Implications for future research and practice are provided.*

7. Stenmark, J. K., & Bush, W. S. (Eds.). (2001). *Mathematics assessment: A practical handbook for grades 3–5, Classroom assessment for school mathematics, K–12 Series.* Reston, VA: National Council of Teachers of Mathematics.

   *An excellent tool for the classroom teacher. Provides scoring rubrics, checklists, and observation forms to assist in monitoring student progress. This is one book in a series linked closely to the NCTM standard related to assessment.*

8. Newman, V. (1994). *Math journals: Tools for authentic assessment.* San Leandro, CA: Watten/Poe Teaching Resource Center.

   *Teachers looking for ways to integrate mathematics into the curriculum will find some great ideas in this book. It is particularly useful in helping students with writing/mathematics connections.*

9. Laughlin, C., & Kepner, H. S. (2001). *Guidelines for the tutor of mathematics* (2nd ed.). Reston, VA: National Council of Teachers of Mathematics.

   *Need support for the volunteer math tutors in your classroom or after-school programs? Here's a practical guide for math tutors. It provides the basics in teaching skills to help your volunteer tutors get started.*

10. Su, H. F. H. (2000). *Strategies? Tricks? See math is not difficult.* Boca Raton, FL: Project MIND, Inc.

    *This book also has an instructional guidebook and teacher activity book. Activities are based on the successful Project MIND initiative developed in Florida. This program is hands-on with lots of motivational activities and a strong parent component.*

# suggested websites

http://nctm.org
This is the official website of the National Council of Teachers of Mathematics and includes information about conferences, publications, standards, and research.

http://askeric.org/cgi-bin/lessons.cgi/
  mathematics
This website contains math lesson plans and ideas (e.g., algebra, measurement).

**www.ofcn.org/cyber.serv/academy/ace/math/elem.html**
This website contains math lesson plans and ideas (e.g., problem solving, geometry, multiplication).

**www.ed.gov/pubs/parents/Math/index.html**
This website provides parents with instructional materials to increase math skills.

**www.ldonline.org/ld_indepth/math_skills/math-1.html**
This website contains an overview of math difficulties of students with LD.

**www.ldonline.org/ld_indepth/math_skills/adapt_cld.html**
This website contains information on instructional adaptation of mathematics for students with learning disabilities in regular classes.

**www.ldonline.org/ld_indepth/math_skills/math_jld.html**
This website contains information on math instruction for secondary students with LD.

**www.ldonline.org/ld_indepth/math_skills/mathld_ mercer.html**
This website provides information on educational aspects of math difficulties (e.g., learner characteristics, effective strategies).

**www.ldonline.org/ld_indepth/math_skills/coopmath.html**
This website contains information on cooperative learning in math instruction.

**www.ldonline.org/ld_indepth/teaching_techniques/ strategies.html#anchor1001355**
This website provides several useful links on math.

**http://users.black-hole.com/users/rsch/indexnew.html**
This website provides worksheets for addition, subtraction, multiplication, division, and word problems.

**www.edbydesign.com/parentres.html**
This website contains practical resources for mathematics.

# Teaching in the Content Areas

# chapter | outline

# focus | questions

1. What are some critical issues that content-area teachers face when promoting learning for all students?

2. What difficulties do students face in content-area learning?

3. What steps can you take to prepare student-friendly demonstrations?

4. How can you promote student participation through questioning and classroom discussion?

5. What procedures can you use to learn the strengths and weaknesses of your textbook?

6. How can you adapt textbooks for students with reading difficulties?

7. How can you promote success in homework, class assignments, and tests for all learners?

8. How can you plan interdisciplinary thematic units to integrate the content areas?

# interview

## Nancy Brice

Nancy Brice is a social studies teacher at South Miami Middle School, a suburban school that is among the most ethnically mixed in the city of Miami, Florida. She teaches approximately 150 seventh- and eighth-graders in six different classes (five civics and one geography). Fifteen of her students have been school-identified as having learning disabilities, seven have been identified as gifted, and two as vision-impaired. Thus, Nancy's classroom has a range of cultural, linguistic, and academic diversity coupled with an extraordinary range of individual needs.

    Nancy puts a lot of energy into her teaching. She is feisty and highly interactive with students. She is constantly on her feet, frequently moving around the room, working with small groups of students, and checking in with individual students. Nancy is positive, upbeat, and full of energy. A visit to her classroom gives you the feeling that she is ready to teach. Despite the challenge of large classes and frequent interruptions during the day, learning happens in her class. Here is Nancy's explanation:

I try to make my class interesting and entertaining. When I was teaching "supply and demand" I made up a game where all students were given play money when they came into class and had to buy their desks. I made up a relay race when it was time to review for a test. When I plan I try to think, "How can I make it fun?"

My particular challenge this year is my geography class. First of all, it is the first time I've taught it. I don't even have a textbook that I like. The real problem is that it is an elective and only one out of three students actually signed up for it. The rest didn't get their first choice for an elective and so were just dumped in this class. Many of the students with disabilities are placed in this class. To make this class work, I really have to do some careful planning and be ready to make adaptations to meet their needs.

With 150 students, I can't make individual plans for each student with special needs. On a day-to-day basis, I don't sit down and plan for Rudy, for example.

But I do spend a great deal of time planning each lesson, and I plan for adaptations. I meet with the spe-

cial education and gifted teachers at the beginning of the school year so that I am aware of individual student needs. I discuss their IEPs and brainstorm with these resource teachers about how I can adapt curriculum. For example, [I give] students with learning disabilities . . . extra time to take tests. In book work we do a lot of cooperative learning so they can work back and forth with each other. When I lecture, I show them how to take notes.

Even though I have too many students, I get to know each one by name. I think my relationship with the kids is excellent. I like to joke and laugh with the students, and I help them see that we're a family in here. But at the same time, I'm pretty strict. There are rules they must follow in the class, but they know I'm fair.

The kids also know that in my class, they have to think and they have to think about their thinking. We have debates, discussions, you name it. I even demonstrate how to think. I'll say something like, "I'm sorry it's taking me so long to think, but it's a tough problem." Then I talk through my thinking to show them how to solve problems. I also make them answer their own questions through research. I'll say, "Find out; do you think I'm the encyclopedia of knowledge?" and then I show them how to find out.

# i n t r o d u c t i o n

How does Nancy Brice ensure that learning takes place in her social studies classes? How does Nancy attend to the needs of special learners while teaching 150 students in a content area in which students with special learning needs are most often included, creating the greatest possible academic diversity?

This chapter begins with a discussion of critical issues in content-area instruction and the learning difficulties students experience in content-area classes. The focus is on teaching strategies you can use to promote learning in your content-area classes.

## ● Critical Issues in Content-Area Instruction

Tony Valenti teaches ninth-grade world history in an urban high school. His teaching responsibilities include six classes a day, with approximately 35 stu-

dents per class. The textbook is Tony's primary tool for planning. Content coverage is his main concern:

I have 38 chapters to cover in 36 weeks. We really have only 30 weeks, when you consider pep rallies and things like that. My biggest problem is trying to fit everything in. My assistant principal, who supervises curriculum and instruction, would like me to teach study skills and to make adaptations for kids who can't read, but frankly I don't see how to cram it into an already impossible schedule.

Tony took a university course on making adaptations for students with special learning needs. He enrolled for the class because he thought that what he learned would help him work with the many students at risk whom he teaches. His classroom teaching was videotaped, and a graduate student served as a peer coach to help him resolve his concerns about content coverage. As he watched the videotape, Tony realized that he was flooding students with information. There was little time for students to ask questions, process the information, or distinguish what information was most important. His overheads were difficult to read, and he had difficulty being specific about what he wanted students to learn. As Tony put it, "I was an information machine gun."

Peer-coaching sessions focused on how Tony could present information more clearly to students and teach them note-taking and test-taking skills. At the end of the course, Tony acknowledged, "I have all the same challenges, but I am more considerate and better at recognizing the scope of special needs. The time spent on process has made me more focused and has made the students more focused."

## Balancing Content and Process

Tony is faced with a common problem of many content-area teachers: the **content and process dilemma**. Vacca and Vacca (1989, p. 9) put it this way: "Teachers who are wedded to a discipline walk a tightrope between content and process. It's a balancing act every time the attempt is made to influence what is learned (content) and how it should be learned (process)." Teachers are often pressured to complete a textbook during a semester or to cover a set of objectives determined by state or school district curriculum guides. This pressure to cover content causes teachers to move steadily through material, even though some students have not learned it.

One critical issue in content-area instruction is to strive for balance between content coverage (subject-centered) and process (student-centered) (Readence et al., 1992). Process includes teacher-directed instructional activities that help students understand

material. For example, by teaching key vocabulary before reading, you can help students zero in on key ideas while they read. Process also includes student-implemented study skills.

## Balancing Text-Driven and Activities-Driven Instruction

Sara Hood teaches social studies to 190 sixth-grade students in their first year of middle school. To prepare for lessons, Sara examines the whole unit in the book and chooses the fundamental ideas that she wants students to learn. She then thinks of ways to give them background information and to teach key vocabulary. Sara uses the state-adopted social studies textbook as the basis of her planning. One major concern in planning is to find activities that will keep her middle-school students involved in learning and thus help her maintain control of the class. As Sara commented, "My college professors encouraged us to use activities-based learning for social studies, but frankly every time I try something 'hands-on,' they freak out!" Consequently, Sara relies heavily on routines such as guided textbook reading and answering the questions at the end of the chapter.

Like Tony, Sara attended the university course on making adaptations for students with special needs. She had a peer coach, and her teaching was videotaped. After watching her first videotaped lesson, Sara realized that her students were not as engaged as she had thought. As she watched the tape, she commented, "When I was going through the lesson, it seemed to be going well. But now that I'm looking at it on the tape, I'm bored to tears. If I'm bored, they must really be bored."

Sara and her peer coach talked about planning in terms of the planning pyramid (refer to Chapter 7) and co-constructed plans. They brainstormed about teaching and learning strategies that would encourage involvement and provide alternatives to the "read the chapter, answer the questions" routines. They talked about how Sara could incorporate cooperative learning groups into her planning and discussed how to place students with different talents and needs together in groups so that they could provide support for each other.

Sara used the planning pyramid to plan a 2½-week unit on Latin American countries. She planned to divide the classes into mixed-ability cooperative learning groups, each of which would select a country and present

These students are giving a group presentation. What decisions did their social studies teacher need to make on the content/process dilemma? How might this presentation reflect an effort to balance text-driven and activities-driven instruction in a content area?

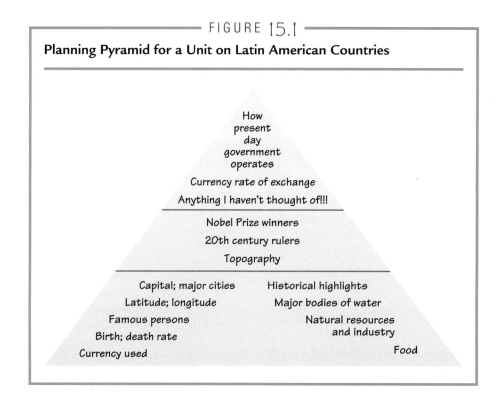

FIGURE 15.1

**Planning Pyramid for a Unit on Latin American Countries**

How
present
day
government
operates

Currency rate of exchange

Anything I haven't thought of!!!

Nobel Prize winners

20th century rulers

Topography

| | |
|---|---|
| Capital; major cities | Historical highlights |
| Latitude; longitude | Major bodies of water |
| Famous persons | Natural resources and industry |
| Birth; death rate | |
| Currency used | Food |

what they learned to the rest of the class. The bottom of the pyramid (see Figure 15.1) listed topics that all groups would research and on which all students would be tested. The middle and top of the pyramid listed student-selected material.

The unit was successful, and Sara began using cooperative learning groups regularly. Students were actively engaged in helping each other and were learning to respect each other's talents. Sara found that students are more engaged in learning when textbook assignments are balanced with other activities.

Sara's experience is not unusual. In social studies and science courses, the trend is toward activities-oriented learning that emphasizes real-world, hands-on experiences. The benefits of activities-oriented learning include increased student engagement in learning and increased opportunities for students who do not read and write well to be actively involved.

Activities-oriented instruction, coupled with effective content-area reading methods, can enable all students to become effective learners.

**r e s e a r c h b r i e f**

## Textbook or Activity Approach: What Works for Students with Learning Disabilities?

For decades, science educators have debated the relative merits of textbook versus activity approaches to science instruction. Some say that a textbook approach prepares students for the rigors of college reading and standardized achievement tests. Others prefer hands-on science instruction, on the premise that students learn by doing. This debate is particularly salient for middle-school students with learning disabilities who have difficulty reading and learning from text.

Thomas Scruggs, Margo Mastropieri, and their colleagues (Scruggs, Mastropieri, Bakken, & Brigham, 1993) conducted a carefully controlled investigation that compared the two approaches for 26 students with learning disabilities in four middle-school special education classrooms. The textbook approach consisted of guided reading coupled with paper-and-pencil vocabulary and comprehension tasks. The activity approach engaged students in experiments and recording observations. All 26 students were exposed to both approaches.

Outcomes were better in the activity approach than in the textbook approach in measures of vocabulary, factual recall, and application of concepts. Moreover, these middle-school students overwhelmingly preferred the activity approach, commenting that it helped them learn more and was more enjoyable.

## Coordinating Content-Area Teaching and Learning Strategies

Another issue in content-area instruction is an emphasis on professional collaboration. One way in which professionals collaborate is by teaching learning strategies. Teachers agree on a core group of learning strategies that will be reinforced from grade to grade and from course to course.

These students are participating in a community-based activity as part of their integrated thematic unit on colonial life. Why are collaborative and integrative curricula desirable in content area learning?

trend is toward integration of all language processes in the content areas. Content-area classes require students to use the basic skills of reading and writing and to speak and listen. Conley (1995, p. 9) suggests that content-area teachers take a **communication approach** by "teaching the student how to (1) communicate with oneself and others and (2) integrate reading with other language skills including writing, speaking, and listening."

The issue of how to integrate subject areas through **interdisciplinary thematic units**—teaching several subject areas around a central theme—is of interest to content-area teachers. For example, in high school, the teaching of marine science, history, geography, and American literature could be centered on a theme of whales (*Moby Dick*).

Al Fabre was able to initiate such a coordinated program at his school, the Louisiana State University Laboratory School. The program was called the Learning Environment and Attitude Program (**LEAP**) for Success (Cowart & Fabre, 1986). All teachers in the middle school agreed to implement four strategies: note taking, test taking, textbook reading, and vocabulary study. Teachers participated in workshops to learn how to teach the strategies, students took a minicourse to learn how to use the strategies, and parents were introduced to the strategies at an open house and through a parent handbook.

## Integrating the Curriculum

Vern Glidden is a sixth-grade science teacher at a large inner-city middle school that is organized by teams. One teacher from each subject area is assigned to a team, and the same cohort of students rotates from teacher to teacher during the day. The team includes several specialists (e.g., English as a Second Language teacher, special education teacher, gifted education teacher) who serve students in the cohort. Vern chairs his team, which meets daily to coordinate planning and to discuss individual student needs. The principal charged each team to set professional development goals for the next two school years. After much deliberation, Vern's team decided on two goals. Their year 1 goal was to learn more about how to incorporate all language processes (reading, writing, listening, and speaking) into content-area instruction. Their year 2 goal was to learn how to plan collaboratively across their content areas to develop interdisciplinary thematic units.

The goals set by Vern's team represent two important trends in content-area learning. The first

## Learning Difficulties in the Content Areas

Why do students have difficulty learning in the content areas? The question is so broad that you might as well ask, "Why do students have difficulty learning?" You could answer that question by summarizing all you have learned about different students, but typical content-area classes pose particular problems for students. These problems include the following:

- Not all subjects are uniformly interesting to all students.
- Not all subjects are consistent with students' cultural backgrounds and prior knowledge.
- Learning in some content areas requires basic skills in reading, writing, and mathematics that some students do not have.
- The pace of instruction in some content areas is too fast for some students.
- The level of conceptual complexity and density in some content areas is overwhelming for some students.
- Textbooks in content-area classes can be dull and encyclopedic.
- Content-area classes require both regular homework and assignments and long-term projects.
- Taking tests is a required component of many content-area classes.

The suggestions in this chapter focus on how to give students who have difficulties in these areas the support they need to succeed in your content-area class.

## Effective Content-Area Instruction for All Learners

Faimon Roberts is a seventh- and eighth-grade science teacher at Louisiana State University Laboratory School. Although Faimon recognizes that his primary responsibility is to teach science, he also understands that his responsibility includes teaching students how to learn in science classes. In Faimon's more than 20 years of teaching experience, he has learned that students need to get ready to listen and to read. Their minds are on a million different things, and prelearning activities help them focus. In addition, Faimon has learned that setting a purpose for learning is essential, especially for students who tend to get lost when they read science textbooks or hear a lecture. Also, Faimon says, some students need to be told, "Here is the structure that the author of your textbook uses to organize the material. Watch for this structure." This section describes ways in which teachers like Faimon Roberts provide effective content-area instruction for all learners, including ways to develop prelearning activities, to structure classroom presentations, and to promote student participation.

> Common misconceptions: (1) students learned to read in elementary school, (2) reading and comprehending content area textbooks is no different from reading and comprehending basal readers, and (3) remedial reading classes will ensure the necessary skills for reading in the content areas (Readence, Bean, & Baldwin, 1992).

### Utilizing Prelearning Activities

**Prelearning activities** are strategies teachers use to activate students' prior knowledge and to preteach vocabulary and concepts—essentially, to prepare students to learn. Faimon typically uses purpose-setting activities, semantic maps, and concept diagrams to help students prepare to learn new information.

**Purpose Setting**    Purpose-setting activities provide students with a reason for completing a reading assignment or for listening to a lecture. For a few students, getting a good grade on a test is reason enough. Other students set their own purposes for reading and listening. For example, a chapter entitled "The Stormy Sixties" might get a student to think, "I really want to know what life was like when my parents were my age." Setting a purpose for learning helps to guide the reading and listening process and helps students to improve the depth of their comprehension. Purpose-setting activities are important for all learners but particularly for students with motivational and attentional problems. Tips for Teachers 15.1 provides guidelines for setting a purpose before you give a lecture or a reading assignment.

**Semantic Maps**    Providing students with visual representations of concepts and vocabulary to be learned is a powerful prelearning tool, particularly for special learners. One visual tool that is commonly used in prelearning activities is a **semantic map** (Pearson & Johnson, 1978), a visual aid that helps students see how ideas are related to each other and to what students already know.

Lists of words prepared in advance by the teacher or generated by students through teacher-guided brainstorming are placed on the board. After discussing the words' meanings, the class discusses

---

# Tips for Teachers

## 15.1    Setting a Purpose for a Lesson

- Keep the purpose brief, but make it powerful. Students become more actively involved in listening, reading, or participating in a classroom activity when they have a reason for doing so.
- Set a single purpose. When students are given too many purposes, they can lose their focus.
- Make certain that the purpose statement is not too narrow in scope and that it does not reveal too much content, which can actually inhibit comprehension.
- Have a regular purpose-setting routine. For example, write the purpose for learning on the board, or demonstrate how the purpose was set.

- After reading, begin discussion with a reiteration of the purpose for reading.
- Help students learn how to set their own purposes. Talk about the importance of setting a purpose and how to develop purpose statements.
- Keep the written purpose statement in full view of students while they are participating in a class activity. Some students may need to be reminded about the purpose of the lesson.

*Source:* Blanton, W. E., Wood, K. D., & Moorman, G. B. (1990). The role of purpose in reading instruction. *The Reading Teacher, 43*(7), 486–493.

FIGURE 15.2

**Example of a Semantic Map**

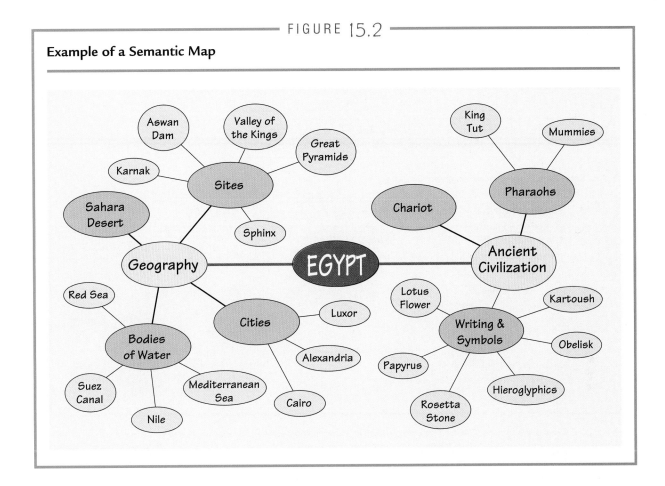

how to cluster the words and works together to develop a map to represent visually the relationships that exist among the ideas. For example, Figure 15.2 shows a semantic map for the following words for a chapter on Egypt:

| | | |
|---|---|---|
| Nile | Karnak | kartoush |
| Cairo | Sphinx | Mediterranean |
| Great | pharaohs | Sea |
|    Pyramids | Sahara Desert | King Tut |
| papyrus | mummy | chariot |
| lotus flower | hieroglyphics | Aswan Dam |
| Red Sea | obelisk | Rosetta Stone |
| Suez Canal | Valley of | Alexandria |
| Luxor |    the Kings | |

Students can use the map as a listening or reading guide. The map can also serve as a framework for postlistening and postreading discussions and an aid for studying for tests or quizzes.

**Concept Diagrams**     Concept diagrams (Bulgren et al., 1988) are another way to introduce a lecture or reading assignment. A **concept diagram** (see Figure 15.3) is similar to a semantic map but also helps students to determine the definitions, characteristics, examples, and nonexamples of a concept.

To create and use a concept diagram, follow these steps:

1. Identify major concepts to teach.
2. List important characteristics of the concepts. Think about whether each characteristic is always present, sometimes present, or never present.
3. Locate examples and nonexamples of the concept.
4. Construct a definition of the concept by naming the superordinate concept, its characteristics, and the relationship among characteristics.
5. Introduce the concept diagram to students, using an advance organizer.
6. Elicit a list of key words or ideas that relate to the concept.
7. Explain or review the parts of the concept diagram and their intended use.
8. With students, name and define the concept.
9. Discuss characteristics that are always present, sometimes present, and never present in the meaning of the concept.
10. Discuss examples and nonexamples of the concept.
11. Link the examples and nonexamples to the characteristics.

─── FIGURE 15.3 ───

### Concept Diagram

Concept Name: | fossils

Definitions: | Fossils are remains or prints of plants or animals who lived thousands of years ago which have been preserved in the earth.

Characteristics Present in the Concept:

| Always | Sometimes | Never |
|---|---|---|
| remains or prints | frozen in ice | still alive |
| plants or animals | trapped in tar | still decaying |
| thousands of years old | crushed by water | |
| preserved in the earth | in volcanic ash | |

Example:

( tigers in La Brea tar pits ) ( petrified forest in Arizona )

( Siberian mammoth ) ( fish skeleton in limestone layers )

Nonexample:

( your pet cat ) ( tree limbs and leaves in your yard )

( elephant in Africa today ) ( fish in supermarket )

*Source:* Bos, C. S., & Vaughn, S. (1994). *Strategies for teaching students with learning and behavior problems,* (3rd ed.). Copyright © 1994 by Allyn & Bacon. Reprinted by permission.

Concept diagramming is time consuming. Select concepts with care. Choose those that are pivotal to the curriculum and that students need to understand thoroughly.

What steps did this presenter follow to develop an effective concept diagram? What other prelearning activities can teachers use to increase success for all learners in the classroom?

## Developing Classroom Presentations

The goal of classroom presentations is to enhance student understanding. One key to enhancing understanding is **instructional clarity**—the clear, direct, explicit presentation of information. McCaleb and White (1980) list the following five components of instructional clarity:

- *Understanding:* connecting new information with what students already know
- *Structuring:* providing a clear format for the presentation, one that students can follow easily
- *Sequencing:* arranging a presentation in a logical order
- *Explaining:* defining key terms and providing examples as necessary
- *Presenting:* delivering material in an articulate and lively manner with correct pacing and using visual aids and multimedia as necessary

In all classroom presentations, clarity should be your goal. Clarity is important for all students but particularly for students who have poor organizational skills, poor language skills, or little prior knowledge of a topic.

Instructional clarity is particularly important during lectures. Lectures are often necessary to generate interest in a topic, to provide information that is not included in textbooks, or to clarify or embellish textbook information. Although lectures tend to be overused, used properly they can be an effective way to teach. By improving your lectures, you help students to improve their note taking.

## Giving Demonstrations

Demonstrations can be used to show students how to perform a skill, complete a task, or solve a problem. Demonstrations can be for the whole class, small groups, or individual students. They can be preplanned or can occur on the spot as part of interactive planning when students need more explanation. The key to demonstrations is that they must engage students, especially passive learners who will watch your demonstration and then forget every step of it. The important thing is to get students involved and thinking about what you are doing.

As with any lesson, before you give a demonstration, be sure to set a purpose, define key vocabulary, and provide an overview or advance organizer of the presentation, including key things to observe (Good & Brophy, 1994). Also provide guidelines for student participation during the presentation. Should they take notes? Should they ask questions before, during, or after the demonstration (Good & Brophy, 1994)?

After the demonstration, ask students to summarize the steps, or have one or two students repeat the demonstration for the class. Rivera and Deutsch-Smith (1988) offer an additional strategy for giving demonstrations to students with learning problems: the **demonstration plus model strategy**. To use this strategy, after completing your demonstration by following the steps outlined in the preceding paragraph, you would add these two steps:

- After the students have viewed the demonstration, have a student perform each step, verbalizing each step as you did.
- Have all students complete additional practice exercises independently, using the steps.

You can also improve a demonstration by describing your thinking as you move through the demonstration. Teacher **think alouds** are a way to model how to think and learn. Davey (1983, p. 45) listed the following five powerful uses of think alouds:

- Making predictions or showing students how to develop hypotheses
- Describing your visual images
- Sharing an analogy or showing how prior knowledge applies
- Verbalizing confusing points or showing how you monitor developing understanding
- Demonstrating fix-up strategies

## Facilitating Student Participation

As you have seen, student engagement can be fostered through cooperative learning groups and involvement in hands-on learning activities. This section includes additional suggestions for facilitating participation of all students in your class through two common content-area practices: questioning and discussion.

**Questioning**   Suellen Cannon teaches fifth grade. To the principal and to her school's special education teacher, Suellen is exemplary in the way she promotes learning for students in her class who have learning and behavior problems. During graduate school, Suellen read a research article by Allington (1983), which reported that instruction for low-achieving students tends to focus on low-level questioning. This article made Suellen rethink her questioning practices in her own class:

> Searfoss and Readence (1989) refer to the typical exchange that goes on in a classroom as *ping-pong discussion*. The teacher asks questions and students answer, back and forth. When teachers "serve the ball" only to students who are most capable of supplying the answer, other students become mere spectators.

I began to realize that not only did I tend to ask more questions of higher-achieving students, but when I did ask questions of lower-achieving students, the questions were low level and didn't make them think very much. Frankly, I just didn't want to embarrass them and put them on the spot. Since that time, I've set six goals for myself:

1. *Distribute questions evenly among all my students.* To get myself started with this, I put a check by a student's name on a class list when I asked him or her a question. I don't need to do that any more, now that I'm in the habit of spreading the questions around.
2. *Make certain that my questions are clearly stated.* Sometimes my questions are clear to me but ambiguous to students. If students seem confused, I try to reword the question so that it comes out right. I've learned that it's OK to say, "Oops, let me try to word that again."

3. *Ask all kinds of students all kinds of questions.* This was really hard to do at first. I want all students to succeed, and I want to make certain that they shine in front of the class. I've found that if I give students enough time to think through an answer, they come up with something that I can build on with follow-up questions and probes.

4. *Give students feedback about their answer.* I let them know when an answer is right and why it is right. I let them know when an answer is wrong and why it is wrong. The trick is trying to do this in positive and constructive ways and to use sensitive language. I'm getting better at this.

5. *Let students explain why an answer is right.* If a student gets an answer right, sometimes I let him or her explain how the answer was determined. This gives everyone a chance to learn how to answer that kind of question the next time.

6. *Let students explain their thinking when they get an answer wrong.* I let my students know that it is OK to make a mistake. When they do, then the important thing is to learn from the mistakes. Sometimes when a student gets an answer wrong, I ask them to tell me how they arrived at the answer. I then say, "I can understand how you were thinking that way. Here's another way to look at it."

Suellen had been under the impression that the best thing to do with low-achieving students and students with disabilities was to leave them alone. She didn't want them to expose what they didn't know to the rest of the class. Suellen has learned to work at involving all students in classroom questioning.

**Classroom Discussions**  One way to involve students is through **vibrant discussions** (Bean, 1985) in which student participation is high, students' thinking is stimulated, and students have opportunities to connect what they are learning to their personal knowledge and experience. Vibrant discussions help students learn how to express ideas, justify positions, listen to the ideas of others, and ask for clarification when they don't understand (Kauchak & Eggen, 1993).

## research brief

### Improving Classroom Discussions

In the early 1990s, Alvermann, O'Brien, and Dillon (1990) conducted classroom observations to learn more about teachers' practices using classroom discussion. Teachers said that classroom discussions are when "students are active participants and thoughtful sharers of information" (p. 306). However, observations indicated that of the 24 classroom discussions observed, the researchers classified 11 as *recitation* (consisting of activities such as answering textbook questions), 6 as *lecture and recitation* (which included long segments of teacher talk), and 7 as *open forum discussions* with exchanges on a variety of issues. Discussions that best matched teachers' definitions of the ideal were not textbook bound. The research also showed that teacher concerns about maintaining control, using class time, and covering content affected the quality of classroom discussion.

Since that time, a number of researchers have developed strategies for helping teachers become more effective in conducting classroom discussions (e.g., conversational discussion groups [O'Flahavan & Stein, 1992b], instructional conversations [Goldenberg, 1992–1993]). One strategy that has been shown to be particularly effective in helping students become engaged in classroom discourse is *questioning the author* (QtA). QtA is based on the idea that little classroom discussion is going to happen if teachers ask questions that prompt simple or one-word responses. The key to high-quality conversations is asking queries that elicit more elaborate and thoughtful responses. Both teachers and students learn how to generate and respond to queries.

The research of Beck and her colleagues (Beck et al., 1996; McKeown, Beck, & Sandora, 1996) found that regular use of QtA helps teachers improve the quality of their responses to student comments and the ways in which they extend classroom conversation. Students who participated in QtA became more active in classroom discussions, more facile in generating questions about text, and more focused on the meaning of text.

What qualities are present in a vibrant discussion group? How can discussion skills be directly taught? What are other ways to facilitate student participation in content-area learning?

# Tips for Teachers

## 15.2    Techniques for Stimulating Discussion without Asking Questions

- *Declarative statements.* Provide information to which students can respond or react.
- *Declarative restatements.* Summarize student comments.
- *Indirect questions.* Ask questions that begin "I wonder..." or "What would happen if ...."
- *Imperatives.* Make statements that encourage students to tell more about what they were thinking or to provide examples.

- *Student questions.* Invite students to ask questions of each other.
- *Deliberate silence.* Give everyone time to think and to gather their thoughts.

---

A thorough explanation of this exciting strategy is beyond the scope of this textbook. For further information, look into Dr. Beck and colleagues' book on QtA referenced in the Read More about It section of this chapter.

Your role in a discussion is that of moderator and encourager. As a moderator, you help the group to establish a focus and stay on the topic. As an encourager, you engage reluctant participants and make certain that students are free to express their points of view. For vibrant discussions, try the alternatives to traditional questioning in Tips for Teachers 15.2 (Dillon, 1979).

The **discussion web** (Alvermann, 1991) is a graphic aid to help students prepare for classroom discussions in content-area classes. As Figure 15.4 shows, the discussion web is designed to help students examine both sides of an issue. It is appropriate for elementary and secondary students and can be used before and after lectures.

FIGURE 15.4

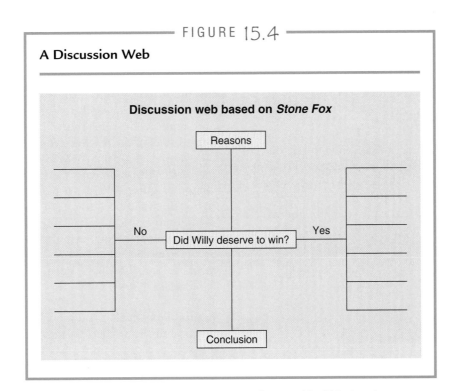

**A Discussion Web**

Discussion web based on *Stone Fox*

Reasons

No — Did Willy deserve to win? — Yes

Conclusion

*Source:* Alvermann, D. E. (1991). The discussion web: A graphic aid for learning across the curriculum. *The Reading Teacher, 45*(2), 92–99. Copyright by the International Reading Association.

Alvermann suggests the following procedure for implementing the discussion web:

- Prepare students for reading or listening by introducing key vocabulary, activating prior knowledge, and setting a purpose for reading.
- After students have read a selection or listened to a lecture, introduce the discussion web with a provocative question. For example, after giving a lecture about the First Amendment, you could ask, "Should rap music be censored?" Students discuss the pros and cons of the issue in pairs and complete the discussion web as a team. Students take turns filling in as many "Yes" and "No" statements as the team can generate.
- Pairs are regrouped into teams of four students, who then compare their discussion webs and build consensus on an answer to the question.
- The group selects and records the strongest argument and the reason for their choice.
- A spokesperson from each group takes three minutes to report the results, and individual students with dissenting or unrepresented points of view are given an opportunity to state their positions.
- As an individual activity, students write a position statement about their point of view on the issue.

The discussion web provides a structure for *critical thinking*—examining both sides of an issue carefully before making a judgment.

## Effective Content-Area Reading Instruction for All Learners

Many content-area teachers continue to rely on the textbook as a primary medium of instruction (Alvermann & Moore, 1991; Muther, 1985; Woodward & Elliott, 1990). This section shows you how to become familiar not only with the strengths and weaknesses of your textbook, but also with the ways in which students interact with and respond to the text. This section also contains effective strategies for making textbook adaptations for special learners and planning content-area reading lessons.

### Familiarizing Yourself with the Textbook

As a classroom teacher, you might not have the opportunity to select the textbook that is used in your content-area classroom. Typically, state selection com-

mittees decide on a limited number of state-adopted textbooks from which school districts can choose. At the district level, the list is shortened by a district committee. At the school level, grade- or committee-level teams frequently choose the textbook. Chances are that, like Nancy Brice, the teacher interviewed at the beginning of this chapter, you will inherit a textbook that someone else has chosen for you.

To familiarize yourself with your textbook, you need to consider the same five factors that textbook-selection committees consider: subject matter content, social content, instructional design, readability level, and friendliness level. You will also need to consider ways to go beyond the textbook.

**Subject Matter Content**   The **subject matter content** refers to the comprehensiveness of content coverage and the currency and accuracy of information (Young & Riegeluth, 1988). Ask the following guiding questions: What is being taught? Is the content complete, accurate, and up to date? Is the content consistent with our state and district curriculum guides? If the textbook is lacking in any of these areas, you will need to supplement the textbook with other materials.

**Social Content**   The values represented in a textbook are part of its **social content**, which also includes the textbook's portrayal of ethnic groups, genders, age groups, and individuals with disabilities. Young and Riegeluth (1988) suggest that curricular materials be examined closely and systematically to detect subtle biases. If the textbook has poor social content, it is your responsibility as a teacher to supplement the text.

**Instructional Design**   The way content is taught—how skills and concepts are introduced, developed, and reinforced—reflects the **instructional design**. Suggestions in the teacher's edition and supplemental materials (such as worksheets, workbooks, sample tests, transparencies, audiovisual aids, and computer software) also are part of instructional design. You might need to create or collect additional or alternative instructional materials. You might also need to adapt textbook materials for special learners; as an example, you might need to add graphic organizers to help students learn important concepts (Chambliss, 1994).

**Readability Level**   Traditionally, a textbook's level of difficulty is gauged by its **readability level**, expressed as a grade level. For example, you might hear a teacher say, "This history book is a sixth-grade book, but the readability level is seventh grade." Readability levels are determined by applying to the text one or more readability formulas (e.g.,

Dale & Chall, 1948; Fry, 1977; Raygor, 1977). Such formulas are based on sentence complexity (measured by sentence length) and word difficulty (measured by word length and frequency).

> "Students who are behind their peers in textbook reading do not need 'watered down' textbooks, nor do they need 'different' or 'slower' instruction. Rather, they need instructors to help them discover how to gain or regain confidence in their abilities and control their learning lost through years of an accumulation of academic frustration and failure" (Ciborowski, 1995, p. 90).

Textbook publishers typically supply readability information. Software programs that calculate the readability level of the text you type in are available, as are word-processing programs, such as Microsoft Word, that analyze readability. People who use readability formulas must understand not only that these formulas measure only two of the many factors that affect the difficulty of a text, but also that they are not exact. Different formulas yield different grade levels. Finally, the typical standard error of measurement for readability formulas is plus or minus approximately 1.5 grade levels (Singer & Donlan, 1989). For example, a text with readability predicted at grade 6.5 ranges by chance from grades 5.0 to 8.0.

Some textbooks are written to match a readability formula by using shorter sentences and simpler words. Simplified texts do not always convey ideas meaningfully, however, and force the reader to make connections that words normally provide.

**Friendliness Level**   Friendly text or considerate text is written and formatted in such a way that information can be extracted easily and support is available when the reader does not understand (Armbruster & Anderson, 1988; Singer, 1986). The degree to which text is considered friendly or considerate to the reader is determined by the number of features that promote learning (such as headings and subheadings, vocabulary in boldface type, and chapter summaries) included in text.

Familiarize yourself with the textbook you plan to use, and learn to recognize friendly text features that support student learning as well as areas in which you will need to intervene. Friendly text has the following characteristics:

- **Organization:** how the author orders information in the text. Organization includes the general structure of the text as well as consistency and connectedness of ideas.
- **Explication:** how the author explains ideas and teaches the reader. Explication includes necessary background information and examples.
- **Conceptual density:** the number of new vocabulary terms or concepts the author introduces.
- **Metadiscourse:** the degree to which the author "talks" to the reader. Metadiscourse includes di-

rect explanations of how to learn from the text and how to connect ideas from one part of the text to another.

- **Instructional devices:** the number of learning tools the author provides. Examples of learning tools are a table of contents, marginal annotations, and a glossary.

## Understanding How Students Interact with and Respond to Text

Your examination of the textbook helps you anticipate how you will need to supplement it. The ultimate judge of the readability and friendliness of a textbook is the reader. The **FLIP chart strategy** helps students learn to evaluate text on their own (Schumm & Mangrum, 1991). ("FLIP" stands for Friendliness, Language, Interest, Prior knowledge.) By filling out charts like the one shown in Figure 15.5, students learn what is comfortable for them individually as readers. After students have completed the FLIP chart, you can learn (through class discussions and individual conferences) about what is difficult for them in terms of text friendliness, language, interest, and prior knowledge. Students with reading and learning problems especially need to learn how to talk about the textbook and any problems they have with it. Classroom discussions based on the FLIP chart strategy also help students think as a group about effective strategies for coping with text they find difficult.

## Making Textbook Adaptations

Suppose you learn that the textbook is too difficult for some of your students. What will you do? Research indicates that most content-area teachers seldom implement many adaptations for a number of reasons (Schumm & Vaughn, 1992a; Schumm, Vaughn, & Saumell, 1992). First, adapting textbooks takes time, and teachers' time for planning and preparing for instruction is already limited. Second, textbook adaptations often slow down instruction, and teachers cannot cover as much material as they would like. Third, some teachers think that making adaptations for the few students who need them is not fair to the higher-achieving students who are ready to work at a faster pace.

Despite these concerns, research indicates that students at all achievement levels feel that they need textbook adaptations and are not getting the adaptations they need (Schumm et al., 1992). Also, adaptations can be helpful to all students and therefore are worth your planning time. Tips for Teachers 15.3 lists textbook adaptations you might consider, three of which are discussed here in greater depth.

FIGURE 15.5

## The FLIP Chart

Title of assignment _____

Number of pages _____

General directions: Rate each of the four FLIP categories on a 1–5 scale (5 = high).
Then determine your purpose for reading and appropriate reading rate, and budget
your reading/study time.

**F  =  Friendliness: How friendly is my reading assignment?**

Directions: Examine your assignment to see if it includes the friendly elements listed below.

*Friendly text features*

| | | |
|---|---|---|
| Table of contents | Index | Glossary |
| Chapter introductions | Headings | Subheadings |
| Margin notes | Study questions | Chapter summary |
| Key terms highlighted | Graphs | Charts |
| Pictures | Signal words | Lists of key facts |

1 ——————— 2 ——————— 3 ——————— 4 ——————— 5

No friendly text features          Some friendly text features          Many friendly text features

Friendliness rating _____

**L  =  Language: How difficult is the language in my reading assignment?**

Directions: Skim the chapter quickly to determine the number of new terms. Read
three random paragraphs to get a feel for the vocabulary level and number of long,
complicated sentences.

1 ——————— 2 ——————— 3 ——————— 4 ——————— 5

Many new words;                     Some new words;                     No new words;
complicated sentences          somewhat complicated sentences          clear sentences

Language rating _____

**I  =  Interest: How interesting is my reading assignment?**

Directions: Read the title, introduction, headings/subheadings, and summary. Examine the
pictures and graphics included.

1 ——————— 2 ——————— 3 ——————— 4 ——————— 5

Boring                     Somewhat interesting                     Very interesting

Interest rating _____

**P  =  Prior knowledge: What do I already know about the material covered in my reading assignment?**

Directions: Think about the title, introduction, headings/subheadings, and summary.

1 ——————— 2 ——————— 3 ——————— 4 ——————— 5

Mostly new information          Some new information          Mostly familiar information

Prior knowledge rating _____

Overall, this reading assignment appears to be at:

☐ a comfortable reading level for me

☐ a somewhat comfortable reading level for me

☐ an uncomfortable reading level for me

*Source:* Schumm, J. S., & Mangrum, C. T. (1991). FLIP: A framework for textbook thinking. *Journal of Reading, 35,* 120–124. Copyright by the International Reading Association.

# Tips for Teachers

## 15.3    Guidelines for Adapting Content-Area Textbooks

*Substitute the textbook* for students who have severe word-recognition problems:
- Audiotape textbook content.
- Read textbook aloud to students.
- Pair students to master textbook content.
- Use direct experiences, films, videotapes, recorders, and computer programs as substitutes for textbook reading.
- Work with students individually or in small groups to master textbook material.

*Simplify the textbook* for students whose reading level is far below that of the textbook used in class:
- Construct abridged versions of the textbook content or use the publisher's abridged version.
- Provide students with chapter outlines or summaries.
- Use a multilevel, multimaterial approach.

*Highlight key concepts* for students who have difficulty comprehending textbook material:
- Preview reading assignments with students to orient them to the topic and provide guidelines for budgeting reading and study time.
- Provide students with a purpose for reading.
- Provide an overview of an assignment before reading.
- Structure opportunities for students to activate prior knowledge before starting a reading assignment.
- Introduce key vocabulary before assigning reading.

- Develop a study guide to direct learning.
- Summarize or reduce textbook information to guide classroom discussions and independent reading.
- Color-code or highlight textbooks.
- Reduce length of assignments.
- Slow down the pace of reading assignments.
- Provide assistance in answering text-based questions.
- Demonstrate or model effective reading strategies.
- Place students in cooperative learning groups to master textbook content.
- Teach comprehension-monitoring techniques to improve ongoing understanding of text material.
- Teach students to use graphic aids to understand textbook information.

*Increase idea retention* for students who have difficulty with long-term memory:
- Structure postreading activities to increase retention of content.
- Teach reading strategies to improve retention.
- Teach students to record key concepts and terms for study purposes.
- Teach memory strategies to improve retention of text material.

*Source:* Schumm, J. S., & Strickler, K. (1991). Guidelines for adapting content area textbooks: Keeping teachers and students content. *Intervention in School and Clinic, 27*(2), 79–84. Copyright © 1991 by PRO-ED, Inc. Reprinted by permission.

**Study Guides**    **Study guides** are tools that teachers can use to lead students through a reading assignment. A typical study guide is a series of questions or activities that students complete while they read a selection. As Wood, Lapp, and Flood (1992, p. 1) put it, "Study guides are designed to accompany reading, not follow it." Study guides help to direct students to the key points to be learned. They also provide structure for students to reflect about what they are reading and to engage in higher-order thinking. In short, study guides can help tutor a student through a chapter.

Commercially prepared study guides can be purchased as supplements to some textbooks. For example, with a chemistry text, you may be able to purchase a blackline master book or individual workbooks for students that include study guides for each chapter. The advantage of commercially prepared study guides is that they are already done and so are real time savers. The disadvantage is that the publisher does not know your style of teaching, your emphasis, or your school district's requirements. Moreover, the publisher

does not know your students. Many teachers elect to construct their own study guides.

Study guides are appealing to all students but particularly to students with learning and behavior problems (Hudson et al., 1994). The guides help students to stay focused on what they need to learn. Students can use study guides independently or in conjunction with cooperative learning activities.

Many types of study guides exist. Some are designed to help students activate prior knowledge, others to help students understand literal or inferential information in the textbook, others to foster peer interaction and discussion, and still others to help students recognize meaning patterns in text (e.g., cause and effect, comparison and contrast). Following are some general suggestions for developing study guides (Wood, Lapp, & Flood, 1992):

- *Decide whether a guide is needed.* Is textbook information particularly dense? Are there few considerate features? Will students with special needs need support and guidance to get through the chapter and to grasp the most important ideas?

● *Analyze the chapter.* Can some parts be omitted? Are some parts easier to understand than others? What skills will your students need to read and understand this material?

● *Decide how you want to structure your study guide.* Create one that includes the suggested components.

All study guides should also include the following components (Hudson et al., 1994):

● Specific information about the reading assignment (page numbers, title)
● Learning objectives of the assignment
● Purpose statement for the assignment
● Introduction of key terms or vocabulary
● Activities for students to complete
● Questions for students to answer as they read

**Text Highlighting**    Students with comprehension problems have difficulty sifting out important information. Underlining or highlighting key points in the textbooks can help students attend to the most salient information (Wood & Wooley, 1986). As you read the textbook, highlight the information you think is most important. Then student or adult volunteers can use your book as a guide to highlight the same information in books for students with reading and learning disabilities. Keep in mind that this is an intermediate step. Students should also be taught how to highlight and identify key information on their own.

**Using Alternative Reading Materials**    After you and your students have taken a careful look at your textbook, you might realize that you will need to go

beyond the textbook to provide your students with alternative reading material. Here's how Steve Beaumont, a fifth-grade teacher, selects reading material for his science and social studies classes:

> My textbook is actually very good, and I use it regularly, but I find that there are such marvelous reading materials out there that I feel a strong responsibility to expose my students to materials beyond the textbook. My three students who are nonreaders need to have exposure to text, and they simply can't read the textbook. I have some other students who are ready for more challenging material. So I use a lot of informational trade books. I find that the quality of writing and the illustrations of these books are fabulous. My local public library lets teachers check out 25 books at a time. When I start a new unit, on astronomy, for example, I load up with books from the library. I make certain that books represent a range of reading levels. I find picture books and books written in easy text for students who have trouble reading.
>
> I have also started using novels and biographies in teaching science and social studies. Students often get tired of the informational style of writing in the textbook. Novels and biographies make science, history, and geography come alive.
>
> Finally, I collect articles from the newspaper and magazines related to whatever I'm teaching in science and social studies. My students collect articles as well! These articles usually have catchy titles, summarize information clearly, and are written in an engaging style. The pictures in magazines are also appealing. I've found that articles are a good way to "hook" my reluctant readers.

Like Steve, more and more content-area teachers are using trade books (both fiction and nonfic-

# TechTalk

## Using the Internet in Content-Area Instruction

Thanks to the advent of the computer age, a world of information is available to you and your students. In their book *Teaching with the Internet: Lessons from the Classroom,* Donald J. Leu and Deborah Diadiun Leu (2000) explore the realm of possibilities that the computer can offer the classroom teacher. The book provides excellent suggestions for using the Internet for instructional purposes and gives specific websites for teachers and students. In addition to their book, Leu and Leu maintain a website to update websites mentioned in their book (www.sp.uconn.edu/~djleu/

third.html). Leu and Leu list seven general ways in which the Internet can be used to enhance instruction (2000, pp. 13–16):

1. Send an e mail message to anyone in the world.
2. Discover great lesson plans and teaching ideas.
3. Acquire content-area information.
4. Communicate with others who have a similar interest.
5. Acquire new software.
6. Conduct a video conference.
7. Publish a page on the World Wide Web for your school and your class.

tion) and other reading materials (e.g., magazines and journals) to supplement content-area textbooks. It's no secret that some textbooks are dry and uninteresting. Trade books and other alternative reading sources can be used to spark interest and to help students develop lifelong reading habits.

Yopp and Yopp (2000) argue that using informational trade books should not be limited to the intermediate grades and above. The rich array of informational books for primary students and beyond is simply too good to be missed. Yopp and Yopp point out that both informational books and narrative text are important for young children so that they are not shocked by the format of expository text when they hit the upper grades.

Informational picture books (i.e., books that can be understood with only minimal text) and high-interest, low-vocabulary-level books have been used successfully with older students who are English language learners (Hadaway & Mundy, 2000), struggling or reluctant readers (Cassady, 2000), and teen parents with challenges in learning to read (Johnson et al., 2000) and in cross-age tutoring programs (Ellis & Preston, 1984). Picture books can also be used as prompts for student writing; for example, students can create captions for pictures in their own words.

In addition to informational books, historical fiction, biographies, and autobiographies can be included as part of your planning in the content areas. You can elect to read material aloud to students, have all students read and react to the same book or article, or assign books or articles to small groups or individual students to share in presentations to the class as a whole. Regardless of how you choose to integrate trade books in content-area instruction, try to select (or help your students select) books that are engaging and that will grab their interest, and don't forget to share your own enthusiasm for reading and learning beyond the textbook.

**Audiotaping Text Content**  Students who have low reading skills or vision impairments can listen to chapters that have been audiotaped by classmates or volunteers. Recordings for the Blind and Dyslexic (800-221-4792) is a nonprofit organization that records trade books and textbooks for individuals who are blind, have low vision, or have learning disabilities. This organization provides on-loan recorded books at all academic levels.

Audiotaped books are increasingly popular and acceptable to students. Students can listen to the tapes in a listening center in elementary classrooms, resource

What instructional considerations will enhance the effectiveness of audiotaped books?

rooms, or school libraries or at home. Here are some suggestions for audiotaping reading assignments:

- Instead of recording an entire chapter verbatim, read the key sections and paraphrase the less important sections.
- Code the text so that readers or listeners will know whether the person on the tape is reading or paraphrasing.
- Provide a short advanced organizer on the tape to help students get ready to read and listen.
- Insert questions that readers or listeners can stop and think about.
- Remind readers or listeners to stop periodically and think about what they have read.
- Use a natural tone of voice and a comfortable reading rate. Have students experiment with taped texts to see whether they comprehend better with or without the accompanying printed text.

## Effective Content-Area Assignments, Homework, and Tests for All Learners

Students' success or failure in a content-area class is often based on their performance on assignments, homework, and tests. But what about students with learning and behavior problems? Should they have the same assignments and tests as everyone else? What if a student cannot read? What if a student cannot work under timed conditions?

Interestingly, as mentioned previously, teacher surveys, interviews, and classroom observations indicate that teachers of all grade levels (elementary through high school) do not often make individual adaptations in homework, assignments, and tests

making a
# Difference
through **Action Teaching**

## Content-Area Instructional Activities for All Learners

### Right on Time

**Objective:** To provide students with a way to visualize and sequence content-area information

**Grades:** Adapted for all grades

**Materials:** Writing/drawing materials

**Teaching Procedures:** Timelines are not just for social studies anymore! As Donahue and Baumgartner (1997) point out, timelines can be used in math (e.g., sequence of events in word problems), science (e.g., seasons of the year), reading (e.g., biographies or story plots), and art (e.g., timeline of classic art) and as a study skills tool (e.g., assignments for the month and activities needed to complete each assignment).

Timelines can be more than simple listings of facts on a horizontal black line. They can be illustrated or can include photographs as well.

Often, timelines are reserved for intermediate grades and above. However, Donahue and Baumgartner (1997) used timelines with students with learning disabilities as early as age 7. They used timelines as a vehicle for a home/school collaborative activity. This activity required students to work with their parents to create a personal timeline. The authors found this to be a valuable activity in triggering memory of past events and in building self-esteem.

*Source:* Donahue, M. L., & Baumgartner, D. (1997). Having the timeline of my life! *Teaching Exceptional Children, 29,* 38–41.

### Conversational Discussion Groups

**Objective:** To help students become comfortable in classroom discussions

**Grades:** Intermediate and above

**Teaching Procedures:** The idea behind conversational discussion groups is that discourse about reading assignments and lectures should be more like conversations—the type of conversation two friends might have about a book or movie (O'Flahavan, 1989). Discussion groups can be held after reading a book or other selection, listening to a lecture, hearing a guest speaker, or viewing a video in class. There

are three steps to implementing conversational discussion groups:

1. *Introduce/review rules.* Before dividing students into conversation groups, either introduce or review rules. You'll need to determine rules in advance or perhaps have the group generate rules related to etiquette for speaking in a group, participation, staying on task, and behavior.
2. *Lines of thought.* During the discussion time, the teacher presents students with three questions—one at a time. When students finish with one question, the teacher goes to the group to hear and respond to their answer and then gives a second question. Questions are related to background knowledge, summarizing the story or lecture, and making personal reactions or reflections.
3. *Debriefing.* Students then spend some time to reflect on and evaluate their experiences in the conversational discussion group. The reflection is guided by three questions: (a) How did we go about getting our answers today? (b) How did we do? (c) What can we do to improve next time?

Depending on the group of students, they may need more or less teacher direction and modeling in how to discuss what they have read or heard. The real goal of conversational discussion groups is to get beyond a formalized structure and to encourage students to have productive, personally meaningful discussions with their peers.

### Jigsaw Puzzle Method

**Objective:** To help students work cooperatively to learn content-area material (Aronson, Stephan, Sikes, Blaney, & Snapp, 1978)

**Grades:** Intermediate and up

**Materials:** Expert sheets

**Teaching Procedures:**

1. Select a unit of material for students to learn that can be broken up into four sections. For example, a social studies chapter on Italy might be broken up into imports and exports, natural resources, famous sights, and native foods.
2. Assign students to four different "expert" groups. The members of each group are responsible for learning the material in their assigned section—they must become experts.

(Schumm & Vaughn, 1991, 1992a; Schumm et al., 1995a). Constructing individual assignments and tests may not be feasible on a day-to-day basis and may not even be necessary. In this section, you'll learn about ways to prepare effective assignments, homework, and tests for all students.

## Making and Adapting Class Assignments and Homework

After conducting a comprehensive review of the literature, Cooper and Nye (1994) concluded that homework assignments for students with disabili-

3. Allow expert groups enough time to complete "expert sheets." Expert sheets are handouts you have prepared for students to record important information that they have learned.

4. Prepare a quiz (two or three questions) that each group member must pass to truly become an "expert." Students who do not pass the test can work with you or with group mates to learn the information. You can decide whether or not students can use their expert sheets to take the quiz.

5. Move the students into their jigsaw groups. A jigsaw group consists of one expert from each of the four different groups.

6. Each expert then teaches the content he or she learned to members of the jigsaw group.

### Library Scavenger Hunts

**Objective:** To help improve research skills

**Grades:** Intermediate and above

**Materials:** Scavenger hunt lists

**Teaching Procedures:**

1. Divide students into groups of three or four students. Assign students to groups so that each group has a mixture of students in respect to research skills.

2. Provide each group with a list of questions to answer by finding information in the library. You might want to include hints or clues about where the items might be located. Make certain that a variety of research resources are used.

3. Discuss rules for the scavenger hunt—for example, talk only to your team members and only about the hunt, use soft voices, and answer the question and document your sources.

4. Give a time limit for the hunt.

5. At the end of the time limit, collect all documentation from the groups.

6. At the next opportunity, discuss what information was found and how it was found.

Eventually, individuals or groups of students in your class might want to write scavenger hunt lists for their classmates.

### Send a Problem

**Objective:** To help students learn content-area material

**Grades:** Intermediate and above

**Materials:** Index cards

**Teaching Procedures:**

1. Students work individually to generate questions about a reading assignment or lecture.

2. Questions are recorded on the front of an index card; answers are recorded on the back of the same card.

3. Students are assigned to work in groups of three or four students to review the questions and answers for accuracy of the answers. Answers are revised if needed.

4. The stack of question cards is then passed to another group of students. Members of the group take turns asking and answering questions.

5. The process of passing continues until time is up or until all groups have had the opportunity to review the cards of every group.

### K–W–E–L

**Objective:** To help students develop an awareness of school district standards and learner outcomes

**Grading:** Intermediate and above

**Teaching Procedures:** K–W–L (Ogle, 1986) is a popular teaching method used to help students activate prior knowledge before reading and to reflect about what they learned after reading (see Chapter 12 for a description of K–W–L). What is missing from K–W–L is a clear description of school district standards and learner outcomes that are used in many schools today. In other words, students may be missing out on finding out what they are *expected* to learn. Laura Alatorre-Parks devised K–W–E–L to teach her high-school English students what they were expected by the school district to learn by weaving those expectations into the K–W–E–L strategy.

K–W–E–L is essentially the same as K–W–L. The critical difference is that the extended version includes an in-depth discussion about district objectives or standards after the brainstorming (what I *know* and what I *want* to learn). Alatorre-Parks also engages her students in planning how to merge their interests and wants with what they are expected to learn. She reports that this simple extension helps students to become more aware of what is expected of them and to develop a sense of ownership about their learning.

*Source:* Alatorre-Parks, L. (2001). Aligning student interests with district mandates. *Journal of Adolescent and Adult Literacy, 44,* 330–332.

ties should be brief, focused on reinforcement rather than new material, monitored carefully, and supported through parental involvement.

The most important aspect of making assignments is to give complete information. You need to let students know why the assignment is important,

when it is due, what support they will have for completing the task, and the steps necessary for getting the job done. Having complete information helps to motivate students. The procedure in Tips for Teachers 15.4 can help you provide students with a complete set of directions.

## Tips for Teachers

### 15.4 A Strategy for Giving Assignments

1. Explain the purpose of the assignment. Stress what you expect students to learn and why learning the skill or concept is important. Connect the skill or concept to real-life applications.

2. Explain in detail the procedures for completing the assignment. Ask one or two students to summarize the procedures, to check for understanding.

3. Get students started by modeling one or two problems or by providing an example.

4. Describe the equipment and materials needed to complete the assignment.

5. Anticipate trouble spots, and ask students how they might tackle difficult parts in the assignment.

6. Explain when the assignment is due.

7. Explain how the assignment will be graded and how it will affect students' grades.

8. Describe appropriate ways to get help or support in completing the assignment.

9. For an in-class assignment, explain your expectations for student behavior while they complete the assignment and what students who finish early should do.

10. Address student questions.

---

In a survey of students in grades 6 through 8 (48 with learning disabilities and 48 without), the students with learning disabilities had greater difficulty completing homework assignments because of problems with attention, motivation, and study skills (Gajria & Salend, 1995).

Class assignments and homework can be adapted for special learners so that they can experience success without undue attention being brought to their learning difficulties. The key to success is to make assignments appropriate in content, length, time required to complete, and skill level needed to accomplish the task. It is also important that students know how and where to get help when they get stuck.

## Progress Monitoring

Tests are a way to find out what students have learned. The best way to discover what students have learned is to construct student-friendly tests, adapt test administration and scoring as necessary, consider alternatives to testing (such as assessment portfolios), and teach test-taking skills.

Student-friendly tests are considerate to the test taker in content and format. The content has been covered in class or assigned readings, and students have been told explicitly that they are responsible for learning it. The format is clear and easy to understand.

To construct student-friendly tests, you must first decide what skills and concepts to include. The lesson and unit planning pyramids can be particularly helpful here; to complete them, you decide which concepts are most important and prioritize

those concepts for instructional purposes. You know what you want all, most, and some of your students to know, and you have told them your expectations. You can cover those skills and concepts on the test.

In a test format, directions should be clear and unambiguous, and items should be legible and properly spaced. Students should have sufficient room to place their answers and specific guidelines if answers are to be written on a separate sheet (Salend, 1994). Attention to format is important for all students but particularly for those who have difficulty reading and taking tests and who are very anxious about test taking.

Even with student-friendly tests, students with learning problems may have difficulty reading tests, working within time constraints, or resisting distractions during a test. Other special learners may have physical needs (they may tire easily, for example) that inhibit performance on a test. Tips for Teachers 15.5 suggests adaptations in test administration and scoring. As you decide which, if any, adaptations to use, consider the material to be covered by the test, the test's task requirements (e.g., reading, taking dictation), and the particular needs of special learners. Consult with the special education teacher and other specialists in your school to get advice about the most appropriate adaptations for individual students.

In one study of middle- and high-school content-area teachers, test scores, including those for students with disabilities, represented about half of the students' grade (45.9 percent). The percentage was lower (37.3 percent) for English classes, higher for mathematics (53.6 percent) (Putnam, 1992).

## Tips for Teachers

### 15.5   Testing Adaptations

- Teach students test-taking skills.
- Give frequent quizzes rather than only exams.
- Give take-home tests.
- Test on less content than the rest of the class.
- Change types of questions (e.g., essay to multiple choice).
- Use tests with enlarged print.
- Use black-and-white copies (versus dittos).
- Highlight key words in questions.
- Provide extra space on tests for answering.
- Simplify wording of test questions.
- Allow students to answer fewer questions.
- Give extra help preparing for tests.
- Give the actual test as a study guide.
- Give practice questions as a study guide.
- Give open-book and note tests.

- Give tests to small groups.
- Give extended time to finish tests.
- Read test questions to students.
- Allow use of learning aids during tests (e.g., calculators).
- Give individual help with directions during tests.
- Allow oral instead of written answers (e.g., tape recorders).
- Allow answers in outline format.
- Allow word processors.
- Give feedback to individual students during test.

*Source:* Jayanthi, M., Epstein, M. H., Polloway, E. A., & Bursuck, W. D. (1996). Testing adaptions: A national survey of the testing practices of general education teachers. *Journal of Special Education, 30,* 99–155.

In addition to or instead of tests, consider using portfolios as an assessment tool. **Assessment portfolios** are collections of work samples that document a student's progress in a content area. You can use portfolios to provide tangible evidence of student performance over a period of time. Portfolios can include writing samples of all stages of the writing process in all genres. Suggestions for developing assessment portfolios are included in Tips for Teachers 15.6.

## Tips for Teachers

### 15.6   Development of Assessment Portfolios

- Develop a portfolio plan consistent with your purposes for the assignment.
- Clarify what work will go into portfolios.
- Start with only a couple of different kinds of entries and expand gradually.
- Compare notes with other teachers as you experiment with portfolios.
- Have as a long-term goal the inclusion of a variety of assessments that address content, process, and attitude goals across the curriculum.
- Make portfolios accessible in the classroom. Students and teachers should be able to add to the collection quickly and easily.
- Develop summary sheets or graphs that help to describe a body of information (e.g., "I can do" lists, lists of books read, or pieces of writing completed). Let students record these data when possible.

- Work with the student to choose a few representative samples that demonstrate the student's progress.
- Review portfolios with students periodically (at least four times during the school year). The review should be a time to celebrate progress and to set future goals.
- Encourage students to review portfolios with a classmate before reviewing with the teacher. Students should help make decisions about what to keep.
- In preparation for a parent conference, have students develop a table of contents for the portfolio.

*Source:* Radencich, M. C., Beers, P. C., & Schumm, J. S. (1993). *A handbook for the K–12 reading resource specialist* (pp. 119–120). Boston: Allyn & Bacon.

Examples of items you can include in a portfolio are as follows (Radencich et al., 1993):

| | |
|---|---|
| Student interviews | Interest and attitude |
| Self-assessments | inventories |
| Audiotapes | Photographs |
| Videotapes | Copies of passages |
| Diagnostic tests | read fluently |
| Achievement tests | Contributions |
| Teacher-made tests | from parents |
| Pages from journals | Report cards |
| Awards | List of accomplishments |
| Personal reading and | Observation |
| writing records | checklists |
| Peer assessments | |

## Planning Interdisciplinary Thematic Units

As you may recall, increasing numbers of educators are planning interdisciplinary thematic units as a way to provide more holistic instruction (see Figure 15.6). Meinbach, Rothlein, and Fredericks (1995, p. 5) describe a **thematic interdisciplinary approach,** as follows:

> A thematic approach to learning combines structured, sequential, and well-organized strategies, activities, children's literature, and materials used to expand a particular concept. A thematic unit is multidisciplinary and multidimensional; it knows no boundaries. It is responsive to the interests, abilities, and needs of children and is respectful of their developing aptitudes and attitudes. In essence, a thematic approach to learning offers students a realistic arena in which they can pursue learning using a host of contexts and a panorama of literature.

Thematic units are increasingly popular in elementary and secondary settings because they help students explore topics in depth, see connections between subject areas, and see the connection between what they learn in school and real life. They are particularly appropriate for diverse classrooms because the emphasis is on providing a variety of learning activities. Thematic units also help to consolidate areas in a crowded curriculum and make the teaching of curriculum more efficient (Shanahan et al., 1995).

A thematic unit can last for a few days or for weeks. The unit can involve a single classroom teacher, multiple grades, or several teachers in a

grade. In any case, interdisciplinary units take careful planning and organization to avoid confusion and chaos. Meinbach, Rothlein, and Fredericks (1995) identified the following five steps in planning a thematic unit:

1. *Selecting the theme:* A theme can be derived from curricular objectives, current events and issues, special events or holidays, and student interests.
2. *Organizing the theme:* A theme web can be used to show what content areas will be represented and what objectives and activities will be associated with each content area.
3. *Gathering materials and resources:* Thematic units extend beyond a single textbook. Both print and nonprint resources are used to make the unit come alive. Materials with a variety of reading levels should be included as well as multisensory resources. Students and parents can become actively involved in gathering materials.
4. *Designing activities and projects:* To avoid making a thematic unit no more than a set of isolated activities around a single theme, activities must be selected that are purposeful and lead to an integrated experience.
5. *Implementing the unit:* Decide how long the unit will last and how it will be merged with your ongoing curriculum plans.

Figure 15.6 shows the sample thematic unit plan in these five steps.

When teachers are working as a team to plan an interdisciplinary unit, trying to come up with a theme can be a challenge. Fogarty (1994) suggested the following strategy, organized around the acronym **THEMES,** for deciding on a theme:

- *Think of themes.* Brainstorm 20–50 themes.
- *Hone the list.* Divide the list into three groups: topics, concepts, and problems. Have each group member select one "champion theme" from each group. Agree on a final three.
- *Extrapolate criteria.* Think of why the final three were chosen, and record those reasons for future thinking. Decide on the final theme.
- *Manipulate the theme.* Generate as many questions as you can about the theme to give it further depth and direction.
- *Expand into activities.* List activities that can be planned to teach skills and introduce concepts.
- *Select valued outcomes.* Decide what outcomes are desired. How will these outcomes be observed and recorded?

FIGURE 15.6

**Interdisciplinary Thematic Unit Planning Form**

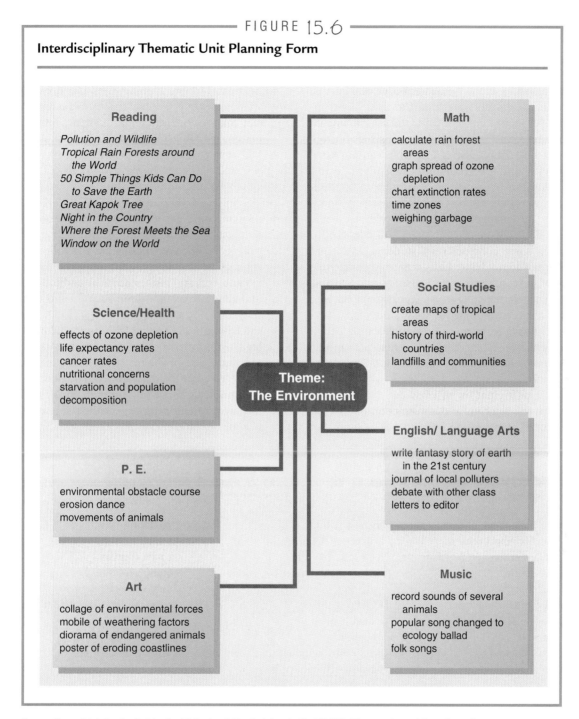

**Reading**

*Pollution and Wildlife*
*Tropical Rain Forests around*
*   the World*
*50 Simple Things Kids Can Do*
*   to Save the Earth*
*Great Kapok Tree*
*Night in the Country*
*Where the Forest Meets the Sea*
*Window on the World*

**Science/Health**

effects of ozone depletion
life expectancy rates
cancer rates
nutritional concerns
starvation and population
decomposition

**P. E.**

environmental obstacle course
erosion dance
movements of animals

**Art**

collage of environmental forces
mobile of weathering factors
diorama of endangered animals
poster of eroding coastlines

**Theme:
The Environment**

**Math**

calculate rain forest
   areas
graph spread of ozone
   depletion
chart extinction rates
time zones
weighing garbage

**Social Studies**

create maps of tropical
   areas
history of third-world
   countries
landfills and communities

**English/ Language Arts**

write fantasy story of earth
   in the 21st century
journal of local polluters
debate with other class
letters to editor

**Music**

record sounds of several
   animals
popular song changed to
   ecology ballad
folk songs

*Source:* From Meinbach, A. M., Rothlein, L., & Fredericks, A. D. (1995). *The complete guide to thematic units: Creating the integrated curriculum,* p. 15. Norwood, MA: Christopher-Gordon. Used with permission of the publisher.

The last step is particularly important. With thematic units, it is easy to get caught up in the activity and forget what student outcomes were desired. This is especially true for students with learning problems. It is important not only to identify valued concepts using the planning pyramid, but also to communicate those outcomes to students and to monitor student progress in meeting those outcomes during the implementation of the unit.

# summary

- Critical issues faced by content-area teachers as they try to promote learning for all students include balancing content and process, balancing text-driven and activities-driven instruction, coordinating content-area teaching and learning strategies, and integrating the curriculum.
- Students can have difficulty learning in content-area classrooms because not all subjects are uniformly interesting or consistent with students' cultural background and prior knowledge. To learn in some content areas, students need basic skills they do not have. The pacing and conceptual load of some subjects is cumbersome, and learning tasks such as textbook reading, assignments, and tests are overwhelming for some students.
- Content-area teachers can use prelearning activities such as purpose setting and semantic mapping to improve students' comprehension and depth of learning.
- Student participation in class can be improved through the planning and implementation of well-structured questions and vibrant discussions.

- You can become familiar with the strengths and weaknesses of your textbook by evaluating its subject matter content, social content, instructional design, readability level, and friendliness level.
- One way to learn how your students interact and respond to the textbook is to use the FLIP Chart.
- Textbook adaptations include study guides, highlighting, and alternative reading materials.
- As you construct class assignments, homework, and tests for students with learning and behavior problems, be sure to consider the following factors: clarity of assignments, appropriateness of assignments and tests, student-friendliness of tests, and adaptations for administration and scoring of tests.
- Interdisciplinary thematic units can be used to integrate the curriculum. For students with learning and behavior problems, however, care must be taken to identify desired student outcomes, to communicate those outcomes to students, and to monitor student progress during the implementation of the unit.

# key terms and concepts

assessment portfolios
communication approach
concept diagram
conceptual density
considerate text
content and process dilemma
demonstration plus model strategy
discussion web
explication
FLIP chart strategy

friendly text
instructional clarity
instructional design
instructional devices
interdisciplinary thematic units
LEAP
metadiscourse
organization
prelearning activities
purpose-setting activities

readability level
semantic map
social content
study guides
subject matter content
thematic interdisciplinary approach
THEMES
think alouds
vibrant discussions

# think and apply

1. Now that you have read Chapter 15, think about how Nancy Brice planned and made adaptations for special learners in her classroom. What practices did she use? What additional strategies would you use in your own class?
2. Plan a lesson using a prelearning activity. What would you plan as a follow up?
3. Plan and deliver a demonstration using the suggestions provided in this chapter.
4. Lead a class discussion or questioning session using one of the formats provided in this chapter.

5. Familiarize yourself with a content-area textbook. Include in your analysis an evaluation of subject matter content, social content, instructional design, readability level, and considerateness level. What are the strengths of the textbook? How friendly is the textbook? What adaptations would you need to plan for students who are nonreaders or low-level readers?
6. Construct a student-friendly test for a lesson or unit. What adaptations would you need to plan for students with learning or behavior problems?

# read more about it

1. Alvermann, D. E., Dillon, D. R., & O'Brien, D. G. (1987). *Using discussion to promote reading comprehension.* Newark, DE: International Reading Association.

   *This monograph provides examples of ways to implement vibrant discussions in your classroom.*

2. Anders, P. L., & Guzzetti. B. J. (1996). *Literacy instruction in the content areas.* Fort Worth, TX: Harcourt Brace.

   *An excellent resource for helping teachers plan and implement reading and writing instruction in the content areas.*

3. Farr, R., & Tone, B. (1998). *Portfolio performance and assessment* (2nd ed.). Fort Worth, TX: Harcourt Brace.

   *This extensive, user-friendly guide to portfolio assessment includes detailed explanations of portfolio conferences and scoring systems.*

4. Meinbach, A. M., Rothlein, L., & Fredericks, A. D. (2000). *The complete guide to thematic units: Creating the integrated curriculum* (2nd ed.). Norwood, MA: Christopher-Gordon.

   *A brief but comprehensive guide to planning and implementing thematic units.*

5. Moore, D. W., Readence, J. E., & Rickelman R. J. (2000). *Prereading activities for content area reading and learning* (3rd ed.). Newark, DE: International Reading Association.

   *This monograph provides an excellent collection of prereading and prelistening activities.*

6. Readence, J. E., Bean, T. W., & Baldwin R. S. (2000). *Content area literacy: An integrated approach* (7th ed.). Dubuque, IA: Kendall/Hunt.

   *This comprehensive book includes excellent suggestions for determining the appropriateness of textbooks for your students, as well as instructional activities for learning technical vocabulary and for helping students comprehend content area textbooks. Contains a CD-ROM supplement with suggestions for technology integration.*

7. Wood, K. D., Lapp, D., & Flood, J. (1992). *Guiding readers through text: A review of study guides.* Newark, DE: International Reading Association.

   *Explains 14 types of study guides, with examples and suggested applications.*

8. Lenz, K., & Schumaker, J. (1999). *Adapting language arts, social studies, and science materials for the inclusive classroom.* Reston, VA: Council for Exceptional Children.

   *This monograph provides an outstanding collection of suggestions for adapting materials, mediating existing materials, and selecting alternative materials. The target group for the monograph is for teachers in grades 6 through 8, but high-school teachers will find this to be a valuable resources as well.*

9. McCarnery, S. B., Wunderlich, K. C., & Bauer, A. M. (1993). *The pre-referral intervention manual* (2nd ed.). Columbia, MO: Hawthorne.

   *Guessing about what to do during the prereferral period? This tool can help. This manual provides doable suggestions for most common learning and behavior problems the general education teacher is likely to encounter.*

10. Moore, D. W., Alverman, D. E., & Hinchman, K. A. (Eds.). (2000). *Struggling adolescent readers: A collection of teaching strategies.* Newark, DE: International Reading Association.

    *This edited book contains chapters written by experts in reading instruction for secondary students. Chapters include excellent strategies for content-area reading, writing, and inquiry as well as suggestions for using literature for content area instruction.*

11. Beck, I. L., McKeown, M. G., Hamilton, R. L., & Kucan, L. (1997). *Questioning the author.* Newark, DE: International Reading Association.

    *This monograph provides a thorough description of the questioning the author (QtA) strategy for improving the quality of classroom discussion about text. The authors include many examples of queries and dialogues of classroom discussions to help the reader construct a vision of how to use QtA.*

# suggested websites

**www.enc.org**
This website provides a wealth of resources from the Eisenhower National Clearinghouse for Mathematics and Science Education.

**www.sciencegems.com**
This website is entitled Frank Potter's Science Gems and provides links to thousands of science resources.

**www.exploratorium.edu**
This is the website of the Museum of Science, Art, and Human Perception, a great site to get students excited about science.

**http://www.nasa.gov**
NASA's website can open the universe to your students and to you.

**www.nytimes.com/learning**
This website provides information on current events, daily lesson plans, and suggestions for thematic units.

**www.nationalgeographic.com**
This website can open the world for your students and provide you with a wealth of resources for geography lessons.

**www.loc.gov**
Help your students learn about a national treasure: The Library of Congress. This website includes a site for children, exhibitions, and resources regarding American history and beyond.

**www.ncss.org/home2.html**
This website is home of the National Council for the Social Studies.

**www.si.edu**
Want to take a virtual tour of another national treasure? Go to the Smithsonian Institution website.

# Making a Difference through Action Learning: Teaching Study Skills, Learning Strategies, and Self-Advocacy

**appendix**

## introduction

As a middle- or high-school teacher, one of your major challenges is to balance teaching content (e.g., American government, chemistry, earth science, English, history) with teaching learning strategies and study skills. Teachers are pressured to complete the textbook or cover a set of objectives specified in state or district curricula, but many students with disabilities and those who are at risk need to be taught how to study and learn more effectively. This appendix describes active learning activities you can integrate into content-area classes. The activities are grouped in the following action learning areas:

- Effective time management
- Organizing your studying
- Setting goals, self-monitoring, and self-advocacy
- Listening and taking notes
- Remembering information
- Studying and taking tests

When you teach learning strategies and study skills, keep in mind several general principles or stages of teaching. By using these principles (Deshler et al., 1996), you help to ensure that students become proficient in using the skill or strategy and that they generalize its use to different situations.

- *Develop the rationale for learning the study skill or learning strategy.* With students, establish why learning to use the skill or strategy is worthwhile.

- *Analyze the skill or strategy, and, if possible, determine the steps students can use to develop the skill or strategy.*
- *Develop a memory device, such as an acronym, to help students remember the steps in the skill or strategy.* For editing written work, for example, use COPS—for Capitalization, Organization, Punctuation, and Spelling (Schumaker et al., 1985).
- *Demonstrate or model each step in the skill or strategy. Use "thinking aloud" to model what you are thinking.* It is important to demonstrate not only what you are doing but also what you are thinking. Cue students with a phrase such as "When I do (describe action), what I am thinking is (describe thinking)."
- *Help students memorize the steps in the skill or strategy.* Use of a memory device can be quite helpful in memorizing the strategy.
- *Provide ample opportunity for students to practice the skills or strategy.* Start by applying the skill or strategy to easy tasks, then to more difficult ones.
- *Cue students to use the skill or strategy.*
- *Throughout the teaching process, discuss when, where, and how the skill or strategy can be used in different situations, such as different classes, tasks, and settings (school and job).* This principle is important for students to generalize the skill or strategy.

461

- *Have students monitor their success in using the skill or strategy and the way it affects their learning.*

The approach you use to teach study skills and learning strategies can vary. You can present the skill or strategy and its steps, or you can have students develop their own steps in cooperative groups, through class discussion, or independently. Whatever your approach, an important key to success is to use the preceding principles.

 ## Resources

For more information about teaching study skills, learning strategies, and self-advocacy, see the following books:

- Bos, C. S., & Vaughn, S. (2001). *Teaching students with learning and behavior problems* (5th ed.). Boston: Allyn & Bacon.
- Bragstad, B. J., & Stumpf, S. M. (1987). *A guidebook for teaching study skills and motivation* (2nd ed.). Boston: Allyn & Bacon.
- Bulgren, J., & Scanlon, D. (1997). Instructional routines and learning strategies that promote understanding of content area concepts. *Journal of Adolescent & Adult Literacy, 41,* 292–302.
- Deshler, D. D., Ellis, E. S., & Lenz, B. K. (1996). *Teaching adolescents with learning disabilities* (2nd ed.). Denver: Love.
- Ellis, D. B. (1985). *Becoming a master student* (5th ed.). Rapid City, SD: College Survival, Inc.
- Lenz, B. K., Ellis, E. S., & Scanlon, D. (1996). *Teaching learning strategies to adolescents and adults with learning disabilities.* Austin, TX: PRO-ED.
- Strichart, S. S., Mangrum, C. T., II, & Iannuzzi, I. (2002). *Teaching study skills and strategies to students with LD, ADD, or special needs* (3rd ed.). Boston: Allyn & Bacon.

 ## Action Learning Area: Effective Time Management

*Time management* is the organization and monitoring of time so that tasks can be scheduled and completed in an efficient and timely manner. Effective time management includes the following steps:

- Identifying the tasks to be completed
- Estimating the time needed to complete the tasks
- Prioritizing tasks and estimating time
- Scheduling the time
- Working toward meeting deadlines
- Monitoring progress and adjusting deadlines or tasks

- Reviewing deadlines after task completion and adjusting schedules and priorities based on past performance

Use the following four activities to teach effective time management.

## Interviewing Others about Time Management

**Objective:** To help students learn the importance of managing their time.

**Grades:** Middle school, high school, and postsecondary classes

**Teaching Procedures:** Have students interview a parent and one other adult they consider a successful manager of time, asking questions such as the following:

- Describe your schedule or what you do for two typical days during the week and one typical weekend day.
- What strategies do you use to schedule your time so that your tasks get completed?
- What strategies do you use to help you remember what you have to do?
- Do you think that managing your time is important? Why or why not?

Have students work in cooperative groups to compile lists of strategies for scheduling and monitoring schedules. Also have them compile a list of reasons for managing time, such as the following (Bragstad & Stumpf, 1982), making sure that they add their own ideas.

### Why Bother with a Schedule?
- Parents will "get off your back" when you have regular study times.
- Writing down what you have to do gives you less to remember.
- When you give yourself a set amount of time to do an assignment, you concentrate more.
- With a schedule, you are less likely to extend your breaks longer than scheduled.
- You feel more satisfied when you are in control of your life and know what you plan to do when.
- Organizing your time helps you come to class prepared.
- Scheduling your time is the smart way to operate if you want to have more time for fun and friends.

**Content Class Integration:** A unit on time management is easily integrated into any class. It can be the first unit of the year in a math class, emphasizing time use and computation of time. It can be integrated into an economics class, emphasizing how time relates to productivity, or into a life skills class.

## Determining How You Spend Your Time

**Objective:** To have students determine how they currently spend their time and how much time it takes to complete usual activities.

**Grades:** Middle school and above

**Teaching Procedures:** Have student groups identify usual activities and estimate the time it takes to complete them. Distribute a schedule form (see Figure A.1) to students, and have them use the form to keep track of their activities for one week. Also have students list each school assignment and note whether they had "too much time" (+), "the right amount of time" (x), or "too little time" (–) to complete it.

At the end of the week, have student groups review their schedules and compare how much time they spent on different activities such as sleeping, eating, studying, attending class, and so on. Also have students compare their estimates with the actual time it took to complete the activities. Usually students underestimate their time by about 50 percent.

## Planning a Schedule

**Objective:** To have students plan their weekly schedules and develop to-do lists.

**Grades:** Middle school and above

**Teaching Procedures:** Have students list due dates for assignments, tests, and other important projects. Help them divide complex tasks or projects into smaller tasks and determine the due dates for each smaller task. Next, have students make a to-do list for each day (refer to Figure A.1) so that they can

FIGURE A.1

### Sample Weekly Schedule and To-Do List

Name: _____      Week of: _____

| Time | Monday | Tuesday | Wednesday | Thursday | Friday | Saturday | Sunday |
|------|--------|---------|-----------|----------|--------|----------|--------|
| 6 – 7 AM | | | | | | | |
| 7 – 8 AM | | | | | | | |
| 8 – 9 AM | | | | | | | |
| 9 – 10 AM | | | | | | | |
| 10 – 11 AM | | | | | | | |
| 11 – 12 | | | | | | | |
| 12 – 1 PM | | | | | | | |
| 1 – 2 PM | | | | | | | |
| 2 – 3 PM | | | | | | | |
| 3 – 4 PM | | | | | | | |
| 4 – 5 PM | | | | | | | |
| 5 – 6 PM | | | | | | | |
| 6 – 7 PM | | | | | | | |
| 7 – 8 PM | | | | | | | |
| 8 – 9 PM | | | | | | | |
| 9 – 10 PM | | | | | | | |

| To-Do List | | | | | | |
|------------|--------|---------|-----------|----------|--------|----------|--------|
| Monday | Tuesday | Wednesday | Thursday | Friday | Saturday | Sunday |
| | | | | | | |

*Source:* Adapted from Bos, C. S., & Vaughn, S. (1988). *Teaching students with learning and behavior problems* (4th ed., p. 308). Boston: Allyn & Bacon.

see how they need to plan their time, particularly their study time.

Have students plan their weekly schedules, using the following guidelines (Bos & Vaughn, 2002):

- Plan regular study times with at least one-hour blocks.
- Use daytime or early evening for studying, if possible.
- When studying for longer than an hour, plan breaks and stick to the time allowed.
- Determine which assignments you are going to work on.
- For each assignment, take a few minutes to review what you have done and learned and to plan what you are going to accomplish.
- Work on your more difficult assignments when you are most alert (usually first).
- Distribute your study time for a test instead of cramming for it.
- Plan time for recreational activities.
- Reward yourself by crossing off items on your to-do list when you complete them.

## Monitoring Your Schedule

**Objective:**   To have students monitor their schedules and task completion and adjust their schedules.

**Grades:**   Middle school and above

**Teaching Procedures:**   Monitoring task completion is the key to successful use of schedules and to-do lists. Following are some suggestions for monitoring:

- Have students spend about five minutes during the class period to update their schedules and cross off tasks they have completed. This can be done at the beginning of class when you are taking roll.
- Meet with students as necessary to review their schedules and their monitoring.
- Have students adjust their schedules as necessary.

## ● Action Learning Area: Organizing Your Studying

In addition to organizing and using a schedule, students need to organize their study environment and notebook and develop positive study habits. The three activities in this section can help students get organized. All the activities can be integrated into a first unit for any content-area class.

## Organizing Your Study Environment

**Objective:**   To have students assess their study environment at home and modify it to promote studying.

**Grades:**   Middle school and above

**Teaching Procedures:**   Let parents know that students will be assessing and thinking about modifying their home study environment to promote studying. After students complete a study environment checklist (see Figure A.2), have them meet in groups to dis-

---

FIGURE A.2

**Study Environment Checklist**

Name _____    Date _____

Evaluate each statement by checking the column that describes the place where you study.

| Statement | Rarely | Generally | Almost Always |
|---|---|---|---|
| 1. I study in a consistent place. | | | |
| 2. The place where I study is quiet. | | | |
| 3. It has good light. | | | |
| 4. There are no visual distractions. | | | |
| 5. There are a comfortable desk/table and a chair. | | | |
| 6. The materials I need are at my desk. | | | |
| 7. The study area is available when I need it. | | | |

*Source:* Adapted from Strichart, S. S., & Mangrum, C. T., II (1993). *Teaching study strategies to students with learning disabilities* (p. 356). Boston: Allyn & Bacon.

cuss the results and their ideas for modifying their study environments.

Meet with each student individually to summarize the results and to write one to three goals for improving the study environment if warranted. Have students report on their progress toward meeting their goals.

## Shaping Up Your Study Habits

**Objective:** To help students assess their study habits and modify them to promote studying.

**Grades:** Middle school and above

**Teaching Procedures:** Let parents know that students will be assessing and thinking about modifying their study habits to promote studying. After students complete a study habits checklist like the one shown in Figure A.3, have them meet in groups to discuss the results and their ideas for changing their study habits to promote studying at home.

Next, meet with each student individually to summarize the results and to write one to three goals for improving study habits. Finally, have students report on their progress toward meeting their goals.

## Organizing Your Notebook

**Objective:** To teach students to organize their notebooks so that materials and information are easy to retrieve and use.

**Grades:** Middle school and above

**Teaching Procedures:** Alert parents that students will be reviewing their notebooks for organization, and send home a list of recommended materials, including the following:

- Three-ring notebook, so that pages can be added easily
- Supply pouch and school supplies such as pens, pencils, erasers, computer disks, calculator, hole punch, package of file cards, ruler

---

FIGURE A.3

### Study Habits Checklist

Name _____  Date _____

Evaluate each statement by checking the column that describes your study habits.

| Statement | Rarely | Generally | Almost Always |
|---|---|---|---|
| 1. I set aside a regular time to study. | | | |
| 2. I do not take calls or allow interruptions during study time. | | | |
| 3. I take short breaks when I get tired but return to work. | | | |
| 4. I take a few minutes at the beginning to organize my study time. | | | |
| 5. I begin with the hardest assignments. | | | |
| 6. I finish one assignment before going on to the next one. | | | |
| 7. I break long projects down into short tasks and work on the tasks over time. | | | |
| 8. I begin studying for a test at least three days before the test. | | | |
| 9. I have someone I can contact when I get stuck. | | | |
| 10. I write down questions I need to ask the teacher. | | | |

*Source:* Adapted from Strichart, S. S., & Mangrum, C. T., II (1993). *Teaching study strategies to students with learning disabilities* (p. 356). Boston: Allyn & Bacon.

- Labeled dividers—one for each class, plus others labeled "Schedules and Calendar," "Reference Information," "Notebook Dictionary," "Personal Word List," "Notebook Paper," "Graph Paper," "Computer Paper"

Have students look at their notebooks to determine how they have organized information for each class, their assignments, schedules, and materials. Work with students to organize their notebooks, using the following suggestions:

- Include a semester calendar, weekly schedules, and to-do lists in the section on schedules and calendar.
- After the divider for each class, organize materials for that class (starting with class outline or syllabus).
- Date notes and place them in order.
- In the personal word list, alphabetically list frequently misspelled words.

## Action Learning Area: Goal Setting, Self-Monitoring, and Self-Advocacy

One way to get students actively involved in learning is to plan activities in which students learn to set goals, monitor their accomplishments, and advocate for what they want and need. The two activities in this section set the stage for active learning.

## Goal Setting and Self-Monitoring

**Objective:**   To have students learn to set, plan, and monitor their goals.

**Grades:**   Middle school and above

**Teaching Procedures:**   Whether you are working on finishing a term paper or saving enough money to buy a car, it is important to set goals, make a plan to accomplish the goals, and monitor your progress. Van Reusen and Bos (1992) developed a strategy that students can use for setting goals and monitoring progress. The strategy uses the acronym *MARKER* (it gives students a *mark* to work toward and is a *marker* of their progress) and includes the following steps:

Make a list of goals, set the order, and set the dates.

Arrange a plan for each goal, and predict your success.

Run your plan for each goal, and adjust if necessary.

Keep records of your progress.

Evaluate your progress toward each goal.

Reward yourself when you reach a goal, and set a new goal.

For each goal, students use a Goal-Planning Sheet (see Figure A.4) to answer the following questions:

- Can I describe my goal?
- What is the reason or purpose for the goal?
- Where am I going to work on and complete this goal?
- How much time do I have to complete the goal?
- What materials do I need to complete the goal?
- Can I divide the goal into steps or parts? If so, in what order should I complete each step or part?
- How am I going to keep records of my progress?
- How will I reward myself for reaching my goal?

Students usually work on one to three goals at a time, keeping progress data on each goal.

**Content Class Integration:**   This strategy can be taught as a unit in almost any class but is particularly appropriate for social studies and life skills classes. When Van Reusen and Bos (1992) used this strategy with middle- and high-school students with learning disabilities and behavior disorders, they found that students accomplished more goals and gained a more informed perspective on their educational and personal goals.

**Resources:**   For more information, see:

- Lenz, B. K., Ehren, B. J., & Smiley, L. (1991). A goal attainment approach to improve completion of project-type assignments by adolescents with learning disabilities. *Learning Disabilities Research and Practice, 6,* 166–176.
- Van Reusen, A. K., & Bos, C. S. (1992). *Use of the goal-regulation strategy to improve the goal attainment of students with learning disabilities* (Final Report). Tucson, AZ: University of Arizona.

## Self-Advocacy

**Objective:**   To help students inventory their learning strengths, weaknesses they need to improve, goals, and interests, and then advocate for themselves with key adults (e.g., parents, teachers, counselors).

**Grades:**   Middle school and above

─────────── FIGURE A.4 ───────────

## Goal-Planning and Monitoring Sheet

Name: _____          Class: _____          Date: _____

1. Goal: _____

2. Reason(s) for working on goal: _____

   _____

3. Goal will be worked on at: _____

4. Date to reach goal (due date): _____

5. Materials needed: _____

   _____

6. Steps used to reach the goal: _____

   _____

7. Progress toward the goal: Record in each box the date and progress rating.

   3—Goal reached          2—Good progress made          1—Some progress made          0—No progress made

   | Date / Rating | | | | |
   |---|---|---|---|---|
   | Date / Rating | | | | |
   | Date / Rating | | | | |

8. Reward for reaching goal: _____

*Source:* Adapted from Van Reusen, A. K., & Bos, C. S. (1992). *Use of the goal-regulation strategy to improve the goal attainment of students with learning disabilities* (Final Report). Tucson, AZ: University of Arizona.

**Teaching Procedures:** *Self-advocacy* occurs when individuals effectively communicate and negotiate for their interests, desires, needs, and rights. It involves making informed decisions and taking responsibility for those decisions (Van Reusen et al., 1994). The I PLAN self-advocacy strategy is one way to help students develop their advocacy skills.

During the first (Inventory) step, students work in instructional groups to develop their own personal inventories. Each student examines the following items:

● Strengths
● Areas to improve or learn
● Goals
● Choice for learning or accommodations

If the emphasis is on career and transition planning, students also think about areas related to jobs and adult life. The major components of an education inventory and a transition inventory are presented in Table A.1.

The remaining four steps in the strategy focus on the communication skills needed to present the information and advocate with teachers, parents, counselors, and others. These steps are presented, discussed, and then practiced through simulations:

Provide your inventory information.
Listen and respond.
Ask questions.
Name your goals.

—— TABLE A.1 ——

## Components of Education and Transition Inventories

| | |
|---|---|
| Strengths | Reading<br>Writing<br>Math<br>Study skills<br>Social skills<br>Career and employment skills<br>Independent living skills<br>Leisure and recreation skills |
| Areas to Improve or Learn | Based on learning strengths and needs |
| Goals | Academic<br>Social<br>Extracurricular/recreation<br>Career/employment<br>Independent living |
| Choices for Learning | Helpful activities<br>Learning preferences<br>Helpful materials<br>Testing preferences |
| Accommodations | Changes that need to be made so that student can succeed |

*Source:* Adapted from Van Reusen, A. K., Bos, C. S., Schumaker, J. B., & Deshler, D. D. (1994). *The self-advocacy strategy for education and transition planning.* Lawrence, KS: Edge Enterprises.

Students also learn the following SHARE behaviors to promote positive communication:

Sit up straight.
Have a pleasant tone of voice.
Activate your thinking.
• Tell yourself to pay attention.
• Tell yourself to participate.
• Tell yourself to compare ideas.

Relax
• Don't look uptight.
• Tell yourself to stay calm.

Engage in eye communication.

**Content Class Integration:** This activity can be integrated into most content classes but is particularly suited for social studies and life skills classes.

**Resources:** For additional information, see *The self-advocacy strategy for education and transition planning,* by A. K. Van Reusen, C. S. Bos, J. B. Schumaker, and D. D. Deshler, published (1994) by Edge Enterprises, Lawrence, Kansas.

## ● Action Learning Area: Listening and Taking Notes

Listening to lectures, asking questions, and taking notes are skills critical for success in school. Teachers generally are more willing to accommodate students who actively participate in class, and these students tend to be more successful academically (Schumm & Vaughn, 1991). The six activities in this section can be used to promote active listening, note taking, and class participation.

## Creating Rationales for Effective Note Taking

**Objective:** To teach students how to develop rationales for taking notes.

**Grades:** Upper elementary and above

**Teaching Procedures:** On the average, teachers in secondary settings spend at least half their class time presenting information through lectures, and base a significant number of test items on information presented in class discussion and lectures (Putnam et al., 1993). Note taking is one of the most efficient ways to record this information.

Using class discussion or cooperative groups, have students generate a rationale for the importance of taking notes to success in school. If students do not mention the following reasons, make sure that you do:

● Note taking increases attention.
● Note taking requires a deeper level of thinking than just listening, because students must make sense of the information and write the ideas.
● Because students must process information on a deeper level, note taking makes learning and remembering information easier.

With class discussion or cooperative groups, have students create a list of requirements for effective note taking. If the following items are not part of the list, be sure to mention them:

- Paying attention
- Writing fast and legibly
- Using abbreviations
- Deciding what to write
- Spelling
- Making sense of notes after the lecture

Finally, through class discussion or cooperative groups, develop a list of ideas for accommodations for each requirement in the list (e.g., for "spelling," teacher could write difficult words on board, transparency, or handout).

Post the three lists so that students can review them.

**Content Class Integration:** Completing a unit on listening and note taking can be valuable in any content class. Such a unit not only improves students' note taking, but also makes them aware of your style of presenting information.

## Using Listener-Friendly Lectures

**Objective:** To use strategies that make it easier for students to understand and take notes on the information you present during lectures.

**Grades:** Upper elementary and above

**Teaching Procedures:** As you plan your teaching, the following guidelines can make your lectures listener-friendly:

- Use advance organizers.
- Use cue words or phrases to let students know what information is important (e.g., "It is important that you know . . . ," "The key information to remember is . . . ," "In summary . . .").
- Repeat important information.
- Write important information on board, transparency, and handout.
- Stress key points by varying the tone and quality of your voice.
- Number ideas or points (e.g., first, second, next, then, finally).
- Write technical words or words that are difficult to spell.
- Use a study guide that lists the major concepts, with space for students to add other information.
- Use pictures, diagrams, and semantic maps to show relationships among ideas.

- Provide examples and nonexamples of the concepts you are discussing.
- Ask questions or encourage discussion that requires students to relate the new information to ideas they already know (from their own background or your previous lectures).
- Stop frequently and have students work with partners and discuss what they have learned.
- Allow time at the end of a lecture for students to look over their notes, summarize, and ask questions.

By using these guidelines, you will naturally incorporate cues that indicate what information is important.

**Content Class Integration:** Whenever you give a lecture in any content course, make sure it is listener-friendly.

## Pause Procedure

**Objective:** To give students frequent opportunities to review notes, check for understanding, and ask questions.

**Grades:** Upper elementary and above

**Teaching Procedures:** The pause procedure is a technique that helps students learn more from lectures. During logical breaks in a lecture (approximately every ten minutes), the teacher pauses for two minutes. During that time, pairs of students compare their notes to make certain that key concepts have been recorded. Students also ask each other questions to check for understanding.

At the end of the two minutes, ask students whether they have any questions or concepts that need further discussion or clarification. Then resume lecturing.

**Resources:** For additional information, see the following publications:

- Ruhl, K. L., Hughes, C. A., & Gajar, A. H. (1990). Efficacy of the pause procedure for enhancing learning disabled and nondisabled college students' long- and short-term recall of facts presented through lecture. *Learning Disability Quarterly, 13,* 55–64.
- Ruhl, K. L., Hughes, C. A., & Schloss, P. J. (1987). Using the pause procedure to enhance lecture recall. *Teacher Education and Special Education, 10,* 14–18.

## Teaching Note Taking

**Objective:** To help students evaluate their notes and improve their note-taking strategies.

**Grades:** Middle school and above

**Teaching Procedures:** Teaching note-taking skills to students in your class is a good investment of time and effort. As you teach a content unit you can use the following procedure to evaluate your students' note-taking skills and to introduce and teach alternative ways to take notes:

1. *Have students evaluate the effectiveness of their current note-taking skills.* Give a lecture from the content unit, and have students take notes as usual. The next day, give students a quiz. Have them evaluate the completeness, format, and legibility of their notes, as well as their ease of use for review.
2. *Use videotaped lectures to teach students to listen effectively and take notes.* Use a videotape of your lecture so that students can listen and watch for cues you give to note important information. When students notice a cue, stop the videotape and replay it so that all the students can hear and see it.
3. *Control the difficulty of the lectures.* Select the first unit of the year to teach note taking. This unit usually contains simple information that was presented the previous year.
4. *Discuss with students ways to record notes* (i.e., record key ideas, not sentences; use consistent abbreviations; use an outline format; spell a word the way it looks or sounds). As a class, have students develop a set of abbreviations to be posted on a wall chart.
5. *Teach students how to review their notes,* add missing information, and clarify information that is unclear. Have students, working as partners or cooperative groups, use their notes to study for tests. Teach students how to use their notes to create questions and then check to see that they can answer them.
6. *Have students monitor their note taking.* Have them keep track of how often they use their note-taking skills in your class (and others), and record how they are doing on tests and assignments (and the effect of their improved note-taking skills).

**Content Class Integration:** You can integrate teaching how to take notes into any content class.

Teaching these skills early in the year improves the atmosphere and student learning throughout the year.

## Using Cues When Listening to Lectures

**Objective:** To help students learn to listen and watch for cues during lectures and to record important information.

**Grades:** Middle school and above

**Teaching Procedures:** Use the following list of cues to help students learn how to listen and watch for important information:

| Type of Cue | Examples |
| --- | --- |
| Organizational Cues | Today, we will be discussing . . . <br> The topic I want to cover today . . . <br> There are (number) points I want you to be sure to learn. . . . <br> The important relationship is . . . <br> The main point of this discussion is . . . <br> Any statement that signals a number or position (e.g., first, last, next, then). <br> To review/summarize/recap . . . |
| Emphasis Cues | |
| Verbal | You need to know/understand/remember . . . <br> This is important/key/basic/critical . . . <br> Let me repeat this, . . . <br> Let me check, now do you understand . . . <br> Any statement repeated. <br> Words are emphasized. <br> Teacher speaks more slowly, loudly, or with more emphasis. <br> Teacher stresses certain words. <br> Teacher spells words. <br> Teacher asks rhetorical question. |
| Nonverbal | Information written on overhead or board. <br> Information handed out in study guide. <br> Teacher emphasizes point by using gestures. |

---

## FIGURE A.5

**Sample Two-Column Note-Taking Format**

Date: _____                                      Page: _____

Topic: _____

| Key Concepts/Questions | Notes |
|---|---|
|  |  |

---

Encourage students to listen and watch for additional cues and add them to the list.

**Content Class Integration:** When integrating a content unit with a unit on note taking, the information presented in this activity can be placed on a handout and posted on a wall chart.

**Resources:** For more information, see:

- Suritsky, S. K., & Hughes, C. A. (1996). Note-taking strategy instruction. In D. D. Deshler, E. S. Ellis, & B. K. Lenz, *Teaching adolescents with learning disabilities* (2nd ed.), pp. 267–312. Denver: Love.

## Guidelines for Effective Note Taking

**Objective:** To teach students to use a note-taking system that is effective for recording and studying information.

**Grades:** Middle school and above

**Teaching Procedures:** Teach the specifics of note taking, using the following guidelines:

- Use a two- or three-column system for taking notes, with one column for recording key concepts and questions (see Figure A.5).
- Date and number each page of notes, and label the topic.

- Use a modified outline format, leaving space in which to add information when notes are reviewed.
- Write key ideas or phrases. (Paraphrase; do not write complete sentences.)
- Use pictures and diagrams to relate ideas.
- Use consistent abbreviations.
- Record information that the lecturer writes on the board or transparency.
- Underline, highlight, or use asterisks to mark key information.
- If you miss information, draw a blank and fill it in later.
- If you cannot spell a word, spell it the way you think it looks or sounds.
- As soon as possible, review your notes and fill in any missing information. Check with your teacher or other students if you have questions.

## Action Learning Area: Remembering Information

Using memory strategies to remember information is critical for success in school. Students, particularly students with disabilities and those who are at risk, often have difficulty memorizing information. Sometimes students do not understand the information, but in other cases, students may not perform well because they have difficulties retrieving information or because they do not use deliberate memory strategies. This section highlights two activities you can use to teach memory strategies.

## Guidelines for Remembering Information

**Objective:** To use general guidelines to increase the amount of information students remember.

**Grades:** Upper elementary and above

**Teaching Procedures:** When you present information, make it easier to remember by following these guidelines:

- Cue students when important information is being presented.
- Activate prior knowledge and help students make connections between old and new knowledge.
- Use visual aids such as semantic maps and diagrams to make the information more memorable.
- Limit the amount of information presented; group related ideas.
- Control the rate at which information is presented.
- Provide time to review, rehearse, and elaborate on the information.
- Teach students how to use and apply memory strategies and devices.
- Provide opportunities for distributed review of information and encourage over learning.

## Generating Acronyms and Acrostics

**Objective:** To teach students to generate acronyms and acrostics that help them remember information.

**Grades:** Middle school and above

**Teaching Procedures:** *Mnemonics* are memory-triggering devices that help us remember and retrieve information by forming associations that do not exist naturally in the content. Two types of mnemonics are acronyms and acrostics. *Acronyms* are words created by joining the first letters of a series of words. Examples are *radar* (**ra**dio **d**etecting **a**nd **r**anging), *scuba* (**s**elf-**c**ontained **u**nderwater **b**reathing apparatus), and *laser* (**l**ight **a**mplification by **s**timulated **e**mission of **r**adiation). *Acrostics* are sentences created by words that begin with the first letters of a series of words. A popular example of an acrostic is "Every good boy does fine," which represents the notes on the lines of the treble clef staff: E, G, B, D, F. By teaching students to construct acronyms and acrostics, sharing them in class, and then cueing students to use them when they study and take tests, you help them to learn and retrieve information.

The FIRST-letter mnemonic strategy is one strategy you can teach to help students construct lists of information to memorize and develop an acronym or acrostic for learning and remembering the information. The strategy includes an overall strategy (LISTS) and a substrategy for making the mnemonic device (FIRST). The steps in the overall strategy include the following:

*Look for clues.* (In class notes and textbooks, look for lists of information that are important to learn. Name or give a heading to each list.)
*Investigate the items.* (Decide which items should be included in the list.)
*Select a mnemonic device, using FIRST.* (Use the FIRST substrategy, explained shortly, to construct a mnemonic.)
*Transfer the information to a card.* (Write the mnemonic and the list on one side of a card and the name of the list on the other side of the card.)
*Self-test.* (Study by looking at the name of the list, using the mnemonic to recall the list.)

To complete the Select step, students use the FIRST substrategy to design an acronym or acrostic:

Form a word. Using uppercase letters, write the first letter of each word in the list; see whether an acronym—a recognizable word or nonsense word—can be made.
Insert a letter(s). Insert letter(s) to see whether a word can be made. (Be sure to use lowercase letters so that you know they do not represent an item on the list—BACk, for example.)
Rearrange the letters. Rearrange the letters to see whether a word can be made.
Shape a sentence. Using the first letter of each word in the list, try to construct a sentence (an acrostic).
Try combinations. Try combinations of these above steps to generate the mnemonic.

**Content Class Integration:** This strategy can be taught in any content class but is particularly effective in science and social studies classes in which lists of information are to be learned. The strategy provides a systematic method for students to review text and class notes, construct lists, and develop acronyms and acrostics that help them remember and retrieve information.

**Resources:** For more information, read *The FIRST-letter mnemonic strategy* (Learning Strategies Curriculum), by B. R. Nagel, J. B. Schumaker, and D. D. Deshler (1986), published by Edge Enterprises, Lawrence, Kansas.

## Action Learning Area: Studying and Taking Tests

Tests are the primary means that teachers use to determine whether students have learned new concepts and can apply them. If your goal in testing is to measure what students have learned (and not test-taking skills), then teaching test-taking strategies as part of the curriculum is important. This section contains five activities for teaching strategies for studying and taking tests.

## Guidelines for Studying for Tests

**Objective:**    To help students use general strategies when studying for tests.

**Grades:**    Middle school and above

**Teaching Procedures:**    Teach the following general guidelines to help students develop positive study habits when studying for tests.

- *Manage your study time.* Keep up with assignments and do daily and weekly reviews. Plan five minutes each day for students to review the material. On Monday, take an extra five minutes, and have students review the previous week's material. Use partners, cooperative groups, and whole-class discussion to review.
- *Create study aids.* Create a semantic map, study guide, mnemonic, and other study aids to help students remember key information. Use an ongoing map or study guide that students add to daily.
- *Create flashcards.* Teach students how to create and use flashcards. When students are learning vocabulary, have them put the word on one side and the definition and an example on the other. For other information, have students put the question on one side and the answer on the other. In math or science, have students put a formula on one side and examples of its use on the other. Have students keep index cards in their notebooks and on their desks during class. Cue students to make a card when they learn about a key concept or idea.

- *Use flashcards to review.* One advantage of flashcards is that each item or piece of information is on a separate card. Have students sort cards into categories, arrange the cards in a semantic map, or review them in random order.
- *Learn about the test.* Rather than telling students about the test, have them learn about it by asking questions. Start the discussion with, "Let's talk about the test. What do you want to ask me?" Use the following checklist to guide the students' questioning:

  - Format of test; types of questions
  - Date of test
  - Time allotted for test
  - Whether books and notes are allowed
  - How much test counts toward the class grade
  - Information covered
  - Teacher's recommendations for how to study
  - Teacher's recommendations for what to study

- *Predict questions.* Show students how they can predict what questions will be asked. Have students predict questions by using what they know about the teacher's testing style, class notes and textbook, and study aids. Two days before a test, have students—working as partners or in cooperative groups—write (and then answer) the questions they think will be on the test.
- *Think positive.* Help students develop a positive attitude by asking the following questions during each day's review:

  - What have you learned today?
  - How does it relate to what you already know?
  - What will you be working on tomorrow?
  - How well have you learned the information?

  Have students rate how well they think they will do on the test and think about what they can do to improve their ratings.

- *Review test-taking strategies and visualize success.* Just before a test, review test-taking strategies and have students visualize themselves being successful as they take the test.

**Content Class Integration:**    Guidelines for studying for tests are easily taught in any content class. Students learn not only about effective ways to study in general, but also about your views on developing, studying for, and giving tests.

## Guidelines for Taking Tests

**Objective:**    To teach students general strategies for taking tests.

**Grades:** Middle school and above

**Teaching Procedures:** Teach students the following general guidelines for taking tests:

● Bring the necessary materials.

● Be on time and sit where you will not be disturbed.

● Survey the test.

● Read the directions carefully and make sure that you understand them. If not, ask for assistance.

● Schedule your time.

● Be sure you understand the scoring system (i.e., is guessing penalized?).

● If you have memorized specific outlines, formulas, mnemonics, and so on, write that information before you forget it.

● When answering questions, place a mark in the margin next to questions about which you are unsure or that you want to review.

● Avoid changing answers arbitrarily.

● Review your answers and proofread written responses.

## Using a Test-Taking Strategy

**Objective:** To teach students to use a test-taking strategy.

**Grades:** Middle school and above

**Teaching Procedures:** Some students may profit from learning a specific test-taking strategy that they can use when taking objective tests. Introduce the PIRATES strategy, letting students know that its use generally improves test scores by 10–30 percent. Then model the steps in the following strategy:

1. Prepare to succeed.
   Put your name and the word PIRATES on the test.
   Allot time and order the sections.
   Say affirmations.
   Start within two minutes.

2. Inspect the instructions.
   Read instructions carefully.
   Underline what to do and where to respond.
   Notice special requirements.

3. Read, remember, reduce.
   Read the whole question.
   Remember what you studied.
   Reduce your choices.

4. Answer or abandon.
   Answer the question.
   Abandon the question for the moment.

5. Turn back.

6. Estimate your answer.
   Avoid absolutes.
   Choose the longest or most detailed choice.
   Eliminate similar choices.

7. Survey.
   Survey to ensure all questions are answered.
   Switch an answer only if you're sure.

Tell students to repeat the second, third, and fourth steps (i.e., **I**nspect the instructions; **R**ead, remember, reduce; **A**nswer or abandon) for each section of the test.

Give students the opportunity to learn the mnemonic (PIRATES) and the steps in the strategy, as well as the opportunity for practice. Cue students to use the strategy and discuss when, where, and how it can be used. Have students monitor their success in using the strategy and how it affects their test scores.

**Content Class Integration:** Teaching a test-taking strategy takes time but is worthwhile if you use objective tests as the major way to grade students.

**Resources:** For more information, see the following publications:

● Hughes, C. A., & Schumaker, J. B. (1991). Test-taking strategy instruction for adolescents with learning disabilities. *Exceptionality, 2,* 205–221.
● Hughes, C. A., Schumaker, J. B., Deshler, D. D., & Mercer, C. D. (1988). *The test-taking strategy.* Lawrence, KS: Edge Enterprises.

## Tips for Answering Objective Questions

**Objective:** To teach students tips for answering objective questions.

**Grades:** Middle school and above

**Teaching Procedures:** Discuss the following tips with students and give them a handout. In your discussion, include ideas that you and the students generate. Allow students to use the handout when they answer objective questions.

### True–False Questions

● Remember, *everything* in a true statement must be true. One false detail makes it false.

● Look for qualifying words that tend to make statements false, such as *all, always, everyone, everybody, never, no, none, no one, only.*

● Look for qualifying words that tend to make statements true, such as *generally, most, often, probably, some, sometimes, usually.*

● Simplify questions that contain double negatives by crossing out both negatives and then determining whether the statement is true or false.

● Don't change an answer unless you have a good reason. Your first impression is usually correct.

### Matching Questions

● Read directions carefully. Determine whether each column contains an equal number of items and whether items can be used more than once.

● Read both columns before you start matching, to get a sense of the items.

● Focus on each item in one column and look for its match in the other column.

● If you can use items only once, cross out each item as you use it.

### Multiple-Choice Questions

● Determine whether you are penalized for guessing.

● Answer the questions you know, putting a check mark in the margin next to items you want to return to later.

● Read all possible options, even when you are pretty sure of the right answer.

● See whether multiple options are available (e.g., c. A and B; d. All of the above).

● Minimize the risk of guessing by reading the stem with each option to see which option is most logical.

● Use a process of elimination, crossing out options you know are wrong.

● When you do not know the answer and you are not penalized for guessing, use the following signals to help you select the right option:
 • The longest option is often correct.
 • The most complete answer is often correct.
 • The first time the option "all of the above" or "none of the above" is used, it is usually correct.
 • The option in the middle, particularly if it is the longest, is often correct.

• Answers with qualifiers such as *generally, probably, sometimes,* and *usually* are frequently correct.

### Completion Questions

● Determine whether more than one word can be put in one blank.

● If blanks are of different lengths, use length as a clue for the length of the answer.

● Read the question to yourself so that you can hear what is being asked.

● If more than one answer comes to mind, write them down; then reread the question with each answer to see which one fits best.

● Makes sure that the answer you provide fits grammatically and logically.

**Content Class Integration:** In any content class, you can teach students to use tips for taking objective tests. You may want to modify the list to better match the type of objective tests you give in your class.

**Resources:** For more information, read J. Lagan's *Reading and study skills* (2nd ed.), 1982, published by McGraw-Hill, New York.

## Using Instruction Cue Words for Answering Essay Questions

**Objective:** To help students learn and apply the meaning of instruction cue words when they answer essay questions.

**Grades:** Middle school and above

**Teaching Procedures:** When you teach strategies for answering essay questions, discuss the meanings of different instruction cue words such as those in Table A.2. In your discussion, add other cue words and meanings generated by you and the students. Develop a handout, and have students use it when they answer essay questions. Ask students to underline the instruction cue words in each essay question.

**Content Class Integration:** This activity gives students an opportunity to learn how instruction cue words determine what information to include in an answer. For example, as a social studies teacher you can demonstrate how taking one concept, such as *democracy,* and using different instruction cue words (*define* versus *illustrate*) will change the answer.

TABLE A.2

## Instruction Cue Words for Answering Essay Questions

| Cue | Meaning | Cue | Meaning |
|-----|---------|-----|---------|
| Analyze | Break into parts and examine each part. | Interpret | Explain and share your own judgment. |
| Apply | Discuss how the principles would apply to a situation. | Justify | Provide reasons for your statements or conclusion. |
| Compare | Discuss differences and similarities. | List | Provide a numbered list of items or points. |
| Contrast | Discuss differences and similarities, stressing the differences. | Outline | Organize your answer into main points and supporting details. If appropriate, use outline format. |
| Critique | Analyze and evaluate, using criteria. | | |
| Define | Provide a clear, concise statement that explains the concept. | Prove | Provide factual evidence to support your logic or position. |
| Describe | Give a detailed account, listing characteristics, qualities, and components as appropriate. | Relate | Show the connection among ideas. |
| | | Review | Provide a critical summary in which you summarize and present your comments. |
| Diagram | Provide a drawing. | State | Explain precisely. |
| Discuss | Provide an in-depth explanation. Be analytical. | Summarize | Provide a synopsis that does not include your comments. |
| Explain | Give a logical development that discusses reasons or causes. | Trace | Describe the development or progress of the idea. |
| Illustrate | Use examples or, when appropriate, provide a diagram or picture. | **Add your own instruction cue words and definitions!!!** | |

*Source:* Adapted from Bos, C. S., & Vaughn, S. (1998). *Teaching students with learning and behavior problems* (4th ed., p. 326). Boston: Allyn & Bacon.

**Absence seizures (petit mal).** A type of seizure characterized by short lapses in consciousness

**Academic language.** Refers to the more cognitively demanding language skills required for the new learning that occurs in school

**Acquired immunodeficiency syndrome (AIDS).** A viral infection transmitted through bodily fluids that may eventually cause a loss of stamina, developmental delays, motor problems, progressive neurological defects, repeated bacterial infections, psychological stresses, and death

**Activity reinforcers.** Reinforcers such as free time, extra time on the computer, or time to listen to a CD

**Adaptive behavior.** Refers to the effectiveness or degree with which individuals meet the standards of personal independence and social responsibility expected for the person's age and cultural group

**Additive approach.** A strategy characterized by the addition of content, concepts, themes, and perspectives without changing the basic structure of the curriculum

**Add-on programs.** Services provided in time slots typically not allocated to regular instruction

**Advance organizer.** Information presented in advance of and at a higher level of generality, inclusiveness, and abstraction than the learning task itself

**Advocacy.** One of the primary characteristics of the Individuals with Disabilities Education Act, which involves the assignment of representatives (advocates) for individuals with disabilities who lack parents or guardians

**African American Vernacular English (AAVE).** Articulation used by some African Americans, and the most prevalent native English vernacular dialect used in the United States. It reflects the complex racial and economic history of African Americans in the United States

**Alliteration.** Identification of similarities or differences in word beginnings

**Alphabetic principle.** The use of the letters of the alphabet to form words

**American Sign Language (ASL).** A visual, gestural language

**Anxiety-withdrawal.** A type of problem behavior involving extreme worry, anxiousness, or depression

**AOK strategy.** A way to help students learn to read and reread for different purposes during revising and editing for meaning, paragraphs, sentences, words, and neatness

**Articulation disorders.** Occur when students are unable to produce the sounds and sound combinations of language

**Asperger's syndrome.** A disorder in which the individual has a normal IQ and language development but also exhibits autisticlike behaviors and marked deficiencies in social and communication skills

**Assessment portfolios.** Collections of work samples that document student progress in one or more subject areas

**ASSET.** A social skills program for adolescents, designed to effectively teach students strategies to enhance their social functioning

**Assistive listening devices.** Tools that aid in the process of hearing

**Attention deficit hyperactivity disorder (ADHD).** A disorder consisting of two subtypes of behavior: inattention and hyperactivity-impulsivity

**Audiogram.** A visual representation of an individual's ability to hear sound

**Augmentative or alternative communication (AAC).** Systems that attempt to facilitate and compensate for, temporarily or permanently, the impairment and disability patterns of individuals with severe expressive and/or language comprehension disorders

**Authentic learning.** Takes place when students can construct meaning by connecting new information to what they already know and have experienced, recognize the value of what they are learning beyond grades and success in school, and connect what they learn in school to the real world

**Authoring cycle.** A cycle of prewriting, composing (drafting), and postwriting (revising, editing, and publishing)

**Autism.** A developmental disability characterized by extreme withdrawal and communication difficulties

**Automaticity.** Automaticity in decoding refers to recognizing the words on sight

**Balanced bilingual.** Characterized by fluency in two languages or social language

**Basic interpersonal communication skills (BICS).** Refer to the conversational competencies that develop with a second language

**Behavioral inhibition.** The ability to withhold a planned response, interrupt a response that has been started, protect an ongoing activity from interfering activities, or delay a response

**Behavior support plans.** A written plan to describe the target problem behaviors and the ways the environment will change to improve the social behavior of the target student

**Biased responding.** The tendency of students to respond with "yes" because of a desire to please the teacher or in an effort to hide their confusion

**Big books.** Books with large pictures and words that can be seen by a whole class and used for shared reading activities

**Bilingual education.** An educational program involving instruction in two languages, the goal being to promote bilingualism (proficiency in both languages)

**Blending.** Putting sounds or phonemes together to form words

**Blind.** Describes an individual who is unable to see and therefore uses tactual (touch) and auditory (hearing) abilities to access the environment

**Braille.** A system of embossed or raised dots that can be read with the tips of the fingers

**Cerebral palsy.** Results from damage to the brain before or during birth; conditions are classified according to the areas affected and the types of symptoms

**Child find.** A requirement that each state identify and track the number of students with disabilities and plan for their educational needs

**Childhood disintegrative disorder.** A neurologic condition generally classified in the pervasive developmental disorders (PDDs) that is characterized by normal development through age 2 followed by a severe deterioration of mental and social functioning, with regression to a state suggestive of autism

**Class meetings.** Meetings that include all students in the class, as well as the teacher; used to foster students' involvement in the management of their classes

**Classification.** The ability to group or sort objects by one or more common properties

**Classwide peer tutoring.** Students of different reading levels are paired (one average or high and one low) and read materials that can be easily read by the less able reader in the pair

**Cluster grouping.** A group of five to eight students qualifying for services as gifted or talented placed together in the same general education setting

**Cognitive academic language performance (CALP).** Refers to the more cognitively demanding language skills required for the new learning that is characteristic of school settings

**Cognitive strategies.** Thinking processes used by students to complete their academic work

**Cognates.** Words in different languages that sound alike (homophones) or that look alike (homographs) and have roughly the same meaning

**Collaboration.** A style for direct interaction between at least two coequal parties voluntarily engaged in shared decision making as they work toward a common goal

**Collaborative open-note quizzes.** Tests given after students have had an opportunity to compare and further develop their notes in collaborative groups; students have the opportunity to answer test questions as a collaborative group

**Collaborative strategic reading (CSR).** A multicomponent learning strategy that combines essential reading comprehension strategies that have been demonstrated as effective in improving students' understanding of text

**Common underlying proficiency.** The phenomenon that the better developed the students' first language proficiency and conceptual foundation, the more likely they are to develop similarly high levels of proficiency and conceptual ability in the second language

**Communication approach.** Teaching the student how to (1) communicate with oneself and others and (2) integrate reading with other language skills including writing, speaking, and listening

**Communication board.** An example of augmentative communication that includes the board itself and symbols or pictures

**Communication disorders.** Difficulties with the transfer of knowledge, ideas, opinions, and feelings

**Compensatory education.** Instruction designed to compensate (make up) for prior lack of educational opportunities and intervention or prevention programs

**Compensatory skills.** Skills needed for independence, which may include the use of Braille, a slate and stylus, and an abacus

**Composing.** Process in which the author attempts to get ideas on paper in the form of a draft

**Comprehensible input.** Refers to input received and made understandable when listening to or reading in a second language

**Comprehensible output.** Output that is transmitted and made understandable when speaking

**Comprehension.** A person's ability to understand what is being communicated

**Comprehension monitoring.** Refers to monitoring understanding

**Comprehension strategies.** Techniques designed to improve students' understanding of text

**Computational Arithmetic Program.** Provides 314 worksheets to teach basic math skills in grades 1 through 6

**Computer-assisted instruction (CAI).** Involves learning through the use of computers and/or multimedia systems

**Computer equity.** Equal access to computers in the home and in the school

**Concept diagram.** A way to introduce a lecture or reading assignment (similar to a semantic map) that also helps students determine the definitions, characteristics, examples, and nonexamples of a concept

**Conceptual density.** The number of new vocabulary terms or concepts the author introduces

**Conduct disorder.** Includes behaviors such as hitting, fighting, throwing, temper tantrums, acting defiant or disobedient, and being irritable or overactive, difficult to get along with, uncooperative, inconsiderate, resistive, jealous, quarrelsome, distractible, teasing, irresponsible, and inattentive

**Cone of experience.** Classifies experience on a scale from concrete to abstract, from action to observation to representation

**Conferencing.** An ongoing student–teacher meeting prepared to read the student's writing piece, to describe problem areas, and to respond to questions

**Confidentiality of records.** The Individuals with Disabilities Education Act requires that all records and documents regarding students with disabilities remain undisclosed to the public but accessible to parents

**Conflict resolution.** A strategy for resolving conflicts between students and between students and teachers

**Consequences.** The ramifications of not following classroom guidelines

**Considerate text.** Text that is written and formatted in such a way that information can be extracted easily, with support available when the reader does not understand

**Constant time delay.** A procedure for teaching math facts that provides for the systematic introduction of teacher assistance

**Consultation model.** An interactive process that enables people with diverse expertise to generate creative solutions to mutually defined problems

**Content.** The semantics of language

**Content acceleration.** The practice of rapid movement through the curriculum

**Content and process dilemma.** The conflict between covering sufficient material (content) or altering instruction so that students with special needs master the learning process (sometimes by covering less material)

**Content integration.** Focused use of examples and content from different cultures and groups to illustrate concepts, principles, generalizations, and theories

**Context-embedded communication and instruction.** Providing a link between students' culture, the instruction they receive, and the mode in which they receive it

**Continuum of services.** A full range of service options for students with disabilities, provided by the school system

**Contributions approach.** Characterized by the insertion of ethnic heroes and discrete cultural artifacts into the curriculum

**Cooperative learning groups.** Groups of students work together toward a common goal, usually to help one another learn academic material

**Cooperative teaching.** General and special education teachers working together to coordinate curriculum and instruction and teach heterogeneous groups of students in the general education classroom setting

**Corrective Mathematics Program.** A math program that requires only minimal reading skills and provides remedial math for students in grades 3 through 12

**Course Planning Routine.** A long-range planning guide for classrooms with diverse learners; includes procedures for setting goals for the course, getting the course off on the right foot, monitoring and managing the course during the year, and closing the course

**Creatively gifted or talented.** Describes students who display their unique abilities within the framework of the visual or performing arts and who usually demonstrate a superior ability to express ideas through various forms of communication (drawing, music, singing, writing, and acting)

**Cross-age pairing.** A method of pairing older students with younger students for reading instruction

**Cultural characteristics.** Traits or aspects that characterize a particular culture

**Cultural inversion.** The tendency to regard certain forms of behavior, events, symbols, and meanings as inappropriate because they are characteristic of European-American culture

**Curriculum-based measurement (CBM).** A means of measuring student progress that highlights the close tie between curriculum and student performance

**Curriculum compacting.** Provides students with the opportunity to demonstrate what they already know about a subject by eliminating repetitive or review content and replacing it with advanced learning experiences

**Deaf.** Describes a person with a severe or profound loss of hearing

**Deafness–blindness.** Also known as dual sensory impairment; involves impairments in the two main channels (auditory and visual) of receptive communication and learning

**Decodable books.** Books that primarily use words that reflect the phonic and word patterns already learned

**Decodable text.** Text in which most of the words are comprised of letter–sound correspondences that have been taught

**Decoding.** A strategy for recognizing words

**Degrees of learning.** This primary component of the planning pyramid is based on the premise that although all students are capable of learning, not all students will learn all the covered content

**Demonstration plus model strategy.** A strategy for giving demonstrations to students with learning problems that includes completion of the demonstration, having a student perform each step, verbalizing each step as the teacher did, and having all students complete additional practice exercises independently, using the steps

**Developmental arithmetic disorder.** Refers to students who have significant difficulties learning arithmetic (difficulties that are unexpected, given the students' overall cognitive functioning and/or academic performance in other subject areas)

**Developmental disability.** Refers to a disability that is attributable to mental retardation or related conditions that include cerebral palsy, epilepsy, autism, or other neurological conditions when such conditions result in impairment of general intellectual functioning or adaptive behavior similar to that of a person with mental retardation

**Developmental pathways.** The etiologies associated with specific disorders

**Developmental period.** A period before the age of 18 years during which the bulk of human development occurs

***Diagnostic and Statistical Manual of Mental Disorders.*** A reference book published by the American Psychiatric Association

**Dialect.** Refers to language variations associated with a regional or social group of people

**Dialogue journal.** An ongoing written conversation between two students (or in some cases between a student and an adult)

**Difficulty with zero.** Refers to students' misunderstanding of the multiple meanings and uses of zero that causes errors in arithmetic

**Discrepancy analysis.** A review of each specific step or skill and determination of how a student does the step or skill compared to what is expected

**Discussion web.** A graphic aid to help students prepare for classroom discussions in content-area classes

**DISSECT.** A learning strategy for secondary students with learning disabilities to approach a multisyllable word in a strategic way

**DISTAR Arithmetic Program.** Stresses direct instruction through a highly sequenced format that provides immediate feedback to students

**Down syndrome.** One of the most common chromosomal disorders, usually associated with mental retardation

**Drafting.** (See *Composing*)

**Dropouts.** Students who do not complete high school

**Dual sensory impairments.** Refers to impairments in the two main channels (auditory and visual) of receptive communication and learning

**Due process.** Ensures that everyone with a stake in the student's educational success has a voice; also addresses written notification to parents for referral and testing for special education, parental consent, and guidelines for appeals and record keeping

**Dyscalculia.** Severe disability in learning mathematical concepts and computation

**Dysgraphia.** Severe difficulty learning to write (including handwriting)

**Dyslexia.** Severe difficulty learning to read, particularly as it relates to decoding

**Early intervention programs.** Special learning programs provided during the preprimary and early primary grades

**Early intervention services.** Comprehensive services that incorporate goals in education, health care, and social services

**Echolalia.** A repetition of what was said without necessarily understanding the meaning

**Ecological inventories.** Analyses of the different skills a student needs in relation to his or her specific environments

**Editing.** The process that takes place as the author reviews the written work line by line to determine whether the overall content is appropriate and the mechanics are correct

**Educational interventions.** Special strategies for meeting the diverse needs of students

**Educational placement.** The type of educational setting in which a particular student is instructed; examples include general education classrooms, resource rooms, special schools, and other types of settings

**Effective listening.** Requires hearing the message being sent and often requires asking questions to clarify the true message being sent

**Emotional or behavioral disorders.** Behavior that falls considerably outside the norm

**Empowering school culture.** A culture that promotes gender, racial, and social class equity

**Encode.** To change written language to symbols; to write

**English as a Second Language (ESL) instruction.** Students are taught English as a second language, with limited emphasis on maintaining or developing proficiency in their first language

**Enrichment.** Adding breadth and depth to the traditional curriculum

**Environmental accommodations.** Changes made to the physical learning environment so that each student can participate successfully

**Environment-related factors.** Factors that pertain to the context in which one teaches (including state, local, and class factors) and that can influence the planning process

**Epilepsy.** A condition characterized by the tendency to have recurrent seizures caused by sudden, excessive, spontaneous, and abnormal discharges of neurons accompanied by alteration in motor function and/or sensory function and/or consciousness

**Equity pedagogy.** The teacher attends to different teaching and learning styles and modifies teaching to facilitate the academic achievement of students from diverse cultures

**Exceptionalities.** Refers to students who represent a range of disability categories (e.g., students with emotional disorders, learning disabilities, physical impairments, and students who are gifted)

**Executive functioning.** Refers to the ability to regulate one's thinking and behavior through the use of working memory, inner speech, control of emotions and arousal levels, and analysis of problems and communication of problem solutions to others

**Expansion.** A technique used to facilitate the development of more complex language form and content

**Explication.** How the author explains ideas and teaches the reader, including the provision of background information and examples

**Expository writing.** Informational writing

**Expressive language.** A person's ability to convey the intended message

**Externalizing behaviors.** Behaviors such as aggression, hitting, and shouting that are readily observable and tend to affect others

**Extinction.** The elimination of a student's undesirable behavior by removing reinforcers

**Facilitator.** The teacher who guides his or her peer through the process and helps to generate solutions

**Failure to shift operations.** Occurs when the student fails to move to the next operation after completing a previous operation

**Family adjustment.** A family's changes in response to having a child with severe disabilities, mental retardation, or physical disabilities

**FAST.** A strategy designed to teach students to consider problems, identify alternatives, and evaluate consequences to their interpersonal problems

**FAST DRAW.** A type of mnemonic used to teach the concrete-representational-abstract teaching principle advocated in mathematics instruction (Find what you're solving for; Ask yourself "What are the parts of the problem?"; Set up the numbers; Tie down the sign; Discover the sign; Read the problem; Answer or draw a conceptual representation of the problem, using lines and tallies, and check; Write the answer)

**Fetal alcohol syndrome (FAS).** Refers to a spectrum of birth defects caused by the mother's drinking during pregnancy

**Figurative language.** Represents abstract concepts and usually requires an inferential rather than literal interpretation

**Finger spelling.** A system for manually representing the English alphabet

**FLIP Chart Strategy.** Helps students learn to evaluate the difficulty of text on their own by examining text friendliness and language as well as their interest in and prior knowledge of the topic

**Flow of the Planning Process Model.** A model that indicates the sequence and relationships among three types of planning and the factors that influence planning

**Fluency.** The ability to recognize printed words quickly

**Fluency disorders.** Refers to difficulty with the rate and flow of speech

**Form.** The phonology, morphology, and syntax of language

**Free appropriate public education.** Mandatory legislation provides that all children with disabilities be given a free and appropriate public education

**Friendly text.** A text that features elements that support student learning

**Frustration reading level.** The reading level at which students have difficulty reading even with assistance, because reading materials are too difficult

**Full inclusion.** A movement that advocates educating all students with disabilities in the general education classroom full-time

**Full-service school.** A school that serves as a hub for educational, psychological, physical, financial, social, and health-related services for a community by housing a health center, social service and employment agencies, and adult education organizations

**Functional assessment.** Involves analyses of the skills needed to complete a particular activity or task

**Functional behavior assessment.** A method of gathering data to design the most effective positive support plans and to monitor their progress

**Functional practice.** Relevant practice that helps students to easily see the connection between what they are practicing and its use in real life

**Functional vision.** Refers to both the way an individual uses his or her vision as well as the amount of vision the individual has

**Funds of knowledge.** The information and resources available in the student's home community

**Gangs.** Groups of individuals working to unlawful or antisocial ends

**Giftedness.** Evidence of high performance capability in areas such as intelligence, creativity, art, or leadership or in specific academic fields that, to be more fully developed, requires services or activities not ordinarily provided by the school

**Group behavior.** Behaviors displayed in the presence of other group members

**Hanover method.** A system for teaching cursive writing based on the similarities of letters or letter families

**Hard of hearing.** Describes a person with a mild to moderate loss of hearing

**Higher-order thinking.** Involves problem solving, decision making, creative thinking, critical thinking, and investigation

**High-frequency words.** Words that occur frequently in spoken language and in written text

**Homogeneous grouping.** The practice of putting students at approximately the same achievement level together for instruction (also called same-ability grouping)

**Human immunodeficiency virus (HIV).** A virus that infects and eventually destroys cells in the immune system that protect the body from disease

**Hyperactivity–impulsivity.** Refers to a group of behaviors associated with restlessness, excess motor activity, and an inability to control one's own actions

**Ignoring on purpose.** A method of eliminating a student's undesirable behavior by purposely removing the teacher's and other students' attention to that behavior

**Immaturity.** Behaviors that include lack of perseverance, failure to finish tasks, short attention span, poor concentration, and frequent daydreaming or preoccupation

**Inattention.** Refers to difficulty sustaining attention

**In-class programs.** Programs that use the general education classroom as the primary setting for instruction (sometimes called *pull-in programs*)

**Inclusion.** The situation in which students with disabilities are educated with their nondisabled peers, with special education supports and services provided as needed

**Inclusion support teacher.** A teacher whose responsibilities include supporting students with disabilities (e.g., mental retardation, severe disabilities, physical disabilities, visual impairments) in general education classrooms

**Independent learning.** Occurs when students work and learn without assistance from others

**Independent reading level.** The reading level at which students read on their own without support from others

**Individualized education program (IEP).** A written plan, developed to meet the special learning needs of each student with disabilities

**Individualized family service plan (IFSP).** A plan, for children from birth to 3 years of age, developed to meet not only the special needs of each student with disabilities but also those of his or her family

**Individualized transition plans.** A plan, for students from 16 years of age (or 14 years and even younger, if appropriate) to age 21, that states what transition services are necessary and, when appropriate, includes a statement of the interagency responsibilities and linkages

**Individuals with Disabilities Education Act (IDEA).** Legislation designed to ensure that all children with disabilities receive an appropriate education through special education and related services

**Informal member checks.** A form of monitoring student understanding that involves frequent, quick observations by teachers to determine whether students are comprehending the current lesson

**Informal reading inventory.** An individually administered reading assessment designed to help a teacher determine a student's reading instructional needs. The student reads lists of words and passages that are leveled by grade and retells or answers comprehension questions about the passages

**Initiator.** The teacher who addresses the problems to his or her peer

**Inner speech.** Talking to one's self about various solutions when in the midst of solving a problem

**Instructional clarity.** The clear, direct, and explicit presentation of information

**Instructional congruence.** Occurs between general education and remedial programs and is necessary for determining what type of remedial instruction is most appropriate for an individual student

**Instructional conversations.** Conversations between students and teachers on the reading process (e.g., sharing the strategies the students use to decode words and construct meaning)

**Instructional design.** The way the content is taught; how skills and concepts are introduced, developed, and reinforced

**Instructional devices.** The number of learning tools an author provides (examples include a table of contents, marginal annotations, and a glossary)

**Instructional reading level.** The reading level at which instruction should occur and at which students are challenged by the reading but still need some support

**Instructional unit.** A series of lessons related to the same topic

**Intellectual functioning.** An individual's overall mental abilities

**Intellectually gifted.** Refers to students who are exceptional learners and tend to excel both in the classroom and on standardized tests but are not homogeneous in their thinking strategies

**Interactive planning.** Involves monitoring students' learning and making adaptations in response to their needs

**Interdisciplinary thematic units.** The teaching of several subject areas around a central theme

**Internalizing behaviors.** Behaviors such as shyness, withdrawal, or depression that tend to be less readily observable that negatively affect the individual exhibiting the behaviors

**Interpersonal problem solving.** A strategy for teaching students to identify their problems, goals, and a wide range of alternatives for effectively solving their problems

**Invented spelling.** Children's early attempts to spell in their own way

**Invisible gifted.** Underidentified gifted and talented students from minority groups

**Key Math Teach and Practice.** A program designed to provide remedial practice in, and diagnosis of, math difficulties

**Knowledge construction.** Refers to students' learning about how implicit cultural assumptions, frames of reference, perspectives, and biases influence the ways that knowledge is constructed

**K–W–L strategy.** A strategy (based on research underscoring the importance of activating prior knowledge before reading) to help students become actively engaged in comprehension before, during, and after reading

**Language disorders.** A major area of communication disorders

**Language variation.** Refers to the fact that language varies from place to place and from group to group

**LEAP.** A coordinated program to emphasize professional collaboration (Learning Environment and Attitude Program)

**Learner characteristics.** The third factor affecting second language acquisition or output; includes the age at which students learn a second language, their aptitude for learning language, their purposes and degree of motivation for learning the second language, their self-confidence in language learning, and the learning strategies they have for learning language

**Learning and developmental process.** In the learning and developmental process of second language acquisition and learning, students generally acquire competency in the basic interpersonal communication skills (BICS) before becoming competent with cognitive academic language proficiency (CALP)

**Least restrictive environment.** The instructional setting most like that of nondisabled peers that also meets the educational needs of each student with disabilities

**Legal blindness.** Describes an individual who with the best possible correction in the better eye has a measured visual acuity of 20/200 or worse or a visual field restricted to 20 degrees or less

**Lesson co-planning.** General and special education teachers working together to plan activities for students

**Lesson co-teaching.** Teaching in which the special education and general education teachers are both in the classroom during the same lesson and both participate in the instruction

**Level system.** An approach to controlling behavior by providing a guide for managing student behavior through an organized framework based on token economies and the application of behavioral principles whereby students are provided with privileges based on their behavior

**Life-space intervention (LSI).** An intervention used to help students with emotional and behavioral problems cope with a crisis situation

**Linguistic input.** Refers to the type of input received when listening or reading in a second language

**Long range co-planning.** Planning in which the general education and special education teachers broadly plan their overall goals and desired outcomes for the class and for specific students with disabilities in the class

**Long-term planning.** Planning for the term or the entire school year

**Low vision.** Describes an individual who is either partially sighted or legally blind

**Macroculture.** The core culture in a school

**Magnet schools.** Designated elementary or secondary schools that serve as centers for the education of gifted and talented students

**Mainstreaming.** The participation of students with disabilities in general education classrooms to the extent appropriate for meeting their needs

**Maintenance bilingual education.** Attempts to foster the students' first language and strengthen their sense of cultural identity

**Making words.** A whole-class guided activity that helps students develop phonological awareness and become more sensitive to common spelling patterns

**Manipulating.** A type of phonological awareness skills: deleting, adding, and substituting syllables and sounds

**Manuscript writing.** Print writing

**Mastery.** Occurs when accuracy, speed, and knowledge have met expectations

**McGill Action Planning System (MAPS).** A planning activity that fosters relationships in order to improve the quality of life for persons with severe disabilities while facilitating participation in inclusive settings

**Medically fragile.** A subgroup that has emerged within the health disabilities, characterized by an individual being at risk for medical emergencies on a regular basis and often requiring life support or specialized support systems such as ventilators

**Memory problems.** Occur when students forget or misremember a fact; lead to errors in arithmetic calculation and other areas

**Memory strategies.** Mental techniques for increasing students' abilities to memorize information and utilize information in memory

**Mental retardation.** Characterizes individuals who have limited intellectual functioning that affects their learning

**Mentoring programs.** Volunteer efforts that structure partnerships between a student and an adult who can offer guidance and support

**Metadiscourse.** The degree to which the author "talks" to the reader; includes direct explanations of how to learn from the text and how to connect ideas from one part of the text to another

**Metalinguistics.** Involves thinking about, analyzing, and reflecting on language as an object in much the same way one reflects on a table or a friend

**Microcultures.** Home cultures based on such factors as national origin, ethnicity, socioeconomic class, religion, gender, age, and disability

**Milliken Wordmath.** Uses computer programs to teach problem-solving strategies within the mathematics curriculum to students in fourth grade and up who have been unsuccessful in adequately learning problem-solving skills

**Mistaken goal.** Evidenced when students display inappropriate behavior because they believe it will get them the recognition and acceptance they desire

**Mixed-ability grouping.** (See *Heterogeneous grouping*)

**Mobility skills.** Skills such as going up and down stairs, crossing streets, and using public transportation

**Modeling.** A technique for teaching language that involves following examples illustrated by others

**Morpheme.** The smallest unit of language that conveys meaning

**Morphology.** Focuses on the rule system that governs the structure of words and word forms

**Motoric problems.** Difficulty of writing and reading numbers

**Moving model.** Modeling for students how to form letters and words in order to develop their legibility

**Multicultural education.** An educational reform movement whose major goal is to change the structure of educational institutions so that male and female students, exceptional students, and students who are members of diverse racial, ethnic, and cultural groups have an equal chance to achieve in school

**Multidimensional traits.** The concept that a variety of individual characteristics and traits define intelligence

**Multidisciplinary team (MDT).** This group of individuals usually includes a representative of the local education agency, the classroom teacher, the special education teacher, parents or guardians, and, when appropriate, the student, who together develop and implement the IEP

**Multiple causation theory.** A theory that suggests that although some students may be at risk owing to one primary condition, quite often multiple conditions interact to compound learning challenges

**Multiple disabilities.** Describes individuals who have severe or profound mental retardation and one or more significant motor or sensory impairments and/or special health needs

**Multiple grouping formats.** The use of a variety of grouping patterns

**Multiple intelligence.** The theory that human beings are capable of exhibiting intelligence in eight domains: linguistic, logical-mathematical, spatial, musical, bodily–kinesthetic, interpersonal (i.e., discerning and responding to the needs of others), intrapersonal (i.e., having detailed and accurate self-knowledge), and naturalistic (i.e., differentiating between living things and accurate knowledge of the natural world)

**Multiple meanings.** Applies to words that have more than one meaning

**Muscular dystrophy.** A chronic disorder characterized by the weakening and wasting of the body's muscles

**Narrative writing.** Writing stories

**NCTM Navigation Series.** Refers to a series of graded and topical books that focus on teaching of algebra, geometry, numbers, and operations based on the NCTM principles and standards

**Negative reinforcement.** The removal of a stimulus to increase responding

**Neurological impairment.** A disability caused by a dysfunction of the brain, spinal cord, and nerves, thereby creating transmission of improper instructions, uncontrolled bursts of instructions from the brain, or incorrect interpretation of feedback to the brain

**Neuromuscular diseases.** Disorders that involve both the nerves and muscles

**Noncompliance.** Failure to comply with the law; the Individuals with Disabilities Act requires that states mandate consequences for noncompliance

**Nondiscriminatory evaluation.** An evaluation that does not discriminate on the basis of language, culture, and student's background; must be provided for each individual who is assessed for special education

**Nonverbal math disabilities.** Students who display good reading and verbal expression but who have extreme difficulty with mathematics

**One-to-one correspondence.** A situation in which each object corresponds to another object

**Onset-rime.** Onset is the word's initial consonant or consonant combination (e.g., g-), and rime is the rhyming part of the word (e.g., -et)

**Open question.** A question that allows a full range of responses and discourages short "yes" or "no" answers

**Organization.** How the author orders information in the text; includes the general structure of the text as well as the consistency and connectedness of ideas

**Orientation skills.** Includes understanding one's own body, one's position in space, and abstract concepts such as the layout of a city block

**Orthopedic impairment.** Includes deficits caused by congenital anomaly (e.g., clubfoot, absence of some member), impairments caused by disease (e.g., poliomyelitis, bone tuberculosis), and impairments from other causes (e.g., cerebral palsy, amputations, and fractures or burns that cause contractures)

**Other health impairments (OHI).** Limited strength, vitality, or alertness (caused by chronic or acute health problems such as heart condition, tuberculosis, rheumatic fever, nephritis, asthma, sickle-cell anemia, hemophilia, epilepsy, lead poisoning, leukemia, or diabetes) that adversely affects a student's educational performance

**Pairs.** Two students of the same ability level working together

**Parallel talk.** A process in which the teacher describes what students are doing or thinking

**Parent participation.** Involvement of parents in all aspects of identifying and evaluating students with disabilities, including decision making

**Partial participation.** A concept that assumes that an individual has the right to participate, to the extent possible, in all activities

**Partial sight.** Describes an individual who with best possible correction in the better eye has a measured visual acuity between 20/70 and 20/200

**Peer Collaboration Model.** Developed to help classroom teachers solve problems by providing time and structure to do so

**Peer editing.** Process in which students revise and edit each other's work

**Peer tutoring.** One student in a pair acts as a teacher for the other student

**Pervasive developmental disorder (PDD).** Characterized by students who express farfetched, unusual, or unbelievable ideas

**Pervasive developmental disorder–not otherwise specified.** A disorder in which a child exhibits stereotypical behaviors or delays in social interaction or communication, but does not meet the criteria for another PDD

**Phoneme.** The smallest unit of speech sound

**Phonemic awareness.** The understanding of how to listen to and produce sounds

**Phonemic pairs.** A strategy designed to help students learn to read and spell words; pairs of students work together to analyze words by looking at alliteration and rhyme

**Phonic analysis.** Identifying and blending letter–sound correspondences into words

**Phonics.** The systematic teaching of the alphabetic principle and the way spelling patterns relate to sound patterns

**Phonological awareness.** Possession of skills such as rhyming, alliteration, blending, and segmentation

**Phonology.** Focuses on the sounds of language and the rules that determine how the sounds fit together

**P.L. 94–142.** This legislation, designed to ensure that all children with disabilities receive an appropriate education through special education and related services, was originally referred to as the Education for All Handicapped Children Act, enacted in 1975, and later reauthorized and expanded as the Individuals with Disabilities Education Act (IDEA)

**Planned ignoring.** A strategy to eliminate (extinguish) a student's undesirable behavior, which is being reinforced through attention, by ignoring

**Planning pyramid.** A framework for unit planning, aimed at meeting diverse student needs

**PLEASE strategy.** A strategy developed to provide students with a step-by-step procedure for paragraph writing

**Positive behavioral support.** The modification of behavior management principles applied in various community settings with supports to reduce problem behaviors and develop appropriate behaviors that lead to enhanced social relations and lifestyle

**Positive feedback.** Recognizing a student behavior by providing some judgment about the appropriateness of the behavior

**Positive reinforcement.** The presentation of a stimulus (verbal response, physical response such as touching, or tangible response such as a reward) following the target behavior to maintain or increase the target behavior

**Postplanning.** Follow-up planning that comes at the end of a lesson and allows teachers to reflect about how students performed and to use this information to guide their planning for subsequent instruction

**Postwriting.** Process in which authors revise, edit, and publish their written work

**Pragmatics.** Refers to the purposes or functions of communication or how we use language to communicate

**Prelearning activities.** Strategies teachers use to activate students' prior knowledge and to preteach vocabulary and concepts—essentially, to prepare students to learn

**Premack principle.** Provides the opportunity for behaviors that are desirable to both teachers and students to serve as reinforcers for other behaviors that are more desirable to teachers than to students

**Preplanning.** Advanced preparation that involves decisions about what to teach and how to teach it

**Prereferral assistance team (PAT).** A group of teachers from the same school who meet regularly to discuss the specific progress of students brought to their attention by other teachers in the school

**Prewriting.** Process in which a writer collects information about a topic through observing, remembering, interviewing, and reading

**Print-rich environment.** The physical environment of the classroom communicates to students that the classroom is a place to read

**Procedural congruence.** A common understanding of the schedules and policies between classroom and remedial teachers that allows for improved communication

**Procedural error.** Occurs when a student misapplies a procedure from one arithmetic operation to another

**Production.** A person's ability to convey the intended message

**Project Math.** A math curriculum designed specifically for students with mild disabilities

**Publishing.** Preparing a written work in a way that enables others to read it

**Pull-out programs.** Programs in which children are pulled out of their general education classroom for supplemental instruction in basic skills

**Punishment.** The opposite of reinforcement, in that it follows a behavior and decreases the strength of the behavior or the likelihood the behavior will continue to occur

**Purpose-setting activities.** Give students a reason to complete a reading assignment or listen to a lecture

**Question–answering relationships strategy.** A strategy for teaching students how to answer different types of comprehension questions

**Rapid naming.** Tasks such as naming a series of random numbers or letters

**Readability level.** The level of difficulty of a textbook

**Reading comprehension.** The ability to understand individual words, phrases and clauses, sentences, paragraphs, and larger units of text

**Real content.** The main idea or key information that someone wants to convey

**Real-Life Math Program.** Focuses on teaching students with learning difficulties the mathematics skills they need for daily life

**Receptive language.** A person's ability to understand what is being communicated

**Reciprocal causation.** The combination of factors related to a student's reading problems

**Register.** A language style the speaker uses to communicate to meet the needs or expectations of the speaker; includes such features as choice of words, sentences, intonation, and formality

**Regular Education Initiative (REI).** A concept that promotes coordination of services between regular and special education

**Related services.** The types of services to which students with disabilities are entitled, including speech therapy, audiology, psychological services, physical therapy, occupational therapy, recreation, early identification and assessment, counseling, medical services for diagnostic or evaluation purposes, school health services, transportation, and social work services

**Remediation.** Additional instruction for students who do not demonstrate, at an expected rate, competency in basic skills in reading, writing, and mathematics

**Repeated readings.** Process of reading passages over and over again to develop fluency in reading

**Residual hearing.** Usable hearing

**Retention.** The practice of having a student repeat a grade level because of low academic performance

**Rett's syndrome.** An extremely rare disorder that affects only females, characterized by the following symptoms occurring between 5 and 48 months: deceleration of head growth, loss of hand skills with subsequent development of stereotyped hand movements, loss of social engagement, poor gait or trunk movements, and severely impaired receptive and expressive communication

**Revising.** Stage of writing during which points are explored further, ideas are elaborated on, and further connections are made

**Rhyming.** Identifying similarities and differences in word endings

**Roots and Wings.** A learning program that adds guidelines for an integrated approach to other content areas, such as science and social studies

**Same-ability grouping.** (See *Homogeneous grouping*)

**Schoolwide enrichment model.** Learning strategy in which a large portion of the school population is given the opportunity to participate in enrichment activities

**Schoolwide programs.** Policies that affect every classroom and student in a school

**SCORE A.** A type of mnemonic used to identify the writing steps (Select a topic; Create categories; Obtain reference tools; Read and take notes; Evenly organize the information using notecards; Apply writing process steps)

**Secondary language output.** The level of proficiency in producing (speaking and writing) a language

**Segmenting.** Process of dividing ideas into words and words into syllables and individual phonemes

**Self-injurious behavior.** A behavior that may consist of head banging, scratching, or biting oneself

**Self-management.** Skills that enable students to be more aware of their own behaviors and to govern the reinforcers for their behaviors

**Self-monitoring.** Refers to keeping track of how well one is understanding or performing by oneself

**Self-talk.** A technique in which the teacher describes what he or she is doing or thinking

**Semantic feature analysis.** A vocabulary-enhancement procedure that involves the placement of categories or critical features along one axis and the specific vocabulary along the other axis

**Semantic map.** A prelearning activity for increasing students' comprehension

**Semantics.** The content of language

**Seriation.** The ability to rank objects according to the degree to which they possess a certain common characteristic

**Severe disabilities.** Conditions that significantly affect typical life activities

**Sheltered English.** A type of ESL instruction in which the goal is to teach English language skills at the same time that students are learning content-area information

**Sight word.** Words that are recognized immediately upon seeing them

**Sight word association procedure.** A learning technique that helps students associate spoken words with their printed forms

**Silent or nonverbal period.** A time during which children are absorbing information and language that they cannot demonstrate or do not yet feel comfortable demonstrating

**Situational factors.** Factors related to the context or situation in which the second language learning occurs

**SLAM.** A strategy for teaching students to act and respond appropriately to negative feedback from others

**SMARTER.** The acronym used to remember the six steps of the Course Planning Routine

**Social action approach.** Incorporates all the elements of the transformation approach but also includes cultural critique and problem solving that require students to make decisions and take actions related to the concept, issue, or problem being studied

**Social competence.** Those responses that prove effective in a given situation or, in other words, maximize the probability of producing, maintaining, or enhancing positive effects for the interactor

**Social content.** The values represented in a textbook

**Socialized aggression.** Refers to students who routinely engage in antisocial behavior

**Social language.** Refers to the conversational competencies we develop with a second language—the greetings and "small talk" between peers, which generally do not require much cognitive effort or social problem solving

**Social learning.** Involves observing and modeling or imitating the behavior of others

**Social reinforcers.** Reinforcers such as notes of congratulations, handshakes, or positive notes home to parents

**Special education resource room.** A placement outside the general education classroom where students with disabilities receive specialized, individualized, and intensive instruction to meet their needs

**Specific learning disabilities (LD).** Represents a heterogeneous group of students who, despite adequate cognitive functioning and the ability to learn some skills and strategies quickly and easily, have great difficulty learning other skills and strategies

**Speech disorders.** Disorders that involve unintelligible or unpleasant communication

**Spelling patterns.** Common word patterns such as base words, prefixes, suffixes, consonants, consonant blends, digraphs, and vowel sound–symbol associations

**Spina bifida.** A birth defect that occurs when the spinal cord fails to close properly

**Spiral curriculum.** Occurs when the same skills (e.g., mathematics skills) are woven into every year of school and students continually repeat knowledge acquisition in the same area

**Stereotypic behavior.** Behaviors that characterize a disorder or condition such as rocking, flapping fingers, twirling or spinning objects, and grinding teeth

**Stimulant medications.** Medications that are frequently used in the treatment of attention-deficit and hyperactivity disorders

**Stimulus.** Something that incites activity or attention

**Story retelling.** Technique that actively involves students in the oral or written reconstruction of stories they have read or heard

**Story webs.** Developed as visual displays to help students understand the structure of the stories they read

**Structural analysis.** Involves the use of root words, prefixes, and suffixes to determine the pronunciation and meaning of a word, including multisyllable words and merged words such as compounds (buttermilk, pancake) and contractions (don't, can't)

**Student acceleration.** The rapid movement of students through their years of schooling

**Student-centered model.** An educational model in which students have ample opportunity to create personal meaning from what they are reading and writing

**Student-related factors.** Factors (which can and should influence the planning process) that pertain to who individual students are, how they learn, and how they respond to instruction, both academically and socially

**Students at risk.** Students who fail to succeed academically and who require additional instruction

**Study guides.** Tools teachers can use to lead students through a reading assignment

**Stuttering.** The most common fluency disorder, involving an interruption of the forward flow of speech

**Subject matter content.** Refers to comprehensiveness of content coverage and the currency and accuracy of information

**Substandard basic skills.** The ability to read, write, and compute at levels below those regarded as necessary for working in high-performance workplaces

**Syllabication.** Dividing words by common syllable types

**Syntax.** Focuses on the rules that govern the order of words in sentences

**Systems of support.** Refers to the coordinated set of services and accommodations matched to the student's needs

**TAG.** A strategy for students to provide each other with feedback about their writing

**Talent pool approach.** Procedure used to avoid overlooking students with exceptional talents and abilities who might not be identified through IQ tests or teacher nominations alone

**Tangible reinforcers.** Reinforcers such as food, magazines, clothes, or toys

**Task analysis.** A breakdown of each individual step or skill, with the necessary adaptations, that will be used as a guide for teaching the step or skill to the student

**Teacher assistance team (TAT).** A group of teachers who provide initial strategies and support for fellow classroom teachers before referring a student for assessment for special education services

**Teacher-related factors.** Factors that pertain to teachers as planners for their classes as a whole, as well as for students with special needs

**Team-Assisted Individualization.** Provision of individualized instruction within a cooperative learning model

**Thematic interdisciplinary approach.** An approach to learning that combines structured, sequential, and well-organized strategies, activities, children's literature, and materials used to expand a particular concept.

**THEMES.** A type of mnemonic used to plan an interdisciplinary unit (Think of themes; Hone the list; Extrapolate criteria; Manipulate the theme; Expand into activities; Select valued outcomes)

**Think alouds.** A way to model how to think and learn

**Think–pair–share.** A method that can be used during monitoring activities and that yields high student involvement and verbal interaction

**Time out.** Time during which the student is removed from the opportunity to receive reinforcement

**Token reinforcers.** Reinforcers such as smiley faces, stars, or check marks

**Token system.** A system in which students receive tokens in exchange for meeting classroom objectives and can exchange the tokens for rewards

**Tonic-clonic seizures.** A type of seizure that is characterized by convulsions followed by loss of consciousness

**Topic-related factors.** Factors that directly concern the topic of instruction

**Total blindness.** Refers to a very small minority of individuals who have visual impairments and who are unable to see anything, including objects or light sources

**Touch Math.** A program for teaching students math skills through math strategies (including the touch-point, counting-on, count-off, and count-by strategies)

**Tracking.** The practice of placing students with similar needs together for extended periods of the school day

**Transdisciplinary teaming.** Refers to a group of experts working together and viewing the student as a whole instead of working independently in a single specialty area

**Transformation approach.** The basic core of the curriculum is changed, and goals focus on viewing events, concepts, and themes from multiple perspectives, based on diversity

**Transitional bilingual education.** A program that helps students shift from the home language to the dominant language

**Traumatic brain injury.** An injury to the brain, caused by an external physical force, that causes total or partial functional disability or psychosocial impairment, or both, which adversely affects a student's educational performance

**TREE method.** A type of mnemonic used to plan the essay, (write a Topic sentence; think of Reasons to support the topic sentence; Examine your reasons; think of an Ending or conclusion)

**Tutoring.** A systematic plan for supplementing the student's educational program

**Two-way bilingual programs.** A program in which half the students are native speakers of English and the other half speak another language, usually Spanish. Instruction is delivered in English half the time and in the other language the other half

**Underachievers.** Individuals who have high academic or creative potential but low academic or creative performance

**Unidimensional traits.** The concept that human intelligence is made up of a unitary element

**Vibrant discussions.** Discussions in which student participation is high, students' thinking is stimulated, and students have opportunities to connect what they are learning to their personal knowledge and experience

**Visual acuity.** The clarity with which an individual can see an object from a distance of 20 feet

**Visual detail.** Ability to perceive details in the visual field. Difficulties in this area may lead to academic problems such as misreading an aspect of an arithmetic problem

**Visual field.** How well an individual can see using peripheral or side vision

**Vocabulary.** An individual's working knowledge of words

**Vocational Rehabilitation Act.** This act (P.L. 93–112) prevents any private organization that uses federal funds, or any local or state organization, from discriminating against persons with disabilities solely on the basis of those disabilities

**Voice disorders.** Disorders that relate to the quality of the voice itself

**Wait time.** Time provided to allow students to understand what has been said and to construct a response

**Whole-class grouping.** A grouping strategy in which the group comprises all students in the class

**Within-class same-ability grouping.** Occurs when students with the same abilities and from the same classroom are placed together for instruction

**Word identification.** A strategy for recognizing words involved in reading

**Word retrieval.** Finding words from memory

**Word wall.** A large, permanent bulletin board to which words are added each week and grouped in alphabetical order; used for word recognition and spelling

**Zero reject.** An element of IDEA that states that no child with disabilities can be excluded from receiving a free and appropriate education

Abikoff, H., Courtney, M. E., Szeibel, P. J., & Koplewicz, H. S. (1996). The effects of auditory stimulation on the arithmetic performance of children with ADHD and nondisabled children. *Journal of Learning Disabilities, 29*(3), 238–246.

Accardo, P., Blondis, T., & Whitman, B. (1991). *Attentional deficit disorders and hyperactivity in children.* New York: Marcel Dekker.

Achenbach, T. M. (2000). *Achenbach system of empirically based assessment.* Burlington: University of Vermont.

Achenbach, T. M., & Edelbrock, C. S. (1981). Behavior problems and competencies reported by parents of normal and disturbed children aged four through sixteen. *Monographs of the Society for Research in Child Development, 46* (1 Serial No. 188).

Adams, M. J. (1990). *Beginning to read: Thinking and learning about print.* Cambridge, MA: MIT Press.

Adderholdt-Eliot, M., Algozzine, K., Algozzine, B., & Haney, K. (1991). Current state practices in educating students who are gifted and talented. *Roeper Review, 14*(1), 20–23.

Adreon, D., & Stella, J. (2001). Transition to middle and high school: Increasing the success of students with Asperger syndrome. *Intervention in School and Clinic, 36,* 266–271.

Ahlberg, J., & Ahlberg, A. (1979). *Each peach pear plum.* New York: Viking Press.

Alarcon, M., DeFries, J. C., Light, J. G., & Pennington, B. F. (1997). A twin study of mathematics disability. *Journal of Learning Disabilities, 30*(6), 617–623.

Allan, S. D. (1991). Ability-grouping research reviews: What do they say about grouping and the gifted? *Educational Leadership, 48*(6), 60–65.

Allington, R. L. (1983). The reading instruction provided readers of differing ability. *Elementary School Journal, 83,* 548–559.

Allsopp, D. H. (1997). Using classwide peer tutoring to teach beginning algebra problem-solving skills in heterogeneous classrooms. *Remedial and Special Education, 18*(6), 367–379.

Alper, S., Schloss, P., & Schloss, C. (1994). *Families of students with disabilities.* Boston: Allyn & Bacon.

Alvermann, D. E. (1991). The discussion web: A graphic aid for learning across the curriculum. *The Reading Teacher, 45*(2), 92–99.

Alvermann, D. E., & Moore, D. W. (1991). Secondary school reading. In R. Barr, M. L. Kamil, P. B. Mosenthal, & P. D. Pearson (Eds.), *Handbook of reading research* (Vol. 2, pp. 951–983). New York: Longman.

Alvermann, D. E., O'Brien, D. G., & Dillon, D. R. (1989). What teachers do when they say they're having discussion of content reading assignments: A qualitative analysis. *Reading Research Quarterly, 25,* 296–322.

American Association on Mental Retardation. (1992). *Mental retardation: Definition, classification, and systems of supports* (9th ed.). Washington, DC: Author.

American Printing House for the Blind. (1999). *Distribution of eligible students based on the federal quota census of January 4, 1999.* Available: http://www.aph.org/fedquotpgm/dist99.html.

American Psychiatric Association. (1994). *Diagnostic and statistical manual of mental disorders: DSM-IV* (4th ed.). Washington, DC: American Psychiatric Association.

American Psychiatric Association. (2000). *Diagnostic and Statistical Manual of Mental Disorders: DSM-IV-TR* (4th ed., Text Rev.). Washington, DC: American Psychiatric Association.

American Speech-Language-Hearing Association. (1993). Definitions: Communicative disorders and variations. *ASHA, 35* (Suppl. 10), 40–41.

American Speech-Language-Hearing Association Committee on Prevention of Speech-Language and Hearing Problems. (1984). Prevention: A challenge for the profession. *ASHA, 26,* 35–37.

Amish, P. L., Gesten, E. L., Smith, J. K., Clark, H. B., & Stark, C. (1988). Social problem-solving training for severely emotionally and behaviorally disturbed children. *Behavioral Disorders, 13*(3), 175–186.

Andersen, E., Dunlea, A., & Kekelis, L. S. (1984). Blind children's language: Resolving some differences. *Journal of Student Language, 11*(3), 645–664.

Anderson, R. C. (1977). The notion of schemata and the educational enterprise. In R. C. Anderson, R. J. Spiro, & W. E. Montague (Eds.), *Schooling and the acquisition of knowledge* (pp. 415–431). Hillsdale, NJ: Erlbaum.

Anderson, R. C., Hiebert, E. H., Scott, J. A., & Wilkinson, I. A. (1985). *Becoming a nation of readers. The report of the commission on reading* (p. 7). Washington, DC: National Institute of Education.

Anderson, R. C., & Pearson, P. D. (1984). A schema-theoretic view of basic processes in reading. In P. D. Pearson (Ed.), *Handbook of reading research* (pp. 255–201). New York: Longman.

Appleton, N. (1983). *Cultural pluralism in education.* New York: Longman.

Arguelles, M. E., Schumm, J. S., & Vaughn, S. (1996). *Executive summaries for ESE/FEFP pilot program.* Report submitted to the Florida Department of Education.

Armbruster, B. B., & Anderson, T. H. (1988). On selecting "considerate" content area textbooks. *Remedial and Special Education, 9,* 47–52.

Aronson, E., Stephan, C., Sikes, J., Blaney, N., and Snapp, M. (1978). *The jigsaw classroom.* Beverly Hills, CA: Sage.

Asperger, H. (1944). Die "Autistischen Psychopathen" im Kindesalter. *Archiv für Psychiatrie und Nervenkrankheiten, 117,* 76–136.

Atwell, N. (1984). Writing and reading literature from the inside out. *Language Arts, 61,* 240–252.

Atwell, N. (1985). Writing and reading from the inside out. In J. Hansen, T. Newkirk, & D. Graves (Eds.), *Breaking ground: Teachers relate reading and writing in the elementary school* (pp. 147–168). Portsmouth, NH: Heinemann.

Atwell, N. (1987). *In the middle: Writing, reading, and learning with adolescents.* Portsmouth, NH: Boynton/Cook.

Au, K. (1993). *Literacy instruction in multicultural settings.* Fort Worth, TX: Harcourt Brace Jovanovich.

August, D., & Hakuta, K. (1997). *Improving schooling for language-minority children.* Washington, DC: National Academy Press.

Axelrod, S., & Hall, R. V. (1999). *Behavior modification: Basic principles.* Austin, TX: PRO-ED.

Ayllon, T. (1999). *How to use token economies and point systems.* Austin, TX: PRO-ED.

Babad, E., Bernieri, F., & Rosenthal, R. (1991). Students as judges of teachers' verbal and nonverbal behavior. *American Educational Research Journal, 28,* 211–234.

Babbitt, B. C., & Miller, S. P. (1996). Using hypermedia to improve the mathematics problem-solving skills of students with learning disabilities. *Journal of Learning Disabilities, 29*(4), 391–401.

Baca, L. M., & Cervantes, H. T. (1998). *The bilingual special education interface* (3rd ed.). Columbus, OH: Merrill.

Badian, N. A., & Ghublikian, M. (1983). The personal-social characteristics of children with poor mathematical computation skills. *Journal of Learning Disabilities, 16*(3), 154–157.

Baker, C. (1993). *Foundations of bilingual education and bilingualism.* Clevedon, England: Multilingual Matters.

Baker, J. M., & Zigmond, N. (1990). Are regular education classes equipped to accommodate students with learning disabilities? *Exceptional Children, 56,* 515–526.

Balla, D. A., & Zigler, E. (1979). Personality development in retarded persons. In N. R. Ellis (Ed.), *Handbook of mental deficiency: Psychological theory and research* (2nd ed., pp. 154–168). Hillsdale, NJ: Erlbaum.

Ballard, W. S., & Tighe, P. L. (Eds.). (1987). *Idea language proficiency test* (Level I & II). Brea, CA: Ballard & Tighe.

Bandura, A. (1971). *Psychological modeling.* Chicago: Aldine/Atherton.

Bandura, A. (1973). *Aggression: A social learning analysis.* Englewood Cliffs, NJ: Prentice-Hall.

Banks, J. A. (Ed.). (1981). *Education in the 80s: Multiethnic education.* Washington, DC: National Education Association.

Banks, J. A. (Ed.). (1996). *Multicultural education, transformative knowledge, & action: Historical and contemporary perspectives.* New York: Teachers College Press.

Banks, J. A. (1997a). Multicultural education: Characteristics and goals. In J. A. Banks and C. A. Banks (Eds.), *Multicultural education: Issues and perspectives* (3rd ed., pp. 1–28). Boston: Allyn & Bacon.

Banks, J. A. (1997b). Approaches to multicultural curriculum reform. In J. A. Banks and C. A. Banks (Eds.), *Multicultural education: Issues and perspectives* (3rd ed., pp. 195–214). Boston: Allyn & Bacon.

Banks, J. A. (1997c). *Teaching strategies for ethnic studies* (6th ed.). Boston: Allyn & Bacon.

Banks, J. A., & Banks, C. A. M. (Eds.). (1995). *Handbook of research on multicultural education.* New York: Macmillan.

Barkley, R. A. (1997). *Attention-deficit hyperactivity disorder and the nature of self-control.* New York: Guilford Press.

Barkley, R. A. (2000). *Taking charge of ADHD: The complete, authoritative guide for parents* (rev. ed.). New York: Guilford.

Barkley, R. A. (1998). *Attention-deficit hyperactivity disorder: A handbook for diagnosis and treatment* (2nd ed.). New York: Guilford Press.

Barkley, R. A., & Murphy, K. R. (1998). *Attention-deficit hyperactivity disorder: A clinical workbook* (2nd ed.). New York: Guilford Press.

Barnett, D. W., Carey, K. T., & Hall, J. D. (1993). Naturalistic intervention design for young children: Foundations, rationales, and strategies. *Topics in Early Childhood Special Education, 13*(4), 430–444.

Barr, R. (1995). What research says about grouping in the past and present and what it suggests about the future. In M. C. Radencich & L. J. McKay (Eds.), *Flexible grouping for literacy in the elementary grades* (pp. 1–24). Boston: Allyn & Bacon.

Barr, R., & Dreeben, R. (1991). Grouping students for reading instruction. In R. Barr, M. Kamil, P. Mosenthal, & P. D. Pearson (Eds.), *Handbook of reading research: Vol. 2. Literacy and schooling* (pp. 885–910). New York: Longman.

Barraga, N. C., & Erin, J. N. (2001). *Visual handicaps and learning* (3rd ed.). Austin, TX: PRO-ED.

Baumeister, J. J. (1995). ADD and Hispanic (Puerto-Rican) children: Some thoughts and research findings. *Attention, 2*(1), 16–19.

Bauwens, J., & Hourcade, J. J. (1995). *Cooperative teaching: Rebuilding the schoolhouse for all students.* Austin, TX: PRO-ED.

Bean, T. W. (1985). Classroom questioning: Directions for applied research. In A. C. Graesser & J. Black (Eds.), *Psychology of questions* (pp. 335–358). Hillsdale, NJ: Erlbaum.

Beck, A. R., & Dennis, M. (1997). Speech-language pathologists' and teachers' perceptions of classroom-based interventions. *Speech, Language, and Hearing Services in the Schools, 28,* 146–153.

Beck, I., & McKeown, M. G. (1981). Developing questions that promote comprehension: The story map. *Language Arts, 58,* 913–918.

Beck, I. L., McKeown, M.G., Worthy, J., Sandora, C. A., & Kucan, L. (1996). Questioning the author: A year-long classroom implementation to engage students with text. *The Elementary School Journal, 96*(4), 385–414.

Beirne-Smith, M. (1991). Peer tutoring in arithmetic for children with learning disabilities. *Exceptional Children, 57*(4), 330–337.

Beirne-Smith, M., Ittenbach, R., & Patton, J. (1998). *Mental retardation* (5th ed.). New York: Prentice-Hall Merrill Education.

Belenky, M. F., Clinchy, B. M., Goldberger, N. R., & Tarule, J. M. (1986). *Women's ways of knowing: The development of self, voice, and mind.* New York: Basic Books.

Bennett, T., Deluca, D., & Bruns, D. (1997). Putting inclusion into practice: Perspectives of teachers and parents. *Exceptional Children, 64*(1), 115–131.

Bereiter, C., & Scardamalia, M. (1982). From conversation to composition. In R. Glaser (Ed.), *Advances in instructional psychology* (Vol. 2). Hillsdale, NJ: Erlbaum.

Berger, S. L. (1994). *College planning for gifted students.* Reston, VA: Council for Exceptional Children.

Bergeron, B. (1990). What does the term whole language mean? Constructing a definition from the literature. *Journal of Reading Behavior, 22,* 301–329.

Bergstein, B. (1996, April). *Smoking linked to retarded babies.* Seattle, WA: The Seattle Times Company.

Berk, L. E. (2000). *Child development* (5th ed.). Boston: Allyn & Bacon.

Berko Gleason, J. (2001). *The development of language* (5th ed.). Boston: Allyn & Bacon.

Berler, E. S., Gross, A. M., & Drabman, R. S. (1982). Social skills training with children: Proceed with caution. *Journal of Applied Behavior Analysis, 15,* 41–53.

Berliner, D. C., & Biddle, B. J. (1995). The manufactured crisis: Myths, fraud, and the attack on America's public schools. Reading, MA: Addison-Wesley.

Berliner, D. C., & Casanova, U. (1993). *Putting research to work in your school.* New York: Scholastic.

Berner, R. (1977). What parents and teachers should know about death education. *DOPHHH Journal, 3,* 17–21.

Berninger, V., Abbott, R., Rogan, L., Reed, E., Abbott, S., Brooks, A., Vaughan, K., & Graham, S. (1998). Teaching spelling to children with specific learning disabilities: The mind's ear and eye beat the computer or pencil. *Learning Disability Quarterly, 21*(2), 106–122.

Bernstein, D. K., & Tiegerman, E. (2002). *Language and communication disorders in children* (5th ed.). New York: Macmillan.

Bernthal, J. E., & Bankson, N. W. (1998). *Articulation and phonological disorders* (4th ed.). Boston: Allyn & Bacon.

Beverly, C. L., & Thomas, S. B. (1997). Developmental and psycho-social effects of HIV in school-aged population: Educational implications. *Education and Training in Mental Retardation and Developmental Disabilities, 32,* 32–41.

Bierman, K. L., & Furman, W. (1984). The effects of social skills training and peer involvement on the social adjustment of preadolescents. *Child Development, 55,* 151–162.

Bishop, D. V. M., & Adams, C. (1992). Comprehension problems in children with specific language impairments: Literal and inferential meaning. *Journal of Speech and Hearing Research, 35,* 119–129.

Blachman, B. A. (Ed.). (1997). *Foundations of reading acquisition and dyslexia: Implications for early intervention.* Mahwah, NJ: Erlbaum Associates.

Blachman, B. A. (2000). Phonological awareness. In M. L. Kamil, P. B. Mosenthal, P. D. Pearson, & R. Barr (Eds.), *Handbook of reading research* (vol. 3, pp. 251–284). Mahwah, NJ: Erlbaum.

Blankenship, T. (1984). Update: These school systems swear by the four-day school week because students work harder and face fewer distractions. *American School Board Journal, 171*(8), 32–33.

Bliatout, B., Downing, B., Lewis, J., & Yang, D. (1988). *Handbook for teaching Hmong-speaking students.* Folsom, CA: Folsom Cordova Unified School District, Southeast Asia Community Resource Center.

Bliss, C. (1965). *Semantography.* Sydney, Austrialia: Semantography Publications.

Bloom, L., & Lahey, M. (1978). *Language development and language disorders.* New York: John Wiley.

Bode, B. A. (1989). Dialogue journal writing. *The Reading Teacher, 42,* 568–571.

Boothroyd, A. (1988). *Hearing impairments in young children.* Washington, DC: A.G. Bell Association for the Deaf.

Borkowski, J. G., Estrada, M. T., Milstead, M., & Hale, C. A. (1989). General problem-solving skills: Relations between metacognition and strategic processing. *Learning Disability Quarterly, 12,* 57–70.

Borkowski, J. G., & Turner, L. A. (1990). Transsituational characteristics of metacognition. In W. Schneider & F. E. Weinert (Eds.), *Interactions among aptitudes, strategies, and knowledge in cognitive performance* (pp. 159–176). New York: Springer-Verlag.

Borland, J. H. (1989). *Planning and implementing programs for the gifted.* New York: Teachers College Press.

Bos, C. S. (1987). *Promoting story comprehension using a story retelling strategy*. Paper presented at the annual meeting of the Arizona Association for Children with Learning Disabilities Conference, Phoenix.

Bos, C., Coleman, M., & Vaughn, S. (2002). Reading and students with E/BD: What do we know and recommend? In K. L. Lane, F. M. Gresham, & T. E. O'Shaughnessy (Eds.), *Interventions for children with or at risk for emotional and behavioral disorders* (pp. 87–103). Boston, MA: Allyn & Bacon.

Bos, C. S., & Filip, D. (1984). Comprehension monitoring in learning disabled and average students. *Journal of Learning Disabilities, 17*, 229–233.

Bos, C. S., & Vaughn, S. (2002). *Strategies for teaching students with learning and behavior problems* (5th ed.). Boston: Allyn & Bacon.

Bos, C. S., Nahmias, M. L., & Urban, M. A. (1999). Targeting home-school collaboration for students with ADHD. *Teaching Exceptional Children, 31*(6), 4–11.

Bouchard, D., & Tetreault, S. (2000). The motor development of sighted children and children with moderate low vision aged 8–13. *Journal of Visual Impairment and Blindness, 94*(9), 564–573.

Bradley, J. M. (1975). *Sight word association procedure*. Unpublished manuscript, College of Education, University of Arizona, Tucson.

Bragstad, B. J., & Stumpf, S. M. (1982). *A guidebook for teaching study skills and motivation*. Boston: Allyn & Bacon.

Brandenburg, N. A., Friedman, R. M., & Silver, S. E. (1990). The epidemiology of childhood psychiatric disorders: Prevalence findings from recent studies. *Journal of the American Academy of Child and Adolescent Psychiatry, 29*, 76–83.

Bricker, D. D., & Cripe, J. W. (1992). *An activity-based approach to early intervention*. Baltimore: Paul H. Brookes.

Brigance, A. H. (1981). *Brigance Diagnostic Inventory of Essential Skills*. North Billerica, MA: Curriculum Associates.

Briggs, A., Austin, R., & Underwood, G. (1984). Phonological coding in good and poor readers. *Reading Research Quarterly, 20*, 54–66.

Brimer, R. W. (1990). *Students with severe disabilities: Current perspectives and practices*. Mountain View, CA: Mayfield Publishing.

Brooke, M. H. (1986). *A clinician's view of neuromuscular diseases* (2nd ed.). Baltimore: Williams & Wilkins.

Brophy, J. (1981). Teacher praise: A functional analysis. *Review of Educational Research, 51*, 5–32.

Brophy, J. (1988). Educating teachers about managing classrooms and students. *Teacher and Teacher Education, 4*, 1–18.

Browder, D. M., & Shear, S. M. (1996). Interspersal of known items in a treatment package to teach sight words to students with behavior disorders. *The Journal of Special Education, 29*(4), 400–413.

Brown, W. H., McEvoy, M. A., & Bishop, N. (1991). Incidental teaching of social behavior. *Teaching Exceptional Children, 24*(1), 35–38.

Brozo, W. G. (1990). Hiding out in the secondary classroom: Coping strategies of unsuccessful readers. *Journal of Reading, 33*, 324–328.

Bryan, T., Pearl, R., & Herzog, A. (1989). Learning disabled adolescents' vulnerability to crime: Attitudes, anxieties, experiences. *Learning Disability Quarterly, 5*, 51–60.

Bryant, B. R., & Rivera, D. P. (1997). Educational assessment of mathematics skills and abilities. *Journal of Learning Disabilities, 30*(1), 57–68.

Bryant, D. P., & Bryant, B. R. (1998). Using assistive technology adaptations to include students with learning disabilities in cooperative learning activities. *Journal of Learning Disabilities, 31*(1), 41–54.

Bryant, N. D., Drabin, I. R., & Gettinger, M. (1981). Effects of varying unit size on spelling achievement in learning disabled children. *Journal of Learning Disabilities, 14*(4), 200–203.

Budden, S. S. (1996). Intrauterine exposure to drugs and alcohol: How do the children fare? *Medscape Women's Health, 1*(10). Retrieved November 20, 1996, from http://www.unhooked.com/sep/intrauter.htm

Buhrow, M. M., Hartshorne, T. S., & Bradley-Johnson, S. (1998). Parents' and teachers' rating of social skills of elementary-aged students who are blind. *Journal of Visual Impairment and Blindness, 92*(7), 503–511.

Bulgren, J., Schumaker, J. B., & Deshler, D. D. (1988). Effectiveness of a concept teaching routine in enhancing the performance of LD students in secondary-level mainstream classes. *Learning Disabilities Quarterly, 11*, 3–17.

Bullis, M., & Walker, H. M. (1994). *Comprehensive school-based systems for troubled youth*. Eugene, OR: University of Oregon, Center on Human Development.

Bullock, J. (1991). *Touch Math*. Colorado Springs: Innovative Learning Concepts.

Burcham, B. G., & DeMers, S. T. (1995). Comprehensive assessment of children and youth with ADHD. *Intervention in School and Clinic, 34*, 211–220.

Burke, J. C. (1992). *Decreasing classroom behavior problems: Practical guidelines for teachers*. San Diego, CA: Singular.

Burt, M., Dulay, H., & Hernández-Chávez, E. (1975, 1980). *Bilingual syntax measure* (Level I & II). San Antonio, TX: The Psychological Corporation.

Bussing, R., Zima, B. T., Belin, T. R., & Forness, S. R. (1998). Children who qualify for LD and SED programs: Do they differ in level of ADHD symptoms and comorbid psychiatric conditions? *Behavioral Disorders, 23*(2), 85–97.

Button, H. W., & Provenzo, E. F. (1983). *History of education and culture in America*. Englewood Cliffs, NJ: Prentice-Hall.

California State Department of Education. (1996). *The California Reading Initiative*. Sacramento, CA: Author.

Calkins, L. M. (1991). *Living between the lines*. Portsmouth, NH: Heinemann.

Campbell, L. (1997). Variations on a theme: How teachers interpret MI theory. *Educational Leadership, 55*, 14–19.

Candlelighters Childhood Cancer Foundation. (1993). Advice to educators (adapted from a survey by A Wish with Wings). In *Educating the child with cancer* (pp. 21–22). Bethesda, MD: Author.

Canfield, J., & Wells, H. C. (1994). *100 ways to enhance self-concept in the classroom*. Boston: Allyn & Bacon.

Carlberg, C., & Kavale, K. (1980). The efficacy of special versus regular class placement for exceptional children: A meta-analysis. *The Journal of Special Education, 14*, 295–309.

Carlson, R. (1984). *Picsyms categorical dictionary*. Lawrence, KS: Baggeboda Press.

Carnine, D. (1990). New research on the brain: Implications for instruction. *Phi Delta Kappan, 71*(5), 372–377.

Carnine, D. (1991). Curricular interventions for teaching higher order thinking to all students: Introduction to the special series. *Journal of Learning Disabilities, 24*(5), 261–269.

Carnine, D. (1997). Instructional design in mathematics for students with learning disabilities. *Journal of Learning Disabilities, 30*(2), 130–141.

Carpenter, D., & Miller, L. J. (1982). Spelling ability of reading disabled LD students and able readers. *Learning Disabilities Quarterly, 5*, 65–70.

Carpenter, S. L., & McKee-Higgins, E. (1996). Behavior management in inclusive classrooms. *Remedial and Special Education, 17*(4), 195–203.

Carr, E. G. (1977). The motivation of self-injurious behavior: A review of some hypotheses. *Psychological Bulletin, 84*, 800–816.

Carr, E. G., Levin, L., McConnachie, G., Carlson, J. I., Kemp, D. C., & Smith, C. E. (1994). *Communication-based intervention for problem behavior*. Baltimore: Brookes.

Carreker, S. (1999). Teaching spelling. In J. R. Birsh (Ed.), *Multisensory teaching of basic language skills* (pp. 217–256). Baltimore: Paul H. Brookes.

Carroll, J. (1964). *Language and thought*. Englewood Cliffs, NJ: Prentice-Hall.

Carter, T. P., & Chatfield, M. L. (1986). Effective bilingual schools: Implications for policy and practice. *American Journal of Education, 5*(1), 200–234.

Cartwright, G. P., Cartwright, C. A., & Ward, M. E. (1995). *Educating special learners*. Belmont, CA: Wadsworth.

Caspi, A., Henry, B., McGee, R. O., Moffitt, T. E., & Silva, P. A. (1995). Temperamental origins of child and adolescent behavior problems: From age 3 to age 15. *Child Development, 66*, 55–68.

Cassady, J. K. (2000). Wordless books: No-risk tools for inclusive middle-grade classrooms. In D. W. Moore, D. E. Alvermann, & K. A. Hinchman (Eds.), *Struggling adolescent readers: A collection of teaching strategies* (pp. 251–256). Newark, DE: International Reading Association.

Cassini, K. K., & Rogers, J. L. (1990). *Death in the classroom*. Cincinnati, OH: Griefwork.

Catts, H., Fey, M., Zhang, X., Tomblin, B. (2001). Estimating the risk of future reading difficulties in kindergarten children: A research-based model and its clinical implementation. *Language, Speech, and Hearing Services in Schools, 32*(1), 38–50.

Cawley, J. F. (1984). Selection, adaptation and development of curriculum and instructional materials. In J. F. Cawley (Ed.), *Developmental teaching of mathematics for the learning disabled* (pp. 227–251). Austin, TX: PRO-ED.

Cawley, J. F., Fitzmaurice, A. M., Sedlak, R., & Althaus, V. (1976). *Project Math*. Tulsa, OK: Educational Progress.

Cawley, J. F., Miller, J. H., & School, B. A. (1987). A brief inquiry of arithmetic word-problem-solving among learning disabled secondary students. *Learning Disabilities Focus, 2*(2), 87–93.

Cawley, J., Parmar, R., Foley, T. E., Salmon, S., & Roy, S. (2001). Arithmetic performance of students: Implications for standards and programming. *Exceptional Children, 67*, 311–328.

Cawley, J. F., Parmar, R. S., Yan, W. F., & Miller, J. H. (1996). Arithmetic computation abilities of students with learning disabilities: Implications for instruction. *Learning Disabilities Research and Practice, 11*(4), 230–237.

Chalfant, J. C., & Pysh, M. V. (1989). Teacher assistance teams: Five descriptive studies on 96 teams. *Remedial and Special Education, 10*(6), 49–58.

Chalfant, J. C., & Pysh, M. V. (1993). Teacher assistance teams: Implications for the gifted. In C. J. Maker (Ed.), *Critical issues in gifted education: Vol III. Gifted students in the regular classroom* (pp. 32–48). Austin, TX: PRO-ED.

Chalfant, J. C., Pysh, M. V., & Moultrie, R. (1979). Teacher assistance teams: A model for within—Building problem solving. *Learning Disability Quarterly, 2*, 85–96.

Chambliss, M. J. (1994). Evaluating the quality of textbooks for diverse learners. *Remedial and Special Education, 15*(6), 348–362.

Chamot, A. U. (1998). Effective instruction for high school English language learners. In R. M. Gersten & R. T. Jimenez (Eds.), *Promoting learning for culturally and linguistically diverse students* (pp. 186–209). Belmont, CA: Wadsworth.

Chamot, A., & O'Malley, J. M. (1994). *The CALLA handbook: Implementing the cognitive academic language learning approach*. Reading, MA: Addison-Wesley.

Chaney, C. (1998). Preschool language and metalinguistic skills are links to reading success. *Applied Psycholinguistics, 19*(3), 433–446.

Chappell, G. (1985). Description and assessment of language disabilities of junior high school students. In C. Simon (Ed.), *Communication skills and classroom success: Assessment of language-learning disabled students.* San Diego, CA: College-Hill.

Chard, D. J., & Dickson, S. V. (1999). Phonological awareness: Instructional and assessment guidelines. *Intervention in Clinic and School, 34*(5), 261–270.

Charles, C. M. (1989). *Building classroom discipline: From models to practice.* White Plains, NY: Longman.

Checkley, K. (1997). The first seven . . . and the eighth: A conversation with Howard Gardner. *Educational Leadership, 55,* 8–13.

Cheng, L. L. (1991). *Assessing Asian language performance.* Oceanside, CA: Academic Communication Associates.

Children and Adults with Attention Deficit Disorders. (1992). Testimony to the Senate and U.S. House of Representatives Subcommittee on Appropriations. *CH.A.D.D.ER, 6*(2), 24.

Children's Defense Fund. (2001). *Key facts: The uninsured.* Available: http://www.childrensdefensefund.org/

Chomsky, C. (1979). Approaching reading through invented spelling. In L. Resnick & P. Weaver (Eds.), *Theory and practice of early reading,* (Vol. 2, pp. 43–65). Hillsdale, NJ: Erlbaum.

Christensen, K. M., & Delgado, G. L. (Eds.). (1993). *Multicultural issues in deafness.* White Plains, NY: Longman.

Christenson, S., Thurlow, M., Ysseldyke, J., & McVicar, R. (1989). Written language instruction for students with mild handicaps: Is there enough quantity to ensure quality? *Learning Disability Quarterly, 12,* 219–229.

Christenson, S. L., Ysseldyke, J. E., & Thurlow, M. L. (1989). Critical instruction factors for students with mild handicaps: An integrative review. *Remedial and Special Education, 10*(5), 21–31.

Chung, J. P-L. (1992). *The out-of-class language and social experience of a clique of Chinese immigrant students: An ethnography of a process of social identity information.* Unpublished doctoral dissertation, State University of New York at Buffalo.

Ciborowski, J. (1995). Using textbooks with students who cannot read them. *Remedial and Special Education, 16*(2), 90–101.

Clarizio, H. F., & McCoy, G. F. (1983). *Behavior disorders in children.* New York: Crowell.

Clay, M. (1985). *Early detection of reading difficulties.* Portsmouth, NH: Heinemann.

Coelho, E. (1994). Social integration of immigrant and refugee children. In F. Genesee (Ed.), *Educating second language children: The whole child, the whole curriculum, the whole community* (pp. 301–328). Cambridge, England: Cambridge University Press.

Cohen, E., Conway, R., & Gow, L. (1988). Mainstreaming special class students with mild handicaps through group instruction. *Remedial and Special Education, 9*(5), 34–41.

Cohn, S. J. (1981). What is giftedness? A multidimensional approach. In A. H. Karmer (Ed.), *Gifted children: Challenging their potential.* New York: Trillium.

Coldwell, J. (1997). *Introducing word families through literature.* Greensboro, NC: Carson-Dellosa.

Coleman, M., Webber, J., & Algozzine, B. (1999). Inclusion and students with emotional/behavioral disorders. *Special Services in the Schools, 15*(1/2), 25–47.

Coleman, M. C., & Webber, J. (2002). *Emotional and behavioral disorders: Theory and practice.* Boston: Allyn & Bacon.

Coleman, M. R., & Gallagher, J. J. (1995). The successful blending of gifted education with middle schools and cooperative learning: Two studies. *Journal for the Education of the Gifted, 18*(4), 363–384.

Coleman, P., Koppenhaver, D. A., & Yoder, D. E. (1991). *Emerging literacy activities for preschool augmentative communicators.* Unpublished manuscript.

Collier, V. P. (1989, April). *Academic achievement, attitudes, and occupations among graduates of two-way bilingual classes.* Paper presented at the annual meeting of the American Educational Research Association, San Francisco.

Collins, R. A., & Goldinher, M. R. (1984). *Evaluative Summary of the Dade County Public Schools Elementary Gifted Program.*

Colson, S. E., & Carlson, J. K. (1993). HIV/AIDS education for students with special needs. *Intervention in School and Clinic, 28*(5), 262–274.

Come, B., & Fredericks, A. D. (1995). Family literacy in urban schools: Meeting the needs of at-risk children. *The Reading Teacher, 48,* 566–570.

Conley, M. W. (1995). *Content reading instruction: A communication approach* (2nd ed.). New York: McGraw-Hill.

Conners, C. K. (1989). *Conners teachers rating scale.* Lawrence, KS: CS Pearson.

Connolly, A. J. (1985). *Key Math Teach and Practice.* Circle Pines, MN: American Guidance Service.

Cook, L., & Friend, M. (1995). Co-teaching: Guidelines for creating effective practices. *Focus on Exceptional Children, 28*(3), 1–16.

Cooper, H., & Nye, B. (1994). Homework for students with learning disabilities: The implications of research for policy and practice. *Journal of Learning Disabilities, 27*(8), 470–479.

Corkill, A. J. (1992). Advance organizers: Facilitators of recall. *Educational Psychology Review, 4,* 33–67.

Corn, A. L., & Koenig, A. J. (1996). Perspectives on low vision. In A. L. Corn & A. J. Koenig (Eds.), *Foundations of low vision: clinical and functional perspectives* (pp. 3–25). New York: American Foundation for the Blind.

Corn, A. L., Wall, R., & Bell, J. (2000). Impact of optical devices on reading rates and expectations for visual functioning of school aged children and youth with low vision. *Visual Impairment Research, 2,* 33–41.

Cortes, C. E. (1978). Chicano culture, experience and learning. In L. Morris, G. Sather, & S. Schull (Eds.), *Extracting learning styles from social/cultural diversity: A study of five American minorities.* Norman, OK: Southwest Teachers Corps Network.

Coulter, D. L. (Ed.). (1993). Special issue: Epilepsy and mental retardation. *American Journal of Mental Retardation, 98* (supplement), 1–62.

Council for Exceptional Children. (1991). Some statistical clues to today's realities and tomorrow's trends. *Teaching Exceptional Children, 24,* 80.

Cowart, D., & Fabre, A. (1986, March). *LEAP for success.* Paper presented at the meeting of the National Association of Laboratory Schools, New Orleans.

Cox, A. R. (1992). *Foundations for literacy: Structures and techniques for multisensory teaching of basic written English language skills (Alphabetic Phonics).* Cambridge, MA: Educators Publishing Service.

Crawford, J. (1995). *Bilingual education: History, politics, theory, and practice* (3rd ed.). Los Angeles: Bilingual Educational Services.

Crosby, E. A. (1993). The "at risk" decade. *Phi Delta Kappan, 74*(8), 598–604.

Cuccaro, K. (April 3, 1996). Teacher observations key in bilingual assessment. *Special Education Report, 22,* 1, 3.

Cummins, J. (1981). *Bilingualism and minority language children.* Toronto, Ontario: Institute for Studies in Education.

Cummins, J. (1984). *Bilingualism and special education: Issues in assessment and pedagogy.* Clevedon, England: Multilingual Matters.

Cummins, J. (1989). A theoretical framework for bilingual special education. *Exceptional Children, 56,* 111–119.

Cummins, J. (1991). Interdependence of first- and second-language proficiency in bilingual children. In E. Bialystok (Ed.), *Language processing in bilingual children.* Cambridge, England: Cambridge University Press.

Cummins, J. (1992). The empowerment of Indian students. In J. Reyhner (Ed.), *Teaching American Indian students* (pp. 1–12). Norman, OK: University of Oklahoma Press.

Cunningham, A. E., & Stanovich, K. E. (1991). Tracking the unique effects of print exposure in children: Associations with vocabulary, general knowledge, and spelling. *Journal of Educational Psychology, 83,* 264–274.

Cunningham, P. M. (1995). *Phonics they use: Words for reading and writing* (2nd ed.). New York: HarperCollins.

Cunningham, P. M. (2000a). *Phonics they use: Words for reading and writing* (3rd ed.). New York: Longman.

Cunningham, P. M. (2000b). *Systematic sequential phonics they use: For beginning readers of any age.* Greensboro, NC: Carson-Dellosa.

Cunningham, P. M., & Cunningham, J. W. (1992). Making words: Enhancing the invented spelling-decoding connection. *The Reading Teacher, 46*(2), 106–115.

Cunningham, P., & Hall, D. (1994). *Making words.* Parsippany, NY: Good Apple.

Dale, E. (1969). *Audio visual methods in teaching* (3rd ed.). New York: Holt, Rinehart & Winston.

Dale, E., & Chall, J. (1948). A formula for predicting readability. *Educational Research Bulletin, 27,* 37–54.

D'Andrea, F. M., & Farrenkopf, C. (2000). *Looking to learn: Promoting literacy for students with low vision.* New York: AFB Press.

Darling-Hammond, L. (1997). *The right to learn: A blueprint for creating schools that work.* San Francisco: Jossey-Bass.

Davey, B. (1983). Think-aloud: Modeling the cognitive processes of reading comprehension. *Journal of Reading, 27,* 44–47.

Davis, G. A., & Rimm, S. B. (1989). *Education of the gifted and talented* (2nd ed.). Englewood Cliffs, NJ: Prentice-Hall.

De Avila, E., & Duncan, S. E. (1986). *Language assessment scales* (Includes PreLAS). Monterey, CA: McGraw-Hill.

De La Paz, S., & Graham, S. (1997). Strategy instruction in planning: Effects on the writing performance and behavior of students with learning difficulties. *Exceptional Children, 63*(2), 167–183.

De La Paz, S., Swanson, P. N., & Graham, S. (1998). The contribution of executive control to the revising by students with writing and learning difficulties. *Journal of Educational Psychology, 90*(3), 448–460.

Delquadri, J., Greenwood, C. R., Whorton, D., Carta, J. J., & Hall, R. V. (1986). Classwide peer tutoring. *Exceptional Children, 52*(6), 535–542.

Deno, S. L. (1985). Curriculum-based measurement: The emerging alternative. *Exceptional Children, 52,* 219–232.

Deshler, D. D., Ellis, E. S., & Lenz, B. K. (1996). *Teaching adolescents with learning disabilities* (2nd ed.). Denver, CO: Love.

Dettmer, P., Dyck, N., & Thurston, L. P. (1999). *Consultation, collaboration, and teamwork for students with special needs* (3rd ed.). Boston: Allyn & Bacon.

Diaz, R. (1983). Thought and two languages: The impact of bilingualism on cognitive development. *Review of Research in Education, 10,* 23–34.

Díaz-Rico, L., & Weed, K. Z. (1995). *The crosscultural, language, and academic development handbook: A complete K–12 reference guide.* Boston: Allyn & Bacon.

Dillon, J. (1979). Alternatives to questioning. *High School Journal, 62,* 217–222.

Di Vesta, F. J., & Smith, D. A. (1979). The pausing principle: Increasing the efficiency of memory for ongoing events. *Contemporary Educational Psychology, 4,* 288–296.

Donahue, M. L., & Baumgartner, D. (1997). Having the timeline of my life! *Teaching Exceptional Children, 29,* 38–41.

Donahue, P. L., Voelkl, K. E., Campbell, J. R., & Mazzeo, J. (1999). *NAEP 1998 reading report card for the nation and the states.* Available: http://nces.ed.gov/nationsreportcard/pubs/main1998/1999500.asp.

Doss, L., & Reichle, J. (1991). Replacing excess behavior with an initial communicative repertoire. In J. Reichle, J. York, & J. Sigafoos (Eds.), *Implementing augmentative and alternative communication: Strategies for learners with severe disabilities* (pp. 215–238). Baltimore: Paul H. Brookes.

Downing, J. E. (1996). *Including students with severe and multiple disabilities in typical classrooms: Practical strategies for teachers.* Baltimore: Brookes.

Downing, J., & Bailey, B. R. (1990). Sharing the responsibility: Using a transdisciplinary team approach to enhance the learning of students with severe disabilities. *Journal of Educational and Psychological Consultation, 1,* 259–278.

Downing, J., & Eichinger, J. (1990). Instructional strategies for learners with dual sensory impairments in integrated settings. *Journal of the Association for Persons with Severe Handicaps, 15*(2), 98–105.

Dreikurs, R., & Cassel, P. (1972). *Discipline without tears.* New York: Hawthorn.

Dreikurs, R., Grunwalk, B., & Pepper, F. (1982). *Maintaining sanity in the classroom.* New York: Harper & Row.

Drew, C. J., & Hardman, M. L. (2000). *Mental retardation: A life cycle approach* (7th ed.). Upper Saddle River, NJ: Merrill.

Drew, C. J., Hardman, M. L., & Logan, D. R. (1996). *Mental retardation: A life cycle approach* (6th ed.). Englewood Cliffs, NJ: Merrill/Prentice-Hall.

Dryfoos, J. G. (1994). *Full-service schools: A revolution in health and social services for children, youth, and families.* San Francisco: Jossey-Bass.

DuPaul, G. J., Power, T. J., Anatopoulos, A., D., & Reid, R. (1998). *ADHD Rating Scale IV: Checklists, norms, and clinical interpretation.* New York: Guilford.

Durand, V. M. (1990). *Severe behavior problems: A functional communication approach.* New York: Guilford.

Durden, W. G., Tangherlini, A. E. (1993). *Smart kids: How academic talents are developed and nurtured in America.* Kirkland, WA: Hogrefe & Huber Publishers.

Durkin, D. D. (1978–1979). What classroom observations reveal about reading comprehension instruction. *Reading Research Quarterly, 14,* 481–533.

Dusek, J. B., & Joseph, G. (1983). The bases of teacher expectancies: A meta-analysis. *Journal of Educational Psychology, 75*(3), 327–346.

Dweck, C. S., Kamins, M. L., & Person V. (1999). Process praise and criticism: Implications for contingent self-worth and coping. *Developmental Psychology, 35*(3), 835–847.

Dziwulski, M. (1994). *Developing literacy skills for persons with developmental disabilities: Some considerations.* Chapel Hill, NC: University of North Carolina, Clinical Center for the Study of Development and Learning.

Eber, L., Nelson, C. M., & Miles, P. (1997). School-based wraparound for students with emotional and behavioral challenges. *Exceptional Children, 63*(4), 539–555.

Echevarria, J. (1995). Interactive reading instruction: A comparison of proximal and distal effects of instructional conversations. *Exceptional Children, 61*(6), 536–552.

Echevarria, J., & Graves, A. (1998). *Sheltered content instruction: Teaching English-language learners with diverse abilities.* Boston: Allyn & Bacon.

Ehri, L. C. (1998). Grapheme-phoneme knowledge is essential for learning to read words in English. In J. Methsala & L. Ehri (Eds.), *Word recognition in beginning literacy* (pp. 3–40). Mahwah, NJ: Erlbaum Associates.

Ehri, L. D., & Wilce, L. S. (1983). Development of word identification speed in skilled and less skilled beginning readers. *Journal of Educational Psychology, 75,* 3–18.

Eiserman, W. D. (1988). Three types of peer tutoring: Effects on the attitudes of students with learning disabilities and their regular class peers. *Journal of Learning Disabilities, 21*(4), 249–252.

Elam, S. M., & Gallup, A. M. (1989). The 21st annual Gallup poll of the public's attitudes toward the public schools. *Phi Delta Kappan, 71,* 41–54.

Elbaum, B. E., Schumm, J. S., & Vaughn, S. (1995). *Students' perceptions of grouping formats for reading instruction.* Paper presented at the American Educational Research Association Conference, San Francisco.

Elbaum, B., & Vaughn, S. (2001). School-based interventions to enhance the self-concept of students with learning disabilities: A meta-analysis. *Elementary School Journal, 101*(3), 303–329.

Elbaum, B., Vaughn, S., Hughes, M., & Moody, S. W. (1999). Grouping practices for reading outcomes for students with disabilities. *Exceptional Children, 65*(3), 399–415.

Elbaum, B. E., Vaughn, S., Hughes, M. T., & Moody, S. W. (2000). How effective are one-to-one tutoring programs in reading for elementary students at risk for reading failure? *Journal of Educational Psychology, 92*(4), 605–619.

Elbaum, B., Vaughn, S., Hughes, M., Moody, S. W., & Schumm, J. S. (2000). How reading outcomes of students with disabilities are related to instructional grouping formats: A meta-analytic review. In R. Gersten, E. Schiller, & S. Vaughn (Eds.), *Contemporary special education research* (pp. 105–135). Mahwah, NJ: Lawrence Erlbaum Associates.

Elkonin, D. B. (1973). U.S.S.R. In J. Downing (Ed.), *Comparative reading* (pp. 551–579). New York: Macmillan.

Ellis, D. W., & Preston, F. W. (1984). Enhancing beginning reading using wordless picture books in a cross-age tutoring program. *The Reading Teacher, 37*(8), 692–698.

Ellis, E. (1991). *SLANT: A starter strategy for participation.* Lawrence, KS: Edge Enterprises.

Ellis, E. S. (1994). Integrating writing strategy instruction with content-area instruction: Part II—writing process. *Intervention in School and Clinic, 29,* 219–228.

Ellis, R. (1985). *Understanding second language acquisition.* Oxford, England: Oxford University Press.

Ellis, R. (1994). *The study of second language acquisition.* Oxford, England: Oxford University Press.

Emmer, E. T., Evertson, C. M., Sanford, J. P., Clements, B. S., & Worsham, M. E. (1989). *Classroom management for secondary teachers* (2nd ed.). Englewood Cliffs, NJ: Prentice-Hall.

Engelmann, S., Meyer, L., Carnine, L., Becker, W., Eisele, J., & Johnson, G. (1999). *Corrective reading program.* Columbus, OH: SRA/McGraw-Hill.

Engelmann, S., & Carnine, D. (1972). *DISTAR: Arithmetic Level III.* Chicago: Science Research Associates.

Engelmann, S., & Carnine, D. (1975). *DISTAR: Arithmetic Level I.* Chicago: Science Research Associates.

Engelmann, S., & Carnine, D. (1976). *DISTAR: Arithmetic Level II.* Chicago: Science Research Associates.

Engelmann, S., & Carnine, D. (1982). *Corrective mathematics program.* Chicago: Science Research Associates.

Englert, C. S., Berry, R., & Dunsmore, K. (2001). A case study of the apprenticeship process: Another perspective on the apprentice and the scaffolding metaphor. *Journal of Learning Disabilities, 34*(2), 152–171.

Englert, C. S., & Raphael, T. E. (1988). Constructive well-formed prose: Process, structure, and metacognitive knowledge. *Exceptional Children, 54,* 513–520.

Englert, C. S., Raphael, T. E., Anderson, L. M., Anthony, H. M., Fear, K. L., & Gregg, D. D. (1988). A case for writing intervention: Strategies for writing informational text. *Learning Disabilities Focus, 3*(2), 98–113.

Englert, C. S., Raphael, R. E., & Mariage, T. V. (1994). Developing a school-based discourse for literacy learning: A principled search for understanding. *Learning Disability Quarterly, 17,* 2–32.

Epstein, J. L., & Becker, J. H. (1982). Teacher practices of parent involvement. *The Elementary School Journal, 83,* 103–113.

Erickson, F., & Mohatt, G. (1982). Cultural organization and participation structures in two classrooms of Indian students. In G. Spindler (Ed.), *Doing the ethnography of schooling* (pp. 141–174). New York: Holt, Rinehart & Winston.

Ervin-Tripp, S. (1974). Is second language learning like the first? *TESOL Quarterly, 8* (June), 111–127.

Evans, I. M., & Meyer, L. H. (1985). *An educative approach to behavior problems: A practical decision model for interventions with severely handicapped learners.* Baltimore: Brookes.

Falvey, M. A. (1995). *Inclusive and heterogeneous schooling: Assessment, curriculum, and instruction.* Baltimore: Brookes.

Farrell, D. T., Smith, S. W., & Brownell, M. T. (1998). Teacher perceptions of level system effectiveness on the behavior of students with emotional or behavioral disorder. *Journal of Special Education, 32*(2), 89–98.

Fearn, L., & Farnam, N. (1998). *Writing effectively: Helping children master the conventions of writing.* Boston: Allyn & Bacon.

Feldhusen, J. F. (1998, June). Programs for the gifted few or talent development for the many? *Phi Delta Kappan, 79,* 735–738.

Feldhusen, J., Van Tassel-Baska, J., & Seeley, K. (1989). *Excellence in educating the gifted.* Denver, CO: Love.

Feldman, S. (1997). Passing on failure. *American Educator, 21*(3), 4–10.

Ferguson, D. L., & Baumgart, D. (1991). Partial participation revisited. *Journal for the Association for Persons with Severe Handicaps, 16,* 218–227.

Ferrara, R. A. (1987). Learning mathematics in the zone of proximal development: The importance of flexible use of knowledge. Unpublished doctoral dissertation, University of Illinois, Urbana-Champaign.

Ferrell, K. A. (1996). Your child's development. In M. C. Holbrook (Ed.), *Children with visual impairments* (pp. 73–96). Bethesda, MD: Woodbine House.

Ferrell, K. A. (2000). Growth and development of young children. In M. C. Holbrook & A. J. Koenig (1993), *Foundations of education: Instructional strategies for teaching children and youth with visual impairments* (Vol. I, 135–160, 2nd ed.). New York: AFB Press.

Fettler, F., & Tokar, E. (1982). Getting a handle on teacher stress. *Educational Leadership, 39,* 456–457.

Fimian, M. J., Zoback, M. S., & D'Alonzo, B. J. (1983). Classroom organization and synthesization. In B. J. D'Alonzo (Ed.), *Educating adolescents with learning and behavior problems* (pp. 123–151). Rockville, MD: Aspen.

Flannery, K. B., & Horner, R. H. (1994). The relationship between predictability and problem behavior for students with severe disabilities. *Journal of Behavioral Education, 4,* 157–176.

Fletcher, J. B., Francis, D. J., Shaywitz, S. E., Lyon, G. R., Foorman, B. R., Stuebing, K. K., & Shaywitz, B. A. (1998). Intelligent testing and the discrepancy model for children with learning disabilities. *Learning Disabilities Research and Practice, 13,* 186–203.

Flexer, C. (2000). The startling possibility of sound field. *Advance for Speech-Language Pathologists and Audiologists, 36,* 5, 13.

Floyd, C. (1954). Meeting children's reading needs in the middle grades: A preliminary report. *Elementary School Journal, 55,* 99–103.

Fogarty, R. (1994). Thinking about themes: Hundreds of themes. *Middle School Journal, 25*(4), 30–31.

Fombonne, E. (1999). The epidemiology of autism: A review. *Psychological Medicine, 29,* 769–786.

Foorman, B. R., Francis, D. J., Fletcher, J. M., Schatschneider, C., & Mehta, P. (1998). The role of instruction in learning to read: Preventing reading failure in at-risk children. *Journal of Educational Psychology, 90,* 38–57.

Ford, D. Y. (1992). An American achievement ideology and achievement differentials among preadolescent gifted and non-gifted African American males and females. *Journal of Negro Education, 61,* 45–64.

Ford, D. Y. (1998). The underrepresentation of minority students in gifted education: Problems and promises in recruitment and retention. *The Journal of Special Education, 32*(1), 4–14.

Forest, M., & Lusthaus, E. (1989). Promoting educational equality for all students: Circles and maps. In S. Stainback, W. Stainback, and M. Forest (Eds.), *Educating all students in the mainstream of regular education* (pp. 45–57). Baltimore: Brookes.

Forness, S. R. (1973). The reinforcement hierarchy. *Psychology in the Schools, 10*(2), 168–177.

Forness, S. R. (1988). School characteristics of children and adolescents with depression. In R. B. Rutherford, C. M. Nelson, & S. R. Forness (Eds.), *Bases of severe behavioral disorders of children and youth.* Boston: Little, Brown.

Forness, S. R., & Kavale, K. A. (1993). The Balkanization of special education: Proliferation of categories and sub-categories for "new" disorders. *The Oregon Conference Monograph, 5,* ix–xii.

Forness, S. R., & Knitzer, J. (1992). A new proposed definition and terminology to replace "serious emotional disturbance" in Individuals with Disabilities Education Act. *School Psychology Review, 21,* 12–20.

Forness, S., & Kavale, K. (1999). Teaching social skills in children with learning disabilities: A meta-analysis of the research. *Learning Disability Quarterly, 19,* 2–13.

Foster, S. L., & Ritchey, W. L. (1979). Issues in assessment of social competence in children. *Journal of Applied Behavior Analysis, 12,* 625–638.

Fowler, M. (1992). *CH.A.D.D. educators manual: An indepth look at attention deficit disorders from an educational perspective.* Plantation, FL: Children and Adults with Attention Deficit Disorders.

Fowler, S. A., Schwartz, I., & Atwater, J. (1991). Perspective on the transition from preschool to kindergarten for children with disabilities and their families. *Exceptional Children, 58,* 136–145.

Fradd, S. H., & Lee, O. (2001). Needed: A framework for integrating standardized and informal assessment for students developing academic language proficiency in English. In S. R. Hurley, & J. V. Tinajero (Eds.), *Literacy assessment of second language learners* (pp. 130–148). Boston: Allyn & Bacon.

Friend, M. (2000). Perspective: Myths and misunderstandings about professional collaboration. *Remedial and Special Education, 21*(3), 130–132.

Friend, M., & Cook, L. (2000). *Interactions: Collaboration skills for school professionals* (3rd ed.). New York: Addison Wesley Longman.

Frisbee, K., & Libby, J. (1992). *All together now.* Concord, NH: Chubb Life America.

Frith, U. (1980). *Cognitive processes in spelling.* London: Academic Press.

Frose, V. (1981). Handwriting: Practice, pragmatism, and progress. In V. Frose & S. B. Straw (Eds.), *Research in the language arts: Language and schooling* (pp. 227–243). Baltimore: University Park Press.

Fry, E. B. (1977). Fry's readability graph: Clarifications, validity, and extension to level 17. *Journal of Reading, 21,* 242–252.

Fry, E. B., Fountoukidis, D. L., & Polk, J. L. (1985). *The new reading teacher's book of lists.* Englewood Cliffs, NJ: Prentice-Hall.

Frymier, J. (1992). Children who hurt, children who fail. *Phi Delta Kappan, 74*(3), 257–259.

Fuchs, D., & Fuchs, L. S. (1988). Mainstream assistance teams to accommodate difficult to teach students in general education. In J. L. Graden, J. E. Zins, & M. J. Curtis (Eds.), *Alternative educational delivery systems: Enhancing instructional options for all students* (pp. 49–70). Washington, DC: National Association of School Psychologists.

Fuchs, D., & Fuchs, L. S. (1994). Inclusive school movement and radicalization of special education reform. *Exceptional Children, 60,* 294–309.

Fuchs, D., Fuchs, L. S., & Bahr, M. W. (1990). Mainstream assistance teams: A scientific basis for the art of consultation. *Exceptional Children, 57*(2), 128–139.

Fuchs, D., Fuchs, L. S., & Burish, P. (2000). Peer-assisted learning strategies: An evidence-based practice to promote reading achievement. *Learning Disabilities Research and Practice, 15*(2), 85–91.

Fuchs, L. S., Bahr, C. M., & Reith, H. J. (1988). *Effects of goal structures and performance contingencies on the math performance of adolescents with learning disabilities.* Paper presented at the annual meeting of the American Association of Educational Research, New Orleans, LA.

Fuchs, L. S., & Fuchs, D. (1998). Treatment validity: A unifying concept for reconceptualizing the identification of learning disabilities. *Learning Disability Research and Practice, 13,* 201–219.

Fuchs, L. S., Fuchs, D., Hamlett, C. L., Phillips, N. B., & Bentz, J. (1994). Classwide curriculum-based assessment: Helping general educators meet the challenge of student diversity. *Exceptional Children, 60,* 518–537.

Fuchs, L. S., Fuchs, D., Hamlett, C. L., Walz, L., & Germann, G. (1993). Formative evaluation of academic progress: How much growth can we expect? *School Psychology Review, 22,* 27–48.

Fugate, D. J., Clarizio, H. F., & Phillips, S. E. (1993). Referral-to-placement ratio: A finding in need of reassessment? *Journal of Learning Disabilities, 26,* 413–416.

Furey, P. (1986). A framework for cross-cultural analysis of teaching methods. In P. Byrd (Ed.), *Teaching across cultures in the university ESL program.* Washington, DC: National Association of Foreign Student Advisors.

Gagne, F. (1991). Toward a differentiated model of giftedness and talent. In N. Colangelo & G. A. Davis (Eds.), *Handbook of gifted education* (pp. 65–80). Boston: Allyn & Bacon.

Gajria, M., & Salend, S. J. (1995). Homework practices of students with and without learning disabilities: A comparison. *Journal of Learning Disabilities, 28*(5), 291–296.

Galambos, S., & Goldin-Meadow, S. (1990). The effects of learning two languages on metalinguistic development. *Cognition, 34,* 1–56.

Gallagher, J. (1998, June). Accountability for gifted students. *Phi Delta Kappan, 79,* 739–742.

Gallagher, J. J., & Gallagher, S. A. (1994). *Teaching the gifted child* (4th ed.). Boston: Allyn & Bacon.

Gambrell, L. B. (1985). Dialogue journals: Reading-writing interaction. *The Reading Teacher, 38,* 512–515.

Garbarino, J. (1997). Educating children in a socially toxic environment. *Educational Leadership, 54*(7), 12–16.

Garcia, E. E. (1991). Effective instruction for language minority students: The teacher. *Journal of Education, 173*(2), 130–141.

Gardner, D. P. (1983). *A nation at risk: The imperative for education reform.* Washington, DC: U.S. Department of Education.

Gardner, H. (1983). *Frames of mind.* New York: Basic Books.

Gardner, H., & Hatch, T. (1989). Multiple intelligences go to school: Educational implications of the theory of multiple intelligences. *Educational Researcher, 18*(8), 4–9.

Garnett, K. (1992). Developing fluency with basic number facts: Intervention for students with learning disabilities. *Learning Disabilities Research and Practice, 7*(4), 210–216.

Garnett, K., & Fleischner, J. E. (1983). Automatization and basic fact performance of normal and learning disabled children. *Learning Disability Quarterly, 6*(2), 223–230.

Gaskins, I. W. (1996). *Word detectives: Benchmark extended word identification program for beginning readers.* Media, PA: Benchmark School.

Gast, D., Ault, M., Wolery, M., Doyle, P., & Belanger, S. (1988). Comparison of constant time delay and the system of least prompts in teaching sight word reading to students with moderate retardation. *Education and Training in Mental Retardation, 23,* 117–128.

Gearheart, B. R., Mullen, R. C., & Gearheart, C. J. (1993). *Exceptional individuals: An introduction.* Pacific Grove, CA: Brooks/Cole.

Geary, D. C. (1993). Mathematical disabilities: Cognitive neuropsychological, and genetic components. *Psychological Bulletin, 114,* 345–362.

Geary, D. C., Brown, S. C., & Samaranayake, V. A. (1991). Cognitive addition: A short longitudinal study of strategy choice and speed-of-processing differences in normal and mathematically disabled children. *Developmental Psychology, 27*(5), 787–797.

Gentry, J. R. (1982). An analysis of developmental spellings in GYNS AT WRK. *The Reading Teacher, 36,* 192–200.

Gerber, A. (1993). *Language related learning disabilities: Their nature and treatment.* Baltimore: Brookes.

Gerber, P. J., Ginsberg, R., & Reiff, H. B. (1992). Identifying alterable patterns in employment success for highly successful adults with learning disabilities. *Journal of Learning Disabilities, 25,* 475–487.

Gerber, P. J., & Popp, P. A. (1999, September/October). Consumer perspectives on the collaborative teaching model: Views of students with and without LD and their parents. *Remedial and Special Education, 20*(5), 288–296.

German, D. J. (1992). Word-finding intervention for children and adolescents. *Topics in Language Disorders, 13*(1), 33–50.

German, D. J. (1993). *Word finding intervention program.* Austin, TX: PRO-ED.

Gersons-Wolfensberger, D. C. M., & Ruijssenaars, W. A. J. J. M. (1997). Definition and treatment of dyslexia: A report by the committee on dyslexia of the Health Council of the Netherlands. *Journal of Learning Disabilities, 30*(2), 209–213.

Gersten, R., & Baker, S. (in press). Teaching expressive writing to students with learning disabilities: A meta-analysis. *Journal of Special Education.*

Gersten, R. M., & Jiménez, R. T. (Eds.). (1998). *Promoting learning for culturally and linguistically diverse students.* Belmont, CA: Wadsworth.

Gersten, R., Marks, S. U., Keating, T., & Baker, S. (1998). Recent research on effective instructional practices for content areas ESOL. In R. M. Gersten & R. T. Jiménez (Eds.), *Promoting learning for culturally and linguistically diverse students* (pp. 57–72). Belmont, CA: Wadsworth.

Gersten, R., Williams, J., Fuchs, L., & Baker, S. (1998). *Improving reading comprehension for children with disabilities: A review of research.* Final Report: Section 1, U.S. Department of Education Contract HS 921700.

Getch, Y. Q., & Neuharth-Pritchett, S. (1999). Children with asthma: Strategies for educators. *Teaching Exceptional Children, 31*(3), 30–36.

Giangreco, M. F., Cloninger, C. J., & Iverson, V. (1998). *Choosing outcomes and accommodations for children: A guide to educational planning for students with disabilities (COACH)* (2nd ed.). Baltimore: Brookes.

Giangreco, M. F., Edelman, S., Cloninger, C., & Dennis, R. (1993). My child has a classmate with severe disabilities: What parents of nondisabled children think about full inclusion. *Developmental Disabilities Bulletin, 21*(1), 77–91.

Gillies, R. M., & Ashman, A. F. (2000). The effects of cooperative learning on students with learning difficulties in the lower elementary school. *The Journal of Special Education, 34*(1), 19–27.

Gilligan, C. (1982). *In a different voice: Psychological theory and women's development.* Cambridge, MA: Harvard University Press.

Ginsburg, H. P. (1997). Mathematics learning disabilities: A view from development psychology. *Journal of Learning Disabilities, 30*(1), 20–33.

Glatthorn, A. A. (1990). Cooperative professional development: Facilitating the growth of the special education teacher and the classroom teacher. *Remedial and Special Education, 11*(3), 29–34, 50.

Gold, M., & Mann, D. (1972). Delinquency as a defense. *American Journal of Orthopsychiatry, 42,* 463–479.

Goldman, L. S., Genel, M., Bezman, R. J., & Slanetz, P. J. (1998). Report on MPH for the Council on Scientific Affairs, American Medial Association. *Journal of the American Medical Association, 279,* 1100–1107.

Goldman, S. R., Hasselbring, T. S., & The Cognition and Technology Group of Vanderbilt. (1997). Achieving meaningful mathematics literacy for students with learning disabilities. *Journal of Learning Disabilities, 30*(2), 198–208.

Goldman, S. R., Pellegrino, J. W., & Mertz, D. L. (1988). Extended practice of basic addition facts: Strategy changes in learning disabled students. *Cognition & Instruction, 5,* 223–265.

Goldstein, A. P., & Huff, C. R. (1993). *The gang intervention handbook.* Champaign, IL: Research Press.

Goldstein, S., & Goldstein, M. (1990). *Managing attention disorders in children.* New York: Wiley.

Gollnick, D. M., & Chinn, P. C. (1990). *Multicultural education in a pluralistic society* (3rd ed.). New York: Merrill.

Gonzalez, N., Moll, L. C., Floyd-Tenery, M. Rivera, A., Rendón, P., Gonzales, R., & Amati, C. (1995). Teacher research on funds of knowledge: Learning from households. *Urban Education, 29,* 443–470.

Good, T. L., & Brophy, J. E. (1994). *Looking in classrooms* (6th ed.). New York: HarperCollins College Publishers.

Goodlad, J. I. (1984). *A place called school.* New York: McGraw-Hill.

Goor, M. B., & Schwenn, J. O. (1993). Accommodating diversity and disability with cooperative learning. *Intervention in School and Clinic, 29*(1), 6–16.

Gordon, J., Vaughn, S., & Schumm, J. S. (1993). Spelling interventions: A review of literature and implications for instruction for students with learning disabilities. *Learning Disabilities Research & Practice, 8*(3), 175–181.

Gough, P. B. (1996). How children learn to read and why they fail. *Annals of Dyslexia, 46,* 3–19.

Graham, S., (1999). Handwriting and spelling instruction for students with learning disabilities. *Learning Disability Quarterly, 22,* 78–98.

Graham, S. (1992). Helping students with LD progress as writers. *Intervention in School and Clinic, 27,* 134–144.

Graham, S., & Freeman, S. (1986). Strategy training and teacher vs. student-controlled study conditions: Effects on LD students' spelling performance. *Learning Disability Quarterly, 9,* 15–22.

Graham, S., & Harris, K. (1989a). Cognitive training: Implications for written language. In J. Hughes & R. Hall (Eds.), *Cognitive behavioral psychology in the schools: A comprehensive handbook* (pp. 247–279). New York: Guilford.

Graham, S., & Harris, K. R. (1989b). Improving learning disabled students' skills at composing essays: Self-instructional strategy training. *Exceptional Children, 56,* 201–214.

Graham, S., & Harris, K. (1997). Self-regulation and writing: Where do we go from here? *Contemporary Educational Psychology, 22,* 102–114.

Graham, S., Harris, K. R., MacArthur, C. A., & Schwartz, S. (1991). Writing and writing instruction for students with learning disabilities: Review of a research program. *Learning Disability Quarterly, 19,* 2–89.

Graham, S., & Miller, L. (1979). Spelling research and practice: A unified approach. *Focus on Exceptional Children, 13*(2), 1–16.

Graham, S., & Miller, L. (1980). Handwriting research and practice: A unified approach. *Focus on Exceptional Children, 13*(2), 1–16.

Grant, C. A., & Sleeter, C. E. (1993). Race, class, gender, and disability in the classroom. In J. A. Banks and C. A. Banks (Eds.), *Multicultural education: Issues and perspectives* (2nd ed., pp. 48–67). Boston: Allyn & Bacon.

Graves, A. W., Valles, E. C., & Rueda, R. (2000). Variations in interactive writing instruction: A study in four bilingual special education settings. *Learning Disabilities Research & Practice, 15*(3), 1–9.

Graves, D. H. (1983). *Writing: Teachers and children at work.* Portsmouth, NH: Heinemann Educational Books.

Graves, D. H. (1985). All children can write. *Learning Disability Focus, 1*(1), 36–43.

Graves, D. H. (1994). *A fresh look at writing.* Portsmouth, NH: Heinemann.

Greenbaum, S. (1989). *Set straight on bullies.* Encino, CA: National School Safety Center.

Greenwood, C. R., Carta, J. J., Arreaga-Mayer, C., & Rager, A. (1991). The behavior analyst consulting model: Identifying and validating naturally effective instructional models. *Journal of Behavioral Education, 1,* 165–191.

Greenwood, C. R., & Delquadri, J. (1995). Classwide peer tutoring and the prevention of school failure. *Preventing School Failure, 39*(4), 21–25.

Gresham, F. M., Sugai, G., & Horner, R. H. (2001). Interpreting outcomes of social skills training for students with high-incidence disabilities. *Exceptional Children, 67*(3), 331–344.

Griffin-Shirley, N., Trusty, S., & Rickard, R. (2000). Orientation and mobility. In A. J. Koenig & M. C. Holbrook (Eds.), *Foundations of education: Instructional strategies for teaching children and youth with visual impairments* (2nd ed., Vol. 2, pp. 529–568). New York: AFB Press.

Griffith, P. L., Rogers-Adkinson, D. L., & Cusick, G. M. (1997). Comparing language disorders in two groups of students with severe behavioral disorders. *Behavioral Disorders, 22*(3), 160–166.

Grossman, H. (1995). *Special education in a diverse society.* Boston: Allyn & Bacon.

Grossman, H. J. (1983). *Classification in mental retardation.* Washington, DC: American Association on Mental Deficiency (now Retardation).

Gulland, D. M., & Hinds-Howell, D. G. (1986). *The Penguin dictionary of English idioms.* London: Penguin.

Gunning, T. G. (1998). *Assessing and correcting reading and writing difficulties.* Boston: Allyn & Bacon.

Gunning, T. G. (2000). *Creating literacy instruction for all children* (3rd ed.). Boston: Allyn and Bacon.

Guyer, B. P. (Ed.). (2001). *ADHD: Achieving success in school and life.* Boston: Allyn & Bacon.

Haager, D., & Vaughn, S. (1995). Parent, teacher, peer, and self-reports of the social competence of students with learning disabilities. *Journal of Learning Disabilities, 28*(4), 205–215.

Hadaway, N. L., & Mundy, J. (2000). Children's informational picture books visit a secondary ESL classroom. In D. W. Moore, D. E. Alvermann, & K. A. Hinchman (Eds.), *Struggling adolescent readers: A collection of teaching strategies* (pp. 83–95). Newark, DE: International Reading Association.

Hagin, R. A. (1983). Write right or left: A practical approach to handwriting. *Journal of Learning Disabilities, 16,* 266–271.

Hakuta, K. (1974). A report on the development of grammatical morphemes in a Japanese girl learning English as a second language. *Working Papers in Bilingualism* (Vol. 4, pp. 18–44). Toronto: OISE Press.

Hale-Benson, J. E. (1986). *Black children: Their roots, culture, and learning styles* (rev. ed.). Baltimore, MD: Johns Hopkins University Press.

Hall, R. V., & Hall, M. L. (1999a). *How to use planned ignoring (extinction).* Austin, TX: PRO-ED.

Hall, R. V., & Hall, M. L. (1999b). *How to use time-out.* Austin, TX: PRO-ED.

Hallahan, D. P. (1992). Some thoughts on why the prevalence of learning disabilities has increased. *Journal of Learning Disabilities, 25*(8), 523–528.

Hallahan, D. P., & Kauffman, J. M. (1991). *Exceptional children: Introduction to special education* (5th ed.). Englewood Cliffs, NJ: Prentice-Hall.

Hallenbeck, B. A., & Kauffman, J. A. (1995). How does observational learning affect the behavior of students with emotional or behavioral disorders? A review of research. *The Journal of Special Education, 29*, 45–71.

Hallinan, M. T., & Sorensen, A. B. (1985). Ability grouping and student friendships. *American Educational Research Journal, 22*(4), 485–499.

Hallowell, E. M., & Ratey, J. J. (1995). *Driven to distraction: Recognizing and coping with attention deficit disorder from childhood through adulthood.* New York: Touchstone.

Hamre-Nietupski, S. Nietupski, J., & Strathe, J. (1992). Functional life skills, academic skills, and friendship/social relationship development: What do parents of students with moderate/severe/profound disabilities value? *Journal for the Association for Persons with Severe Handicaps, 17*, 53–58.

Hamstra-Bletz, L., & Blote, A. W. (1993). A longitudinal study on dysgraphic handwriting in primary school. *Journal of Learning Disabilities, 26*, 689–699.

Hanline, M. F., & Knowlton, A. (1988). A collaborative model for providing support to parents during their child's transition from infant intervention to preschool special education public school programs. *Journal of the Division for Early Childhood, 12*, 116–125.

Hanover, S. (1983). Handwriting comes naturally? *Academic Therapy, 18*, 407–412.

Hansen, J. (1985). Skills. In J. Hansen, T. Newkirk, and D. Graves (Eds.), *Breaking ground: Teachers relate reading and writing in the elementary school* (pp. 147–168). Portsmouth, NH: Heinemann.

Hanson, C. J., & Carta, J. J. (1996). Addressing the challenges of families with multiple risks. *Exceptional Children, 62*(3), 201–212.

Hanson, M. J., & Lynch, E. W. (1989). *Early intervention.* Austin, TX: PRO-ED.

Harper, G. F., Mallete, B., & Moore, J. (1991). Peer-mediated instruction: Teaching spelling to primary school children with mild disabilities. *Reading, Writing and Learning Disabilities, 7*, 137–151.

Harris, K. R., & Graham, S. (1992). *Helping young writers master the craft: Strategy instruction and self-regulation in the writing process.* Boston: Brookline Books.

Harris, K. R., Graham, S., Reid, R., McElroy, K., & Hamby, R. S. (1994). Self-monitoring of attention versus self-monitoring of performance: Replication and cross-task comparison studies. *Learning Disability Quarterly, 17*, 121–139.

Harris, L., & Associates. (1994). *National organization on disability/Harris survey of Americans with disabilities.* New York: Author.

Harry, B., Allen, N., & McLaughlin, M. (1995). Communication versus compliance: African-American parents' involvement in special education. *Exceptional Children, 6*(4), 364–377.

Hart, B. (1985). Naturalistic language training techniques. In S. F. Warren & A. Rogers-Warren (Eds.), *Teaching functional language* (pp. 63–85). Austin, TX: PRO-ED.

Hart, B., & Risley, T. R. (1982). *How to use incidental teaching for elaborating language.* Austin, TX: PRO-ED.

Hasazi, S. B., Johnson, R. E., Hasazi, J., Gordon, L. R., & Hull, M. (1989). A statewide follow-up of high school exiters: A comparison of former students with and without handicaps. *Journal of Special Education, 23*, 243–255.

Hasbrouck, J. E., & Tindal, G. (1992). Curriculum-based oral reading fluency norms for students in grades 2 through 5. *Teaching Exceptional Children, 24*(3), 41–44.

Hazel, J. S., Schumaker, J. B., Sherman, J. A., & Sheldon-Wildgen, J. (1982). Group training for social skills: A program for court-adjudicated, probationary youths. *Criminal Justice and Behavior, 9*, 35–53.

Heald-Taylor, B. G. (1984). Scribble in first grade writing. *The Reading Teacher, 38*(1), 4–9.

Healy, M. K., & Barr, M. (1991). Language across the curriculum. In J. Flood, J. M. Jensen, D. Lapp, & J. R. Squire (Eds.), *Handbook of research on teaching the English language arts* (pp. 820–826). New York: Macmillan.

Hechtman, L., Weiss, G., & Perlman, T. (1980). Hyperactives as young adults: Self-esteem and social skills. *Canadian Journal of Psychiatry, 25*(6), 478–483.

Hedge, M. N. (1996). *A coursebook on language disorders in children.* San Diego: Singular Publishing Group.

Helmstetter, E., & Durand, V. M. (1991). Nonaversive interventions for severe behavior problems. In L. Meyer, C. Peck, & L. Brown (Eds.), *Critical issues in the lives of people with severe disabilities* (pp. 559–600). Baltimore: Brookes.

Hendrickson, J. M., Shokoohi-Yekta, M., Hamre-Nietupski, S., & Gable, R. A. (1996). Middle- and high-school students' perceptions on being friends with peers with severe disabilities. *Exceptional Children, 63*, 19–28.

Henley, M., Ramsey, R. S., & Algozzine, R. (1993). *Characteristics of and strategies for teaching students with mild disabilities.* Boston: Allyn & Bacon.

Henry, M. (1997). The decoding/spelling curriculum: Integrated decoding and spelling instruction from preschool to early secondary school. *Dyslexia, 3*, 178–189.

Hepting, N. H., & Goldstein, H. (1996). What's natural about naturalistic language interventions? *Journal of Early Intervention, 20*(3), 249–265.

Heumman, J. E., & Hehir, T. (1997). Believing in children: A great IDEA for the future. *Exceptional Parent, 27*, 38–42.

Heward, W. L. (2000). *Exceptional children: An introduction to special education* (7th ed.). Englewood Cliffs, NJ: Prentice-Hall.

Hiebert, E. H. (1983). An examination of ability grouping for reading instruction. *Reading Research Quarterly, 18,* 231–235.

Hill, E. W., & Ponder, P. (1976). *Orientation and mobility techniques.* New York: American Foundation for the Blind.

Hill, J. L. (1999). *Meeting the needs of students with special physical and health care needs.* Upper Saddle River, NJ: Merrill.

Hilton, A., & Henderson, C. J. (1993). Parent involvement: A best practice or forgotten practice? *Education and Training in Mental Retardation, 28,* 199–211.

Hoctor, M., & Kaplan, S. (1989). *Developing policies for a gifted/talented program: A handbook.* Canoga Park, CA: California Association of the Gifted.

Hodges, R. E. (1991). The conventions of writing. In J. Flood, J. M. Jensen, D. Lapp, & J. R. Squire (Eds.), *Handbook of research on teaching the English language arts* (pp. 775–786). New York: Macmillan.

Hoff, K. E., & DuPaul, G. J. (1998). Reducing disruptive behavior in general education classrooms: The use of self-management strategies. *School Psychology Review, 27,* 290–303.

Hofmeister, A. M. (1989). Teaching problem-solving skills with technology. *Educational Technology, 29*(9), 26–29.

Hofmeister, A. M. (1993). Elitism and reform in school mathematics. *Remedial and Special Education, 14*(6), 8–13.

Holmes, C. T., & Matthews, K. M. (1984). The effects of nonpromotion on elementary and junior high school pupils: A meta-analysis. *Review of Educational Research, 54,* 225–236.

Horner, R., Sugai, G., Todd, A. W., & Lewis-Palmer, T. (1999–2000). Elements of behavior support plans: A technical brief. *Exceptionality, 8*(3), 205–215.

Hudson, F., Ormsbee, C. K., & Myles, B. S. (1994). Study guides: An instructional tool for equalizing student achievement. *Intervention in School and Clinic, 30*(2), 99–102.

Hudson, P., & Glomb, N. (1997). If it takes two to tango, then why not teach both partners to dance? Collaboration instruction for all educators. *Journal of Learning Disabilities, 30*(4), 442–448.

Hughes, M. T. (1995). *Parental involvement in literacy instruction: Perceptions and practices of Hispanic parents of children with learning disabilities.* Unpublished doctoral dissertation, University of Miami, Coral Gables, FL.

Hughes, M. T., Schumm, J. S., & Vaughn, S. (1999). Home literacy activities: Perceptions and practices of Hispanic parents of children with learning disabilities. *Learning Disability Quarterly, 22,* 209–222.

Hulit, L. M., & Howard, M. R. (1997). *Born to talk: An introduction to speech and language development* (2nd ed.). New York: Macmillan.

Hunt, P., Staub, D., Alwell, M., & Goetz, L. (1994). Achievement by all students within the context of cooperative learning groups. *Journal for the Association for Persons with Severe Handicaps, 19,* 290–301.

Hunter, M. (1982). *Mastery teaching.* El Segundo, CA: TIP.

Huntington, D. D., & Bender, W. N. (1993). Adolescents with learning disabilities at risk? Emotional well-being, depression, suicide. *Journal of Learning Disabilities, 26*(3), 159–166.

Hurley, S. R., & Tinajero, J. V. (Eds.). (2001). *Literacy assessment of second language learners.* Boston: Allyn & Bacon.

Hutchins, M. P., & Renzaglia, A. (1998). Interviewing families for effective transition to employment. *Teaching Exceptional Children, 30*(4), 72–78.

Hutchinson, N. L. (1993). Effects of cognitive strategy instruction on algebra problem solving of adolescents with learning disabilities. *Learning Disability Quarterly, 16,* 34–63.

Idol, L. (1987). Group story mapping: A comprehension strategy for both skilled and unskilled readers. *Journal of Learning Disabilities, 20,* 196–205.

Idol, L., Nevin, A., & Paolucci-Whitcomb, P. (2000). *Collaborative Consultation* (3rd ed.). Austin, TX: PRO-ED.

Idol, L., Paolucci-Whitcomb, P., & Nevin, A. (1986). *Collaborative consultation.* Rockville, MD: Aspen.

*Individuals with Disabilities Education Act.* (1990). Washington, DC: U.S. Government Printing Office.

Individuals with Disabilities Education Act. (1997 Amendments). Washington, DC: U.S. Government Printing Office.

Irvine, J. J. (1991). *Black students and school failure: Policies, practices, and prescriptions.* New York: Praeger.

Isaacson, S., & Gleason, M. M. (1997). Mechanical obstacles to writing: What can teachers do to help students with learning problems? *Learning Disabilities Research and Practice, 12*(3), 188–194.

Jacobs, D. H. (1994). Environmental failure: Oppression is the only cause of psychopathology. *Journal of Mind and Behavior, 15*(1–2), 1–18.

Jankowski, M. S. (1991). *Islands in the street: Gangs and American urban society.* Berkeley, CA: University of California Press.

Janney, R., & Snell, M. E. (2000) *Behavior supports.* Baltimore: Brookes.

Janney, R. E., Snell, M. E., Beers, M. K., & Raynes, M. (1995). Integrating students with moderate and severe disabilities into general education classes. *Exceptional Children, 61*(5), 425–439.

Jayanthi, M., Bursuck, W. D., Epstein, M. H., & Cumblad, C. (1992). [School reform: Impact of homework, testing, and grading on students with disabilities and their families]. Unpublished raw data.

Johnson, D. J., & Myklebust, H. R. (1967). *Learning disabilities: Educational principles and practices* (Report No. EC–001–107). New York: Grune & Stratton, Inc. (ERIC Document Reproduction Service No. ED 021 352).

Johnson, D., & Johnson, R. (1989). Cooperative learning: What special education teachers need to know. *Pointer, 33*(2), 5–10.

Johnson, D. T. (2000, April). *Teaching mathematics to gifted students in a mixed-ability classroom.* ERIC EC Digest #E 594.

Johnson, H. L., Pflaum, S., Sherman, E. Taylor, P., & Poole, P. (2000). Focus on teenage parents: Using children's literature to strengthen teenage literacy. In D. W. Moore, D. E. Alvermann, & K. A. Hinchman (Eds.), *Struggling adolescent readers: A collection of teaching strategies* (pp. 257–264). Newark, DE: International Reading Association.

Johnson, J. M., Baumgart, D., Helmstetter, E., & Curry, C. A. (1996). *Augmenting basic communication in natural contexts.* Baltimore: Brookes.

Johnson, L. J., & Pugach, M. C. (1991). Peer collaboration: Accommodating students with mild learning and behavior problems. *Exceptional Children, 57*(5), 454–461.

Johnson, R. (1985). *The picture communication symbols: Book II.* Solana Beach, CA: Mayer-Johnson.

Johnson, T. E., Chandler, L. K., Kerns, G. M., & Fowler, S. A. (1986). What are parents saying about family involvement in school transitions: A retrospective transition interview. *Journal of the Division for Early Childhood, 11,* 10–17.

Johnston, D. (1985). *Core picture vocabulary.* Wauconda, IL: Don Johnston Developmental Equipment.

Johnston, P., & Allington, R. (1991). Remediation. In R. Barr, M. L. Kamil, P. Mosenthal, & P. D. Pearson (Eds.), *Handbook of reading research* (Vol. 2, pp. 984–1012). New York: Longman.

Jones, E. D., Wilson, R., & Bhojwani, S. (1997). Mathematics instruction for secondary students with learning disabilities. *Journal of Learning Disabilities, 30*(2), 151–163.

Jordan, C. (1985). Translating culture: From ethnographic information to educational program. *Anthropology and Education Quarterly, 16,* 105–123.

Kagan, S., Zahn, G. L., Widaman, K. F., Schwarzwald, J., & Tyrell, G. (1985). Classroom structural bias: Impact of cooperative and competitive classroom structures on cooperative and competitive individuals and groups. In R. E. Slavin, S. Sharan, S. Kagan, R. Hertz-Lazarowitz, C. Webb, & R. Schmuck (Eds.), *Learning to cooperate, cooperating to learn* (pp. 177–209). New York: Plenum.

Kameenui, E. J., & Simmons, D. C. (1990). *Designing instructional strategies: The prevention of academic learning problems.* Columbus, OH: Merrill.

Kamhi, A. G. (1987). Metalinguistic abilities in language-impaired children. *Topics in Language Disorders, 7*(2), 1–12.

Kauffman, J. M. (1989). *Characteristics of children's behavior disorders* (4th ed.). Columbus, OH: Merrill.

Kauffman, J. M. (1993). *Characteristics of emotional and behavioral disorders of children and youth* (5th ed.). Columbus, OH: Merrill/Macmillan.

Kauffman, J. M., & Hallahan, D. P. (1995). *The illusion of full inclusion: A comprehensive critique of a special education bandwagon.* Austin, TX: PRO-ED.

Kazdin, A. (1993). Treatment of conduct disorder: Progress and directions in psychotherapy research. *Development and Psychopathology, 5*(1/2), 277–310.

Keilitz, I., & Dunivant, N. (1986). The relationship between learning disability and juvenile delinquency: Current state of knowledge. *Remedial and Special Education, 7*(3), 18–26.

Kelker, K., Hecimovic, A., & LeRoy, C. H. (1994). Designing a classroom and school environment for students with AIDS: A checklist for teachers. *Teaching Exceptional Children, 26*(4), 52–55.

Kelly, B., Carnine, D., Gersten, R., & Grossen, B. (1987). The effectiveness of videodisc instruction in teaching fractions to learning handicapped and remedial high school students. *Journal of Special Education Technology, 8*(2), 5–17.

Kelly, B., Gersten, R., & Carnine, D. (1990). Student error patterns as a function of curriculum design: Teaching fractions to remedial high school students and high school students with learning disabilities. *Journal of Learning Disabilities, 23,* 23–29.

Kelly, M. (1990). *School–home notes: Promoting children's classroom success.* New York: Guilford Press.

Kennedy, M. M., Birman, B. F., & Demaline, R. E. (1986). *The effectiveness of Chapter I services.* Washington, DC: U.S. Government Printing Office.

Keogh, B. K. (1993). Linking purpose and practice: Social-political and developmental perspectives on classification. In G. R. Lyon, D. B. Gray, J. R. Kavanagh, & N. A. Krasnegor (Eds.), *Better understanding learning disabilities* (pp. 311–323). Baltimore: Paul H. Brookes.

Kern, L., & Vorndran, C. M. (2000). Functional assessment and intervention for transition difficulties. *Journal of the Association for Persons with Severe Handicaps, 25,* 212–216.

King, T. W. (1999). *Assistive technology: Essential human factors.* Boston: Allyn & Bacon.

Kirk, S. (1963). *Behavior diagnosis of the perceptually handicapped children.* Proceedings of the Conference on Exploration into the Problems of the Perceptually Handicapped Children. Evanston, IL: Fund for the Perceptually Handicapped Child, Inc.

Kirk, S. A., Kirk, W. D., & Minskoff, E. (1985). *Phonic remedial reading lessons.* Octova, CA: Academic Therapy.

Kirstein, I., & Bernstein, C. (1981). *Oakland schools picture dictionary.* Pontiac, MI: Oakland Schools Communication Enhancement Center.

Kitano, M. K. (1973). Highlights of Institute on Language and Culture: Asian component. In L. A. Bransford, L. M. Baca, & K. Lane (Eds.), *Cultural diversity and the exceptional child* (pp. 14–15). Reston, VA: Council for Exceptional Children.

Kitzinger, M. (1984). The role of repeated and echoed utterances in communication with a blind child. *British Journal of Disorders of Communication, 19,* 135–146.

Klein, R. G., & Last, C. G. (1989). *Anxiety disorders in children.* Newbury Park, CA: Sage.

Klingner, J. K., & Vaughn, S. (1998). Using collaborative strategic reading. *Teaching Exceptional Children, 30*(6), 32–37.

Klingner, J. K., & Vaughn, S. (1999). Promoting reading comprehension, content learning, and English acquisition through collaborative strategic reading. *The Reading Teacher, 52*(7), 738–747.

Klingner, J. K., & Vaughn, S. (2000). The helping behaviors of fifth-graders while using collaborative strategic reading during ESL content classes. *TESOL Quarterly, 34*(1), 69–98.

Klingner, J. K., Vaughn, S., & Schumm, J. S. (1998a). Collaborative strategic reading during social studies in heterogeneous fourth-grade classrooms. *Elementary School Journal, 99,* 3–22.

Klingner, J. K., Vaughn, S., Hughes, M. T., Schumm, J. S., & Elbaum, B. (1998b). Outcomes for students with and without learning disabilities. *Learning Disabilities Research and Practice, 13*(3), 153–161.

Kloomok, S., & Cosden, M. (1994). Self-concept in children with learning disabilities: The relationship between global self-concept, academic "discounting," nonacademic self-concept, and perceived social support. *Learning Disability Quarterly, 17*(2), 140–153.

Knapp, M. S., & Turnbull, B. J. (1991). Alternatives to conventional wisdom. In M. S. Knapp & P. M. Shields (Eds.), *Better schooling for the children of poverty: Alternatives to conventional wisdom* (pp. 329–353). Richmond, CA: McCutchan Publishing Corporation.

Knapp, M. S., Turnbull, B. J., & Shields, P. M. (1990). New directions for educating the children of poverty. *Educational Leadership, 49*(1), 4–8.

Knitzer, J., Steinberg, Z., & Fleisch, B. (1990). *At the schoolhouse door.* New York: Bank Street College of Education.

Knoblauch, B. (1998). *Rights and responsibilities of parents of children with disabilities.* (ERIC Document Reproduction Service No. ED 419 326).

Kokaska, C. J., & Brolin, D. E. (1985). *Career education for handicapped individuals* (2nd ed.). New York: Merrill/Macmillan.

Kollott, P. B. (1991). Special residential high schools. In N. Colangelo & G. A. Davis (Eds.), *Handbook of gifted education.* Boston: Allyn & Bacon.

Korinek, L., & Bulls, J. A. (1996). SCOREA: A student research paper writing strategy. *Teaching Exceptional Children, 28,* 60–63.

Kortering, L., Haring, N., & Klockars, A. (1992). The identification of high-school dropouts identified as learning disabled: Evaluating the utility of a discriminant analysis function. *Exceptional Children, 58*(2), 422–435.

Kosc, D. (1981). Neuropsychological implications of and treatment of mathematical learning disabilities. *Topics in Learning and Learning Disabilities, 1*(3), 19–30.

Koskinen, P. S., Blum, I H., Bisson, S. A., Phillips, S. M., Creamer, T. S., & Baker, T. K. (1999). Shared reading, books, and audiotapes: Supporting diverse students in school and at home. *The Reading Teacher, 52,* 430–444.

Kovacs, M., Paulauskas, S., Gatsonis, C., & Richards, C. (1988). Depressive disorders in childhood: A longitudinal study of comorbidity with and risk for conduct disorders. *Journal of Affective Disorders, 15,* 205–217.

Koziol, S. (1973). The development of noun plural rules during the primary grades. *Research in the Teaching of English, 7,* 30–50.

Kozma, C., & Stock, J. S. (1993). What is mental retardation? In R. Smith (Ed.), *Children with mental retardation* (pp. 1–49). Rockville, MD: Woodbine House.

Krashen, S. (1985) *The input hypothesis: Issues and implications.* London: Longman.

LaBerge, D., & Samuels, S. J. (1974). Toward a theory of automatic information processing in reading. *Cognitive Psychology, 6,* 293–323.

Labov, W., Cohen, P., Robins, C., & Lewis, J. (1968). *A study of the non-standard English of Negro and Puerto Rican speakers in New York City* (Report on Cooperative Research Project 3288). New York: Columbia University.

Ladson-Billings, G. (1995). Toward a theory of culturally relevant pedagogy. *American Educational Research Journal, 32,* 465–491.

Lahey, M. (1988). *Language disorders and language development.* New York: Macmillan.

Lambert, N., Nihira, K., & Leland, H. (1993). *AAMR Adaptive Behavior Scale—School: Examiner's manual* (2nd ed.). Austin, TX: PRO-ED.

Lampert, M., & Clark, C. (1990). Expert knowledge and expert thinking in teachers: A response to Floden and Klinzing. *Educational Researcher, 19,* 18–25.

Lanauze, M., & Snow, C. (1989). The relation between first- and second-language writing skills. *Linguistics and Education, 1,* 323–339.

Lancelotta, G. X., & Vaughn, S. (1989). Relation between types of aggression and sociometric status: Peer and teacher perceptions. *Journal of Educational Psychology, 81,* 86–90.

Landau, S., Mangione, C., & Pryor, J. B. (1997). HIV & AIDS. In G. G. Bear, K. M. Minke, & A. Thomas (Eds.), *Children's needs II: Development, problems, and alternatives* (pp. 761–791). Bethesda, MD: National Association of School Psychologists.

Larson, C. N., & Slaughter, H. (1984). The use of manipulatives and games in selected elementary school classrooms, from an ethnographic study. In A. E. Uprichard & J. V. Perez (Eds.), *Focus on learning problems in mathematics* (pp. 31–49). Framingham, MA: Center for Teaching/Learning of Mathematics.

Lash, M. H. (2000). *Resource guide: Children, adolescents and young adults with brain injuries.* Wake Forest, NC: L & A Publishing/Training.

Lazar, R. T., Warr-Leeper, G. A., Nicholson, C. B., & Johnson, S. (1989). Elementary school teachers' use of multiple meaning expressions. *Language, Speech, and Hearing Services in Schools, 20,* 420–430.

Leavell, A., & Ioannides, A. (1993). Using character development to improve story writing. *Teaching Exceptional Children, 25,* 41–45.

Leff, S., & Leff, R. (1978). *Talking pictures.* Milwaukee, WI: Crestwood Company.

Lefkowitz, M. M., & Tesiny, E. P. (1985). Depression in children: Prevalence and correlates. *Journal of Consulting and Clinical Psychology, 53*(5), 647–656.

Lenz, B. K. (1983). Promoting active learning through effective instruction: Using advance organizers. *Pointer, 27*(2), 11–13.

Lenz, B. K., Alley, G. R., & Schumaker, J. B. (1987). Activating the inactive learner: Advance organizers in the secondary content classroom. *Learning Disability Quarterly, 10*, 53–67.

Lenz, B. K., Ehren, B. J., & Smiley, L. (1991). A goal attainment approach to improve completion of project-type assignments by adolescents with learning disabilities. *Learning Disabilities Research and Practice, 6*, 166–176.

Lenz, B. K., Schumaker, J. B., Deshler, D. D., & Beals, V. L. (1984). *The word identification strategy* (Learning Strategies Curriculum). Lawrence, KS: University of Kansas.

Lenz, K., et al. (1993). *The course planning routine: A guide for inclusive planning* (Research Report). Lawrence, KS: University of Kansas Center for Research on Learning.

Leon, J. A., & Pepe, H. J. (1983). Self-instructional training: Cognitive behavior modification for remediating arithmetic deficits. *Exceptional Children, 50*, 54–60.

Lerner, J. W., Lowenthal, B., & Lerner S. R. (1995). *Attention deficit disorders: Assessment and teaching.* Pacific Grove, CA: Brooks/Cole.

Leske, C. M. (1981). Prevalence estimates of communication disorders in the U.S.: Speech disorders. *ASHA, 23*(3), 217–225.

Lessow-Hurley, J. (1996). *The foundations of dual language instruction.* White Plains, NY: Longman.

Leu, D. J., & Leu, D. D. (2000). *Teaching with the internet: Lessons from the classroom* (3rd ed.). Norwood, MA: Christopher-Gordon Publishers.

Levin, J., & Nolan, J. F. (1991). *Principles of classroom management: A hierarchical approach.* Englewood Cliffs, NJ: Prentice-Hall.

Lewis, R. B. (1993). *Special education technology: Classroom applications.* Pacific Grove, CA: Brooks Cole.

Lewis, R. B., & Doorlag, D. H. (1995). *Teaching special students in the mainstream.* New York: Merrill.

Light, J., & Kelford-Smith, A. (1993). Home literacy experiences of preschoolers who use AAC systems and of their nondisabled peers. *Augmentative and Alternative Communication, 9*, 10–22.

Lindamood, P. A., & Lindamood, P. (1998). *The Lindamood phoneme sequencing program for reading, spelling, and speech: The LiPS program.* Austin, TX: PRO-ED.

Lloyd, J., Saltzman, N. J., & Kauffman, J. M. (1981). Predictable generalization in academic learning as a result of preskills and strategy training. *Learning Disability Quarterly, 4*, 203–216.

Lobovits, D. A., & Handal, P. J. (1985). Childhood depression: Prevalence using DSM-III criteria and validity of parent and child depression scales. *Journal of Pediatric Psychology, 10*, 45–54.

Lockwood, A. T. (1992). The de facto curriculum. *Focus in Change, 6.*

Loeber, R., Wung, P., Keenan, K., Giroux, B., Stouthamer-Loeber, M., Van Kammen, W., & Maughan, B. (1993). Developmental pathways in disruptive child behavior. *Development and Psychopathology, 51*(1/2), 103–134.

Logan, D. R., & Malone, D. M. (1998). Comparing instructional contexts of students with and without severe disabilities in general education classrooms. *Exceptional Children, 64*, 343–358.

Lombroso, P. J., Pauls, D. L., & Leckman, J. F. (1994). Genetic mechanisms in childhood psychiatric disorders. *Journal of the American Academy of Child and Adolescent Psychiatry, 33*(7), 921–936.

Long, N. J., Morse, W. C., & Newman, R. G. (1980). *Conflict in the classroom.* Belmont, CA: Wadsworth.

Longstreet, E. (1978). *Aspects of ethnicity.* New York: Teachers College Press.

Longwill, A. W., & Kleinert, H. L. (1998). The unexpected benefits of high-school peer tutoring. *Teaching Exceptional Children, 30*(4), 60–65.

Lou, Y., Abrami, P. C., Spence, J. C., Poulsen, C., Chambers, B., & d'Appolonia, S. (1996). Within-class grouping: A meta-analysis. *Review of Educational Research, 66*, 423–458.

Lucangeli, D., Coi, G., & Bosco, P. (1997). Metacognitive awareness in good and poor math problem solvers. *Learning Disabilities Research and Practice, 12*(4), 209–212.

Lucas, T., Henze, R., & Donato, R. (1990). Promoting the success for Latino language minority students: An exploratory study of six high schools. *Harvard Educational Review, 60*, 315–334.

Lue, M. S. (2001). *A survey of communication disorders for the classroom teacher.* Boston: Allyn & Bacon.

Lusthaus, E., & Forest, M. (1987). The kaleidoscope: A challenge to the cascade. In M. Forest (Ed.), *More education integration* (pp. 1–17). Downsview, Ontario: G. Allan Roeher Institute.

Lynch, E. W., & Hanson, M. J. (1992). *Developing cross-cultural competence: A guide for working with young children and their families.* Baltimore: Brookes.

Lyon, G. R. (1998a). *Congressional testimony: Reading research.* Washington, DC: Committee on Labor and Human Resources.

Lyon, G. R. (1998b). *Overview of reading and literacy initiatives.* Statement prepared for the National Institutes of Health, Bethesda, MD.

Lyon, G. R. (1999). *The NICHD research program in reading development, reading disorders and reading instruction.* Washington, DC: National Center for Learning Disabilities.

Lyon, G. R., Fletcher, J. M., Shaywitz, S. E., Shaywitz, B. A., Torgesen, J. K., Wood, F. B., Schulte, A., & Olson, R. (2001). Rethinking learning disabilities. In C. Finn, A. Rotherham, & C. Hokanson, Jr. (Eds.), *Rethinking special education for a new century* (pp. 259–287). Washington, DC: Fordham Foundation.

Maccini, P., & Hughes, C. A. (1997). Mathematics interventions for adolescents with learning disabilities.

*Learning Disabilities Research and Practice, 12*(3), 168–176.

MacLeod, J. (1987). *Ain't no makin' it: Leveled aspirations in a low-income neighborhood.* Boulder, CO: Westview.

Madden, N. A., Slavin, R. E., Karweit, N. L., Dolan, L., & Wasik, B. A. (1991). Success for all. *Phi Delta Kappan, 72,* 593–599.

Maddux, C. D., Johnson, D. L., & Willis, J. W. (1992). *Educational computing: Learning with tomorrow's technologies.* Boston: Allyn & Bacon.

Maheady, L. (1997). Preparing teachers for instructing multiple ability groups. *Teacher Education and Special Education, 20*(4), 322–339.

Maheady, L., Harper, G. F., & Sacca, M. K. (1988). Peer mediated instruction: A promising approach to meeting the needs of learning disabled adolescents. *Learning Disability Quarterly, 11,* 108–113.

Mahr, G, & Leith, W. (1992). Psychogenic stuttering of adult onset. *Journal of Speech and Hearing Research, 35,* 283–286.

Majsterek, D. J. (1990). Writing disabilities: Is word processing the answer? *Intervention in School and Clinic, 26,* 93–97.

Mallory, B. L., & Kerns, G. M. (1988). Consequences of categorical labeling of preschool children. *Topics in Early Childhood Special Education, 8,* 39–50.

Mandler, J. M., & Johnson, N. S. (1977). Remembrance of things passed: Story structure and recall. *Cognitive Psychology, 9,* 111–151.

Mann, V. A. (1984). Longitudinal prediction and prevention of early reading difficulty. *Annals of Dyslexia, 34,* 117–135.

Manset, G., & Semmel, M. I. (1997). Are inclusive programs for students with mild disabilities effective? A comparative review of model programs. *The Journal of Special Education, 31*(2), 155–180.

March of Dimes. (1993). *Substance abuse: Statbook.* White Plains, NY: March of Dimes Birth Defects Foundation.

Mariage, T. V. (2000). Constructing educational possibilities: A sociolinguistic examination of meaning-making in "sharing chair." *Learning Disability Quarterly, 23,* 79–103.

Marland, S. (1972). *Education of the gifted and talented.* Report to the Congress of the United States by the U.S. Commissioner of Education. Washington, DC: U.S. Government Printing Office.

Marsh, L. G., & Cooke, N. L. (1996). The effects of using manipulatives in teaching math problem solving to students with learning disabilities. *Learning Disabilities Research and Practice, 11*(1), 58–65.

Marshall, R. M., Hynd, G. W., Handwerk, M. J., & Hall, J. (1997). Academic underachievement in ADHD subtypes. *Journal of Learning Disabilities, 30*(6), 635–642.

Marston, D. (1996). A comparison of inclusion only, pull-out only, and combined service models for students with mild disabilities. *The Journal of Special Education, 30*(2), 121–132.

Martin, K. F., & Manno, C. (1995). Use of a check-off system to improve middle school students' story compositions. *Journal of Learning Disabilities, 28,* 139–149.

Masten, W. G. (1981). *Approaches to the identification of gifted minority students.* Paper for U.S. Department of Education, National Institute of Education. Education Resources Information Center. (ED 234578)

Mastropieri, M. A., Leinart, A., & Scruggs, T. E. (1999). Strategies to increase reading fluency. *Intervention in School and Clinic, 34*(5), 278–283.

Mastropieri, M. A., & Scruggs, T. E. (1997). Best practices in promoting reading comprehension in students with learning disabilities: 1976–1996. *Remedial and Special Education, 18,* 197–213.

Mastropieri, M. A., Scruggs, T. E., & Shiah, S. (1991). Mathematics instruction for learning disabled students: A review of research. *Learning Disabilities Research and Practice, 6*(2), 89–98.

Mather, N., & Lackowicz, B. L. (1992). Shared writing: An instructional approach for reluctant writers. *Teaching Exceptional Children, 25*(1), 26–30.

Mather, N., & Roberts, R. (1995). *Informal assessment and instruction in written language.* Brandon, VT: Clinical Psychology Publishing Company.

Mathes, P. G., & Babyak, A. E. (2001). The effects of peer-assisted learning strategies for first-grade readers with and without additional mini-skills lessons. *Learning Disabilities Research and Practice, 16,* 18–27.

Mathes, P. G., Fuchs, D., Roberts, P. H., & Fuchs, L. S. (1998). Preparing students with special needs for reintegration: Curriculum-based measurement's impact on transenvironmental programming. *Journal of Learning Disabilities 31,* 615–624.

Mathes, P. G., Fuchs, L. S., Fuchs, D., Hanley, A. M., & Sanders, A. (1994). Increasing strategic reading practice with Peabody Classwide Peer Tutoring. *Learning Disabilities Research and Practice, 9*(1), 44–48.

Mattingly, J. C., & Bott, D. A. (1990). Teaching multiplication facts to students with learning problems. *Exceptional Children, 56*(5), 438–449.

McBurnett, K., Lahey, B., & Pfifner, L. (1993). Diagnosis of attention deficit disorders in DSM-IV: Scientific basis and implications for education. *Exceptional Children, 60*(2), 108–177.

McCaleb, J., & White, J. (1980). Critical dimensions in evaluating teacher clarity. *Journal of Classroom Interaction, 15,* 27–30.

McGregor, K. K., & Leonard, L. B. (1995). Intervention for word-finding deficits in children. In M. E. Fey, J. Windsor, & S. F. Warren (Eds.), *Language intervention: Preschool through the elementary years* (pp. 85–105). Baltimore: Paul H. Brookes.

McGuffin, P., Asherson, P., Owen, M. J., & Farmer, A. (1994). The strength of the genetic effect: Is there room for an environmental influence in the etiology of schizophrenia? *British Journal of Psychiatry, 164*(5), 593–599.

McIntosh, R., Vaughn, S., & Bennerson, D. (1995). FAST social skills with a SLAM and a RAP: Providing social skills training for students with learning disabilities. *Teaching Exceptional Children, 28*(1), 37–41.

McIntosh, R., Vaughn, S., Schumm, J. S., Haager, D., & Lee, O. (1993). Observations of students with learning disabilities in general education classrooms. *Exceptional Children, 60*(3), 249–261.

McIntyre, T. (1992). *The behavior management handbook: Setting up effective management systems.* Boston: Allyn & Bacon.

McKeown, M. G., Beck, I. L., & Sandora, C. A. (1996). Questioning the author: An approach to developing meaningful classroom discourse. In M. G. Graves, P. van den Broek, & B. M. Taylor (Eds.), *The first R: Every child's right to read* (pp. 97–119). New York: Teachers College Press; Newark, DE: International Reading Association.

McKinley, N., & Larson, V. Lord. (1991, November). *Seventh, eighth, and ninth graders' conversations in two experimental conditions.* Paper presented at the annual convention of the American Speech-Language-Hearing Association, Atlanta, GA.

McKinney, J., Montague, M., & Hocutt, A. (1993). Educational assessment of students with attention deficit disorder. *Exceptional Children, 60*, 125–131.

McLaren, J., & Bryson, S. E. (1987). Review of recent epidemiological studies of mental retardation: Prevalence, associated disorders & etiology. *American Journal of Mental Retardation, 92*, 243–254.

McLaughlin, M. J., & Owings, M. F. (1992). Relationships among states' fiscal and demographic data and the implementation of P.L. 94–142. *Exceptional Children, 59*(3), 247–261.

McLaughlin, S. (1998). *Introduction to language development.* San Diego, CA: Singular Publishing Group.

McLeod, T. M., & Armstrong, S. W. (1982). Learning disabilities in mathematics: Skill deficits and remedial approaches at the intermediate and secondary level. *Learning Disability Quarterly, 5*(3), 305–311.

McLeskey, J., Henry, D., & Axelrod, M. I. (1999). Inclusion of students with learning disabilities: An examination of data from reports to Congress. *Exceptional Children, 66*(1), 55–66.

McNeill, D. (1970). *The acquisition of language: The study of developmental psycholinguistics.* New York: Harper and Row.

McTighe, J., & Lyman, F. T., Jr. (1988). Cueing thinking in the classroom: The promise of theory-embedded tools. *Educational Leadership, 45*(7), 18–24.

Medical Research and Training Center in Rehabilitation and Childhood Trauma. (1993). *Facts from the National Pediatric Trauma Registry: Fact sheet 2.* Washington, DC: U.S. Department of Education.

Meinbach, A. M., Rothlein, L., & Fredericks, A. D. (1995). *The complete guide to thematic units: Creating the integrated curriculum.* Norwood, MA: Christopher-Gordon.

Menolascino, F. J., & Stark, J. A. (Eds.). (1988). *Preventive and curative intervention in mental retardation.* Baltimore: Brookes.

Menyuk, P. (1971). *The acquisition and development of language.* Englewood Cliffs, NJ: Prentice-Hall.

Merbler, J. B., Hadadian, A., & Ulman, J. (1999). Using assistive technology in the inclusive classroom. *Preventing School Failure, 32*, 113–117.

Mercer, C. D., Jordan, L., & Miller, S. P. (1994). Implications of constructivism for teaching math to students with moderate to mild disabilities. *Journal of Special Education, 28*(3), 290–306.

Mercer, C. D., & Miller, S. P. (1992). Teaching students with learning problems in math to acquire, understand, and apply basic math facts. *Remedial and Special Education, 13*(3), 19–35, 61.

Merritt, D., & Culatta, B. (1998). *Language intervention in the classroom.* San Diego, CA: Singular.

Meyen, E. L., & Skrtic, T. M. (1995). *Special education and student disability: An introduction* (4th ed.). Denver, CO: Love.

Meyer, L. H., Peck, C. A., & Brown, L. (1991). *Critical issues in the lives of people with severe disabilities.* Baltimore: Brookes.

Meyer, M. S., & Felton, R. H. (1999). Repeated reading to enhance fluency: Old approaches and new direction. *Annals of Dyslexia, 49*, 283–306.

Michelson, L., & Mannarino, A. (1986). Social skills training with children: Research and clinical application. In P. S. Strain, M. J. Guralnick, & H. M. Walker (Eds.), *Children's social behavior* (pp. 373–406). Orlando, FL: Academic Press.

Miller, D. (1993). Sexual and physical abuse among adolescents with behavioral disorders: Profiles and implications. *Behavioral Disorders, 20*(1), 61–68.

Miller, J. A. (1991, May 22). Chapter I: An educational revolution. *Education Week*, pp. 1–7, 9–10.

Miller, S. P., Butler, F. M., & Lee, K. (1998). Validated practices for teaching mathematics to students with learning disabilities: A review. *Focus on Exceptional Children, 31*, 1–24.

Miller, S. P., & Mercer, C. D. (1997). Educational aspects of mathematics disabilities. *Journal of Learning Disabilities, 30*(1), 47–56.

Miller, W. S., & Otto, J. (1930). Analysis of experimental studies in homogeneous grouping. *Journal of Educational Research, 21*, 95–102.

Miner, C. A., & Bates, P. E. (1997). Person-centered transition planning. *Teaching Exceptional Children, 30*(1), 66–69.

Moats, L. C., & Smith, C. (1992). Derivational morphology: Why it should be included in language assessment and instruction. *Language, Speech, and Hearing Services in Schools, 23*, 312–319.

Mobbs, F., Reed, V. A., & McAllister, I. (1993, May). *Rankings of the relative importance of selected communication skills in adolescent peer interactions.* Paper presented at the annual conference of the Australian Association of Speech and Hearing, Darwin, Australia.

Moeller, M. P. (2000). Early intervention and language development in children who are deaf and hard of hearing. *Pediatrics, 106*(2), 43–62.

Moll, L. C. (Ed.). (1990). *Vygotsky and education: Implications and applications of sociohistorical psychology.* Cambridge, England: Cambridge University Press.

Moll, L. C., & Greenberg, J. B. (1990). Creating zones of possibilities: Combining social contexts for instruction. In L. C. Moll (Ed.), *Vygotsky and education* (pp. 319–348). Cambridge, England: Cambridge University Press.

Montague, M. (1992). The effects of cognitive and metacognitive strategy instruction on the mathematical problem solving of middle school students with learning disabilities. *Journal of Learning Disabilities, 25,* 230–248.

Montague, M., & Applegate, B. (1993). Mathematical problem-solving characteristics of middle-school students with learning disabilities. *The Journal of Special Education, 27,* 175–201.

Montague, M., & Bos, C. S. (1986). Verbal mathematical problem solving and learning disabilities: A review. *Focus on Learning Problems in Mathematics, 8*(2), 7–21.

Montague, M., & Graves, A. (1993). Improving students' story writing. *Teaching Exceptional Children, 25,* 36–37.

Morales, D. (1992, June). Report examines gang activity. *Newsletter of Texas Commission on Alcohol and Drug Abuse, 1,* 8.

Morgan, H. (1980). How schools fail black children. *Social Policy, 10*(4), 49–54.

Morgan, S. R., & Reinhart, J. A. (1991). *Interventions for students with emotional disorders.* Austin, TX: PRO-ED.

Morrice, C., & Simmons, M. (1991). Beyond reading buddies: A whole language cross-age program. *The Reading Teacher, 44*(8), 572–577.

Morrow, L. M. (1985). Retelling stories: A strategy for improving children's comprehension, concept of story structure and oral language complexity. *Elementary School Journal, 85,* 647–661.

Morrow, L. M., & Smith, J. K. (1990). The effects of group size on interactive storybook reading. *Reading Research Quarterly, 25*(3), 213–231.

Mtetwa, D., & Garofalo, J. (1989). Beliefs about mathematics: An overlooked aspect of student difficulties. *Academic Therapy, 24,* 611–618.

Muscular Dystrophy Association (2000). *Facts about muscular dystrophy.* Available: http://www.mdausa.org/publications/fa-md.html

Muse, N. J. (1990). *Depression and suicide in children and adolescents.* Austin, TX: PRO-ED.

Muther, C. (1985). What every textbook evaluator should know. *Educational Leadership, 42*(7), 87–90.

Nahmias, M. (1995). *Project ADEPT.* Tucson, AZ: University of Arizona, Department of Special Education and Rehabilitation.

National Advisory Neurological Disorders and Stroke Council. (1990). *Implementation plan: Decade of the brain.* Bethesda, MD: National Institutes of Health.

National Center for Education Statistics. (2000). Executive summary. *Dropout rates in the United States: 1999.* Available: http://nces.ed.gov/pubs2001/dropout/

National Center for Hearing Assessment and Management. (2001). Available: http://www.infanthearing.org/ehdi/screening.html

National Coalition for the Homeless. (1999). *Making the grade: Successes and challenges in providing educational opportunities to homeless children and youth.* Washington, DC: National Coalition for the Homeless.

National Council of Teachers of Mathematics. (1989). *Curriculum and evaluation standards for school mathematics* (Report No. SE–050–418). Reston, VA: National Council of Teachers of Mathematics. (ERIC Document Reproduction Service No. ED 304 338).

National Education Goals Panel. (1994). *National education goals report.* Washington, DC: Author.

National Institute of Mental Health. (2000). *Interdisciplinary research on attention deficit hyperactivity disorder.* Washington, DC: NIMH. Available: http://www.nimh.nih.gov/research/interadhd.cfm

National Institute of Neurological Disorders and Stroke. (1988). *Developmental speech and language disorders: Hope through research* (NIH Publication No. Pamphlet 88–2757). Bethesda, MD: Author.

National Joint Committee on Learning Disabilities. (1990). *Learning disabilities: Issues on definition. Collective perspectives on issues affecting learning disabilities.* Position papers and statements (pp. 61–66). Austin, TX: PRO-ED.

National Literacy Summit. (2000). *From margins to the mainstream: An action agenda for literacy.* Washington, DC: National Literacy Summit.

National Mental Health Association. (1986). *Severely emotionally disturbed children: Improving services under Education of the Handicapped Act (P.L. 94–142).* Washington, DC: Author.

National Reading Panel. (2000). *Teaching children to read: An evidence-based assessment of the scientific research literature on reading and its implications for reading instruction.* Bethesda, MD: National Institutes of Health, National Institute of Child Health and Human Development.

Natrillo, G., McDill, E. L., & Pallas A. M. (1990). *Schooling disadvantaged children: Racing against catastrophe.* New York: Teachers College Press.

Neal, L. V. I., McCray, A. D., & Webb-Johnson, G. (2001). Teachers' reactions to African American students' movement styles. *Intervention in Clinic and Schools, 36,* 168–174.

Neilsen, S. L., Olive, M. L., Donovan, A. L., McEvoy, M. A. (1998). Challenging behavior in your classroom? Don't respond—teach instead! *Young Exceptional Children, 2,* 2–10.

Nelson, J. S., Epstein, M. H., Bursuck, W. D., Jayanthi, M., & Sawyer, V. (1998). The preferences of middle-school students for homework adaptations made by general education teachers. *Learning Disabilities Research & Practice, 13*(2), 109–117.

Nelson, J., Lott, L., & Glenn, H. S. (1993). *Positive discipline in the classroom.* Rocklin, CA: Prima.

Nelson, N. W. (1998). *Childhood language disorders in context: Infancy through adolescence* (2nd ed.). Boston: Allyn & Bacon.

Newland, E. (1932). An analytic study of the development of illegibilities in handwriting from the lower grades to adulthood. *Journal of Educational Research, 26,* 249–258.

Newman, F. M., & Wehlage, G. G. (1992–1993). Five standards of authentic instruction. *Educational Leadership, 50*(4), 8–12.

Nieto, S. (1992). *Affirming diversity: The sociopolitical context of multicultural education.* New York: Longman.

Nieto, S. (1994). Lessons from students on creating a chance to dream. *Harvard Educational Review, 64,* 392–426.

Nieto, S. (1996). *Affirming diversity: The sociopolitical context of multicultural education* (2nd ed.). New York: Longman.

Nippold, M. A. (1998). *Later language development: The school-age and adolescent years* (2nd ed.). Austin, TX: PRO-ED.

Noonan, M., & Siegel-Causey, E. (1990). Special needs of students with severe handicaps. In L. McCormick & R. L. Schiefelbusch (Eds.), *Early language intervention: An introduction* (2nd ed., pp. 383–425). Columbus, OH: Merrill.

Northcutt, L., & Watson, D. (1986). *Sheltered English teaching handbook.* San Marcos, CA: AM Graphics & Printing.

Oakes, J. (1985). *Keeping track: How schools structure inequality.* New Haven, CT: Yale University Press.

Oakes, J. (1990). *Multiplying inequalities: The effects of race, social class, and tracking on opportunities to learn math and science.* Santa Monica, CA: RAND.

Oakes, J. (1992). Can tracking research inform practice? Technical, normative, and political considerations. *Educational Researcher, 21*(4), 12–21.

Oakes, J., Gamoran, A., & Page, R. (1991). Curriculum differentiation: Opportunities, consequences, and meanings. In P. Jackson (Ed.), *Handbook of research on curriculum.* New York: Macmillan.

O'Connor, R. (2000). Increasing the intensity of intervention in kindergarten and first grade. *Learning Disabilities Research and Practice, 15,* 43–54.

Office of Vocational and Educational Services for Individuals with Disabilities. (2001). *Special education in New York state for children ages 3–21: A parent's guide.* Albany, NY: The University of the State of New York.

O'Flahavan, J. F., & Stein, C. (1992a, December). *Interpretive development in peer discussion about literature: An exploration of the teacher's role.* Paper presented at the Forty-first Annual Meeting of the National Reading Conference, San Antonio, TX.

O'Flahavan, J. F., & Stein, C. (1992b, December). The conversational discussion groups project. In K. Jongsma (Chair), *Understanding and enhancing literature discussion in elementary classrooms.* Symposium conducted at the 42nd Annual Meeting of the National Reading Conference, San Antonio, TX.

O'Flahavan, J. (1989). *An exploration of the effects of participant structure upon literacy development in reading group discussion.* Unpublished doctoral dissertation. University of Illinois–Urbana-Champaign.

Ogbu, J. U. (1978). *Minority education and caste: The American system in cross-cultural perspective.* New York: Academic Press.

Ogbu, J. U. (1990). Minority education in comparative perspective. *Journal of Negro Education, 59,* 45–57.

Ogbu, J. U. (1992). Understanding cultural diversity and learning. *Educational Researcher, 21*(8), 5–14.

Ogle, D. (1986). KWL: A teaching model that develops active reading of expository text. *The Reading Teacher, 39,* 564–570.

Ogle, D. (1989). Implementing strategic teaching. *Educational Leadership, 46*(4), 47–48, 57–60.

Oishi, S., Slavin, R. E., & Madden, N. A. (1983, April). *Effects of student teams and individualized instruction on cross-race and cross-sex friendships.* Paper presented at the annual meeting of the American Educational Research Association, Montreal, Canada.

Okolo, C. M. (1992). The effect of computer-assisted instruction format and initial attitude on the arithmetic facts proficiency and continuing motivation of students with learning disabilities. *Exceptionality: A Research Journal, 3*(4), 195–211.

Olenckak, F. R., & Renzulli, J. S. (1989). The effectiveness of the schoolwide enrichment model on selected aspects of elementary school change. *Gifted Child Quarterly, 33,* 36–46.

Olsen, L. (1988). *Crossing the schoolhouse border: Immigrant students and the California public schools.* San Francisco: California Tomorrow.

Olson, M. R., Chalmers, L., & Hoover, J. H. (1997). Attitudes and attributes of general education teachers identified as effective inclusionists. *Remedial and Special Education, 18,* 28–35.

Olson, R. (1999). Genes, environment, and reading disabilities. In R. J. Sternberg & L. Spear-Swerling (Eds.), *Perspectives on learning disabilities* (pp. 3–22). Oxford, England: Westview Press.

O'Neill, R. E., Horner, R. H., Albin, R. W., Storey, K., Sprague, J. R. (1997). *Functional assessment and program development for problem behavior: A practical handbook.* Sycamore, IL: Sycamore Publishing Company.

Opitz, M. F. (1998). Children's books to develop phonemic awareness—for you and parents, too! *The Reading Teacher, 51,* 526–528.

Orelove, F. P., & Sobsey, D. (1996). *Educating children with multiple disabilities: A transdisciplinary approach* (3rd ed.). Baltimore: Brookes.

Ormrod, J. E. (1995). *Educational psychology: Principles and applications.* Englewood Cliffs, NJ: Prentice-Hall.

Osborne, A. G., & DiMattia, P. (1994). The IDEA's least restrictive environment mandate: Legal implications. *Exceptional Children, 61,* 6–14.

O'Shea, D. J., & O'Shea, L. J. (1997). Collaboration and school reform: A twenty-first-century perspective. *Journal of Learning Disabilities, 30*(4), 449–462.

Otto, W., Wolf, A., & Eldrige, R. G. (1984). Managing instruction. In P. D. Pearson (Ed.), *Handbook of reading research* (pp. 799–828). New York: Longman.

Ovando, C. J., & Collier, V. P. (1998). *Bilingual and ESL classrooms: Teaching in multicultural contexts* (2nd ed.). Boston: McGraw-Hill.

Owens, Jr., R. E. (1995). *Language disorders: A functional approach to assessment and intervention* (2nd ed.). Boston: Allyn & Bacon.

Owens, Jr., R. E. (1996). *Language development: An introduction* (4th ed.). Columbus, OH: Merrill.

Owens, Jr., R. E. (1998). Development of communication, language, and speech. In G. H. Shames, E. H. Wiig, & W. A. Secord (Eds.), *Human communication disorders: An introduction* (5th ed., pp. 27–68). Boston: Allyn & Bacon.

Owens, R. (2001). *Language development: An introduction* (5th ed.). Boston: Allyn & Bacon.

Oyer, H. J., Crowe, B., & Haas, W. H. (1987). *Speech, language, and hearing disorders: A guide for teachers.* Austin, TX: PRO-ED.

Palincsar, A. S. (1986). The role of dialogue in providing scaffolded instruction. *Educational Psychologist, 21* (1/2), 73–98.

Palinscsar, A. S., & Brown, A. L. (1984). The reciprocal teaching of comprehension-fostering and comprehension-monitoring activities. *Cognition and Instruction, 1,* 117–175.

Palmer, D. S., Borthwick-Duffy, S. A., & Widaman, K. (1998). Parent perceptions of inclusive practices for their children with significant disabilities. *Exceptional Children, 64,* 271–282.

Palmer, J. M., & Yantis, P. A. (1990). *Survey of communication disorders.* Baltimore: Williams & Wilkins.

Parette, H. P., & Angelo, D. H. (1996). Augmentative and alternative communication impact on families: Trends and future directions. *The Journal of Special Education, 30,* 77–98.

Passenger, T., Stuart, M., & Terrell, C. (2000). Phonological processing and early literacy. *Journal of Research in Reading, 23*(1), 55–66.

Pavri, S., & Monda-Amaya, L. (2000). Loneliness and students with learning disabilities in inclusive classrooms: Self-perceptions, coping strategies, and preferred interventions. *Learning Disabilities Research and Practice, 6,* 12–16.

Payne, K. T., & Taylor, O. L. (1998). Communication differences and disorders. In G. H. Shames, E. H. Wiig, & W. A. Secord (Eds.), *Human communication disorders: An introduction* (5th ed., pp. 118–154). Boston: Allyn & Bacon.

Peal, E., & Lambert, W. (1962). The relation of bilingualism to intelligence. *Psychological Monographs, 7*(546), 1–12.

Pearson, P. D., & Johnson, D. D. (1978). *Teaching reading comprehension.* New York: Holt, Rinehart & Winston.

Pecyna-Rhyner, P., Lehr, D., & Pudlas, K. (1990). An analysis of teacher responsiveness to communicative initiations of children with handicaps. *Language, Speech, and Hearing Services in Schools, 21,* 91–97.

Pellegrini, A., & Galda, L. (1982). The effects of thematic fantasy plan training on the development of children's story comprehension. *American Educational Research Journal, 19,* 443–452.

Pennington, B. F., Groisser, D., & Welsh, M. C. (1993). Contrasting cognitive deficits in attention deficit hyperactivity disorder versus reading disability. *Developmental Psychology, 29,* 511–523.

Pennington, R. K. (1999). Dyslexia as a neurodevelopmental disorder. In H. Tager-Flusberg (Ed.), *Neurodevelopmental disorders* (pp. 307–330). Cambridge, MA: MIT Press.

Pepper, E. C. (1976). Teaching the American Indian child in mainstream settings. In R. L. Jones (Ed.), *Mainstreaming and the minority child* (pp. 135–136). Reston, VA: Council for Exceptional Children.

Perfect, K. A. (2000). Rhyme and reason: Poetry for the heart and head. *The Reading Teacher, 52,* 728–737.

Peterson, S. K., Mercer, C. D., & O'Shea, L. (1988). Teaching learning disabled students place value using the concrete to abstract sequence. *Learning Disabilities Research, 4,* 52–56.

Phillips, N. B., Fuchs, L. S., & Fuchs, D. (1995). Effects of classwide curriculum-based measurement and peer tutoring: A collaborative researcher–practitioner interview study. *Journal of Learning Disabilities, 27,* 420–434.

Phillips, N. B., Hamlett, C. L., Fuchs, L. S., & Fuchs, D. (1993). Combining classwide curriculum-based measurement and peer tutoring to help general educators provide adaptive education. *Learning Disabilities Research & Practice, 8,* 148–156.

Pinnell, G. S. (1990). Success for low achievers through reading recovery. *Educational Leadership, 48*(1), 17–21.

Pinnell, G. S., & Fountas, I. C. (1997). *Help America read: A handbook for volunteers.* Portsmouth, NH: Heinemann.

Pinnell, G. S., Fried, M. D., & Estice, R. M. (1990). Reading recovery: Learning how to make a difference. *The Reading Teacher, 43*(4), 282–295.

Pisecco, S. Baker, D. B., Silva, P. A., & Brooke, M. (2001). Boys with reading disabilities and/or ADHD: Distinctions in early childhood. *Journal of Learning Disabilities, 34,* 98–106.

Platt, J. J., & Spivack, G. (1972). Social competence and effective problem solving thinking in psychiatric patients. *Journal of Clinical Psychiatry, 28,* 3–5.

Pomplun, M. (1997). When students with disabilities participate in cooperative groups. *Exceptional Children, 64*(1), 49–58.

Powers, M. D. (1989). *Children with autism: A parents' guide*. Rockville, MD: Woodbine House.

Prater, M. A., & Sileo, N. M. (2001). Using juvenile literature about HIV/AIDS. *Teaching Exceptional Children, 33*(6), 34–45.

Pressley, M. J., Rankin, J., & Yokoi, L. (1996). A survey of instructional practices of outstanding primary-level literacy teachers. *Elementary School Journal, 96,* 363–384.

Pressley, M., Wharton-McDonald, R., Allington, R., Block, C. C., Morrow, L., Tracey, D., Baker, K., Brooks, G., Cronin, J., Nelson, E., & Woo, D. (2001). A study of effective first-grade literacy instruction. *Scientific Studies of Reading, 5,* 35–58.

Prewitt-Diaz, J. O., Trotter, R. T., & Rivera, V. A. (1990). Effects of migration on children. *The Education Digest, 55,* 26–29.

Pugach, M. C., & Johnson, L. J. (1995). *Collaborative practitioners, collaborative schools*. Denver, CO: Love.

Putnam, M. L. (1992). Testing practices of mainstreamed secondary classroom teachers. *Remedial and Special Education, 13*(5), 11–21.

Putnam, M. L., Deshler, D. D., & Schumaker, J. S. (1993). The investigation of setting demands: A missing link in learning strategy instruction. In L. S. Meltzer (Ed.), *Strategy assessment and instruction for students with learning disabilities* (pp. 325–354). Austin, TX: PRO-ED.

Putnam, S. W. (Ed.). (1998). *Cooperative learning and strategies for inclusion: Celebrating diversity in the classroom* (3rd ed.). Baltimore: Brookes.

Quay, H. C., & Peterson, D. R. (1987). *Manual for the Revised Behavior Problem Checklist*. Coral Gables, FL: Author.

Quay, H. C., & Werry, J. S. (1986). *Psychopathological disorders of childhood*. New York: Wiley.

Radencich, M. C., Beers, P. C., & Schumm, J. S. (1993). *A handbook for the K–12 reading resource specialist* (pp. 119–120). Boston: Allyn & Bacon.

Radencich, M. C., & McKay, L. J. (Eds.). (1995). *Flexible grouping for literacy in the elementary grades*. Boston: Allyn & Bacon.

Rafferty, Y., & Rollins, N. (1989). *Learning in limbo: Educational deprivation of homeless children*. New York: Advocates for Children of New York.

Ramirez, J. D., & Merino, B. J. (1990). Classroom talk in English immersion, early-exit & late-exit transition bilingual education programs. In R. Jacobson & C. Faltis (Eds.), *Language distribution issues in bilingual schooling*. Clevedon, England: Multilingual Matters.

Ramirez, M. (1992, Winter/Spring). Executive summary, final report: Longitudinal study of structured English immersion strategy, early-exit and late-exit transitional bilingual education programs for language-minority children. *Bilingual Research Journal, 16*(1, 2), 1–62.

Ramirez, M., & Castaneda, A. (1974). *Cultural democracy, bicognitive development and education*. New York: Academic Press.

Raphael, T. E. (1982). Question-answering strategies for children. *The Reading Teacher, 36,* 188.

Raphael, T. E. (1984). Teaching learners about sources of information for answering comprehension questions. *Journal of Reading, 27,* 303–311.

Raphael, T. E. (1986). Teaching question-answer relationships revisited. *The Reading Teacher, 39*(6), 516–523.

Raskind, M. H., Goldberg, R. J., Higgins, E. L., & Herman, K. L. (1999). Patterns of change and predictors of success in individuals with learning disabilities: Results from a twenty-year longitudinal study. *Learning Disabilities Researach and Practice, 14*(1), 35–49.

Ratleff, J. E. (1989). *Instructional strategies for crosscultural students with special education needs*. Sacramento, CA: Resources in Special Education.

Raygor, A. L. (1977). The Raygor readability estimate: A quick and easy way to determine difficulty. In P. D. Pearson (Ed.), *Reading: Theory, research, and practice: Twenty-sixth yearbook of the National Reading Conference* (pp. 259–263). Clemson, SC: National Reading Conference.

Read, C. (1971). Pre-school children's knowledge of English phonology. *Harvard Educational Review, 41,* 1–34.

Readence, J. E., Bean, T. W., & Baldwin R. S. (1992). *Content area reading: An integrated approach* (4th ed.). Dubuque, IA: Kendall/Hunt.

Readence, J. E., Bean, T. W., & Baldwin R. S. (1998). *Content area literacy: An integrated approach* (6th ed.). Dubuque, IA: Kendall/Hunt.

Redl, F. (1959). The concept of the Life–Space Interview. *American Journal of Orthopsychiatry, 29,* 1–18.

Reid, R. (1995). Assessment of ADHD with culturally different groups: The use of behavioral rating scales. *School Psychology Review, 24,* 537–560.

Reid, R., Maag, J. W., & Vasa, S. F. (1993). Attention deficit hyperactivity disorder as a disability category: A critique. *Exceptional Children, 60,* 198–214.

Reiff, J. C. (1997). Multiple intelligences, culture, and equitable learning. *Childhood Education, 73,* 301–304.

Reis, S. M., & McCoach, D. B. (2000, Summer). The underachievement of gifted students: What do we know and where do we go? *Gifted Child Quarterly, 44*(3), 152–170.

Reisner, H. (1988). *Children with seizure disorder: A parent's guide*. Kensington, UK: Woodbine House.

Renzulli, J. S., & Delcourt, M. A. B. (1986). The legacy and logic of research on the identification of gifted persons. *Gifted Child Quarterly, 30*(1), 20–23.

Renzulli, J. S., & Reis, S. M. (1991). The Schoolwide Enrichment Model: A comprehensive plan for the development of creative productivity. In N. C. Colangelo & G. A. Davis (Eds.), *Handbook of gifted education* (pp. 111–141). Boston: Allyn & Bacon.

Renzulli, J. S., & Smith, L. H. (1979). *A guidebook for developing individualized educational programs for gifted and talented students.* Mansfield Center, CN: Creative Learning Press.

Renzulli, J. S., Smith, L. H., & Reis, S. M. (1982). Curriculum compacting: An essential strategy for working with gifted students. *Elementary School Journal, 82,* 185–194.

Reutzel, D. R., & Hollingsworth, P. M. (1993). Effects of fluency training on second graders' reading comprehension. *Journal of Educational Research, 86,* 325–331.

Rex, E. J., Koenig, A. J., Wormsley, D. P., & Baker, A. J. (1994). *Foundations of Braille literacy.* New York: American Foundation for the Blind.

Reyes, E. I., & Bos, C. S. (1998). Interactive semantic mapping and charting: Enhancing content-area learning for language-minority students. In R. M. Gersten & R. T. Jimenez (Eds.), *Promoting learning for culturally and linguistically diverse students* (pp. 133–150). Belmont, CA: Wadsworth.

Reyhner, J. (1992). American Indian bilingual education: The White House conference on Indian education and tribal college movement. *NABE News, 15*(7), 7–18.

Richard-Amato, P. (1996). *Making it happen: Interaction in the second language classroom* (2nd ed.). Reading, MA: Addison-Wesley.

Richard-Amato, P. A., & Snow, M. A. (1992). Strategies for content-area teachers. In P. A. Richard-Amato & M. A. Snow (Eds.), *The multicultural classroom: Readings for content-area teachers* (pp. 145–163). White Plains, NY: Longman.

Richards, M. (2000). Be a good detective: Solve the case of oral reading fluency. *The Reading Teacher, 53,* 534–539.

Richters, J. E., Arnold, L. E., Abikoff, H., Conners, C. K., Greenhill, I. L., Hechtman, L., Hinshaw, S. P., Pelham, W. E., & Swanson, J. M. (1995). NIMH collaborative multisite multimodal treatment study of children with ADHD: Background and rationale. *Journal of the Academy of Child and Adolescent Psychiatry, 34,* 987–1000.

Ridley, C. A., & Vaughn, S. R. (1982). Interpersonal problem solving: An intervention program for preschool children. *Journal of Applied Developmental Psychology, 3,* 177–190.

Rivera, D. P., Smith, R. G., Goodwin, M. W., & Bryant, B. R. (1998). Mathematical word problem solving: A synthesis of intervention research for students with learning disabilities. In T. E. Scruggs & M. A. Mastropieri (Eds.), *Advances in learning and behavioral disabilities* (pp. 245–285). Greenwich, CT: JAI.

Robertson, P., Kushner, M. I., Starks, J., & Drescher, C. (1994). An update of participation rates of culturally and linguistically diverse students in special education: The need for a research and policy agenda. *The Bilingual Special Education Perspective, 14,* 2–9.

Robinson, R. (1993, February 25). P. C. Anderson students try hand at problem-solving. *Dallas Examiner,* pp. 1, 8.

Rochelle, N. (2001). Barriers to serious parent involvement. *The Education Digest, 66*(5), 33–7.

Rock, E. E., Fessler, M. A., & Church, R. P. (1997). The concomitance of learning disabilities and emotional/behavioral disorders: A conceptual model. *Journal of Learning Disabilities, 30*(3), 245–263.

Rodríguez-Brown, F. V. (2001). Home-school connections in a community where English is the second language: Project FLAME. In V. J. Risko, & K. Bromley (Eds.), *Collaboration for diverse learners* (pp. 273–288). Newark, DE: International Reading Association.

Rogers-Warren, A., & Warren, S. F. (1980). Mands for verbalization: Facilitative effects of incidental teaching on preposition use by autistic children. *Journal of Applied Behavior Analysis, 18,* 17–31.

Rogoff, B., & Morelli, G. (1989). Culture and American children. *American Psychologist, 44,* 341–342.

Roisen, N. J., Blondis, T. A., Irwin, M., & Stein, M. (1994). Adaptive functioning in children with attention-deficit hyperactivity disorder. *Archives of Pediatric and Adolescent Medicine, 148,* 1037–1088.

Romberg, T. A. (1993). NCTM's standards: A rallying flag for mathematics teachers. *Educational Leadership, 50*(5), 36–41.

Rosenberg, M. S., Wilson, R., Maheady, L., & Sindelar, P. T. (1997). *Educating students with behavior disorders* (2nd ed.). Boston: Allyn & Bacon.

Rosenshine, B., & Meister, C. (1994). Reciprocal teaching: A review of the research. *Review of Educational Research, 64,* 479–530.

Rosenshine, B., & Stevens, R. (1986). Teaching functions. In M. C. Wittrock (Ed.), *Handbook of research on teaching* (3rd ed., pp. 376–391). New York: Macmillan.

Rosman, N. P. (1994). Acute head trauma. In F. A. Oski, C. D. DeAngelis, R. D. Feigin, J. A. McMillan, & J. B. Warshaw (Eds.), *Principles and practices of pediatrics* (2nd ed., pp. 2030–2048). Philadelphia: J. B. Lippincott.

Rourke, B. P. (1993). Arithmetic disabilities, specific and otherwise: A neuropsychological perspective. *Journal of Learning Disabilities, 26*(4), 214–226.

Routman, R. (1991). *Invitations: Changing as teachers and learners K–12.* Portsmouth, NH: Heinemann.

Rubalcava, M. (1991). *Locating transformative teaching in multicultural education.* Unpublished manuscript. University of California–Berkeley, Department of Anthropology, Special Project.

Rubia, K., Oosterlaan, J., Sergeant, J. A., Brandeis, D., & van Leeuwen, T. (1998). Attention deficit/hyperactivity disorder—from brain dysfunctions to behavior. *Behavioral Brain Research, 94,* 1–10.

Rubin, H. (1988). Morphological knowledge and early writing ability. *Language and Speech, 31,* 337–355.

Ruhl, K. L., Hughes, C. A., & Gajar, A. H. (1990). Efficacy of the pause procedure for enhancing learning disabled and nondisabled college students' long- and short-term recall of facts presented through lecture. *Learning Disability Quarterly, 13,* 55–64.

Ruiz, N. T., Garcia, E., & Figueroa, R. A. (1996). *The OLE curriculum guide: Creating optimal learning environments for students from diverse backgrounds in special and general education.* Sacramento, CA: California Department of Education, Specialized Programs Branch.

Rule, S., Losardo, A., Dinnebeil, L., Kaiser, A., & Rowland, C. (1998). Translating research on naturalistic instruction into practice. *Journal of Early Intervention, 21*(4), 283–293.

Rumberger, R. W. (1987). High school drop outs: A review of issues and evidence. *Review of Educational Research, 57*(2), 101–121.

Russo, D. C. (1991, November). *Behavioral treatment of pediatric head injury: Issues and outcomes.* Paper presented at conference on neurogenic developmental disorders, Niskayuna, NY.

Rutter, M. (1991). Age changes in depressive disorders: Some developmental considerations. In J. Garber & K. A. Dodge (Eds.), *The development of emotion regulation and dysregulation* (pp. 273–300). New York: Cambridge University Press.

Sacks, S. Z., & Wolffe, K. E. (1998). Lifestyles of adolescents with visual impairments: An ethnographic analysis. *Journal of Visual Impairment and Blindness, 92*(1), 7–17.

Safran, S. P. (1998). Disability portrayal in film: Reflecting the past, directing the future. *Exceptional Children, 64*(2), 227–238.

Salend, S. J. (1994). *Effective mainstreaming: Creative inclusive classrooms* (2nd ed.). New York: Macmillan.

Salend, S. J., Johansen, M., Mumper, J., Chase, A. S., Pike, K. M., & Dorney, J. A. (1997). Cooperative teaching: The voices of two teachers. *Remedial and Special Education, 18*(1), 3–11.

Salisbury, C., Galucci, C., Palombaro, M., & Peck, C. (1995). Strategies that promote social relations among elementary students with and without severe disabilities in inclusive schools. *Exceptional Children, 62*, 125–137.

Sanson, A., Smart, D., Prior, M., & Oberklaid, F. (1993). Precursors of hyperactivity and aggression. *Journal of the American Academy of Child and Adolescent Psychiatry, 32*(6), 1207–1216.

Santa, C. (1988). *Content reading including secondary systems.* Dubuque, IA: Kendall Hunt.

Sarcco, W. P., & Graves, D. J. (1985). Correspondence between teacher ratings of childhood depression and child self-ratings. *Journal of Clinical Child Psychology, 14*, 353–355.

Savage, R. C. (1993). Children with traumatic brain injury. *TBI Challenge!, 1*(3), 4–5.

Schloss, P. J., Alper, S., & Jayne, D. (1993). Self-determination for persons with disabilities: Choice, risk, and dignity. *Exceptional Children, 60*, 215–225.

Schmidt, P. R. (1999). KWLQ: Inquiry and literacy learning in science. *The Reading Teacher, 52*(7), 789–792.

Schnorr, R. (1990). "Peter? He comes and goes . . .": First graders' perspectives of a part-time mainstream student. *Journal of the Association for Persons with Severe Handicaps, 15*, 132–240.

Schroeder, H. (1993). Cerebral trauma: Accidental injury or shaken impact syndrome? *Headlines, 4*(5), 18–21.

Schumaker, J. B., Nolan, S. M., & Deshler, D. D. (1985). *The error monitoring strategy.* Lawrence, KS: Center for Research on Learning, University of Kansas.

Schumm, J. S. (1987). AOK: A reading for revision strategy. *Reading: Exploration and Discovery, 10*, 26–34.

Schumm, J. S., Hughes, M. T., & Arguelles. (2001). Co-teaching: It takes more than ESP. In V. J. Risko & K. Bromley (Eds.), *Collaboration for diverse learners* (pp. 52–69). Newark, DE: International Reading Association.

Schumm, J. S., & Lopate, K. (1989). An 8-step instructional plan for teaching notetaking skills to middle school students. *Florida Reading Quarterly, 26*(2), 17–21.

Schumm, J. S., & Mangrum, C. T. (1991). FLIP: A framework for content area reading. *Journal of Reading, 35* (2), 120–124.

Schumm, J. S., Moody, S. W., & Vaughn, S. R. (2000). Grouping for reading instruction: Does one size fit all? *Journal of Learning Disabilities, 33*(5), 477–488.

Schumm, J. S., & Schumm, G. E. (1999). *The reading tutor's handbook: A commonsense guide to helping students read and write.* Minneapolis, MN: Free Spirit.

Schumm, J. S., & Strickler, K. (1991). Guidelines for adapting content area textbooks: Keeping teachers and students content. *Intervention in School and Clinic, 27*(2), 79–84.

Schumm, J. S., & Vaughn, S. (1991). Making adaptations for mainstreamed students: General classroom teachers' perspectives. *Remedial and Special Education, 12*(4), 18–27.

Schumm, J. S., & Vaughn, S. (1992a). Planning for mainstreamed special education students: Perceptions of general classroom teachers. *Exceptionality, 3*, 81–98.

Schumm, J. S., & Vaughn, S. (1992b). Reflections on planning for mainstreamed special education students. *Exceptionality, 3*, 121–126.

Schumm, J. S., & Vaughn, S. (1995). *Using Making Words in heterogeneous classroom.* Unpublished manuscript.

Schumm, J. S., Vaughn, S., Haager, D., McDowell, D., Rothlein, L., & Saumell, L. (1995a). General education teacher planning: What can students with learning disabilities expect? *Exceptional Children, 61*(4), 335–352.

Schumm, J. S., Vaughn, S., Haager, D., McDowell, D., Rothlein, L., & Saumell, L. (1995b). Responsible inclusion for students with learning disabilities. *Journal of Learning Disabilities, 28*(5), 264–270, 290.

Schumm, J. S., Vaughn, S., & Harris, J. (1997). Pyramid power for collaborative planning. *Teaching Exceptional Children, 29*(6), 62–66.

Schumm, J. S., Vaughn, S., & Leavell, A. G. (1994). Planning pyramid: A framework for planning for diverse student needs during content area instruction. *The Reading Teacher, 47*(8), 608–615.

Schumm, J. S., Vaughn, S., & Saumell, L. (1992). What teachers do when the textbook is tough: Students speak out. *Journal of Reading Behavior, 24*(4), 481–503.

Schuster, J. W., Stevens, K. B., & Doak, P. K. (1990). Using constant time delay to teach word definitions. *Journal of Special Education, 24*, 306–318.

Schwartz, S. E. (1977). *Real Life Math Program.* Austin, TX: PRO-ED.

Scruggs, T. E., & Mastropieri, M. A. (1986). Improving the test-taking skills of behaviorally disordered and learning disabled children. *Exceptional Children, 53,* 63–68.

Scruggs, T. E., Mastropieri, M. A., Bakken, J. P., & Brigham, F. (1993). Reading versus doing: The relative effects of textbook-based and inquiry-oriented approaches to science learning in special education classrooms. *Journal of Special Education, 27*(1), 1–15.

Searfoss, L. W., & Readence, J. E. (1989). *Helping children learn to read* (2nd ed.). Englewood Cliffs, NJ: Prentice-Hall.

Seuss, Dr. (1974). *There's a wocket in my pocket.* New York: Random House.

Sexson, S. B., & Madan-Swain, A. (1993). School reentry for the child with chronic illness. *Journal of Learning Disabilities, 26,* 115–125.

Sexton, M., Harris, K. R., & Graham, S. (1998). Self-regulated strategy development and the writing process: Effects on essay writing and attributions. *Exceptional Children, 64*(3), 290–291.

Shanahan, T., Robinson, B., & Schneider, M. (1995). Integrating curriculum. *The Reading Teacher, 48*(8), 718–719.

Share, D. L., & Stanovich, K. E. (1995). Cognitive processes in early reading development: A model of acquisition and individual differences. *Issues in Education: Contributions from Education Psychology, 1,* 1–57.

Shaywitz, S. E., Pugh, K. R., Jenner, A. R., Fulbright, R. K., Fletcher, J. M., Gore, J. C., & Shaywitz, B. A. (2000). The neurobiology of reading and reading disability (dyslexia). In M. L. Kamil, P. B. Mosenthal, P. D. Pearson, and R. Barr (Eds.), *Handbook on reading research* (Vol. 3, pp. 229–249). Mahwah, NJ: Erlbaum.

Shaywitz, S., & Shaywitz, B. (1988). Attention deficit disorder: Current perspectives. In J. Kavanagh & J. Truss (Eds.), *Learning disabilities: Proceedings of the national conference* (pp. 369–567). Parkton, MD: York Press.

Shaywitz, S., Shaywitz, B., Fletcher, J. M., & Escobar, M. D. (1990). Prevalence of reading disability in boys and girls: Results of the Connecticut longitudinal study. *Journal of the American Medical Association, 264,* 998–1020.

Shea, T. M., & Bauer, A. M. (1991). *Parents and teachers of children with exceptionalities: A handbook for collaboration.* Boston: Allyn & Bacon.

Sherman, A. (1994). *Wasting America's future: The Children's Defense Fund report on the costs of child poverty.* Boston: Beacon Press.

Shiah, R. L., Mastropieri, M. A., Scruggs, T. E., & Fulk, B. J. (1994). The effects of computer-assisted instruction on the mathematical problem solving of students with learning disabilities. *Exceptionality, 5*(3), 131–161.

Shure, M. B., & Spivack, G. (1978). *Problem-solving techniques in childrearing.* San Francisco: Jossey-Bass.

Siegel-Causey, E., Guy, B., & Guess, D. (1995). Severe and multiple disabilities. In E. L. Meyen & T. M. Skrtic (Eds.), *Special education and student disability, an introduction* (4th ed.). Denver, CO: Love.

Sigelman, C. K., Budd, E. C., Spanhel, C. L., & Schoenrock, C. J. (1981). When in doubt, say yes: Acquiescence in interviews with mentally retarded persons. *Mental Retardation, 19,* 53–58.

Simmerman, S., & Swanson, H. L. (2001). Treatment outcomes of students with learning disabilities: How important are internal and external validity? *Journal of Learning Disabilities, 34*(3), 221–226.

Simpson, R. L. (1988). Needs of parents and families whose children have learning and behavior problems. *Behavioral Disorders, 14,* 40–47.

Singer, H. (1986). Friendly texts: Description and criteria. In E. K. Dishner, T. W. Bean, J. E. Readence, & D. W. Moore (Eds.), *Reading in the content areas: Improving classroom instruction* (2nd ed., pp. 112–128). Dubuque, IA: Kendall Hunt.

Skiba, R. J., & Peterson, R. L. (2000). School discipline at a crossroads: From zero tolerance to early response. *Exceptional Children, 66*(3), 335–346.

Skutnabb-Kangas, T. (1981, February). *Linguistic genocide and bilingual education.* Paper presented at the California Association for Bilingual Education, Anaheim, California.

Slavin, R. E. (1987). Ability grouping and student achievement in elementary schools: A best-evidence synthesis. *Review of Educational Research, 57*(3), 293–336.

Slavin, R. E. (1991). Synthesis of research on cooperative learning. *Educational Leadership, 48*(5), 71–82.

Slavin, R. E. (1995). *Cooperative learning: Theory, practice, and research* (2nd ed.). Boston: Allyn & Bacon.

Slavin, R. E. (2000). *Educational psychology: Theory and practice.* Boston: Allyn & Bacon.

Slavin, R. E., Karweit, N. L., & Madden, N. A. (1989). *Effective programs for students at risk.* Boston: Allyn & Bacon.

Slavin, R. E., Madden, N. A., Dolan, L. J., & Wasik, B. A. (1994). Roots and wings: Inspiring academic excellence. *Educational Leadership, 52*(3), 10–14.

Slavin, R. E., Madden, N. A., & Leavey, M. (1984). Effects of team assisted individualization on the mathematics achievement of academically handicapped and non-handicapped students. *Journal of Educational Psychology, 76*(5), 813–819.

Smit, A. B. (1993). Phonological error distributions in the Iowa-Nebraska articulation norms project: Word-initial consonant clusters. *Journal of Speech and Hearing Research, 36,* 931–947.

Smith, C. R. (1998). From gibberish to phonemic awareness: Effective decoding instruction. *Teaching Exceptional Children, 30*(6), 20–25.

Smith, J. O., & Lovitt, T. C. (1982). *Computational arithmetic program.* Austin, TX: PRO-ED.

Snow, C. E., Burns, M. S., & Griffin, P. (1998). *Preventing reading difficulties in young children.* Washington, DC: National Academy Press.

Snyder, T. D. (1993). Trends in education. *Principal, 73*(1), 9–14.

Sobsey, D., & Wolf-Schein, E. G., (1996). Sensory impairments. In F. P. Orelove & D. Sobsey (Eds.), *Educating children with multiple disabilities: A transdisciplinary approach* (3rd ed.). Baltimore: Brookes.

Speckman, N. J., Goldberg, R. J., & Herman, K. L. (1993). A exploration of risk and resilience in the lives of individuals with learning disabilities. *Learning Disabilities Research and Practice, 8,* 11–18.

Speece, D. L. (1994). The role of classification in learning disabilities. In S. Vaughn & C. S. Bos (Eds.), *Research issues in learning disabilities: Theory, methodology, assessment, and ethics* (pp. 69–82). New York: Springer-Verlag.

Spivack, G., Platt, J. J., & Shure, M. (1976). *The problem-solving approach to adjustment.* San Francisco: Jossey-Bass.

Sprague, J., & Walker, H. (2000). Early identification and intervention for youth with antisocial and violent behavior. *Exceptional Children, 66*(3), 367–380.

Spreen, O. (1988). *Learning disabled children growing up: A follow-up into adulthood.* New York: Oxford University Press.

Stach, B. (1998). *Clinical audiology: An introduction.* San Diego, CA: Singular Publications.

Stainback, S., & Stainback, W. (1992). *Curriculum consideration in inclusive classrooms: Facilitating learning for all students.* Baltimore: Paul H. Brookes.

Stallings, J. (1975). *Relationships between classroom instructional practices and child development* (Report No. PLEDE–C–75). Menlo Park, CA: Stanford Research Institute. (ERIC Document Reproduction Service No. ED 110 200).

Stanovich, K. E. (1986). Cognitive processes and the reading problems of learning-disabled children: Evaluating the assumption of specificity. In J. K. Torgesen & B. Y. L. Wong (Eds.), *Psychological and educational perspectives on learning disabilities* (pp. 87–131). Orlando, FL: Academic Press.

Stanovitch, K. E. (1991). Discrepancy definitions of reading disability: Has intelligence led us astray? *Reading Research Quarterly, 26,* 1–29.

Stanovich, K. I. (1992). Speculations on the causes and consequences of individual differences in early reading acquisition. In P. B. Gough, L. D. Ehri, & R. Treiman (Eds.), *Reading acquisition* (pp. 307–342). Mawah, NJ: Erlbaum Associates.

Stanovich, K. E., & Siegel, L. S. (1994). Phenotypic performance profile of children with reading disabilities: A regression-based test of the phonological-core variable-difference model. *Journal of Educational Psychology, 86*(1), 24–53.

Stein, N. L., & Glenn, C. G. (1979). An analysis of story comprehension in elementary school children. In R. O. Freedle (Ed.), *New directions in discourse processing* (Vol. 2, pp. 53–120). Norwood, NJ: Ablex.

Stephen, V. P., Varble, M. E., & Taitt, H. (1993). Instructional and organizational change to meet minority and at risk students' needs. *Journal of Staff Development, 14*(4), 40–43.

Stephens, K. R., & Karnes, F. A. (2000, Winter). State definitions for the gifted and talented revisited. *Exceptional Children, 66*(2), 219–238.

Stevens, K. B., & Schuster, J. W. (1987). Effects of a constant time delay procedure on the written spelling performance of a learning disabled student. *Learning Disability Quarterly, 10,* 9–16.

Stevens, K. B., & Schuster, J. W. (1988). Time delay: Systematic instruction for academic tasks. *Remedial and Special Education, 9*(5), 16–21.

Stevens, L. J., & Price, M. (1992). Meeting the challenge of educating children at risk. *Phi Delta Kappan, 74*(1), 18–23.

Stevens, S. (2001). A teacher looks at the elementary child with ADHD. In B. P. Guyer (Ed.), *ADHD: Achieving success in school and in life* (pp. 67–80). Boston: Allyn & Bacon.

Stiles, S., & Knox, R. (1996). Medical issues, treatments, and professionals. In M. C. Holbrook (Ed.), *Children with visual impairments: a parent's guide* (pp. 21–48). Bethesda, MD: Woodbine House.

Still, G. F. (1902). Some abnormal psychical conditions in children. *Lancet, 1,* 1008–1012, 1077–1082, 1163–1168.

Stires, S. (1983). Real audiences and contexts for LD writers. *Academic Therapy, 18*(5), 561–568.

Strickland, B. B., & Turnbull, A. P. (1990). *Developing and implementing individual education programs* (3rd ed.). Columbus, OH: Merrill.

Sugai, G., Horner, R. H., Dunlap, G., Hieneman, M., Lewis, T. J., Nelson, C. M., Scott, T., Liaupsin, C., Sailor, W., Turnbull, A. P., Turnbull, H. R. III, Wickham, D., Reuf, M., & Wilcox, B. (2000). Applying positive behavioral support and functional behavioral assessment in schools. *Journal of Positive Behavioral Interventions and Support, 2,* 131–143.

Sullivan, P. (1992). *ESL in context.* New York: Corwin Press.

Svenson, O., & Broquist, S. (1975). Strategies for solving simple addition problems: A comparison of normal and subnormal children. *Scandinavian Journal of Psychology, 16,* 143–151.

Swain, M. (1986). Communicative competence: Some roles of comprehensible input & comprehensible output in its development. In J. Cummins & M. Swain (Eds.), *Bilingualism in education.* New York: Longman.

Swanson, H. L. (1993). Working memory in learning disability subgroups. *Journal of Experimental Child Psychology, 56,* 87–114.

Swanson, H. L. (2001). Research on interventions for adolescents with learning disabilities: A meta-analysis of outcomes related to higher-order processing. *Elementary School Journal, 101*(3), 331–348.

Swanson, H. L., & Cooney, J. B. (1991). Learning disabilities and memory. In B. Y. L. Wong (Ed.), *Learning about learning disabilities* (pp. 103–127). Orlando, FL: Academic Press.

Swanson, H. L., & Hoskyn, M. (1998). Experimental intervention research on students with learning disabilities. A meta-analysis of treatment outcomes. *Review of Educational Research, 68,* 277–321.

Swanson, H. L., with Hoskyn, M., & Lee, C. (1999). *Interventions for students with learning disabilities: A meta-analysis of treatment outcomes.* New York: Guilford.

Swanson, M., McBurnett, K., Wigal, T., Pfiffner, L., Lerner, M., Williams, L., Christian, D., Tamm, L., Willcutt, E., Crowley, K., Clevenger, W., Khouzam, N., Woo, C., Crinella, F., & Fisher, T. (1993). Effect of stimulant medication on children with attention deficit disorder: A "review of reviews." *Exceptional Children, 60*(2), 154–162.

Swenson, A. M. (1999). *Beginning with braille: Firsthand experiences with a balanced approach to literacy.* New York: AFB Press.

Swisher, K., & Deyhle, D. (1992). Adapting instruction to culture. In J. Reyhner (Ed.), *Teaching American Indian students* (pp. 81–95). Norman, OK: University of Oklahoma Press.

Tangel, D. M., & Blachman, B. A. (1995). Effect of phoneme awareness instruction on the invented spelling of first-grade children: A one-year follow-up. *Journal of Reading Behavior, 27,* 153–185.

Tarnowski, K. J., & Rohrbeck, C. A. (1993). Disadvantaged children and families. In T. H. Ollendick & R. J. Prinz (Eds.), *Advances in clinical psychology* (Vol. 15, pp. 41–80). New York: Plenum Press.

Taylor, B., Harris, L. A., & Pearson, P. D. (1988). *Reading difficulties: Instruction and assessment.* New York: Random House.

Taylor, B. M., Pearson, P. D., Clark, K. F., & Walpole, S. (1999). Effective schools/accomplished teachers. *The Reading Teacher, 53*(2), 156–159.

Taylor, M. (1971). *Roll of thunder, hear my cry.* New York: Dial.

Texas Education Agency. (1996). *The Texas reading initiative.* Austin, TX: Author.

Tharp, R. G., Estrada, P., Dalton, S. S., & Yamaguchi, L. (1999). *Teaching transformed: Achieving excellence, fairness, inclusion, and harmony.* Boulder, CO: Westview Press.

Tharp, R. G., & Gallimore, R. (1988). *Rousing minds to life: Teaching, learning, and schooling in social context.* Cambridge, England: Cambridge University Press.

Thomas, C. H., & Patton, J. R. (1990). Mild and moderate retardation. In J. R. Patton, M. Beirne-Smith, & J. S. Payne (Eds.), *Mental retardation* (2nd ed., pp. 197–226). New York: Merrill/Macmillan.

Thomas, W. P., & Collier, V. P. (1997). Two languages are better than one. *Educational Leadership, 55*(4), 23–26.

Thornburg, K. R., Hoffman, S., & Remeika, C. (1991). Youth at risk: Society at risk. *The Elementary School Journal, 91*(3), 199–208.

Tiedt, P. L., & Tiedt, I. M. (1995). *Multicultural teaching: A handbook of activities, information, and resources* (4th ed.). Boston: Allyn & Bacon.

Tikunoff, W. J. (1983). *Compatibility of the SBIF features with other research instruction of LEP students.* San Francisco: Far West Laboratory.

Todd, A. W., Horner, R. H., Sugai, G. (2000). Self-monitoring and self-recruited praise: Effects on problem behavior, academic engagement, and work completion in a typical classroom. *Journal of Positive Behavioral Interventions, 1,* 66–76.

Torgesen, J. K. (1999). Assessment and instruction for phonemic awareness and word recognition skills. In H. W. Catts & A. G. Kamhi (Eds.), *Language and reading disabilities* (pp. 128–153). Boston: Allyn & Bacon.

Torgesen, J. K., & Burgess, S. R. (1998). Consistency of reading-related phonological processes throughout early childhood: Evidence from longitudinal, correlational and instructional studies. In J. Methsala & L. Ehri (Eds.), *Word recognition in beginning literacy* (pp. 161–188). Mahwah, NJ: Erlbaum Associates.

Torgesen, J. K., & Goldman, T. (1977). Rehearsal and short-term memory in second grade reading disabled children. *Child Development, 48,* 56–61.

Torgesen, J. K., Wagner, R. K., & Rashotte, C. A. (1994). Longitudinal studies of phonological processing and reading. *Journal of Learning Disabilities, 27,* 276–286.

Towell, J., & Wink, J. (1993). *Strategies for monolingual teachers in multilingual classrooms.* Turlock, CA: California State University, Stanislaus. (ERIC Document Reproduction Service No. ED 359 797).

Townsend, B. L. (2000). The disproportionate discipline of African American learners: Reducing school suspensions and expulsions. *Exceptional Children, 66*(3), 381–391.

Trammel, D. L., Schloss, P. J., & Alper, S. (1994). Using self-recording, evaluation, and graphing to increase completion of homework assignments. *Journal of Learning Disabilities, 27,* 75–81.

Treffinger, D. J. (1982). Gifted students, regular students: Sixty ingredients for a better blend. *Elementary School Journal, 82,* 267–273.

Trelease, J. (1995). *The new read-aloud handbook* (4th ed.). New York: Penguin.

Trent, S. C., Pernell, E., Mungai, A., & Chimedza, R. (1998). Using concept maps to measure conceptual change in preservice teachers enrolled in a multicultural education/special education course. *Remedial and Special Education, 19*(1), 16–31.

Troia, G. A., Graham, S., & Harris, K. R. (2000). Teaching students with learning disabilities to mindfully plan when writing. *Exceptional Children, 65*(2), 235–252.

Tucker, B. F., & Colson, S. E. (1992). Traumatic brain injury: An overview of school reentry. *Intervention in School and Clinic, 27*(4), 196–206.

Turnbull, A. P., & Turnbull, H. R. (1990). *Families, professionals, and exceptionality: A special partnership* (2nd ed.). Columbus, OH: Merrill.

Turnbull, H. R. (1990). *Free appropriate public education: The law and children with disabilities.* Denver, CO: Love.

Tuttle, F. B., Becker, L. A., & Sousa, J. A. (1988). *Characteristics and identification of gifted and talented students.* Washington, DC: National Education Association.

Tyler, J. S. (1990). *Traumatic head injury in school-aged children: A training manual for educational personnel.* Kansas City, KS: Children's Rehabilitation Unit, University of Kansas Medical Center.

Tyler, J. S., & Myles, B. S. (1990). Serving students with traumatic brain injury: A new challenge for teachers of students with learning disabilities. *LD Forum, 16*(1), 69–74.

Umansky, W., & Hooper, S. R. (1998). *Young children with special needs* (3rd ed.). Upper Saddle River, NJ: Prentice-Hall.

Unsworth, L. (1984). Meeting individual needs through flexible within-class grouping of pupils. *The Reading Teacher, 38*(3), 298–304.

U.S. Bureau of the Census. (1993). *Current population reports* (Series P–60, No. 181). Education Statistics on Disk. Washington, DC: U.S. Department of Education, Office of Educational Research and Improvement, National Center for Education Statistics.

U.S. Department of Education. (1992). Rules and regulations. *Federal Register, 57*(189), 44,800–44,824.

U.S. Department of Education. (1994b). *Sixteenth annual report to Congress on the implementation of the Education for All Handicapped Children Act.* Washington, DC: U.S. Government Printing Office.

U.S. Department of Education. (1995). *Seventeenth annual report to Congress on the implementation of the Individuals with Disabilities Education Act.* Washington, DC: Author.

U.S. Department of Education. (1997). *Nineteenth annual report to Congress on the implementation of the Individuals with Disabilities Education Act.* Washington, DC: Author.

U.S. Department of Education (1998). *Twentieth annual report to Congress on the implementation of the Individuals with Disabilities Act.* Washington, DC: U.S. Government Printing Office.

U.S. Department of Education (2000). *Twenty-second annual report to Congress on the implementation of the Individuals with Disabilities Act.* Washington, DC: U.S. Government Printing Office.

Vacca, R. T., & Vacca, J. L. (1989). *Content area reading* (3rd ed.). Glenview, IL: Scott, Foresman and Company.

Vandercook, T., York, J., & Forest, M. (1989). The McGill action planning system (MAPS): A strategy for building the vision. *Journal for the Association for Persons with Severe Handicaps, 14,* 205–215.

Van Kleeck, A. (1990). Emergent literacy: Learning about print before learning to read. *Topics in Language Disorders, 10,* 25–45.

Van Kleek, A. (1995). Emphasizing form and meaning repeatedly in prereading and early reading instruction. *Topics in Language Disorders, 16,* 27–49.

Van Reusen, A. K., & Bos, C. S. (1990). I PLAN: Helping students communicate in planning conference. *Teaching Exceptional Children, 22*(4), 30–32.

Van Reusen, A. K., & Bos, C. S. (1992). *Use of the goal-regulation strategy to improve the goal attainment of students with learning disabilities* (Final Report). Tucson, AZ: University of Arizona.

Van Reusen, A. K., & Bos, C. S. (1994). Facilitating student participation in individualized education programs through motivation strategy instruction. *Exceptional Children, 60*(5), 466–475.

Van Reusen, A. K., Bos, C. S., Schumaker, J. B., & Deshler, D. D. (1994). *The self-advocacy strategy for education and transition planning.* Lawrence, KS: Edge Enterprises.

Van Riper, C., & Emerick, L. (1984). *Speech correction: Principles and methods* (7th ed.). Englewood Cliffs, NJ: Prentice-Hall.

Van Tassel-Baska, J. (1992). *Planning effective curriculum for gifted learners.* Denver, CO: Love.

Van Tassel-Baska, J., Patton, J. M., & Prillaman, D. (1991). *Gifted youth at risk: A report of a national study.* Reston, VA: Council for Exceptional Children.

Vaughn, B. J., & Horner, R. H. (1997). Identifying instructional tasks that occasion problem behaviors and assessing the effects of student versus teacher choice among these tasks. *Journal of Applied Behavior Analysis, 30,* 299–312.

Vaughn, S., Bos, C., Harrell, J. E., & Lasky, B. A. (1988b). Parent participation in the initial placement/IEP conference ten years after mandated involvement. *Journal of Learning Disabilities, 21*(2), 82–89.

Vaughn, S. R., Bos, C. S., & Lund, K. A. (1986). . . . But they can do it in my room: Strategies for promoting generalization. *Teaching Exceptional Children, 18,* 176–180.

Vaughn, S., & Gersten, R. (1998). Productive teaching of English language learners: What we know and still need to know. In R. M. Gersten & R. T. Jimenez (Eds.), *Promoting learning for culturally and linguistically diverse students* (pp. 230–238). Belmont, CA: Wadsworth.

Vaughn, S., Gersten, R., & Chard, D. J. (2000). The underlying message in LD intervention research: Findings from research syntheses. *Exceptional Children, 67*(1), 99–114.

Vaughn, S., Hughes, M. T., Moody, S. W., & Elbaum, B. (2001a). Instructional grouping for reading for students with LD: Implications for practice. *Intervention in School and Clinic, 36*(3), 131–137.

Vaughn, S., Hughes, M. T., Schumm, J. S., & Klingner, J. K. (1998). A collaborative effort to enhance reading and writing instruction in inclusion classrooms. *Learning Disability Quarterly, 21*(1), 57–74.

Vaughn, S., Klingner, J. K., & Bryant, D. P. (2001b). Collaborative strategic reading as a means to enhance peer-mediated instruction for reading comprehension and content area learning. *Remedial and Special Education, 22,* 24–38.

Vaughn, S., & Lancelotta, G. X. (1990). Teaching interpersonal social skills to low accepted students: Peer-pairing versus no peer-pairing. *Journal of School Psychology, 28*(3), 181–188.

Vaughn, S. R., Lancelotta, G. X., & Minnis, S. (1988a). Social strategy training and peer involvement: Increasing peer acceptance of a female, LD student. *Learning Disabilities Focus, 4,* 32–37.

Vaughn, S., Linan-Thompson, S., Khouzekanani, K., Bryant, D., & Dickson, S. (n.d.). *Grouping for reading instruction: Students with reading difficulties who are monolingual English speakers or English language learners.* Unpublished manuscript.

Vaughn, S., McIntosh, R., & Spencer-Rowe, J. (1991). Peer rejection is a stubborn thing: Increasing peer acceptance of rejected students with learning disabilities. *Learning Disabilities Research and Practice, 6*(2), 83–88.

Vaughn, S. R., & Ridley, C. A. (1983). A preschool interpersonal problem solving program: Does it affect behavior in the classroom? *Child Study Journal, 13,* 1–12.

Vaughn, S. R., Ridley, C. A., & Bullock, D. D. (1984). Interpersonal problem-solving skills training with aggressive young children. *Journal of Applied Developmental Psychology, 5,* 213–223.

Vaughn, S. R., Ridley, C. A., & Cox, J. (1983). Evaluating the efficacy of an interpersonal skills training program with children who are mentally retarded. *Education and Training of the Mentally Retarded, 18,* 191–196.

Vaughn, S., & Schumm, J. S. (1994). Middle school teachers' planning for students with learning disabilities. *Remedial and Special Education, 15*(3), 152–161.

Vaughn, S., & Schumm, J. S. (1995). Responsible inclusion for students with learning disabilities. *Journal of Learning Disabilities, 28*(5), 264–270, 290.

Vaughn, S., Schumm, J. S., & Arguelles, M. E. (1997). The ABCDEs of co-teaching. *Teaching Exceptional Children, 30*(2), 4–10.

Vellutino, F. R., Scanlon, D. M., Sipay, E. R., Small, S. G., Pratt, A., Chen, R., & Denckla, M. B. (1996). Cognitive profiles of difficult-to-remediate and readily remediated poor readers: Early intervention as a vehicle for distinguishing between cognitive and experiential deficits as basic causes of specific reading disability. *Journal of Educational Psychology, 88,* 601–638.

Vogel, S. A., Hruby, P. J., & Adelman, P. B. (1993). Educational and psychological factors in successful and unsuccessful college students with learning disabilities. *Learning Disabilities Research and Practice, 8,* 35–43.

Vygotsky, L. S. (1978). *Mind in society: The development of higher psychological processes.* Cambridge, MA: MIT Press.

Walberg, H. J. (1984). Improving the productivity of America's schools. *Educational Leadership, 41,* 19–27.

Waldie, K., & Spreen, O. (1993). The relationship between learning disabilities and persisting delinquency. *Journal of Learning Disabilities, 26,* 417–423.

Waldron, N. L., & McLeskey, J. (1998). The effects of an inclusive school program on students with mild and severe learning disabilities. *Exceptional Children, 64,* 395–405.

Walker, H. M., Colvin, G., & Ramsey, E. (1995). *Antisocial behavior in school: Strategies and best practices.* Pacific Grove, CA: Brooks/Cole.

Wallach, G. P., & Miller, L. (1988). *Language intervention and academic success.* San Diego, CA: College Hill.

Wallerstein, J. S., & Blakeslee, S. (1989). *Second chances: Men, women and children a decade after divorce. Who wins, who loses—and why.* New York: Ticknor & Fields.

Walp, T. P., & Walmsley, S. A. (1989). Instructional and philosophical congruence: Neglected aspects of coordination. *The Reading Teacher, 42,* 364–368.

Walther-Thomas, C. (1997). Co-teaching experiences: The benefits and problems that teachers and principals report over time. *Journal of Learning Disabilities, 30*(4), 395–407.

Warren, D. W. (1994). *Blindness and children: An individual differences approach.* New York: Cambridge University Press.

Warren, S. F. (1991). Enhancing communication and language development with milieu teaching procedures. In E. Cipani (Ed.), *A guide for developing language competence in preschool children with severe and moderate handicaps* (pp. 68–93). Springfield, IL: Charles C. Thomas.

Wasik, B. A. (1998). Using volunteers as reading tutors: Guidelines for successful practices. *The Reading Teacher, 51,* 562–570.

Waxman, H. S. (1991). Reversing the cycle of educational failure for students in at-risk school environments. In H. C. Waxman, J. W. de Felix, J. E. Anderson, & H. P. Baptise (Eds.), *Students at risk in at-risk schools* (pp. 1–10). Newbury Park, CA: Sage.

Webber, J., Anderson, T., & Otey, L. (1991). Teacher mindsets for surviving in BD classrooms. *Intervention in School and Clinic, 26*(5), 288–292.

Webb-Johnson, G., Artiles, A. J., Trent, S. C., Jackson, C. W., & Velox, A. (1998). The status of research on multicultural education in teacher education and special education: Problems, pitfalls, and promises. *Remedial and Special Education, 19*(1), 7–15.

Wehmeyer, M. L. (1995). *Whose future is it anyway?: A student-directed transition planning process.* Arlington, TX: Arc National Headquarters.

Welch, M. (1992). The P.L.E.A.S.E. strategy: A metacognitive learning strategy for improving the paragraph writing of students with mild learning disabilities. *Learning Disability Quarterly, 15,* 119–128.

Welch, M., & Link, D. P. (1989). *Write, P.L.E.A.S.E.: A strategy for efficient learning and functioning in written expression* (video cassette). Salt Lake City, UT: University of Utah, Department of Special Education, Educational Tele-Communications.

Werner, O., & Begishe, K. (1968). *Styles of learning: The evidence for Navajo.* Paper presented at a conference on styles of learning in American Indian children, Stanford University, Stanford, CA.

West, J. F., & Idol, L. (1990). Collaborative consultation in the education of mildly handicapped and at-risk students. *Remedial and Special Education, 11,* 22–31.

West, J. F., Idol, L., & Cannon, G. (1988). *Collaboration in the schools: Communicating, interacting, and problem solving.* Austin, TX: PRO-ED.

Westling, D. L., & Fox, L. (2000). *Teaching students with severe disabilities* (2nd ed.). Englewood, NJ: Prentice-Hall.

Weyandt, L. L (2001). *An ADHD Primer.* Boston: Allyn & Bacon.

Whipple, G. M. (1936). *The grouping of pupils. Thirty-fifth yearbook of the National Society for the Study of*

*Education (Part 1)*. Chicago: University of Chicago Press.

White, B. (1975). Critical influences in the origins of competence. *Merrill-Palmer Quarterly, 2,* 243–266.

Wiig, E. H., & Semel, E. (1984). *Language assessment and intervention for the learning disabled* (2nd ed.). Columbus, OH: Merrill.

Wilcox, J., Sbardellati, E., & Nevin, A. (1987). Cooperative learning groups aid integration. *Teaching Exceptional Children, 20*(1), 61–63.

Willcutt, E. G., & Pennington, B. R. (2000). Co-morbidity of reading disability and attention-deficit/hyperactivity disorder: Differences by gender and subtype. *Journal of Learning Disabilities, 33,* 179–191.

Willman, A. T. (1999). "Hello, Mrs. Willman, it's me!" Keep kids reading over the summer by using voice mail. *The Reading Teacher, 52,* 788–789.

Wilson, B. A. (1996). *Wilson Reading System*. Millbury, MA: Wilson Language Training Corporation.

Winebrenner, S. (1992). *Teaching gifted kids in the regular classroom*. Minneapolis, MN: Free Spirit Publishing.

Winebrenner, S., & Devlin, B. (1998, January/February). Cluster grouping of gifted students: How to provide full-time services on a part-time budget. *Teaching Exceptional Children, 30*(3), 62–65.

Wishom, P. M., Swaim, J. H., & Huang, A. (1989). AIDS. *Middle School Journal, 20*(3), 3–7.

Witte, R. (1998). Meet Bob, a student with traumatic brain injury. *Teaching Exceptional Children, 30*(3), 56–60.

Wolery, M., Cybriwsky, C. A., Gast, D. L., & Boyle-Gast, K. (1991). Use of constant time delay and attentional responses with adolescents. *Exceptional Children, 57,* 462–474.

Wolery, M. (1989). Transitions in early childhood special education: Issues and procedures. *Focus on Exceptional Children, 22,* 1–16.

Wolery, M., Doyle, P. M., Gast, D. L., & Ault, M. J. (1993). Comparison of progressive time delay and transition-based teaching with preschoolers who have developmental delay. *Journal of Early Intervention, 17*(2), 160–176.

Wolf, M. (1999). What time may tell: Towards a new conceptualization of developmental dyslexia. *Annals of Dyslexia, 49,* 3–28.

Wong, B. Y. L. (1991). The relevance of metacognition to learning disabilities. In B. Y. L. Wong (Ed.), *Learning about learning disabilities* (pp. 231–258). Orlando, FL: Academic Press.

Wong, B. Y. L. (1994). Instructional parameters promoting transfer of learned strategies in students with learning disabilities. *Learning Disability Quarterly, 17,* 110–120.

Wong, B. Y. L., Butler, D. L., Ficzere, S. A., & Kuperis, S. (1997). Teaching adolescents with learning disabilities and low achievers to plan, write, and revise compare-and-contrast essays. *Learning Disabilities Research & Practice, 12*(1), 2–15.

Wood, J. W., & Wooley, J. A. (1986). Adapting textbooks. *The Clearing House, 59,* 332–335.

Wood, K. D., Lapp, D., & Flood, J. (1992). *Guiding readers through text: A review of study guides*. Newark, DE: International Reading Association.

Wood, M. M., & Long, N. J. (1994). *Life–space intervention: Talking with children and youth*. Austin, TX: PRO-ED.

Woodward, A., & Elliott, D. L. (1990). Textbook use and teacher professionalism. In D. L. Elliott and A. Woodward (Eds.), *Textbooks and schooling in the United States: Eighty-ninth yearbook of the National Society for the Study of Education, Part I* (pp. 178–193). Chicago, IL: University of Chicago Press.

Woodward, J., & Rieth, H. (1997). A historical review of technology research in special education. *Review of Educational Research, 67*(4), 503–536.

Wormsley, D. P. (1997). Fostering emergent literacy. In D. P. Wormsley & F. M. D'Andrea, *Instructional strategies for braille literacy* (pp. 17–55). New York: AFB Press.

Wright, C., & Bigge, J. L. (1991). Avenues to physical participation. In J. L. Bigge (Ed.), *Teaching individuals with multiple and physical disabilities* (3rd ed., pp. 132–174). Englewood Cliffs, NJ: Merrill/Prentice-Hall.

Wright, C. D., & Wright, J. P. (1980). Handwriting: The effectiveness of copying from moving versus still models. *Journal of Educational Research, 74,* 95–98.

Wylie, R. E., & Durrell, D. D. (1970). Teaching vowels through phonograms. *Elementary English, 47,* 787–791.

Wysocki, K., & Jenkins, J. R. (1987). Deriving word meanings through morphological generalization. *Reading Research Quarterly, 22,* 66–81.

Yavas, M. (1998). Phonology development and disorders. San Diego, CA: Singular Publishing Group.

Yee, G. (1991). *The melting pot revisited: A literature review of current literature in multicultural education*. Unpublished manuscript. University of California–Berkeley, Department of Anthropology, Special Projects.

Yell, M. L. (1998). *The law and special education*. Upper Saddle River, NJ: Prentice-Hall.

Yopp, H. (1992). Developing phonemic awareness in young children. *The Reading Teacher, 45,* 696–703.

Yopp, R. H., & Yopp, H. K. (2000, February). Sharing informational text with young children. *The Reading Teacher, 53*(5), 410–423.

York, J., & Vandercook, T. (1991). Designing an integrated program for learners with severe disabilities. *Teaching Exceptional Children, 23*(2), 22–28.

Young, M. J., & Riegeluth, C. (1988). *Improving the textbook selection process*. Bloomington, IN: Phi Delta Kappa Educational Foundation.

Ysseldyke, J. E., & Algozzine, B. (1990). *Introduction to special education* (2nd ed.). Boston: Houghton Mifflin.

Zametkin, A., & Rapaport, J. (1987). Neurobiology of attention deficit disorder with hyperactivity: Where have we come in 50 years? *Journal of American Academy of Child and Adolescent Psychiatry, 26,* 676–686.

Zametkin, A., Liebenauer, L., Fitzgerald, G., King, A., Minkunas, D., Herscovitch, P., Yamada, E. M., &

Cohen, R. M. (1993). Brain metabolism in teenagers with attention-deficit hyperactivity disorder. *Archives of General Psychiatry, 50,* 333–340.

Zaragoza, N. (1987). Process writing for high-risk and learning disabled students. *Reading Research and Instruction, 26*(4), 290–301.

Zaragoza, N., & Vaughn, S. (1992). The effects of process instruction on three second-grade students with different achievement profiles. *Learning Disabilities Research and Practice, 7*(4), 184–193.

Zentall, S. S., & Smith, Y. N. (1993). Mathematical performance and behavior of children with hyperactivity, with and without coexisting aggression. *Behavior Research and Therapy, 31*(7), 701–710.

Zigler, E., & Burack, J. A. (1989). Personality development and the dually diagnosed person. *Research in Developmental Disabilities, 10,* 225–240.

Zigmond, N., & Baker, J. M. (1995). An exploration of the meaning and practice of special education in the context of full inclusion of students with learning disabilities. *Journal of Special Education, 29*(2), 1–25.

Zigmond, N., Jenkins, J., Fuchs, L. S., Deno, S., Fuchs, D., Baker, J., Jenkins, L., & Couthino, M. (1995). Special education in restructured schools: Findings from three multi-year studies. *Phi Delta Kappan, 76,* 531–540.

Zutell, J., & Rasinski, T. V. (1991). Training teachers to attend to their students' oral reading fluency. *Theory into Practice, 30,* 211–217.